Apache Cordova 4 Programming

Apache Cordova 4 Programming

John M. Wargo

Addison-Wesley

Upper Saddle River, NJ • Boston • Indianapolis • San Francisco
New York • Toronto • Montreal • London • Munich • Paris • Madrid
Capetown • Sydney • Tokyo • Singapore • Mexico City

For information about buying this title in bulk quantities, or for special sales opportunities (which may include electronic versions; custom cover designs; and content particular to your business, training goals, marketing focus, or branding interests), please contact our corporate sales department at corpsales@pearsoned.com or [illegible].

For government sales inquiries, please contact governmentsales@pearsoned.com.

For questions about sales outside the United States, please contact international@pearsoned.com.

Visit us on the Web: informit.com/aw

Library of Congress Cataloging-in-Publication Data
Wargo, John M.
Apache Cordova 4 programming / John M Wargo.
pages cm
Includes index.
ISBN 978-0-13-404819-2 (pbk. : alk. paper)
1. Mobile computing—Computer programs. 2. Application program interfaces (Computer software)
3. Application software—Development. 4. Apache Cordova. I. Title.
QA76.59.W368 2015
004.167—dc23
2015003045

ISBN-13: 978-0-13-404819-2
ISBN-10: 0-13-404819-9

Text printed in the United States on recycled paper at RR Donnelley in Crawfordsville, Indiana.
First printing, April 2015

This is yet another book that couldn't exist except for the unwavering support (and extreme patience) of my wife, Anna. Crazy about you!

Not so much direct support, but still a lot of patience from Elizabeth and August as well. I'm sorry I wasn't able to sneak pictures of you guys into the manuscript this time.

Contents

Foreword

It's great to have John Wargo in my classroom and in my teaching, both literally and figuratively!

Apache Cordova 4 Programming (AC4P) will be the fourth John Wargo title employed in my classroom. Surprisingly, this frenetic iteration happens in just two semesters and is testimony to the value of John's work.

The figurative: In preparing for my college's first offering of an upper-level mobile application course, it became evident that I should cover both native and hybrid mobile technologies. For a hybrid technology, PhoneGap immediately rose to the top of my candidate list. The search was on for a meaningful text. A survey of potential materials revealed that no formal college textbooks existed, and that John's *PhoneGap Essentials* was the de facto primer for technology professionals looking to learn about PhoneGap. Perfect, right? I order and review a copy, confirm the book's reputation, and place an order with my college bookstore.

Enter John Wargo. I engage John to explore the possibility of acquiring any supporting materials, the true value-add of a text or reference in any fast-paced course like this. John offers to assist but also immediately cautions that my choice of text is dated and that two newer texts now replace the first. I also learn that a fourth text is in the works [unhappy emoji]. Interactions with the college bookstore and publisher ensue, and the adjustments for text numbers two and three are made.

I'll spare you the unnecessary detail, but fast-forward to today. I anxiously await AC4P for inclusion in my course, later this semester.

Ah, I haven't yet shared the literal connection. Recalling my interactions with John, I add this anecdote. In addition to his assistance with the texts, John agrees to visit my campus when traveling to our area. He offers to visit my class as well as a college-wide venue to speak and to interact with our students. (We have a population of more than a thousand information technology students). What happened was marvelous; his words come off the pages and into life in these forums. This provides a tremendous learning opportunity for Georgia Gwinnett College's students. Conversely, we see that the narratives provided in print are his knowledge and experience captured in prose. My students engaged enthusiastically, commenting that we should do much more with PhoneGap (and its open-source cousin, Cordova) in future semesters. They were hooked!

Again, I welcome John into my classroom figuratively and hope that we can host him literally again, too.

—Bob Lutz, Ph.D.
Georgia Gwinnett College
January 2015

Preface

This is a book about Apache Cordova, the leading framework for building native mobile applications for multiple target platforms using HTML5 (HTML, JavaScript, and CSS). I created the book in order to help web developers and mobile developers understand how to use Apache Cordova to build hybrid applications for mobile devices. The book targets the specific capabilities provided in Apache Cordova 4 and subsequent versions.

As Adobe PhoneGap is just a distribution of Apache Cordova, this book is also about Adobe PhoneGap. You'll find any differences between the two clearly described herein.

The book is written for mobile developers who want to learn about Apache Cordova 4. If you're brand-new to Cordova, this book will be just what you need to get started. If you're experienced with an older version of Cordova, this book can act as a refresher, plus it will show you in detail how to use all of the new stuff that's in Cordova 4. You should have at least some experience with mobile development to directly benefit from this book. For web developers who want to get into mobile development using Apache Cordova, I've included content that shows you how to install and use the native SDKs, but I won't cover many native-specific topics.

What you'll find in the book:

- Lots of detailed information about Apache Cordova, what it does, how it works, and how to use the available tools and APIs
- Lots of examples and code; for even more code, be sure to check out my *Apache Cordova API Cookbook* (www.cordovacookbook.com)

What you won't find in this book:

- Mobile web development and mobile development topics; this is a book about Apache Cordova, not mobile development
- Expressions or phrases in languages other than English (I hate it when authors include expressions from Latin or French)
- Obscure references to pop-culture topics (although there is an overt reference to Douglas Adams's *Hitchhiker's Guide to the Galaxy* and one obscure reference to Monty Python)
- Pictures of my children or my pets

This is not a book for experienced Cordova 4 developers—if you consider yourself an experienced Cordova 4 developer, you probably should not buy this book.

Herein I try to provide complete coverage of Apache Cordova 4, covering enough detail that readers will leave with a complete understanding of what Cordova is, what it does, how it works, and how to use it for their mobile application projects. There's a whole lot more to Cordova—many advanced topics and more detailed coverage of the Cordova APIs, which can be found in the Cordova documentation or in blogs.

This book started many years ago as a book called *PhoneGap Essentials* (www.phonegapessentials.com); the book was all about PhoneGap 2.0 and was published right about the time the project name changed to Apache Cordova. The book came in at about 300 pages. The book's first 150 pages covered the available tools and everything a developer needed to know to configure a development environment, and then create, write, build, and test PhoneGap applications. The second half of the book provided a detailed deep dive into each of the (at the time) PhoneGap APIs. The cool part of this second half was that for each API it included at least one complete, functional sample application that demonstrated each aspect of the API. The framework's documentation was pretty useful in demonstrating how the API worked overall, but *PhoneGap Essentials* provided much more thorough examples.

The book went on to become the best-selling book on the topic, and it was used in university courses around the world. According to Amazon.com, people are still purchasing this book today.

With the release of Apache Cordova 3, I reworked the manuscript and published *Apache Cordova 3 Programming* (www.cordovaprogramming.com). This book also came in at 300 pages but was essentially a rewrite of just the first half of *PhoneGap Essentials* with only cursory coverage of the Cordova APIs provided. This allowed me to go into much more detail on the tools and development process.

Unfortunately, because *Apache Cordova 3 Programming* was available only as an ebook, it was hard to find, and many readers continued to buy *PhoneGap Essentials* even though it covered an older version of the framework.

In order to accommodate those readers who were more interested in the Cordova APIs, I reworked the second half of *PhoneGap Essentials* into another 300 pages called *Apache Cordova API Cookbook* (www.cordovacookbook.com). In this book, the complete example applications from *PhoneGap Essentials* were enhanced and expanded, and all of the book's content was updated for the newer version of Cordova. I'd not covered some topics as well as I would have liked to in the first book, so this update allowed me to really expand the coverage of some topics and include even more complete sample applications (32, I think it was).

Between *Apache Cordova 3 Programming* and *Apache Cordova API Cookbook*, I had written more than 600 pages of coverage of Apache Cordova 3. That's more than twice the size of the original book and a lot of good information for developers.

With this book, I've updated *Apache Cordova 3 Programming* for Apache Cordova 4, plus included new content on a bunch of topics. In my previous books, I focused primarily on PhoneGap and Apache Cordova; I didn't cover many third-party tools and left many mobile development topics uncovered as well. For this book, there were a bevy of additional tools available and some hybrid-focused HTML frameworks, so I decided to cover as many of them as I could in the space available to me. Where this book's predecessor was 300 pages, this one should top out at more than 500 pages, so there's a lot of really good information here for all types of Cordova developers. When bundled with *Apache Cordova API Cookbook,* you'll have more than 800 pages of information about Apache Cordova.

Herein you'll find most of the same topics that were covered in *Apache Cordova 3 Programming.* The only missing topic is coverage of the BlackBerry platform. I wrote the first book on BlackBerry development and had pretty much always carried a BlackBerry device, but between books, BlackBerry experienced a dramatic drop in market share and I started carrying an Android device as my primary device. Additionally, in previous books I had the enthusiastic support of my former colleagues at BlackBerry, but when it came time to get feedback on the BlackBerry chapter in *Apache Cordova 3 Programming,* the development team stopped responding to my inquiries. Because of those two things I decided to drop support for BlackBerry from this book.

So, what new stuff have I added in this book? Coverage of

- Plugman and the PhoneGap CLI
- Cordova's support for Firefox OS and Ubuntu devices
- Automation (Grunt and Gulp) and Cordova CLI hooks
- Microsoft's hybrid toolkit for Visual Studio
- Third-party tools such as AppGyver, GapDebug, THyM, and more
- Third-party HTML frameworks such as Bootstrap, OpenUI5, Ionic, and Onsen UI

There's a lot more, but these are some of the highlights.

The one thing I cover in the book but not in tremendous detail is how to build custom Cordova plugins. I cover the topic and show you how to create two complete plugins, but this isn't a native mobile development book and that's a native mobile development topic. I've learned from my readers that the material I do provide is enough to help a lot of people get started with plugins and create their own plugins; I'll leave it up to another author to write a book dedicated to plugin development so it can get the attention it deserves.

Android Studio versus Android Developer Tools (ADT)

As I wrote the previous edition of this book, Google announced a new development tool called Android Studio. I expected then that Android Studio would be out before I started this manuscript and I'd be able to update the content for the new tool. As I worked through the book, Android Studio was still in beta and it was essentially incompatible with Cordova CLI-generated projects. I thought about hacking through it in order to provide updated content here, but after discussing my situation with Andrew Grieve from Google, I decided that it wasn't yet ready for prime time and I would stick with ADT for this book.

Wouldn't you know it, right after the book went into the editing process, Google finally released Android Studio. Sigh. At this point, I could make minor changes to the manuscript but couldn't rewrite a complete chapter. So, unfortunately, some of the content you'll find in Chapter 7, "Android Development with Cordova," refers to the older version of the SDK. The stuff around the SDK is still valid, but Android Studio installs everything in a different place from what I've shown. The incompatible stuff is everything I showed about using the Eclipse tools. Sorry.

University Use

One of the pleasant surprises you have when delivering technical books is when a book is picked up for use in university courses. From what I can tell, several universities around the world use my Cordova books for their PhoneGap/Cordova class work. I regularly receive emails from university professors asking me questions about the book as they prepare to use it in their classes.

I was fortunate enough to hear from Dr. Robert Lutz from Georgia Gwinnett College. They were using my books (*Apache Cordova 3 Programming* and *Apache Cordova API Cookbook*) in class and they were close enough that I could drive there and see how it was working for them. I arranged a visit to the campus, and Dr. Lutz was kind enough to arrange a campus Tech Talk at the university. I spent about an hour talking about mobile development and the role hybrid applications play in the market. After the session ended, I spent some more time with the class using my book and let the students pick my brain on a number of topics. It was quite a lot of fun and allowed me to learn more about how my work is being used by others. I even signed a few copies of my books.

After this book is finished, my goal is to work with Dr. Lutz to prepare classroom material that can be used in conjunction with the book. Stay tuned on that one.

Cordova as a Moving Target

One of the challenges in writing a book about open-source projects is that if the project is well staffed and busy, it gets regular updates. In Cordova's case, it's one of the fastest-moving open-source projects on the planet, so with their regular updates and yearly major releases, it is definitely a moving target.

I've worked very hard to structure and craft this book so that it can survive the rapid pace of the project, but only time will tell. You may find that something I've written here has changed and the book doesn't align with reality. There's nothing I can do about this except to stay on top of it and post updates to the book's web site (described below) when I find that something has changed enough that it breaks part of the book.

A Comment on Source Code

One of the things you'll notice as you look at the source code included in the book is that I've paid special attention to the formatting of the code so that it can be easily read and understood by the reader. Rather than allowing the publisher to wrap the source code wherever necessary, instead I've forced page breaks in the code wherever possible in order to structure it in a way that should benefit the reader. Because of this, as you copy the source code over into your Cordova applications, you will likely find some extra line breaks that affect the functionality of the code. Sorry.

All of the book's source code is available on GitHub (https://github.com/johnwargo/ac4p); there you'll find the complete application source code in a format that will allow you to quickly copy the code into your apps.

The Book's Web Site

The book has its own web site at www.cordova4programming.com. I will post there any updates and errata to the book. I'll also answer questions I receive from readers. Please feel free to use the contact form on the book's web site to provide feedback and/or suggestions for the next edition as well.

Acknowledgments

This book wouldn't exist without the help of others; as you can see below, I had a lot of help. Thank you to everyone who helped me craft this manuscript, including:

- The Cordova dev team for their patience and support as I asked all of my silly questions.
- Raman Sethi, Bobby Anchanattu, Changhoon Baek, Rob Close, Ashwin Desai, Alan Kinzie, Pete Kong, Jonathan Li, Marcus Pridham, Dan Van Leeuwen, and my other colleagues at SAP for continuing to teach me new things about Apache Cordova every day.
- Colleagues Marcus Pridham and Ashwin Desai for again helping me sort out issues with the plugin examples used in the book.
- Brian LeRoux, Steven Gill, Dave Johnson, and Michael Brooks from Adobe for helping me through some issues and reviewing the PhoneGap-related chapters.
- Andrew Grieve from Google for helping me decide whether to cover ADT or Android Studio in this version of the book. Turns out I made the wrong choice, but there's not much I can do about that now.
- Olivier Block, Eric Mittelette, Parashuram Narasimhan, and Sergey Grebnov from Microsoft for helping me through some issues, reviewing the Windows chapter, and providing me with a device to use for testing applications.
- Piotr Zalewa from Mozilla for answering my questions and reviewing the Firefox OS chapter.
- Gorkem Ercan from Red Hat for getting me started with THyM.
- David Pitkin, David Barth, Maxim Ermilov, and Jean-François Moy from Ubuntu for answering my questions, reviewing the Ubuntu chapter, and providing me with a device to use for application testing.
- Ashwin Desai for doing yet another excellent technical review of the manuscript. You've got to love it when the tech reviewer treats the book like his own work and even makes sure that the comments in the sample source code are correct.
- Greg Doench, Michelle Housley, and Chris Zahn for all their help with this project.
- Julie Nahil, Susan Brown Zahn, Anna Popick, and Barbara Wood for their help producing the book.
- My managers at SAP for supporting this endeavor.

Apologies to anyone I may have missed here.

Acknowledgments

About the Author

John M. Wargo is a professional software developer and a contributor to the Apache Cordova Project. John works for German software company SAP as part of the SAP Mobile Platform Product Management team. He is the product manager for the SAP Mobile Platform's Hybrid SDK, a set of enterprise plugins for Apache Cordova, and the SAP Fiori Client, a Cordova-based native application runtime for the SAP Fiori web application. He also works with the team at SAP building the SAP Web IDE Hybrid App Toolkit (HAT), a set of tools that add support for Apache Cordova applications to the SAP Web IDE (a cloud-based web application designer and editor based on the Apache Orion project).

This is his fourth book on Apache Cordova. He got started with mobile development while working at Research In Motion, now called BlackBerry, and eventually wrote the first book on BlackBerry development. He wrote a series of articles covering methods for mobilizing IBM Domino applications for *The View*, a magazine for IBM Lotus Notes and Domino developers, which was eventually published into an anthology.

You can find him online at www.johnwargo.com and on Twitter at @johnwargo.

1

The What, How, Why, and More of Apache Cordova

This chapter is your introduction to Apache Cordova. I'll cover what it is, how developers use it to develop mobile applications, how it differs from Adobe PhoneGap, why it was created, how it's changed over time, where it's going, and more. You could skip this chapter if you wanted and dig into the more technical (and fun) stuff in the chapters that follow, but it's important to understand the heart of what you're working with before getting to all of the details.

As I read through many support forum posts, it seems clear to me that the developers who are just getting started with Apache Cordova don't really "get" what they're working with. This chapter should answer many of the initial who, what, where, when, how, and why questions you have related to Apache Cordova and Adobe PhoneGap.

An Introduction to Apache Cordova

Apache Cordova (http://cordova.apache.org) is a free, open-source framework for building cross-platform native applications using HTML5. The creators of Apache Cordova wanted a simpler way of building cross-platform mobile applications and decided the best approach was to use a combination of native and web technologies. This type of mobile application is called a *hybrid* application.

To build a Cordova application, you create a web application (using whatever tools and user interface [UI] frameworks you want), then use some tools provided by the Cordova team and the software development kit (SDK) from one or more mobile device manufacturers to package the web application into a native application runtime container for each target platform. That's all there is to it.

Within the native application, the application's user interface consists of a single screen that contains nothing but a single native WebView object that consumes the available screen space on the device. When the application launches, it loads the packaged web application's startup page (typically index.html, but the developer can easily change this to something else) into the WebView, then passes control to the WebView to allow the user to interact with the web application. As the user interacts with the application's content (the web application), links or JavaScript code within the application can load other content from within the resource files packaged with the application or can reach out to the network and pull content down from a web or application server.

You can also skip the packaging process and simply have the Cordova application load a remote web site if you want, although Apple doesn't like that type of application very much. You may find that Apple will reject a Cordova application that operates this way.

> **About WebViews**
>
> A WebView is a native application component that is used to render web content (typically HTML pages) within a native application window or screen. It's essentially a programmatically accessible wrapper around the built-in web browser included with the mobile device.
>
> For some examples, on Android it's implemented using a `WebView` view (using `android.webkit.WebView`), and on iOS it's a `UIWebView` (using `System/Library/Frameworks/UIKit.framework`).

The Cordova application packaging process is illustrated in Figure 1.1.

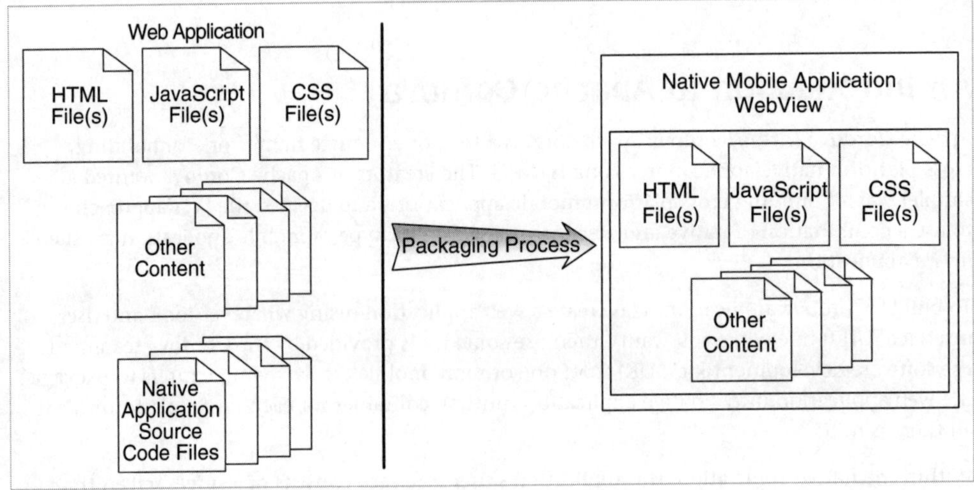

Figure 1.1 Apache Cordova Application Packaging Process

> **Note**
>
> When many developers first learn about this technology, they immediately assume that the web application code is somehow translated into the native language for each supported mobile device platform—converted into Objective-C for iOS or Java for Android, for example—but that's not what's happening here. There are some mobile application frameworks that take that approach, but for Cordova, the web application simply runs unmodified within a native application shell.

For some mobile device platforms such as Firefox OS, a native application is just a web application; there's no concept of a compiled native application that is deployed to devices. Instead, a specially packaged web application is what is executed on the device.

The web application running within the container is just like any other web application that would run within a mobile web browser. It can open other HTML pages (either locally or from a web server sitting somewhere on the network). JavaScript embedded within the application's source files implements needed application logic, loading, hiding, or unhiding content as needed within a page, playing media files, opening new pages, performing calculations, retrieving content from or sending content to a server. The application's look-and-feel is determined by any font settings, lines, spacing, coloring, or shading attributes added directly to HTML elements or implemented through Cascading Style Sheets (CSS). Graphical elements applied to pages can also help provide a theme for the application. Anything a developer can do in a web application hosted on a server can also be done within a Cordova application.

What Is Adobe PhoneGap?

Adobe PhoneGap is simply a distribution of Apache Cordova with some extra stuff added to it. The PhoneGap developers are essentially the same folks from Adobe who work on the Cordova project. At its core are the Cordova container, application programming interface (API) plugins, and tools described throughout this book. As Adobe's primary business is selling tools and services, the PhoneGap implementation of Cordova more tightly integrates the framework with Adobe's other products.

The primary differences between Cordova and PhoneGap are the command-line tools, the PhoneGap Build service, and the recently released PhoneGap Developer App. The PhoneGap command-line tools provide a command-line interface into the PhoneGap Build service; I'll cover the Adobe PhoneGap Build service in Chapter 12, "Using PhoneGap Build." You'll find the PhoneGap command-line interface (CLI) commands described in Chapter 13, "Using the PhoneGap CLI," and the PhoneGap Developer App in Chapter 5, "The Mechanics of Cordova Development."

Throughout the remainder of the book (except in the history section that follows), when I refer to PhoneGap, I'm talking about a specific capability that is available only in the PhoneGap version of Cordova. Both versions are free; PhoneGap simply adds some additional capabilities to Cordova.

A Little PhoneGap/Cordova History

PhoneGap was started at the 2008 iPhoneDevCamp by Nitobi, who started the project as a way to simplify cross-platform mobile development. The project began with a team of developers working through a weekend to create the skeleton of the framework—the core functionality plus the native application container needed to render web application content on the iPhone. After the initial build of the framework, the PhoneGap project team quickly added support for Android with BlackBerry following a short time thereafter.

In 2009, PhoneGap won the People's Choice Award at the Web 2.0 Expo LaunchPad competition. Of course, being a project for geeks, the conference attendees voted for the winner by Short Message Service (SMS) from their mobile phones.

Over time, the PhoneGap developers have added support for additional hardware platforms and worked to ensure parity of API features across platforms. During this period, IBM started contributing to the project as did many other companies.

In late 2011, Nitobi announced that it was donating PhoneGap to the Apache Foundation. Very quickly thereafter, the next day as a matter of fact, Adobe announced that it was acquiring Nitobi. PhoneGap joined the open-source Apache project (www.apache.org) as an incubator project, first as Apache Callback, then briefly as Apache DeviceReady, and finally later (beginning with version 1.4) as Apache Cordova (the name of the street where the Nitobi offices were located when PhoneGap was created).

The acquisition of Nitobi by Adobe (and Adobe's subsequent announcement that it would discontinue support for Adobe Flash on mobile devices) clearly indicates that Adobe saw PhoneGap as an important part of its product portfolio. The folks at Nitobi who were working on PhoneGap in their spare time as a labor of love are now in a position where they can work full-time on the project. The result of this is that Cordova is one of the, if not the, most frequently updated Apache projects. The Cordova team was delivering new releases monthly, which is pretty amazing considering the complexity of the code involved, but the pace has slowed somewhat recently.

Cordova Components

Apache Cordova consists of the following components:

- Source code for a native application container for each of the supported mobile device platforms. The container renders the web application content on the device. On platforms where the native application is a web application, no container exists.
- A suite of APIs, implemented as plugins, that provide a web application running within the container access to native device capabilities (and APIs). More on this in the next section.
- A set of tools used to manage the process of creating application projects, managing plugins, building (using native SDKs) native applications, and testing applications on

mobile device simulators and emulators. The available tools are described in detail in many of the later chapters in the book.

- Documentation for each of the tools and APIs.

Access to Native APIs

At this point, you're probably thinking that this is no big deal; you can already create a web application and save a link to that web application on a mobile device's home screen for easy access. The difference here is in what the web application can do when it is running inside the Cordova container: access native APIs not available in the mobile browser.

At the time all of this started, the best way to build a mobile application that worked on multiple mobile devices was to build it using HTML. Unfortunately, though, for mobile developers, many mobile applications needed to do more than HTML and web browsers could support; building a web application that interacted with the device camera or the local contacts application, for example, simply wasn't possible. To get around this, Cordova implements a suite of APIs that extend native device capabilities to a web application running within the native container.

A typical mobile web browser application does not usually have access to device-side applications, hardware, and native APIs. For example, the contacts application is not accessible to web applications, nor can a web application typically interact with the accelerometer, camera, compass, microphone, and more or determine the status of the device's network connection. The typical native mobile application, on the other hand, makes frequent use of those capabilities. To be an interesting mobile application (interesting to prospective application users anyway), a mobile application will likely need access to those native device capabilities.

Cordova accommodates that need by providing a suite of JavaScript APIs that a developer can leverage to allow a web application running within the Cordova container to access device capabilities outside of the web context. Essentially these APIs are implemented in two parts: a JavaScript library that exposes the native capabilities to the web application and the corresponding native code running in the container that implements the native part of the API. The project team would essentially have one JavaScript library but separate native implementations on each supported mobile device platform. JavaScript access to native APIs is made available through the JavaScript to native bridge built into the Cordova container.

In versions of Apache Cordova prior to Cordova 3.0, all of the Cordova APIs were built into the Cordova container and were automatically available to any application running in the container. Beginning with Cordova 3.0, each of the Cordova APIs was broken into separate plugins; you can use the Cordova CLI or Plugman, the Cordova plugin manager, to add and remove plugins from your Cordova projects. We'll talk more about plugins and the Cordova tools later in this chapter and throughout the book.

The Cordova plugin architecture is illustrated in Figure 1.2—an application with discrete code for each plugin and where only the needed plugins are packaged with the application.

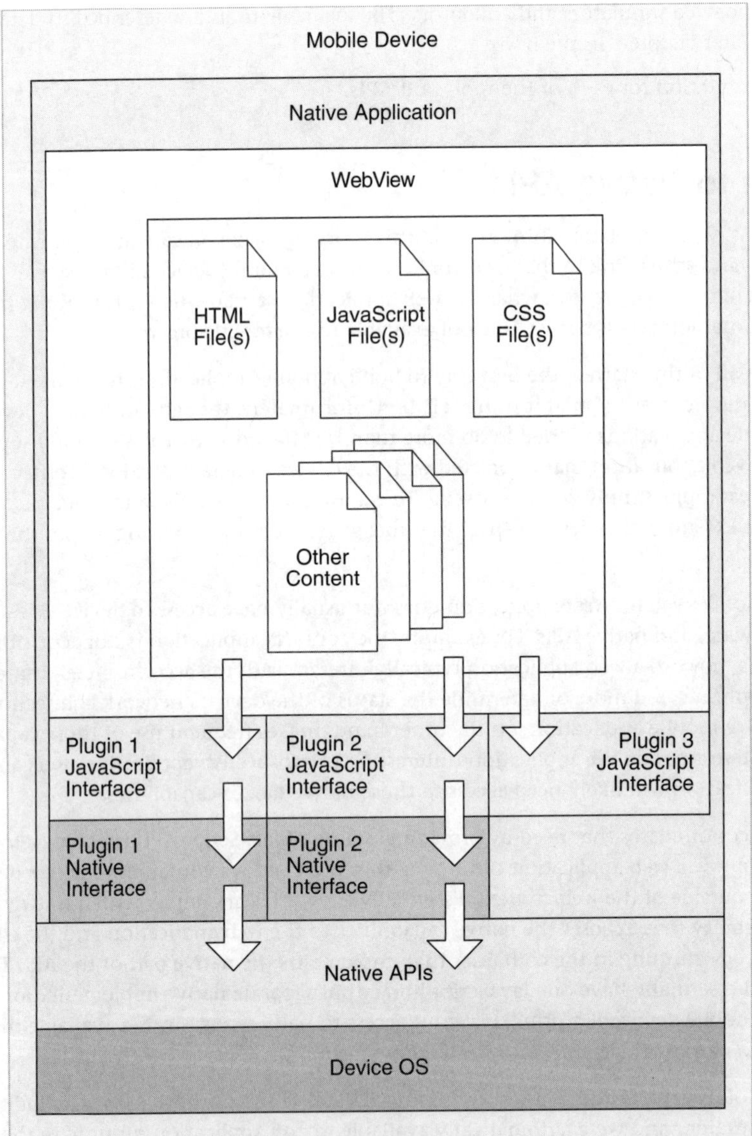

Figure 1.2 Apache Cordova Native Application Architecture

Cordova currently provides the following core APIs:

- Battery Status
- Camera

- Console
- Contacts
- Device
- Device Motion
- Device Orientation
- Dialogs
- FileSystem
- File Transfer
- Geolocation
- Globalization
- InAppBrowser
- Media
- Media Capture
- Network Information
- Splashscreen
- StatusBar
- Vibration

The Device Motion API is commonly referred to as the Accelerometer API, the Device Orientation API is called the Compass API, and the Network Information API is the Connection API. Most of these APIs are described and demonstrated in Chapter 14, "Working with the Cordova APIs"; more complete coverage of each of the Cordova APIs (about 300 pages' worth) can be found in this book's companion: the *Apache Cordova API Cookbook* (www.cordovacookbook.com).

When a developer implements a feature in an application that uses one of the Cordova APIs, the application calls the API using JavaScript, and then a special layer within the application translates the Cordova API call into the appropriate native API for the particular feature. As an example, the way the camera is accessed on an Android device is different from how it's done for iOS, so this common API layer allows a developer to implement a single interface that is translated behind the scenes (within the container application or the plugin's code) into the appropriate native API for each supported mobile platform.

To take a picture in a mobile application using Cordova and the default options for the API, the JavaScript code would look like this:

```
navigator.camera.getPicture(successCallback, errorCallback);
```

As parameters, the application passes in the names of two callback functions, `successCallback` and `errorCallback`, which are called once a picture has been captured or when an error is encountered.

On Android the code being executed by the function might look something like this:

```
camera.takePicture( shutterCallback, rawCallback, jpegCallback );
```

However, on iOS, the code might look like this:

```
UIImagePickerController *imgPckr =
  [[UIImagePickerController alloc] init];
imgPckr.sourceType =
  UIImagePickerControllerSourceTypeCamera;
imgPckr.delegate = self;
imgPckr.allowsImageEditing = NO;
[self presentModalViewController:imgPckr
  animated:YES];
```

The code samples listed here don't cover all aspects of the process of taking a picture (such as dealing with errors or processing the resulting image), but the examples illustrate how Cordova simplifies cross-platform mobile development. A developer makes a single call to a common API available across all supported mobile platforms, and Cordova translates the call into something appropriate for each target platform. This eliminates the need for developers to have intimate knowledge of the underlying technologies, instead allowing them to focus on their application and their application's capabilities rather than how to accomplish the same task across multiple device types.

JavaScript-Only Plugins

In Figure 1.2, you may have noticed that Plugin 3 doesn't have any native code associated with it. For the most part, a Cordova plugin exists to allow a developer to expose a native device API to a web application to use. However, there is no reason why the plugin must include native code. While adding capabilities to a web application through JavaScript can be easily accommodated using a simple JavaScript library loaded by the web application, it can also be accomplished by simply adding the JavaScript code to a plugin and adding the plugin to a Cordova project.

As mentioned previously, for some platforms such as Firefox OS, a mobile application is a web application, so there is no native code that can be executed by the plugin. For these platforms, all plugins are JavaScript-only plugins.

Additionally, over time, more and more native capabilities exposed by Cordova APIs are being implemented as standard features in the browser. For specific features on these platforms, there wouldn't be any need for native code—the plugin might simply contain the JavaScript code needed to initialize the browser capability or translate the Cordova API signature into the appropriate code for the target platform. For platforms that don't support the feature, native code would still be needed, but where the feature is available in the browser natively, only JavaScript code will be needed. If the particular feature aligned with a standard Cordova had already implemented, there would actually be no native code at all as the API would simply already be available within the WebView.

I will show you in Chapter 16, "Creating Cordova Plugins," how to create a JavaScript-only plugin to use in your Cordova applications.

As with any developer tool, there are times when the base functionality provided by the solution just isn't enough for your particular needs. Every developer, it seems, wants that one thing that's not already in there. Even though Cordova provided a solid set of API capabilities through plugins, the Cordova project team published a solid specification for plugins so developers could build their own.

With that in place, developers started creating all sorts of plugins. There's a Facebook plugin (https://github.com/phonegap/phonegap-facebook-plugin), an Urban Airship plugin for push notifications (http://docs.urbanairship.com/build/phonegap.html), and one of the most popular plugins, ChildBrowser, eventually became a part of the core Cordova API as InAppBrowser.

To help developers find plugins, the Cordova team published a Cordova Plugin Registry at http://plugins.cordova.io/. Developers can browse the catalog to locate useful plugins for their applications. They can easily publish plugins to the registry using Plugman; I'll show you how in Chapter 16. Figure 1.3 shows the Plugin Registry web site.

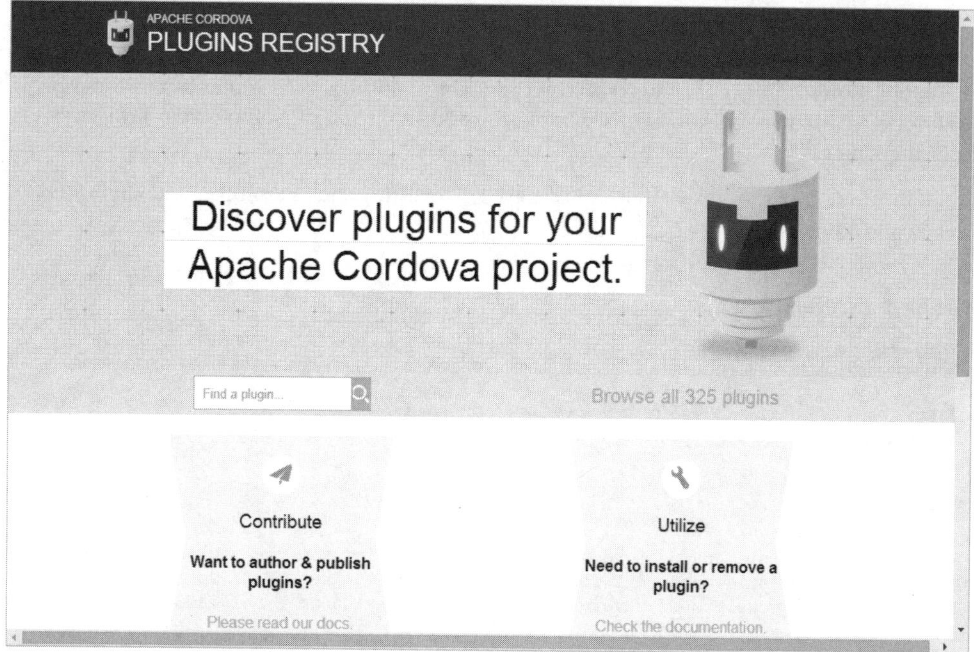

Figure 1.3 Cordova Plugin Registry Home Page

Notice that there aren't many plugins in the registry—only 325 on the day this screen was captured; I expect the list to continue to grow over time. There's also a third-party plugin registry called PlugReg available at www.plugreg.com.

Cordova User Interface Capabilities

One of the things I've noticed from trolling the Cordova and PhoneGap support forums and reading the Cordova dev list is that, from time to time, developers working with Apache Cordova seem to expect the Cordova framework to deliver some sort of UI capability on top of what it already delivers. They seem to be missing the point that Cordova is simply all about web applications running in a native context with access to native capabilities—nothing more.

The UI capabilities provided by Cordova? None . . . mostly.

Here's the deal. If you're a developer, you should already know that developers are pretty picky. They all have their own approach to writing code and what tools and frameworks they like to use. For every tool or framework a developer likes, there are many more that are loathed. When it comes to web application UIs, the public face of the application, developers can be even more critical—they tend to settle on one approach (using a single framework or possibly a collection of tools) and scorn all others. Any UI capabilities implemented by the Cordova team might be used by some developers, but many would ignore them and use whatever other approach they were comfortable with.

For that reason (mostly), the Cordova team focuses its efforts on the container, APIs, and tools and leaves the UI to others.

A Cordova application is a web application, so the UI for the application will be rendered using the application's HTML, CSS, and JavaScript code. The application's UI comes from whatever features of HTML you use, what CSS elements you add, and what capabilities your JavaScript code implements.

As an illustration of this, take a look at Listing 1.1. The listing shows a simple, uncomplicated web application.

Listing 1.1 Example 1.1

```
<!DOCTYPE HTML>
<html>
<head>
  <title>Example 1.1</title>
</head>
<body>
  <h1>Example 1.1</h1>
  <p>This is a sample Apache Cordova application. Notice how the application's UI is
pretty boring. This is because I didn't do anything to make the UI special. Instead,
this application consists of a very simple HTML page with no embellishments.</p>
```

```
  <p>The application UI is implemented using the default settings for the mobile
device's webView.</p>
</body>
</html>
```

When you run the application on a mobile device, you will see something similar to what is shown in Figure 1.4 (in this case the application is running on an Android emulator).

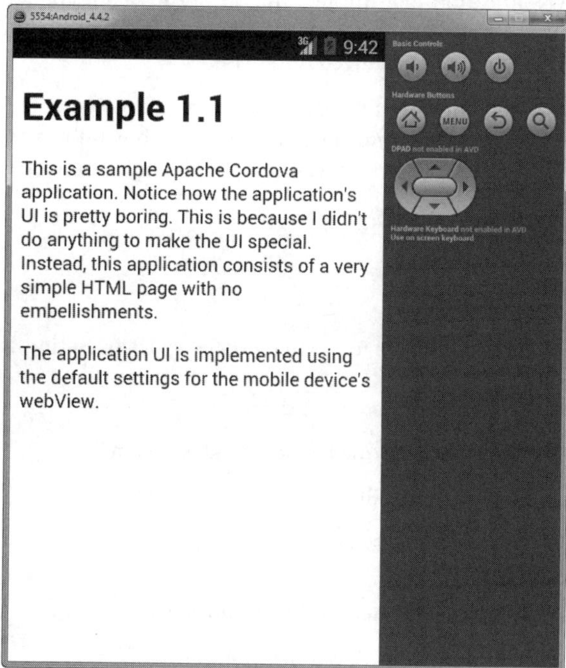

Figure 1.4 A Simple Cordova Application

In this example, the look-and-feel of the application has not been specified, so the browser simply renders it using its standard settings for headings and paragraphs. Not very pretty, right? That's because I've done no work to make the application pretty. This example actually looks much worse on a desktop browser; at least the mobile device browsers have pleasant default fonts and styles.

If I added some CSS to the page, I could dramatically change the look-and-feel of the application. For your applications, you won't want to stick with what the browser gives you; instead, use the UI framework that makes the most sense for you and your application's requirements. There are a ton of them out there to choose from; find one you like and put it to good use since Cordova is not going to do it for you.

In Chapter 17, "Using Third-Party UI Frameworks with Cordova," I'll show you how to use some popular HTML5 frameworks for your Cordova applications and will even highlight some that are especially made for hybrid application development. I've used jQuery Mobile (www.jquerymobile.com) and Topcoat (www.topcoat.io) for application UIs in my previous Cordova books; for this one I'm going to add a few more just so you can easily see what's possible (and to give myself more experience with other frameworks).

Where Cordova does add some UI capabilities is when a particular API needs to show the user something. For example, when using the Camera API to capture a photograph, the API simply invokes the device's Camera application and uses its UI to perform the photo capture. Additionally, the Cordova Notification API (through the use of the Dialogs plugin) implements alert and prompt dialogs an application can use—the content of the dialogs is under programmatic control, but the dialog UI cannot be changed otherwise.

The only other place where I know that the Cordova team has implemented a UI is in the InAppBrowser plugin. InAppBrowser implements a browser sub-window you can use in your applications, and in order to enable certain features, the plugin in some cases renders its own browser chrome.

Supported Platforms

Apache Cordova currently supports the following mobile device operating system platforms:

- Android (Google)—http://developer.android.com
- BlackBerry 10 (BlackBerry)—https://developer.blackberry.com/
- Firefox OS—https://developer.mozilla.org/en-US/Firefox_OS/
- Fire OS (Amazon)—https://developer.amazon.com/appsandservices/solutions/platforms/android-fireos/
- iOS (Apple)—https://developer.apple.com/devcenter/ios/index.action
- Tizen (Linux Foundation)—https://developer.tizen.org
- Ubuntu (Canonical)—http://developer.ubuntu.com/
- Windows Phone 8 (Microsoft)—http://developer.windowsphone.com/en-us
- Windows (Microsoft)—http://msdn.microsoft.com

You can find the complete list of supported operating systems plus the specific capabilities that are supported at http://goo.gl/wKqoZL. Additional platforms are available as well. Cordova has in the past supported WebOS, Samsung bada, and other target platforms; the code for those platforms is still available, usually on GitHub. It seems as if new platforms are constantly being added—I know there is a team working on Google Glass support, and another team is working on implementing Cordova on Sugar Learning Platform (www.sugarlabs.org).

For this book, I'm going to cover what are considered the most popular platforms, Android and iOS, plus some others that I find interesting such as Firefox OS, Windows (including Windows Phone 8), and Ubuntu.

It is important to note that when the Cordova project started, support for different mobile platforms was added primarily by an independent developer who was interested in the framework and wanted it to run on the devices he or she was working on. Over time, as Cordova became more popular and mainstream, the mobile device vendors got on board and helped with the implementation of Cordova on their platforms. The folks at BlackBerry are heavily involved with the BlackBerry implementation of Cordova, Google has a large team working on a bunch of stuff, Intel is involved in the Tizen implementation, and I know that Microsoft has been involved in the Windows implementation as well. What this means for developers is that even though Cordova is an open-source project, the device OS companies are heavily involved and have a vested interest in making this project successful. Sadly, only Apple has chosen not to support the framework directly.

Cordova License

Apache Cordova has been released under the Apache License, Version 2.0. You can find more information about the license at www.apache.org/licenses/LICENSE-2.0.

Working with Cordova

Now that you know a little bit about Cordova, let's dig into how to build mobile applications using the framework. In this section, I'll describe how to design your web application so it will run in the container, then describe how to use the available tools to package your web application into a native mobile application.

In subsequent chapters, I'll give you a detailed analysis of the anatomy of a Cordova application (Chapter 2, "Anatomy of a Cordova Application"), information on how to use third-party frameworks with Apache Cordova (Chapter 17), the mechanics of Apache Cordova development (Chapter 5), and a walk-through of the complete, end-to-end development process (Chapter 15, "Cordova Development End to End").

Designing for the Container

Cordova applications are web applications running inside a client-side native application container. Because of this, web applications running within a Cordova application leverage an HTML5 offline application structure rather than that of a traditional server-based web application.

In old-school, traditional web applications, a web server serves up either static HTML pages or dynamic pages to the requesting user agent (the browser). With dynamic pages, a server-side language or scripting language is used to retrieve dynamic content (from a database, for example) and format it all into HTML before sending it to the browser. When the browser makes a request, the server retrieves the containing page and content, massages it all into HTML, and sends it to the browser to be displayed.

In this example, the browser doesn't need any intelligence with regard to the content; it merely requests a page and the server does most of the work to deliver the requested content. On the browser, the application can leverage client-side JavaScript code to allow the user to interact with the content on the page, but in general, most of the work is done by the server.

With the advent of Web 2.0, a reduced load is placed on the web server and instead, JavaScript code running within the browser manages the requesting and presentation of data. The web server delivers an HTML-based wrapper for the web application, and JavaScript code delivered with the page dynamically manages the content areas of the page, moving data in and out of sections of the page as needed.

What allowed Web 2.0 applications to be successful was the addition of the XMLHTTPRequest (XHR) API in JavaScript. This API allows a web application to submit asynchronous requests to a server and process the data whenever it returns from the server, without interrupting the user's activity within the application.

This approach allows for much more interesting web applications, applications that can easily look and feel like native desktop applications. The web server is still involved, serving up the pages and the content to the browser, but it does less direct manipulation of the data. Google Maps (maps.google.com) and Google Gmail (mail.google.com) are good examples of Web 2.0 applications available today.

Mobile devices need a slightly different approach. Web 1.0 and 2.0 technologies work great on smartphones, but Web 1.0 apps caused a lot of data to be transmitted between server and device; Web 2.0 apps were cooler but still required constant network connectivity to operate.

With HTML5, web applications can make use of new capabilities that allow an application to operate more efficiently on a mobile device (or devices with limited connectivity). With HTML5, web applications can make use of a client-side database to store application data. This makes it easier for mobile devices to operate as they go in and out of wireless coverage. Additionally, HTML5 supports the addition of a manifest file that lists all of the files that constitute the web application. When the web application's index file loads, the browser will read the manifest file, retrieve all of the files listed in the manifest, and download them to the client device. If a mobile device were to lose network connectivity, and the files listed in the manifest are available on-device, the application can continue working—using any data that might be stored locally.

Hybrid applications don't leverage the manifest file I spoke of in the previous paragraph; the reason I brought it up was that typically hybrid applications expect all of their web application assets to be available within the container, similarly to what is enabled in the browser with the manifest file.

To run within a hybrid container like Apache Cordova, a web application should be written so it is able to run completely within the container. The index.html file is typically the only HTML file in the application, and the application's different "screens" are actually just different `<div>` containers that are switched in and out as needed by the application. HTML5 applications will still reach out to a server for data as needed, using XHR to request data asynchronously and store it locally. Cordova applications don't have to be written this way; it's just how it's typically done today.

> **Note**
>
> Web applications coded in PHP, ASP.NET, JSP, and the like will not run unmodified in the Cordova container. Those applications are designed to run on a web server, and the application's pages are preprocessed by special software running on the web server before output (typically HTML) is sent to the browser.
>
> I see a lot of support forum posts where developers ask how to get a server-based web application built with one of those technologies to run in the Cordova container. There's no processor for PHP, ASP.NET, and the other files available in the container, so it simply won't work. Those applications must be rewritten so that there's a stand-alone web application running in the Cordova container that then reaches back to the web server for the dynamic content generated by the server using one of those technologies (PHP, ASP.NET, and so on).

Web developers must rethink their approach to web development to leverage these capabilities. Instead of retrieving a web application from a web server, the HTML5 application running in the Cordova container must be self-contained, making sure it has the files and data it needs to at least launch and display a UI before optionally reaching out to a remote server for additional content and data. As mentioned earlier, when a Cordova application launches, it loads the web application's startup page (typically index.html) and associated content (CSS files, JavaScript files) before passing control to the web app. In order for this to work, the resources the app needs to start have to be located within the container.

There are some Cordova developers who load as little as possible within the container and immediately after startup run off to a server to get the "real" content for the application; I see their questions on the support forums all the time. This approach works, but it's not the best experience for users and may cause you problems with app store submissions—some smartphone platforms (Apple iOS, for example) don't like it when your app doesn't contain content and is merely a shell for a web application being hosted by a web server.

For a great presentation on how to write a web application for Apache Cordova, watch Lyza Danger Gardner's presentation from PhoneGap Day 2013 entitled "PhoneGap Self-defense for Web Devs" (www.youtube.com/watch?v=J0aQoor3OGE)—it was amazing. She did an excellent job of describing the approach one must take to craft a mobile web application that "works" in the Cordova container.

Coding Cordova Applications

As mentioned previously, Cordova applications are built using normal, everyday web technologies such as HTML, CSS, and JavaScript. Whatever you want your application to do, if you can make it work using standard web technologies, you can make it work in a Cordova application. Cordova applications can do more than standard web applications, through the specialized plugins provided by the framework and third-party developers that I discussed earlier.

The Cordova project doesn't currently offer or support any special editor for writing Cordova applications; you simply need to dig out your web content editor of choice and start coding. To keep things simple, you could use default tools like Notepad on Microsoft Windows or TextEdit on a Macintosh. You could even use something more sophisticated such as Adobe Dreamweaver (www.adobe.com/products/dreamweaver.html) or the Eclipse integrated development environment (IDE) (www.eclipse.org).

For my previous Cordova books, I coded all of the sample applications using the open-source Aptana Studio (www.aptana.com); it's an Eclipse-based IDE tailored for web development. It's a little lighter-weight than Eclipse and allowed me to easily format the project source code for easy importing into this manuscript (two spaces instead of tabs, all code properly aligned, and so on).

Adobe offers a free, open-source code editor called Brackets (http://brackets.io) that I've been playing around with. It provides a nice, clean interface for coding web applications. As it's an Adobe product, there are both Cordova and PhoneGap plugins for it. It is a relatively new tool, and it already has a robust set of plugins available for it. For this book, I did all of my web application coding using Brackets. I'll show you how to use Brackets in Chapter 18, "Using Third-Party Tools with Cordova."

Building Cordova Applications

Once you have a completed web application, whether it uses any of the Cordova APIs or not, it has to be packaged into a native application that will run on-device. Each of the mobile device platforms supported by the Cordova project has its own proprietary tools for packaging or building native applications. To build a Cordova application for each supported mobile platform, the application's web content (the HTML, CSS, JavaScript, and other files that constitute the application) must be added to an application project appropriate for each mobile platform, then built using the platform's proprietary tools. What's challenging about this process is that each mobile platform uses completely different tools, and application projects use different configuration files and most likely a different project folder structure.

Additionally, some of the supported mobile platform development tools will run only on certain desktop operating systems. For example:

- The Android SDK runs on Linux, Microsoft Windows, and Macintosh OS X.
- The BlackBerry SDKs (there are several) run on Linux, Microsoft Windows, and Macintosh OS X.
- The iOS SDK runs only on Macintosh OS X (no surprise there).
- The Ubuntu SDK runs only on Linux, most likely only Ubuntu (no surprise there either, I hope).
- The Windows Phone SDK runs only on Microsoft Windows (no surprise there either).

What this means for developers is that to work with the most popular smartphones (you can argue with me later about whether BlackBerry and Windows Phone are popular), you're going to have to have at a minimum development systems running both Windows and Macintosh OS X. This process is highlighted in Figure 1.5.

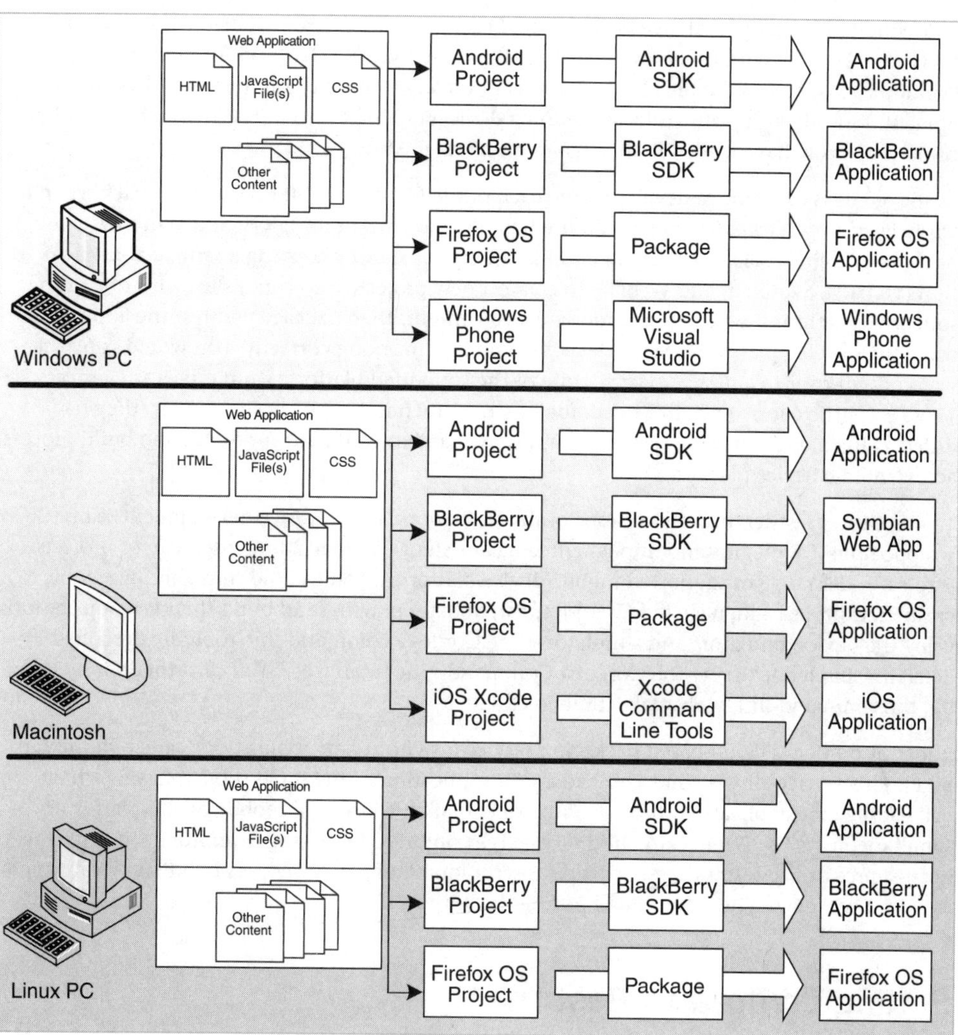

Figure 1.5 Cordova Application Build Process

For my Cordova development work, I use a loaded Macintosh Mini (Intel I7 Quad Core, 16GB memory, 1TB hard drive) running VMware Fusion (http://goo.gl/cd720d); this configuration allows me to easily run both Windows-based and Macintosh-based SDKs and seamlessly share files between both operating systems. I installed the software development kits for Macintosh on the machine's OS X partition: Xcode, Ant, NodeJS, Android Developer Tools (ADT), Firefox (for Firefox OS development), and so on. Next, I configured a virtual machine (VM) for Windows 7 and Windows 8 (using legal, licensed copies of each, of course) and installed the compatible tools and SDKs for Windows as well. Fusion allows me to easily share OS X folders with the Windows VMs, so I could quickly share project files across all of the systems. For Ubuntu development, I installed Ubuntu and the SDK on a dedicated Linux system I have in my office, but I could very easily have loaded it all in a VM on my Mac Mini.

In the old days of Cordova development (back in the PhoneGap 1.0 time frame—back when I wrote *PhoneGap Essentials*), you would use IDE plugins (on Android, iOS, and Windows Phone) or command-line tools (on Android and BlackBerry) or start by copying a sample application (on bada, Symbian, and WebOS) to create a new project. You would start with one of the supported platforms, write the appropriate web content, then package and test the application using the selected platform's SDK. Once you had it all working correctly, you would copy the web content over to a new project for one of the supported platforms and repeat the process. There was little consistency in project folder structure, framework JavaScript files (they had different file names on some platforms and were markedly different for each), and build process across mobile device platforms.

To make things easier, in later versions of the framework, the Cordova development team scrapped the IDE plugins and implemented a consistent command-line interface for projects across a wider range of supported mobile device platforms. You use the command-line tools to create new projects, manage (add, remove, list, update) plugins, and build then test applications using the device emulators and simulators. The Cordova command-line tools are described in detail in Chapter 4, "Using the Cordova Command-Line Interfaces." You can still do it by hand, but the command-line tools make it much easier.

Adobe also offers a cloud-based packaging service for PhoneGap applications called PhoneGap Build. This service allows you to upload a web application to the Build service servers which will package the application into a PhoneGap container for several mobile device platforms simultaneously. The PhoneGap Build service is a commercial offering from Adobe; it's free for open-source projects, but there are paid subscription plans for developers building private applications. I will cover PhoneGap Build in Chapter 12.

Putting Cordova to Best Use

There are people who try to categorize the types of apps you should or should not build with a hybrid container. I really don't approve of that approach. The hybrid application approach used by Cordova has strengths and weaknesses—and you have to assess your particular mobile application needs against them and decide on a case-by-case basis whether the Cordova approach is the right one for your application.

Web applications are likely going to be slower than native applications, but an inexperienced developer can easily build a native application that performs poorly (without even trying very hard it seems). You can read about Facebook ditching HTML5 and switching to native for performance reasons (http://goo.gl/Am4X2s), but then you can read how Sencha was able to build a suitably fast web version of the Facebook application using its HTML5 framework (http://goo.gl/ezXGaH).

Hybrid applications may be slower than a native mobile application in most cases; it's just the nature of the technology being used. On the other hand, there are many games that have been created using Cordova, so if Cordova performs well enough for games, it should be OK for many of the applications you need to write. In the past, both Android and iOS used a different engine in the WebView than they did for their mobile browsers. With the latest Android (Version 4.4.x) and iOS (iOS 8), the WebView used by Cordova uses the same rendering engine, and therefore has the same performance, as the default, built-in browser on the device.

There are a lot of commercial applications available today that were built using Cordova; you can find a list of many of the applications on the PhoneGap web site at www.phonegap.com/app. The framework is used primarily for consumer applications (games, social media applications, utilities, productivity applications, and more) today, but more and more enterprises are looking at Cordova for their employee-facing applications as well. There are many commercial mobile development tools with Cordova inside and likely more in the works.

So where should you use Cordova? Use it anywhere you feel comfortable using it. Do some proofs of concept of your application's most critical and complicated features to make sure you can implement them in HTML and you'll get the performance you need from the framework.

The issues I see are

- Can you implement the app you want using HTML? There are so many JavaScript and CSS frameworks out there to help simplify mobile web development that most things a developer wants to do in an application can be done in HTML.
- Can you get the performance you need from a hybrid application? That you'll have to prove with some testing.

So, where does it fail?

Early on, Cordova would fail when you wanted to build an application that needed access to a native API that wasn't already exposed through the container. Nowadays with all of the plugins available you're likely to find one that suits your application's requirements—if not, write your own plugin and donate it to the community. Cordova doesn't (today) have access to the calendar or email client running on the device, so if your application has requirements for those features, you may be out of luck—although don't forget about plugins.

If your application needs to interface with a particular piece of hardware (either inside the device or outside), Cordova might not be the best choice for you unless there's a plugin for the hardware.

If your application requires heavy-duty offline capabilities such as a large database and offline synchronization, you could run into issues. However, there are several HTML5-based sync engines that should work within a Cordova container, and there is a SQLite plugin for Android, iOS, and Windows Phone at http://goo.gl/SnihFb.

Try it out with some common use cases for your application and see what happens. If you are building an application with a large database and a bunch of heavy data entry forms, Cordova might not be the best choice, but you'll have to try it first and see.

Getting Support

One of the things corporations worry about is getting support for the software products they use for their business applications. An open-source project such as Linux wouldn't be as popular with companies if there weren't support options available to them. Since commercial support for Linux is provided by a wide range of companies including Red Hat, Canonical, SUSE, and others, organizations are much more willing to run their businesses on open-source software products. Cordova is no different.

While there is no Cordova support area, the best place I've found for getting support for the framework is the PhoneGap area in Google Groups (http://groups.google.com/group/phonegap). A lot of experienced developers monitor the list of questions, and you can usually get an answer there pretty quickly. You can even find me up there from time to time answering questions that I can.

There's also a support forum for PhoneGap Build located at http://goo.gl/MTNZIk. The forums are supposed to be for questions related to the PhoneGap Build service, but a lot of developers incorrectly use the forum for general PhoneGap development questions as well. Please do me a favor and use the Build forums for PhoneGap Build–related questions and the Google Groups area for any other PhoneGap-related questions. In my experience, you'll get a faster and sometimes better response to a PhoneGap development question in Google Groups.

Recently, the Cordova development team has started pointing support requests to Stack Overflow (http://stackoverflow.com/questions/tagged/cordova). They've created a special tag for Cordova questions and even map PhoneGap to the Cordova tag as well. Going forward this will be the primary source for Cordova and PhoneGap support.

Nitobi, and later Adobe, used to offer commercial support options for PhoneGap, but that option seems to be no longer available. Adobe recently announced PhoneGap Enterprise (http://enterprise.phonegap.com/), which is supposed to include a support offering, but months after the announcement there is still no information available for the offering.

Resources

There are many places online where you can find information about how to work with the Cordova and PhoneGap frameworks. Table 1.1 lists the different web sites where you can find information about Apache Cordova and Adobe PhoneGap.

To stay informed about what's going on with the project, you can sign up for the mailing lists at http://cordova.apache.org/#mailing-list. It you have some extra time, it is fun to read through the emails as the development team discusses the implementation of a new feature or tracks

Table 1.1 Cordova Resources

Resource	Link(s)
Cordova web site	http://cordova.io or http://cordova.apache.org (both point to the same site)
Cordova Documentation	http://docs.cordova.io
Cordova Wiki	http://wiki.cordova.io
Cordova Issue Tracker	https://issues.apache.org/jira/browse/CB
Cordova Mailing Lists	http://cordova.apache.org/#mailing-list
Cordova Twitter account	http://twitter.com/apachecordova
PhoneGap web site	http://www.phonegap.com
PhoneGap Wiki	http://wiki.phonegap.com
PhoneGap Blog	http://www.phonegap.com/blog
PhoneGap Twitter account	https://twitter.com/phonegap

down a bug. The dev mailing list is used by the developers of the Cordova framework to discuss issues and make decisions about the Cordova implementation. The Commits mailing list is for tracking commit logs for the Cordova repositories, when new or updated code is added to a version of the framework. The Issues mailing list is for conversations around bug and feature requests submitted to the Cordova Jira issue and bug tracking system at http://issues.apache.org/jira/browse/CB.

> **Warning**
>
> Please don't use the dev list to ask questions about Cordova development; use Google Groups or Stack Overflow instead. The dev lists are for the developers building Cordova to discuss feature implementation and so on, while the other options are set up specifically to provide Cordova and PhoneGap developers with answers to their questions.

You'll spend the majority of your time on the Apache Cordova Documentation site, which is shown in Figure 1.6. The site contains a complete reference to all of the Cordova APIs plus additional guides you'll need as you work with the framework.

While you're looking at the Documentation site, if you scroll down within either the left or the right side of the page, you will see the list of guides shown in Figure 1.6. These guides contain a lot of useful information a developer needs to work with the framework, including how to create plugins, using the command-line tools, and most importantly the getting-started guides for each of the supported mobile device platforms.

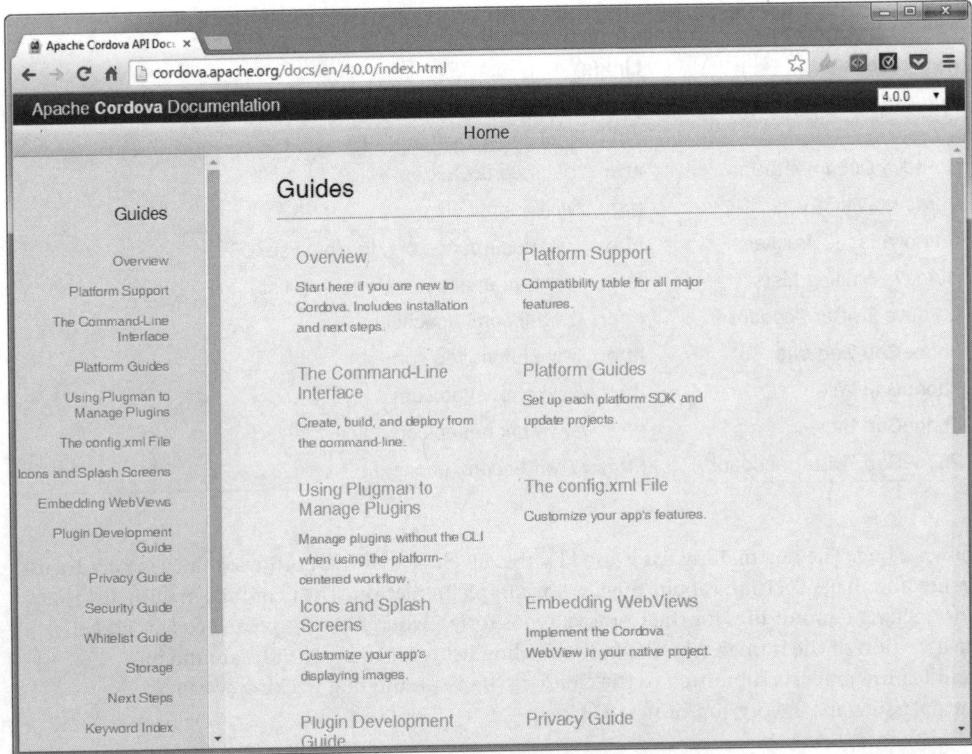

Figure 1.6 Apache Cordova Documentation

The API reference shown in Figure 1.7 includes a complete reference for all of the methods, properties, and events for each of the Cordova APIs. On the API pages, you'll also find sample source code and additional information you will need to make use of the APIs in your applications.

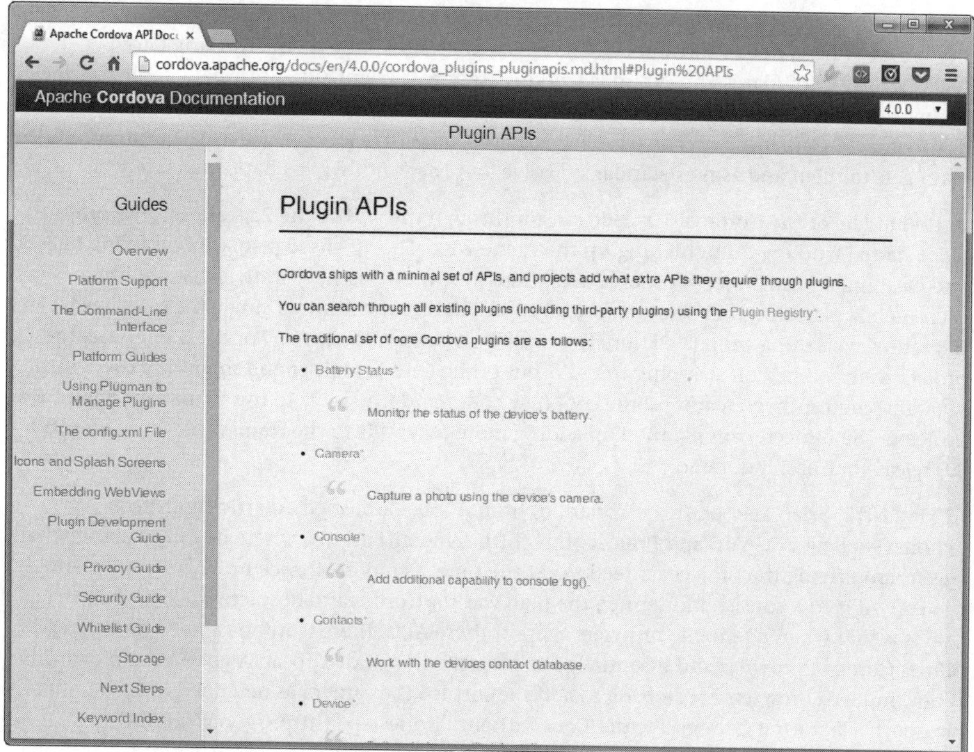

Figure 1.7 Cordova Documentation—Plugin APIs Section

The documentation is so much better than it was when I wrote *PhoneGap Essentials*, so it's probably a good place to start for anything Cordova related. Of course, my *Apache Cordova API Cookbook* (www.cordovacookbook.com) provides more thorough coverage of the APIs (with complete sample applications and detailed descriptions, with examples, of how each of the APIs actually works).

Cordova Going Forward

When you look at the project's description on its Apache project home page (http://cordova.apache.org/#about), you'll see that the project team describes itself almost entirely by the APIs Cordova implements.

The Cordova project's efforts around API implementation were initially guided by the World Wide Web Consortium (W3C) Device APIs and Policy (DAP) Working Group (www.w3.org/2009/dap). This group is working to "create client-side APIs that enable the development of Web Applications and Web Widgets that interact with device services such as Calendar, Contacts, Camera, etc." The plan was for additional APIs to be added as the Cordova project team gets to them and as new standards evolve, but that's not what's happened lately.

In the middle of the Cordova 1.x code stream through the end of the 2.x releases, the project team started working on tightening up the framework. They focused primarily on fixing bugs and cleaning up the project's code. Where there were previously separate JavaScript libraries for each mobile platform, they worked toward consolidating them into a single file (cordova.js) and migrating everything from the PhoneGap to the Cordova namespace. For the 3.0 release, the project team focused on stripping the APIs out of the core container and migrating them into separate plugins, then creating some cool new command-line tools to use to manage application projects. The project team planned on adding more new APIs to the framework soon after the 3.0 release but hasn't done so.

In May 2012, Brian LeRoux (http://brian.io) from Adobe published an article entitled "PhoneGap Beliefs, Goals, and Philosophy" (http://goo.gl/EmqtjA) where he talked about what was (then) driving the project's direction. At the time, as mobile device browsers implemented the DAP APIs in a consistent manner, the plan was for Cordova to obsolete itself. The expectation was that when all mobile browsers support these APIs, there won't be a need for the capabilities Cordova provides and essentially the project will just disappear. A good example of this is how modern browsers are starting to add support for the camera as described in Ray Camden's blog post "Capturing Camera/Picture Data without PhoneGap" (http://goo.gl/RPnD3E).

However, one of the things I noticed as I finished *PhoneGap Essentials* was that plugins were gaining in prominence in the Cordova space. The APIs provided by Cordova were interesting and helpful to developers, but developers wanted more. Where there were first only a few Cordova plugins available, now there are many, and the core APIs are plugins as well. So, Cordova becomes at its core just a hybrid container and everything else is done in plugins.

As the browsers implement additional APIs, the core Cordova APIs will become obsolete, but the Cordova container may live on. Cordova could still obsolete itself, but only in a time when the popular mobile browsers provide a standard interface to native APIs. As each platform's OS and API suite are different, I'm not sure how that would work out. It's the cross-platform development capabilities of Cordova that make it most interesting to the market; there's limited chance that the market will expose native APIs to the browser in a consistent enough way to keep cross-platform development viable.

Hybrid Application Frameworks

The hybrid application approach Cordova uses is not unique to the market. The Cordova project may have started the trend, but there are many other products on the market that use a similar approach. Here is a list of some of the products that use a hybrid application approach. Some are like Cordova and others are built with Cordova inside. This is only a subset of the available options in the hybrid mobile application space:

- Appcelerator Titanium
- AppGyver
- AT&T WorkBench and Antenna Software Volt (they're the same product)
- BlackBerry WebWorks
- IBM Worklight
- Oracle Application Development Framework (ADF) Mobile
- Salesforce Touch
- SAP Mobile Platform Hybrid SDK (Kapsel)
- Strobe (formerly SproutCore and now part of Facebook)
- Tiggr

Wrap-Up

In this chapter, I've given you a thorough (I think) overview of what Apache Cordova and Adobe PhoneGap are and how to work with the framework and the tools that are available. You now know a little bit of the history of the framework, where to get support, and what the future looks like for Cordova. Throughout the rest of the book, I'll start digging into the technical details of how all of this works—I'll dig into the tools and how to use them, talk about developing for some of the most popular mobile platforms, and even build an application or two.

Enjoy!

2

Anatomy of a Cordova Application

In the previous chapter, I provided you with an overview of Apache Cordova; before I start digging into all of the tools, capabilities, APIs, and so on, I want to give you a clear definition of what a Cordova application is. In this chapter, I show you what makes a web application a Cordova application and give you a tour of the sample application the Cordova team provides.

As mentioned at the beginning of the book, a Cordova application can do anything that can be coded in standard, everyday HTML, CSS, and JavaScript. There are web applications and Cordova applications, and the distinctions between them can be minor or can be considerable.

The sections in this chapter highlight different versions of the requisite HelloWorld application found in most any developer book, article, or training class. For the purpose of highlighting aspects of the applications' web content, rather than how they were created, the steps required to create the applications are omitted here (but covered in subsequent chapters).

Hello World!

As in any developer book, we're going to start with the default HelloWorld application, then build upon it to highlight different aspects of what makes a web application into a Cordova application. The HTML content shown in Listing 2.1 describes a very simple web page that displays some text; this application could easily run in a desktop or mobile browser.

Listing 2.1 Hello World #1 Application

```
<!DOCTYPE HTML>
<html>
<head>
  <title>Hello World #1</title>
</head>
<body>
```

```
  <h1>Hello World #1</h1>
  <p>This is a sample Apache Cordova application.</p>
</body>
</html>
```

If you open the web page in the mobile browser on a physical device or on a device emulator or simulator, you will see something similar to what is shown in Figure 2.1 (here it's running in an Android emulator). The browser simply renders the page the best it knows how to, in this case, trying to render it as if it's a full web page scaled to fit the smaller screen of the mobile device. Since it's the browser, the window also displays the browser chrome, the address field, tab controls, and so on from the mobile browser.

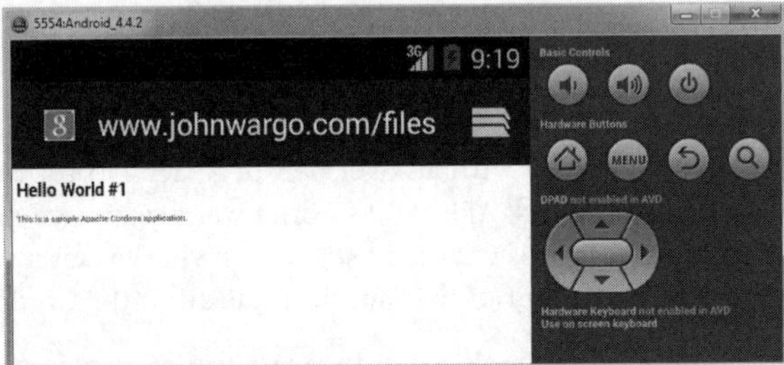

Figure 2.1 Hello World #1 Application Running in the Mobile Browser on an Android Emulator

This is not a Cordova application; it's just a web application running in a mobile browser.

If you package that same index.html file into a Cordova application (using the tools I will discuss throughout the book) and run it on a smartphone device or device emulator, the app will display something similar to what is shown in Figure 2.2.

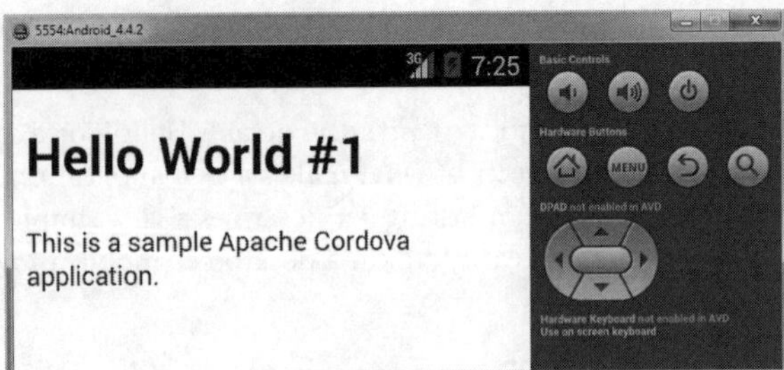

Figure 2.2 Hello World #1 Application Running on an Android Emulator

Here, the container seems to understand a bit about the view it's being rendered within and renders full size, not scaled down, so the whole page fits within the browser window.

In this example, this is a Cordova application because the web application has been packaged into the Cordova native application container. If I hadn't cropped the image, you would see that the web application consumes the entire screen of the emulated Android device. Even though

I'm running a web application, because it's running within a native application, there's no browser UI being displayed and no access to browser features. It's simply a native application rendering web content.

There is, however, nothing Cordova-ish about this application. It's running in the Cordova native container, but it isn't leveraging any of the APIs provided with the Cordova framework. Therefore, any web application can be packaged into a Cordova application—there's nothing forcing you to use the Cordova APIs. If you have a simple web application that simply needs a way to be deployed through a smartphone's native app store, for example, using Cordova is one way to accomplish that goal.

However, the app's not very interesting, is it? It's certainly not very pretty, but I'll show you how to fix that in Chapter 17, "Using Third-Party UI Frameworks with Cordova." For me, it needs to do some cool Cordova stuff before it becomes interesting.

Cordova Initialization

Now let's take the previous example application and add some Cordova-specific stuff to it.

Even though the Cordova container exposes native APIs to the web application running within it, in general (there are a few exceptions) those APIs are not available until the plugin that exposes the API has been added to the project. Additionally, the Cordova container has to do some prep work before any of its APIs can be utilized. To make it easy for developers to know when they can start using APIs exposed by the Cordova container, Cordova fires a specific event, the deviceready event, once it has finished its initialization and it's ready to go. Any application processing that requires the use of the Cordova APIs should be executed by the application only after it has received its notification that the Cordova container is available through the deviceready event.

The Hello World #2 application shown in Listing 2.2 has been updated to include code that uses a deviceready event listener to determine when the Cordova container application has completed its initialization. In this simple example, the application just displays an alert dialog when the event fires.

Listing 2.2 Hello World #2 Application

```
<!DOCTYPE html>
<html>
<head>
  <title>Hello World #2</title>
  <meta charset="utf-8" />
  <meta name="format-detection" content="telephone=no" />
  <meta name="viewport" content="user-scalable=no, initial-scale=1,
    maximum-scale=1, minimum-scale=1, width=device-width,
    height=device-height" />
  <script src="cordova.js"></script>
  <script>
```

```
    function onBodyLoad() {
      console.log("Entering onBodyLoad");
      alert("Body Load");
      document.addEventListener("deviceready", onDeviceReady, false);
    }

    function onDeviceReady() {
      console.log("Cordova is ready");
      navigator.notification.alert("Cordova is ready!");
    }

  </script>
</head>
<body onload="onBodyLoad()">
  <h1>Hello World #2</h1>
  <p>This is a sample Cordova application.</p>
</body>
</html>
```

> **Warning**
>
> If you copy the code from any of the listings in this chapter and try them in your own Cordova applications, you may notice that there are some extra carriage returns in the middle of some of the HTML. This was done to make the code render cleanly in the printed edition of the book. To download clean versions of all of the projects in this book, access the Code section of the book's web site at www.cordova4programming.com or get them from GitHub at https://github.com/johnwargo/ac4p.

On the iPhone simulator, the application will display the screen shown in Figure 2.3.

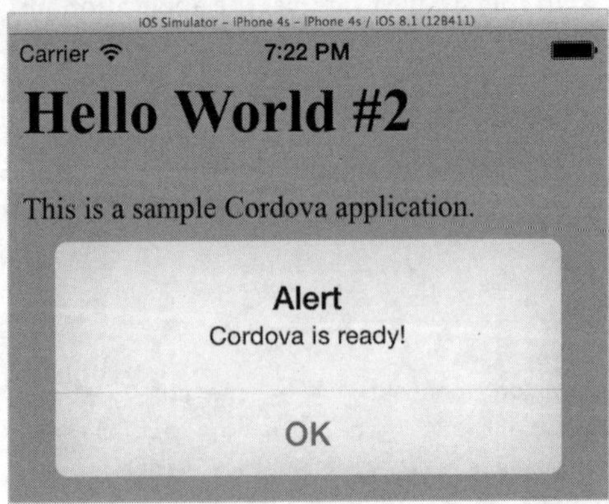

Figure 2.3 Hello World #2 Application Running on an iOS Simulator

Let's take a look at the sample application as there's a lot of new stuff in this example.

Within the `<head>` section of the web page are a few new entries, some meta tags that describe the content type for the application, and some other settings. For the most part, I pulled these meta tags from the default Cordova HelloCordova application described later in the chapter.

The `charset` tag identifies the character encoding used for the HTML document. What I've shown here is the default option; you would change this only if you were using a different character set for the HTML page.

```
<meta charset="utf-8" />
```

The next tag disables the embedded web browser's automatic processing of telephone numbers. With this option disabled, as shown below, the browser won't automatically turn phone numbers on the page into clickable links. You would need to change `telephone=no` to `telephone=yes` to enable this option.

```
<meta name="format-detection" content="telephone=no" />
```

Honestly, I'm really not sure why the Cordova team did this in their sample application; you would probably assume the user was running the application on a smartphone and would want phone numbers to be automatically enabled as links.

The viewport settings shown in the following tell the embedded web browser rendering the content how much of the available screen real estate should be used for the application and how to scale the content on the screen:

```
<meta name="viewport" content="user-scalable=no, initial-scale=1,
  maximum-scale=1, minimum-scale=1, width=device-width,
  height=device-height" />
```

In this case, the HTML page is configured to use the maximum height and width of the screen (through the `width=device-width` and `height=device-height` attributes) and to scale the content at 100% and not allow the user to change that in any way (through the `initial-scale=1`, `maximum-scale=1`, and `user-scalable=no` attributes).

> **Note**
>
> The viewport and associated attributes are not required. If they're omitted, the browser will revert to its default behavior, which may (or may not—who knows?) result in the application's content not consuming the full screen area available to it or zooming beyond it. Because there's not much content in the Hello World #2 application, it could, for example, consume only the upper half of the screen on some devices. You may also find that on some platforms the settings have no effect—all the more reason to test your Cordova applications on a variety of mobile devices before release.

There's also a new script tag in the code that loads the Cordova JavaScript library:

```
<script src="cordova.js"></script>
```

This loads the core Cordova API library and makes any core Cordova APIs available to the program. This file is also responsible for loading and initializing all of the plugins you have added to your Cordova application. You don't have to add the cordova.js file to your project; this is done for you automatically by the Cordova CLI (described in Chapter 4, "Using the Cordova Command-Line Interfaces"), but you do need to add this reference to your application.

To set up the deviceready event listener we need for Cordova, the application adds an `onload` event function to the application's body tag using the following:

```
<body onload="onBodyLoad()">
```

Within the `onBodyLoad` function, the code registers an event listener that instructs the application to call the `onDeviceReady` function when the Cordova container is ready, when the Cordova application container has finished its initialization routines and fired its deviceready event:

```
function onBodyLoad() {
  document.addEventListener("deviceready", onDeviceReady, false);
}
```

In this example application the `onDeviceReady` function simply displays a Cordova alert dialog (which is different from a JavaScript alert dialog) letting the user know everything's OK:

```
navigator.notification.alert("Cordova is ready!")
```

In production applications this function could update the UI with content created through API calls or do whatever other processing is required by the application. (You'll see an example of this in Listing 2.4.)

> **Note**
>
> Cordova applications fail silently when they encounter typos or syntax errors in a web application's code, so when you're testing an application, sometimes nothing will happen and you'll have no clue why. If you look at the complete source code for the application, you'll notice that there are a few things I haven't described yet that I do in every Cordova application I write to help me troubleshoot the application. These tricks help me more quickly understand what's happening in an application as it runs.

One of the things I do during testing is use the web browser console to display status messages as the application runs using code similar to the following:

```
console.log("Entering onBodyLoad");
```

I'll show you how this works in Chapter 5, "The Mechanics of Cordova Development."

In the `onBodyLoad` function, I also make sure to make a call to the JavaScript `alert` function so I can easily tell that the onload event has fired:

```
alert("Body Load");
```

Note

Unfortunately, the JavaScript `alert()` function is not available in universal Windows apps, so you will have to adjust your code when running on that platform. This topic is discussed further in Chapter 11, "Windows Development with Cordova."

As I mentioned earlier, the Cordova container fails silently when it encounters an error with the web application's source code. So, if I have this alert in the code and it doesn't fire, I know very quickly (in the very first code the application executes) that something is wrong with the application.

In the deviceready event handler, I always add a call to `navigator.notification.alert` as shown in the example code. This allows me to confirm visually that the deviceready event has actually fired, plus it allows me to confirm that the Cordova Dialogs plugin has been added to the project and that any other debug alerts I put into the code will be operational. I use the Cordova `alert` instead of the JavaScript `alert` because it's better looking (I can set the title of the dialog, for example, although I didn't do that here); it also gives me access to callback functions I can use to perform extra steps when something interesting happens.

Remember, most of the Cordova APIs have been removed from the container and implemented as plugins. So, to utilize the Cordova `alert` method, you must add the Dialogs plugin to your application by opening a terminal window to your Cordova project folder and issuing the following command:

```
cordova plugin add org.apache.cordova.dialogs
```

You'll learn all about how to use the `cordova` command in Chapter 4. You'll learn more about the Dialogs plugin in Chapter 14, "Working with the Cordova APIs."

The Cordova Navigator

Many of the APIs implemented by Cordova are instantiated from the Navigator object. Unfortunately it's not consistent; some APIs do it that way and some do not. Be sure to check the API documentation before calling an API.

The deviceready event will fire when the Cordova container finishes initializing, but it will also fire any time a new deviceready event listener is added by the application. Listing 2.3 shows this in action.

Listing 2.3 Hello World #3 Application

```
<!DOCTYPE html>
<html>
<head>
```

```
    <title>Hello World #3</title>
    <meta charset="utf-8" />
    <meta name="format-detection" content="telephone=no" />
    <meta name="viewport" content="user-scalable=no, initial-scale=1,
      maximum-scale=1, minimum-scale=1, width=device-width,
      height=device-height" />
    <script src="cordova.js"></script>
    <script>

      function onBodyLoad() {
        console.log("Entering onBodyLoad");
        alert("Body Load");
        document.addEventListener("deviceready", onDeviceReady, false);
      }

      function onDeviceReady() {
        console.log("Entering onDeviceReady");
        navigator.notification.alert("Cordova is ready!");
      }

      function addSecondDeviceReadyListener() {
        console.log("Entering addSecondDeviceReadyListener");
        document.addEventListener("deviceready", someOtherFunction, false);
      }

      function someOtherFunction() {
        console.log("Entering someOtherFunction");
        navigator.notification.alert("Second deviceready Function Fired.");
      }

    </script>
  </head>
  <body onload="onBodyLoad()">
    <h1>Hello World #3</h1>
    <p>This is a sample Cordova application.</p>
    <button onclick="addSecondDeviceReadyListener()">Add deviceready Event Listener</
button>
  </body>
</html>
```

In this example, I've added a button to the application's main page. When the button is tapped, an additional deviceready event listener is defined, and then the callback function for the new listener is immediately executed by the Cordova container. In this case, the `onDeviceReady` function executes once the container completes its initialization, and then the `someOtherFunction` function executes only after the second deviceready event listener has been added.

Leveraging Cordova APIs

Now that we know how to configure an application to wait until the Cordova APIs are available, let's build an application that actually uses some of the Cordova APIs. The Hello World #4 application shown in Listing 2.4 uses the Cordova Device API to allow the application to understand a bit about the environment it is running in.

Listing 2.4 Hello World #4 Application

```
<!DOCTYPE html>
<html>
<head>
  <title>Hello World #4</title>
  <meta charset="utf-8" />
  <meta name="format-detection" content="telephone=no" />
  <meta name="viewport" content="user-scalable=no, initial-scale=1,
    maximum-scale=1, minimum-scale=1, width=device-width,
    height=device-height" />
  <script src="cordova.js"></script>
  <script>
    var br = "<br />";

    function onBodyLoad() {
      console.log("Entering onBodyLoad");
      alert("Body Load");
      document.addEventListener("deviceready", onDeviceReady, false);
    }

    function onDeviceReady() {
      navigator.notification.alert("Cordova is ready!");
      console.log("Cordova: " + device.cordova);
      //Get the appInfo DOM element
      var element = document.getElementById('appInfo');
      //replace it with specific information about the device
      //running the application
      element.innerHTML =
        'Cordova Version: ' + device.cordova + br +
        'Platform: ' + device.platform + br +
        'Model: ' + device.model + br +
        'OS Version ' + device.version;
    }

  </script>
</head>
<body onload="onBodyLoad()">
  <h1>Hello World #4</h1>
```

```
  <p>This is a Cordova application that makes calls to the Cordova Device API.</p>
  <p id="appInfo">Waiting for Cordova Initialization to complete.</p>
</body>
</html>
```

Figure 2.4 shows the Hello World #4 application running on the Windows Phone 8.1 simulator.

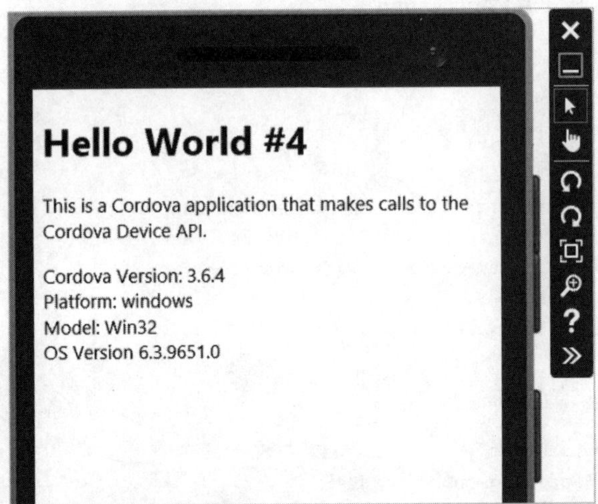

Figure 2.4 Hello World #4 Application Running on a Windows Phone Simulator

In this version of the HelloWorld application, the code in the `onDeviceReady` function has been updated so the program updates a portion of the application's content with an ID of `appInfo` with information about the device running the application and the version of Cordova used to build the application. Device-specific information is available via the Cordova Device API (http://plugins.cordova.io/#/package/org.apache.cordova.device), and this sample application uses a subset of the available properties in this API.

In order for me to be able to call the Device API, I had to add the Device API plugin to the project using the CLI command:

```
cordova plugin add org.apache.cordova.device
```

> **Note**
>
> Remember, Cordova fails silently when it encounters an error in a web application's code. So, if you forget to add the plugin to your application, the code will seem to execute, but nothing will happen. I can't tell you how many times I've tried to use the Device API's methods only to see them not work because I simply forgot to add the plugin to the project.

With the Device API in place, the application can access it using the following code:

```
var element = document.getElementById('appInfo');
element.innerHTML = 'Cordova Version: ' + device.cordova + br +
  'Platform: ' + device.platform + br +
  'Model: ' + device.model + br +
  'OS Version ' + device.version;
```

In the figure, you may have noticed that the Cordova version shows that I'm running Cordova 3.6.4. I actually ran this application using Cordova 4.0, but with this release the Cordova CLI, Cordova container, and Cordova APIs have all been broken out into separate releases. So, even though I'm actually running Cordova 4.0, some of the components may be at a different release.

Listing 2.5 shows a slightly modified version of the application; in this case I added some markup to make the device information into an unordered list so it would render more neatly on the page.

Listing 2.5 Hello World #5 Application

```
<!DOCTYPE html>
<html>
<head>
  <title>Hello World #5</title>
  <meta charset="utf-8" />
  <meta name="format-detection" content="telephone=no" />
  <meta name="viewport" content="user-scalable=no, initial-scale=1,
    maximum-scale=1, minimum-scale=1, width=device-width,
    height=device-height" />
  <script src="cordova.js"></script>
  <script>
    function onBodyLoad() {
      alert("Body Load");
      document.addEventListener("deviceready", onDeviceReady, false);
    }

    function onDeviceReady() {
      navigator.notification.alert("Cordova is ready!");
      console.log("Cordova: " + device.cordova);
      //Get the appInfo DOM element
      var element = document.getElementById('appInfo');
      //replace it with specific information about the device
      //running the application
      element.innerHTML =
        '<ul><li>Cordova Version: ' + device.cordova +
        '</li><li>Platform: ' + device.platform +
        '</li><li>Model: ' + device.model +
```

```
        '</li><li>OS Version ' + device.version + '</li></ul>';
    }
  </script>
</head>

<body onload="onBodyLoad()">
  <h1>Hello World #5</h1>
  <p>This is a Cordova application that makes calls to the Cordova Device API.</p>
  <p id="appInfo">Waiting for Cordova Initialization to complete.</p>
</body>
</html>
```

Just so you can see a Cordova application running on yet another device, Figure 2.5 shows the Hello World #5 application running on a Firefox OS simulator.

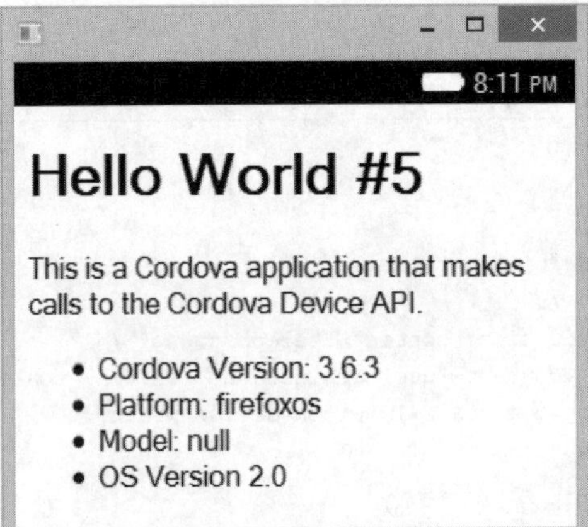

Figure 2.5 Hello World #5 Application Running on a Firefox OS Simulator

Structuring Your Application's Code

The way you structure the code for your web application is a matter of personal style, but for Cordova applications, and for some web applications, there may be a valid reason to use a particular approach. So far in this chapter I've set up my example applications so that everything, the HTML content as well as the JavaScript code, is in the same file. Additionally, I've broken things up a bit so the examples are simple and easy to read. There are a lot of things a developer can do to write more efficient and compact code—here I've deliberately not done them to make the examples as easy to read as possible.

A web developer will usually want to separate an application's HTML from its JavaScript code. In the simple applications I've shown here, there's not much of each, so it's not a big deal. But for more complicated applications, when there's a whole lot of code, separation of the two types of code can make the code easier to maintain and allow multiple developers to work on different parts of the application (UI versus application logic) separately.

There is, however, a Cordova-specific reason why you will likely want to do this. Remember how I explained earlier that the Cordova container needed to initialize itself? Well, if you think about an application that has several Cordova plugins added to it, it might take some time for the Cordova container to initialize itself, and for all of the plugins to initialize themselves as well. What I've found in many sophisticated Cordova applications is that large web applications and/or a bunch of plugins can cause a Cordova application to time out during initialization. It takes so long to load and initialize everything that the Cordova container thinks something's wrong and fails with a timeout error. I've seen this happen most frequently with a large web application using jQuery Mobile.

So, what do you do to avoid this? You structure your web application projects so that the web content and the JavaScript code are separated, and then you take some extra steps to arrange the order in which things happen.

Another reason why you would want an application's JavaScript code broken out into a separate file is to more easily support JavaScript debugging. Throughout the book I'll show you many different tools you can use to test and debug your Cordova applications. What I found in my testing of these tools is that most of them are able to interact with an application's JavaScript code only when the code is not embedded inside the application's HTML content (the application's index.html file, for example).

Listing 2.6 shows a simple application I've created that is structured a little differently from all of the other examples I've shown so far. In this example, two things are different: the application loads all of its JavaScript code after all of the application's HTML has been defined, plus all of the application's logic has been split out into a separate JavaScript file called index.js.

Listing 2.6 Hello World #6 Application index.html

```
<!DOCTYPE html>
<html>
<head>
  <title>Hello World #6</title>
  <meta charset="utf-8" />
  <meta name="format-detection" content="telephone=no" />
  <meta name="viewport" content="user-scalable=no, initial-scale=1,
    maximum-scale=1, minimum-scale=1, width=device-width,
    height=device-height" />
</head>
<body>
  <header>
    <h1>Hello World #6</h1>
  </header>
  <p>This is a simple Cordova application.</p>
  <script src="cordova.js"></script>
```

```
  <script src="index.js"></script>
</body>

</html>
```

When the earlier example applications started up, the cordova.js file was loaded before much else happened on the page. If the cordova.js took a while to load, on a slower device, for example, it might delay the rendering of the page's HTML content while it waited for the JavaScript to load. So, users of the application might see a blank page before the HTML displayed. If this was a large application, and several JavaScript files were being loaded, this might take some time, enough that the user would notice.

In the Hello World #6 application, all of the HTML loads within the browser context before the cordova.js file is loaded. If the index.js file were quite large, or I was loading jQuery Mobile and a bunch of other JavaScript stuff, the user would at least be looking at some sort of UI as the JavaScript was being loaded.

Listing 2.7 shows the application's index.js. It contains all of the JavaScript code the application is using. In this example, the file defines a simple function that self-initializes when the file is loaded, adds the event listener for the deviceready event, and provides a function that is executed when the event fires.

Listing 2.7 Hello World #6 Application index.js

```
var cvaReady;

var someOtherFunction = function () {
  if (cvaReady) {
    //do something

  } else {
    //tell the user why they can't do that

  }
};

(function () {

  var onDeviceReady = function () {
    console.log("Entering onDeviceReady");
    //Let the user know that the deviceReady event has fired
    navigator.notification.alert("Cordova is ready", null,
      "Device Ready", "Continue");
    //Set the variable that lets other parts of the program
    //know that Cordova has initialized
    cvaReady = true;
```

```
    //=====================================================
    //Do whatever other stuff you want to do on startup
    //=====================================================

    console.log("Leaving onDeviceReady");
  };

  //add an event listener for the Cordova deviceReady event.
  document.addEventListener('deviceready', onDeviceReady, false);

}());
```

I've added a new feature in this example as well, a `cvaReady` object that the application can use to tell whether the `onDeviceReady` function has executed. If you don't want to wait to do everything until the deviceready event has fired, you can ignore it and check the `cvaReady` object as needed to see if you are able to do Cordova stuff. I know this is a clunky way to do this; I'm just trying to give you different options for your applications.

When you run into an issue where the Cordova container times out before loading all of your stuff, what some people recommend doing is setting up a timer in your deviceready event listener that waits a few seconds before loading a new page that then loads your application's JavaScript files. This allows all of the Cordova initialization to complete before anything else is done by the application. This is supposedly one way people have gotten around timing issues with using jQuery Mobile with a large Cordova application, but I've never had the need to use this approach.

The Generated Web Application Files

Now that I've shown you how a Cordova application is crafted, let's take a look at the default application generated by the Cordova CLI. In Chapter 4 you'll see that when the CLI creates a new application project, by default it creates a simple HelloCordova web application and places it in the project's www folder. You can override this behavior if you want, but this is the default.

The project folder contains a web application folder structure that is designed to separate the different types of files into separate folders. For example, the web application's CSS files should be placed in the css folder, JavaScript files in the js folder, and so on.

The application's index.html file is shown in Listing 2.8; it contains many of the same HTML elements and attributes as the other examples shown throughout the chapter. What the application does is display a simple page with the Cordova logo and some blinking text, "Connecting to Device," centered beneath the logo.

Listing 2.8 Contents of the HelloCordova index.html File

```
<!DOCTYPE html>
<!--
    Licensed to the Apache Software Foundation (ASF) under one
```

```
    or more contributor license agreements. See the NOTICE file
    distributed with this work for additional information
    regarding copyright ownership. The ASF licenses this file
    to you under the Apache License, Version 2.0 (the
    "License"); you may not use this file except in compliance
    with the License. You may obtain a copy of the License at

    http://www.apache.org/licenses/LICENSE-2.0

    Unless required by applicable law or agreed to in writing,
    software distributed under the License is distributed on an
    "AS IS" BASIS, WITHOUT WARRANTIES OR CONDITIONS OF ANY
     KIND, either express or implied. See the License for the
    specific language governing permissions and limitations
    under the License.
-->

<html>
  <head>
    <meta charset="utf-8" />
    <meta name="format-detection" content="telephone=no" />
    <!-- WARNING: for iOS 7, remove the width=device-width and
      height=device-height attributes.
      See https://issues.apache.org/jira/browse/CB-4323 -->
    <meta name="viewport" content="user-scalable=no,
      initial-scale=1, maximum-scale=1, minimum-scale=1,
      width=device-width, height=device-height,
      target-densitydpi=device-dpi" />
    <link rel="stylesheet" type="text/css" href="css/index.css" />
    <meta name="msapplication-tap-highlight" content="no" />
    <title>Hello World</title>
  </head>
  <body>
    <div class="app">
      <h1>Apache Cordova</h1>
      <div id="deviceready" class="blink">
        <p class="event listening">Connecting to Device</p>
        <p class="event received">Device is Ready</p>
      </div>
    </div>
    <script type="text/javascript" src="cordova.js"></script>
    <script type="text/javascript" src="js/index.js"></script>
    <script type="text/javascript">
      app.initialize();
    </script>
  </body>
</html>
```

Notice that the application loads the cordova.js and other resources at the end of the file as I explained in the previous section. In this application initialization is done a little differently. Rather than having an index.js file that auto-initializes, the index.js exposes an `initialize` method that is called manually in a separate `script` tag in the file.

Listing 2.9 shows the contents of the application's index.js file.

Listing 2.9 Contents of the HelloCordova index.js File

```
/*
 * Licensed to the Apache Software Foundation (ASF) under one
 * or more contributor license agreements. See the NOTICE file
 * distributed with this work for additional information
 * regarding copyright ownership. The ASF licenses this file
 * to you under the Apache License, Version 2.0 (the
 * "License"); you may not use this file except in compliance
 * with the License. You may obtain a copy of the License at
 *
 * http://www.apache.org/licenses/LICENSE-2.0
 *
 * Unless required by applicable law or agreed to in writing,
 * software distributed under the License is distributed on an
 * "AS IS" BASIS, WITHOUT WARRANTIES OR CONDITIONS OF ANY
 * KIND, either express or implied. See the License for the
 * specific language governing permissions and limitations
 * under the License.
 */
var app = {
  // Application Constructor
  initialize: function() {
    this.bindEvents();
  },

  // Bind Event Listeners
  //
  // Bind any events that are required on startup. Common events are:
  // 'load', 'deviceready', 'offline', and 'online'.
  bindEvents: function() {
    document.addEventListener('deviceready', this.onDeviceReady, false);
  },
  // deviceready Event Handler
  //
  // The scope of 'this' is the event. In order to call the 'receivedEvent'
  // function, we must explicitly call 'app.receivedEvent(...);'.
  onDeviceReady: function() {
    app.receivedEvent('deviceready');
  },
```

```
  // Update DOM on a Received Event
  receivedEvent: function(id) {
    var parentElement = document.getElementById(id);
    var listeningElement = parentElement.querySelector('.listening');
    var receivedElement = parentElement.querySelector('.received');

    listeningElement.setAttribute('style', 'display:none;');
    receivedElement.setAttribute('style', 'display:block;');

    console.log('Received Event: ' + id);
  }
};
```

The JavaScript code registers the deviceready listener you've seen in many of the other examples in this chapter. When the `onDeviceReady` function executes, it writes some information to the console (this will be discussed more in Chapter 5) and then updates the page content to indicate that the Cordova container is ready.

This application is much more complicated than it needs to be; as you can see from my previous examples, you can easily do the same thing with much less code. However, it's apparently the way the Cordova team wants to highlight how to build Cordova applications.

> **Note**
>
> In the examples I have provided throughout the chapter, I deliberately simplified the application code to make it easier to teach you what a Cordova application looks like. The sample application generated by the CLI is structured more like modern HTML5 applications.
>
> The approach you take when building your web applications is up to you; there's no right or wrong approach. I think the CLI-generated application is more complicated than it needs to be, but as features are added to an application, it may be easier to use the approach highlighted in this section.

Figure 2.6 shows the default Cordova HelloCordova application running on an Android emulator. When building your Cordova applications, you can start with this sample application and add in your custom code, or you can rip out the HTML and CSS files and start from scratch.

Figure 2.6 HelloCordova Application Running on an Android Emulator

Responsive Design and Cordova

When a smartphone or tablet user rotates a device running a web or Cordova application, the browser needs to be able to react to the change and adjust the page's properties. If it didn't, when the browser window switches from a portrait to a landscape orientation, much of the available screen real estate would go unused. Designing a web application so it properly renders the application's content across varying display widths or changing orientations is called responsive design.

Dealing with responsive design is a mobile web development topic, and I've always tried to limit these books to Cordova-related subjects only, but in this case it seemed to make sense to cover this topic. It didn't fit in other areas of the book, so I decided to add it here.

There are several ways you can approach dealing with browser window size and orientation-related challenges. Bootstrap (http://getbootstrap.com/) and other front-end frameworks provide capabilities web developers can leverage to automatically scale and adjust their web applications' content based on the available screen real estate. Additionally, there are capabilities in CSS and JavaScript that the web developer can leverage directly to accomplish this. I'm not going to cover third-party frameworks in this chapter; I'll cover some of them in Chapter 17. What I will show you is how to build some of these capabilities into your own applications directly.

Using Cascading Style Sheets, an application has the capability to define specific CSS attributes that apply depending on the orientation of the device. In the following example, you see that

I've defined two `body` styles, one that applies when the content is rendered on a screen while the orientation is portrait and the other when rendered on a screen while the orientation is landscape.

```
/* portrait */
@media screen and (orientation: portrait) {
  /* portrait-specific styles */
  body {
    background-color: blue;
    color: white;
  }
}
/* landscape */
@media screen and (orientation: landscape) {
  /* landscape-specific styles */
  body {
    background-color: red;
    color: black;
  }
}
```

In this case, just so I could demonstrate the changes cleanly, if you add this code to your web application (I'll show you an example in a minute), you get white text on a blue background while in portrait orientation and black text on a red background in landscape orientation. For your own applications, you'll want to adjust margins, borders, and so on based on the space available to your application.

Sometimes you want to do a little more when things change; to accommodate this, the web browser exposes events you can listen for and update your application's UI as needed. Two events that matter for Cordova developers are orientationchange and resize. To add event listeners for these events to your Cordova applications, you can use the following:

```
//Set the orientation change event listener
window.addEventListener('orientationchange', onOrientationChange);
//For actions that don't fire the orientationchange event
window.addEventListener("resize", onResize, false);
```

With this code in place, when the device's orientation changes, the `onOrientationChange` function is executed, and when the browser window resizes, the `onResize` function is executed. All your application has to do then is populate those two functions with the code you want executed when those particular events happen. In this example, I simply wrote some screen measurements to the page when the events fire.

To see all of this in action, I've created Example 2.7 shown in Listing 2.10. This application implements both the CSS queries and JavaScript events to create a web application that reacts to changes that occur while the application is running.

Listing 2.10 Example 2.7 Application index.html

```
<!DOCTYPE html>
<html>
<head>
  <title>Example 2.7</title>
  <meta charset="utf-8" />
  <meta name="format-detection" content="telephone=no" />
  <meta name="viewport" content="user-scalable=no, initial-scale=1,
    maximum-scale=1, minimum-scale=1, width=device-width,
    height=device-height" />
  <style>
    /* portrait */
    @media screen and (orientation: portrait) {
      /* portrait-specific styles */
      body {
        background-color: blue;
        color: white;
      }
    }
    /* landscape */
    @media screen and (orientation: landscape) {
      /* landscape-specific styles */
      body {
        background-color: red;
        color: black;
      }
    }
  </style>
  <script src="cordova.js"></script>
  <script>
    br = "<br />";

    function onBodyLoad() {
      alert("Body Load");
      document.addEventListener("deviceready", onDeviceReady, false);
      //set the orientationchange event listener
      window.addEventListener('orientationchange',
        onOrientationChange);
      //for devices that don't fire orientationchange
      window.addEventListener("resize", onResize, false);
      //Fire this at the start to set the initial orientation on
      //the page
      updatePage();
    }

    function onDeviceReady() {
      navigator.notification.alert("Cordova is ready!");

    }
```

```
    function updatePage(msg) {
      //Build an output string consisting of the different screen
      //measurement values
      var strongStart = "<strong>";
      var strongEnd = "</strong>";
      //var StrRes, or, sw, sh, ww, wh;
      or = strongStart + "Orientation: " + strongEnd +
        window.orientation + " degrees";
      console.log(or);
      strRes = or + br;
      sw = strongStart + "Width: " + strongEnd + screen.width;
      console.log(sw);
      strRes += sw + br;
      sh = strongStart + "Height: " + strongEnd + screen.height;
      console.log(sh);
      strRes += sh + br;
      ww = strongStart + "Inner width: " + strongEnd +
        window.innerWidth;
      console.log(ww);
      strRes += ww + br;
      wh = strongStart + "Inner height: " + strongEnd +
        window.innerHeight;
      console.log(wh);
      strRes += wh + br;
      document.getElementById('appInfo').innerHTML = strRes;
    }

    function onOrientationChange() {
      var msg;
      console.log("Orientation has changed");
      switch (abs(window.orientation)) {
      case 90:
        console.log("Device is in Landscape mode");
        break;
      default:
        console.log("Device is in Portrait mode");
        break;
      }
      updatePage();
    }

    function onResize() {
      console.log("Resize event fired");
      updatePage();
    }
  </script>
</head>
```

```
<body onload="onBodyLoad()">
  <h1>Example 2.7</h1>
  <p>This is a Cordova application that responds to device
     orientation and resize events.</p>
  <p id="appInfo">Waiting for Cordova Initialization to complete.</p>
</body>
</html>
```

Figure 2.7 shows the application running on an Android device in portrait orientation.

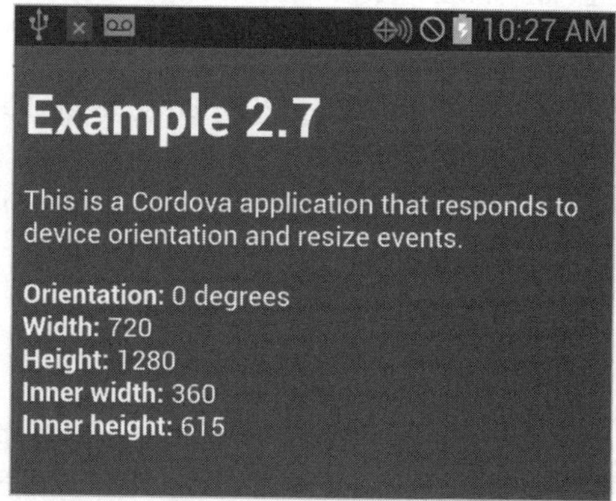

Figure 2.7 Example 2.7 Running on an Android Device in Portrait Orientation

Figure 2.8 shows the application running on an Android device in landscape orientation.

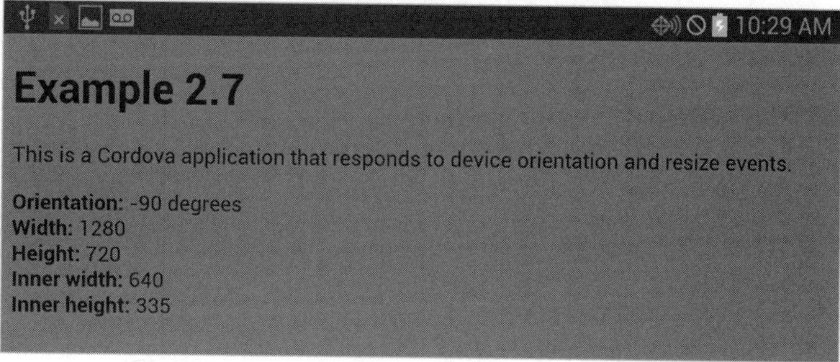

Figure 2.8 Example 2.7 Running on an Android Device in Landscape Orientation

There's a whole lot more that can be said about responsive design and the tools that address it, but that's way beyond the scope of this simple Cordova book. I'm a big fan of *Smashing*

Magazine, and they've published some nice articles on web design and responsive design that might help you with this topic:

- www.smashingmagazine.com/responsive-web-design-guidelines-tutorials/
- www.smashingmagazine.com/2010/07/19/how-to-use-css3-media-queries-to-create-a-mobile-version-of-your-website/
- www.smashingmagazine.com/2012/03/22/device-agnostic-approach-to-responsive-web-design/

There are a lot of web design and development books available that cover this topic in much more detail than I can. For example, take a look at the following Pearson titles:

- Dutson, Phil. *Responsive Mobile Design: Designing for Every Device*. Boston: Addison-Wesley, 2014.
- Kymin, Jennifer. *Sams Teach Yourself Responsive Web Design in 24 Hours*. Indianapolis, IN: Sams Publishing, 2014.

Wrap-Up

In this chapter, I've shown you what makes an application a Cordova application, plus I've shown you the sample application that the Cordova CLI creates for you. You now have the building blocks necessary to start building your own Cordova applications.

In the next chapters, I'll show you how to install Apache Cordova and use the Cordova CLI to create and manage your Cordova projects.

Notice that in this chapter, I didn't do anything to make my applications visually appealing. You can use CSS to do this, which is not something I really want to cover in a Cordova book. In Chapter 17 I'll show you how to use third-party frameworks, some of them specifically designed for hybrid applications, to add pizzazz to your Cordova web applications.

3

Configuring a Cordova Development Environment

To make it easier for developers to manage their projects, the Cordova project team built a single, unified command-line interface (CLI) that works across all of the Cordova supported mobile device platforms. This chapter illustrates how to install the Cordova CLI. The following chapter will show you how to use it to manage your Cordova projects.

The PhoneGap CLI is essentially the Cordova CLI with some additional commands added on. Most everything you learn in this chapter easily applies to the PhoneGap CLI as well. In Chapter 13, "Using the PhoneGap CLI," I describe the additional capabilities provided by the PhoneGap CLI.

The instructions provided in this chapter cover both the Microsoft Windows and Macintosh OS X operating systems. The instructions for Ubuntu are completely different, so I cover them in Chapter 10, "Ubuntu Development with Cordova." The Windows examples I show here are for Windows 8, but the Windows 7 steps are almost identical. Later in the book I have dedicated chapters covering the tooling for Android, Firefox OS, iOS, Ubuntu, and Windows Cordova development, but both Android and iOS have some prerequisites for the CLI to operate properly, so I include the necessary information here. So, if you're going to do some Cordova development for a particular mobile OS beyond Android and iOS, read through the instructions here, and then also take a look at the appropriate chapter for your particular OS.

Installing the Cordova CLI

The Cordova CLI is built using JavaScript code that is exposed through the Node JavaScript runtime engine (www.nodejs.org). Since it is built using JavaScript, it can essentially run anywhere that Node is available (Linux, Macintosh OS X, and Microsoft Windows). The instructions that follow will help you get the CLI installed on your development workstation; there are separate instructions for Macintosh OS X and Microsoft Windows.

The CLI has to be able to create new Cordova projects, so it provides the necessary project files—plus it has to interface with the native SDKs to build projects and load applications in an emulator or simulator. Because of that, you have to make sure that the appropriate SDKs are installed (depending on which platforms you're working with) and that the SDKs are visible to the CLI. As mentioned in the previous section, I'm going to include some up-front information on the installation of the Android and iOS SDKs so you'll leave this chapter with fully functioning development environments for the two most popular mobile platforms.

Android Development Tools

In this section, I will show you how to install the CLI requirements for developing Android applications.

Java Development Kit Installation

One of the requirements for the Android SDK is the Java Development Kit (JDK). On Macintosh, you should have Java already available, although you may have to install it first. Open a terminal window, type `javac` at the command prompt, and press Enter. If you see a bunch of help text scroll by, you're all set. If not, you'll see instructions for how to download and install the appropriate Java files for your system.

On Windows, you will need to point your browser of choice to http://java.oracle.com and download the JDK. On the Java home page, select Java SE, and then download and install the latest version of the JDK. You will want to install a version of the Oracle JDK that matches the processor and Windows version running on your system. Install the 64-bit version of Java if you're running a 64-bit version of Windows and a 32-bit version if you're running a 32-bit version of Windows.

At the conclusion of the JDK installation, there are still a couple more steps to complete—you will need to define the `JAVA_HOME` environment variable and point it to where the JDK is installed. To create the `JAVA_HOME` environment variable on Windows 7, open Windows Explorer, right-click on the Computer icon (it used to be called My Computer in older versions of Windows), then select Properties. On Windows 8, open Windows Explorer, right-click on This PC (highlighted in Figure 3.1), and then select Properties.

In the dialog that appears, select Advanced system settings as highlighted on the left side of Figure 3.2.

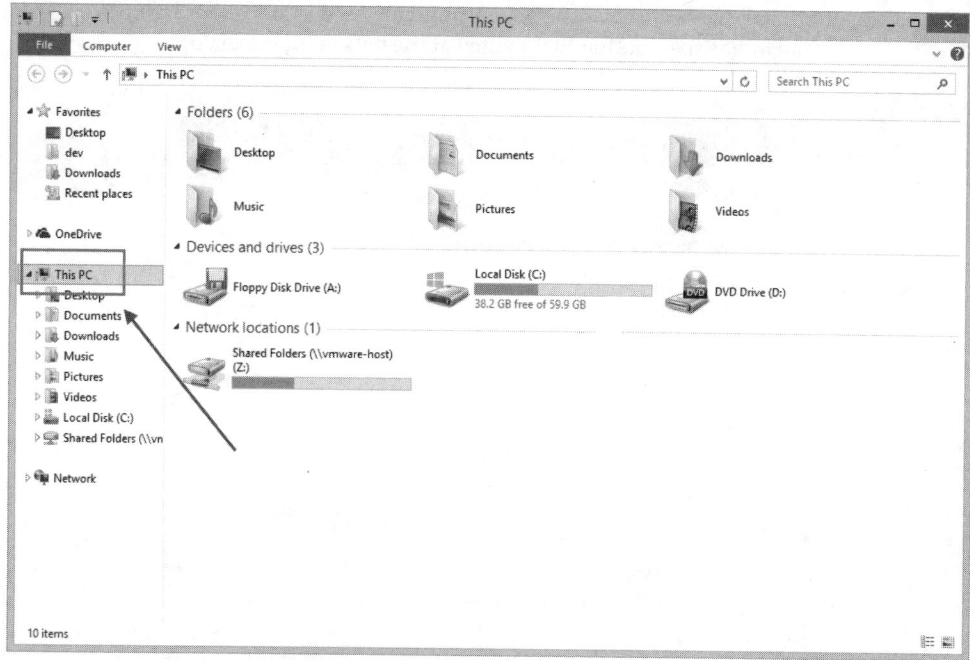

Figure 3.1 Microsoft Windows Explorer

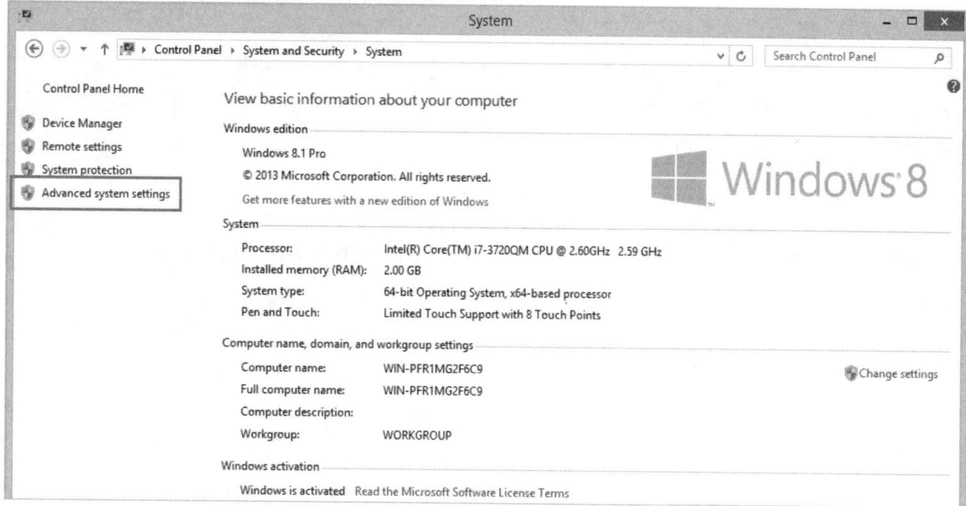

Figure 3.2 Windows Control Panel—System Settings

In the dialog that appears, select the Advanced tab as highlighted in the top of Figure 3.3, then click the Environment Variables button highlighted at the bottom of the dialog.

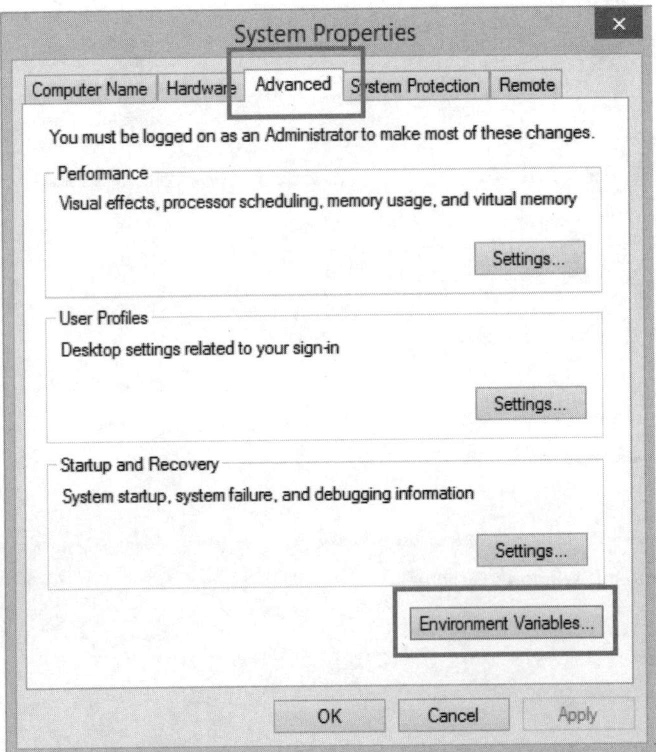

Figure 3.3 Windows System Properties

In the dialog that appears, look for a user variable entry labeled JAVA_HOME; if there's already one there, you can skip this step. If not, click the New button highlighted in Figure 3.4.

In the New User Variable dialog that appears, type `JAVA_HOME` into the Variable name field, then populate the Variable value field with the full path pointing to the JDK installation folder as shown in Figure 3.5. Click the OK button when you're done.

On Macintosh, the Java installation automatically configures the system so you can execute Java commands from the command line, so there is no need to update the system path.

On Windows, we need to configure the system so the Java compiler is available to the command-line tools. The JDK installation doesn't update the Windows system path, so you will have to do it manually. In the dialog shown in Figure 3.4, select the `PATH` variable at the top of the User variables list, then click the Edit button.

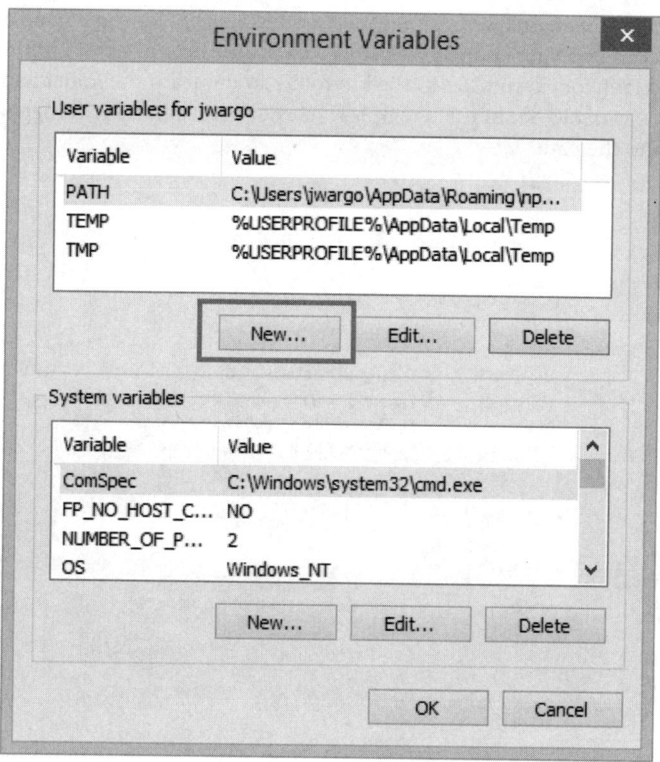

Figure 3.4 Windows Environment Variables Dialog

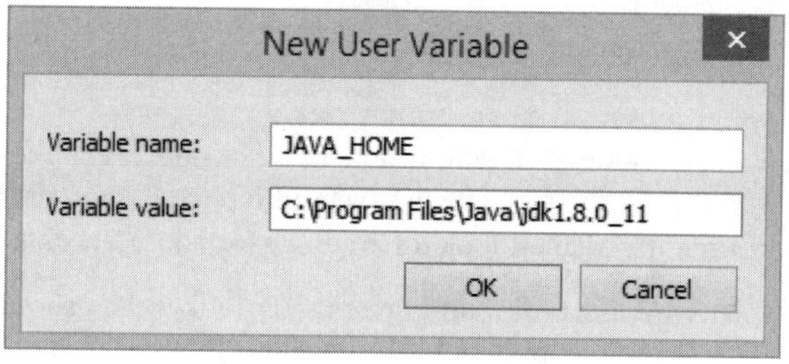

New User Variable

Variable name: JAVA_HOME

Variable value: C:\Program Files\Java\jdk1.8.0_11

OK Cancel

Figure 3.5 Adding the `JAVA_HOME` User Variable

Figure 3.6 shows the dialog that appears. In the Variable value field, add a semicolon at the end of the existing value, then append `%JAVA_HOME%\bin` to the field as shown in the figure. This tells Windows to look for executables in the bin folder underneath the folder name described in the `JAVA_HOME` variable. So, in this example, I'm essentially adding C:\Program Files\Java\jdk1.8.0_11\bin to the path.

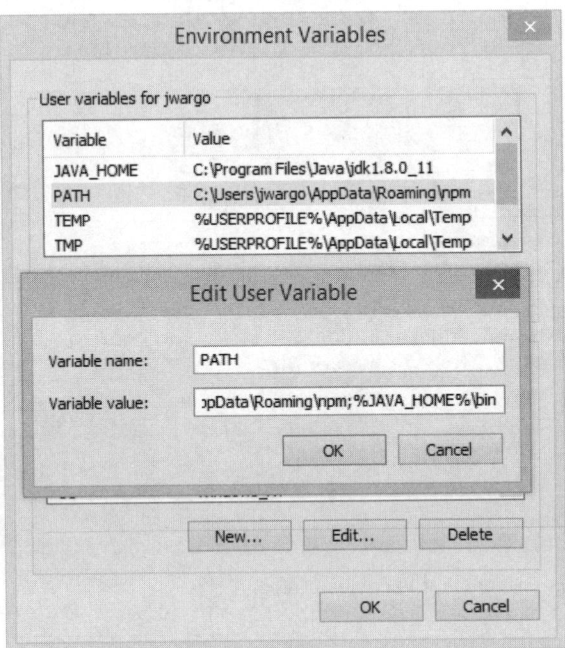

Figure 3.6 Editing the Windows Path Variable

When you're finished, click the series of OK buttons to take you back to the Control Panel. To test the configuration, open a new terminal window and type `set`, then press Enter. You should see a long list of environment variables; look for an entry for your new `JAVA_HOME` variable.

Next, type `javac` in the terminal window and press the Enter key. You should see information about the available Java Compiler commands scroll past on the screen. If you do, the `PATH` variable is configured correctly. If you receive an error message, there is an error in the `PATH` variable configuration that you will have to resolve before continuing.

Java Build Tools (Ant) Installation

The Android SDK, covered in the next section, uses command-line build tools to automate some of the Android project management and build steps. In this section, I will show you how to install Ant (http://ant.apache.org) into your development environment.

Ant versus Gradle

Google is currently in an SDK transition, migrating from the Android Developer Tools (ADT) to Android Studio (still in beta); ADT is based on the Eclipse IDE and uses Ant to manage the build process, while Android Studio is based on IntelliJ IDEA and is implementing Gradle (www.gradle.org) to manage projects and builds.

At the time of this writing, well before the release of Cordova 4.0, the Cordova CLI uses the Android SDK's Ant-based scripts. I imagine that when Android Studio is finally released (it's been in beta for more than a year now), everything will switch over to Gradle. So for now, I'll show you how to install Ant; you may find that you will also need to install Gradle by the time you read this.

There's not much to installing Ant. The project doesn't include an installer; all you need to do is download the latest distribution, unpack the files to an appropriate destination, then modify the system path so that applications, like the Cordova CLI, can execute it. What I typically do is extract the files into the system's Downloads folder, rename the extracted folder to ant, then move the files to an appropriate destination. On Windows I move the folder to the root of my system's primary hard drive (usually C:\) so the Ant files will be found at `C:\ant\`. On Macintosh, I usually drag the files into the system's Applications folder. An example of the Ant installation on my Windows 8 system is shown in Figure 3.7.

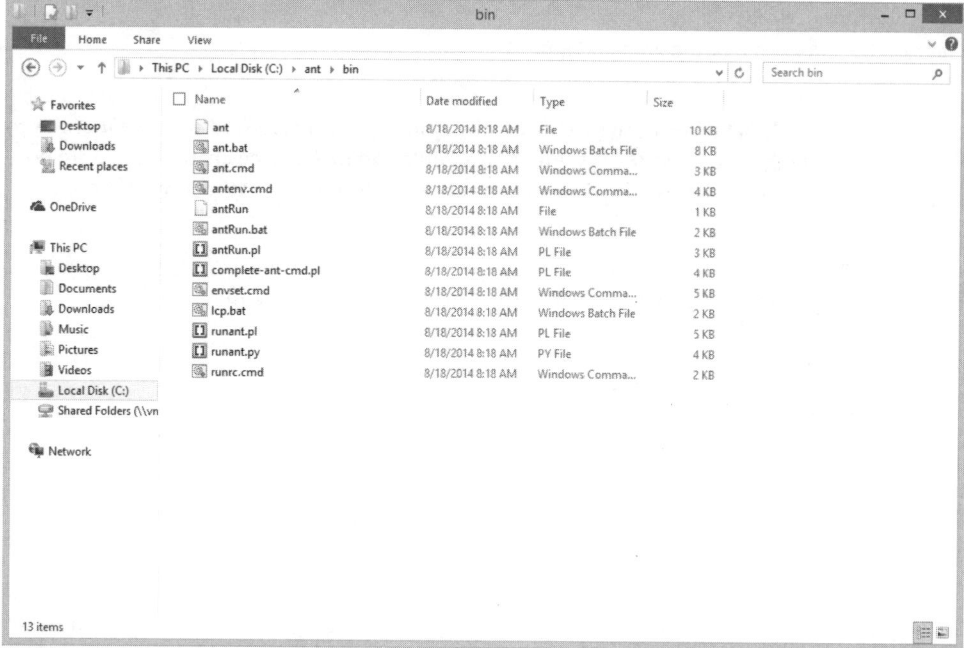

Figure 3.7 Ant Installation Folder

Macintosh users can also install Ant using Homebrew (http://brew.sh). When you install Ant using Homebrew, the system path is updated automatically, so you can skip the following instructions.

The Cordova and Android command-line tools need to be able to execute Ant from any folder, so you will need to update the system path with the Ant installation's bin folder.

On Windows 7, open Windows Explorer, then right-click on the Computer icon (it used to be called My Computer in older versions of Windows) and select Properties. On Windows 8, open Windows Explorer and right-click on This PC (highlighted in Figure 3.1), then select Properties. In the dialog that appears (shown in Figure 3.4), select the `PATH` variable at the top of the User variables list, then click the Edit button.

Append a semicolon and the path to the Ant installation's bin folder to the Variable value field in the dialog as shown in Figure 3.8. Click the OK button to save your changes.

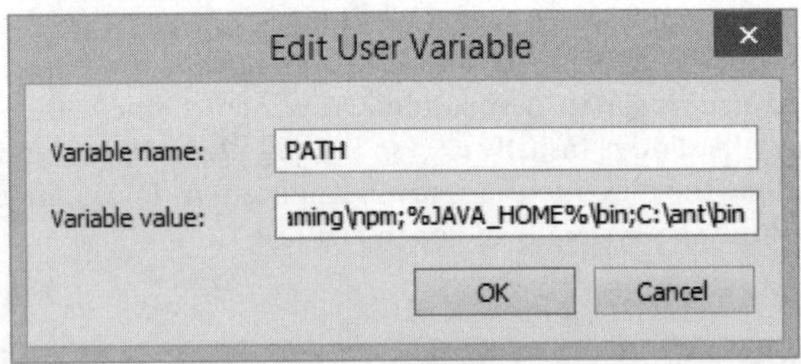

Figure 3.8 Adding Ant to the System Path

On Macintosh, there are several ways to update the system path. The easiest way I've found is to simply use a text editor to open the system's bash profile and make some changes there. To do this, open a terminal window and invoke the default text editor using the following command:

```
open ~/.bash_profile
```

Within the file, add the following lines after the existing content in the file:

```
ANT_HOME=/Applications/ant
PATH=$PATH:$HOME/bin:$ANT_HOME/bin
export ANT_HOME PATH
```

Remember, I dragged the ant folder to the system's Applications folder; if you placed your Ant files in a different location, be sure to update the value associated with the `ANT_HOME` variable in the example with the correct location. Save the changes, then exit the editor. To test the configuration, from a terminal window execute the following command:

```
ant
```

If Ant is installed correctly, you should see a response similar to the one shown in Figure 3.9.

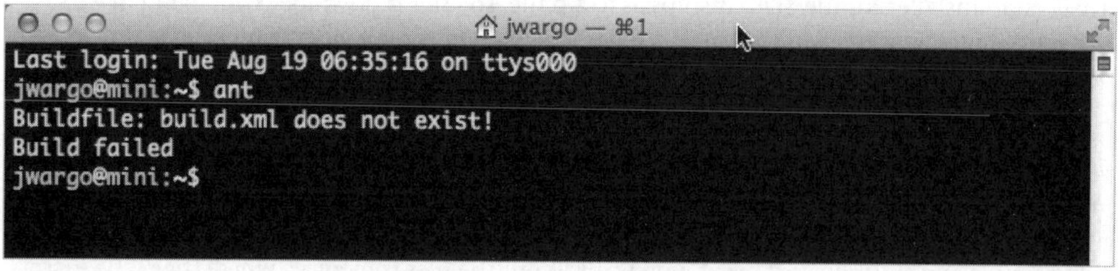

```
Last login: Tue Aug 19 06:35:16 on ttys000
jwargo@mini:~$ ant
Buildfile: build.xml does not exist!
Build failed
jwargo@mini:~$
```

Figure 3.9 Testing the Ant Configuration

This is not an error; it's simply Ant's way of telling you that it did not find the configuration file it needed in the current folder. This is OK as we've not created any projects yet, so the build file we need isn't there (yet)—the Cordova CLI will add it for us later. If you're in a folder that contains a build.xml file, when you execute the command you will see a bunch more text outputted to the screen as Ant reads the build.xml file and starts following the instructions in the file.

If the configuration is not set up correctly, you should get a Command Not Found error or something similar when you execute the `ant` command. If you see this, there's something wrong with the Ant configuration.

Android SDK Installation

With Java installed and configured, it's time to install the Android SDK. Google is currently in transition between developer tools. Since the beginning, Google has offered developers an Eclipse-based IDE (www.eclipse.org) called Android Developer Tools (ADT). More than a year ago, Google announced a new IDE called Android Studio. With Android Studio, Google is moving away from Eclipse to the IntelliJ IDEA IDE (www.jetbrains.com/idea). The Android Studio tools are currently available only as a beta; ideally by the time you read this Google will have released the product. Since there are two options available, I'm going to show you how to install and configure both sets of tools in this section.

Open your browser of choice and point it to http://developers.android.com. On the Android developer home page, click the Develop menu item, then on the page that opens, click the Tools menu. On the page that appears, you can access the SDK directly at http://developer.android.com/sdk/index.html; you have options for downloading ADT or the new Android Studio beta.

For developers who want to use a different IDE, Google offers a separate download, the Android SDK Tools, which include the command-line tools, Android emulators, Monitor, and other tools that a developer will use for developing any Android application (regardless of which IDE is used). Regardless of which IDE you use, it's the SDK that's used by the Cordova CLI. In the sections that follow, I'll quickly show you how to install ADT or Android Studio but then focus my attention on configuring the SDK tools so that the Cordova CLI can use them to manage Android projects. In Chapter 7, "Android Development with Cordova," I show you more about how to use all of these tools for your Android application development and debugging.

Installing ADT

There is no installer for the SDK; it ships as a .zip file, so after it downloads you will have to extract the files to a location that makes sense for you. On some Macintosh OS versions, when you download .zip files using the Safari browser, the files are automatically extracted to the Downloads folder for you.

Once the files have been extracted, you'll notice that they are extracted into a folder with a long and complicated name like adt-bundle-windows-x86_64-20140702. That folder name becomes a little cumbersome when dealing with the system path later, so I always rename the folder to something simple and short like adt. Next, you want to put the files someplace where they'll be easy to work with. I don't like to run stuff from my system's Downloads folder, so on Windows, I move the newly renamed adt folder to the root of the system's main hard drive (C:\adt, for example). On Macintosh OS X, I drag the adt folder to the Applications folder (/Applications/adt).

Install Android Studio

Android Studio has an installer, so to install the application, simply execute the downloaded file and follow the prompts. On Windows, the downloaded application is a standard Windows installer application, so you simply have to follow the installation wizard to complete the installation. On Macintosh OS X, the download is a disk image; you'll have to mount the image, then execute the package file included therein and follow the standard installation procedure to install the software, which is essentially dragging the Android Studio application into the Applications folder.

Configuring the Android SDK

As I said earlier, the Cordova CLI really only cares about the SDK tools, so we have to do some things to make sure the CLI can access its files. Figure 3.10 shows the SDK installation folder for Android Studio on Windows 8.

For the Android Studio installation, on Windows the SDK will be located in C:\Program Files (x86)\Android\Android-studio\sdk. On Macintosh OS X, the SDK will be located in /Applications/Android\ Studio.app/sdk.

> **Note**
>
> If the Android Studio SDK folder path on Macintosh looks a little odd to you, you're right. Because of the way Macintosh OS manages application installations, the SDK is installed in a hidden, application-specific folder within the /Applications folder. Because Application Studio has a space in its name, and a space is normally used as a delimiter between parameters on a command line, you have to use an escape character, the \, to indicate that the space is part of the previous parameter.

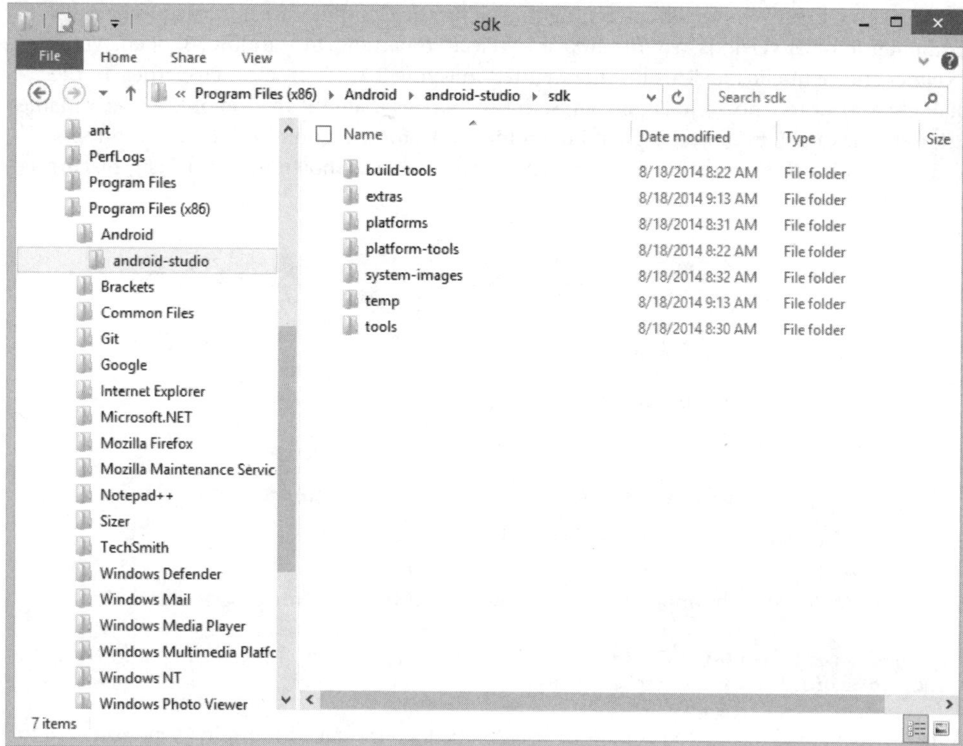

Figure 3.10 Android SDK Installation Folder

If you followed my instructions in the previous sections, for ADT on Windows, the SDK will be located in C:\adt\sdk and on Macintosh OS X it will be located in /Applications/adt/sdk.

The SDK installation contains two folders that matter to the CLI: platform-tools and tools. To use the SDK from the CLI, we have to add these two folders to the system path on the computer running the CLI.

On Macintosh, there are several ways to update the system path. The easiest way I've found is to simply use a text editor to open the system's bash profile and make some changes there. To do this, open a terminal window and invoke the default text editor using the following command:

```
open ~/.bash_profile
```

Assuming you followed the earlier instructions for adding Ant to the system path, add the full paths to the Android SDK tools and platform-tools folders to the path as shown here:

```
ANT_HOME=/Applications/ant
PATH=$PATH:$HOME/bin:$ANT_HOME/bin:/Applications/Android\ Studio.app/sdk/tools:/
Applications/Android\ Studio.app/sdk/platform-tools
export ANT_HOME PATH
```

On Windows, open Windows Explorer, right-click on the Computer icon (it used to be called My Computer in older versions of Windows), and select Properties. On Windows 8, open Windows Explorer and right-click on This PC (highlighted in Figure 3.1), then select Properties. In the dialog that appears, shown in Figure 3.4, select the `PATH` variable at the top of the User variables list, then click the Edit button. Append the folder paths for the Android SDK platform-tools and tools folders to the existing `PATH` environment variable as shown in Figure 3.11, placing a semicolon between each path entry.

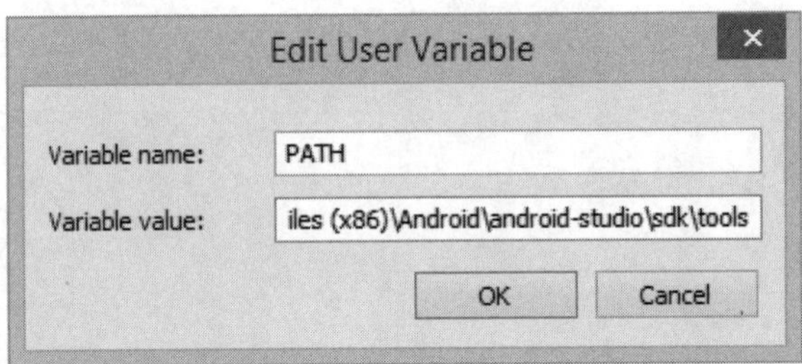

Figure 3.11 Adding the Android SDK Folders to the System Path

For this example, you'll be appending the following text to the existing `PATH` entry:

```
c:\Program Files (x86)\Android\Android-studio\sdk\tools;c:\Program Files (x86)\
Android\Android-studio\sdk\platform-tools
```

After saving your changes, you should be able to open a terminal window and type `android` to run the Android SDK Manager as shown in Figure 3.12. The SDK Manager should look the same regardless of whether you're running on Macintosh OS or Windows.

If you added the two required paths to the system path and the SDK Manager doesn't load when you type `android` at a command prompt, the configuration is incomplete and the CLI will not be able to manipulate Android projects. You'll need to go back and resolve any issues before continuing.

If you know you will need to develop Cordova applications for Android OS versions beyond the default ones installed with the Android SDK Manager, now might be a good time to select the required additional platforms and install those as well.

You will learn more about Android development for Apache Cordova in Chapter 7.

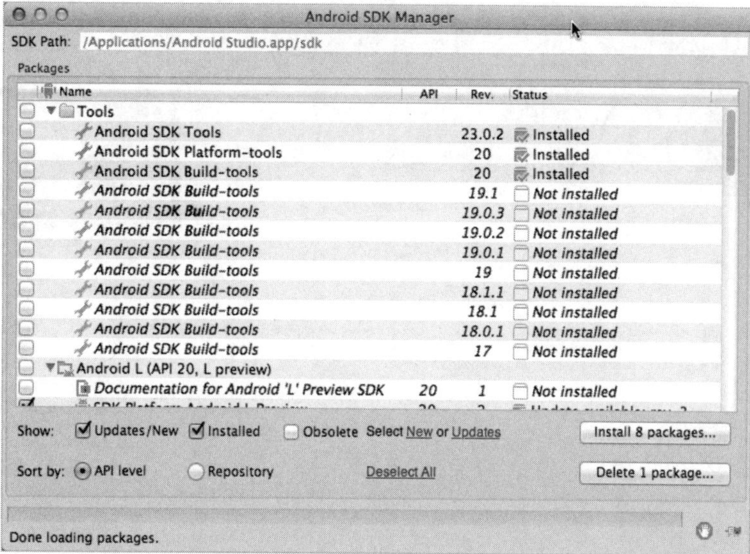

Figure 3.12 Testing the Android Configuration

iOS Development Tools

Before you can do much around iOS development, you must first join the Apple iOS Developer Program. You can find information about the program at https://developer.apple.com/programs/ios/; there's a yearly fee, and different capabilities are available to you depending on which program you choose.

Next, you will want to open the Macintosh App Store, search for "xcode," and install the Xcode IDE as shown in Figure 3.13. Xcode is a huge install, so find something else to do for a while as it downloads.

The Cordova CLI requires access to the Xcode Command Line Tools in order to be able to execute builds. With older versions of Xcode, the Command Line Tools were a separate download performed within the Xcode Preferences dialog. It looks as if the tools are installed automatically with Xcode, but I wasn't able to verify this (I had manually installed the tools before checking to see if they were already there). Open a terminal window and execute the following command:

```
xcodebuild
```

If you see a message similar to what is shown in Figure 3.14, the Xcode Command Line Tools are installed.

Figure 3.13 Macintosh App Store Xcode Entry

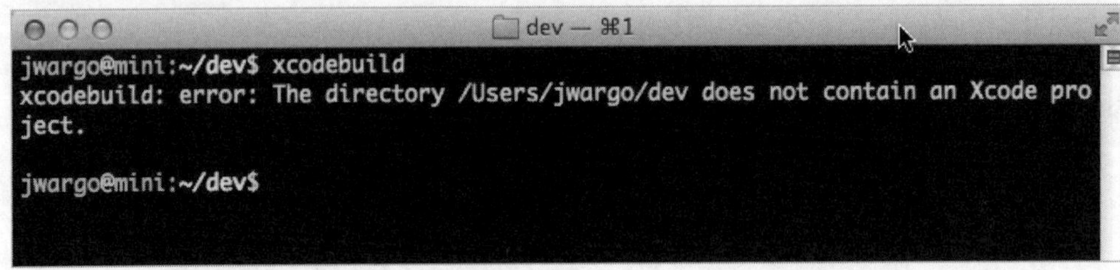

Figure 3.14 Testing the `xcodebuild` Installation

If not, open Xcode, open the Xcode menu, select Open Developer Tools, then select More Developer Tools. On the web page that opens, you will be able to download and install the components you need. Be sure to test that the command works after completing the installation.

You can read more about iOS development for Apache Cordova in Chapter 9, "iOS Development with Cordova."

CLI Installation

OK, now that we have a few of the mobile device platform SDK requirements in place, it's time to start the Cordova CLI installation. A few more installations are required first, so let's get started.

Node Installation

The CLI is written in JavaScript and therefore uses Node as a runtime execution engine. The CLI currently requires Node 0.10 and higher, so if you already have it installed, make sure you update it to the latest version. To install Node, point your browser of choice to www.nodejs.org, then download and install the latest version of the software. The software installs using the standard installers for both Windows and Macintosh, so I'm not going to show you all of the steps here.

By default Node will install in your system path, so you can open a terminal window and type `node` to launch the Node application. If the prompt changes to a "greater than" symbol (>) as shown in Figure 3.15, Node is installed correctly. Press Ctrl-C twice to exit Node.

```
jwargo — ⌘1
Last login: Mon Aug 18 13:43:42 on ttys000
jwargo@mini:~$ node
> _
```

Figure 3.15 Testing the Node Installation

Git Installation

When the CLI was first released, it relied heavily upon GitHub for storage of many of the components it used to manage Cordova application projects. Because of this, you'll need to install a version of Git (http://git-scm.com) before you can use the CLI. The team has since started moving everything to Node Package Manager (NPM; www.npmjs.org). It's possible that by the time you read this, you may not need to do this.

If you're running on Linux or Macintosh OS X, you can install Git using NPM by opening a terminal window and typing

```
npm install -g git
```

On Windows, you should download Git tools and install them on your development workstation from http://git-scm.com. There are some extra Windows Explorer and shell options available through the Windows installer that cannot be installed using NPM.

Once you've completed the installation, open a terminal window (Mac OS X) or command prompt (Windows), type `git`, and press Enter. A bunch of text should scroll by, then you should see a screen similar to the one shown in Figure 3.16.

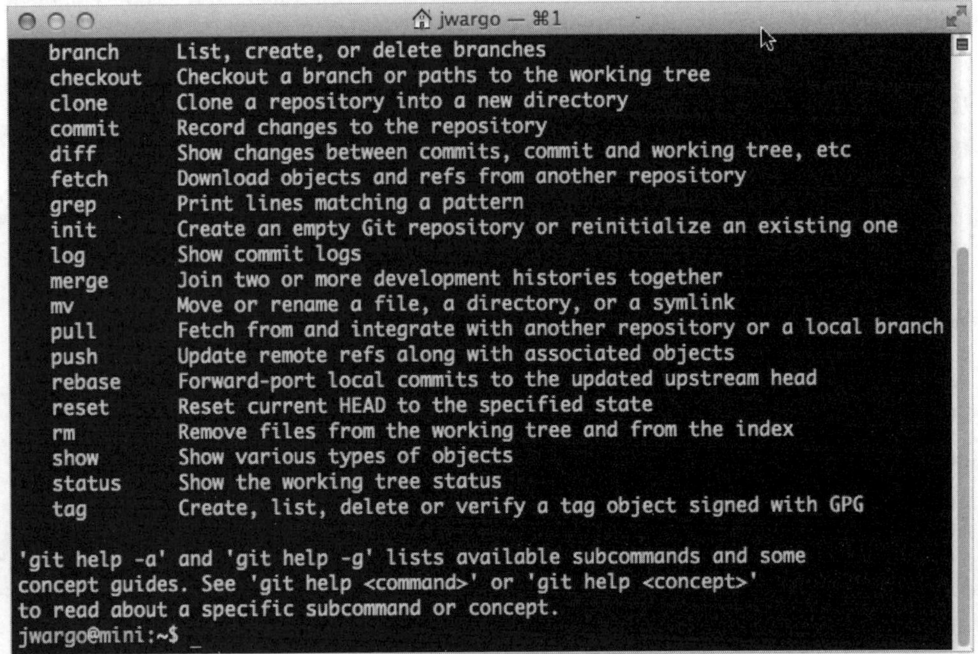

jwargo — ⌘1
branch List, create, or delete branches
checkout Checkout a branch or paths to the working tree
clone Clone a repository into a new directory
commit Record changes to the repository
diff Show changes between commits, commit and working tree, etc
fetch Download objects and refs from another repository
grep Print lines matching a pattern
init Create an empty Git repository or reinitialize an existing one
log Show commit logs
merge Join two or more development histories together
mv Move or rename a file, a directory, or a symlink
pull Fetch from and integrate with another repository or a local branch
push Update remote refs along with associated objects
rebase Forward-port local commits to the updated upstream head
reset Reset current HEAD to the specified state
rm Remove files from the working tree and from the index
show Show various types of objects
status Show the working tree status
tag Create, list, delete or verify a tag object signed with GPG
'git help -a' and 'git help -g' lists available subcommands and some
concept guides. See 'git help <command>' or 'git help <concept>'
to read about a specific subcommand or concept.
jwargo@mini:~$ _

Figure 3.16 Testing the Git Configuration

If you receive an error message indicating that the `git` command couldn't be found, the Git installation didn't complete successfully and you will need to resolve the error before continuing.

Cordova Installation

With Git and Node installed, you're ready to install the Cordova CLI. After all of the work we've done so far, this is going to seem a bit anticlimactic, but here we go. . . .

To install the Cordova CLI on Windows, open a terminal window and issue the following command:

```
npm install -g cordova
```

The `-g` in the command tells NPM to install the Cordova CLI globally; if you did not use this parameter, the CLI will only be available from the current folder.

On Macintosh, you will need to install the CLI using `sudo` with the following command:

```
sudo npm install -g cordova
```

sudo allows you to execute programs with a higher access level, so when you issue the command, you should be prompted for your password before the installation begins. There is supposed to be a way to configure the Macintosh NPM installation so it doesn't require sudo to install modules, but I've not been able to make this work on any of my systems.

NPM will spin for a while, then display the results shown in Figure 3.17.

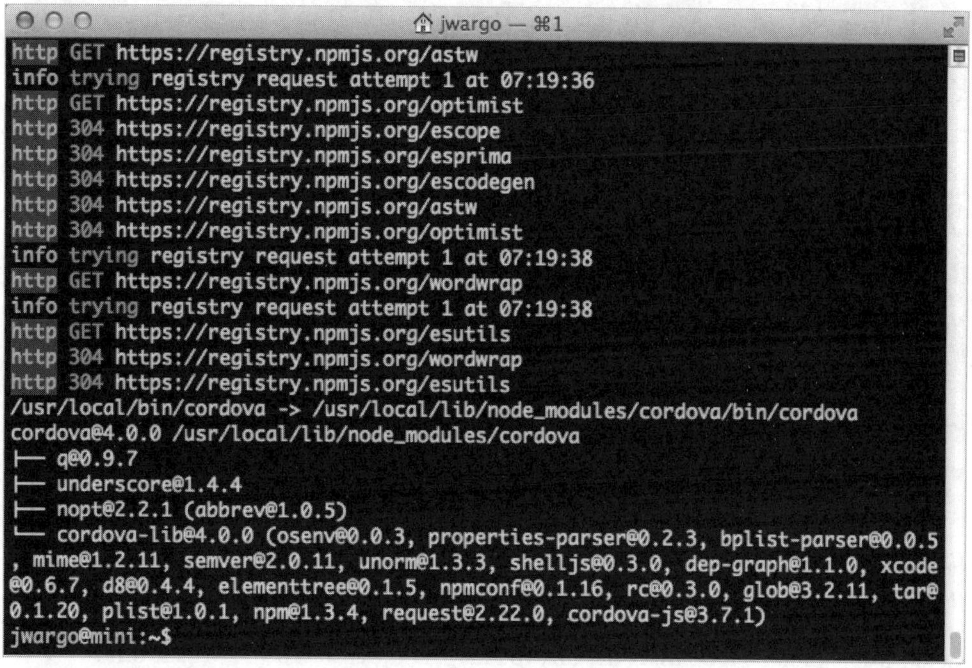

```
jwargo — ⌘1
http GET https://registry.npmjs.org/astw
info trying registry request attempt 1 at 07:19:36
http GET https://registry.npmjs.org/optimist
http 304 https://registry.npmjs.org/escope
http 304 https://registry.npmjs.org/esprima
http 304 https://registry.npmjs.org/escodegen
http 304 https://registry.npmjs.org/astw
http 304 https://registry.npmjs.org/optimist
info trying registry request attempt 1 at 07:19:38
http GET https://registry.npmjs.org/wordwrap
info trying registry request attempt 1 at 07:19:38
http GET https://registry.npmjs.org/esutils
http 304 https://registry.npmjs.org/wordwrap
http 304 https://registry.npmjs.org/esutils
/usr/local/bin/cordova -> /usr/local/lib/node_modules/cordova/bin/cordova
cordova@4.0.0 /usr/local/lib/node_modules/cordova
├── q@0.9.7
├── underscore@1.4.4
├── nopt@2.2.1 (abbrev@1.0.5)
└── cordova-lib@4.0.0 (osenv@0.0.3, properties-parser@0.2.3, bplist-parser@0.0.5
, mime@1.2.11, semver@2.0.11, unorm@1.3.3, shelljs@0.3.0, dep-graph@1.1.0, xcode
@0.6.7, d8@0.4.4, elementtree@0.1.5, npmconf@0.1.16, rc@0.3.0, glob@3.2.11, tar@
0.1.20, plist@1.0.1, npm@1.3.4, request@2.22.0, cordova-js@3.7.1)
jwargo@mini:~$
```

Figure 3.17 Watching the Cordova CLI Installation

That's it; that's all there is to installing the Cordova CLI. To test the installation, open a terminal window, type cordova at the prompt, and press Enter. If everything installed correctly, you should see a screen similar to the one shown in Figure 3.18.

There's a lot of stuff that can go wrong here, but if you've installed all of the prerequisites, it should just work. Where you typically run into problems is with network connectivity or proxy issues. You will have to work through any issues that impact the installation. Refer to the section "Configuring Proxy Settings" in Chapter 4, "Using the Cordova Command-Line Interfaces," for information on how to configure proxy settings.

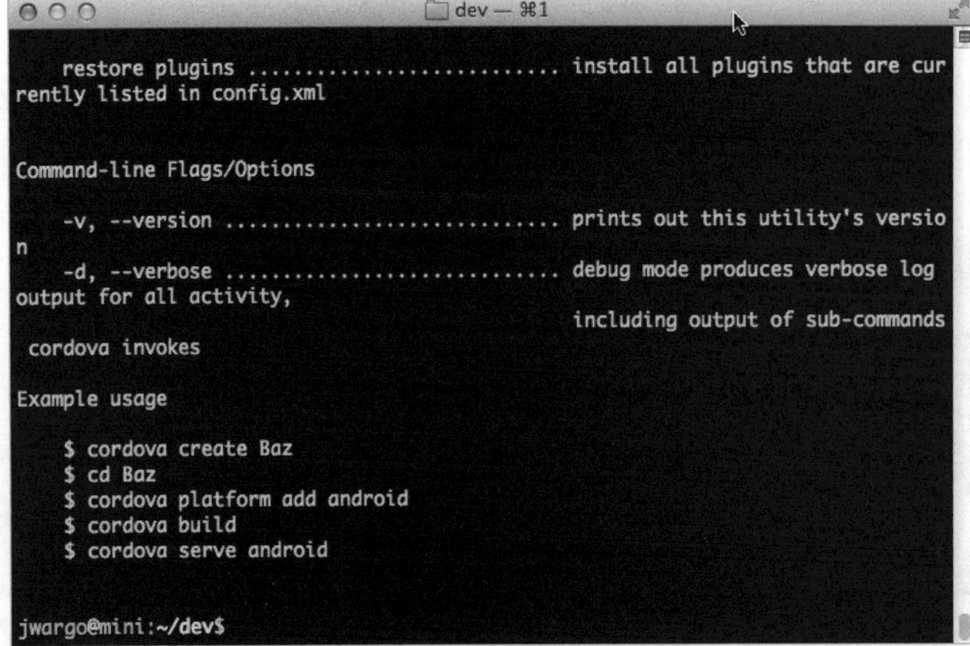

dev — ⌘1
restore plugins .... install all plugins that are cur
rently listed in config.xml
Command-line Flags/Options
-v, --version .... prints out this utility's versio
n
-d, --verbose .... debug mode produces verbose log
output for all activity,
including output of sub-commands
cordova invokes
Example usage
$ cordova create Baz
$ cd Baz
$ cordova platform add android
$ cordova build
$ cordova serve android
jwargo@mini:~/dev$

Figure 3.18 Cordova Help Screen

CLI Requirements for iOS

If you intend to use the CLI to build and test Cordova applications, you may have a few more steps to complete first. Where the installation process is right now, if you attempted to test a Cordova application on iOS using the CLI, you may get the error shown in Figure 3.19.

```
jwargo@mini:~/dev$ cd test
jwargo@mini:~/dev/test$ cordova run ios
Running command: /Users/jwargo/dev/test/platforms/ios/cordova/run
Error: ios-deploy was not found. Please download, build and install version 1.0.
4 or greater from https://github.com/phonegap/ios-deploy into your path. Or 'npm
 install -g ios-deploy' using node.js: http://nodejs.org/
Error: /Users/jwargo/dev/test/platforms/ios/cordova/run: Command failed with exi
t code 1
    at ChildProcess.whenDone (/usr/local/lib/node_modules/cordova/node_modules/c
ordova-lib/src/cordova/superspawn.js:135:23)
    at ChildProcess.emit (events.js:98:17)
    at maybeClose (child_process.js:756:16)
    at Process.ChildProcess._handle.onexit (child_process.js:823:5)
jwargo@mini:~/dev/test$
```

Figure 3.19 Error Running an iOS application from the Command Line

This happens because some of the tools needed for the CLI to launch the iOS simulator aren't included with the Cordova download or the CLI, so you'll have to install them manually. To fix this problem, open a terminal window and enter the following commands:

```
sudo npm install -g ios-deploy
sudo npm install -g ios-sim
```

Notice that there's an error in the error message—the error text is instructing you to execute `npm` to install the required module, but on Macintosh OS X you have to execute `npm` using `sudo` as shown in the example.

> **Note**
>
> This issue affects only the CLI running on Macintosh OS X; you can't run iOS applications on a Windows system.

Installing Plugman

If you're going to be creating your own plugins or will want to manage Cordova projects using Plugman, you will need to install the Plugman CLI on your system. To do this, on Windows, open a terminal window and issue the following command:

```
npm install -g plugman
```

The `-g` in the command tells NPM to install Plugman globally; if you did not use this parameter, Plugman will only be available from the current folder.

On Macintosh, you must install Plugman using `sudo` with the following command:

```
sudo npm install -g plugman
```

To confirm that the installation completed successfully, execute the following command:

```
plugman
```

If Plugman is installed correctly, you should see a help page returned to the console similar to what is shown in Figure 3.20.

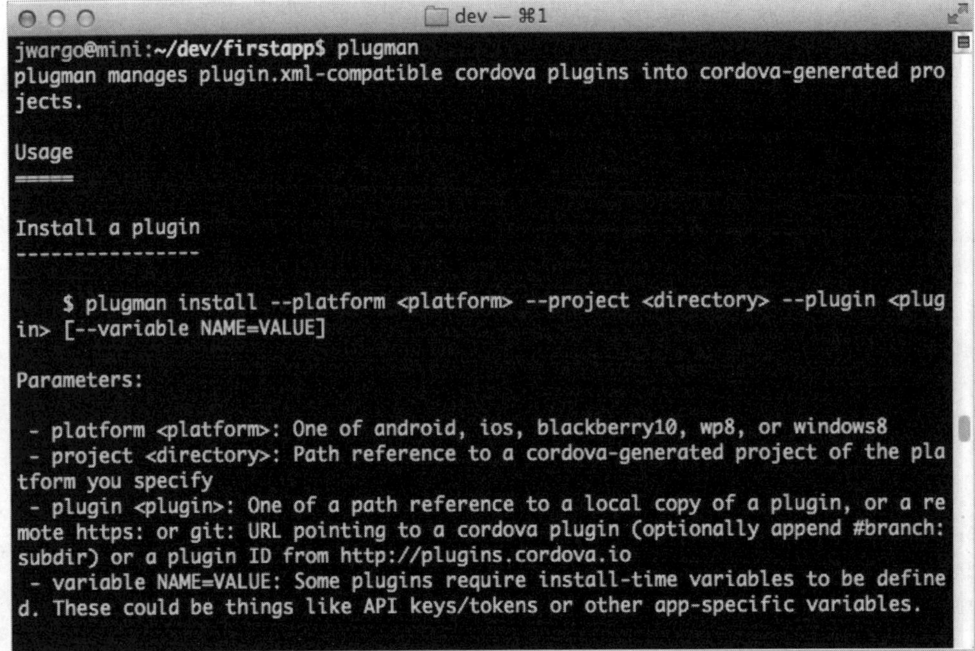

dev — ⌘1
jwargo@mini:~/dev/firstapp$ plugman
plugman manages plugin.xml-compatible cordova plugins into cordova-generated projects.
Usage
=====
Install a plugin

$ plugman install --platform <platform> --project <directory> --plugin <plugin> [--variable NAME=VALUE]
Parameters:
- platform <platform>: One of android, ios, blackberry10, wp8, or windows8
- project <directory>: Path reference to a cordova-generated project of the platform you specify
- plugin <plugin>: One of a path reference to a local copy of a plugin, or a remote https: or git: URL pointing to a cordova plugin (optionally append #branch:subdir) or a plugin ID from http://plugins.cordova.io
- variable NAME=VALUE: Some plugins require install-time variables to be defined. These could be things like API keys/tokens or other app-specific variables.

Figure 3.20 Validating the Plugman Installation

Wrap-Up

In this chapter, I showed you how to install the Cordova CLI on Windows and Macintosh OS X. With these tools in place, you're ready to begin writing your own Cordova applications. In the next chapter, I'll show you how to use the CLI to create and manage your Cordova projects.

4

Using the Cordova Command-Line Interfaces

Rather than have separate processes for each supported mobile platform, the Cordova team created two command-line interfaces (CLIs) developers can use to manage most any aspect of an Apache Cordova project. The primary CLI is the Cordova CLI; the other is Plugman, which is used indirectly by the Cordova CLI to manage plugins and directly by developers creating plugins or doing single-platform development. I will cover both of these tools in this chapter.

PhoneGap has its own CLI—it's basically the Cordova CLI with some additional commands or command parameters added to it. I will cover the additional capabilities of the PhoneGap CLI in Chapter 13, "Using the PhoneGap CLI," after I've introduced you to PhoneGap Build, where most of the additional capabilities apply.

This is an important chapter. I suggest you dig through the Cordova CLI parts of the chapter in order to understand how most developers use Apache Cordova and then come back and take a look at the Plugman stuff when you're creating your own plugins and the PhoneGap stuff if you find you need the special capabilities PhoneGap provides.

CLIs for Different Types of Cordova Developers

When Cordova 3.0 came out, for me the focus was on the Cordova CLI and what it did for Cordova developers. It seemed to me to be a very nice, simple, and elegant solution to the cross-platform development problems Cordova was trying to solve. As I monitored the Cordova dev list, I noticed comments every now and then that indicated that some on the list never used the Cordova CLI. I reached out to the group to see if I could figure out why.

Basically, there are two types of Cordova developers: the web developer building cross-platform mobile applications and the native developer who is either using Cordova to get around some specific problem but is still doing mostly native development or is a plugin developer. I'm a developer of the first type, and all of my Cordova books are targeted at this type of developer.

If you're a developer working on a cross-platform development project, the Cordova CLI takes care of everything. Project, platform, and plugin management are all done by the CLI; all the developer has to do is write his or her web application and compile, test, fix, and distribute. The Cordova CLI is for developers who aren't really mobile developers. They know enough about mobile to get around but primarily leverage their web development skills over their native skills.

Plugman, on the other hand, exists to enable everything related to plugin development and plugin management. Since we're dealing with plugins, and a big part of plugins is native code, it's easy to see that Plugman is more for the native developer. If you're creating new plugins, you can't really use the Cordova CLI. If you're mucking around within the native project settings or customizing the native code, the things that the Cordova CLI does for the Cordova developer are only going to mess up customizations and frustrate the developer.

When I asked Joe Bowser, one of the Cordova committers on the Android platform, about the Cordova CLI, here's what he said:

> The biggest problem with the CLI is the fact that it hides the platforms in the .cordova directory and that if you're an advanced user of Cordova you have no way to make custom modifications to the source code on a per-project basis. We've run into this numerous times where certain things need to be modified on a WebView on 3.0 that you can't easily do anymore. Now, these changes by themselves are individual edge cases, which I don't want to see put in the XML of the project, but if you hide the source, you end up having to do crazy things like declare Java code in XML to override these cases. I think that people should be able to modify the code and use it whichever way they want and that they should be able to do this on a per-project basis if they want, and I view the CLI as something that gets in the way of that, which is why I have such a low opinion of it.

So essentially, there are two different developer workflows, and there are two CLIs in Cordova because each one targets a different developer workflow. The traditional cross-platform Cordova developer workflow will be described in great detail in the next chapter; you can also read more about how the Cordova team views the workflows at http://goo.gl/YYHIWI.

Troubleshooting

It's never good to start a chapter with troubleshooting information, but when working with the CLI, there are a couple of troubleshooting things you will need to know before you get started. The tips highlighted here apply to both the Cordova and Plugman CLIs.

Configuring Proxy Settings

As you saw in the previous chapter, there's no download and installation of software for Cordova; everything you need is installed on the fly as needed. The same is true for activities that happen through usage of the Cordova CLI. When you need something, if you don't already have it cached on your local development system, the CLI will go out to the Internet to grab it for you automatically.

Most home, independent, or small-company developers don't have a lot of corporate networking hardware affecting how they access Internet-based resources. When in a home office, in a coffee shop, or on an airplane, the developer workstation can usually reach out and get what it needs when it needs it, provided the network connectivity is available.

Unfortunately, corporate developers, developers who work for midsize to large organizations, often have extra layers of authentication and access control in place to help protect the corporation. In many of these environments, access to external resources is controlled by a proxy. All outbound requests are forwarded to the proxy; it's the proxy that decides whether you're authorized to access the external resource, and it's the proxy that retrieves the content on behalf of the system.

For the most part, your typical desktop or laptop in a proxied environment will already be configured to use the proxy—the system is preconfigured with the appropriate proxy settings, and most networked applications will automatically leverage those settings. Git and NPM, on the other hand, aren't your typical network applications. In order to operate in a proxied environment, your development workstation may have to have some additional configuration settings changed.

If you know you're operating in an environment with a proxy, or if you try to run Cordova CLI commands that make use of the network and get errors indicating that there's a network access problem, you may need to configure proxy settings for Git and/or NPM.

If you need to set proxy settings, you must first determine what the proxy server configuration is. Typically all you'll need is the proxy server host address and a port number. If you're not sure what these are, reach out to your corporate help desk or IT administrator for help.

Git is configured using the `git config` command and has two settings that affect its proxy configuration: `http.proxy` and `https.proxy`. To configure the proxy settings for Git, open a terminal window and execute the following commands:

```
git config --global http.proxy http://PROXY_ADDRESS[:port]
git config --global https.proxy http://PROXY_ADDRESS[:port]
```

In these examples, replace the `PROXY_ADDRESS` with the host address of the proxy server and, optionally—depending on your environment—`port` with the network port the proxy is listening on. So, if your proxy server host address is http://proxy-srvr, and the proxy server is listening on port number 8080, you would issue the following commands:

```
git config --global http.proxy http://proxy-srvr:8080
git config --global https.proxy http://proxy-srvr:8080
```

NPM, on the other hand, is configured through the `npm config` command, but it essentially works the same way. To configure the proxy settings for NPM, open a terminal window and execute the following commands:

```
npm config set proxy http://PROXY_ADDRESS[:port]
npm config set https-proxy http://PROXY_ADDRESS[:port]
```

For the example used previously, you would use the following commands:

```
npm config set proxy http://proxy-srvr:8080
npm config set https-proxy http://proxy-srvr:8080
```

After you've successfully configured these settings, try your CLI commands again to see if the network errors have gone away.

Enabling Verbose Output

I've been using the Cordova CLI for a very long time. I was working on my *Apache Cordova 3 Programming* book and an enterprise SDK based on Cordova as the CLI was being developed, so I really see myself as part of the early group of beta testers for the CLI. In the first releases, the CLI didn't tell you anything when it ran; it simply did its stuff and returned you to the command prompt when it was done.

When developers ran into problems, they needed some way to get information from the CLI about what happened. The CLI developers added a command-line switch, `-d`, that would cause the CLI to spit out more information about what it was doing as it ran. Eventually, the CLI team changed the CLI so it at least told you something as it ran, then the `-d` switch turned on an even more verbose output.

For example, the following Cordova command returns a little information about the prepare process:

```
cordova prepare
```

In general, as long as the command works before returning to the terminal window, that's OK, but when working with a command that fails silently or fails with an unclear error message, it's useful to be able to see exactly what's happening with the command.

If you issue the following command instead:

```
cordova -d prepare
```

the terminal window will fill with many lines of text (which I won't list here) that show the status of every step performed by the CLI during processing of the command. Some of the information is provided by the CLI commands, but some is generated by any third-party tool that might be called by the CLI.

You can also use `--verbose` as a command-line switch to enable the same verbose output mode.

Overdoing Verbose Output Mode

What I've found is that many developers use the `-d` switch with every CLI command, and that makes no sense to me. The CLI usually works, it simply works most every time, and you really only rarely need to enable debug mode. What I suggest you do is run the commands as you need to and resort to verbose mode only when something fails. You'll do a whole lot less typing that way (three fewer characters for every Cordova CLI command you execute), and you don't have to read all that text on the screen to see that everything worked.

The Cordova CLI

As Cordova applications are web applications and can be coded using any text editor, and the mobile device manufacturers use different IDEs and project structures for building native applications, there isn't a single tool a developer can use to build Cordova applications for multiple target platforms. Instead, the Cordova team created a single tool a developer can use to interface with the tools for each mobile platform: the Cordova CLI. Think of it as a terminal-driven abstraction layer for Cordova development.

Developers use the Cordova CLI to manage most aspects of the Cordova development process. The Cordova CLI is a command-line interface that adds a suite of commands a developer can use to

- Create cross-platform Cordova application projects
- Add support for each of the Cordova supported mobile device platforms
- List supported mobile device platforms
- Remove support for a mobile device platform
- Add a plugin to a project (this can be a core Cordova plugin, a third-party plugin, or a plugin you've created yourself)
- List plugins installed in a project
- Remove a plugin from a project
- Prepare, compile, and build projects
- Save project information so the project can be easily transported to another developer's system or to a version control system
- Serve an application project's web content via a web server
- Launch an application in the appropriate mobile device simulator

With these commands in place, a developer can manage the complete lifecycle of a Cordova application. Each of these options will be described in the remainder of the chapter.

When support for a new platform is added, the development team implementing the platform capabilities simply creates the necessary underlying native and JavaScript code, creates the appropriate core project files, then implements the CLI capabilities for the platform. Each platform operates differently, with its own custom code, but they all respond to the same CLI commands. What happens under the covers when the command executes doesn't matter as long as the results are predictable and help you achieve something.

Cordova CLI Command Summary

Table 4.1 provides a summary of the available CLI commands; the sections that follow describe each of the operations in greater detail.

Table 4.1 Cordova CLI Command Summary

CLI Command	Description
`help`	Displays information about the available CLI commands.
`info`	Displays information about the current project.
`create`	Creates a Cordova project and associated project folders and files.
`platform`	Manages the mobile device platforms associated with a Cordova project.
`plugin`	Manages the installation and uninstallation of Cordova plugins.
`prepare`	Copies the web application content from the Cordova project's www folder into the project's mobile platform project folders.
`compile`	Packages web applications into native Cordova applications.
`build`	Prepares, then packages web applications into native Cordova applications.
`emulate`	Runs a Cordova application in one or more mobile device platforms' device simulators.
`run`	Runs a Cordova application in one or more mobile devices.
`serve`	Serves the web application content so it can be accessed via a web browser.
`save`	Writes plugin information to the project's config.xml so the project can be more easily ported to another developer workstation.
`restore`	Restores the plugins associated with a project after the project has been copied to another developer workstation.

Using the Cordova CLI

In this section, I will show you how to use the commands exposed through the Cordova CLI. I'll cover the mechanics of the commands and what happens when each is executed; look to Chapter 5, "The Mechanics of Cordova Development," for more information about the Cordova application project files and Chapter 15, "Cordova Development End to End," for the end-to-end development process.

As the CLI is a command-line interface, you have to execute the CLI commands from a command line. On Windows, this is the Windows Command Prompt application, and on Macintosh OS X and Linux, this is a Terminal Window. Since the CLI is implemented using Node, which should be automatically added to the system path, you should be able to execute any Cordova CLI command from any location on your system.

Most of the commands operate on an existing Cordova project, so except for the `help` command (described soon) and the `create` command (explained in the following section), all of the Cordova CLI commands must be executed from within a Cordova project folder context. What this means is that your terminal window must be open to the project folder before issuing many of the Cordova CLI commands.

Getting Help

To learn more about what commands are available in the Cordova CLI, you can open a terminal window and get help by typing

```
cordova help
```

You can also check the CLI version number by using the following command:

```
cordova -v
```

or

```
cordova -version
```

The CLI will return to the console window the text describing the version of Cordova running on the system.

Creating a Cordova Project

Before you can do any Cordova development, you must first create an application project. To help you, the Cordova CLI includes a `create` command that is used to create new projects.

To create a new Cordova project, open a terminal window, navigate to the folder where you want the project folder created, then issue the following command:

```
cordova create project_folder
```

This will create a simple Cordova project structure and copy in the base web content files you can use for the application. If you supply only a folder name for the `create` command, the CLI will name your application project HelloCordova automatically.

You can also specify an application ID and application name using the following command:

```
cordova create project_folder app_id app_name
```

What this does is create the same project folder, but it also writes the application ID to the application's configuration file and sets a custom name for the application.

As an example, to create a project in a folder called firstapp but with an application name of FirstApp, you would issue the following command:

```
cordova create firstapp com.ac4p.firstapp FirstApp
```

The terminal window highlighting the command and the results presented by the CLI are shown in Figure 4.1. In this particular example, I executed the command on a Macintosh, but the results would be exactly the same if the command were executed on a Windows or Linux system.

dev — ⌘1
jwargo@mini:~/dev$ cordova create firstapp com.ac4p.firstapp FirstApp
Creating a new cordova project with name "FirstApp" and id "com.ac4p.firstapp" a
t location "/Users/jwargo/dev/firstapp"
jwargo@mini:~/dev$ _

Figure 4.1 Cordova CLI—Creating a New Project

> **Context Reminder**
>
> All of the Cordova CLI commands operate against the current folder. The `create` command creates a folder structure for your Cordova projects while the remaining commands must be issued from within the project folder created by `create`.

When the `create` command runs, CLI will create the folder structure shown in Figure 4.2. The folder structure organizes the Cordova project in a way that simplifies the process of using this application across multiple mobile device platforms. Notice that the www folder is separate; this allows you to create a single web application that's shared across multiple mobile device platforms. I'll talk more about the web project structure and files in the next chapter. Right now all you need to know is that the web application running within your Cordova application is defined by the contents of the www folder shown in the figure.

Figure 4.2 New Cordova Project Folder

The platforms folder is used to store a separate folder for each mobile device platform being supported by this application. I'll talk more about this in the next section. The plugins folder is used to store the source code files and libraries for each plugin used by the application. I'll talk more about this later as well.

The project's config.xml file defines settings that describe the mobile application; this file will be covered in detail in Chapter 5.

The hooks folder may not be there by the time you read this; the Cordova team is thinking of hiding it in order to not confuse users. The functionality exposed through the hooks folder will be described in Chapter 6, "Automation and the Cordova CLI."

Cordova CLI Lazy Loading

Instead of preloading everything the Cordova CLI needs, the CLI uses a process called lazy loading to download the project files it needs to create Cordova projects and add platform support to a project. The files are downloaded only when you need them.

When you create a project, the CLI will download the default Cordova HelloWorld project, extract it, and copy it to the appropriate project folder. When you add a platform to a project, the CLI will download a preconfigured project for the target platform, extract it, and copy it to the platform folder.

The CLI uses a special folder called .cordova for storing its lazy-loaded files. The folder is located immediately under your user's home folder (C:\users\user_name\.cordova on Windows, /users/user_name/.cordova on Macintosh). You can see an example of the folder structure in Figure 4.3. On Macintosh, the folder is hidden, so you can't view it in Finder without first reconfiguring the system to show hidden files and folders in Finder.

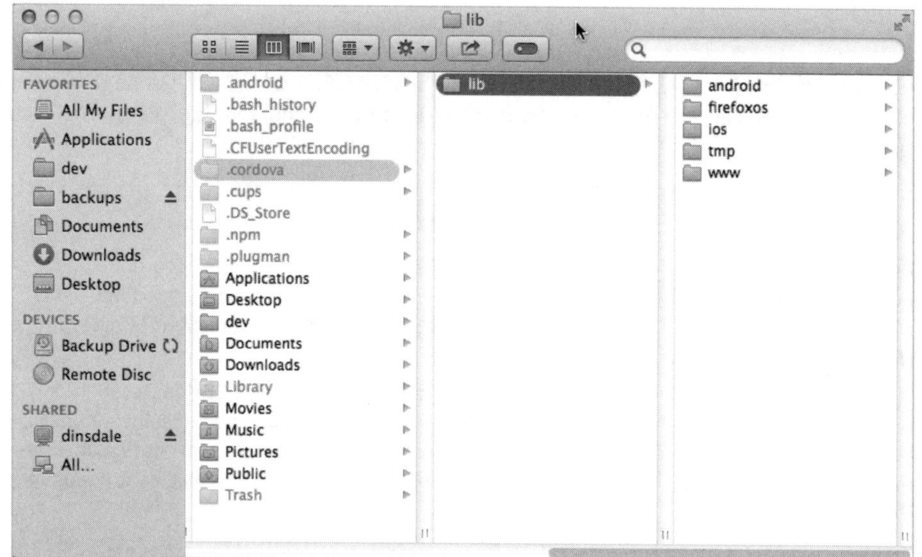

Figure 4.3 CLI .cordova Folder Structure

If you get an error when creating a project or adding a platform, repeat the process using the -d debug flag and look for an indication of what is happening. If you see a message that says the CLI has the files it needs and is skipping the download, take a look in the folder name mentioned in the error message. If there are no files located in the specified location, you should whack the empty folder and try again.

In the sections that follow, I'll describe the remaining CLI commands. The `create` command creates a new project in a subfolder of the folder from where the command was issued. The remaining commands must be issued from a terminal window pointing within the project folder.

In this section, I created a project called FirstApp and the CLI created a folder called firstapp for the project. In order for me to issue CLI commands that manipulate the FirstApp project, I must use the terminal window's `cd` command to change the directory to the firstapp folder before using any of the commands described in the remaining sections.

A Cordova project's CLI configuration is stored in the config.json file located in the project's .cordova folder. The file is not created by default, but you can create it automatically when you first create the project. To do this, append a JSON object to the end of the `create` command; the JSON object should contain the key/value pairs you want written to the file. Here's an example:

```
cordova create test com.ac4p.test test {\"key1\":\"value1\"}
```

In this example, I'm adding a configuration option `key1` with a value of `value1` to the file. When you execute this command, it will create the config.json file in the project's .cordova folder and populate it with the following data:

```
{
  "key1": "value1"
}
```

Notice how I had to escape the quotation marks in the JSON object; if I hadn't done that, the CLI would not have been able to treat the extra text I added to the command line as a JSON object.

Plugin Search Path

I know we haven't covered plugins yet, but there's something I need to tell you about now. For the most part, most of the plugins you'll be working with can be loaded into your Cordova project from a Git repository or, beginning with more recent versions of Cordova, the NPM registry (www.npmjs.org).

If you're working with plugins that are installed as part of a third-party SDK installation or plugins you've created on your local development system, you may have difficulties installing dependent plugins (plugins that are used by plugins you are installing) from your local system. There's a bug in the CLI where it can't seem to locate all of the plugins it needs in this scenario.

The Cordova team implemented an ugly hack developers can use to get around this limitation. It's not pretty, and I really wish they hadn't implemented it this way, but there's nothing I can do about it now and there are currently no plans to fix it. The hack is to configure a `plugin_search_path` configuration option for the Cordova development environment.

Typically, when adding local plugins to a project (I'll show you how in the plugins section), you provide a full path pointing to the plugin's folder. When the CLI goes to add dependent plugins, it fails because it doesn't know how to search the local file system for additional plugins. The search path therefore helps direct the CLI to locate dependent plugins.

You can set the `plugin_search_path` configuration setting when you create your Cordova project. To do so, add some JSON to the end of the `create` command that looks like the following:

```
"{\"plugin_search_path\":\"some_path_name\"}"
```

For example, if you have a set of plugins installed in /Users/dev/mysdk/plugins/, the JSON you add to the end of the `create` command would be

```
"{\"plugin_search_path\":\"/Users/dev/mysdk/plugins/\"}"
```

The complete `create` command would look like the following:

```
cordova create myapp com.ac4p.myapp MyApp
"{\"plugin_search_path\":\"/Users/dev/mysdk/plugins/\"}"
```

The reason why this is such an ugly option is because you shouldn't be passing JSON on a command line, plus, because you're dealing with quotes within a quoted string, you have to escape all quotation marks with the backslash character. It's just way, way too easy to mess up when doing something like this. I hope they'll come up with a better option before you need to use this.

By default, the `create` command will create a new Cordova project and provide a simple base web application for your project in the project's www folder. This approach is nice if you're just getting started with Cordova and want to get up and running as quickly as possible. Most developers simply whack the contents of that folder and replace them with their own web application files.

The Cordova CLI provides a mechanism you can use to copy in your own web application files during project create. To do this, use the `--copy-from` switch and a file path pointing to a folder containing the files you want to use:

```
cordova create firstapp com.ac4p.firstapp FirstApp --copy-from webAppFolder
```

In this example, `webAppFolder` refers to a file path pointing to the folder containing the web application files.

Many developers want to do their web application development using a different folder structure from the one Cordova imposes on them. To accommodate this, you can use the `--link-to` switch to link the Cordova project's www folder to an existing folder:

```
cordova create firstapp com.ac4p.firstapp FirstApp --link-to webAppFolder
```

When you do this, the Cordova project www folder is just a link to the `webAppFolder`; edit the files there, and they will be pulled into the project (through the link) during prepare, build, and so on. With this approach, you can check your web development files into a version control system, and the Cordova project is just an easily replaceable tool used to manage the build/test process.

> **Warning**
>
> On Windows, the CLI needs administrator privileges to create a symbolic link. You'll therefore have to execute the Windows terminal as an administrator. To do this, right-click on the terminal window shortcut and select Run as administrator.

Platform Management

The project structure we've created so far has only a few empty folders plus a web application project. You could start work on your project's web application now, but Cordova doesn't yet know anything about the different mobile device platforms it needs to support for this project. You'll use the Cordova `platform` command to manage the project files for each of the mobile device platforms your application supports.

Adding Platforms

To add support for a particular mobile device platform to your Cordova application, open a terminal window, navigate into the Cordova project folder, then issue the following command:

```
cordova platform add platform_name
```

> **Warning**
>
> The development tools used to create projects for the particular platform must be installed on the system and visible to the CLI before a platform can be added. The CLI may need the platform's native tools to create a new project, so if the tools are not available to the CLI, the command will not work.

For example, if you wanted to add an Android project to your Cordova application, you would issue the following command in a terminal window pointing to the Cordova project folder:

```
cordova platform add android
```

You can also specify multiple target mobile device platforms in a single command as shown in the following example:

```
cordova platform add android firefoxos ios
```

The command will run, create the necessary folder structure for each platform, and then download and extract complete project files for each target platform. Using the project I created in the previous section as an example, I first changed to the firstapp folder, then issued the `platform` command as shown in Figure 4.4.

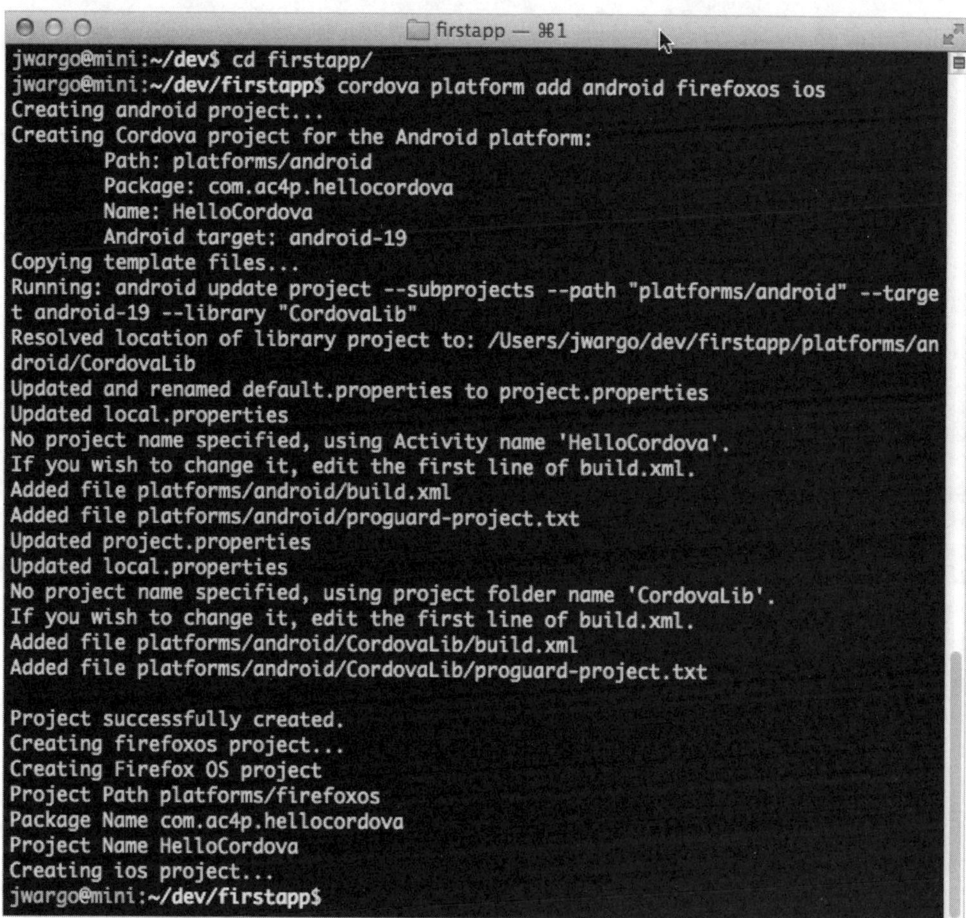

firstapp — ⌘1
jwargo@mini:~/dev$ cd firstapp/
jwargo@mini:~/dev/firstapp$ cordova platform add android firefoxos ios
Creating android project...
Creating Cordova project for the Android platform:
Path: platforms/android
Package: com.ac4p.hellocordova
Name: HelloCordova
Android target: android-19
Copying template files...
Running: android update project --subprojects --path "platforms/android" --targe
t android-19 --library "CordovaLib"
Resolved location of library project to: /Users/jwargo/dev/firstapp/platforms/an
droid/CordovaLib
Updated and renamed default.properties to project.properties
Updated local.properties
No project name specified, using Activity name 'HelloCordova'.
If you wish to change it, edit the first line of build.xml.
Added file platforms/android/build.xml
Added file platforms/android/proguard-project.txt
Updated project.properties
Updated local.properties
No project name specified, using project folder name 'CordovaLib'.
If you wish to change it, edit the first line of build.xml.
Added file platforms/android/CordovaLib/build.xml
Added file platforms/android/CordovaLib/proguard-project.txt
Project successfully created.
Creating firefoxos project...
Creating Firefox OS project
Project Path platforms/firefoxos
Package Name com.ac4p.hellocordova
Project Name HelloCordova
Creating ios project...
jwargo@mini:~/dev/firstapp$

Figure 4.4 Cordova CLI—Adding iOS Support to a Cordova Project

You can see from the console output that the process did quite a few things as it worked. Remember, what happens here is dictated by the tools provided by each target mobile device platform. For Android, you can see that there's a lot going on—that's because the CLI uses the Google-supplied ADT Ant commands to execute project-related tasks, and the Ant scripts output a lot of information about what they're doing as they work. For Firefox OS and iOS, the project uses custom scripts provided by the Cordova platform developers to set up the projects.

If you take a look at Figure 4.5, you'll see that my project has some new folders and files. At this point, you could fire up ADT, Xcode, or the Firefox developer tools, open the project, and run the application.

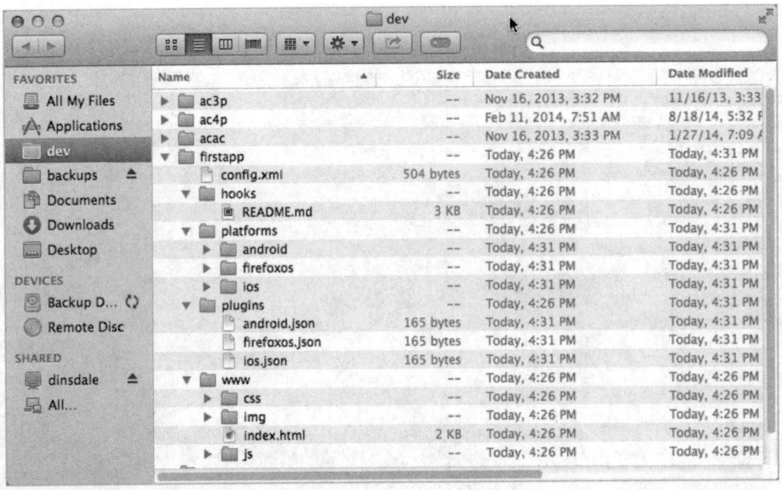

Figure 4.5 Cordova Project Folder with iOS Platform Added

If you now take a look at the firstapp folder we've been working with, you will see that the project's platforms folder now contains an android folder with a complete Android project inside as shown in Figure 4.6.

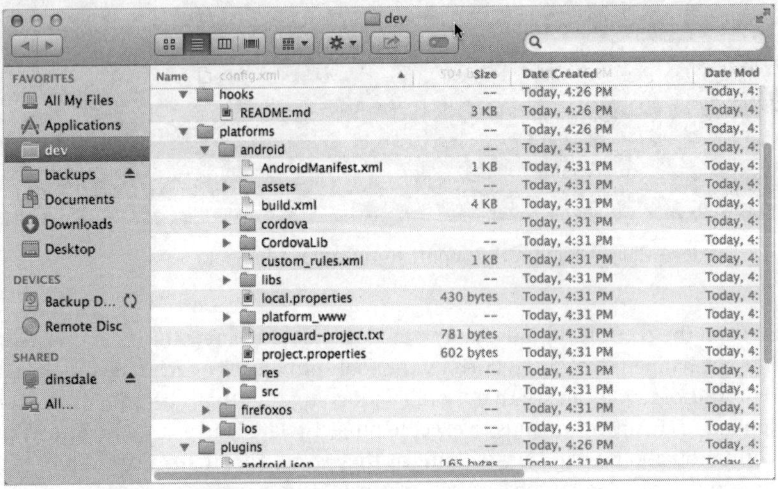

Figure 4.6 Cordova Project Folder with Android Platform Added

You can open the Android project in the Android SDK, then run and debug the application in the Android emulator or on a physical device. I'll show you how to do this in Chapter 7, "Android Development with Cordova."

You don't have to add all of your platforms at the same time; you can add them individually as I've shown here, or in batches. If you are working for a while with a particular set of platforms and later decide you want to add another, simply use the `cordova platform add` command to add your new platform to the existing project.

Listing Platforms

When you're not sure what platforms are associated with a particular project, you can easily look at the project folder structure to figure this out. The Cordova CLI also gives you a command you can use to list the platforms that are associated with a particular Cordova project. To obtain the platform list, simply issue any of the following commands in a terminal window pointing to a Cordova project folder:

```
cordova platforms
cordova platform ls
cordova platform list
```

The CLI will return a list of the names of each of the platforms defined within the project as well as a list of platforms that can be used on this system as shown in Figure 4.7.

```
jwargo@mini:~/dev/firstapp$ cordova platforms
Installed platforms: android 3.5.1, firefoxos 3.5.0, ios 3.5.0
Available platforms: amazon-fireos, blackberry10
jwargo@mini:~/dev/firstapp$
```

Figure 4.7 Cordova CLI—Listing Project Platforms

Removing Platforms

If you decide that your application no longer needs to support a particular mobile platform, you can remove it by issuing the following command:

```
cordova platform remove platform_name
```

You can also use the shortcut `rm` instead of `remove` to remove platforms:

```
cordova platform rm platform_name
```

So, for my test project, if I wanted to remove the project files for the iOS project, I would issue the following command:

```
cordova platform remove ios
```

You can see the results of this operation in Figure 4.8.

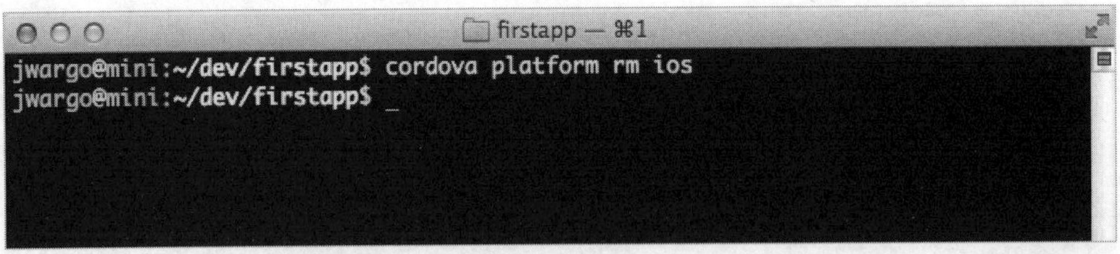

```
firstapp — ⌘1
jwargo@mini:~/dev/firstapp$ cordova platform rm ios
jwargo@mini:~/dev/firstapp$ _
```

Figure 4.8 Cordova CLI—Removing Platforms

As you can see from the figure, the command doesn't return anything to the terminal window on success, so unless you see an error reported, you have to assume that the command worked. If you change your mind and want to add the platform back, just use the `cordova platform add` command to put it back.

Updating Platforms

After Cordova 3.0 was released, the Cordova development team began work to separate the different components of the framework. Instead of the monthly releases that included everything—the CLI, platforms, plugins, and so on—the team started releasing individual components as soon as they were ready. The ultimate goal is to enable you to build Cordova applications using whatever compatible components you want.

In order to accommodate this release strategy, the team added commands to the Cordova CLI that allow a developer to update the platform code within a project. If you have an existing project and want to know whether there is updated code available for the platforms used by the project, you can open a terminal window, navigate to the Cordova project folder, and issue the following command:

```
cordova platforms check
```

The CLI will churn for a little bit, then return the list of platforms that have available updates:

```
android @ 4.0.0 could be updated to: 4.0.1
```

To perform the update, use the following command:

```
cordova platforms update android
```

The CLI will retrieve the updated platform code and update the console as it performs the update:

```
Running: android update project --subprojects --path
"C:\Users\jwargo\dev\ac4p\firstapp\platforms\android" --target android-19
--library "CordovaLib"
Resolved location of library project to:
C:\Users\jwargo\dev\ac4p\firstapp\platforms\android\CordovaLib
Updated project.properties
Updated local.properties
Updated file C:\Users\jwargo\dev\ac4p\firstapp\platforms\android\
proguard-project.txt
Updated project.properties
Updated local.properties
Updated file C:\Users\jwargo\dev\ac4p\firstapp\platforms\android\CordovaLib\
proguard-project.txt

Android project is now at version 4.0.1
```

You can also use the following command format:

```
cordova platforms up android
```

With this command, you must provide the platform you want to update; you can't just issue a generic command and update all of the platforms associated with a project.

Plugin Management

The ability to manage a Cordova project's plugin configuration is one of the best features of the CLI. Instead of your having to manually copy around plugin files and manually edit configuration files, the CLI does it all for you. In this section, I will show you how to use the `cordova plugin` command to manage the plugins used in a Cordova project.

Adding Plugins

To add a plugin to an existing project, open a terminal window, navigate to the Cordova project folder, and issue the following command:

```
cordova plugin add path_to_plugin
```

In this example, the `path_to_plugin` parameter refers to one of the several ways you can point the CLI to a particular plugin's installation files. The CLI can pull plugin code from most any location; if the system can access the location where the plugin files are located, you can install the plugin using the CLI.

> **Warning**
>
> Installing plugins using one of the Cordova CLIs is the only supported way to add plugins to a Cordova project. With previous versions of the framework, plugins were added manually by the developer copying files around and modifying configuration files. If you try to use that approach with Cordova 3.0 and beyond, you run the risk of corrupting your Cordova project.

When Cordova 3.0 was released, all of the core Cordova plugins resided on GitHub, so you would use a GitHub repository URL to point to the plugin's files. In this scenario, to add the Camera plugin to a Cordova application, you would use the following command:

```
cordova plugin add https://git-wip-us.apache.org/repos/asf/cordova-plugin-camera.git
```

The core plugins eventually moved to the Cordova plugin repository and now to npmjs.org, but there still may be times where you need to pull a plugin from GitHub.

Beginning with Cordova 3.1, plugins can be installed directly from the Cordova Plugin Registry (http://plugins.cordova.io) just by specifying the plugin's unique ID. To add the Console plugin to your application, for example, you would issue the following command from a terminal window pointing at your Cordova project folder:

```
cordova plugin add org.apache.cordova.console
```

The CLI will check the Cordova Plugin Registry for a plugin matching the ID specified, pull down the plugin code, and install it into your project. The CLI will show a simple summary of its progress installing the plugin as shown in Figure 4.9. If the plugin you are adding depends on one or more plugins to do its work, those plugins will be installed during this process as well.

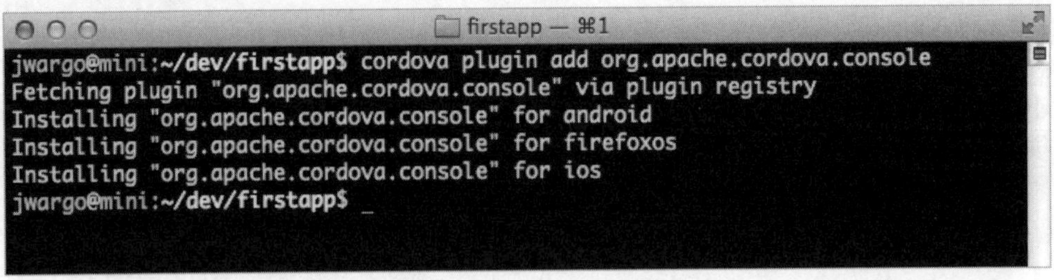

```
firstapp — ⌘1
jwargo@mini:~/dev/firstapp$ cordova plugin add org.apache.cordova.console
Fetching plugin "org.apache.cordova.console" via plugin registry
Installing "org.apache.cordova.console" for android
Installing "org.apache.cordova.console" for firefoxos
Installing "org.apache.cordova.console" for ios
jwargo@mini:~/dev/firstapp$ _
```

Figure 4.9 Cordova CLI—Adding Plugins

If you have a plugin installed locally—for example, if you are working with a third-party plugin or one you created yourself and the files are stored on the local PC—you can pass in the file path pointing to the folder where the plugin's code is located using the following command:

```
cordova plugin add file_path_to_plugin_folder
```

If the plugin's code is located in C:\dev\plugins\my_plugin_name, the command would look like this:

```
cordova plugin add c:\dev\plugins\my_plugin_name
```

If you are installing plugins from the local file system and those plugins have local dependencies, you can specify the plugin search path by adding the `--searchpath` switch to the `plugin add` command:

```
cordova plugin add c:\dev\plugins\my_plugin_name --searchpath c:\dev\plugins
```

You should also be able to install a local plugin by name using the plugin search path:

```
cordova plugin add com.mycompany.myplugin --searchpath c:\dev\plugins
```

You can specify multiple plugin search paths by separating each path with the appropriate delimiter for the OS. Use `;` for Windows and `:` for Macintosh OS X and Linux. You can also use the `--searchpath` switch multiple times within a command, specifying a different path for each instance of the switch.

Figure 4.10 shows a Cordova project folder structure after a plugin has been added using the CLI. All of the plugin code has been added to the plugins folder within the Cordova project's folder structure.

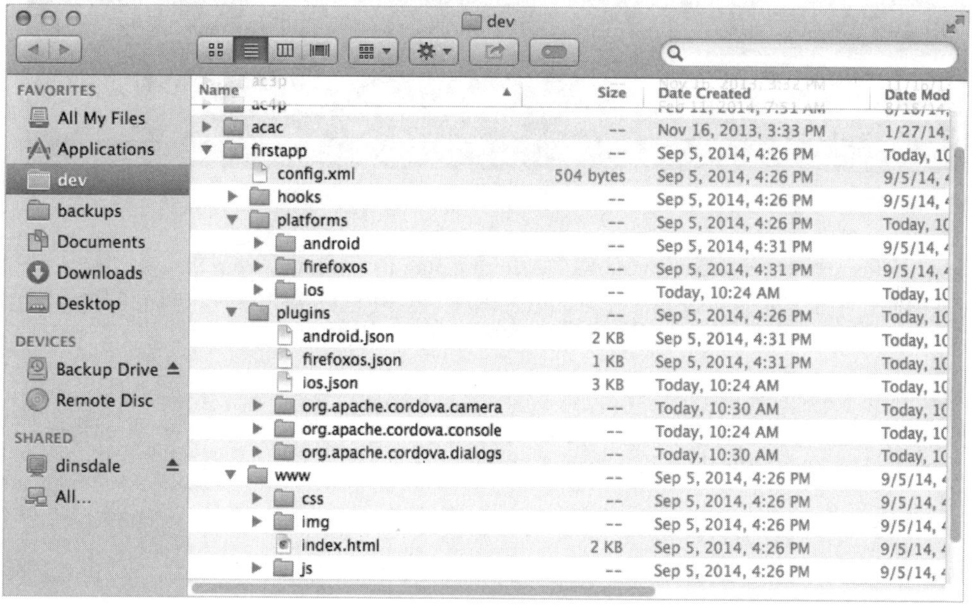

Figure 4.10 Cordova Project plugins Folder Content

Notice that each plugin has a unique namespace built using the reverse-DNS name convention plus the plugin name. All of the Apache Cordova core plugins are referred to by the plugin name added to the end of `org.apache.cordova`. So, we can refer to the Camera plugin we just added to the project via the CLI as `org.apache.cordova.camera`. This approach to plugin naming helps reduce the potential for name conflicts among similar plugins created by different organizations.

Plugins have separate folders for the source code for each supported mobile device platform. Additionally, there are JavaScript files that are consumed by Cordova applications in the www folder. There is a lot more to know about plugins; I'll dig deeper into the plugin project folder structure when I cover plugin development in Chapter 16, "Creating Cordova Plugins."

Listing Plugins

To view a list of the plugins installed in a Cordova project, open a terminal window, navigate to a Cordova project folder, then issue any of the following commands:

```
cordova plugins
cordova plugin ls
cordova plugin list
```

The CLI will scan the project folder and return the list of plugins as shown in Figure 4.11.

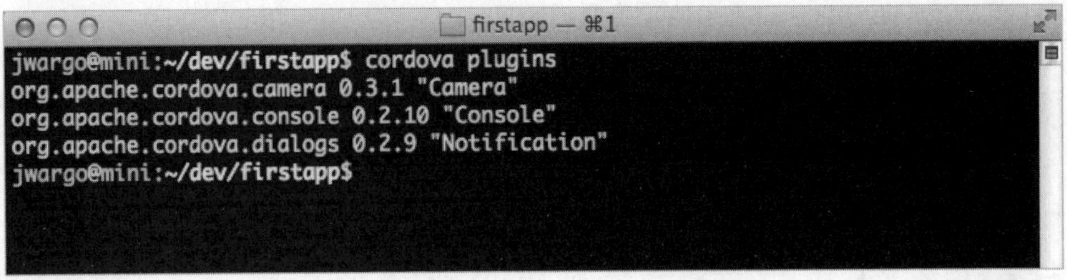

```
firstapp — ⌘1
jwargo@mini:~/dev/firstapp$ cordova plugins
org.apache.cordova.camera 0.3.1 "Camera"
org.apache.cordova.console 0.2.10 "Console"
org.apache.cordova.dialogs 0.2.9 "Notification"
jwargo@mini:~/dev/firstapp$
```

Figure 4.11 Cordova CLI—Plugin List

The Cordova project has recently started versioning plugins separately from the core Cordova releases. To help you better understand your application's environment, the results of the `plugins` command also display the version number for each plugin.

Removing Plugins

To remove a plugin from a Cordova project, open a terminal window, navigate to a Cordova project folder, then issue the following command:

```
cordova plugin remove plugin_id
```

You can also use the shortcut `rm` instead of `remove` to remove plugins:

```
cordova plugin rm plugin_id
```

Regardless of how you installed the plugin, whether from a file path, Git repository, or the Cordova Plugin Registry, a plugin is defined by its ID. So, you will have to know the plugin's ID in order to be able to successfully remove it from the project. For plugins that are added by ID using the Plugin Registry, that won't be much of an issue since you installed the plugin using its ID, but for plugins installed from GitHub or a local file system, you can use the `plugins` command (described in the previous section) to determine the IDs for each of the plugins in your project before trying to remove them.

If a project has the Cordova core File plugin installed, you would remove it from the project by issuing the following command:

```
cordova plugin rm org.apache.cordova.file
```

The CLI will essentially reverse the plugin installation process by removing configuration file entries that point to the plugin and removing the plugin's folder from the project's plugins folder. The CLI will show the status of the process as shown in Figure 4.12.

```
jwargo@mini:~/dev/firstapp$ cordova plugin rm org.apache.cordova.file
Uninstalling org.apache.cordova.file from android
Uninstalling org.apache.cordova.file from firefoxos
Uninstalling org.apache.cordova.file from ios
Removing "org.apache.cordova.file"
jwargo@mini:~/dev/firstapp$ _
```

Figure 4.12 Cordova CLI—Removing Plugins

> **Warning**
>
> For a long time, there has been a known issue with the Cordova CLI related to its capability to successfully remove dependent plugins. You may find that you will have to manually remove dependent plugins after you remove a particular plugin. The Cordova team is aware of this problem and should be preparing a solution.

Search

If you're looking for a particular plugin and can't remember its ID, you can use the `plugin search` command to search the Cordova Plugin Registry (described in Chapter 1, "The What, How, Why, and More of Apache Cordova") for plugins that match a particular search string. For example, if you're looking for a plugin that handles push notifications, you can search the registry for push plugins by opening a terminal window and issuing the following command:

```
cordova plugin search push
```

The CLI will connect to the registry at http://plugins.cordova.io, search for plugins that have "push" in their ID or description, and return the following list:

```
cn.jpush.phonegap - JPush for cordova plugin
cn.jpush.phonegap.jpushplugin - JPush for cordova plugin
```

```
co.realtime.plugins.cordovapush - This Cordova plugin should be used with the
iOS platform together with the Realtime Messaging library (ORTC) for Push
Notifications support.
com.beyond.plugins.jpush - JPush for cordova plugin
com.blackberry.push - BlackBerry 10 Push APIs
com.cmpsoft.mobile.plugin.pushnotification - pushNotification plugin description
com.goldcipher.baidupush - no description provided
com.goldsai.baidupush - no description provided
com.hipmob.android.phonegap.plugin - Hipmob provides an in-app live chat
and helpdesk for mobile apps.
com.hipmob.ios.phonegap.plugin - Hipmob provides in-app live chat and
helpdesk for mobile apps.
com.ibm.mobile.cordova.ibmpush - Cordova IBMPush Plugin
com.infobip.push.cordova - Infobip Push Notification Plugin for Android and iOS
com.metinform.cordova.xmpp - Cordova XMPP Push Plugin for Android
com.phonegap.plugins.pushplugin - This plugin allows your application to
receive push notifications on Android, iOS, WP8 and Windows8 devices.
    Android uses Google Cloud Messaging.
    iOS uses Apple APNS Notifications.
    WP8 uses Microsoft MPNS Notifications.
    Windows8 uses Microsoft WNS Notifications.
org.chromium.gcm - This plugin allows Android apps to send/receive push messages.
org.chromium.pushmessaging - This plugin allows apps to receive push messages.
org.jboss.aerogear.cordova.push - This plugin allows your application to
receive push notifications on both Android and iOS devices. Using the
AeroGear Unified Push Server.
org.pushandplay.cordova.apprate - This plugin provide the "rate this app"
functionality into your Cordova/Phonegap application
re.notifica.cordova - This plugin allows your application to register for,
receive and handle push notifications with Notificare on both Android and iOS
devices.
```

Then, after perusing the list, you can select one (the PhoneGap Push plugin, for example) and add it to your project using the following command:

```
cordova plugin add com.phonegap.plugins.pushplugin
```

Save Plugins

One of the issues the Cordova team has struggled with is how to make a Cordova project transportable, easily transferred from one developer workstation to another. A Cordova project has a lot of build artifacts—the platform code, plugins, configuration files, and so on—that are not part of the app itself. The Cordova team is trying to structure the Cordova project so that it's easy to separate the web application from the native Cordova components needed to build the app.

In the first step in this process the team added a `save plugins` command to the Cordova CLI that allows a developer to capture what plugins are associated with the project. I'll explain this as I show you how it works.

To save the list of plugins, open a terminal window, navigate to a Cordova project folder, and issue the following command:

```
cordova save plugins
```

The Cordova CLI will process the plugins folder:

```
Saved plugin info for "org.apache.cordova.console" to config.xml
Saved plugin info for "org.apache.cordova.device" to config.xml
Saved plugin info for "org.apache.cordova.dialogs" to config.xml
```

A Cordova project uses a configuration file, the config.xml file, to store information about the project; I'll explain the components of this file in the next chapter. Before issuing the `save plugins` command, the file contains the simple application properties shown in Listing 4.1.

Listing 4.1 Cordova Project config.xml File

```
<?xml version='1.0' encoding='utf-8'?>
<widget id="com.ac4p.firstApp" version="0.0.1"
  xmlns="http://www.w3.org/ns/widgets"
  xmlns:cdv="http://cordova.apache.org/ns/1.0">
    <name>FirstApp</name>
    <description>
        A sample Apache Cordova application that responds to the deviceready event.
    </description>
    <author email="dev@cordova.apache.org" href="http://cordova.io">
        Apache Cordova Team
    </author>
    <content src="index.html" />
    <access origin="*" />
</widget>
```

After the `save plugins` command executes, there are some new entries in the configuration file as shown in Listing 4.2.

Listing 4.2 Updated Cordova Project config.xml File

```
<?xml version='1.0' encoding='utf-8'?>
<widget id="com.ac4p.firstApp" version="0.0.1"
  xmlns="http://www.w3.org/ns/widgets"
  xmlns:cdv="http://cordova.apache.org/ns/1.0">
    <name>FirstApp</name>
    <description>
        A sample Apache Cordova application that responds to the deviceready event.
    </description>
    <author email="dev@cordova.apache.org" href="http://cordova.io">
        Apache Cordova Team
```

```
    </author>
    <content src="index.html" />
    <access origin="*" />
    <feature name="Console">
        <param name="id" value="org.apache.cordova.console" />
    </feature>
    <feature name="Device">
        <param name="id" value="org.apache.cordova.device" />
    </feature>
    <feature name="Notification">
        <param name="id" value="org.apache.cordova.dialogs" />
    </feature>
</widget>
```

For each plugin installed into the project, there is a new `feature` entry in the configuration file. With these features defined, if you check the config.xml file and the contents of the project's www folder into a version control system, another developer can check out the files and more easily re-create the full project using the `restore plugins` command described in the following section.

Restore Plugins

After you have saved a project's plugin configuration using the `save plugins` command, you can copy the project to a different system, then restore the plugins to the project by opening a terminal window, navigating to the new Cordova project folder, and issuing the following command:

```
cordova restore plugins
```

The Cordova CLI will read the config.xml file, then download and install the plugins:

```
Discovered org.apache.cordova.console in config.xml. Installing to the project
Discovered org.apache.cordova.device in config.xml. Installing to the project
Discovered org.apache.cordova.dialogs in config.xml. Installing to the project
Fetching plugin "org.apache.cordova.console" via plugin registry
Installing "org.apache.cordova.console" for android
Installing "org.apache.cordova.console" for firefoxos
Fetching plugin "org.apache.cordova.device" via plugin registry
Installing "org.apache.cordova.device" for android
Installing "org.apache.cordova.device" for firefoxos
Fetching plugin "org.apache.cordova.dialogs" via plugin registry
Installing "org.apache.cordova.dialogs" for android
Installing "org.apache.cordova.dialogs" for firefoxos
```

At this point, the new project has been updated to include the plugins from the original project.

Displaying Project Information

There are times when you will want to be able to gather a little information about a particular Cordova project: whether to learn more about it or to provide information to others during troubleshooting. To accommodate this need, the Cordova CLI team added the `info` command.

To obtain information about a particular Cordova project, open a terminal window, navigate to the Cordova project folder, and issue the following command:

```
cordova info
```

The CLI will peruse the project folder structure, collect some information, and display it in the console window. Listing 4.3 shows the results of the command being applied to the FirstApp project created in this chapter.

Listing 4.3 Results of the `cordova info` CLI Command

```
Collecting Data...

Node version: v0.10.32

Cordova version: 4.0.0

Config.xml file:

<?xml version='1.0' encoding='utf-8'?>
<widget id="com.ac4p.firstapp" version="0.0.1"
  xmlns="http://www.w3.org/ns/widgets"
  xmlns:cdv="http://cordova.apache.org/ns/1.0">
    <name>FirstApp</name>
    <description>
        A sample Apache Cordova application that responds to the deviceready event.
    </description>
    <author email="dev@cordova.apache.org" href="http://cordova.io">
        Apache Cordova Team
    </author>
    <content src="index.html" />
    <access origin="*" />
</widget>

Plugins:

org.apache.cordova.camera,org.apache.cordova.console,org.apache.cordova.device,
org.apache.cordova.dialogs

Android platform:
```

```
Available Android targets:
----------
id: 1 or "android-19"
     Name: Android 4.4.2
     Type: Platform
     API level: 19
     Revision: 4
     Skins: HVGA, QVGA, WQVGA400, WQVGA432, WSVGA, WVGA800 (default), WVGA854,
     WXGA720, WXGA800, WXGA800-7in
 Tag/ABIs : default/armeabi-v7a, default/x86
----------
id: 2 or "android-21"
     Name: Android 5.0
     Type: Platform
     API level: 21
     Revision: 1
     Skins: HVGA, QVGA, WQVGA400, WQVGA432, WSVGA, WVGA800 (default), WVGA854,
      WXGA720, WXGA800, WXGA800-7in
 Tag/ABIs : default/armeabi-v7a, default/x86, default/x86_64

iOS platform:

Xcode 6.1
Build version 6A1052d
```

The command returns the Node version, which is very important from a troubleshooting standpoint—the CLI often takes advantage of features of the most recent version of Node, so it's always a good idea to stay with the most recent version.

Beyond those two items, the rest of the information provided is taken directly from the project or from the native SDKs used by the project. The config.xml file is used to configure the project at a high level; I'll show you how it works in Chapter 5.

Build Management

The Cordova CLI has built-in integration with mobile device platform SDKs, so you can use the CLI to manage the application build process. In this section, I'll describe the CLI options for managing the process of building and executing Cordova applications.

`prepare`

The CLI `prepare` command copies a Cordova project's web application content from the www and merges folders into the appropriate platforms folders for the project. This process is described in detail in Chapter 5. You will use this command whenever you make changes to a Cordova web application's content (in the www or merges folder). The `prepare` command is called automatically before some of the operations described throughout the remainder of this chapter.

> **Tip**
>
> Recent testing has shown that the Cordova team is experimenting with the implementation of a folder watch that will allow the Cordova CLI to automatically copy your web application content from the www folder to the appropriate platforms whenever changes are detected. I noticed this as I was doing some testing a few weeks ago, but as I wrote this chapter the "feature" didn't seem to be working. So, as you play around with the CLI, you may find that you don't need to `prepare` as often as you might think.

To use the `prepare` command, open a terminal window, navigate to a Cordova project folder, then issue the following command:

```
cordova prepare
```

This will copy the web application content into the appropriate folders for each of the mobile device platforms that have been added to the project.

To prepare a specific platform's files, use the following command:

```
cordova prepare platform_name
```

So, to prepare the Android platform folder, use the following command:

```
cordova prepare android
```

The command doesn't return anything to the terminal window on success, so unless you see an error reported, the command simply worked.

`compile`

In Figure 4.6, you can see that there's a cordova folder in each platform's folder structure. Within that folder are platform-specific build scripts used to compile a native application for that platform. The `compile` command initiates a compilation process by calling the build script for one or more mobile platforms depending on how you issue the command.

To use the `compile` command, open a terminal window, navigate to a Cordova project folder, then issue the following command:

```
cordova compile
```

To compile a specific platform's native application, use the following command:

```
cordova compile platform_name
```

So, to compile the Android version of an application, use the following command:

```
cordova compile android
```

To compile for multiple platforms, simply pass a list of the platform names to the command:

```
cordova compile android ios
```

build

The `build` command is similar to `compile` except that it first calls `prepare` before executing a `compile`. To use the `build` command, open a terminal window, navigate to a Cordova project folder, then issue the following command:

```
cordova build
```

To build a specific platform's native application, use the following command:

```
cordova build platform_name
```

So, to build the Android version of an application, use the following command:

```
cordova build android
```

To build for multiple platforms, simply pass a list of the platform names to the command:

```
cordova build android ios
```

Executing Cordova Applications

The CLI has built-in integration with mobile device platform simulators, so you can launch Cordova applications directly onto simulators or physical devices. Chapters 7 through 11 provide more detailed information about the simulators and how to configure and launch them, as well as what is required to work with physical devices from the CLI. The following sections provide a high-level overview of the relevant commands for executing a Cordova application.

run

The CLI `run` command automates the process of building an application and deploying it onto a physical device or device emulator. The command will first prepare the application, execute the build process, then deploy the resulting native application package to a connected device.

To run a Cordova application on all platforms that have been added to a project, open a terminal window, navigate to the Cordova project folder, then issue the following command:

```
cordova run
```

When the command executes, it will quickly update the console to let you know what it's going to do:

```
Running command: /Users/jwargo/dev/firstapp/platforms/android/cordova/run
Running command: /Users/jwargo/dev/firstapp/platforms/firefoxos/cordova/run
Running command: /Users/jwargo/dev/firstapp/platforms/ios/cordova/run
run not implemented, please use firefoxos simulator to launch app
```

In this example, the firstapp folder has a Cordova project configured for Android, Firefox OS, and iOS. Notice that for Firefox OS, you can't execute the application on a device or simulator from the command line; you have to use the Firefox browser tools to do so (explained in Chapter 8, "Firefox OS Development with Cordova"). For the other platforms, you'll see a whole bunch of stuff written to the console as the CLI does all the work it needs to do to execute the application on the specified targets.

What happens next depends on what you have connected to the system running the command. If you have physical devices connected to the system using a USB cable, Android and iOS devices in this example, the CLI will deploy the application to each of the devices and launch the application. If you don't have physical devices connected, the CLI will launch the default device emulator or simulator for each platform, then deploy the application to each emulator and launch it.

To run the application for a single platform—Android, for example—you would issue the following command:

```
cordova run android
```

There are also some switches you can pass to the `run` command to control how it works.

You can control which version of a particular application is executed. To run the debug version of the application, use the `--debug` switch:

```
cordova run android --debug
```

To run the release version of the application, use the `--release` switch:

```
cordova run android --release
```

If you have a device and an emulator available, you can tell the CLI which one to use through a command-line switch. To run the application on a connected device, use the `--device` switch:

```
cordova run android --device
```

To run the application on an emulator, use the `--emulator` switch:

```
cordova run android --emulator
```

If you have multiple devices and/or emulators running, you can direct the CLI to run the application on a specific target using the `--target` switch.

For the Android platform, the Android SDK includes a command you can use to determine the list of available devices:

```
adb devices
```

When you issue the command, the console will update with the list of devices and emulators:

```
List of devices attached
emulator-5554   device
```

```
213b4571        device
562a6399        device
```

In this example, I have an emulator running as well as two physical devices connected to the system using USB cables. To run the application on a specific target, just pass the device name to the command using the `--target` switch:

```
cordova run android --target=562a6399
```

The CLI will build the application and deploy it to the specified device.

> **Warning**
>
> For many mobile device platforms, applications will not run on physical devices without first being registered with the manufacturer (Windows Phone 8) or signed by an appropriate signing authority (BlackBerry 10, iOS). I'm deliberately omitting the details of this process from this chapter as it differs among the different supported mobile device platforms and would add some bulk to this book. I'll cover this topic a little bit in the chapters that deal with each mobile device platform separately (Chapters 7 through 11).
>
> Before testing Cordova applications on a physical device, make sure you have followed the manufacturer's instructions for configuring the appropriate environment to do so.

emulate

With the first release of the Cordova CLI, the development team implemented an `emulate` command you could use to run an application on a device emulator. With this in place, you had separate commands to use depending on whether you wanted to execute an application on an emulator or a physical device. Since then, the `emulate` capabilities have been merged into the `run` command, and the `emulate` command is now simply an alias for `run`.

serve

When working with a mobile web application, many developers find that it's better to test the application in a desktop browser before switching to the mobile device. This is especially important when it comes to Cordova applications as there's an extra packaging process that has to happen before the application can be run on a device or simulator.

The CLI includes a `serve` command which a developer can use to launch a local web server that hosts a particular platform's web content. It doesn't expose any of the Cordova APIs to the browser, so all you can really test using this option is your web application's UI. You will need to issue the CLI `prepare` command before launching the server to make sure your web content is up-to-date.

To use the `serve` command, open a terminal window, navigate to a Cordova project folder, then issue the following command:

```
cordova serve
```

Figure 4.13 shows the `serve` command in action. Once the command loads, it will show you what URL you must use to access the web server. Simply open your browser of choice and navigate to the specified URL to access the application content.

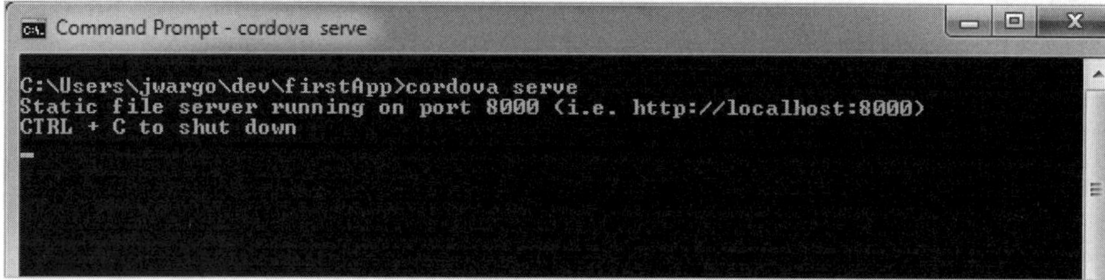

Command Prompt - cordova serve
C:\Users\jwargo\dev\firstApp>cordova serve
Static file server running on port 8000 (i.e. http://localhost:8000)
CTRL + C to shut down

Figure 4.13 Launching a Web Server Using the CLI

When running this process on Microsoft Windows, you may receive a security warning similar to the one shown in Figure 4.14. You will need to click the Allow access button to allow the web server to start.

Figure 4.14 Windows Security Alert

By default, the server will respond to port 8000 as shown in Figure 4.13. If you want to use a different port, you can pass the port number to the CLI as shown in the following example:

```
cordova serve port_number
```

So, for the example shown previously, to serve the web application content on port 8080, you would use the following command:

```
cordova serve 8080
```

To begin using the application, open your browser of choice and navigate to the URL shown in Figure 4.13; the browser will display a page similar to what is shown in Figure 4.15.

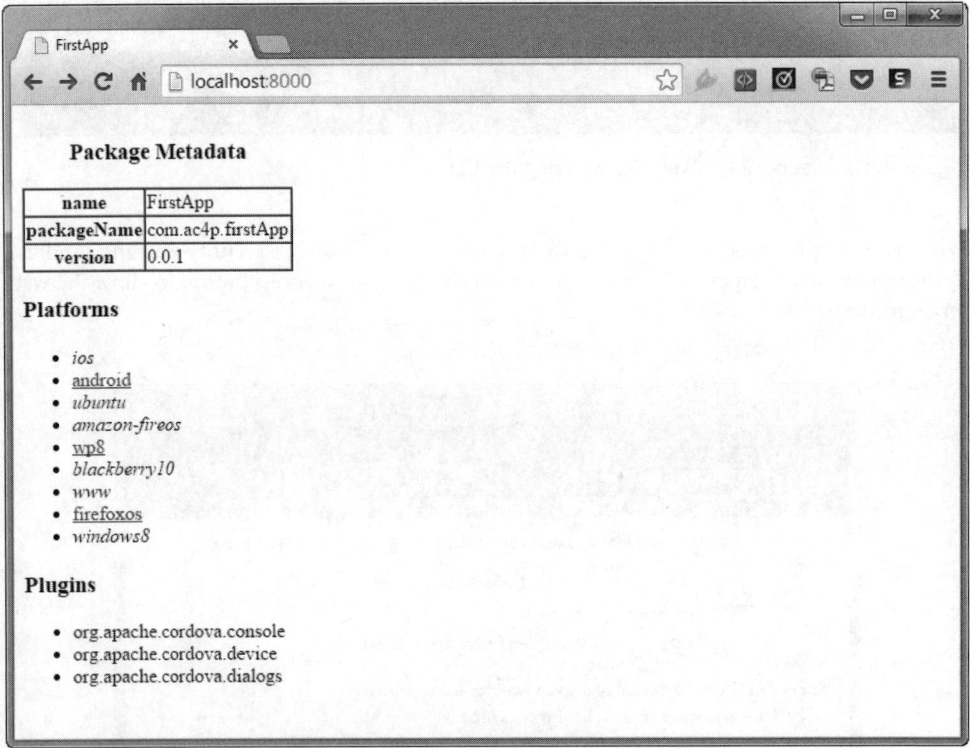

Figure 4.15 Serving a Cordova Application in a Desktop Browser

The browser window will display some information about the application including the version number, package name, and a list of all of the plugins installed into the application.

In the Platforms section of the page, you will see a list of each of the supported platforms. For each of the platforms added to the project, the `serve` command creates a link that takes you to the web content for that platform. This is important because, as you will learn in the next chapter, you can have different content for each target platform; this gives you the ability to test the content for each target platform separately. Nothing is done here to emulate anything about each target platform; this simply gives you access through the browser to each target platform's files.

When you click on one of the platform links, the web application content for that platform will be loaded into the browser. You will then be able to navigate within the application and test your UI and business logic.

As you navigate through the web application in the browser, the terminal window will list each of the web application content files that are loaded by the browser as shown in Figure 4.16.

```
Command Prompt - cordova serve

C:\Users\jwargo\dev\firstApp>cordova serve
Static file server running on port 8000 (i.e. http://localhost:8000)
CTRL + C to shut down
200 /android/www/
200 /android/www/css/index.css
200 /android/www/cordova.js
200 /android/www/js/index.js
200 /android/www/img/logo.png
302 /firefoxos/
200 /firefoxos/www/
200 /firefoxos/www/css/index.css
200 /firefoxos/www/cordova.js
200 /firefoxos/www/js/index.js
200 /firefoxos/www/img/logo.png
200 /firefoxos/www/cordova_plugins.js
200 /firefoxos/www/plugins/org.apache.cordova.dialogs/www/notification.js
200 /firefoxos/www/plugins/org.apache.cordova.dialogs/src/firefoxos/notification
.js
200 /firefoxos/www/plugins/org.apache.cordova.device/www/device.js
200 /firefoxos/www/plugins/org.apache.cordova.device/src/firefoxos/DeviceProxy.j
s
_
```

Figure 4.16 `cordova serve` Console Entries

The `serve` command gives you an easy way to test all of your application's capabilities from the desktop browser. The Cordova team has recently added the browser as a target platform to make this even easier. While it does not fully support all of the Cordova core plugins (today), you can use it to mimic many of the Cordova APIs while testing an application in the browser.

Upgrading Cordova and Cordova Projects

The Cordova team regularly publishes updates to the CLI, the platforms, and plugins, so you'll want to check periodically to see if new stuff is available. The Cordova team doesn't back-port bug fixes, so if you've encountered a bug, the fix won't be made to the version of Cordova you're currently using. It will come in a later version.

To make use of the most recent version of Cordova, the first step is to update the Cordova CLI. To do this for Windows, open a terminal window and issue the following command:

```
npm update -g cordova
```

For Macintosh OS X or Linux, open a terminal window and issue the following command:

```
sudo npm update -g cordova
```

With the Cordova CLI updated, you will want to update any projects you've been working with to the latest version. There is no project-level upgrade, so there are a few steps you have to perform to upgrade a project.

> **Tip**
>
> I've found that it's usually prudent to update many of the dependent tools when performing a Cordova update. Before issuing the commands shown in this section, I usually first install updates to Git and NPM in order to make my life easier.

Remember from the "Platform Management" section of this chapter that there is a command you can use to determine whether updated platforms are available. The first thing you should do is perform a check for updates: open a terminal window, navigate to the Cordova project folder, and issue the following command:

```
cordova platforms check
```

If the Cordova CLI indicates that there are platforms that can be updated, use the `platform update` command to update them:

```
cordova platform update android
```

In this example, the Android platform is being updated. Repeat the command for each of the platforms that have an update available.

With the platforms updated, the next step is to update any plugins you have. The Cordova team recommends that you uninstall the plugins and reinstall them. Remember, though, that there may be a problem with dependent plugins, so be sure to uninstall all plugins before reinstalling them.

> **Note**
>
> When it comes to reinstalling the plugins in a project you are upgrading, don't forget about the `save plugins` command. Before uninstalling any plugins, save the plugin list to the application's config.xml file before uninstalling all plugins. Once you've removed all plugins, you can use the `restore plugins` command to reinstall new versions of all of your application's plugins (and dependencies).

The Plugman CLI

The Plugman CLI is primarily used by developers who are either creating Cordova plugins or working with single-platform native application projects. Plugman is used by the Cordova CLI to manage the plugins in a Cordova application project. In this section, I'll show you how to use all of the available commands exposed by Plugman.

Plugman CLI Command Summary

Table 4.2 provides a summary of the available Plugman CLI commands; the sections that follow describe each of the operations in greater detail.

Table 4.2 Plugman CLI Command Summary

CLI Command	Description
`install`	Used to install a Cordova plugin into a native application project.
`uninstall`	Used to uninstall a Cordova plugin that has been added to a native application project.
`adduser`	Used to define a user account on the Cordova Plugin Registry.
`publish`	Used to publish a plugin to the Cordova Plugin Registry.
`unpublish`	Used to unpublish a plugin from the Cordova Plugin Registry.
`search`	Used to search the Cordova Plugin Registry for plugins that match specific keywords.
`info`	Used to retrieve information about a particular plugin from the Cordova Plugin Registry.
`config`	Used to set Plugin Registry settings for Plugman.
`owner`	Used to manage information about the Cordova Plugin Registry users who are allowed to publish updates to an existing plugin.
`create`	Used to create a new Cordova plugin project.
`platform`	Used to add additional platforms to a Cordova plugin project.

Using the Plugman CLI

In this section, I'll describe how you can use the Plugman CLI to manage different aspects of your Cordova development project.

Creating Plugman Projects

Plugman works against an existing Cordova application project. So, before you can begin using Plugman, you must first create a new project to work with. You can do this either with the Cordova CLI or with the lower-level shell scripts provided by the Cordova project.

Cordova CLI Approach

The easiest way to do this is to use the Cordova CLI. As shown earlier in this chapter, simply open a terminal window, navigate to the folder where you want the project created, and issue the following commands:

```
cordova create project_folder app_id app_name
cd project_folder
cordova platform add platform_name
```

So, to create a project called PlugApp for Android, you would do something like the following:

```
cordova create plugapp com.ac4p.plugapp PlugApp
cd plugapp
cordova platform add android
```

To create the same application for iOS, you would do something like the following:

```
cordova create plugapp com.ac4p.plugapp PlugApp
cd plugapp
cordova platform add ios
```

The problem with this approach is that it creates a lot of unnecessary overhead to your project. As shown in Figure 4.2, a Cordova CLI project has a bunch of extra folders the Cordova CLI uses to help manage the cross-platform nature of the application. For Plugman-driven projects, you don't need all of that stuff. The project folder's hooks, platforms, and www folders add an unnecessary level of complexity to your project. This approach will work, but there's a better way.

Shell Script Approach

As described in Chapter 1, inside of the Cordova CLI are platform-specific scripts that are used behind the scenes to create and manage Cordova application projects. When working with Plugman, it's sometimes easier to simply use these files to create your project. Instructions for how to use these scripts can be found in the Command-line Tools sections of the various Cordova platform guides at http://goo.gl/lyOhju.

To get started with the shell script approach, you must first download a .zip archive containing the latest version of the Cordova tools. Right now, the files can be located at http://goo.gl/D51wGZ. Even though we're working with Cordova 4.0, the latest download might be for an earlier version of Cordova. Once you've extracted the downloaded files, open the folder where you extracted the files. In the folder, you should see a separate .zip file for each supported mobile platform. Select one (or more) of the platforms and extract the files to a folder on your system. Within those extracted files, you will find a folder, typically the bin folder, that contains the script files you'll need. You can see an example of this for Android in Figure 4.17.

For Android, the CLI uses the `create` script to create a new Cordova application project. For Windows, the file is called create.bat, but for Macintosh OS and Linux, it's a shell script called create. Open a terminal window and navigate to the folder where you want to create the new project, then issue the following command:

```
\path_to_script_files\create project_folder app_id app_name
```

For my system, the command would look like this:

```
D:\cordova-3.4.0\cordova-android\create plugapp com.ac4p.plugapp PlugApp
```

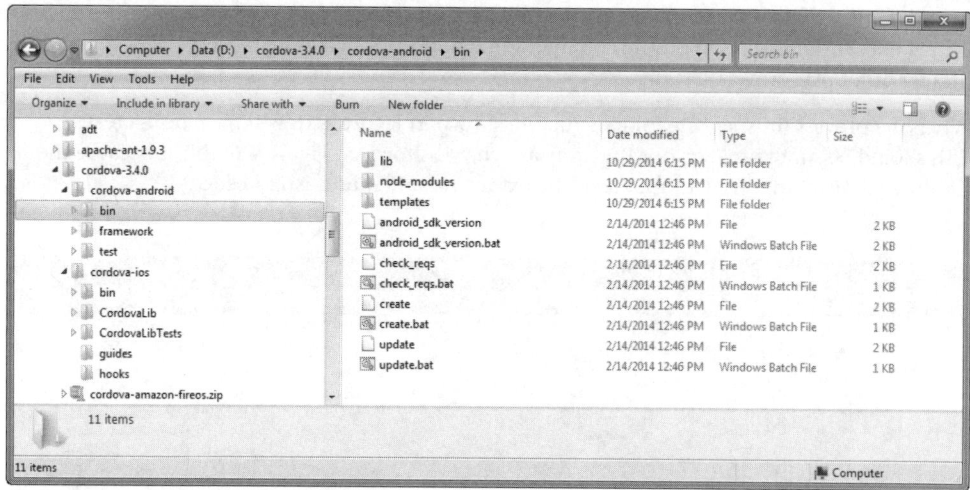

Figure 4.17 Android Shell Script Files

When the script runs, it will send output to the console just like the Cordova CLI does; that's because it's the same code doing it:

```
Creating Cordova project for the Android platform:
    Path: plugtest
    Package: com.ac4p.plugtest
    Name: Plugman Test
    Android target: android-19
Copying template files...
Running: android update project --subprojects --path "plugtest" --target android
-19 --library "CordovaLib"
Resolved location of library project to: C:\Users\jwargo\dev\plugtest\CordovaLib
Updated and renamed default.properties to project.properties
Updated local.properties
No project name specified, using Activity name 'PlugmanTest'.
If you wish to change it, edit the first line of build.xml.
Added file C:\Users\jwargo\dev\plugtest\build.xml
Added file C:\Users\jwargo\dev\plugtest\proguard-project.txt
Updated project.properties
Updated local.properties
No project name specified, using project folder name 'CordovaLib'.
If you wish to change it, edit the first line of build.xml.
Added file C:\Users\jwargo\dev\plugtest\CordovaLib\build.xml
Added file C:\Users\jwargo\dev\plugtest\CordovaLib\proguard-project.txt

Project successfully created.
```

At this point, you have a complete Cordova application project for Android. Refer to the platform guides for information on the command-line options for creating projects using the script files for other platforms.

When the process finishes, the folder structure shown in Figure 4.18 will have been created. This should be similar to, but not the same as, what is shown in Figure 4.6; this is because the Cordova CLI isn't involved and some of the extra structure it uses isn't needed.

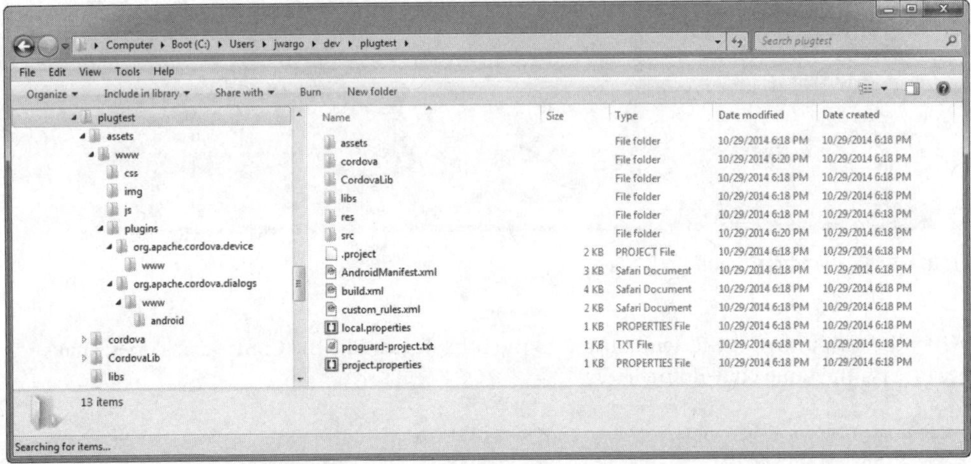

Figure 4.18 Android Project Folder

At this point, you can open ADT and work with the project as a native Android project.

> **Note**
>
> There is no prepare step you need to perform before running this application. The project folder shown in Figure 4.18 is a complete native application project. Simply edit the application's code and begin testing using the Android SDK.

The web application content for the application is located in the assets/www folder as shown in Figure 4.19. You'll edit the content in this folder to customize the content for your application. Notice that the cordova.js file is already in the folder, something that's normally managed for you by the Cordova CLI's `prepare` command.

At this point, you have a complete project and you're ready to go. In the next section, I'll show you how to install and remove Cordova plugins using Plugman.

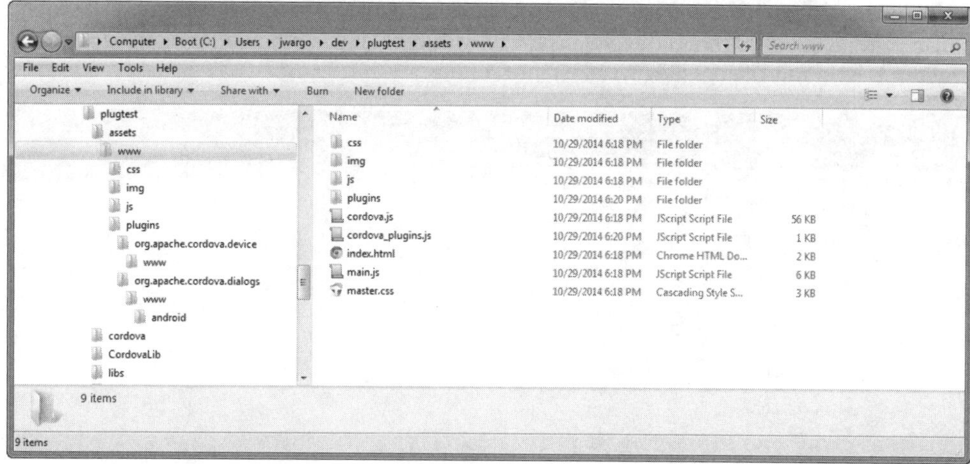

Figure 4.19 Android Project's Web Application Content Folder

Managing Plugins

Plugman can be used to add plugins to and remove plugins from a Cordova application project. In this section, I will describe how to do both.

Installing Plugins

To add plugins to an existing application project, you would open a terminal window and execute the following command:

```
plugman install --platform platform_name --project project_folder --plugin plugin
```

To add the Cordova Camera plugin to the Android project I just created, I would use the following command:

```
plugman install --platform android --project plugtest --plugin org.apache.cordova
.camera
```

When the command runs, it will update the console with details about the steps it is performing:

```
Fetching plugin "org.apache.cordova.camera" via plugin registry
npm http GET http://registry.cordova.io/org.apache.cordova.camera
npm http 304 http://registry.cordova.io/org.apache.cordova.camera
Installing "org.apache.cordova.camera" for android
```

Unlike when you are using the Cordova CLI, you don't have to be in the project folder when issuing the command. In this example, the terminal window is poised at a level right above the project folder, so all I had to do was pass in a relative path to the project folder.

At this point, Plugman has created a plugins folder and populated it with the Android-specific plugin code. Figure 4.20 shows the plugins folder with the Camera plugin I just added, plus the Cordova Device and Dialogs plugins added just for fun.

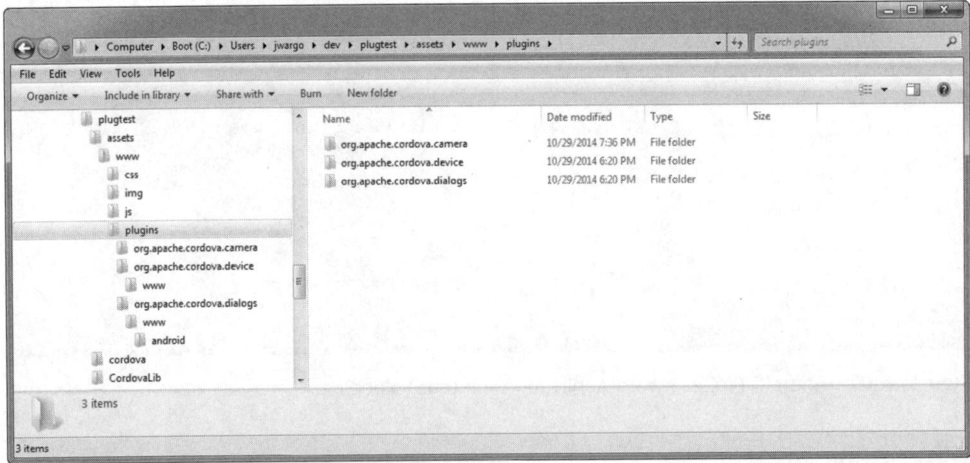

Figure 4.20 Android Project's plugins Folder

In this example, I added plugins directly from the Cordova Plugin Registry; when working on new plugins, you can easily install an in-progress or custom plugin to the project by passing in the plugin folder to the `plugman install` command:

```
plugman install --platform android --project plugtest --plugin c:\dev\myplugins\
plugin_name
```

Uninstalling Plugins

To uninstall a plugin from a project, simply open a terminal window and issue the following command:

```
plugman uninstall --platform platform_name --project project_folder --plugin plugin
```

So, for the Camera example I showed earlier, the command would be

```
plugman uninstall --platform android --project plugtest --plugin
org.apache.cordova.camera
```

As with the Cordova CLI, a plugin can be uninstalled only by using the plugin's ID; you can easily determine the plugin's ID from the folder name shown in Figure 4.20.

Using the Plugin Registry

The Cordova Plugin Registry is an excellent tool for helping you locate plugins for your project. As I write this, the only way to publish plugins to the registry is through Plugman. Plugman offers several commands to help you with managing entries in the registry.

The Cordova Plugin Registry currently doesn't provide the ability for users to log in and manage their plugins using a web interface, so the commands shown here are the only options available to developers.

Add User

Before you can publish plugins to the registry, you must first define a user account. To do this, use the Plugman `adduser` command. Open a terminal window and execute the following command:

```
plugman adduser
```

Plugman will first prompt you for your username, password, and email address, then create the account for you:

```
Username: myusername
Password:
Email: me@somedomain.com
user added
```

Once the process has completed, your account will be created and Plugman will write your account information to a configuration file called config located in the .plugman folder in your home directory.

Publish

With a user account created, you can publish plugins to the Cordova Plugin Registry. To do this, open a terminal window, navigate to the plugin project folder, and issue the following command:

```
plugman publish plugin_folder
```

If the terminal window is open to the folder containing the plugin project, you can publish the current folder's plugin using the following command:

```
plugman publish .
```

Plugman will write content to the console as it works to publish the plugin:

```
attempting to publish plugin to registry
+ com.johnwargo.myplugin@0.0.1
Plugin published
```

All this does is create a simple entry for the plugin in the registry. To enhance the entry with additional information about the plugin, there are two files you will need to work with: the plugin's plugin.xml and readme.md files.

The plugin's plugin.xml file provides information about the plugin and is used by Plugman and the Cordova CLI when managing the plugin's installation and removal from a Cordova project.

I'll describe the file in detail in Chapter 16, but for now, the elements of the file that affect the registry entry are

```
<name>myplugin</name>
<description>John's Plugin</description>
<license>Apache 2.0</license>
<keywords>cordova,puppies,soccer</keywords>
```

These values will be used by the registry to categorize (`keywords`), describe (`description`), and identify the license for (`license`) the plugin.

If you add a file called readme.md to a plugin project's folder, the content of the file will be used in the registry to provide additional information about the plugin.

You can see the results of the publish process in Figure 4.21; notice that the Description, Keywords, and Read Me are all populated with information.

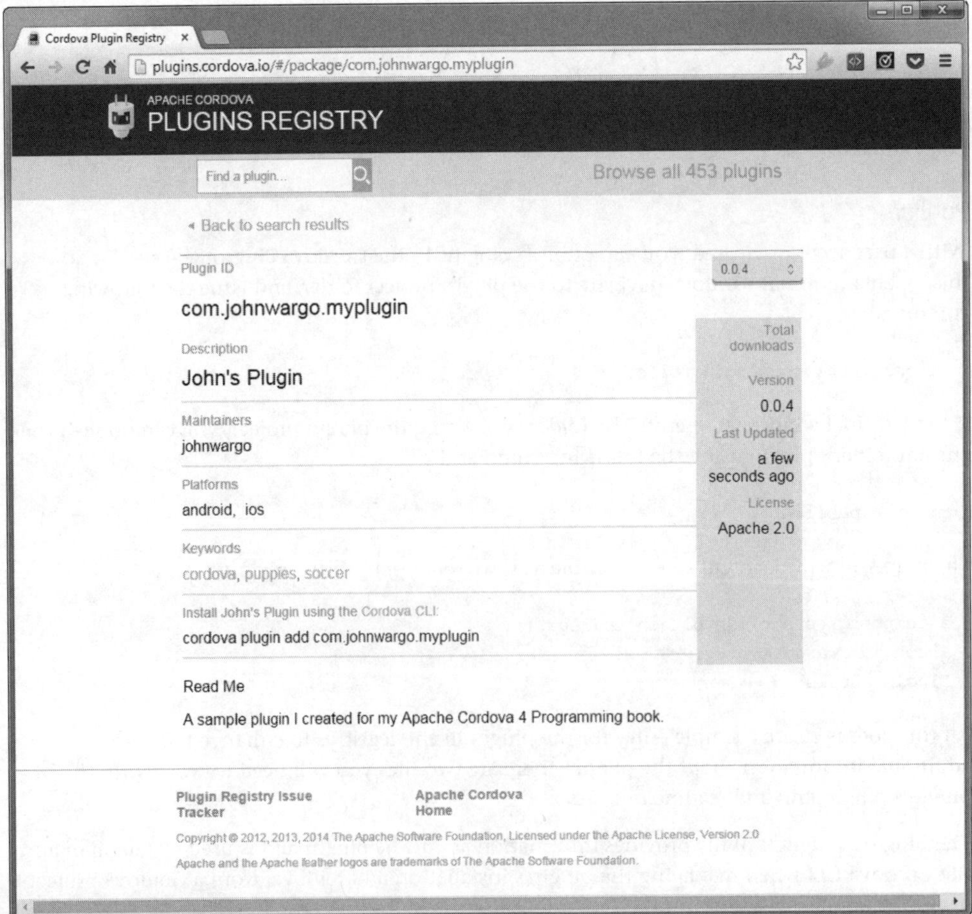

Figure 4.21 Cordova Plugin Registry Entry

With this in place, you or other developers can now install your plugin directly from the registry using the `plugman install` command described previously or the Cordova CLI's `cordova plugin add` command:

```
cordova plugin add com.johnwargo.myplugin
```

To publish an update to the plugin, edit the plugin's version information in the plugin's plugin.xml file and repeat the publish process. The plugin version is stored in the first line of the plugin.xml file:

```
<plugin id="com.johnwargo.myplugin" version="0.0.4"
  xmlns="http://apache.org/cordova/ns/plugins/1.0"
  xmlns:android="http://schemas.android.com/apk/res/android">
```

In this example, you can see that the plugin's current version is 0.0.4, which is also the same value that's shown in Figure 4.21.

Unpublish

If you decide that you no longer want the plugin to be available in the registry, you can unpublish the plugin by opening a terminal window and issuing the following command:

```
plugman unpublish plugin_id
```

So, for the example plugin I've been using throughout this chapter, the command would be

```
plugman unpublish com.johnwargo.myplugin
```

Plugman will write content to the console as it works to unpublish the plugin:

```
attempting to unpublish plugin from registry
Plugin unpublished
```

That's it; there's not much to it.

Search

Sometimes when you're building a Cordova application, you'll want to add some specific functionality to it. You could extend the Cordova container by writing your own plugin, but an easier approach is to see if someone else has already written the plugin you need. You can go to the Cordova Plugin Registry web site (http://plugins.cordova.io) and search for plugins there, or you can use the `plugman search` command to do it directly from a terminal window.

To search using Plugman, open a terminal window and execute the following command:

```
plugman search search_term
```

For example, if I were looking for a push plugin, I would use this command:

```
plugman search push
```

Plugman will connect to the registry and execute the search against the information provided by the registry. An example of the search results is shown earlier in the chapter under the `cordova plugin search` command. With the search results, you can select a plugin, add it to your project, and begin testing.

Info

To view detailed information about a particular plugin, open a terminal window and execute the following command:

```
plugman info plugin_id
```

For the Cordova Camera plugin, the command would be

```
plugman info org.apache.cordova.camera
```

The command returns the contents of the plugin's entry in the registry. Since the plugin's entry contains a lot of information, the results may be difficult to read in the terminal window.

Plugman Configuration

Plugman stores its configuration information in a file located in the user's home folder. To view the current settings for the user, open a terminal window and issue one of the following commands:

```
plugman config get
plugman config ls
```

Plugman will display the current settings in the terminal window:

```
; cli configs
$0 = "node C:\\Users\\jwargo\\AppData\\Roaming\\npm\\node_modules\\plugman\\main.js"
cache = "C:\\Users\\jwargo\\.plugman\\cache"
email = "me@somedomain.com"
registry = "http://registry.cordova.io/"
userconfig = "C:\\Users\\jwargo\\.plugman\\config"
username = "myusername"

; userconfig C:\Users\jwargo\.plugman\config
email = " me@somedomain.com""
username = "myusername"

; node bin location = D:\Program Files\nodejs\node.exe
; cwd = C:\Users\jwargo\dev\myplugin
; HOME = C:\Users\jwargo
; 'npm config ls -l' to show all defaults.

done
```

Of the information presented, the most important item is the `registry` setting. By default, Plugman comes configured to use the Cordova Plugin Registry (http://plugins.cordova.io). If you want to use plugins residing in another repository, you can easily change the registry Plugman uses. You can determine the current `registry` setting by opening a terminal window and issuing the following command:

```
plugman config get registry
```

Plugman will churn for a few seconds, then return

```
http://registry.cordova.io/
```

To change where Plugman gets and puts its plugins, you can use the following command:

```
plugman config set registry http://path_to_registry
```

There's no information in the Cordova documentation that describes what this registry should look like, but the existing registry uses NPM behind the scenes, so I can only assume it looks and feels like npmjs.org.

Owner

Multiple users can have the ability to publish updates to plugins published to the Cordova Plugin Registry. Users who have the ability to publish updates are called owners of the plugin. To manage a particular plugin's owners list, you would use the `plugman owner` command.

To view a list of the current owners for a particular plugin, open a terminal window and issue the following command:

```
plugman owner ls plugin_id
```

For the example plugin I've shown throughout the Plugman section, you would use the following command:

```
plugman owner ls com.johnwargo.myplugin
```

To add a Cordova Plugin Registry user account as an owner of the plugin, you would use the following command:

```
plugman owner add username plugin_id
```

For the example plugin I've shown throughout the Plugman section, you would use the following command:

```
plugman owner add myusername com.johnwargo.myplugin
```

To remove an owner from the plugin, use the following command:

```
plugman owner rm username plugin_id
```

For the example plugin I've shown throughout the Plugman section, you would use the following command:

```
plugman owner rm myusername com.johnwargo.myplugin
```

Creating Plugins

As you'll learn in Chapter 16, a Cordova plugin is typically a project with some JavaScript code and native application code for each supported platform. A developer has to create the JavaScript code, then add the native code to support the JavaScript interface and update a configuration file describing all of it.

Plugman has commands that can help you with the process of creating plugins, including setting up the necessary folder structure and creating (and updating) the configuration file. The commands described in this section help you create plugins and add support for additional mobile platforms to your new plugin.

Create

To create a new Cordova plugin, open a terminal window, navigate to the folder where you want the plugin project created, then issue the following command:

```
plugman create --name plugin_name --plugin_id plugin_id --plugin_version 0.0.1
```

As an example, I created a new plugin using the following command:

```
plugman create --name myplugin --plugin_id com.johnwargo.myplugin
--plugin_version 0.0.1
```

What Plugman did was create a new subfolder called myplugin, then add the folder structure and files shown in Figure 4.22. One of the first things you'll want to do is add a readme.md file to the project folder.

The plugin.xml file is an XML file that describes the plugin; Plugman and the Cordova CLI will use this file to determine what files to install for each supported platform plus what interfaces the plugin exposes to an application using the plugin. Listing 4.4 shows the plugin's default plugin.xml file with `description`, `license`, and `keywords` elements added to the file as described previously.

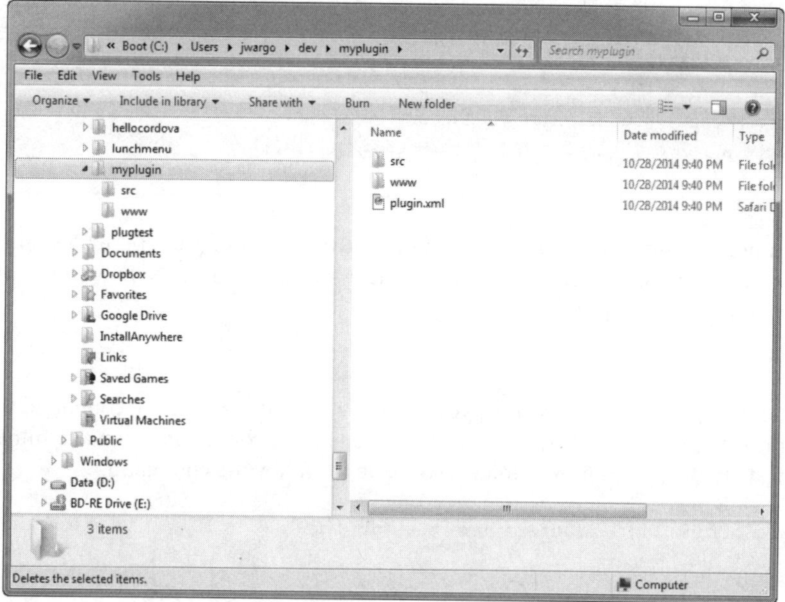

Figure 4.22 Plugin Project Folder

Listing 4.4 plugin.xml File

```
<?xml version='1.0' encoding='utf-8'?>
<plugin id="com.johnwargo.myplugin" version="0.0.1" xmlns="http://apache.org/cordova/
ns/plugins/1.0" xmlns:android="http://schemas.android.com/apk/res/android">
  <name>myplugin</name>
  <description>John's Plugin</description>
  <license>Apache 2.0</license>
  <keywords>cordova,puppies,soccer</keywords>
  <js-module name="myplugin" src="www/myplugin.js">
    <clobbers target="cordova.plugins.myplugin" />
  </js-module>
</plugin>
```

I'll describe the contents of this file in greater detail when I cover creating plugins in Chapter 16.

The plugin's www folder contains a single file called myplugin.js, shown in Listing 4.5. This file is intended to describe the interface your application interacts with when using the plugin. The sample file created by Plugman simply creates a function called `coolMethod` which you can extend, or replace, depending on your plugin's requirements. Again, see Chapter 16 for details on what you should do next.

Listing 4.5 myplugin.js File

```
var exec = require('cordova/exec');

exports.coolMethod = function(arg0, success, error) {
  exec(success, error, "myplugin", "coolMethod", [arg0]);
};
```

The plugin project's src folder should contain the native code your plugin uses. When you first create the project, the src folder is empty. In the next section, I'll describe how to add platform support to your plugin project.

Platform

Once you have a plugin project created, you'll use the `plugman platform` command to add support for one or more mobile device platforms. To use this command, open a terminal window, navigate to the plugin project folder, and issue the following command:

```
plugman platform add --platform_name platformName
```

> **Note**
>
> Notice that this is one of the few Plugman commands that works on the current folder; most other commands accept a folder as a parameter. Be sure you're in the right folder when issuing this command.

So, to add support for the Android platform to your plugin, you would use the following command:

```
plugman platform add --platform_name android
```

Unlike when you use the Cordova CLI, you can't add multiple platforms at the same time, so to add another platform such as iOS, you would use the following command:

```
plugman platform add --platform_name ios
```

Each time you add a platform, Plugman will add a folder for the specified platform to the src folder as shown in Figure 4.23. Inside the folder, you'll find a starter file for the plugin's native source code. In this case, since it's for an Android plugin, Plugman has created a myplugin.java file for you to extend for your plugin. For iOS, Plugman will create a myplugin.m file for you to flesh out for your plugin.

Refer to Chapter 16 for information on how to write the code for your plugin.

As Plugman adds platform support to your plugin project, it also updates the plugin.xml file with information about each platform as shown in Listing 4.6. Sorry to say this again, but you'll learn more about this in Chapter 16.

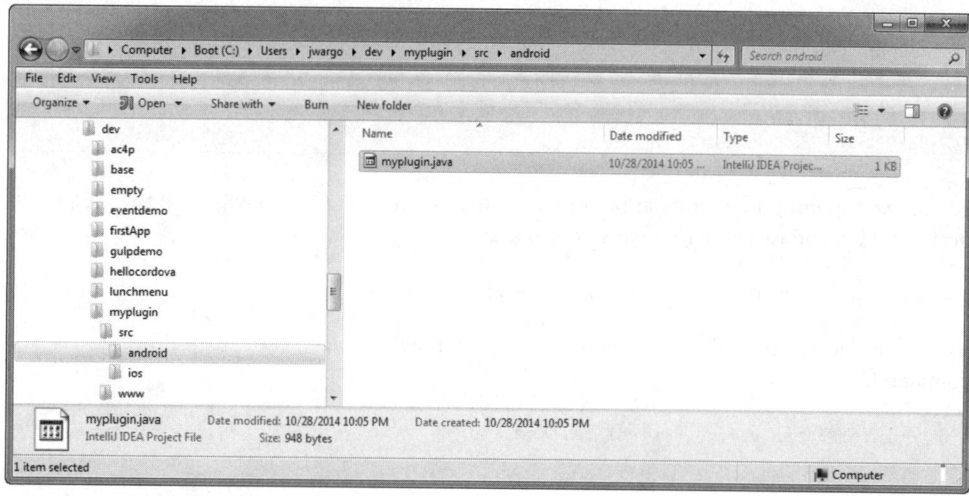

Figure 4.23 Plugin src Folder for Android

Listing 4.6 Updated plugin.xml File

```
<?xml version='1.0' encoding='utf-8' ?>
<plugin id="com.johnwargo.myplugin" version="0.0.1"
  xmlns="http://apache.org/cordova/ns/plugins/1.0"
  xmlns:android="http://schemas.android.com/apk/res/android">
  <name>myplugin</name>
  <description>John's Plugin</description>
  <license>Apache 2.0</license>
  <keywords>cordova,puppies,soccer</keywords>
  <js-module name="myplugin" src="www/myplugin.js">
    <clobbers target="cordova.plugins.myplugin" />
  </js-module>
  <platform name="android">
    <config-file parent="/*" target="res/xml/config.xml">
      <feature name="myplugin">
        <param name="android-package"
          value="com.johnwargo.myplugin.myplugin" />
      </feature>
    </config-file>
    <config-file parent="/*" target="AndroidManifest.xml" />
    <source-file src="src/android/myplugin.java"
      target-dir="src/com/johnwargo/myplugin/myplugin" />
  </platform>
  <platform name="ios">
    <config-file parent="/*" target="config.xml">
      <feature name="myplugin">
        <param name="ios-package" value="myplugin" />
```

```
      </feature>
    </config-file>
    <source-file src="src/ios/myplugin.m" />
  </platform>
</plugin>
```

To remove support for a particular platform, open a terminal window, navigate to the plugin project folder, and issue the following command:

```
plugman platform remove --platform_name platformName
```

As an example, to remove support for iOS from your plugin project, issue the following command:

```
plugman platform remove --platform_name ios
```

Wrap-Up

In this chapter, I showed you how to utilize the Cordova CLI to manage your Cordova application projects and how to use Plugman to manage plugins, interact with the Cordova Plugin Registry, and create your own plugins. The capabilities provided by the CLI dramatically simplify the cross-platform development process and managing your Cordova application's plugin configuration.

In the next chapter, I'll describe the mechanics of Cordova development: how you'll interact with Cordova and your application projects using the CLI and other tools available to Cordova developers.

5

The Mechanics of Cordova Development

Now that you have a Cordova development environment configured and you know all about the CLI commands available to you, it's time to show you the process of developing, testing, and debugging Apache Cordova applications.

There are some processes and capabilities that apply across all supported mobile device platforms. In this chapter, I'll address the mechanics of Apache Cordova development. I'll begin the chapter by addressing some of the issues a Cordova developer must deal with, then I'll cover the development process and some of the tools you can use to test and debug your Cordova applications. I'll even show you how to customize the web application content for your application for different mobile device platforms.

Cordova Development Issues

Before we start discussing how to develop Cordova applications, let's first address some of the issues that you will face as you work with the framework. The Cordova project is supported by developers from all over the world, developers who may have experience with only one or a small number of mobile platforms, developers who have a strong opinion about how something should be done. The problem with this is that when you try to collect development projects written by different people into a single framework, you will likely bump up against some inconsistencies. Add to this the fact that every mobile platform supported by Cordova is different and has different ways of doing things, and you have a difficult task to make everything work cleanly and seamlessly.

The good news is that over time, the Cordova development team has done an amazing job in eliminating most of the cross-platform issues. All that's left are two, and they're not that complicated.

Dealing with API Inconsistency

Figure 5.1 shows the supported feature matrix from the PhoneGap web site (the Cordova team doesn't seem to publish a matrix); you can find the page at http://phonegap.com/about/feature. As you can see, the table is pretty complete; there are some gaps, but it's more full than empty. If a particular feature you want to use in your application is supported only on some mobile platforms, you'll have to make special accommodation within your application for platforms that do not support the particular API (or you can write the code to support it and contribute it to the project ☺).

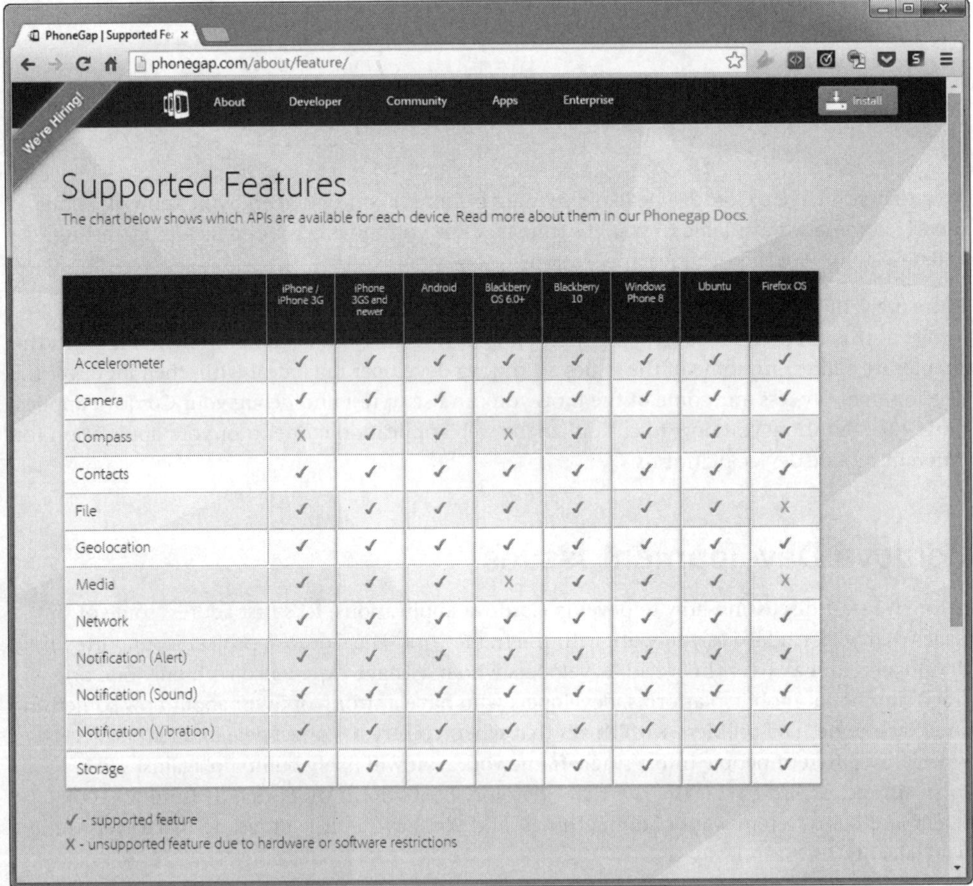

Supported Features

The chart below shows which APIs are available for each device. Read more about them in our Phonegap Docs.

	iPhone / iPhone 3G	iPhone 3GS and newer	Android	Blackberry OS 6.0+	Blackberry 10	Windows Phone 8	Ubuntu	Firefox OS
Accelerometer	✓	✓	✓	✓	✓	✓	✓	✓
Camera	✓	✓	✓	✓	✓	✓	✓	✓
Compass	X	✓	✓	X	✓	✓	✓	✓
Contacts	✓	✓	✓	✓	✓	✓	✓	✓
File	✓	✓	✓	✓	✓	✓	✓	X
Geolocation	✓	✓	✓	✓	✓	✓	✓	✓
Media	✓	✓	✓	X	✓	✓	✓	X
Network	✓	✓	✓	✓	✓	✓	✓	✓
Notification (Alert)	✓	✓	✓	✓	✓	✓	✓	✓
Notification (Sound)	✓	✓	✓	✓	✓	✓	✓	✓
Notification (Vibration)	✓	✓	✓	✓	✓	✓	✓	✓
Storage	✓	✓	✓	✓	✓	✓	✓	✓

✓ - supported feature

X - unsupported feature due to hardware or software restrictions

Figure 5.1 Supported Features Matrix

> **Warning**
>
> Keep in mind that the table is not updated as often as the API, so you may want to validate through the API documentation or through actual testing of an API whether or not it works on a platform for which there's an X in the figure.

One of the things you can do is check for the existence of the API object your application will be calling:

```
if (navigator.camera) {
  //We have a Camera, so do something with it

} else {
  //No Camera, sorry, warn the user or take an alternate path

}
```

If your application uses an API that isn't supported on all of the mobile devices that your application will target, your application's code can use the Device API discussed in Chapter 13, "Using the PhoneGap CLI," to try to figure that out. Your application should use `device.platform` and, as necessary, `device.version` to determine which platform and OS the application is running on and disable an unsupported feature if the application is running on a device that doesn't support the API.

Another option is to simply wrap the call to a particular API with a JavaScript try/catch block and deal directly with any failures that occur. Unfortunately, most Cordova APIs fail silently, so you may not see an exception to catch.

Application Graphics, Splash Screens, and Icons

Each mobile platform and often different versions of a particular device OS have different requirements for application icons and splash screens. Developers building Cordova applications for multiple device platforms need to be prepared to create a suite of graphics for their applications that address the specific requirements for each target device platform and/or device OS.

Additionally, for some devices on some carriers (older BlackBerry devices, for example), the mobile carrier applies a specific theming to the OS in order to help distinguish itself in the market. Any application icon designed for one of these devices will need to accommodate, as much as possible, rendering pleasantly within different themes.

Fortunately with the merges capabilities described later in this chapter, you have the ability to easily merge in the appropriate graphics files (and other content as needed) depending on which mobile platform you are building for.

For application icons, the PhoneGap project maintains a wiki page listing the icon requirements for the different supported operating systems here: http://goo.gl/rfPULW.

Creating splash screens and application icons is a pain since you have to deal with many different screen and icon resolutions. Several developers have built Node modules you can use to generate splash screens and/or application icons for multiple mobile device platforms:

- Cordova Media Generator (www.npmjs.org/package/cordova-media-generator)
- Cordova Gen (www.npmjs.org/package/cordova-gen)
- Cordova Gen Icon (www.npmjs.org/package/cordova-gen-icon)

As the default folder structure for Cordova projects has changed for Cordova 4, these modules may have some issues. Ideally each will be updated by the time you read this.

I'm not going to cover how to set up the application icons for your Cordova projects since a Cordova application is just a native mobile application, and the way you configure your icons has nothing to do with Apache Cordova—it's just the way native application projects are configured. Refer to the documentation for the mobile device SDK for information on how to configure application icons for the platforms you use.

Developing Cordova Applications

Now it's time to start working through the process of how to create Cordova applications. In this section, I'll describe the process for coding a Cordova application. In later sections, I'll show you how to test and debug applications.

To create a new project using the Cordova CLI, you will need to open a terminal window, navigate to the folder where you want the project folder created, and use the `cordova create` command. Next, you will need to change directories (using the OS `cd` command) to the folder created by the `cordova create` command. Once there, you can add platforms and plugins to your project as needed; the series of commands will look something like the following:

```
cordova create app_name
cd app_name
cordova platform add platform_name
cordova plugin add plugin_name
```

In this example, `app_name` refers to the name of the application you are creating, and `platform_name` refers to the mobile device platform you will be working with. So, if I were creating an Android application called lunch_menu, I would issue the following commands:

```
cordova create lunch_menu
cd lunch_menu
cordova platform add android
```

You can also specify more information about your application by using the following:

```
cordova create lunch_menu com.ac4p.lunchmenu "Lunch Menu"
cd lunch_menu
cordova platform add android
```

At this point, the CLI would create the Cordova project folder shown in Figure 5.2, and all you would need to do is open your code editor of choice and start coding and testing your new Cordova application.

The question, though, is where to edit the web application content. If you look at the project folder structure shown in Figure 5.2, you will see that there are two folders called www: one in the Android platform folder structure and another off the project root folder.

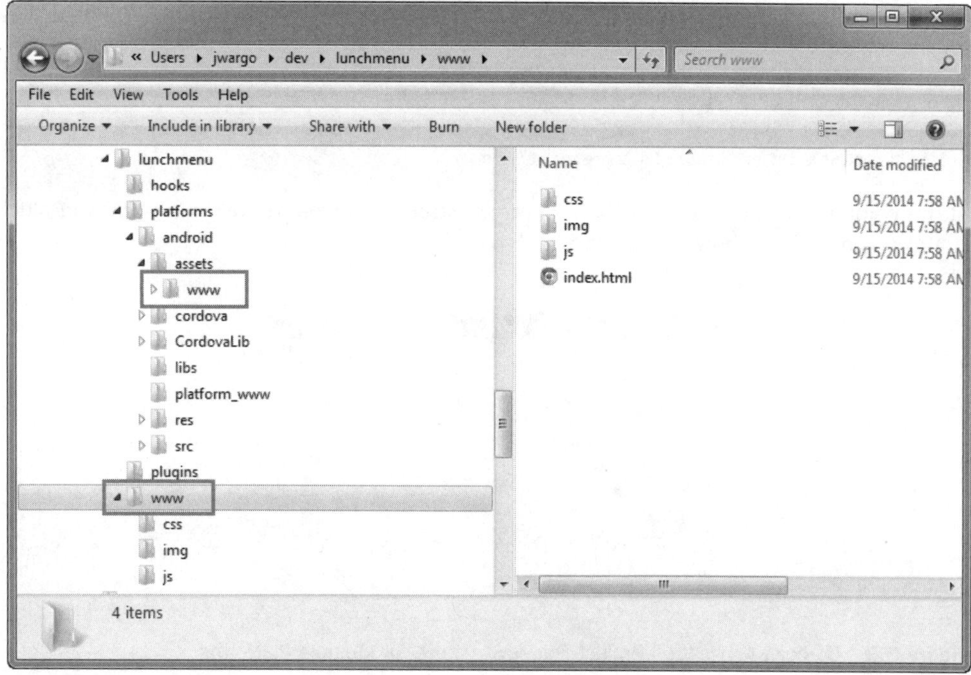

Figure 5.2 Cordova Application Project Folder Structure—Android Application

The project's www folder (the www folder highlighted in the lower half of Figure 5.2) contains the web application files that you will create for your application. During the prepare step, all of the files in the folder are copied to the platform-specific www folder(s) (in this case, the Android project folder highlighted in the top of Figure 5.2). I'll explain a little more about how this works later in the chapter.

> **Note**
>
> You may be asking yourself, "Why can't I edit the web application content in the platform-specific www folder?"
>
> You can, but when you run the `cordova prepare` command, or execute any other Cordova CLI command that performs a `prepare`, the content in the platform-specific folder will be overwritten by the content from the project's www folder. Because of this, it's always best to edit the content in the project's www folder.
>
> If you have platform-specific content you want to add to your project, use the merges capability described later in the chapter.

Because Cordova is all about cross-platform mobile development, you're probably going to want to target multiple mobile device platforms. In that case, if you were, for example, building an app for Android and iOS, you would open up a terminal window and do something like the following:

```
cordova create lunch_menu
cd lunch_menu
cordova platform add android firefoxos ios
```

At this point, what you'd have is a Cordova project structure with separate projects for Android, Firefox OS, and iOS as shown in Figure 5.3.

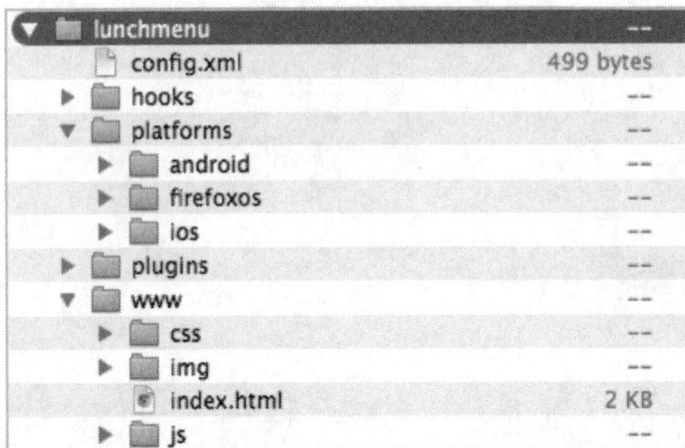

Figure 5.3 Cordova Application Project Folder Structure for Multiple Platforms

> **Note**
>
> Notice that in the last two figures I'm switching between Windows and OS X—that's because this works exactly the same no matter what OS you are running on.

You will still work with the web content stored in the project's www folder shown at the bottom of the folder structure in Figure 5.3. When you have the web application content in that folder ready for testing, you will use the `cordova prepare` command to copy the code into the platforms subfolders shown in the figure.

What I do while working on a Cordova project is keep my web content files open in an HTML editor like Adobe Brackets (www.brackets.io) or Aptana Studio (www.aptana.com), then use the CLI to manage my mobile device platform projects for me. As I edit the files, adding the web content to the .html file and my application's code to the application's .js files, when I'm ready to test (and debug) the applications I switch over to a terminal window that I keep open and pointed to the Cordova project's root folder (the lunch_menu folder I created a while back) and issue the commands I need to prepare my content and execute the application in a simulator or on a device.

To copy the web application content to each target platform, I would use the following:

```
cordova prepare
```

What this command does is copy all of the files from the www folder into the appropriate folder for each specified mobile platform project as shown in Figure 5.4. In this example, it copies the content files to the Android project's assets/www folder, the Firefox OS project's www folder, and the iOS project's www folder.

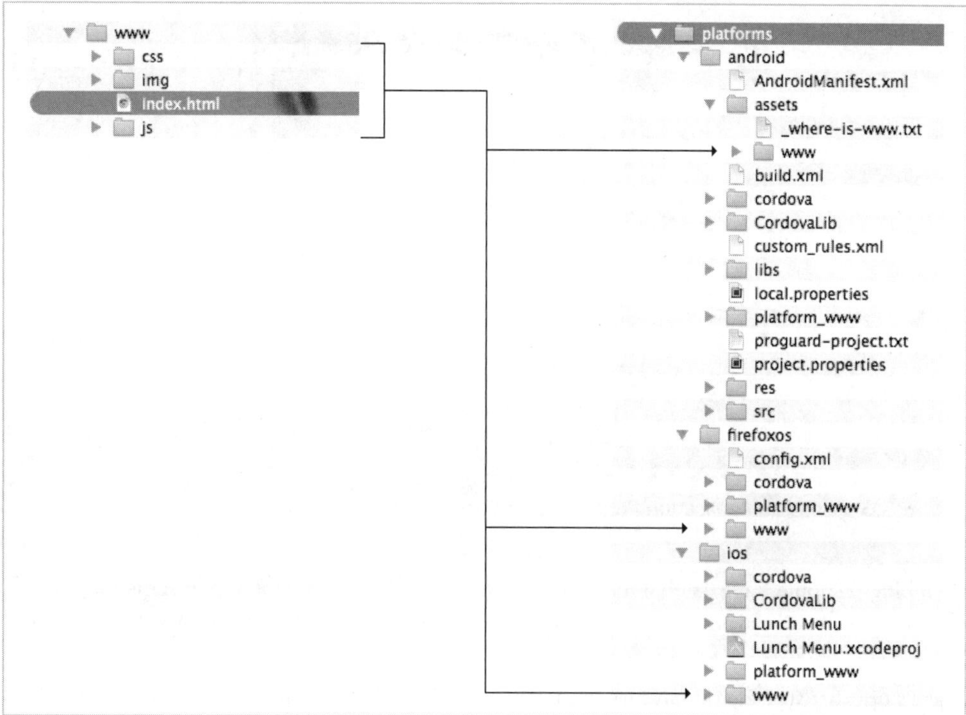

Figure 5.4 Copying Web Content to the Platform Projects Folders

To copy the web application content to the project folder for a specific platform, I would specify the target platform on the command line:

```
cordova prepare android
```

Or, if I will be testing and debugging both the Android and Firefox OS versions of the application, I issue the following command:

```
cordova prepare android firefoxos
```

Now, so far in this process, I've not added any plugins to this project. While you can build a Cordova application and not use any plugins, most developers choose Apache Cordova because it provides a web application with access to native APIs. So, for my project, I'm going to add some plugins by returning to my terminal window and issuing the following commands:

```
cordova plugin add org.apache.cordova.console
cordova plugin add org.apache.cordova.device
cordova plugin add org.apache.cordova.dialogs
```

This will add the Console, Device, and Dialogs plugins to the project (described in Chapter 14, "Working with the Cordova APIs"). When you look at the project folder structure, you should see that there's now some new stuff in the project's plugins folder as shown in Figure 5.5.

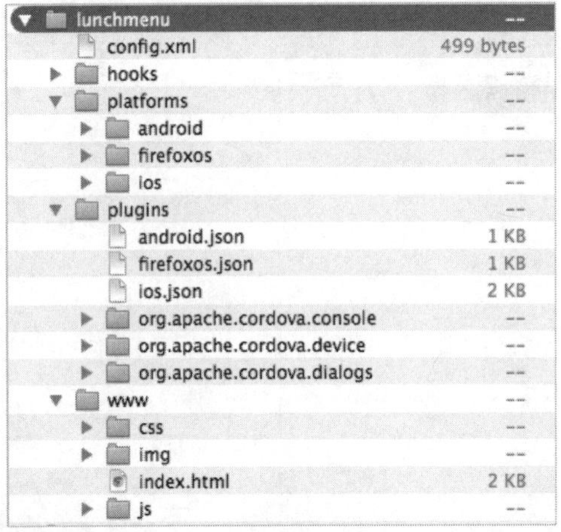

Figure 5.5 Cordova Application Project Folder Structure with Plugins

Each plugin should have its own folder as shown in the figure. Remember that some plugins depend on other plugins, so if you see more plugins listed there than you know you installed, it's probably because the CLI installed any required plugins automatically.

There's nothing special you have to do to use these plugins; simply make the appropriate calls to the associated APIs and you're all set.

The plugins folder contains individual .json configuration files for each target platform supported by the project; you can see an example of the android.json file in Listing 5.1. The files contain metadata used by Plugman to manage the plugins.

Listing 5.1 android.json File

```
{
  "prepare_queue": {
    "installed": [],
    "uninstalled": []
  },
  "config_munge": {
    "files": {
      "res/xml/config.xml": {
        "parents": {
          "/*": [
            { "xml": "<feature name=\"Notification\"><param name=\"android-package\"
            value=\"org.apache.cordova.dialogs.Notification\" /></feature>",
```

```
            "count": 1 },
            { "xml": "<feature name=\"Device\"><param name=\"android-package\"
            value=\"org.apache.cordova.device.Device\" /></feature>",
            "count": 1 }
                ]
        }
      }
    }
  },
  "installed_plugins": {
    "org.apache.cordova.console": {
      "PACKAGE_NAME": "com.ac4p.lunchmenu"
    },
    "org.apache.cordova.dialogs": {
      "PACKAGE_NAME": "com.ac4p.lunchmenu"
    },
    "org.apache.cordova.device": {
      "PACKAGE_NAME": "com.ac4p.lunchmenu"
    }
  },
  "dependent_plugins": {}
}
```

Now, any self-respecting mobile web project may have some icons, screen graphics, CSS, and/or JavaScript files that are unique to each target platform. Since each mobile device has its own theme and icon requirements, it's likely that at a minimum those will be required. In older versions of Cordova, the developer had to manage all of that manually; with the CLI that's all taken care of for you.

To support platform-specific resources, what you'll need is some way to tell the Cordova CLI what files belong to which platform. The www folder you've been working in is not the right place for this as having an extra level of folders in your project folder would further complicate things when you simply want the Android files in the Android project, the iOS files in the iOS project, and so on.

To accommodate this need, the Cordova CLI uses a special folder called merges to manage the platform-specific files. To implement this, add a folder called merges to your Cordova project folder, then create subfolders (under merges) for each target platform. With the folders in place, place the platform-specific content (images, HTML pages, JavaScript files, whatever) in the appropriate folder. Figure 5.6 shows the merges folder structure in my Cordova Lunch Menu project.

With the merges folder structure in place, you're ready to go. When you issue the `cordova prepare` commands shown earlier, the CLI will copy the custom content for each of the platforms into the appropriate web content folder for each platform's project folder as shown in Figure 5.7.

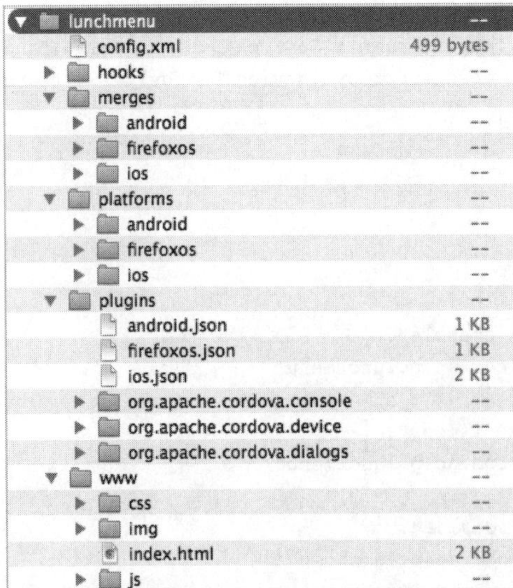

Figure 5.6 Cordova Application Project Folder Structure with Merges

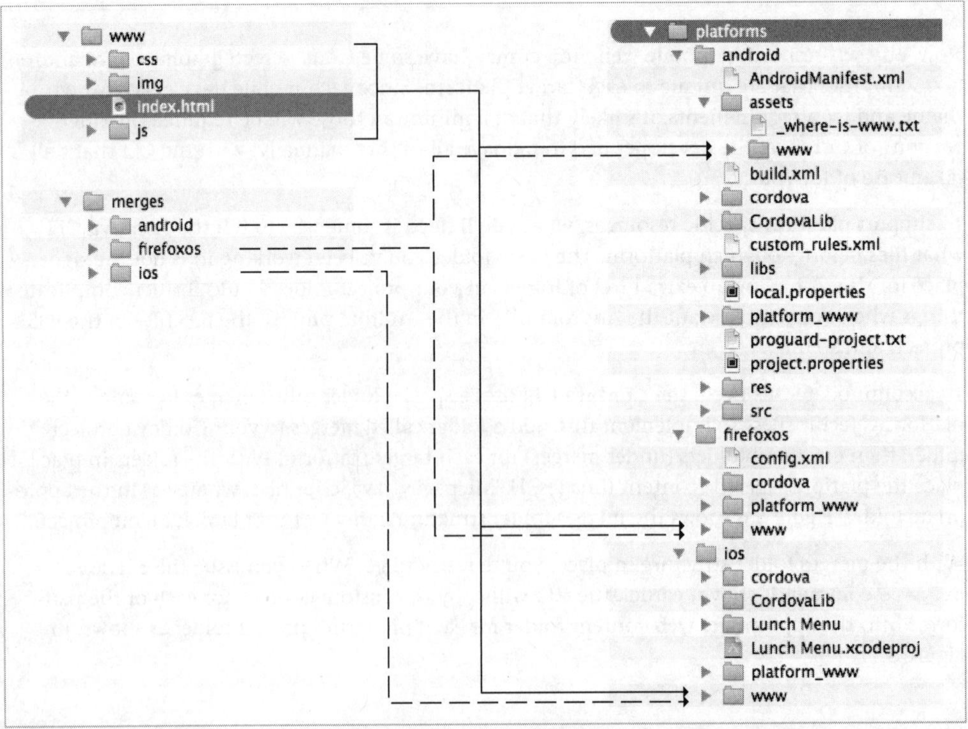

Figure 5.7 Copying Web Content and Platform-Specific Content to the Platform Projects Folders

As shown in the figure, custom content for the Android platform stored in the merges\android folder will be copied into the Android platform project's assets\www folder. Custom content for iOS applications will be copied from merges\ios to the iOS project's www folder.

> **Note**
>
> In earlier versions of Apache Cordova, the merges folder was automatically created. For some bizarre reason, the Cordova dev team decided to remove the folder from the default project in order to avoid confusing users. So, instead of seeing the folder there and being able to quickly determine what it's for (by reading the documentation, for example), you now have to know the capability exists and manually create the necessary folder structure to implement this feature for your applications. Sigh. In Chapter 6, "Automation and the Cordova CLI," I'll give you some tools you can use to automate creation of the necessary merges folder.

With all of the application's content copied into the appropriate project folders, you can open the appropriate IDE (Eclipse for Android, Firefox for Firefox OS, and Xcode for iOS) and begin the testing process. For information on how to import the Cordova projects into each IDE and use the platform's debugging tools, refer to Chapters 7 through 11.

One of the things I've not covered yet is the concept of hooks. You may have noticed that most of the figures in this section show a hooks folder. You use the hooks folder to provide code that executes at different times during the CLI's processing of your project. I am not going to cover this now; instead, I show how hooks work in Chapter 6.

Configuring a Cordova Application

At the top of Figure 5.6, you can see the config.xml file; it's the configuration file for a Cordova project. The file is a standard XML file and originally aligned with the W3C's Widget specification (www.w3.org/TR/widgets/). Over time, the Cordova development team has moved away from the specification and started allowing additional capabilities to be added to the file.

The config.xml file is primarily used to define project-level settings for the application. There are platform-specific config.xml files used by Cordova as well. I'm not going to cover every aspect of the config.xml here, only the project-level settings; refer to the Cordova documentation for additional details at http://goo.gl/86AQeU.

Listing 5.2 shows the default project config.xml file updated with information for my Lunch Menu application.

Listing 5.2 Cordova Project config.xml File

```
<?xml version='1.0' encoding='utf-8'?>
<widget id="com.ac4p.lunchmenu" version="0.0.1"
  xmlns="http://www.w3.org/ns/widgets"
  xmlns:cdv="http://cordova.apache.org/ns/1.0">
  <name>Lunch Menu</name>
```

```
  <description>
    Company lunch menu application.
  </description>
  <author email="anything@my-email.com" href="http://www.johnwargo.com">
    John M. Wargo
  </author>
  <content src="index.html" />
  <access origin="*" />
</widget>
```

Table 5.1 provides a description of each of the properties of the config.xml file shown in Listing 5.2.

Table 5.1 config.xml Options

Option	Description
`name`	The name for the application. This is the text string that appears with the application icon on a mobile device's home screen. This value is added to the file by the Cordova CLI when creating a project; the value is passed to the `create` command as the third parameter to the command. You should be able to have spaces in your application name, although older versions of the Android tools had a problem with this.
`description`	A brief description of the application. The value for this property may be used to display information about the application within the mobile device's application manager.
`author`	The name of the developer who created the application. Notice that it supports `email` and `href` attributes.
`content`	The `src` attribute specifies the startup page for the application. By default it is set to index.html, but if you use an HTML file with a different name, you would specify the file name here, such as startup.html.
`access`	One or more `access` elements specify the external domains the application can access. This is a security feature that allows a developer to whitelist all of the external domains the application is authorized to access. The default option of `origin="*"` indicates that any server can be accessed. This is configured this way during development; you should remove this entry and replace it with one or more specific domains as needed before releasing the application into production. For more information about how to configure your application's whitelist refer to the Cordova Whitelist Guide at http://goo.gl/IG4UQj.

Regarding the `content` element, there's nothing saying you can't populate it with an external URL:

```
<content src="https://www.cordova4programming.com/" />
```

With this in place, when the application starts, it will connect to the specified URL (this book's web site) and load the content from that server into the WebView. With this approach, you're essentially creating a browser application that points to a specific site. As much fun as this is, keep in mind that Apple will likely not allow you to publish an application that does this to the Apple App Store. They tend to frown upon applications that don't have any content of their own.

There are some additional preferences elements that can be added to the file as well. These preferences apply to all mobile device platforms.

The `Fullscreen` preference is used to control visibility of the status bar. The default value is `false`, so if the preference is missing, the status bar will be shown at the top of the screen. To hide the status bar, add the following `preference` element to the project's config.xml:

```
<preference name="Fullscreen" value="true" />
```

Using the `Orientation` preference, you can lock the device orientation; this allows you to prevent the interface from rotating in response to changes in orientation. Possible values for this preference are `default`, `landscape`, and `portrait`. With the `default` setting, or with the preference omitted, the application will respond, and change layout, when the device is in portrait or landscape mode. To lock the application into landscape mode, add the following `preference` element to the config.xml:

```
<preference name="Orientation" value="landscape" />
```

There are some other preferences that apply to a subset of mobile device platforms.

On Android and BlackBerry, you can force the application background color, overriding CSS settings, for the application using the `BackgroundColor` preference:

```
<preference name="BackgroundColor" value="0xff0000ff"/>
```

For this preference, set the `value` property to a 4-byte hexadecimal color value. In this value, the first byte represents the alpha channel and the subsequent 3 bytes the RGB values. In the example shown, the background color is being set to blue (`0000ff`).

For Android and iOS devices, you can control what happens in the application when the user tries to scroll past the beginning or end of the page content using the `DisallowOverscroll` preference:

```
<preference name="DisallowOverscroll" value="true"/>
```

The default setting for this preference is `false`. On iOS, when the user scrolls past the top or bottom of the content, the page will bounce back to its original position. On Android, the top or bottom edge of the content will be highlighted with a glowing effect.

Set this preference to `true` as shown in the example to configure the application so it does not display any feedback when the user tries to scroll past the top or bottom of the page.

On BlackBerry and iOS, you can use the `HideKeyboardFormAccessoryBar` preference to hide an additional toolbar that appears above the default keyboard which provides options to help users navigate from one input field to another.

```
<preference name="HideKeyboardFormAccessoryBar" value="true"/>
```

The default for this preference is `false`.

Listing 5.3 shows an example config.xml file with several of these preferences elements added.

Listing 5.3 Cordova Project config.xml File with Preferences

```
<?xml version='1.0' encoding='utf-8'?>
<widget id="com.ac4p.lunchmenu" version="0.0.1"
  xmlns="http://www.w3.org/ns/widgets"
  xmlns:cdv="http://cordova.apache.org/ns/1.0">
  <name>Lunch Menu</name>
  <description>
    Company lunch menu application.
  </description>
  <author email="anything@my-email.com" href="http://www.johnwargo.com">
    John M. Wargo
  </author>
  <content src="index.html" />
  <access origin="http://myserver.com" />
  <preference name="Fullscreen" value="true" />
  <preference name="Orientation" value="default" />
</widget>
```

The config.xml file is also used to configure PhoneGap Build projects; you will learn more about this topic in Chapter 12, "Using PhoneGap Build."

Testing Cordova Applications

Each of the mobile platforms supported by Cordova has processes and tools a developer can use to test and, in the unlikely event your code has bugs, debug Cordova applications.

Most mobile device manufacturers provide a software program that emulates or simulates a mobile device. This allows developers to easily test their mobile applications when they don't have a physical device. Performance isn't usually the same, but they look and act like real devices as much as they can. In some cases what's provided is generic and simply mimics the capabilities of the specific OS version, while for other mobile platforms the emulator or simulator might mimic specific devices. Either way, there's a software-only solution available that developers can use to test Cordova applications in an almost real-world scenario. Google, for example, provides Android emulators, and Apple and BlackBerry provide simulators of their devices.

Simulator versus Emulator

There is a technical difference between the two that I'm not going to get into here. In order to make things simpler for me (and you), I'm going to dispense with calling out whether I'm referring to an emulator or a simulator for the remainder of the book and simply refer to both as simulators. If you see that word going forward, know that I mean either emulator or simulator.

In Chapter 4, "Using the Cordova Command-Line Interfaces," I showed you how to run your applications on physical devices or simulators using the Cordova CLI `run` command. There are also third-party solutions you can use to test your Cordova applications within a desktop browser interface. In Chapters 7 through 11 I'll show you how to use the tools provided by the mobile device manufacturers.

Leveraging Cordova Debugging Capabilities

As you test your Cordova applications, you're likely to run into issues that you'll need to resolve. The purpose of this section is to highlight some of the debugging capabilities that are available to you outside of an IDE.

Using `alert()`

One of the simplest, and often most annoying, ways to debug a Cordova application is to use the JavaScript `alert()` function to let you know what part of the code you're running or to quickly display the contents of a variable. I've always called this approach "the poor man's debugger," but it works quite well for certain types of application debugging tasks. If you see an event that's not firing within your application or some variable that's not being set or read correctly, you can simply insert an `alert()` that displays a relevant message and use that to see what's going on.

As I started working with PhoneGap and PhoneGap Build, I noticed that there were many times when the deviceready event wasn't firing in my applications. I would write my application and start testing it only to find that none of the PhoneGap APIs were working. In some cases, it was because the PhoneGap Build service wasn't packaging the phonegap.js file with the application. In other cases it was simply because I had some stupid typo in the application that I couldn't see.

> **Warning**
>
> Cordova fails silently when it encounters a JavaScript error, so if you have a typo in your code, the code will simply not run.

If you look at some of the example applications in Chapter 2, "Anatomy of a Cordova Application," you'll notice that most of the applications I show there have a call to `alert` in the `onBodyLoad` function. This allows me to know for sure that the deviceready event is firing; I always remove the `alert` before putting the application into production.

When I was writing all of the sample applications for *PhoneGap Essentials*, I even went as far as to put an alert at the beginning of every function in the application. As I figured out how and when each event fired, I would use the alerts to help me tell what was going on. Now, there are easier ways to do that, which I will show you in the next section, but this was just a simple approach to help me as I got started with each API.

> **Warning**
>
> Those of you who know a little bit about the Cordova APIs might be asking yourselves why I am talking about using `alert()` rather than the Cordova `navigator.notification.alert()` function.
>
> Well, in the `onBodyLoad()` function, it is highly likely that cordova.js hasn't loaded yet, so I can't be sure that the Cordova `navigator.notification.alert()` will even be available. I can use `navigator.notification.alert()` in the `onDeviceReady()` function because the only time that function runs is when the Cordova deviceready event has fired. If you look at the sample applications throughout this book, you'll notice that I always use the JavaScript `alert` method until I know for sure the deviceready event has fired, then switch to the Cordova `alert` for all other notifications.

Writing to the Console

The problem with using the approach described in the previous section is that when you fill your buggy code with alerts, you're constantly interrupting the application flow to dismiss the alerts as they come up. For a simple problem, this approach works pretty well, but when debugging more troublesome errors, you will need an approach that allows you to let the application run, then analyze what is happening in real time or after the application or a process within the application has completed, without interrupting the application. Cordova applications can do this through the JavaScript `console` object implemented by the browser.

Using the `console` object, developers can write messages to the browser's console which can be viewed outside of the running program through capabilities provided by the native SDKs or device simulators. The `console` object has scope at the window level, so it's essentially a global object accessible by any JavaScript code within the application. Cordova supports several options; the most common ones used are

- `console.log("message");`
- `console.warn("message");`
- `console.error("message");`

Beginning with Cordova 3.0, the console has been removed from the core Cordova APIs and is instead available as a plugin. To add console capabilities to your Cordova project, you should open a terminal window, navigate to the project folder, and issue the following command:

```
cordova plugin add org.apache.cordova.console
```

However, most device browsers support this by default anyway, so you may find that for some platforms it is not necessary.

Now, let's take a look at a sample application that illustrates the use of this feature as shown in Listing 5.4.

Listing 5.4 Example Application That Writes to the Console

```
<!DOCTYPE html>
<html>
  <head>
    <meta name="viewport" content="width=device-width,
      height=device-height, initial-scale=1.0,
      maximum-scale=1.0, user-scalable=no;" />
    <meta http-equiv="Content-type" content="text/html;
      charset=utf-8">
    <script src="cordova.js"></script>
    <script>
      function onBodyLoad() {
        document.addEventListener("deviceready", onDeviceReady,
          false);
      }
      function onDeviceReady() {
        //Just writing some console messages
        console.warn("This is a warning message!");
        console.log("This is a log message!");
        console.error("And this is an error message!");
      }
    </script>
  </head>
  <body onload="onBodyLoad()">
    <h1>Debug Example</h1>
    <p>Look at the console to see the messages the application
    has outputted</p>
  </body>
</html>
```

As you can see from the code, all the application has to do is call the appropriate method and pass in the text of the message that is supposed to be written to the console.

Figure 5.8 shows the messages highlighted in the Xcode console window. This window is accessible while the program is running on an iOS simulator, so you can debug applications in real time. Xcode adds the word `WARN` to the output for warning messages and adds `ERROR` to any error messages, so you can more easily locate these messages in the console.

```
2014-09-16 19:56:37.806 Ex5.2[10319:60b] Resetting plugins due to page load.
2014-09-16 19:56:37.972 Ex5.2[10319:60b] Finished load of: file:///Users/jwargo/Library/Application%20Support/iPhone%20Simulator/
7.1/Applications/575210F7-061C-42CB-839C-D8854EF84C1C/Ex5.2.app/www/index.html
2014-09-16 19:56:37.997 Ex5.2[10319:60b] WARN: This is a warning message!
2014-09-16 19:56:37.997 Ex5.2[10319:60b] This is a log message!
2014-09-16 19:56:37.998 Ex5.2[10319:60b] ERROR: And this is an error message!
```

Figure 5.8 Cordova iOS Application Output Log in Xcode

In the Android SDK LogCat (explained in Chapter 7, "Android Development with Cordova"), console messages are highlighted (in green) as shown in Figure 5.9. Older versions of the SDK would color-code each message type in a different color—yellow for warnings and red for errors—but that feature seems to have been removed.

```
Search for messages. Accepts Java regexes. Prefix with pid:, app:, tag: or text: to limit scope.   verbose

Le Time                 PID   TID   Application      Tag              Text
D 09-16 19:55:33.060  1033  1033  com.ac4p.ex052   CordovaActivity  onMessage(spinner,stop)
W 09-16 19:55:33.110  1033  1033  com.ac4p.ex052   AwContents       nativeOnDraw failed; clearing to background color.
D 09-16 19:55:33.310  1033  1033  com.ac4p.ex052   CordovaLog       file:///android_asset/www/index.html: Line 16 : This is a warning m
                                                                    essage!
I 09-16 19:55:33.310  1033  1033  com.ac4p.ex052   chromium         [INFO:CONSOLE(16)] "This is a warning message!", source: file:///an
                                                                    droid_asset/www/index.html (16)
D 09-16 19:55:33.310  1033  1033  com.ac4p.ex052   CordovaLog       file:///android_asset/www/index.html: Line 17 : This is a log messa
                                                                    ge!
I 09-16 19:55:33.310  1033  1033  com.ac4p.ex052   chromium         [INFO:CONSOLE(17)] "This is a log message!", source: file:///androi
                                                                    d_asset/www/index.html (17)
D 09-16 19:55:33.320  1033  1033  com.ac4p.ex052   CordovaLog       file:///android_asset/www/index.html: Line 18 : And this is an erro
                                                                    r message!
I 09-16 19:55:33.320  1033  1033  com.ac4p.ex052   chromium         [INFO:CONSOLE(18)] "And this is an error message!", source: file://
                                                                    /android_asset/www/index.html (18)
D 09-16 19:55:34.780  1033  1033  com.ac4p.ex052   CordovaActivity  onMessage(spinner,stop)
```

Figure 5.9 Cordova Android Application LogCat Output in Eclipse

Remember that in the previous section I mentioned that the JavaScript code in a Cordova application fails silently? Well, you can also wrap the code in a try/catch block so your application will at least have the chance to write its error to the console as shown in the following example:

```
try {
  console.log("Validating the meaning of life");
  someBogusFunction("42");
} catch (e) {
  console.error("Hmmm, not sure why this happened here: " +
    e.message);
}
```

Notice that in Figure 5.9 for Android the LogCat shows the line number where the console message was generated. This will at least help you identify information about where the application is failing. You could also use an alert here, but that's slightly less elegant.

You can also format your output without having to add strings together:

```
console.error("Hmmm, received an error (%s)", e.message);
```

In this case, the `%s` is replaced by the string stored in `e.message`. This isn't a Cordova thing; it's just how the `console` object works in the browser. You can pass multiple values into the string, using `%s` for strings, `%i` for numbers, and so on.

Debugging and Testing Using External Tools

There's a very active partner community supporting Cordova with additional tools for Cordova developers. In this section, I'll introduce a couple of the more popular tools that help developers test and debug Cordova applications. This is by no means a complete list of options; refer to the PhoneGap Tools page (http://phonegap.com/tool/) for information on additional tools that might be available. There are also some built-in debugging tools available with several of the mobile SDKs. These tools will be covered in the individual chapters for each mobile OS (Chapters 7 through 11).

> **Tip**
>
> One of the things I realized as I worked on this chapter as well as some of the other chapters that cover remote debuggers (Chapters 7 through 10) is that the format of a web application project matters. In most of my sample Cordova applications, I typically coded the application's HTML and JavaScript code in the same file. If the application wasn't that large, having everything in the same file made it easier for me to edit and debug my applications. As you'll see next, weinre, and many of the other remote debugging tools, aren't able to set breakpoints and debug JavaScript code embedded in an HTML file.
>
> So, to make your work easier, be sure to split out your web application's JavaScript into a separate file (index.js, for example) wherever possible. You'll be glad you did later.

Weinre

Web Inspector Remote (weinre) is a community-built remote debugger for web pages. It was donated to the PhoneGap project and is currently implemented as part of the PhoneGap Build service. You can find the download files and instructions at http://goo.gl/hG7r0L.

For Cordova development, it allows a developer to remotely debug a web application running in a Cordova container on a physical device or a device simulator. Weinre consists of a debug server, debug client, and debug target. The debug server runs on Macintosh or Windows, and the debug client runs in any compatible desktop browser. Throughout this section I'll demonstrate what you can do with weinre.

To configure weinre, you need to perform a series of steps. The process begins with the server installation. Weinre is Node-based, and since we already have Node installed for the Cordova CLI, you can install the weinre server using the following command:

```
npm install -g weinre
```

Unfortunately on Macintosh weinre may not like your security configuration, so even though it's not recommended, you may have to install weinre using sudo with the following command:

```
sudo npm install -g weinre
```

After the installation completes, you should see a message similar to the following:

```
C:\Users\jwargo\AppData\Roaming\npm\weinre ->
C:\Users\jwargo\AppData\Roaming\npm\node_modules\weinre\weinre
weinre@2.0.0-pre-HZO3BMNG C:\Users\jwargo\AppData\Roaming\npm\node_modules\weinre
+-- underscore@1.7.0
+-- nopt@3.0.1 (abbrev@1.0.5)
+-- express@2.5.11 (mime@1.2.4, qs@0.4.2, mkdirp@0.3.0, connect@1.9.2)
```

With the installation completed, you can start weinre by issuing the following command in the terminal window:

```
weinre
```

When the server starts, it will indicate that it is running by displaying a message in the terminal window similar to the following:

```
2013-06-22T17:00:50.564Z weinre: starting server at http://localhost:8080
```

> **Note**
>
> There are some command-line options you can pass to the weinre server at startup. I chose not to cover them here, but you can find detailed information on the weinre web site at http://goo.gl/DSzqwm.

With the weinre server started, you use a browser-based client application to interact with the server and Cordova client application. Open your browser of choice (I recommend using Safari or Chrome) and point it to the URL shown on the server console when the weinre server started. For my development environment I simply use

```
http://localhost:8080
```

The browser will connect to the weinre server, which will display a page similar to the one shown in Figure 5.10. To start the debug client, click on the debug client user interface link shown at the top of the page in Figure 5.10; the browser will open a page similar to what is shown in Figure 5.11.

So far, we've done nothing to allow a Cordova application to use the capabilities exposed by weinre, so let's get to that now. A Cordova application interacts with the weinre server (and debug client) through some JavaScript code that is deployed with the server. To configure a Cordova application to execute this JavaScript code, add the following script tag to the Cordova application's index.html file:

```
<script src="http://debug_server:8080/target/target-script-min.js"></script>
```

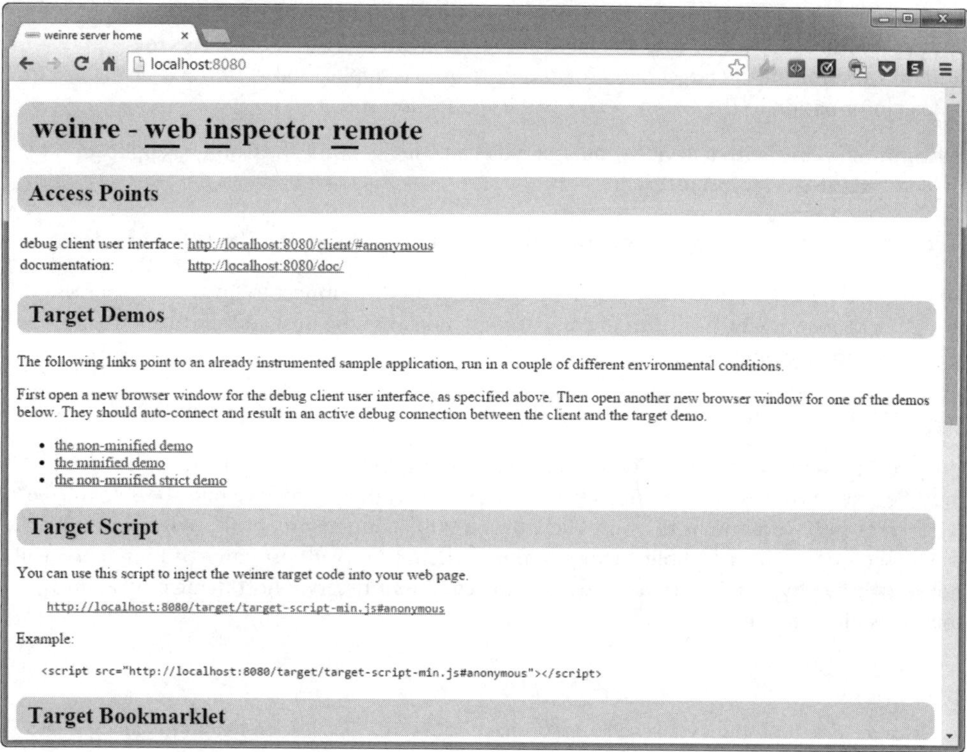

Figure 5.10 Weinre Debug Server

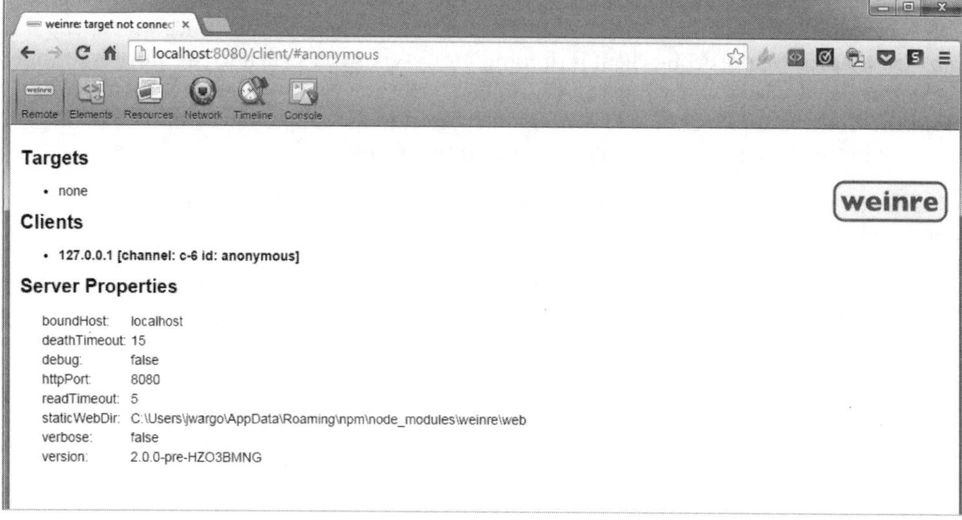

Figure 5.11 Weinre Debug Client

You need to replace the debug_server portion of the URL with the correct host name or IP address for the debug server (the system running the weinre server). This makes the application into a weinre debug target and provides the Cordova application with the code needed to upload information to the weinre server as the application runs.

When using weinre with a device simulator, you can usually point the Cordova application to the local weinre server instance using

```
<script src="http://localhost:8080/target/target-script-min.js"></script>
```

The Android emulator, however, does not have the ability to connect to host-side resources using localhost, so for the Android emulator you must use the host address http://10.0.2.2 as shown in the following example:

```
<script src="http://10.0.2.2:8080/target/target-script-min.js"></script>
```

When using weinre to debug a Cordova application running on a physical device, the device must be able to connect to your debug server. That means that the device must be able to "see" the server on the local network (most likely over a Wi-Fi connection), or the system running the weinre server must have a public-facing IP address. Using a server host name of localhost will not work on a physical device; you must use an actual weinre server host name or IP address that is visible to the device.

> **Warning**
>
> Be sure to remove the weinre script tag from your Cordova application before releasing it into production. The application will likely hang if attempting to connect to a debug server that isn't available.

After you have added the script tag to the Cordova application's index.html file, run the application in the simulator or on a device. Nothing special will appear on the device screen; you can't tell that the weinre debug client is running. However, if you switch to the browser running the weinre debug client, you will see a page similar to the one shown in Figure 5.12. As soon as I start the Cordova application, as long as it can connect to the weinre server, the debug client page will update and display the content shown in the figure.

The debug client provides the means to view and optionally manipulate many of the page elements and other aspects of your application's web content.

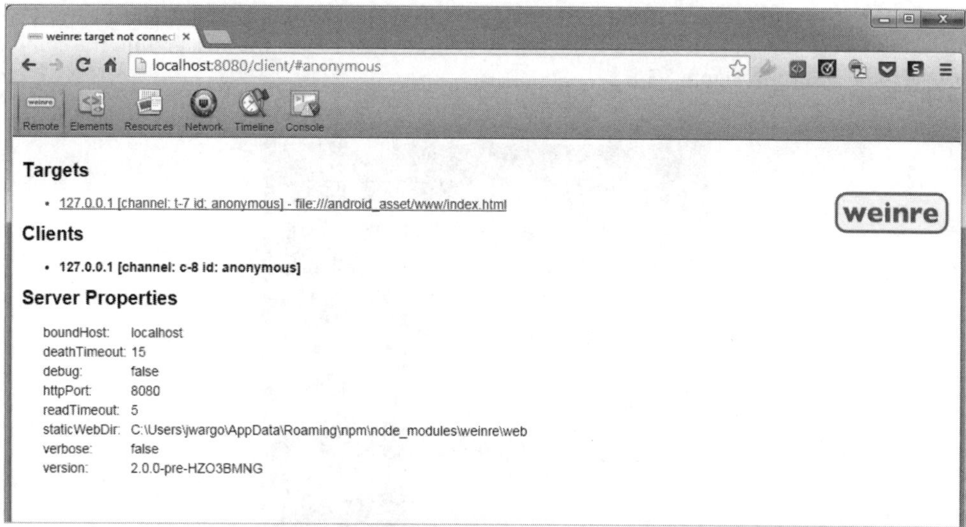

Figure 5.12 Weinre Debug Client with an Application Activated

At this point, the different buttons across the top of the debug client are available to provide you with information about the debug target. For example, in Figure 5.13 you see the contents of the Elements page; it shows you the current HTML5 content running within the debug target.

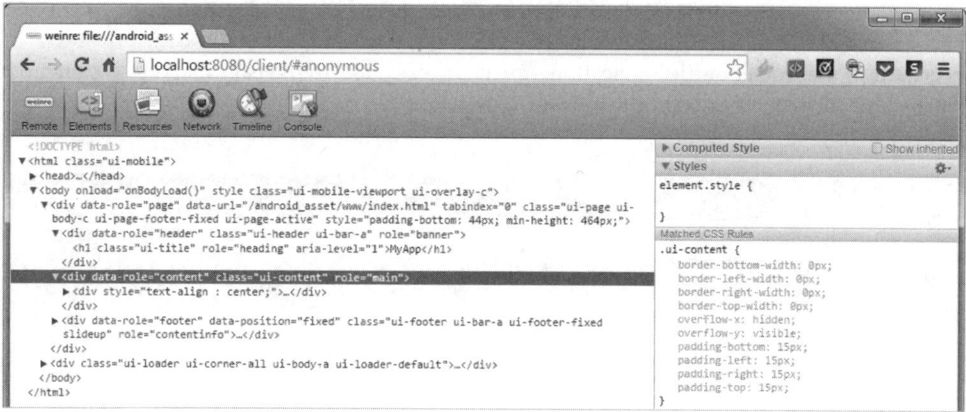

Figure 5.13 Weinre Debug Client Elements Area

One of the cool features of weinre is that as you highlight the different code sections shown in Figure 5.13, weinre will highlight the corresponding content within the web application. This allows you to see what part of your application's UI is affected by the code you're highlighting. So, for the Hello World #3 application shown in Figure 5.13, since I'm highlighting the content div tag, in the debug target you will see that section of the page highlighted as shown in

Figure 5.14. The application I'm demonstrating here is the sample application from Chapter 15, "Cordova Development End to End." The highlighted content area is the area around the compass graphic shown in Figure 5.14.

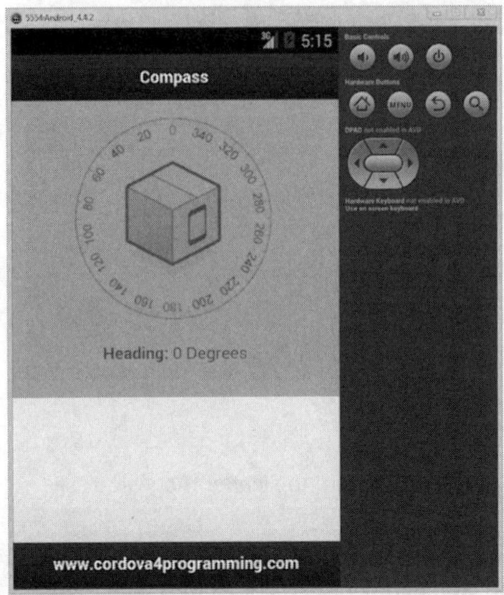

Figure 5.14 Weinre Target Highlighting HTML Content

You can't debug the application's JavaScript code using weinre, but you can edit the content and markup of the application as it runs. In Figure 5.15, you can see that I've edited the text displayed in the header of the application. Any changes I make to the page markup or content will be immediately reflected in the running application.

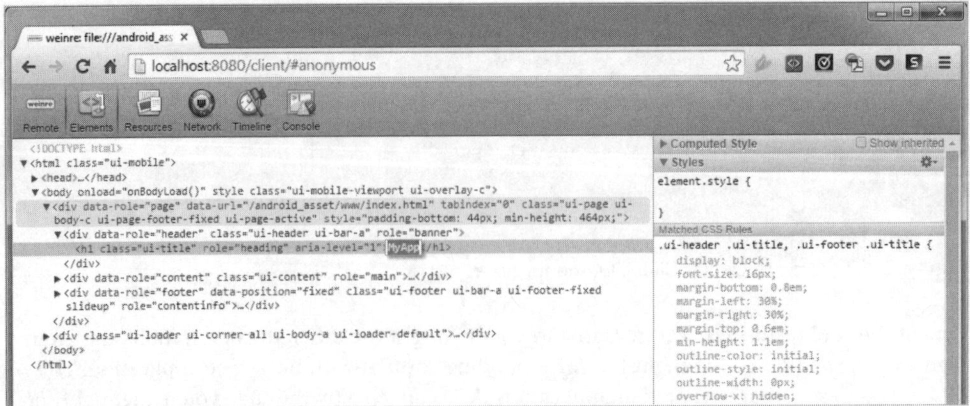

Figure 5.15 Changing Page Content in the Weinre Debug Client

Additionally, on the right side of the figure is a style browser; you can double-click any of the CSS properties and change their values. This allows you to play around with CSS settings in order to get the application looking exactly as you want it to look using a real device (or at least a simulator) in real time.

You can use the Console tab to monitor the application's console output as shown in Figure 5.16. This is where you will be able to view the content generated by calls to `console.log`, `console.error`, and `console.warn` described earlier in this chapter.

Figure 5.16 Monitoring Console Output in the Weinre Debug Client

Using the debug client, you can access the following content areas:

- Elements: the HTML, CSS, and JavaScript code for the application
- Resources: local resources used by the application such as databases, local storage, and session storage
- Network: information about requests made using XMLHTTPRequests (XHR)
- Timeline: events that occur within the target application
- Console: information written to the console using the `console` object described earlier in the chapter

The available documentation for weinre is pretty light, but since the project's capabilities are based upon the Google Chrome Developer Tools, you can find additional information on the Google Chrome web site at http://goo.gl/7f6mf1.

The weinre team refers developers who need to step through their JavaScript code in a remote debugger to Aardwolf (http://lexandera.com/aardwolf/), but I've not used that tool as it's currently considered experimental code.

Ripple Emulator

The Ripple Emulator (now called Apache Ripple—http://ripple.incubator.apache.org/) is a tool you can use to help with the initial testing of your Cordova application. Ripple is a browser-based emulator that can be used to emulate several different systems.

Originally created by Tiny Hippos, which was then acquired by BlackBerry, Ripple is now an incubator project at Apache with independent developers working on it. The problem with Ripple is that it seems to be ignored for long stretches of time. As you'll be able to see in the screen shots in this section, it's in beta and has been in beta for a very long time (almost three years now by my counting). Typically, Ripple is way behind on its Cordova support—supporting Cordova 3.0 when Cordova 3.6 was just released, for example. Because of those limitations, I'm not going to go into too much detail about how Ripple works. If you like what you see, install it and play around with it to see what it can do.

What's interesting is that Ripple has started showing up in several Cordova development tools. The Intel XDK uses it as well as the Microsoft hybrid toolkit. Perhaps it will get some attention going forward.

Ripple emulates the execution of many of the Cordova APIs within the browser container. You can use Ripple for quick testing of Cordova application features and UI during development, then switch to packaging/building Cordova applications and testing them on actual devices or device simulators for more thorough testing. Keep in mind, though, that Ripple is not designed to replace testing on real devices or simulators.

Ripple doesn't provide access to application internals as weinre does. You can learn more about Ripple's capabilities at http://ripple.incubator.apache.org.

The emulator uses Google Chrome, so you will need to install Chrome from www.google.com/chrome before you begin.

The current iteration of Ripple is Node based, so you install the package using NPM. On a Windows system, open a terminal window, then install Ripple using

```
npm install -g ripple-emulator
```

For Macintosh OS X and Linux, install Ripple using

```
sudo npm install -g ripple-emulator
```

NPM will churn for a little while, then display the installation results in the terminal window:

```
C:\Users\jwargo\AppData\Roaming\npm\ripple -> C:\Users\jwargo\AppData\Roaming\np
m\node_modules\ripple-emulator\bin\ripple
ripple-emulator@0.9.23 C:\Users\jwargo\AppData\Roaming\npm\node_modules\ripple-e
mulator
├── connect-xcors@0.5.2
├── colors@0.6.0-1
├── open@0.0.3
├── accounting@0.4.1
├── request@2.12.0
├── moment@1.7.2
└── express@3.1.0 (methods@0.0.1, fresh@0.1.0, range-parser@0.0.4, cookie-signat
ure@0.0.1, buffer-crc32@0.1.1, cookie@0.0.5, commander@0.6.1, mkdirp@0.3.3, send
@0.1.0, debug@2.0.0, connect@2.7.2)
```

At this point, Ripple is installed and ready to go. To use the emulator, in the terminal window navigate to a Cordova application project and issue the following command:

```
ripple emulate
```

Ripple will launch Chrome and launch the Cordova application within the emulator as shown in Figure 5.17. Wrapped around the simulated smartphone are properties panes that can be used to configure options and status for the simulated smartphone such as simulated device screen resolution, accelerometer, network, geolocation, and more.

Figure 5.17 Ripple Emulator Running a Cordova Application

You can click on each of the tabs to expand the options for the tab and make changes to the simulated device's configuration. At this point, you would simply click around within the simulated smartphone screen and interact with the options presented within your application. When you find a problem or a change you want to make within the Cordova application, simply return to your HTML editor, make the necessary changes, write the changes to disk, then reload the page in the Chrome browser to continue with testing.

When Ripple encounters a problem, it will display an error page like the one shown in Figure 5.18. Remember, this is a very old piece of beta software, so this may happen from time to time. You can click Wait and see what happens, or you can reset Ripple and try again. Simply reload the page in the browser to eliminate many problems.

Figure 5.18 Ripple Error Page

PhoneGap Developer App

A recent addition to the suite of testing tools available to Cordova (actually PhoneGap in this case) developers is the PhoneGap Developer app. The application is a free application, available in the Android, iOS, and Windows app stores today, that provides developers with a quick and easy way to test their applications on mobile devices. You can see an example of the app's Google Play app store entry in Figure 5.19.

The application is essentially a PhoneGap application with all of the PhoneGap plugins added and some extra code required to open an AJAX connection to the local server to retrieve and load web application content from the server. The application also sends some information back to the server as you'll see in a little while.

The way this is works is that you install the application on one or more mobile devices, then create a local PhoneGap application project and use the PhoneGap CLI's `serve` command to serve the particular application to the mobile devices running the PhoneGap Developer app. Figure 5.20 shows the results of issuing the `serve` command, in this case serving a PhoneGap application I've created in a folder called test.

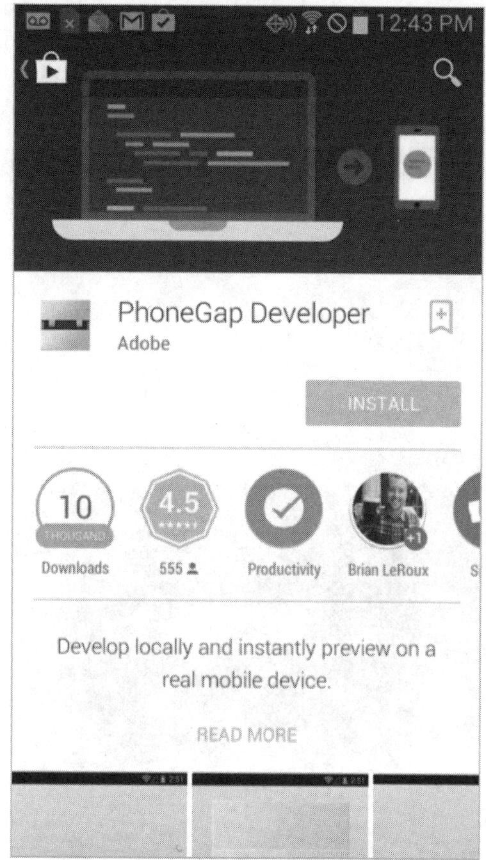

Figure 5.19 PhoneGap Developer App in the Google Play Store

```
Command Prompt - phonegap serve

C:\Users\jwargo\dev\test>phonegap serve
cp: no such file or directory: C:\Users\jwargo\dev\test\icon.png

cp: no such file or directory: C:\Users\jwargo\dev\test\res\icon\ios\icon-72.png


[phonegap] starting app server...
[phonegap] listening on 192.168.1.29:3000
[phonegap]
[phonegap] ctrl-c to stop the server
[phonegap]
```

Figure 5.20 PhoneGap Server Started

The terminal window shown in Figure 5.20 shows you the IP address (192.168.1.29) and port number (3000) the application is being served from. With that information, you can open the PhoneGap Developer app and populate the server address as shown in Figure 5.21.

Figure 5.21 PhoneGap Developer App Running on an Android Device

At this point, the web application you've created will be downloaded from the server and launched within the PhoneGap Developer app. You can interact with the application as needed to verify that it is operating correctly. When you make changes to the local mobile application, the PhoneGap Developer app will automatically detect the changes, update itself, and reload the app.

This provides you with an easy way to iterate through the develop and test process—completely eliminating the time you'd normally waste waiting for a prepare, build, and deploy to be completed by the Cordova CLI.

Remember, though, that the PhoneGap Developer app doesn't provide you with insight into the web application running within the application as weinre does. Console entries, however, are pushed to the server, and you can view them on the console as shown in Figure 5.22. So, if you've identified a problem with the application, you can use the `console` object to send information to the server console to help you troubleshoot the application.

```
Command Prompt - phonegap serve
[phonegap] 200 /plugins/org.apache.cordova.globalization/www/GlobalizationError.
js
[phonegap] 200 /plugins/org.apache.cordova.globalization/www/globalization.js
[phonegap] 200 /plugins/org.apache.cordova.media/www/MediaError.js
[phonegap] 200 /plugins/org.apache.cordova.dialogs/www/notification.js
[phonegap] 200 /plugins/org.apache.cordova.media/www/Media.js
[phonegap] 200 /plugins/org.apache.cordova.vibration/www/vibration.js
[phonegap] 200 /plugins/org.apache.cordova.dialogs/www/android/notification.js
[phonegap] 200 /plugins/org.apache.cordova.splashscreen/www/splashscreen.js
[phonegap] 200 /plugins/org.apache.cordova.inappbrowser/www/InAppBrowser.js
[phonegap] [console.log] body load
[phonegap] 200 /socket.io/?EIO=2&transport=polling&t=1410972935336-3&sid=MMyMqfT
cCfqPZnxJAAAB
[phonegap] [console.log] Entering onDeviceReady
[phonegap] 200 /socket.io/?EIO=2&transport=polling&t=1410972936854-4&sid=MMyMqfT
cCfqPZnxJAAAB
[phonegap] 200 /__api__/autoreload
[phonegap] 200 /__api__/autoreload
[phonegap] 200 /__api__/autoreload
[phonegap] 200 /__api__/autoreload
[phonegap] 200 /__api__/autoreload
[phonegap] 200 /__api__/autoreload
[phonegap] 200 /__api__/autoreload
```

Figure 5.22 PhoneGap Server Console

> **Warning**
>
> The system serving the mobile application must be visible to the mobile devices running the PhoneGap Developer app. In most cases, the system running the PhoneGap `serve` command won't be on the public Internet, so cellular-only devices won't be able to access the server. Any mobile devices running the PhoneGap Developer app will need to be on the same network as the server—most likely connected to a Wi-Fi network that is used by the server or connects to a wired network used by the server.

GapDebug

Another recent entry into the Cordova debugging tools category is GapDebug (http://goo.gl/rsWWrj) from Genuitec. GapDebug is a Chrome-based debugging tool similar to what's available with weinre, Google Chrome (described in Chapter 7), and Apple Safari (described in Chapter 9, "iOS Development with Cordova"). Unlike weinre, it requires that a physical device be connected to the development system via a USB cable. I could not find information about what mobile device platforms GapDebug supports. I know it supports Android and iOS, but I do not know if support for other devices is planned.

The tool is pretty new and is still in beta as I write this, so I'm not going to go too deeply into how it works as how it works is still being decided. The tool's web site says, "GapDebug will always be free for local debugging," so I assume there will be some sort of commercial offering available someday.

On iOS devices, GapDebug makes use of the remote Web Inspector capabilities of the device. Before you can debug applications, you must first enable the Web Inspector. To do this, open the iOS Settings application, select Safari, then at the very bottom of the Settings page select Advanced. Finally, enable the Web Inspector switch as shown in Figure 5.23.

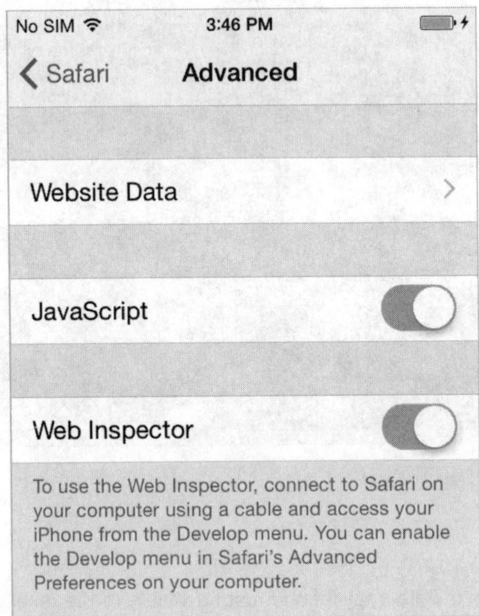

Figure 5.23 Enabling Web Inspector on iOS

GapDebug has an installer for Microsoft Windows and Macintosh OS X—simply go to the web site, then download and install the correct version for your development workstation OS. It uses Google Chrome, so you'll need to download and install the Google Chrome browser (www.google.com/chrome) as well.

After you install GabDebug, you can launch it using the application shortcut created by the installer. It will open Chrome and display a page similar to what is shown in Figure 5.24.

You can't do anything here yet because GapDebug doesn't see any devices connected to the computer. When you connect one or more devices, the page will update and show a list of available devices in the left pane as shown in Figure 5.25.

After you launch a "debug-enabled" Cordova application on one of the connected devices, you can click on the application in the left pane and GapDebug will open the application in the right pane, allowing you to interact with the application running on the device.

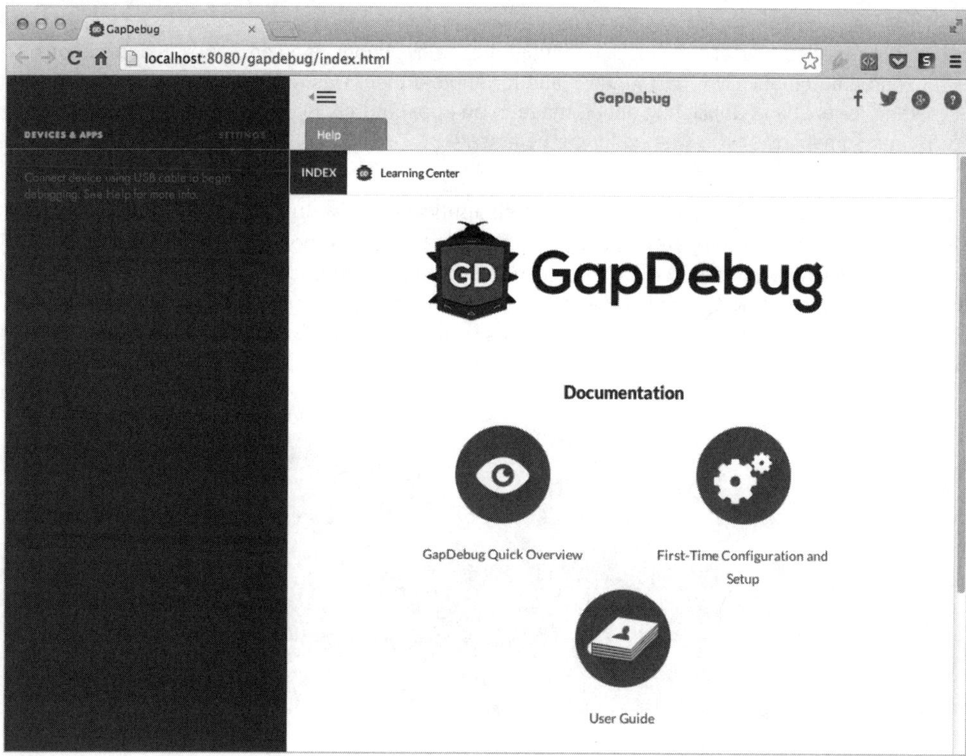

Figure 5.24 GapDebug Startup Page

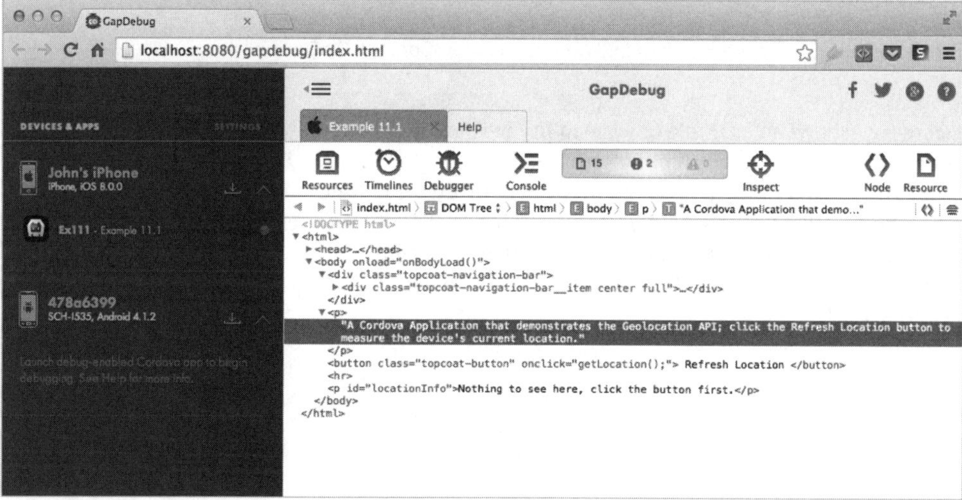

Figure 5.25 GapDebug Page with an Application Open

> **Note**
>
> I'm not really sure what the GapDebug team means by "debug-enabled." My iOS applications appeared automatically in the window, and for Android there was supposed to be a special setting for enabling GapDebug debug mode in an app, but I couldn't make it work and in the forums somebody said it was no longer necessary.

GapDebug highlights HTML content in the web application as weinre does. In Figure 5.25 I've highlighted one of the paragraph tags in the app; when you look at the application running on the device (shown in Figure 5.26), you can see the content highlighted on the screen. This shows you what part of the application's UI is affected by the code you're highlighting. Example 11.1 is one of the example applications from my *Apache Cordova API Cookbook* (www.cordovacookbook.com).

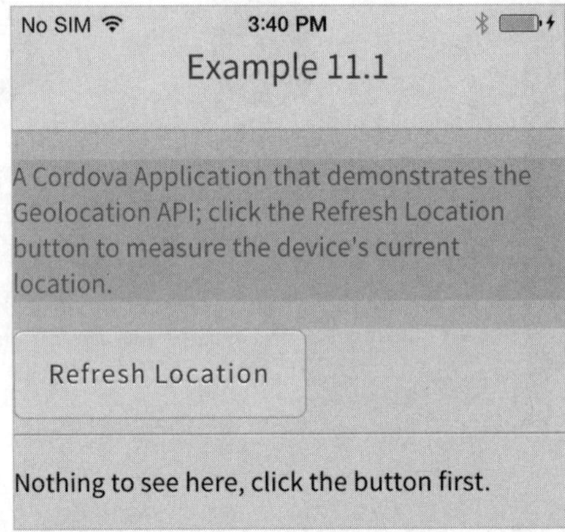

Figure 5.26 GapDebug Highlighting Web Application Content On-Device

Figure 5.27 shows an example of a capability of GapDebug that allows you to set breakpoints in your JavaScript code, then step through the code as it executes just like traditional debugging tools. This is something that you cannot currently do using weinre. In my testing, setting breakpoints and working closely with an application's JavaScript code seems to work only when the application's JavaScript code is its own file rather than being embedded within a page's HTML. I didn't expect it to work that way, so I hope this is something that will be fixed before the product is released.

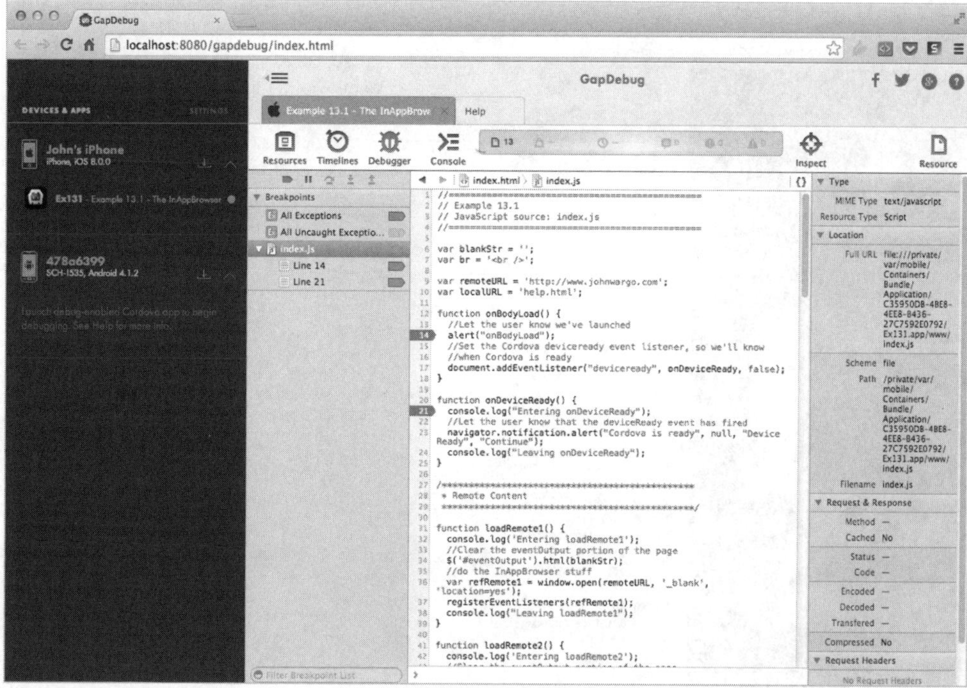

Figure 5.27 Setting Breakpoints in an Application's JavaScript Code

And finally, always important for the type of applications I write, GapDebug gives you the ability to view an application's console output as shown in Figure 5.28. You can filter the console messages, see only debug or warning messages, and clear the log from the interface GapDebug provides.

GapDebug is an interesting tool, and a lot of Cordova developers seem to be taking a look at it. There's a lot more you can do with it than I've shown here; it really simplifies Cordova debugging.

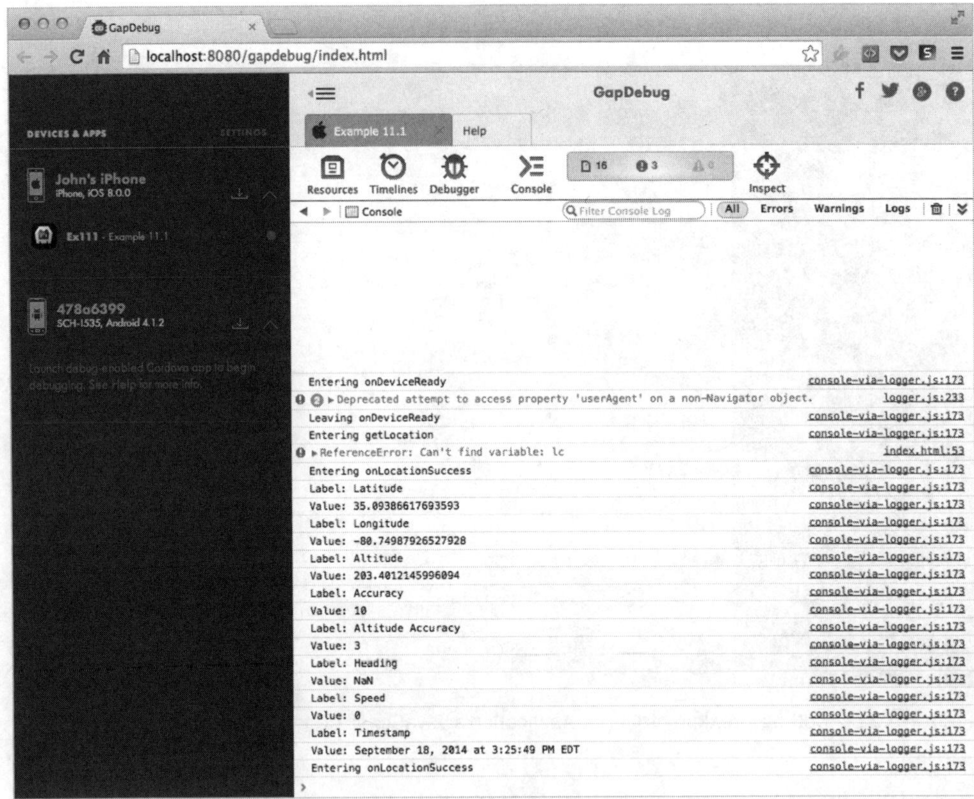

Figure 5.28 Viewing an Application's Console Output in GapDebug

Wrap-Up

By now you should have a pretty good idea of how to build and debug Cordova applications. This chapter highlighted a bit about the development process, then showed you how to test and debug your Cordova applications using some tools that apply across multiple mobile device platforms.

In the next chapter, I'll show you how to add some automation to the Cordova CLI.

6

Automation and the Cordova CLI

As you may have noticed from the last two chapters, the typical Cordova developer spends a lot of time at the command prompt. In this chapter, I'm going to show you how to add a little automation to your Cordova projects.

As I worked on each of my Cordova books (this is my fourth), I found myself typing in the same commands over and over for each Cordova project I created, and I created a lot of apps. In the first half of this chapter, I'll show you how to automate some of the repetitive tasks you perform with the CLI. In the second half of the chapter, I'll show you how to add additional actions to the activities that Cordova performs while it's managing your projects.

Automating the Project Setup Step

For every Cordova application project I create, I always execute the same commands in a terminal window:

```
cordova create project_folder appID AppName
cd project_folder
cordova platform add list_of_platforms
cordova plugin add org.apache.cordova.console
cordova plugin add org.apache.cordova.dialogs
cordova plugin add org.apache.cordova.device
```

After doing this so many times, I started looking for a way to automate those steps so I can type in only one command and get all of that stuff done. In this section, I'll show you several ways to automate this process; there are probably other ways you can do this, but I'm going to show you the ones I know of.

Windows Command File

Microsoft DOS has always had the capability that enabled savvy users to automate a series of tasks using batch files. A batch file is a file with the .bat file extension (make-project.bat, for example) that contains a sequence of DOS commands that are executed in order. Microsoft Windows is "based" on DOS, so the same capability is available here, but it's now command files (a file with a .cmd extension—make-project.cmd, for example) rather than batch files.

To create a command file, open your text editor of choice, copy in those Cordova CLI commands I showed earlier, and save the file to an appropriate location with the appropriate file name plus the .cmd extension. If you then open a terminal window and execute the command file, those steps will execute sequentially and your Cordova project will be created for you.

Unfortunately, each Cordova project is stored in a different folder, and each has a unique ID and a unique name. To accommodate this, Windows applications can accept command-line arguments, so all we need to do is update our process so it accepts the arguments we need like this:

```
command-file.cmd param1 param2 param3
```

So, assuming I've created a command file called cva-create.cmd, I could execute it and pass in my Cordova project arguments like this:

```
cva-create.cmd lunchmenu com.ac4p.lunchmenu LunchMenu
```

All that's needed is to have some way to grab those arguments and use them in the execution of the command file.

Within a Windows command file, arguments passed to the program are automatically assigned to variables called %1, %2, %3, and so on. So, whenever I want to use one of the arguments in the code, all I have to do is refer to it by the variable name. With that information, we have everything we need to make a Windows command file that can be used over and over and over again to create new Cordova application projects.

Listing 6.1 shows a Windows command file I created called cva-create.cmd that operates using the command-line arguments I showed in my previous example. You can create the same file, copy it to your development system, and use it to make new projects.

Listing 6.1 cva-create.cmd

```
REM Turn off writing commands to the console
ECHO off

REM Clear the screen so we start at the top
REM when we run
cls

echo ===================================
echo  Creating the Cordova Project
echo ===================================
call cordova create %1 %2 %3
REM change to the new project folder that
REM was just created
cd %1
echo.

echo ===================================
echo  Adding Platforms
echo ===================================
call cordova platform add android firefoxos wp8
echo.

echo ===================================
echo  Adding Plugins
echo ===================================
call cordova plugin add org.apache.cordova.console
call cordova plugin add org.apache.cordova.device
call cordova plugin add org.apache.cordova.dialogs

REM Tell the user that we're done
echo.
echo Finished!
```

The `echo` commands simply write the content to the console. An `echo` with a period behind it will simply write a blank line to the console.

There's one problem with what I've created here: you can't pass in an application name that contains a space. I tested this several ways, and I wasn't able to get it to work; for everything I tried, it would treat the space between the two words (I tried "Lunch Menu") as a delimiter and a project would get created named Lunch. Perhaps one of you will figure this out and send me the fix.

When you run the command file from a Windows terminal window, it will generate the output shown in Figure 6.1 and, of course, create a new Cordova project for you.

Command Prompt
===================================
Creating the Cordova Project
===================================
Creating a new cordova project with name "LunchMenu" and id "com.ac4p.lunchmenu" at location "C:\Users\jwargo\dev\lunchmenu"
===================================
Adding Platforms
===================================
Creating android project...
Creating Cordova project for the Android platform:
Path: platforms\android
Package: com.ac4p.lunchmenu
Name: LunchMenu
Android target: android-19
Copying template files...
Running: android update project --subprojects --path "platforms\android" --target android-19 --library "CordovaLib"
Resolved location of library project to: C:\Users\jwargo\dev\lunchmenu\platforms\android\CordovaLib
Updated and renamed default.properties to project.properties
Updated local.properties
No project name specified, using Activity name 'LunchMenu'.
If you wish to change it, edit the first line of build.xml.
Added file C:\Users\jwargo\dev\lunchmenu\platforms\android\build.xml
Added file C:\Users\jwargo\dev\lunchmenu\platforms\android\proguard-project.txt
Updated project.properties
Updated local.properties
No project name specified, using project folder name 'CordovaLib'.
If you wish to change it, edit the first line of build.xml.
Added file C:\Users\jwargo\dev\lunchmenu\platforms\android\CordovaLib\build.xml
Added file C:\Users\jwargo\dev\lunchmenu\platforms\android\CordovaLib\proguard-project.txt
Project successfully created.
Creating firefoxos project...
Creating Firefox OS project
Project Path platforms\firefoxos
Package Name com.ac4p.lunchmenu
Project Name LunchMenu
Checking wp8 requirements...
Creating wp8 project...
platformRoot = C:\Users\jwargo\.cordova\lib\wp\cordova\3.5.0\wp8
repoRoot = C:\Users\jwargo\.cordova\lib\wp\cordova\3.5.0
Creating Cordova-WP8 Project:
App Name : LunchMenu
Namespace : com.ac4p.lunchmenu
Path : C:\Users\jwargo\dev\lunchmenu\platforms\wp8
CREATE SUCCESS : C:\Users\jwargo\dev\lunchmenu\platforms\wp8
===================================
Adding Plugins
===================================
Fetching plugin "org.apache.cordova.console" via plugin registry
Installing "org.apache.cordova.console" for android
Installing "org.apache.cordova.console" for firefoxos
Installing "org.apache.cordova.console" for wp8
Fetching plugin "org.apache.cordova.device" via plugin registry
Installing "org.apache.cordova.device" for android
Installing "org.apache.cordova.device" for firefoxos
Installing "org.apache.cordova.device" for wp8
Fetching plugin "org.apache.cordova.dialogs" via plugin registry
Installing "org.apache.cordova.dialogs" for android
Installing "org.apache.cordova.dialogs" for firefoxos
Installing "org.apache.cordova.dialogs" for wp8
Finished!
C:\Users\jwargo\dev\lunchmenu>_

Figure 6.1 Creating a Cordova Application Project Using a Windows Command File

Bash Script

Macintosh OS X and Linux of course don't support Windows command files; instead, you need to write a bash script. Bash scripts are just like Windows command files, but there is a slightly different command syntax to use in some cases. In Listing 6.2 I show the same cva-create process, only in a bash script.

Listing 6.2 cva-create.sh

```
#!/bin/sh

# Clear the screen, so we start at the top
# when we run
clear

# Create the Cordova project
echo ================================
echo  Creating the Cordova Project
echo ================================
cordova create $1 $2 "$3"

# Change to the new project folder
cd $1

echo
echo ================================
echo  Adding Platforms
echo ================================
cordova platform add android ios

echo
echo ================================
echo  Adding Plugins
echo ================================
cordova plugin add org.apache.cordova.console
cordova plugin add org.apache.cordova.dialogs
cordova plugin add org.apache.cordova.device

# Tell the user we're done
echo
echo "Finished!"
```

The bash script starts with a `#!/bin/sh` that tells the operating system we're executing a bash script; otherwise it's pretty much the same as the example in Listing 6.1. Notice that the bash script uses $1, $2, and so on to describe the arguments passed to the script.

If you're running the script in a terminal window from the folder where the script resides, you will execute the script using

```
./cva-create.sh project_folder appID AppName
```

Otherwise, for both examples you'll need to put the file in a folder that is located on the system path, or you will need to type a full path pointing to the file location every time you execute the command. I simply put the script files in my system's dev folder since I create all applications under that folder structure.

Cross-Platform Approach Using NodeJS

As interesting as the command file and bash script options are for automating the creation of a new Cordova project, the implementation requires that you have a different solution for Windows than for OS X. You could install a bash shell on Windows and use the bash script on both, but there's a better solution.

Since the Cordova CLI runs on multiple platforms and uses Node, you could build a Node application that manages the Cordova application creation process for you. This is the solution I picked for myself when I first started looking for a solution to this particular problem. So, instead of having to write the Node application yourself, I've already done it for you. I've created a Node module called `cdva-create` and, rather than show all of the code here, I've already published the source code to my GitHub account at https://github.com/johnwargo/cdva-create and published the module to NPM (www.npmjs.com/package/cdva-create) so you can quickly install the module and put it to work.

To install the module on Windows, open a terminal window and execute the following command:

```
npm install -g cdva-create
```

Macintosh OS X and Linux users should open a terminal window and execute the following command:

```
sudo npm install -g cdva-create
```

NPM will churn for a little while, then let you know it installed the module correctly when it displays something similar to the following:

```
C:\Users\jwargo\AppData\Roaming\npm\cdva-create ->
C:\Users\jwargo\AppData\Roaming\npm\node_modules\cdva-create\cordova-create.js
cdva-create@0.0.12 C:\Users\jwargo\AppData\Roaming\npm\node_modules\cdva-create
├── colors@0.6.2
└── shelljs@0.3.0
```

To use the module, simply open a terminal window, navigate to the folder where you want the application project created, and execute a command similar to the following:

```
cdva-create folder app_id app_name [platform list]
```

To create the Lunch Menu application we've been using lately, I would use the following command:

```
cdva-create lunchmenu com.ac4p. lunchmenu "Lunch Menu" android
```

Notice that I put the application name, Lunch Menu, in quotes; that's because there's a space in the application name and the module needs to know to treat both words as one parameter. Without a space, it would look like this:

```
cdva-create lunchmenu com.ac4p. lunchmenu LunchMenu android
```

To create the same project, but include an iOS project as well, you would use the following command:

```
cdva-create lunchmenu com.ac4p. lunchmenu "Lunch Menu" android ios
```

Figure 6.2 shows the output from the module in the Windows terminal.

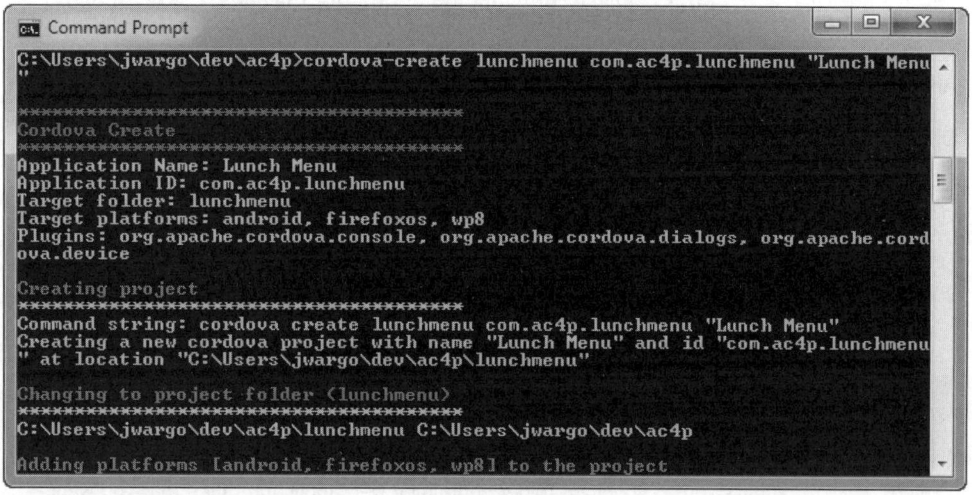

Figure 6.2 Executing the `cdva-create` Module

When you run the module, you will notice that it's preconfigured with a specific set of platforms and plugins. Don't worry; you can easily customize the module.

When the module runs the first time, it creates a configuration file called cdva-create.json in the current user's home folder. The home folder will usually be in C:\Users\user_name on Windows and /Users/user_name on OS X. To customize the module, simply edit the configuration file and adjust the parameters there to suit your specific requirements. The next time you execute the module, your changes will apply.

A sample cdva-create.json file is shown in Listing 6.3.

Listing 6.3 cdva-create.json File

```
{
    "platformList": [
        "android",
        "firefoxos",
        "wp8"
    ],
    "pluginList": [
        "org.apache.cordova.console",
        "org.apache.cordova.dialogs",
        "org.apache.cordova.device"
```

```
    ],
    "enableDebug": false,
    "copyFrom": ""
    "linkTo": ""
}
```

Table 6.1 describes each of the available configuration options for the `cdva-create` module.

Table 6.1 `cdva-create` Configuration Options

Option	Description
`copyFrom`	Allows you to specify a folder containing web application files that you want used as a starter for the Cordova project being created. Populate this value with an absolute or relative folder path pointing to a folder that contains web application content. When this value is non-blank, the module will add the `-copy-from` parameter and the folder path to the parameter list passed to the `cordova create` command. This will cause the web application source files to be copied to the Cordova project's www folder during the `create` process.
`enableDebug`	When this value is `true`, the module will enable verbose mode by adding the `-d` parameter for each Cordova CLI command executed by the module.
`linkTo`	Allows you to specify a folder containing web application files that you want used as a starter for the Cordova project being created. Populate this value with an absolute or relative folder path pointing to a folder that contains web application content. When this value is non-blank, the module will add the `-link-to` parameter and the folder path to the parameter list passed to the `cordova create` command. This will cause the specified folder to be used through a symbolic link in the Cordova project's www folder during the `create` process. With this in place, any edits made to the project's www folder will automatically be reflected in the source folder.
`platformList`	A JSON array specifying each of the platforms that will be added to the project. Add or remove platforms as needed for your environment.
`pluginList`	A JSON array specifying each of the plugins that will be added to the project. Add or remove platforms as needed for your environment.

Automating the Cordova Process

The Cordova CLI does a lot of work for you, managing most everything about your Cordova projects. However, as you've read through Chapter 4, "Using the Cordova Command-Line Interfaces," or worked with your own Cordova projects, I bet you've wondered if it's possible to add your own processes to the steps the Cordova CLI performs when it's doing its work. Well, you can, and in this chapter I'll show you how it works.

With the Cordova CLI, you can enhance most of the CLI commands using the hooks folder. With the hooks folder, you create a folder for each event you want to enhance and add to the folder any executable code you want executed on the event and the CLI will execute it for you automatically.

From an event standpoint, you usually have two options for each event: before and after. As an example, one of the events that you can expose through the hooks folder is `prepare`. Using hooks, you create before_prepare and after_prepare folders within the hooks folder and add any executable code (applications, shell scripts, Node applications, and more) to each folder and the CLI will execute each of them at the appropriate time in any supported CLI process.

The executables or applications in the before_prepare folder will be executed by the CLI before the prepare process starts, and the executables or applications in the after_prepare folder will execute after the prepare process has completed.

> **Warning**
>
> Remember from Chapter 5, "The Mechanics of Cordova Development," that I mentioned the hooks folder; at the time I wrote this, the hooks folder was included with the base Cordova project folder structure, but as the Cordova dev team recently removed the merges folder, I wouldn't be surprised if they whack the hooks folder as well someday. So, if your Cordova project doesn't contain the hooks folder, simply create it and you'll be ready to go.

Hooks aren't supported for the Cordova CLI `create` command, because the hooks folder is created during the create process, so it simply wouldn't work. Hooks, however, support most other Cordova CLI commands; here is the complete list of the current hooks options:

- after_build
- after_compile
- after_docs
- after_emulate
- after_platform_add
- after_platform_ls
- after_platform_rm
- after_plugin_add
- after_plugin_ls
- after_plugin_rm
- after_plugin_search

- after_prepare
- after_run
- after_serve
- before_build
- before_compile
- before_docs
- before_emulate
- before_platform_add
- before_platform_ls
- before_platform_rm
- before_plugin_add
- before_plugin_ls
- before_plugin_rm
- before_plugin_search
- before_prepare
- before_run
- before_serve
- pre_package

The pre_package option (and folder) applies only to the Windows 8 and Windows Phone target platforms. There is some talk about expanding this to allow for custom processes during the packaging and signing process.

Unfortunately, the Cordova CLI doesn't make the hooks folders for you; you'll have to do this yourself. To make things easier for you, I created a command file for Windows and a bash script for OS X and Linux that you can use to create the folders; you can find the files in the Chapter 6 folder of the book's GitHub repository at https://github.com/johnwargo/ac4p. Simply open a terminal window, navigate to a Cordova project folder, and execute the appropriate make-hooks script and it will create the hooks folder (if it's not there), then create each of the subfolders listed above.

Hooks will run in alphabetical order, so if you want your hooks applications to run in a particular order, be sure to name them alphabetically. Most developers begin the hooks files with numeric values; that's the easiest way to list them in a particular order: 1-hook.cmd, 2-hook .cmd, and so on.

Holly Schinsky, an Adobe Evangelist, wrote a blog post that introduces hooks at http://goo.gl/Ggr64k. She includes a few example hooks you can use to better understand your options. One of the examples she gives is for a Node application that would automatically add an application's plugins to a project during the `platform add` step; I'm not sure I agree with this as a good example. Essentially to use this hook, you'd have to create a Cordova project, then create the necessary hooks folder (after_platform_add) and copy in your hook code before executing the Cordova CLI `platform add` command. I really don't see that this approach is less complicated than simply adding the platforms and issuing a few `platform add` commands manually. It's up to you to see if this option works for your projects.

The big question you're probably asking yourself right about now is why you would need to use hooks for your projects. I'm really not sure since I've not encountered a situation where a problem I had could be easily solved using a hook. I imagine that if you needed to copy in some files from another location during some part of the process or process some image files (optimizing or resizing them), hooks would be very useful.

You could easily use hooks to minify your source code or compile CoffeeScript to JavaScript during the before_prepare event, but most developers will most likely use something like Grunt or Gulp to manage these types of processes; I'll show you how to use these tools with your Cordova projects in Chapter 18, "Using Third-Party Tools with Cordova."

The problem for me is that there's not currently a way to automate getting the hooks files into position through the CLI. The Cordova CLI allows me to copy web application project files into the project's www folder through the `--copy-from` switch passed to the `create` command (described in Chapter 4). However, there's no counterpart for hooks files. So, if you have a regular set of hooks you use for your projects, there's no easy way to get them into place except to manually copy them after you create the project.

> **Note**
>
> After I submitted this chapter for editing, I created Node modules to automate the creation of the hooks and merges folders. The module for automating the creation of the hooks folders is called `cdva-hooks` (www.npmjs.com/package/cdva-hooks) and the module for automating the creation of the merges folders is called `cdva-merges` (www.npmjs.com/package/cdva-merges).

Wrap-Up

In this chapter, I've shown you a few ways to automate Cordova CLI commands and how you can insert your own code or applications into many of the Cordova CLI processes. With this information, you should be able to simplify many of your Cordova development processes.

In the next five chapters, I'll show you how to use the native SDKs for several mobile device platforms to build, test, and debug Cordova applications for those platforms.

7

Android Development with Cordova

The Cordova CLI takes care of the process of creating and managing Cordova Android application projects for you. For testing, it can launch a Cordova application on a physical device or on an emulator. Google provides a suite of tools you can use to help you build, test, and debug your Cordova applications for Android. This chapter shows you how to use those tools with your Cordova applications.

When you need to debug your application, you can use weinre (described in Chapter 5, "The Mechanics of Cordova Development") or the Chrome debugger (described later in this chapter) to debug your Cordova web application as it runs on a device or in a device emulator. There are times, however, when you will want to use an IDE to manage your development efforts. Google provides such an environment in the ADT. You would use ADT when you want to customize the Cordova application project or when you are writing, testing, and debugging native plugins.

If you're not developing for Android or you plan on using only the CLI and/or PhoneGap Build to build and test your applications, you can likely skip over this chapter. However, there are some cool tools included with ADT, so what you learn in this chapter should simplify your Android application testing and debugging efforts.

ADT versus Android Studio

Google currently offers two different tools for managing Android development projects: Android Developer Tools (ADT) and Android Studio (beta). ADT is the general-purpose Eclipse and SDK bundle that has been around since the early days of Android. Android Studio, on the other hand, is a new set of tools that were announced when I was working on *Apache Cordova 3 Programming*.

I wrote about ADT in *Apache Cordova 3 Programming* and had intended to cover Android Studio in this edition, but as I started working on the manuscript, Android Studio was still in beta (now more than a year later) and that complicates things. I thought perhaps that I could still write about it, even in its beta state, but as I started digging into it I noticed that Studio, and Studio's support for Cordova, was still in flux; features and capabilities were simply not yet finalized.

At this point, Cordova 4 has been released and I have to finish the manuscript within a deadline. I chatted with the folks at Google, and they couldn't give me any insight into when Studio would actually be "ready." They gave me some workarounds I could use to write this chapter, but they would help me produce a chapter that contained information that would not be useful once the final product was released. Because of this, I've decided to ignore Android Studio until it has reached a state where I can write about it with a reasonable expectation that the content I write will be useful to the book's readers. I'm sorry.

Using the Android Developer Tools

In Chapter 3, "Configuring a Cordova Development Environment," I briefly showed how to install the Android Developer Tools on your Cordova development system. I really didn't cover the topic too deeply or show you how to use the tools to work with your Cordova applications. In this section, I'll show you how to use the ADT IDE as well as the command-line tools Google provides.

Managing the Android SDK

Before we start digging into the tools, we have to talk a bit about the details of the SDK installation. As the Android SDK and tools are updated on a regular basis, Google provides a tool you can use to configure the SDK and to check for and install SDK updates. The tool is the SDK Manager, and you can launch it by opening a terminal window and executing the following command:

```
android
```

On Windows, you can also navigate to the SDK installation folder (I showed how to put the files in C:\adt\sdk in Chapter 3; your location may be different) and execute the application executable (it's called SDK Manager.exe on Windows).

When the application launches, you will see the Android SDK Manager (ASM) screen like the one shown in Figure 7.1.

In this window, you can check or uncheck components of the Android SDK to install or uninstall them on your development system. When you select one or more items in this window, you can then install them by clicking the Install packages button or delete them by clicking the Delete packages button. Be careful, though, since there is no option for installing some and deleting others at the same time; you have to do all of your installing and deleting separately.

What you see in the figure are the options for managing the SDK Tools, Platform tools, and Build tools (the Build tools are used by the Cordova CLI). As you can see, there have been a lot

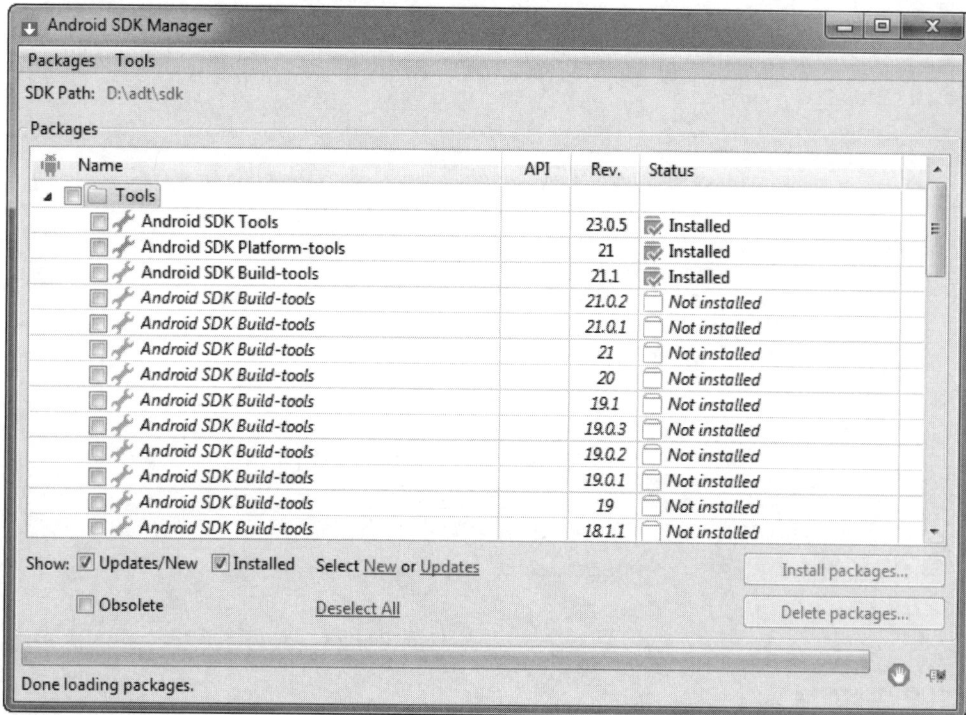

Figure 7.1 Android SDK Manager

of Build tool releases over the years. You can also use the ASM to install the SDK components for specific versions of the Android operating system as shown in Figure 7.2.

What I typically do is install the SDK platform and emulator images for each of the target OSs I will be working with. Notice in the figure that there is an SDK option as well as one for Google APIs; the Google APIs option is the same as the SDK platform but also includes Google applications such as Google Maps and other Google-specific libraries.

As you can see, there are also different types of system devices (emulators) offered; I'll explain them in the next section. I don't install the source code (sources) as I don't ever spend time poking around within the Android source code.

What you should do here is select the appropriate components for each target OS you will be supporting for your application so that you have what you need to build and debug for each target OS version as you develop your application. In the next section, I'll show you how to manage emulator configurations so you have the right set of emulators to test your application against.

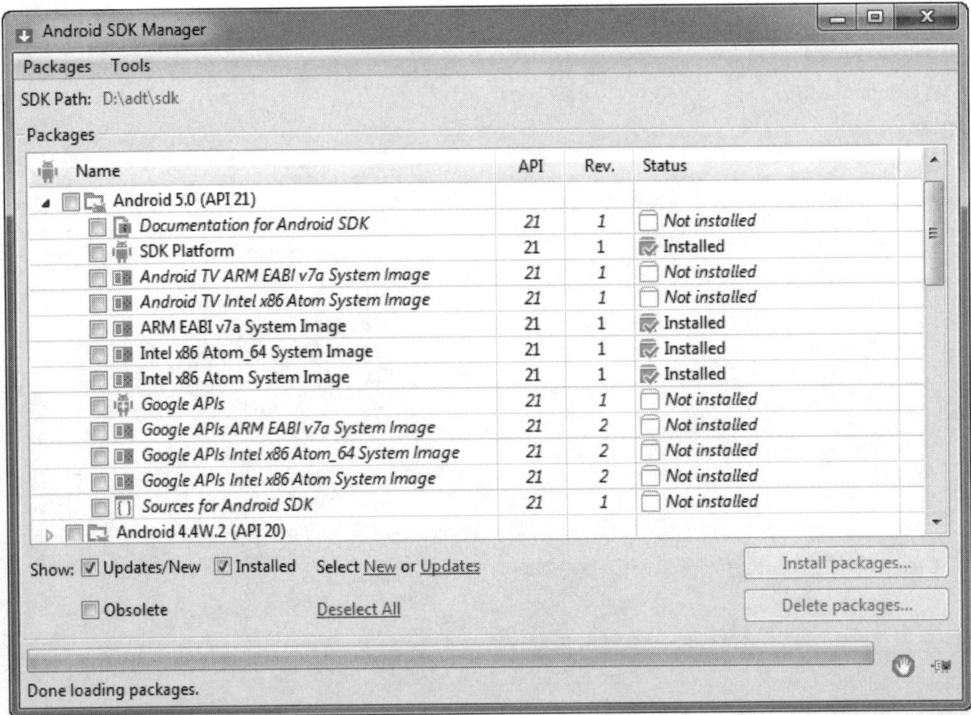

Figure 7.2 Android SDK Manager: Android 5 Platform

Using the Android Virtual Device Manager

For most mobile platforms, the vendor's SDK includes a stock set of device simulators with little variety. Because Android devices are available from a wider variety of vendors and each supports different screen resolutions, hardware, and so on, applications have to be able to run on all of them. Google refers to the Android emulators as Android Virtual Devices (AVDs). To make it easier for you to test your Android applications on different configurations, Google provides an Android Virtual Device Manager application you can use to define the complete set of emulator configurations you need to test your applications.

Android devices are offered on two different processor families: ARM and Intel. In order to allow you to test your applications on both, Google provides emulator system images for each. It's important to note that the Android emulators are very slow; they take a long time to start up, and even on modern hardware you'll find the emulators to be not as responsive as physical devices. That's why it's usually much easier to test your Android applications on a physical device.

Between the two options, the Intel device emulators perform better than the ARM-based emulators. Since both Microsoft Windows and Macintosh OS run on Intel hardware, there must be some internal benefit from emulating the Intel emulators on an Intel processor. Because of this, I usually try to use the Intel-based emulators when testing my applications. There are, however, some additional steps you must follow in order to be able to use the Intel-based emulators; I'm going to cover these steps here, but they are also described on Intel's web site at http://goo.gl/gzMbYY.

In order to be able to use the Intel-based Android emulators, you have to install the Intel Hardware Accelerated Execution Manager (HAXM). If you scrolled down in the Android SDK Manager window, described in the previous section, you would have seen an entry for the HAXM installer at the very bottom as shown in Figure 7.3.

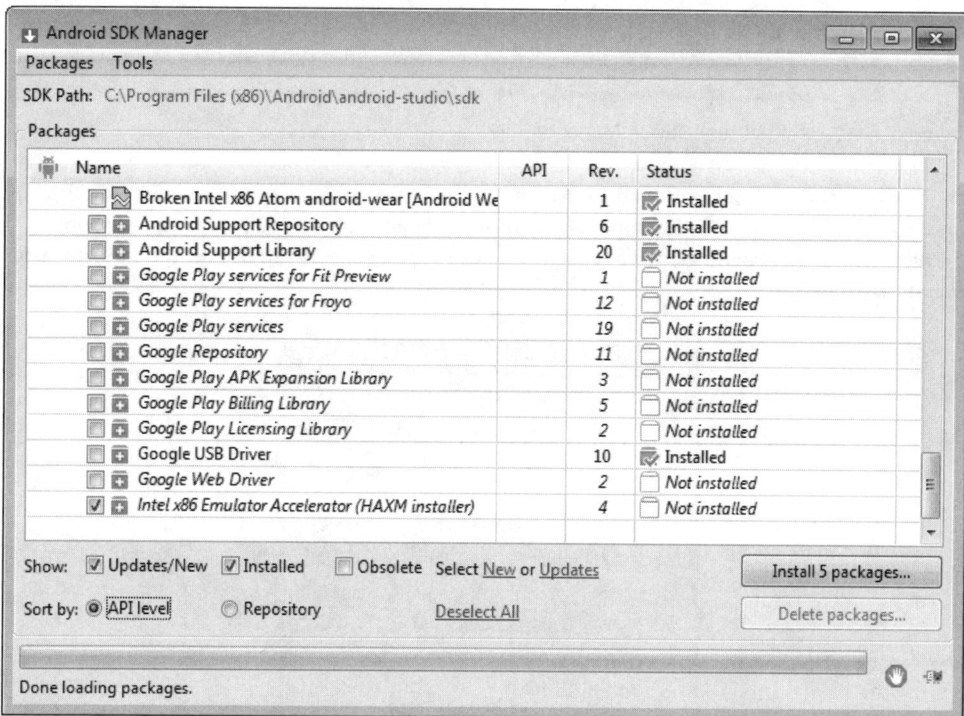

Figure 7.3 Android SDK Manager: HAXM Installer Option

When you select this option as shown and install it, it will place a copy of the HAXM installer into the SDK's extras/intel/Hardware_Accelerated_Execution_Manager folder (this would be in D:\adt\sdk\extras\intel\Hardware_Accelerated_Execution_Manager on my system). Once the file is there, you can launch the installer application in that folder and install the HAXM components required to run the Intel-based emulators.

Now it's time to start defining some emulator configurations. Make sure that you have at least one of the Android platforms installed on your system (shown in Figure 7.2). From the SDK Manager, open the Tools menu, then select Manage AVDs. The SDK Manager will open the window shown in Figure 7.4.

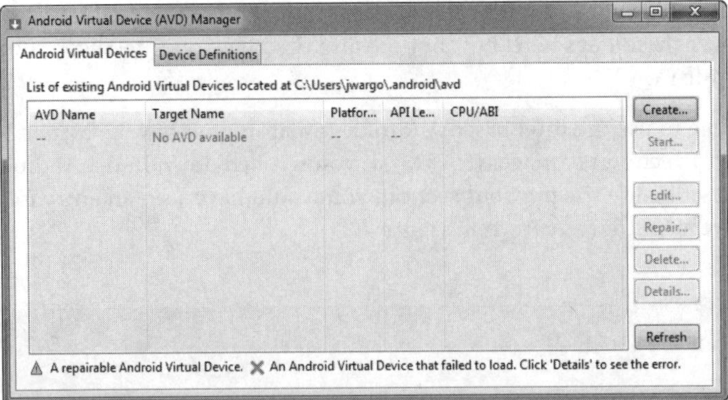

Figure 7.4 Android Virtual Device Manager

This is where the Android SDK manages the AVDs for this system. To create a new AVD, click the Create button shown in the upper-right corner of Figure 7.4. The AVD Manager will open the dialog shown in Figure 7.5. Here you will set the settings specific to the device emulator you want to create.

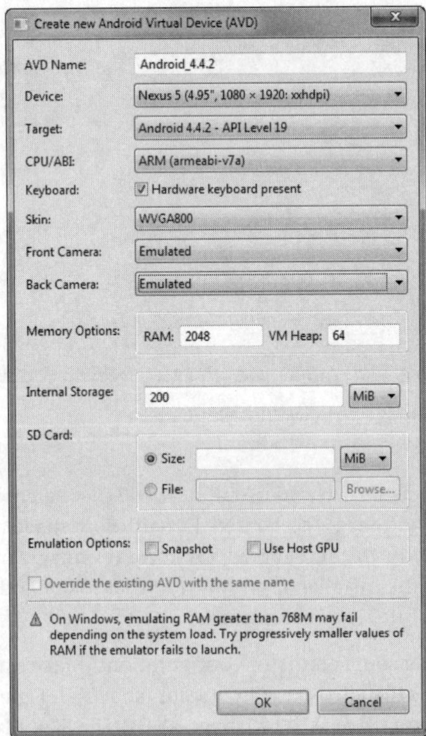

Figure 7.5 Create New Android Virtual Device

You'll have to give the AVD a name (without any spaces) and select the device form factor, target OS, and more. Google doesn't provide any indicators to tell you which fields are required; most of them are, so simply populate the dialog as you see fit and click the OK button when you're done.

After you have saved your changes, the AVD will appear in the list shown in Figure 7.4. Now you'll be able to start the AVD, edit it, delete it, and more. To run the AVD, click the Start button and the AVD Manager will display the dialog shown in Figure 7.6. In this dialog, you can adjust some of the settings for the AVD before launching it.

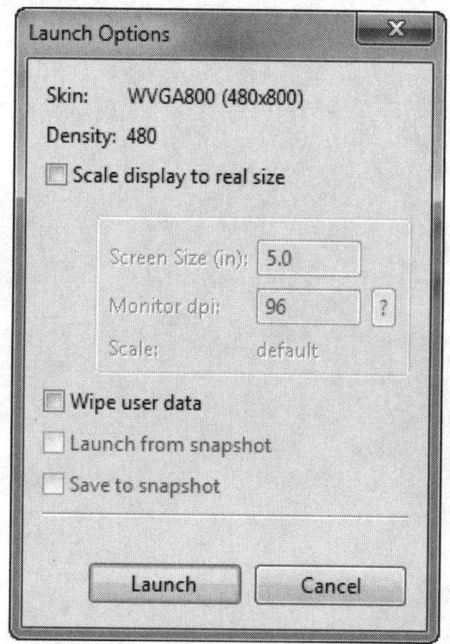

Figure 7.6 Android Virtual Device Launch Options

When you're testing an application's initial load operation or when you've made dramatic changes to the application's configuration options, you may want to wipe any existing user data on the AVD before starting it. To do this, check the Wipe user data checkbox before clicking the Launch button. I'll do this if I have an application or emulator that's misbehaving or after I've been working with a particular AVD for a while. This gives me a clean slate to work with and sometimes fixes weird problems I've encountered. You'll also want to do this if your application installs one or more datasets or changes the device configuration somehow and you want to test that part of the code against a clean image.

When you click the Launch button, a new window will appear showing progress of the AVD launch. After a while, quite a long while usually, the window will close and the emulator will open. Eventually you will see the emulator running in its own window as shown in Figure 7.7.

Figure 7.7 Android Virtual Device

You can also run an AVD directly from the command line. Before you can do this, you'll need to obtain the name of the AVD you want to launch. To do this, open a terminal window and issue the following command:

```
android list avd
```

The SDK Manager application will churn for a little while, then display the list of AVDs defined on the system:

```
Available Android Virtual Devices:
    Name: Android_4.4.2
  Device: Nexus 5 (Google)
    Path: C:\Users\jwargo\.android\avd\Android_4.4.2.avd
  Target: Android 4.4.2 (API level 19)
 Tag/ABI: default/armeabi-v7a
    Skin: WVGA800
---------
    Name: Android_5.0
  Device: Nexus 5 (Google)
    Path: C:\Users\jwargo\.android\avd\Android_5.0.avd
  Target: Android 5.0 (API level 21)
 Tag/ABI: default/armeabi-v7a
    Skin: WVGA800
```

Once you know the name of the AVD, you can launch it from the terminal window using the following command:

```
emulator @avd_name
```

Or you can also use

```
emulator -avd avd_name
```

So, for my environment, to launch my Android 4.4.2 AVD, I would use the following:

```
emulator @android_4.4.2
```

Or I could also use

```
emulator -avd android_4.4.2
```

You won't see any progress window appear with this approach; simply wait a few minutes and the AVD will launch.

Using the ADT IDE

By default, ADT ships with a preconfigured version of the open-source Eclipse IDE. You can use this IDE to edit, compile, run, and debug Android Java applications; you can learn more about and download ADT at the Android Developer web site at http://goo.gl/f0DTPu.

If you're already using Eclipse for other development work, you can add ADT to an existing Eclipse installation using instructions found at http://goo.gl/wIlbtT. The process is pretty easy and doesn't take a lot of time. Be sure to check the system requirements to make sure the version of Eclipse you are using is compatible before attempting to add ADT. Google is really good about keeping up with Eclipse and supports a wide range of Eclipse versions.

To start the ADT IDE, navigate to the folder where you extracted the Android SDK and launch the Eclipse application located in the eclipse folder. The application will be called eclipse on Macintosh OS and eclipse.exe on Microsoft Windows. When you first start ADT, you will see the standard Eclipse UI shown in Figure 7.8.

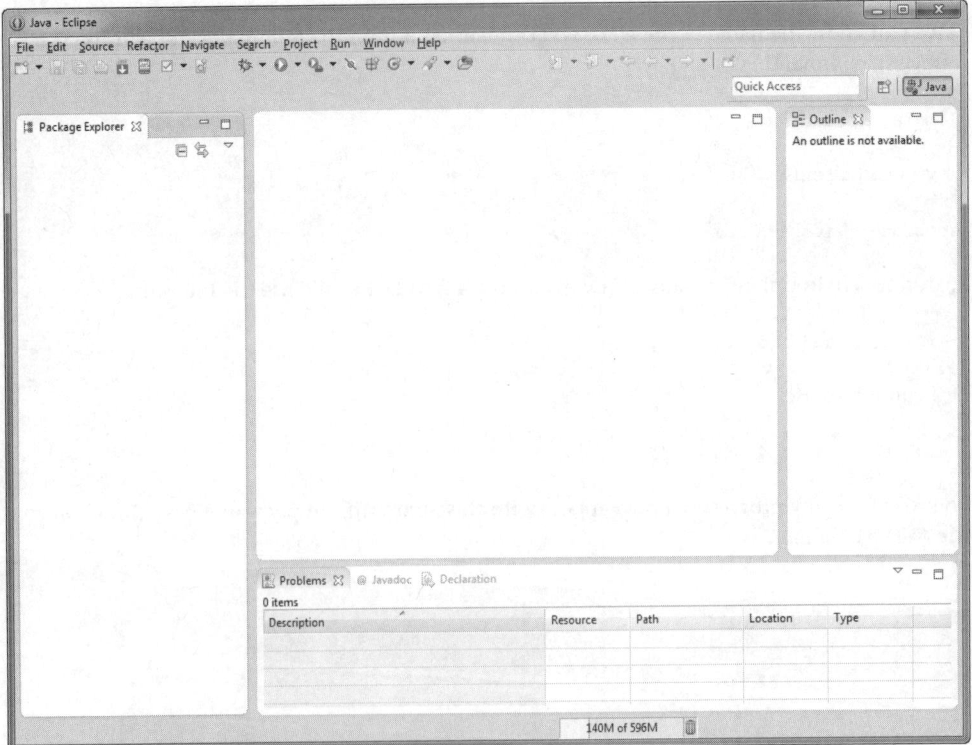

Figure 7.8 Android Development Tools (ADT) IDE

Editing Cordova Application Content Files

Android applications are built using Java, but developers can also code portions of their applications in C or C++. Since Android supports only these limited options for application development, ADT does not include tools specifically designed to help with debugging web applications like those that run within the Cordova container. So, you won't be able to step through an application's JavaScript code, set breakpoints, configure watch expressions, and so on within the ADT IDE. To debug Android applications, you can use the debugging approaches highlighted in Chapter 5 or the Chrome debugger described later in this chapter.

Although the CLI is designed for managing a Cordova application's web application source code in the www folder rather than within one of a Cordova project's platform folders, you will likely use an external web content editor such as Adobe Dreamweaver, Adobe Brackets, or some other tool. A Cordova project for Android has some special features that make it easy for you to edit your web application content in Eclipse. But, since ADT is configured for editing Java and C applications, it doesn't include editors that help with editing the HTML, CSS, and JavaScript files your Cordova application will use. Because of this limitation, if you want to use Eclipse to edit your Cordova application content, you will need to install web content editing capabilities into ADT. The default tools for web content editing in Eclipse are from the Eclipse Web Developer Tools Project, and you can install them in ADT in a few minutes.

Within ADT, open the Help menu and select Install New Software; ADT will display the Install wizard shown in Figure 7.9. In the Work with drop-down field shown in the figure, select the Juno option. Juno is the version of Eclipse that ADT is currently using. After you make the selection, Eclipse will connect to the update site and pull down a list of available options. Scroll through the list and select Eclipse Web Developer Tools as enabled in the figure, then step through the wizard to complete the installation.

With the Eclipse Web Developer Tools in place, you will now be able to edit your Cordova application's web application content in Eclipse.

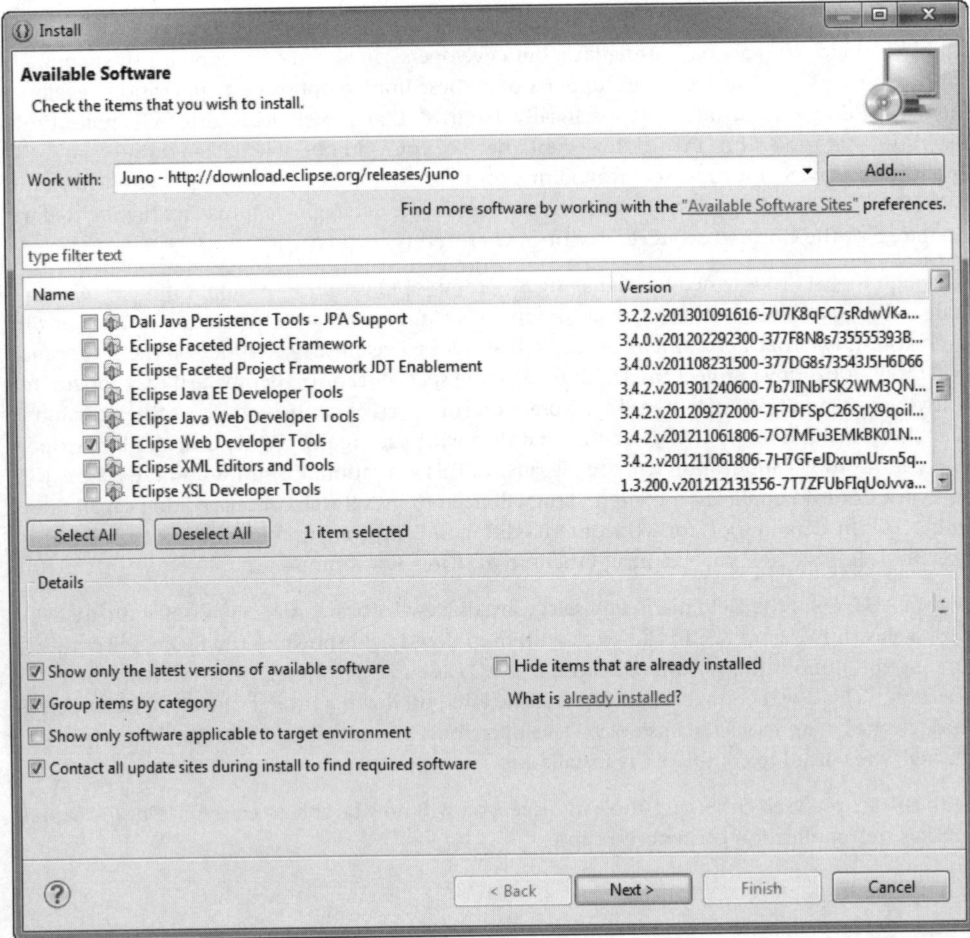

Figure 7.9 Eclipse Available Software Wizard

Importing the Cordova Project

Assuming you followed the instructions in Chapter 4, "Using the Cordova Command-Line Interfaces," to create an Android project, you should have a Cordova application project ready to be opened in the ADT IDE. If you haven't already done so, copy the project's web content from its www folder to the Android project's folder by opening a terminal window, navigating to the Cordova project folder, then issuing the following command:

```
cordova prepare android
```

With the project files in place, you must import the project into ADT before you can work with it. To start the import process, in the ADT IDE open the File menu, then select Import. The ADT IDE will display the Import wizard shown in Figure 7.10. Expand the General option and select Existing Projects into Workspace as shown in the figure, then click the Next button.

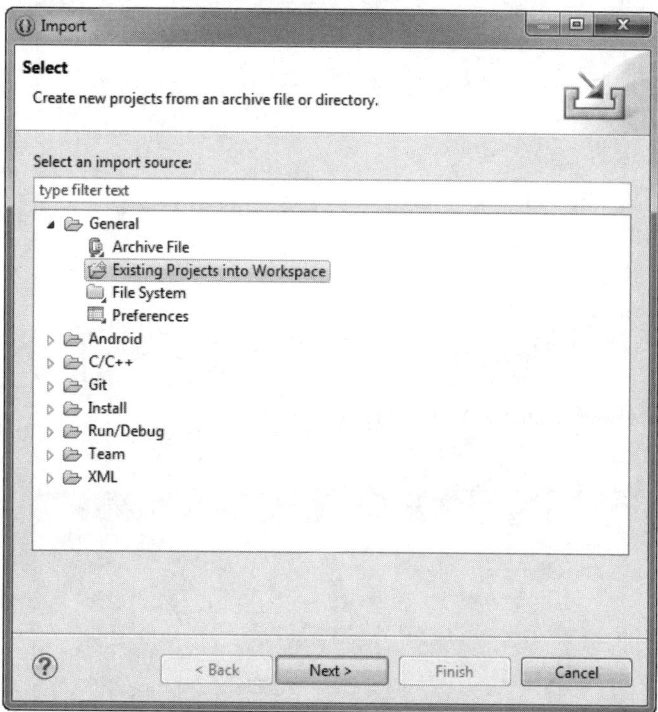

Figure 7.10 ADT IDE Import Wizard

ADT will display the next page in the wizard. In this dialog, you need to populate the Root Directory field with the location where the Cordova project's Android project files are located. Click the Browse button and navigate to the android folder highlighted in Figure 7.11, then click the OK button.

The wizard should automatically add the HelloCordova project to the list of available projects as shown in Figure 7.12.

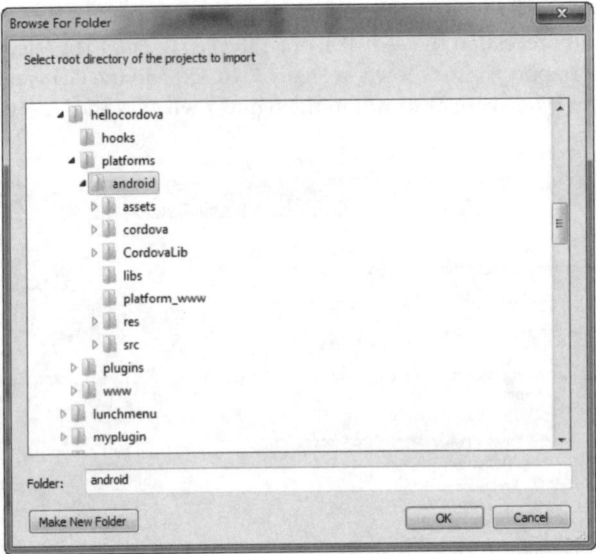

Figure 7.11 Browse for Cordova Android Project Folder

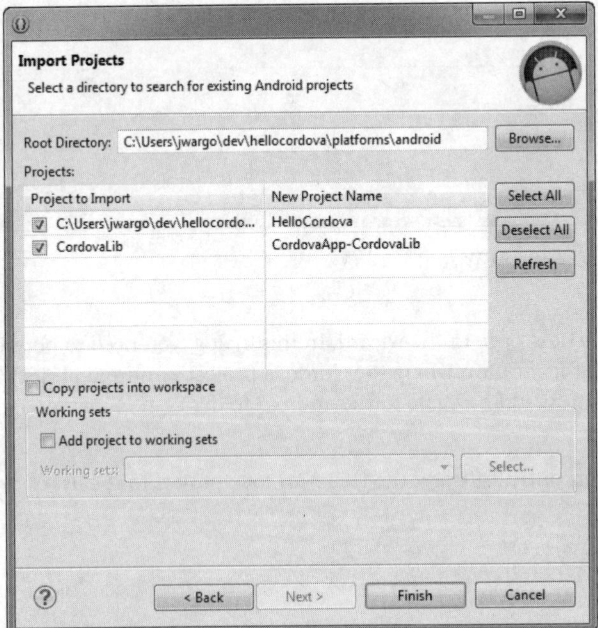

Figure 7.12 ADT IDE Import Projects

When you click the Finish button, ADT should complete the import process and open the imported project in the IDE as shown in Figure 7.13. Since the Cordova project consists of both a native Java Android application and the web content that will execute within the application, you will see a blending of a default Android project structure plus the Cordova www folder discussed in previous chapters.

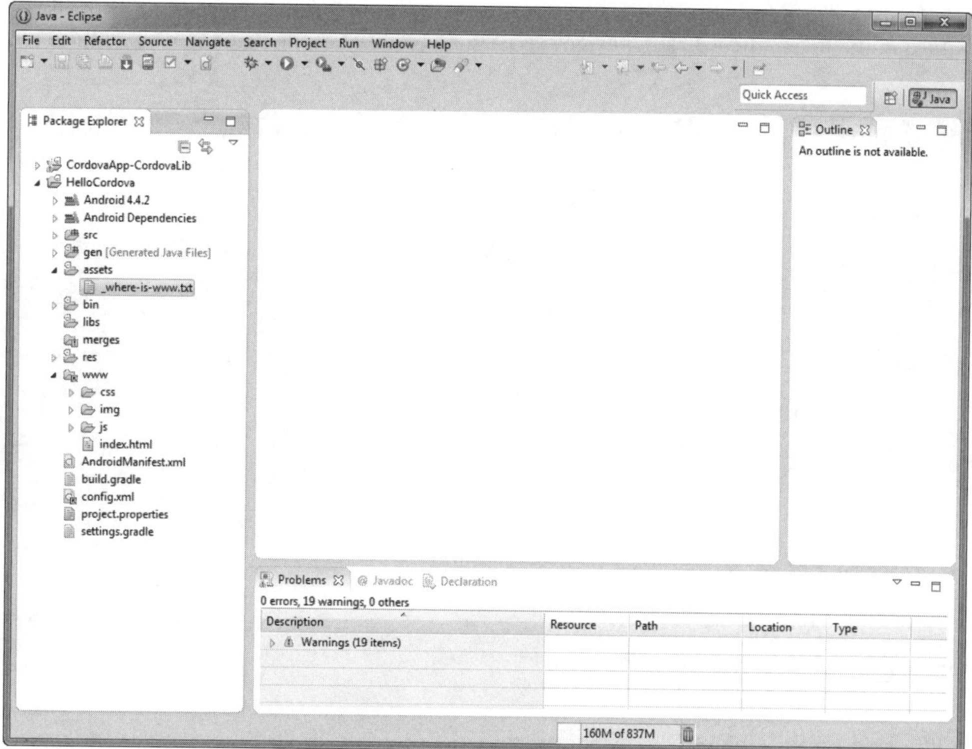

Figure 7.13 ADT IDE: Imported Project

Notice in the figure how I've highlighted the _where-is-www.txt file in the Package Explorer's assets folder. Remember from Chapter 5 that I explained that an Android Cordova project stores the project's web application content in the assets/www folder. If you edit the web application content in that folder, those changes will not be reflected back into the Cordova project's www folder.

To protect you from this, the Cordova team hid the assets/www folder, then created a symbolic link in the Android project structure that points to the Cordova project's www folder (it's the www folder shown expanded further down in the Package Explorer pane). This way, you'll be able to edit the web application content in the right place, then use the `cordova prepare` command to copy the files into the Android project before testing it within the IDE.

You likely don't need to see these files, but if you want to, the highlighted file in the figure contains instructions for unhiding the assets/www folder:

```
To show 'assets/www' or 'res/xml/config.xml', go to:
    Project -> Properties -> Resource -> Resource Filters
And delete the exclusion filter.
```

If you follow the instructions, you will see the dialog shown in Figure 7.14. Select the line highlighted in the figure, then click the Remove button highlighted in the figure to remove the filter.

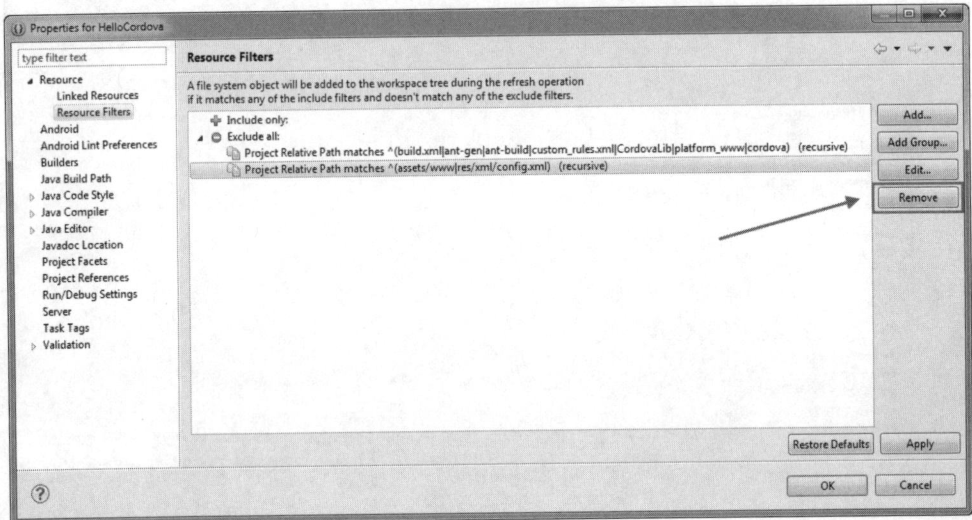

Figure 7.14 Project Properties: Resource Filters

With that completed, you will be able to see the contents of the project's assets/www folder as shown in Figure 7.15.

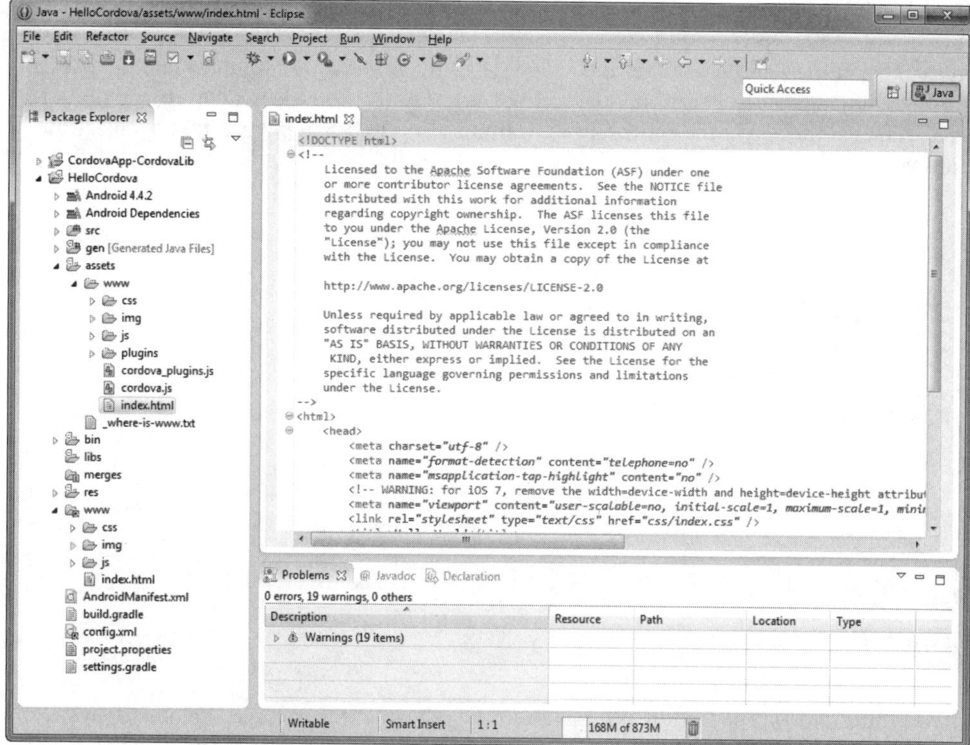

Figure 7.15 ADT IDE: index.html

Running Your Cordova Application

Now that the Cordova project has been imported, you probably want to run it to see how it works. Before doing that, it helps me to have a few extra panes open in the ADT IDE. Open the Window menu and select Show View. In the menu that appears, select Progress; Eclipse will open the new panel at the bottom of the window shown in Figure 7.16. This window will show you what's happening in the IDE when it's building the application and deploying it to a device or device emulator.

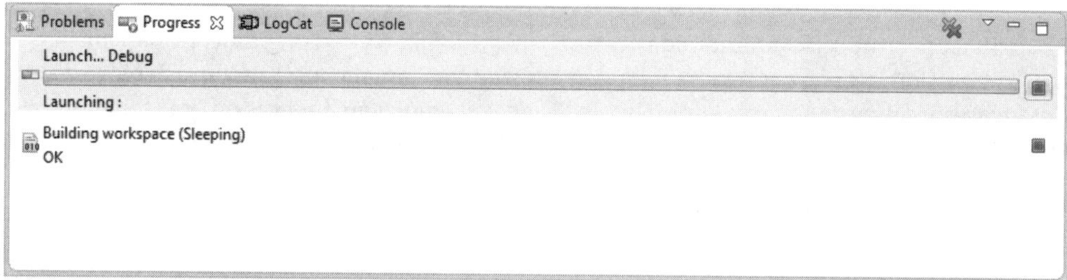

Figure 7.16 ADT IDE Progress Panel

There is also a Console panel that will show you the status of the Android SDK tools as they run. To open the panel, open the Window menu, select Show View, then select Console. You can see an example of the Console's output in Figure 7.17. If the ADT IDE has trouble building, packaging, or deploying your application, it will let you know in the Console window. If you think you have launched the app in the emulator but nothing seems to be happening, take a look at the Console.

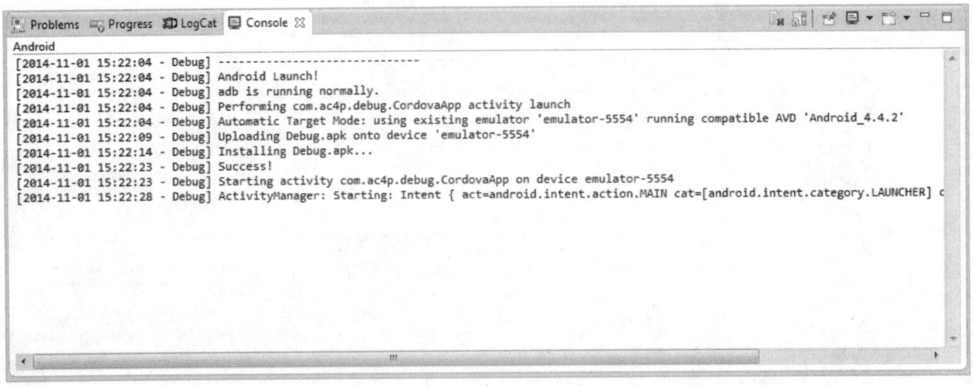

```
Android
[2014-11-01 15:22:04 - Debug] ----------------------------
[2014-11-01 15:22:04 - Debug] Android Launch!
[2014-11-01 15:22:04 - Debug] adb is running normally.
[2014-11-01 15:22:04 - Debug] Performing com.ac4p.debug.CordovaApp activity launch
[2014-11-01 15:22:04 - Debug] Automatic Target Mode: using existing emulator 'emulator-5554' running compatible AVD 'Android_4.4.2'
[2014-11-01 15:22:09 - Debug] Uploading Debug.apk onto device 'emulator-5554'
[2014-11-01 15:22:14 - Debug] Installing Debug.apk...
[2014-11-01 15:22:23 - Debug] Success!
[2014-11-01 15:22:23 - Debug] Starting activity com.ac4p.debug.CordovaApp on device emulator-5554
[2014-11-01 15:22:28 - Debug] ActivityManager: Starting: Intent { act=android.intent.action.MAIN cat=[android.intent.category.LAUNCHER] c
```

Figure 7.17 ADT IDE Console Window

To run your Cordova application, right-click on the project in the Package Explorer, then select Run As. Another menu will appear as shown in Figure 7.18; select Android Application.

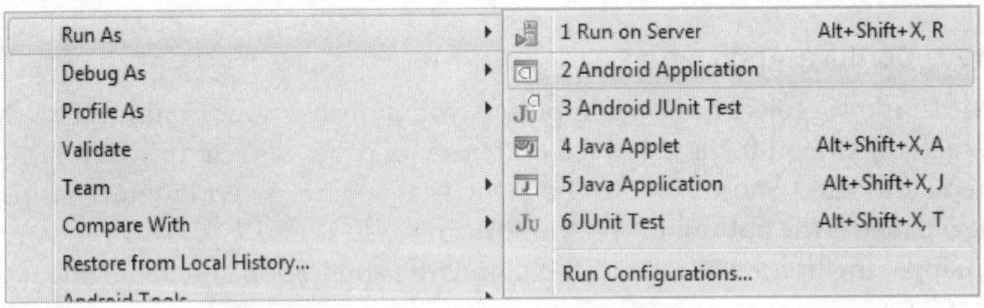

Figure 7.18 ADT IDE Run As Menu

ADT will launch the selected Android emulator (this will take a very long time; be patient—the Android emulators are not known for being fast), then compile, package, and deploy the Cordova application to the emulator. The first time you launch an application, you will be prompted to enable automatic loading of the LogCat panel as shown in Figure 7.19.

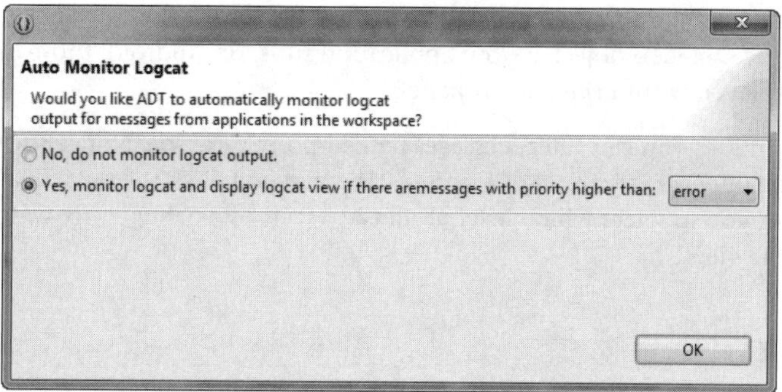

Figure 7.19 ADT IDE: Auto Monitor LogCat Prompt

LogCat is part of the Android SDK and collects log information from different applications running on an Android device. For some reason, Google refers to it as LogCat in some places and Logcat in others. It exists as a stand-alone application, part of the SDK, but its output is also exposed through the ADT IDE using the LogCat panel. When you enable this option, ADT will open the panel shown in Figure 7.20. For Java applications and other types of applications, the IDE offers real-time debugging and the ability to step through your code; this is not available for Cordova applications. You will want this option enabled as it's the only way for you to be able to see what is happening with your Cordova application running within the IDE.

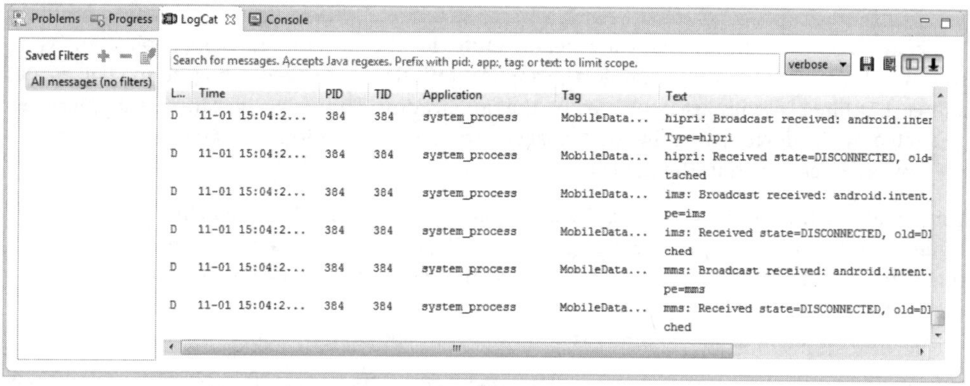

Figure 7.20 ADT IDE: LogCat Panel as Emulator Launches

If the panel gets closed for any reason, you can open it by opening the Window menu, selecting Show View, then selecting Other. In the dialog that appears, select LogCat, then click the OK button to open the view.

The LogCat window will show a multitude of messages as the emulator completes its startup process and as you interact with any part of the Android OS. Look to LogCat for any error messages when you're having trouble with an emulator or device or a running Android application.

Remember from Chapter 5 that I mentioned you could have your Cordova applications write information to the `console` object as your application runs; on Android, those `console` object messages are displayed within the LogCat panel.

In the LogCat window, you can filter messages based upon their type. Notice the verbose button shown in the upper-right corner of Figure 7.21; when you click the button, a drop-down appears, allowing you to select which level of message (verbose, debug, info, warning, or error) is displayed in the view.

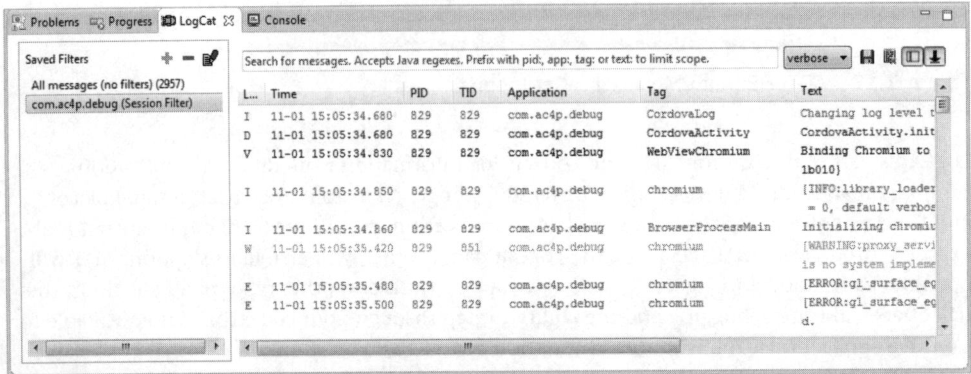

Figure 7.21 ADT IDE LogCat Panel: Session Filter

By default, the ADT IDE automatically creates a filter for the currently running application as shown in Figure 7.21. In this example, the application's ID is com.ac4p.debug, so the IDE creates a filter that filters all message generated by that application. This way, you can view all messages generated by the device using the All messages option, or application-specific messages using the Session Filter shown in the figure.

You can also define your own filters. Click the plus sign shown in the Saved Filters window in Figure 7.21; the IDE will open the dialog shown in Figure 7.22. In this dialog, enter the values that define the filter that suits your particular requirements, then click the OK button to save the changes. The Saved Filters list will update to show your new filter, and you can switch between the different available filters as you work with your application.

When you launched the application, the IDE used its default configuration for running Android applications. As I described earlier in the chapter, you can have multiple emulator configurations, and you have multiple application execution configurations as well; these configurations are called Run Configurations.

To create your own Run Configurations, in the menu shown in Figure 7.18, select the Run Configurations option at the bottom of the second menu. In the dialog that appears, select Android Applications, then click the New button described in Figure 7.23.

Logcat Message Filter Settings

Filter logcat messages by the source's tag, pid or minimum log level.
Empty fields will match all messages.

Filter Name: AC4P

by Log Tag:

by Log Message:

by PID:

by Application Name: com.ac4p

by Log Level: verbose

OK Cancel

Figure 7.22 LogCat Message Filter Settings Dialog

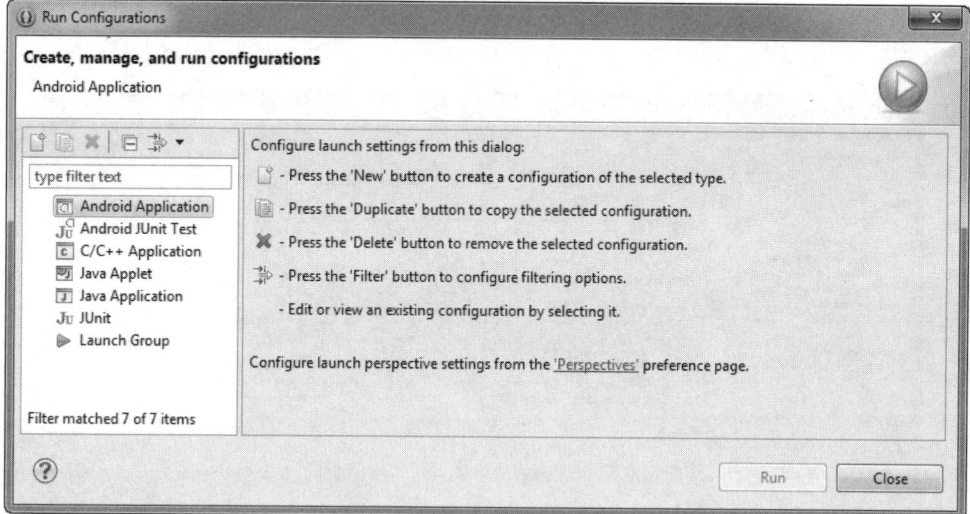

Figure 7.23 ADT IDE Run Configurations

Define the settings for the Run Configuration, assign an application to it, and determine parameters around how it launches one or more Android device emulators when it runs. In the new Run Configuration's Android tab shown in Figure 7.24, you define settings around the application that's executed by this Run Configuration.

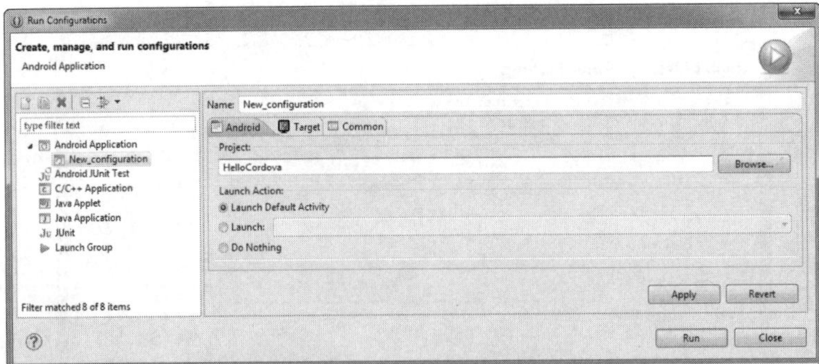

Figure 7.24 ADT IDE Run Configurations: Android Settings

In the Target tab shown in Figure 7.25, you can select which AVD is loaded or configure it so the IDE will prompt you to select the AVD at runtime. You can also configure emulator network speed simulation, wipe the emulator, and more. Click the Manager button to open the AVD Manager to create and manage the system's emulator definitions.

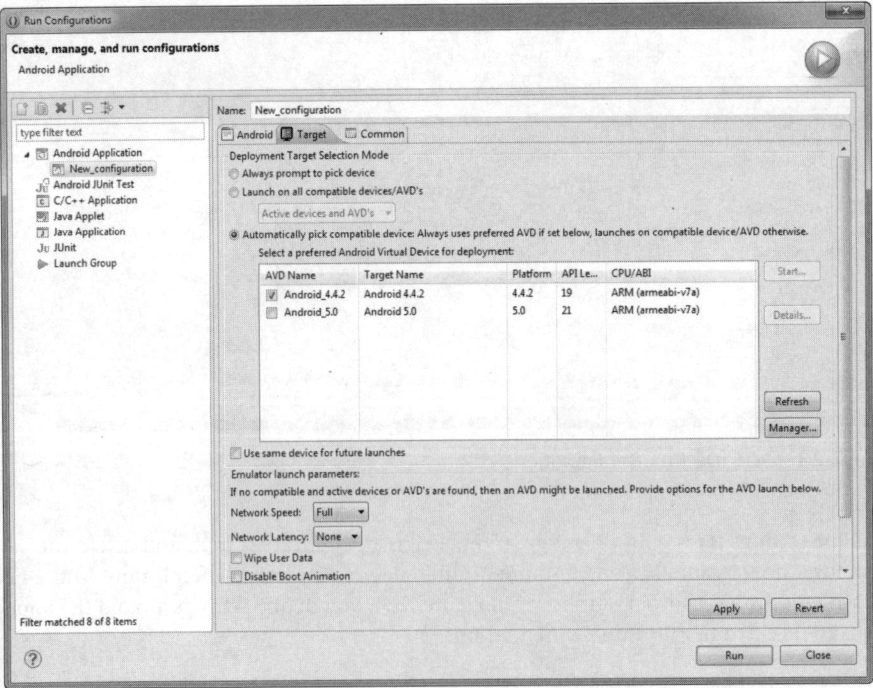

Figure 7.25 ADT IDE Run Configurations: Target Settings

With one or more Run Configurations defined, you can click the Run button shown at the bottom of the figure to launch the emulator and run your application. You can also close this dialog, then run the application on the selected Android emulator by making the appropriate selection from the Run menu or by right-clicking on the application project in the Package Explorer (shown on the left side of Figure 7.13), selecting Run As, then selecting Android Application.

Monitoring Application Activity Outside of the ADT IDE

If you don't want to use the ADT IDE, you can run the ADT debugging tools outside of the IDE. The stand-alone version of LogCat and associated tools can be found in the Android Device Monitor (ADM) utility, which is started by opening a terminal window and executing the `monitor` command.

When the ADM launches, it will display a window similar to the one shown in Figure 7.26. I'm not going to cover all of the options available here, but you can see that there's a lot of information available. The lower half of the application's window displays the same LogCat window from the ADT IDE. In the figure, you can see that I've connected the ADM to an Android device emulator; I'll show you how to connect to a physical device a little later.

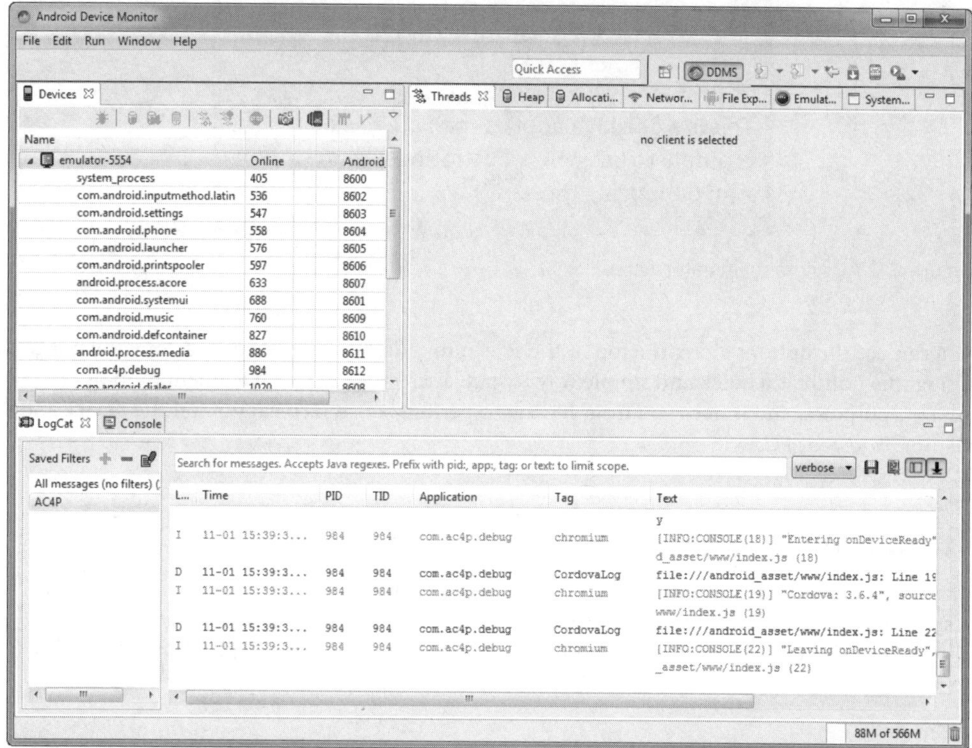

Figure 7.26 Android Device Monitor Application

Notice that the session filter shown in Figure 7.21 isn't created automatically when using ADM.

You should spend some time poking around within the ADM; there's a lot of power in what it provides developers.

Grabbing a Screen Shot

While not critical for developers, it's sometimes useful to be able to pull a screen shot off of an emulator or physical device. If you look at Figure 7.26, within the Devices area in the upper-left corner of the ADM, you will see a little camera icon. With a device connected, you can click that button and grab a screen capture from the connected device. When you click the button, the ADM will display a screen similar to the one shown in Figure 7.27 (I've cropped the image to reduce the amount of space used for the figure).

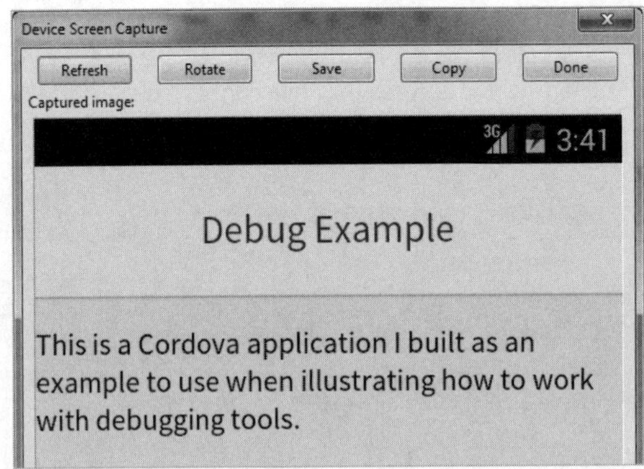

Figure 7.27 Android Emulator Screen Shot

You can use the buttons along the top of the screen to refresh, rotate, save, and copy the image. Using this feature is a quick and simple way to grab a screen image for documentation or support purposes, and it frees you from having to perform the screen capture on the device and transfer it to your PC.

Testing on a Physical Device

The ADM can also interact with a physical device just as it can with a device emulator. Initial testing of an application can be done on an emulator, but before any application is released, it should be tested on a representative sample of the physical devices the application is expected to run on.

To use a physical device with ADM, you must connect the device to the computer system running ADM using a USB cable. Before you can do that, you must first enable USB debugging on the device. The way you enable this setting will vary depending on which type of Android device you are using. On some devices, enabling developer options is accomplished by simply opening the on-device Android Settings application and making some selections. On other devices, it's a little harder. You're just going to have to figure this one out on your own. Sorry.

> **Warning**
>
> In order to be able to test on a live device, your computer system must be able to recognize an Android device when it's connected to the system via a USB cable. If you connect a device and it's not recognized by the system, you must resolve any connectivity issues before continuing.
>
> In my testing on Windows, I had to manually install the Google USB driver from the SDK Manager, then in Windows Device Manager force the installation of the right driver. You can read about the steps at http://goo.gl/MYcGxD.
>
> For a Samsung device you may need to download and install the USB drivers separately before the device will get picked up correctly by Windows. See http://goo.gl/2bBVkB for additional information.

For a Google Nexus 7 tablet, for example, you have to do some special steps before you can even access the developer settings. To enable developer mode on the Nexus 7, you have to open the Settings application and select About Tablet (it will be the very last item on the list of options on the Settings page). On the About Tablet page, scroll down until you see the Build Number item in the list. Tap on the Build Number item seven times to enable the developer options on the device. As you tap, Android will pop up a little window indicating how many more times you need to tap to enable developer mode.

With that process completed, when you open the Settings application, you should be able to scroll down to the bottom of the list of options and see a Developer options option available as shown in Figure 7.28.

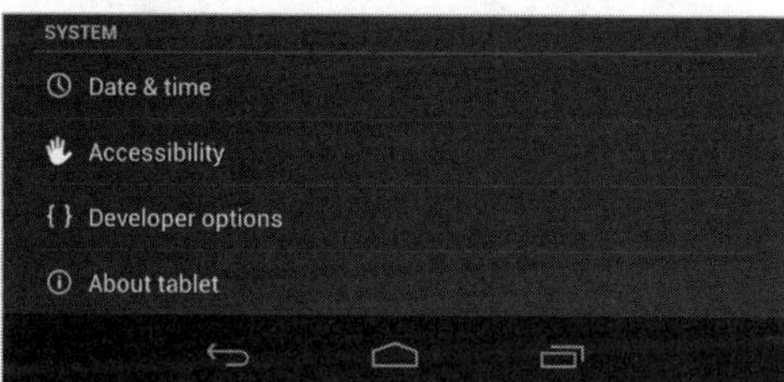

Figure 7.28 Developer Options Enabled in the Android Settings Application

Click on Developer options and you will see a screen similar to the one shown in Figure 7.29; from here you can enable USB debugging as shown at the bottom of the figure.

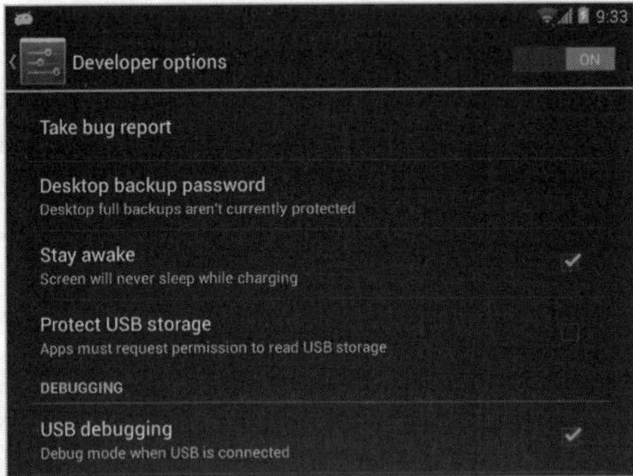

Figure 7.29 Enabling USB Debugging

With USB debugging enabled, launch the ADM, then connect the Android device to the computer system using a USB cable. After the necessary device drivers initialize (see the previous warning for information about how to deal with driver issues), ADM should connect to your device and show the connected device in its list of connected devices as shown in Figure 7.30. In this example, I've connected Samsung Galaxy SIII and Samsung Galaxy S4 devices.

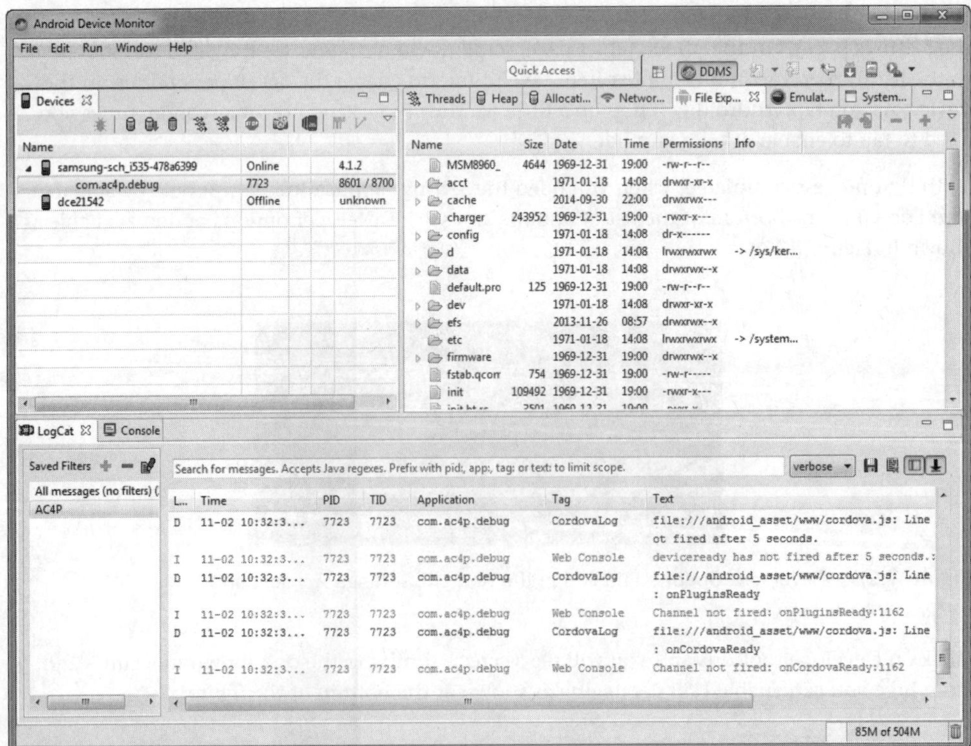

Figure 7.30 Android Device Monitor Monitoring a Cordova Application

In ADM, you have access to many of the same capabilities with a physical device as you do with a device emulator, but there are differences. Refer to the Android documentation for more information about the capabilities of ADM with a physical device. ADM is a good way to pull files from or push files to a device for testing purposes. However, much of the file structure is protected, so you won't be able to access all file locations.

Using the Chrome Debugging Tools

Although the ADT IDE doesn't support debugging Cordova applications, Google does provide tools that do. The Google Chrome browser includes the Chrome DevTools, which is a feature-rich web application debugger that supports debugging web applications running in a browser tab or in a WebView. Since a Cordova application runs in a WebView, Cordova applications running on Android 4.4 and higher can easily be debugged using Google Chrome. You can read more about these tools and how to use them for debugging Android web or WebView applications at http://goo.gl/hj95OR. In this section, I will show you how to debug your Cordova applications using the Chrome DevTools.

Before you can begin, you have to enable remote debugging on an Android device through Developer options in the Settings application. On Android 4.2 and later, the developer options are hidden by default, so you'll have to unhide the option before starting. To do this, open the Settings application on the device and select About Phone. In the screen that appears, scroll down to Build Number and tap on the Build Number item seven times. When that's done, you should have a new Developer options option in the Settings app.

Next, you will need to enable USB debugging. Open the new Developer options option and you will see an option for enabling USB debugging as shown at the bottom of Figure 7.31. Enable this option as shown in the figure and you're ready to go.

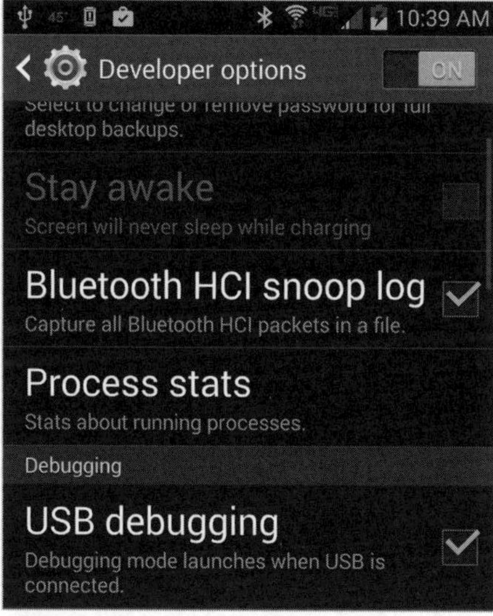

Figure 7.31 Enabling USB Remote Debugging

Next, you need to open the latest version of the Chrome browser; you can download the browser from www.google.com/chrome. After you have installed the browser, you should open the Tools menu and select the Inspect devices option shown in Figure 7.32.

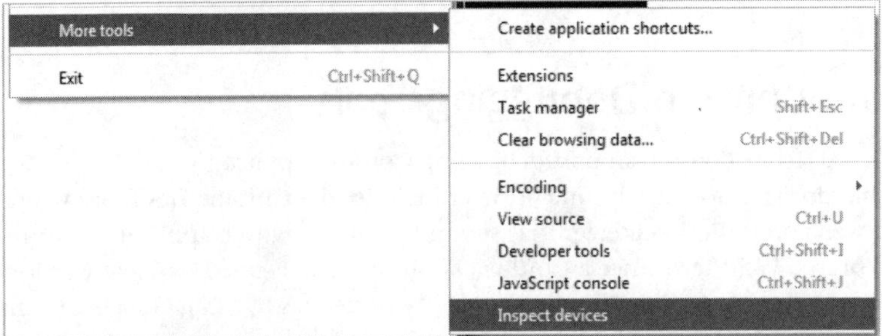

Figure 7.32 Chrome Tools Menu

When you do this, Chrome will open a new browser window and display the page shown in Figure 7.33. Enable the Discover USB devices option shown in the figure and Chrome will try to connect to your device. When Chrome is able to connect to your device, it will display the device information on the page as shown in the figure.

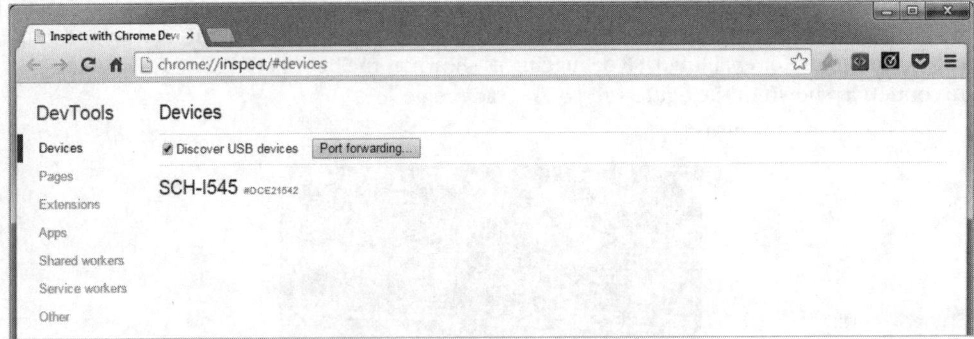

Figure 7.33 USB Debugging Prompt

When Chrome connects to the device, the device will prompt you to accept the connection as shown in Figure 7.34. You will need to accept the connection in order to be able to remotely debug Cordova applications running on the device.

Figure 7.34 Chrome: Inspect Devices

In Figure 7.33, there are no web applications running on the device. If you launch a Cordova application on the device, the browser page will update to show the running application as shown in Figure 7.35. In this example, the device is running the debug application I've shown in other chapters in the book.

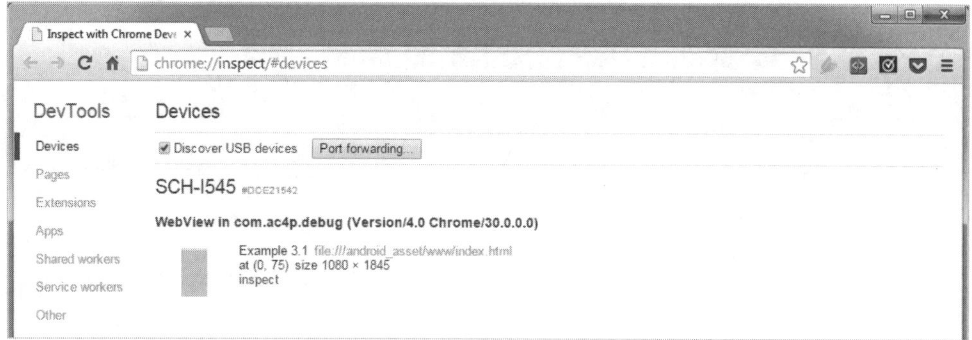

Figure 7.35 Chrome: Inspect Devices Application List

If you click on the inspect link shown beneath the application listing in Figure 7.35, a new browser window will open and display the remote debugger shown in Figure 7.36. The inspector consists of several tabs displayed across the top of the window. Initially, the inspector launches the Console page where you can view any output from the browser `console` object described in Chapter 5.

Developer Tools - file:///android_asset/www/index.html

Elements Resources Network Sources Timeline Profiles Audits Console

```
Entering onDeviceReady                                   index.js:18
Cordova: 3.6.4                                           index.js:19
Leaving onDeviceReady                                    index.js:22
>
```

Figure 7.36 Chrome Developer Tools: Console Pane

The Elements tab, shown in Figure 7.37, allows you to view, edit, and interact with the HTML content of the WebView. In the figure, you can see that I've highlighted one of the buttons within the application I'm running on the device. You can click into the Elements window, edit the HTML content, and see it render in real time on the device.

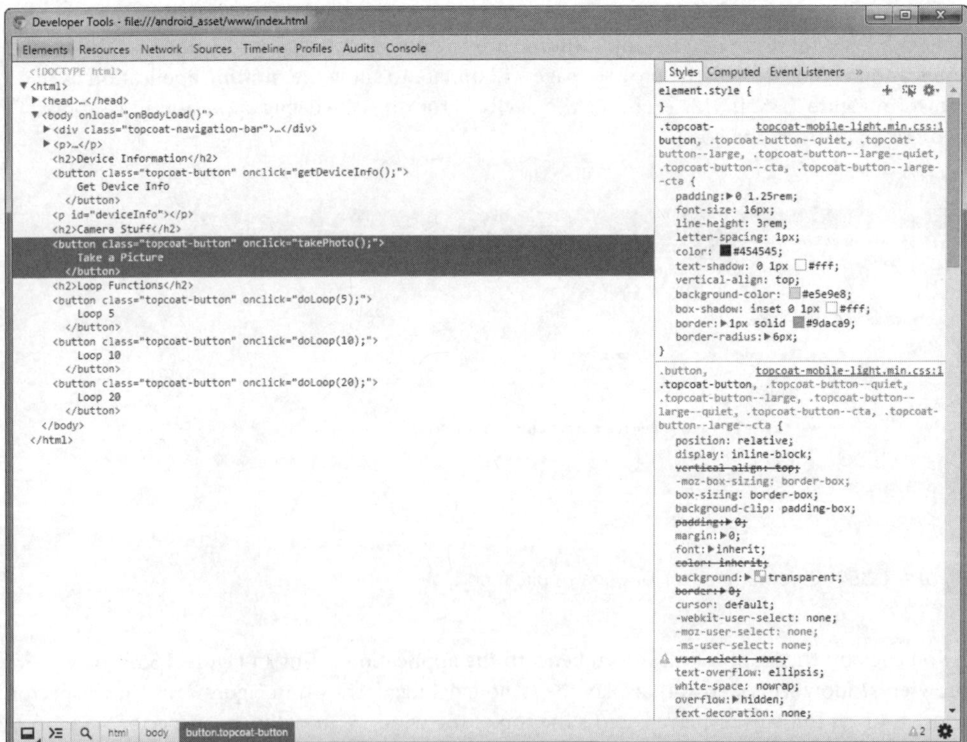

Figure 7.37 Chrome Developer Tools: Elements Pane

When you highlight portions of HTML content in the Elements pane, the corresponding HTML content will be highlighted on the device as shown in Figure 7.38. This gives you an easy way to see what parts of the application are affected by the application's markup and quickly change it to see how the application is affected.

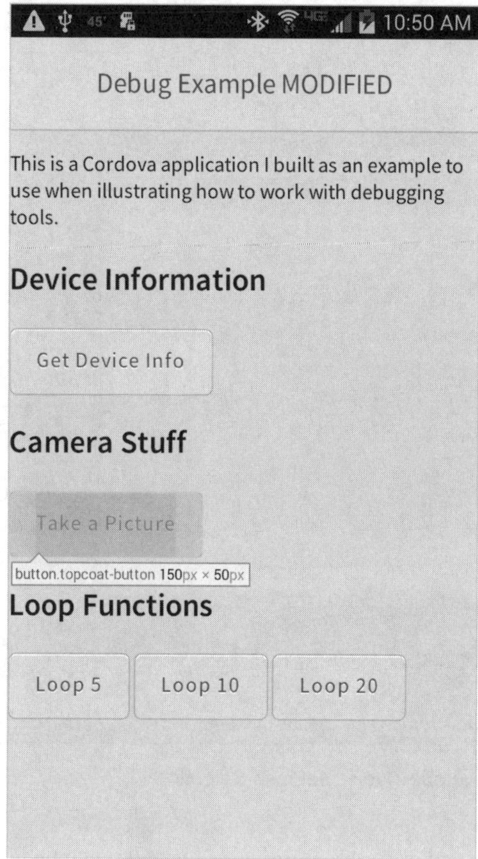

Figure 7.38 Cordova Application: Highlighted Content

The Sources tab allows you to interact with the web application's JavaScript code. When you first select the tab, a blank window is displayed with instructions to press Ctrl-O to open a file. When you press the Ctrl-O keyboard combination, a list of the application's source code files will open as displayed in Figure 7.39. Select one of the files to open it in the inspector.

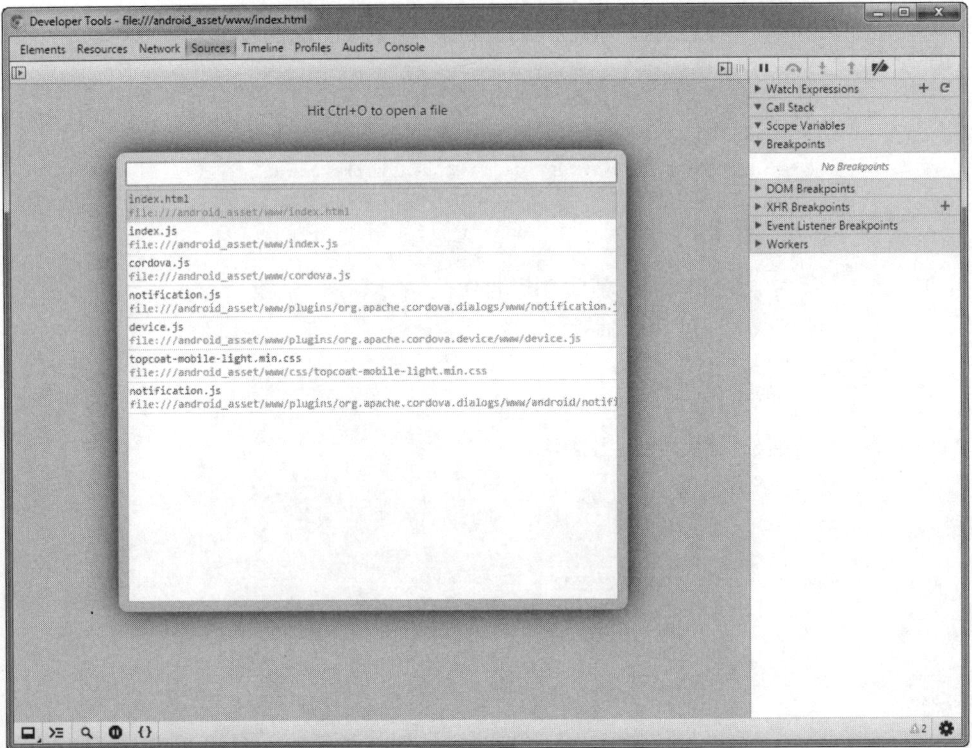

Figure 7.39 Chrome Developer Tools: Sources Selection

At this point, the browser will open the source code file and you'll be in a standard JavaScript debugger. You can set breakpoints as I've done in Figure 7.40 by clicking in the margin next to the line number. With these in place, the inspector will stop execution of the application when it reaches any of those lines.

On the right side of the browser window are expandable areas you can use to interact with the web application running on the device. You can toggle the breakpoints using the expanded area shown in the figure, view variable contents, define watches, and more. Google provides a very capable debugger that can really save you some time when you're trying to locate and fix bugs in a Cordova application.

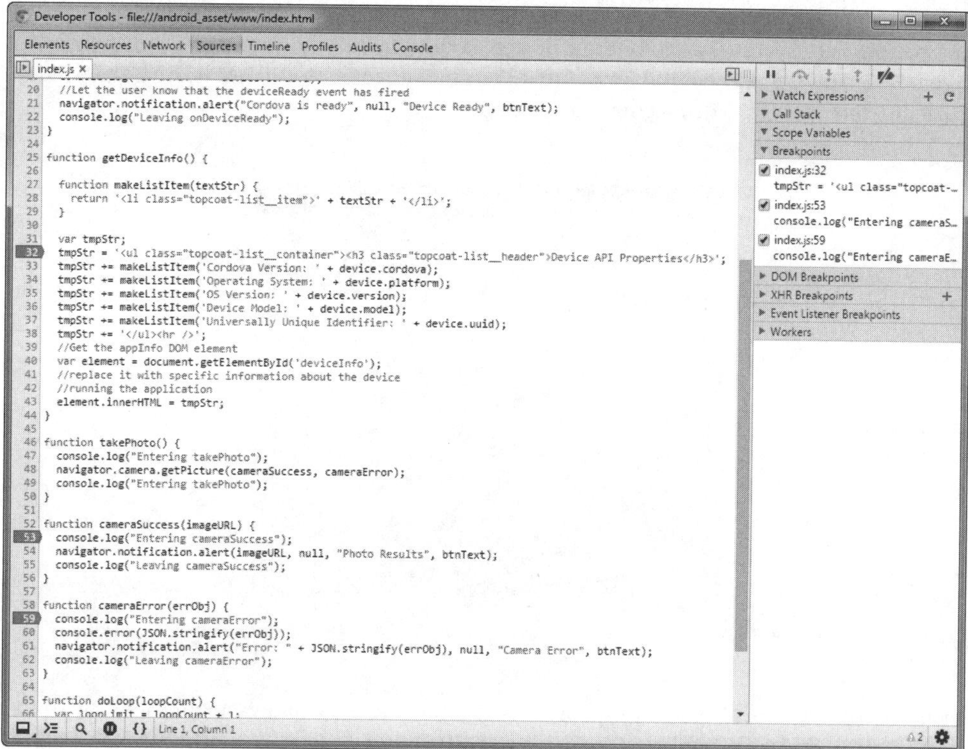

Figure 7.40 Chrome Developer Tools: Sources Pane with Some Breakpoints Set

I experienced this myself as I was making the screen shots for this chapter. My debug application uses the camera, and when I tried to execute the application, it failed and the inspector showed the error highlighted in Figure 7.41. Even though I knew the application required the Camera plugin, apparently I forgot to add it to my application before trying to run it. Even though Cordova applications fail silently, as I've described elsewhere within this book, the inspector quickly caught the error and told me what was going on. I added the plugin to the application and was quickly back in business.

```
function takePhoto() {
  console.log("Entering takePhoto");
  navigator.camera.getPicture(cameraSuccess, cameraError);
  ⊗ Uncaught TypeError: Cannot call method 'getPicture' of undefined
  console.log("Entering takePhoto");
}
```

Figure 7.41 Chrome Developer Tools: JavaScript Error

When an application is paused by the debugger, the on-device application displays a message and buttons the user can use to continue or step around the current function as shown in Figure 7.42. This is a very helpful feature that I've not seen in other debuggers; it's a client-side capability that makes the debugging process simpler.

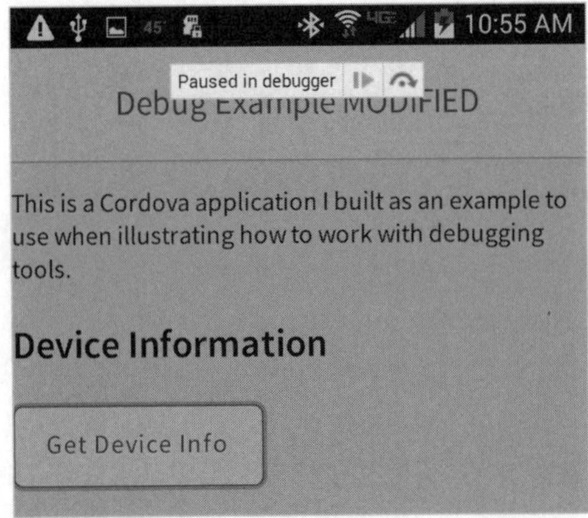

Figure 7.42 Paused Application

In all, Google has provided a very capable debugger for Android Cordova applications. I've only touched the surface of everything the Chrome DevTools can do for a developer working with web applications. Refer to the first link in this section for a more detailed explanation of the capabilities of this tool.

Wrap-Up

In this chapter, I showed you how to use the free tools available from Google that help simplify Android development for Cordova. Using these tools, you can more easily determine what's going on within your Cordova applications and fix them.

8

Firefox OS Development with Cordova

Of the modern, Cordova-supported mobile device platforms, Firefox OS is one of the easiest ones to use. Firefox OS applications are web applications, so there's really no SDK to install or any special tools you need. Everything you need to package Cordova applications for deployment is handled by the Cordova CLI. Everything you need to test and debug Firefox OS applications in a simulator or on a physical device is handled by the Firefox browser.

In this chapter, I show you how to use the Firefox browser tools for working with Firefox OS applications.

> **Note**
>
> When working with physical devices, the Firefox App Manager works only with devices running Firefox OS 1.3 or higher. If you are using Firefox OS devices running older OSs, you will need to use the Firefox OS Simulator (http://goo.gl/NIQxqa), which is not covered in this chapter. However, it works pretty much the same way and runs in the browser like the tools I show here.

Firefox OS Developer Tools

For Cordova developers working on the Firefox OS platform, there is no SDK from Mozilla (the producer of Firefox OS); Firefox OS apps are simply web applications. Instead, most testing and debugging tasks are performed using the Firefox browser and a special tool, called the App Manager, which comes pre-installed in more recent versions of the Firefox browser. In this section, I'll show you how to access the App Manager and install some additional tools you'll need to work with Firefox OS applications in App Manager.

> **Note**
>
> Beginning with Firefox 34, the App Manager highlighted in this chapter will be replaced by a new tool called Web IDE. The Web IDE should have similar testing and debugging capabilities to those described here; Firefox is simply adding editing capabilities that will allow a developer to create new projects and edit existing ones with this update.

To start, you'll need to install a copy of the Firefox desktop browser Version 26 or higher. You can download the latest version at http://goo.gl/WfY4v3. Once you have the browser installed, launch it and go through any of the initial setup steps the browser wants you to perform. When you're all installed and looking at a browser window, click the Menu button in the upper-right corner of the browser window; the button has three horizontal lines on it as highlighted in Figure 8.1. In the window that opens, select the Developer option in the lower-left corner of the menu. On some older versions of the browser, this will be a standard text-based menu rather than the graphical one shown in the figure.

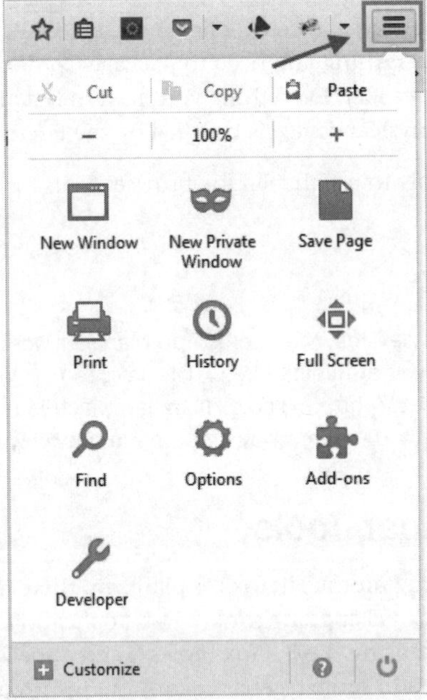

Figure 8.1 Firefox Menu

From the menu that appears, select App Manager as shown in Figure 8.2.

Firefox will open the App Manager window shown in Figure 8.3. This is where you will manage deploying, testing, and debugging Firefox OS applications on Firefox OS simulators or physical devices.

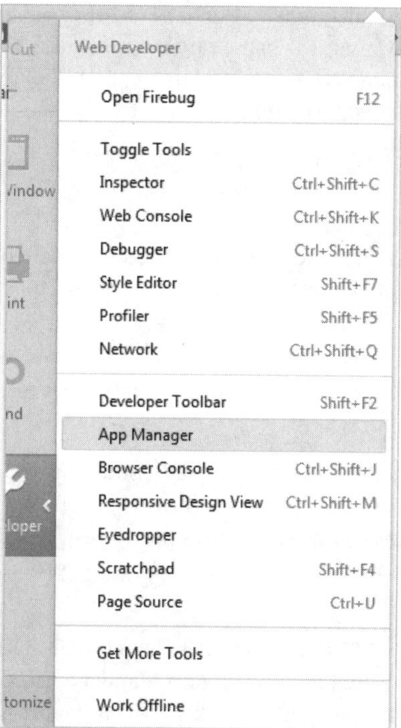

Figure 8.2 Firefox Web Developer Menu

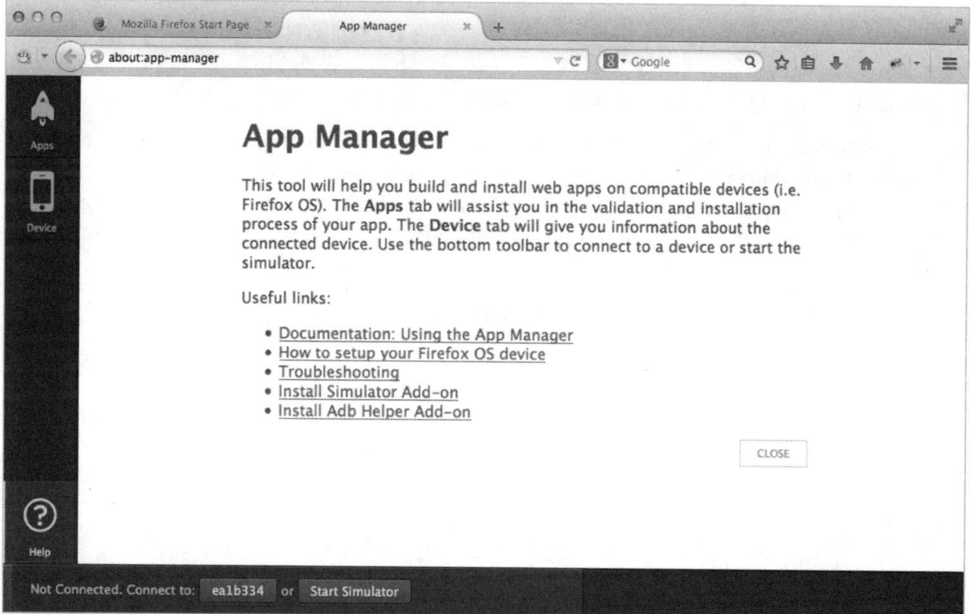

Figure 8.3 Firefox App Manager Help Window

Another way to open the App Manager is to type `about:app-manager` in the Firefox address bar and press Enter. The App Manager is just a target application as far as Firefox is concerned, reachable by a URL. You can also save the App Manager as a bookmark so you can easily reach it again without having to go through the menus.

> **Warning**
>
> The Firefox App Manager uses part of the Android SDK to allow it to communicate with physical devices. So, you will need to have completed the Android SDK installation described in Chapter 4, "Using the Cordova Command-Line Interfaces," to work with physical Firefox OS devices.

At this point, you have two more steps to complete: install one or more Firefox OS simulators and install the ADB Helper add-on.

To install the Firefox OS simulators, click the Install Simulator Add-on link on the help page. You will be taken to a page with information on how to install the simulators. Fortunately, the simulators are just Firefox browser add-ons, so it's pretty easy to install them—just click on the link for the simulator you want to install and follow the prompts to add the add-on to the browser.

Another browser add-on you will need is the ADB Helper. ADB stands for Android Debug Bridge and is part of the Android SDK that allows the App Manager's debug tools to talk to a mobile device. Click the Install ADB Helper Add-on link shown in Figure 8.3. (For some reason Mozilla isn't treating ADB like the acronym it is and has it listed as Adb on the page shown in the figure.) You will be taken to a page with information about how to install the add-on. Remember, it's a browser add-on, so it will install just like the simulator add-ons you've already installed.

When you've completed the installation, click the Close button to close the App Manager help page. The browser will display the App Manager screen shown in Figure 8.4. You can open the help page again by clicking the Help button shown in the lower-left corner of Figure 8.3.

Notice the buttons at the bottom of the App Manager window: the first button, labeled ea1b334, will connect App Manager with a physical device connected to the system via a USB cable. The device has a physical ID of ea1b334; in this example, it's a ZTE Open device I have connected to the system. The Start Simulator button will launch the Firefox OS simulator in a separate window.

In the next section, I'll show you how to use App Manager to interact with the simulator.

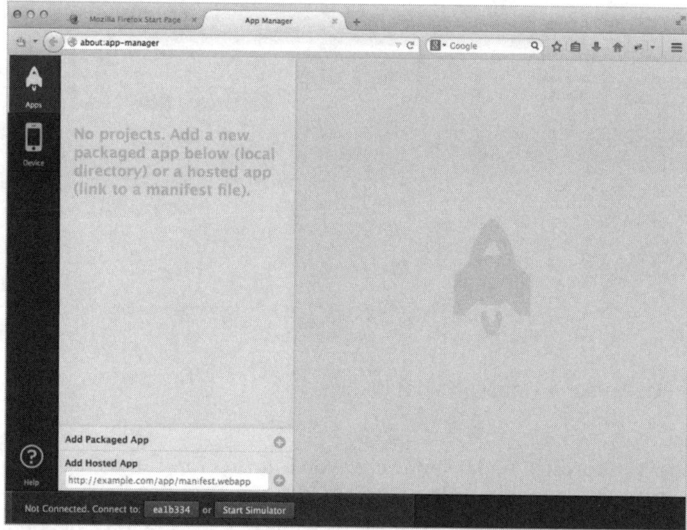

Figure 8.4 Firefox App Manager

Debugging with the Firefox OS Simulator

The Mozilla team has worked really hard to make testing Firefox OS applications in a simulator a very easy process. In this section, I'll show you how to launch the simulator and leverage the Firefox App Manager debugging tools to interact with your application as it runs in the simulator. In the section that follows, I'll show how to do this with a physical device; the debugging process is the same, so the skills you learn here will apply there as well.

> **Note**
>
> In Chapter 4 I showed you how to use the Cordova CLI `run` or `emulate` command to execute Cordova applications on a device or a device simulator. Unfortunately, the `emulate` command won't work for Firefox OS applications; you have to keep a Firefox browser window open and run your applications through it.

After you've created a new Cordova application for Firefox OS and edited the application content, you're ready to test the application. Before you begin, be sure to open a terminal window, navigate to the Cordova application folder, and issue the `cordova prepare` command which will copy the web application content to the necessary mobile device platform folders as described in Chapter 5, "The Mechanics of Cordova Development." With the web application content copied into the project's platforms/firefoxos folder, you're ready to begin testing.

In the Firefox App Manager, click the Add Packaged App item shown in the lower-left corner of Figure 8.4. The system's standard folder browser window will appear; navigate to the project's platforms/firefoxos/www folder and click the Open button as shown in Figure 8.5.

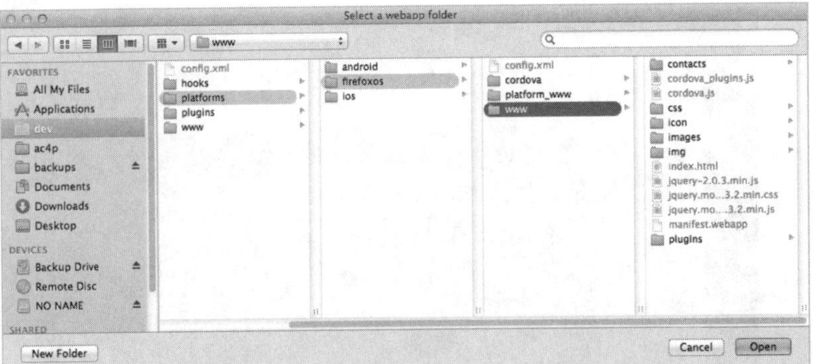

Figure 8.5 Firefox Select a Webapp Folder Dialog

The App Manager window will update and show you information about the Cordova application you selected as shown in Figure 8.6. On the far left is a navigator that allows you to switch between apps and devices. In the remainder of the window's space is a list of applications that have been loaded, in this case one, and on the far right is information about the selected application.

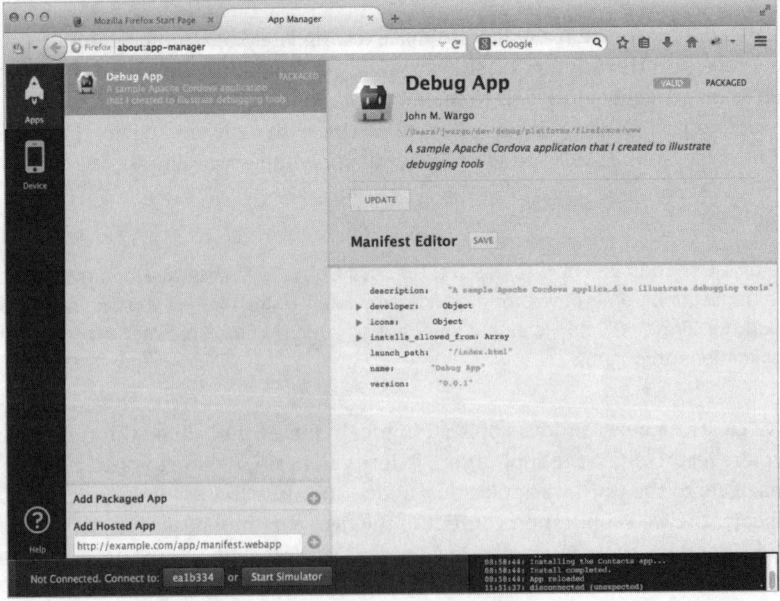

Figure 8.6 Firefox App Manager with a Cordova Application Open

The Manifest Editor (bottom portion of the application screen) allows you to configure properties for the application. The manifest file is created for you automatically during the Cordova CLI's prepare step; information from the Cordova project's config.xml file is copied into the Firefox OS project's manifest.webapp file and displayed here.

You shouldn't make changes to the file here since those changes will be overwritten the next time you execute `prepare`. Instead, make the changes in the Cordova project's config.xml and let the properties propagate to the different platforms' projects through `prepare`.

On Windows you may notice that App Manager displays a warning indicating that the icons are missing from the manifest. This error appeared on Windows but not OS X; it's a bug that should be fixed by the time you read this.

Right now there's not a lot you can do with this application since App Manager hasn't connected to a simulator or physical device. So, since this section of the chapter is about the simulator, let's start one. At the bottom of Figure 8.6 are two buttons; click the one that says Start Simulator. Some options will appear as shown in Figure 8.7. Essentially what this shows is a list of the different Firefox OS simulator add-ons you installed earlier.

Figure 8.7 Launching a Firefox OS Simulator

> **Warning**
>
> I had issues with Norton Antivirus on Windows blocking some of the simulator files. You may find that you will need to disable your antivirus software when debugging using the simulator.

It doesn't really matter which one you pick; for my system I clicked the Firefox OS 1.4 button. The Firefox App Manager will open the browser window shown in Figure 8.8.

Figure 8.8 Firefox Simulator

With the App Manager connected to a device or a simulator, you can click on the Device icon in the navigator in the left side of the App Manager window. The pane that opens will show the list of applications installed on the device as shown in Figure 8.9. You can also start the application from here by clicking the Start button next to the application.

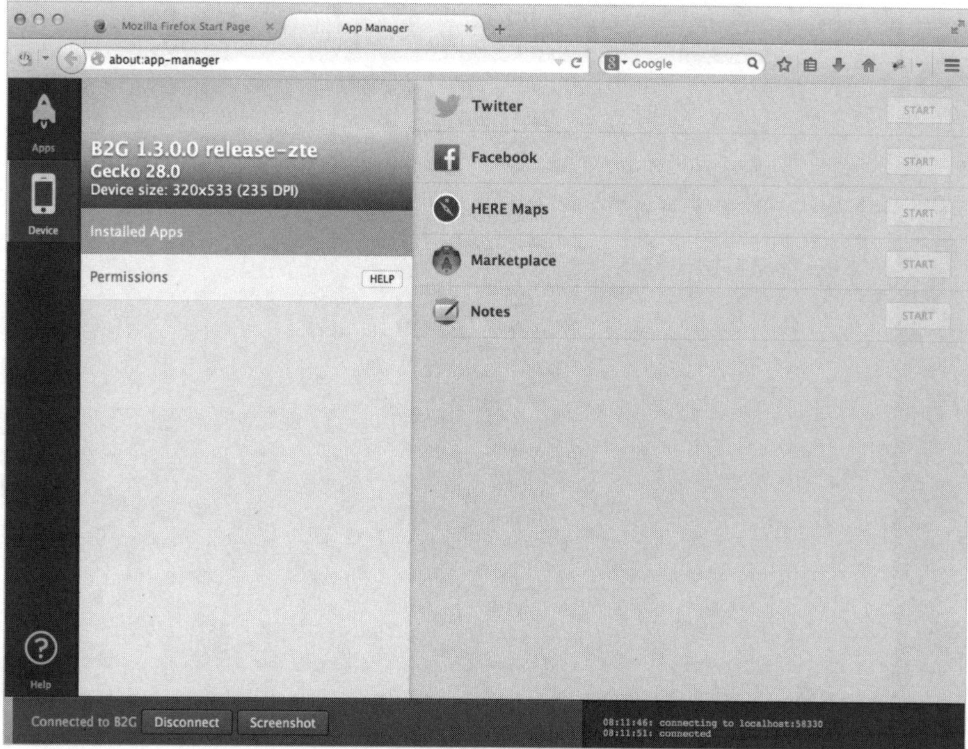

Figure 8.9 Firefox App Manager Device Applications Pane

When you click the Permissions button, App Manager will open a pane that lists all of the application permission settings as shown in Figure 8.10. You can edit permissions here; if you need to make any permission changes, you'll have to make them in the application's manifest. You can learn more about Firefox OS App Permissions at http://goo.gl/yVMwBV.

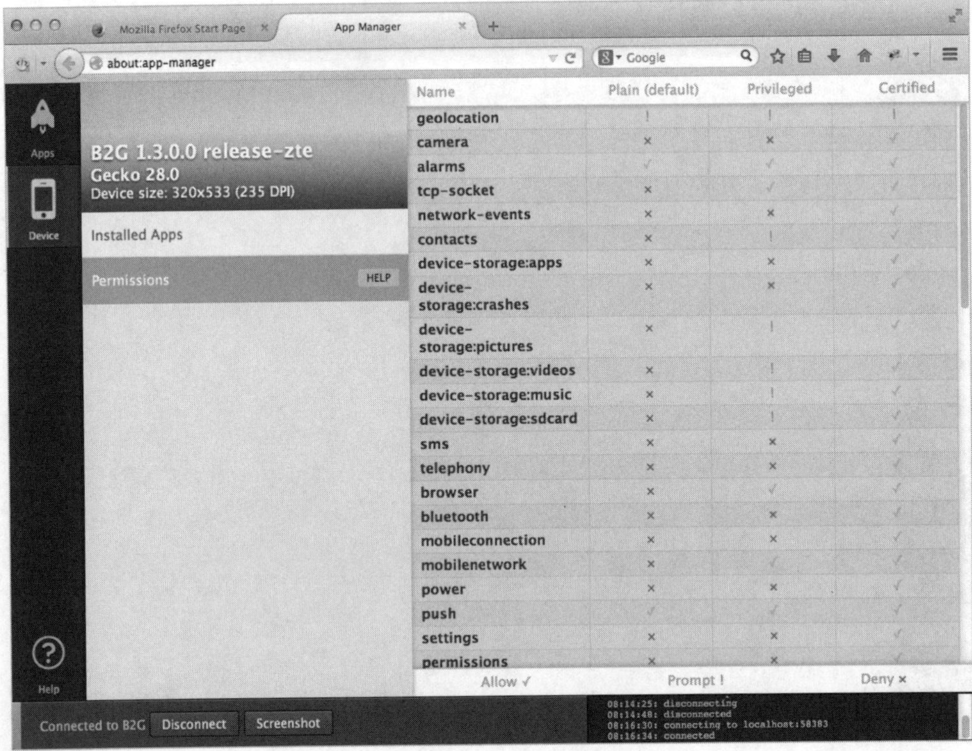

Figure 8.10 Firefox App Manager Device Permissions Pane

If you click the Update button shown in Figure 8.6, the selected application will deploy to the simulator and you will be able to view the application's icon on the home screen as shown in Figure 8.11.

Figure 8.11 Firefox OS 2.0 Simulator Home Screen with an Application Installed

Now that there's a device connected (it's only a simulated one now, but that's enough), the UI for the App Manager will update as shown in Figure 8.12. The Debug button is used to initiate a debug session with the device running the application.

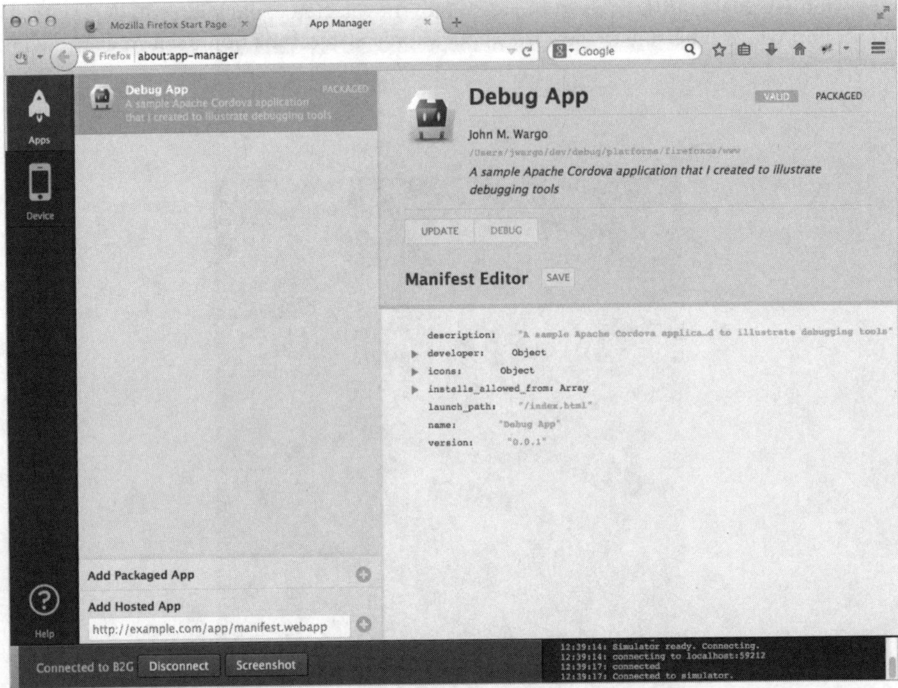

Figure 8.12 Firefox App Manager Apps List

When you click the Debug button, the App Manager will open a new icon in the navigation area on the left for the application that is running on the simulator as shown in Figure 8.13. The main portion of the browser window will open a set of tabs you will use to interact with the application. In the Console tab shown in the figure, you can see the console output written by the application and the simulator as it does its work. In this example, you can see that the simulator has installed proxies for three of the plugins I've added to my application. You can also see the output from the index.js shown in the window—that is the content outputted by my application code to help me understand what the application is doing as it runs.

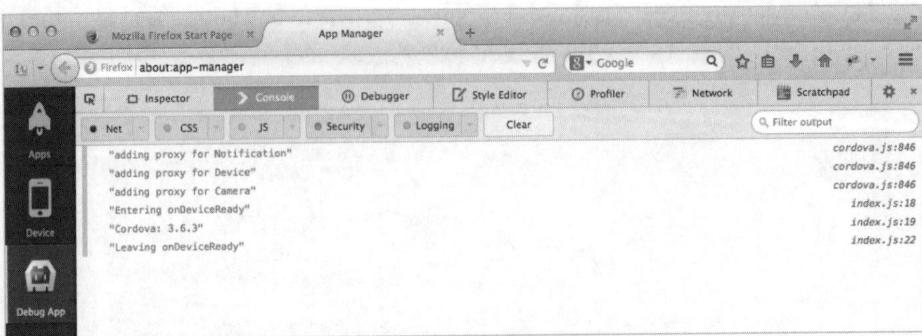

Figure 8.13 Firefox App Manager Console Window

The buttons above the Console window can be used to filter the content displayed in the window. If you click the drop-down indicator next to the JS button, you will be able to select whether to display error and/or warning messages.

The Inspector window shown in Figure 8.14 allows you view the application's HTML content and edit it just as you were able to do with weinre and GapDebug (described in Chapter 5). In the figure, you can see that I've highlighted the div that encloses the main image on the page; in the simulator it draws a red dashed line around the selected element in the application.

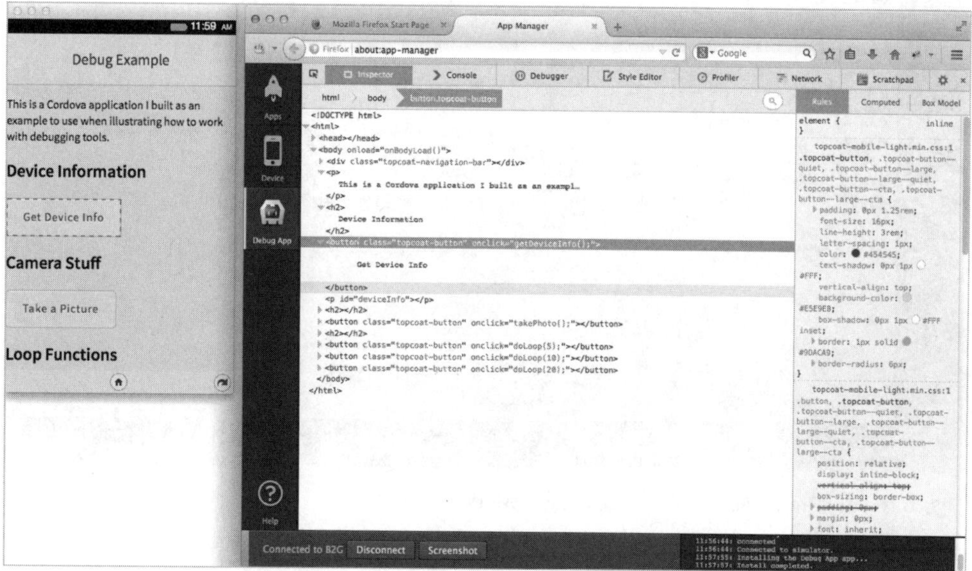

Figure 8.14 Firefox App Manager Inspector Window

In the Debugger window shown in Figure 8.15, you can view the application's JavaScript files and interact with them. In this example, I've set breakpoints inside of several of the functions in the application's JavaScript code by clicking in the margin next to the lines where I want to set the breakpoints.

When the application runs, JavaScript execution will halt on each of the marked lines; then I can use the buttons highlighted in the upper-left corner of the Debugger window to step through the code as needed. The first button is the Pause button, followed by Step Over, Step Into, and Step Out buttons.

The Pause button halts application execution; it will change to a Continue button once the code is halted, allowing you to continue execution. The Step Over button allows you to execute a function without stepping through the code in the function; the function executes and returns to the debugger once execution has completed. The Step Into button allows you to execute the code in a function by stepping through each line individually, and the Step Out button will complete execution of the current function.

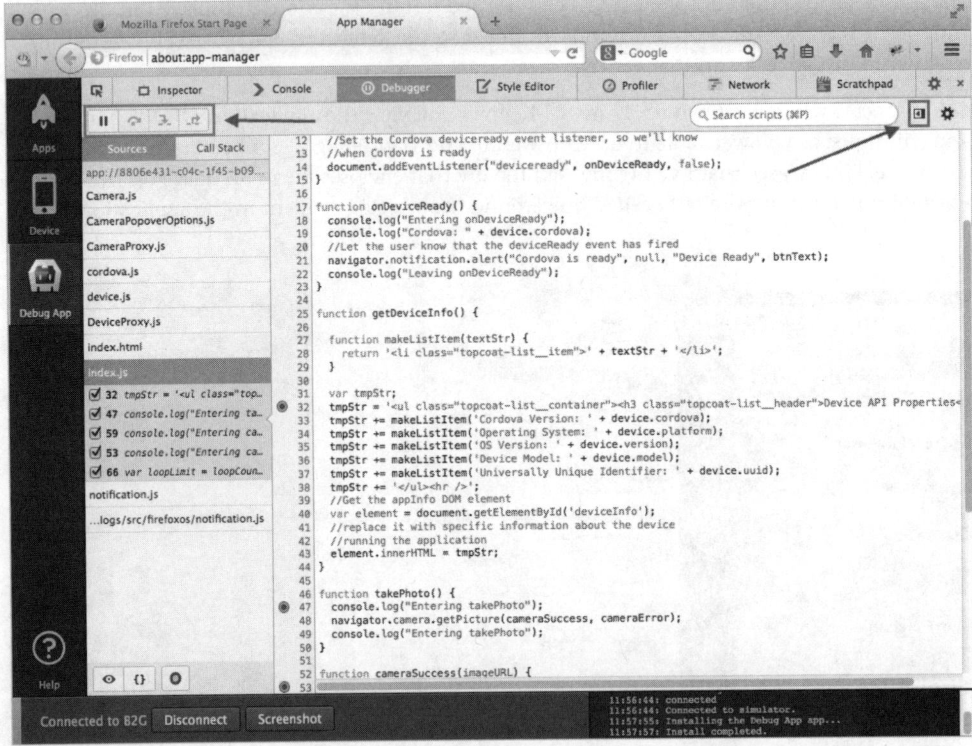

Figure 8.15 Firefox App Manager Debugger Window

Click the icon highlighted on the upper-right corner of the Debugger window to open a panel that provides options for defining watches, viewing variable values, and viewing DOM events bound by your code. These tools give you detailed information about what's happening within your code and should enable you to quickly get to the root of any issues.

> **Warning**
>
> In my testing, I found that the Sources pane in the Debugger window would not list any files until I reloaded the application by clicking the Update button shown in Figure 8.6. Ideally this will be fixed by the time you read this.

When running an application on Firefox OS, dialogs look much different from the way they do on other platforms. Figure 8.16 shows the results of using the JavaScript `alert` function in a Cordova application. Notice how the "dialog" covers the entire window.

Figure 8.16 JavaScript `alert` on a Firefox OS Device Simulator

Calls to the Cordova `alert` method will display the results shown in Figure 8.17.

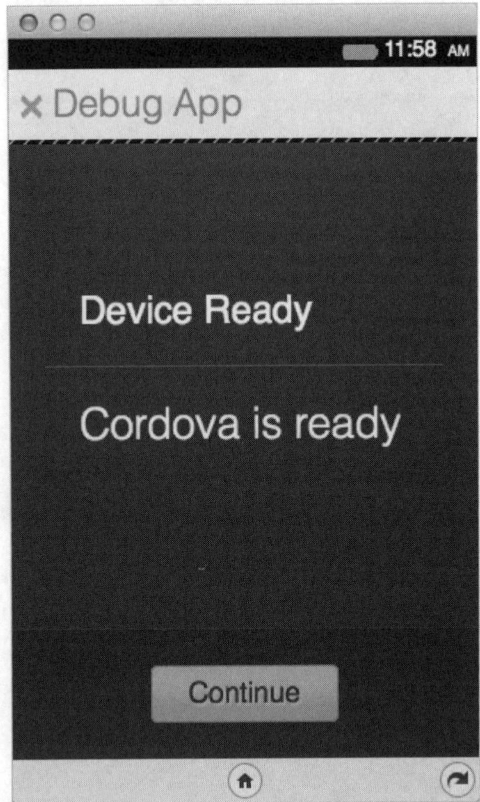

Figure 8.17 Cordova `alert` on a Firefox OS Device Simulator

I've hit only some of the highlights of this tool; there's a whole lot more the Firefox App Manager can do to help you test and debug your Cordova applications. You can find much more detailed instructions on how to use all of the features of App Manager at http://goo.gl/JzSXQQ.

Debugging Applications on a Firefox OS Device

Debugging Firefox OS applications on a physical device is no different from what you have already seen; the capabilities available to you are exactly the same. The only difference is in the initial setup and how you connect the device to the debugger.

Before you can use a physical device with the App Manager's debugging tools, you must first enable remote debugging on the device. To do this, open the device's Settings application, then Device Information. In the Device Information page, tap on More Information. On the More Information page is an option for Developer settings as shown at the bottom of Figure 8.18.

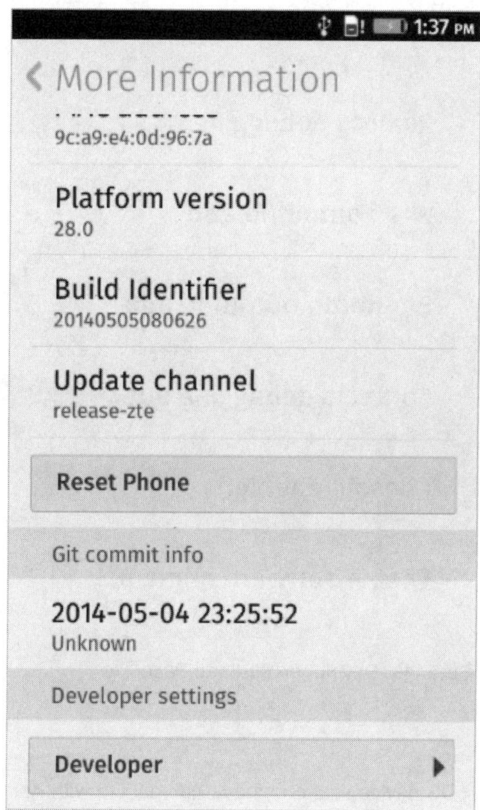

Figure 8.18 Firefox OS Settings: More Information Page

On the Developer page shown in Figure 8.19, enable the Remote debugging checkbox; with this enabled, you're ready to start debugging Cordova applications on the device.

To use a physical device with App Manager, simply connect the device to the system running App Manager using a USB cable. After the device drivers install, you should see the device listed as one of the options in the bottom of the App Manager window as shown in Figure 8.3. In this case, my device is a ZTE Open C, Firefox OS 1.3 device called ea1b334.

When you click the Device button, App Manager will connect to the device, and all of the other testing and debugging capabilities I described in the previous section will be available to you.

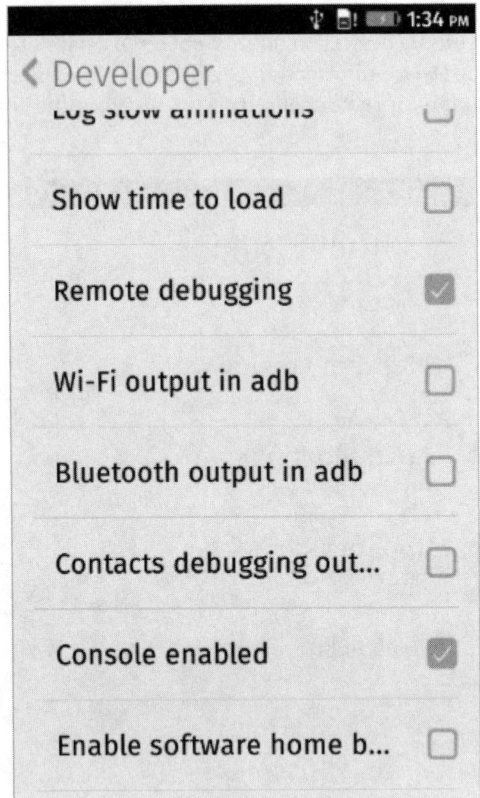

Figure 8.19 Firefox OS Settings: Developer Settings Page

> **Warning**
>
> Be sure that the Firefox OS device you're using is compatible with App Manager. As I started this chapter, I had a Firefox OS device lying around that I used for some application testing for *Apache Cordova 3 Programming*. I plugged it in and spent hours trying to figure out why the App Manager saw the device but wouldn't connect to it. The device I had was a Firefox OS 1.0 device, and App Manager requires Firefox OS 1.2 or higher. Save yourself some trouble and check the device's OS version before trying to make it work with App Manager.

Wrap-Up

In this chapter, I showed you how to use the free tools available from Mozilla to test and debug your Cordova applications for Firefox OS. You now have the information you need to test Firefox OS applications using the Firefox OS simulator or a physical device.

9

iOS Development with Cordova

For developers building Cordova applications for the iOS platform, Apple provides a suite of tools used to design, package, and deploy iOS applications. Even though the Cordova CLI takes care of most of the process of creating, managing, and testing iOS applications, there will be times when you will want to have more control over the process. Even though the CLI can launch a Cordova application in the iOS simulator, when you encounter problems with an application, and you want to know more about what's going on as the application runs, you'll need to use the development tools that Apple provides. Additionally, when coding, testing, and debugging native plugins for iOS, you'll do the majority of your work using Apple's tools.

In this chapter, I'll show you how to use Xcode, Apple's IDE for iOS development, to test Cordova applications for iOS devices. I'll also show you how to use the Safari browser to debug Cordova applications.

Working with Xcode

Assuming you've used the Cordova CLI to create a project and added the iOS platform to it, working with a Cordova application in Xcode is pretty straightforward. When you have your web application's content all ready, use the `cordova prepare` command to copy the project's web application source code over to the project folder for each target platform.

The Cordova CLI creates a project that can be opened directly in Xcode. Simply start Xcode, open the project, and go to work. If the Xcode welcome page is configured to open on startup, you'll open a project by selecting the Open another project option on the welcome page. If not, simply open the File menu and select Open.

In the Open dialog that appears, navigate to the Cordova project's platforms/ios folder as shown in Figure 9.1, then select the file with the .xcodeproj extension and click Open.

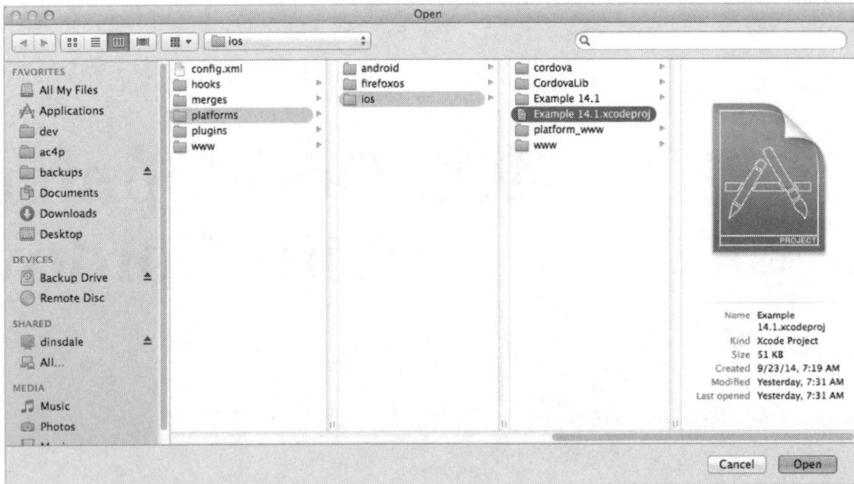

Figure 9.1 Opening a Cordova Xcode Project

When the project opens, you should see a screen similar to the one shown in Figure 9.2. From here, you can run the application in any of the iOS simulators as you would for any other iOS application.

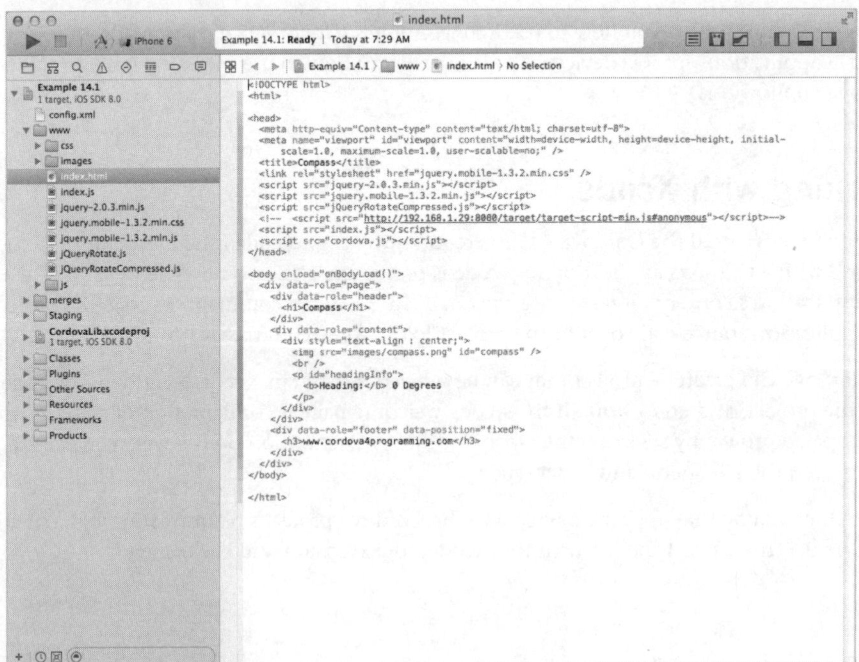

Figure 9.2 Cordova Project Open in Xcode

Xcode isn't designed to be used to edit web applications—Apple created Dashcode for that purpose—so you're not going to get a lot of context-aware editing help with Xcode. That's why I use Adobe Brackets to edit my web applications and switch to Xcode only when I need to be able to see what's happening as the application runs.

For the most part, you can run the Cordova application as is; the default settings in Xcode should be sufficient for your application. By default, though, a Cordova project for iOS is configured only for portrait operation; if you're expecting the user to be able to rotate the device and have the screen update accordingly, you're going to have to make one small change. In Xcode, click on the application project title in the upper-left corner of the project navigation pane shown in Figure 9.2—it's "Example 14.1" in the figure. When you do that, general properties of the application project will open as shown in Figure 9.3.

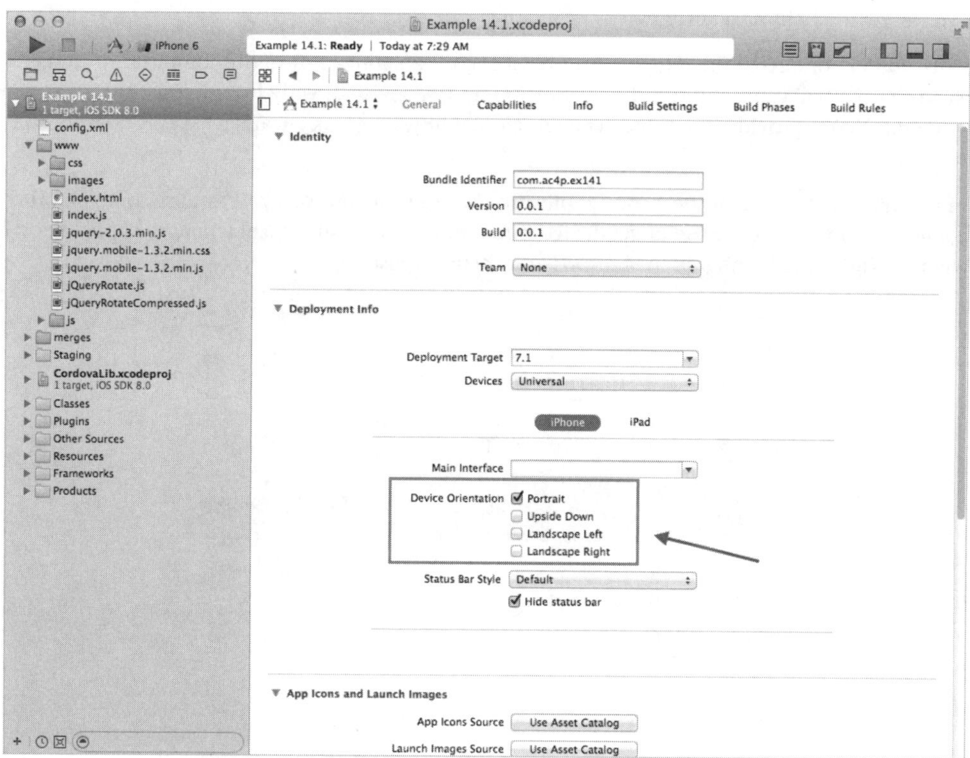

Figure 9.3 Xcode Application Properties

Notice the Device Orientation option highlighted in the figure; to support additional orientations, enable the appropriate checkboxes, such as Landscape Left and Landscape Right to enable landscape orientation, for example.

When it's time to test the application, Xcode can launch an iOS device simulator and deploy the application to it once it launches, or you can deploy the application to a physical device connected to the development system via a USB cable.

There are a few differences between debugging on a simulator and a physical device. So at some point in your development process, you are going to want to run your app on a device. Apple has some complicated processes you must follow before you can run an application on a physical device. As there are hundreds of books and web sites dedicated to iOS development, I'm not going to dig into the details here. You can find detailed instructions on the Apple Developer web site at http://goo.gl/SF2qNV. You'll have to follow the instructions provided there before you can work with a physical device.

Once you've completed the setup of your device, you can connect it to the computer running Xcode with a USB cable and run the application on the device directly from Xcode. In this environment, Xcode provides the same debugging capabilities for a physical device as it does for the simulators.

In the upper-left corner of the Xcode application window are buttons you can use to launch the application and to specify the target device (simulator or physical device) where the application will run. Figure 9.4 highlights the buttons and their purpose.

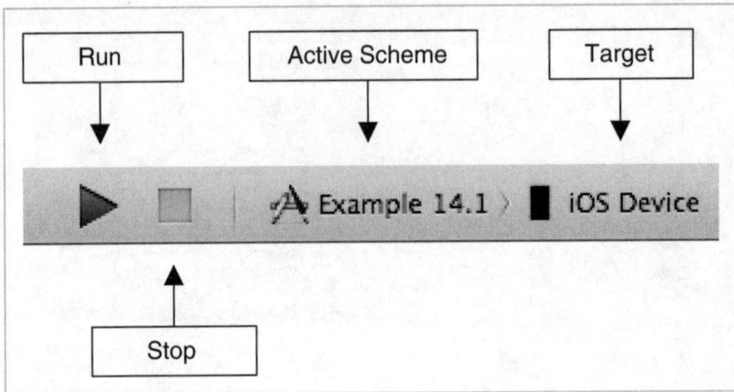

Figure 9.4 Xcode Run Tools

To compile and run the current application project, click the Run button highlighted in the figure. Xcode will build the application, then, depending on the selected target, will deploy the application to a physical device or launch the specified simulator and deploy the application to the simulator.

While the application is running, you can click the Stop button to terminate the application on the target device.

The Active Scheme button is used to select the scheme, a collection of build targets, defined for the application. You can find more information about this option at http://goo.gl/GJ8rlM.

The Target option shown in Figure 9.4 opens a list of available target devices available in Xcode. The list will show any physical devices attached to the system running Xcode, plus it will list any simulators installed in Xcode. A sample list of targets is shown in Figure 9.5, in this case a list of all targets on my development workstation.

Figure 9.5 Xcode Available Device Targets

When you're ready to test the Cordova application, click the Target button, select the device where you want the application to run, then click the Run button to build and deploy the application. That's all there is to it.

Testing Cordova Applications in Xcode

iOS applications are written in Objective-C, a variant of C that was used by NeXT to develop applications for the NeXTSTEP operating system back in the 1980s. While Xcode will let you edit HTML5 source files, because iOS applications are written in C, Xcode does not have the ability to debug web applications running in the Cordova container. You can use weinre or the `console` object to help debug applications as described in Chapter 5, "The Mechanics of Cordova Development," to debug your iOS applications. Later in this chapter, I'll show you how to debug a Cordova application using the Safari browser.

Using Xcode, you can debug native application code, so you'll be able to work directly with the native Cordova container and any native plugin the application is running. As this is a book on Cordova development and not Xcode development, I'm not going to cover native application debugging. Refer to Chapter 28 of Fritz Anderson's *Xcode 6 Start to Finish* (Boston: Addison-Wesley, 2015) for details on how to debug a native iOS application using Xcode. In reality, when you're debugging native plugins, you'll most likely use two debuggers: the Xcode native debugger for the plugin's native code and the Safari browser for the application's HTML and JavaScript code.

When you run an iOS application in Xcode, the IDE opens up a console window at the bottom of the screen where you can see messages generated by the simulator as well as the Cordova application. Using the sample application from Chapter 14, "Working with the Cordova APIs," you can see the output from the code that uses the `console` object written to the IDE console screen in Figure 9.6.

```
No Selection
2014-09-24 07:33:19.020 Example 14.1[4944:162736] onDeviceReady fired.
2014-09-24 07:33:19.020 Example 14.1[4944:162736] Compass - Creating watch: {"frequency":1000}
2014-09-24 07:34:25.156 Example 14.1[4944:162736] THREAD WARNING: ['Compass'] took '65135.086182' ms. Plugin
should use a background thread.
2014-09-24 07:34:25.160 Example 14.1[4944:162927] void SendDelegateMessage(NSInvocation *): delegate
(webView:decidePolicyForNavigationAction:request:frame:decisionListener:) failed to return after waiting 10
seconds. main run loop mode: kCFRunLoopDefaultMode
2014-09-24 07:34:25.163 Example 14.1[4944:162736] ERROR: Compass - Heading Error
2014-09-24 07:34:25.163 Example 14.1[4944:162736] ERROR: Compass - Error: {"code":20}
All Output
```

Figure 9.6 Xcode Console Output Window

Notice how error messages are tagged with additional text so you can identify them more clearly in the console window; the same is true for warning messages. Unfortunately, Xcode doesn't color-code them to make them easier to see; perhaps Apple will add more robust capabilities in the future.

On many other platforms, you can filter the console messages based on type, application ID, or other properties, but that's not possible in the Xcode console window. The only thing you can really do here is click the arrow button shown in the top of the figure to have Xcode push a specific location to the simulator (for testing applications that make use of the device's geolocation capabilities).

If you look at the console output shown in Figure 9.6, you should see that the Compass API returned an error (we'll cover the Compass API in Chapter 14, and I'll show you more about the sample application in Chapter 15, "Cordova Development End to End"). That's because the iOS simulator doesn't provide support for the compass and several other native capabilities; you can find detailed information about the iOS simulator limitations at http://goo.gl/vs3Hi4.

In order to make it easier for the user of the application, I had the application display an alert whenever an error was detected within the application as shown in Figure 9.7. You could, using the Cordova Device API, detect whether the application is running on a simulator and disable features within the application in that situation as well, to avoid showing the user an error dialog.

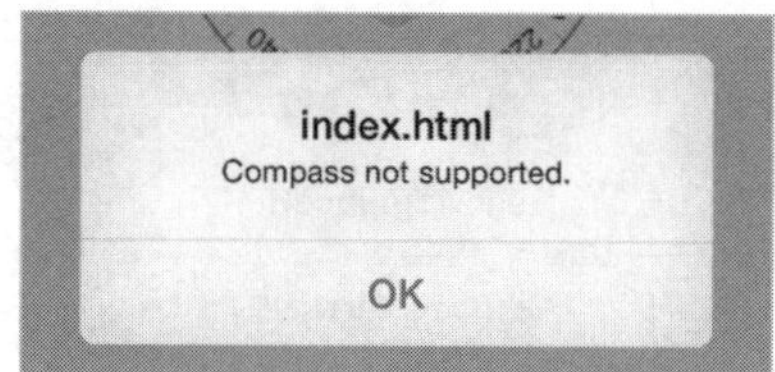

Figure 9.7 Application Error on iOS

When working with iOS device simulators, you can easily grab screen shots using any Macintosh-compatible screen capture utility. When working with a physical device connected to the system running Xcode, you can use the Devices utility to grab screen shots from the device. To access the Devices utility, in Xcode open the Window menu and select Devices; Xcode will open a window similar to the one shown in Figure 9.8. Click the Take Screenshot button to capture the current device's screen. Images captured this way will be automatically saved directly to the desktop.

Figure 9.8 Xcode Devices Utility

Using the Safari Web Inspector

Beginning with iOS 6, Apple added some capabilities to Safari (both on the desktop and in iOS) that allow a web application to be remotely debugged in the desktop Safari browser. The cool thing about this capability is that it works with the `UIWebView` used within a Cordova application. You can find detailed information about this remote debugging capability on Apple's web site at http://goo.gl/XP3Gai.

The first thing you must do is enable the developer menu in the desktop version of Safari for Macintosh OS (this process doesn't work on Windows and probably never will). Open the Safari application preferences and select the Advanced tab as shown in Figure 9.9. Enable the checkbox at the bottom of the figure labeled Show Develop menu in menu bar.

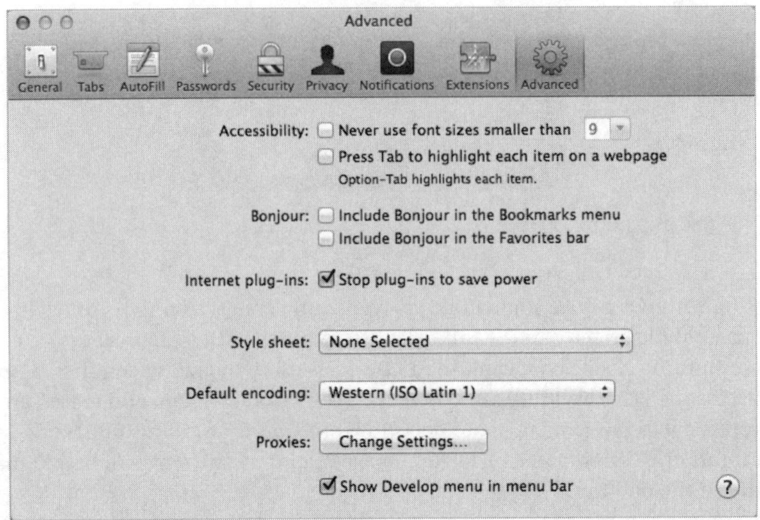

Figure 9.9 Safari Preferences on Macintosh OS X

What this does is add a Develop menu item to Safari that you can use to interact with a device or even a device simulator. With that change in place, close preferences and you should see the new menu in Safari.

Next, you need to enable the Web Inspector on the device on which you will be doing your debugging. On an iOS device (or iOS simulator) open the Settings application, select Safari, then click the Advanced option at the bottom of the Settings screen. On the screen that appears, enable the Web Inspector option shown in Figure 9.10.

> **Note**
>
> With the initial implementation of this feature, Web Inspector was supported only on physical devices, but in my testing, I could access some of the capabilities on a simulator, although I couldn't step through my application's JavaScript code.

With those settings in place, launch the simulator or connect the device to the computer with a USB cable, then launch the Cordova application. You can run the Cordova application from Xcode or preload the application on the device and run it manually from the device's home screen.

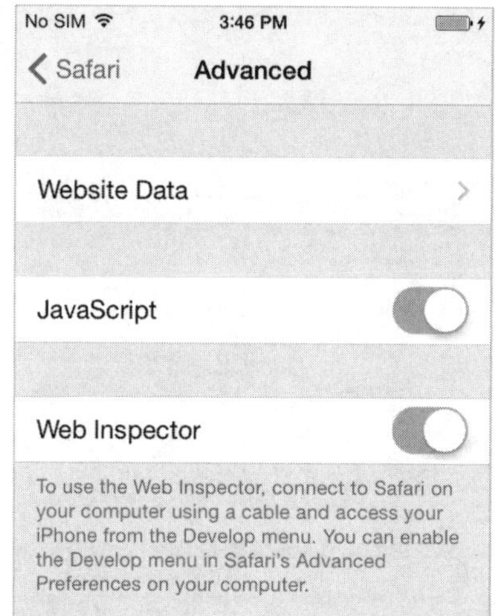

Figure 9.10 Safari Advanced Settings on iOS

With the Cordova application running, switch to your desktop computer, fire up the Safari browser (remember, this works only on Macintosh OS X), and open the Develop menu. You should see your simulator or iOS device listed in the menu that appears. Figure 9.11 shows an example of this; my iPhone, appropriately named John's iPhone, shows as an option in the menu. You should see the application running; select the index.html file as shown in the figure.

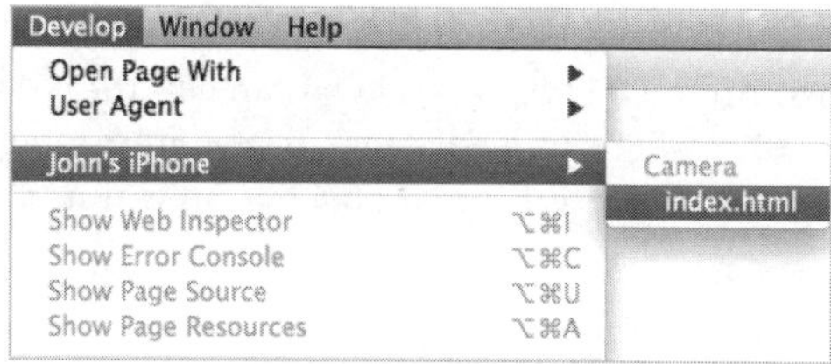

Figure 9.11 Connecting the Remote Web Inspector to the Cordova Application

Safari will connect to the remote application, then open a new window as shown in Figure 9.12. From this new window, you have access to the code running within the Cordova container and the ability to interact with different parts of the application as it runs. In this example, I'm showing you one of the example camera applications from my *Apache Cordova API Cookbook*.

Figure 9.12 shows the contents of the index.html file; you can expand the different parts of the page and even edit the contents on the fly. As with the other examples I've shown in this book, when you highlight content in the HTML editor, the corresponding element will be highlighted on the screen. You can also view console output in the Console tab shown at the top of the figure.

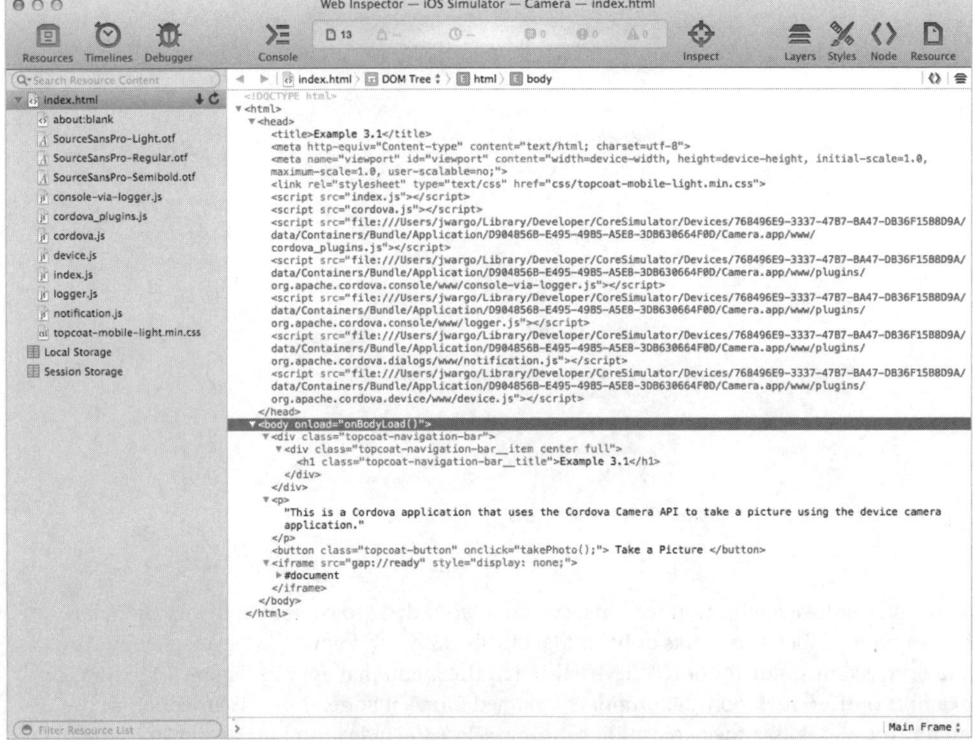

Figure 9.12 Safari Remote Web Inspector Window

Click on any of the code within the HTML file and you can edit the content directly. When you complete the changes, they will be immediately reflected in the mobile application. In Figure 9.13 you can see that I've changed the text on a button within the application while the application is running.

```
▼<p>
    "This is a Cordova application that uses the Cordova Camera API to take a picture using the device camera
    application."
  </p>
  <button class="topcoat-button" onclick="takePhoto();">Changed Button</button>
▼<iframe src="gap://ready" style="display: none;">
  ▶#document
  </iframe>
</body>
```

Figure 9.13 Updating HTML Content in the Web Inspector

In real time, on the device, the Cordova application will update to show the new content as shown in Figure 9.14.

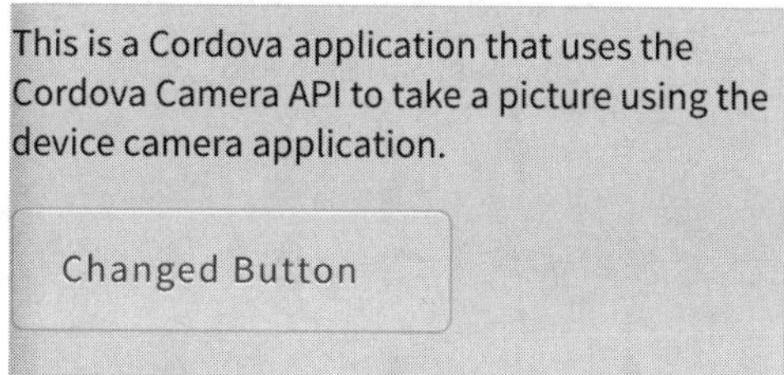

Figure 9.14 Modified Cordova Application

Very important to Cordova developers and something that's not available on most other platforms is the ability to set breakpoints and step through the JavaScript code in a Cordova application. Figure 9.15 shows the application's index.js with some breakpoints set.

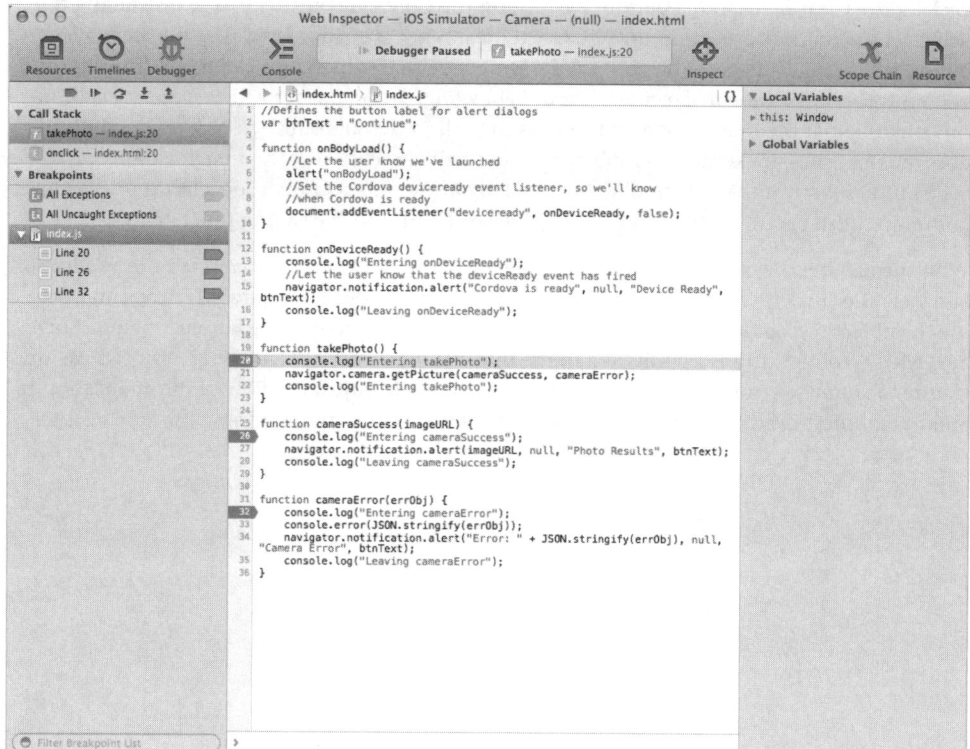

Figure 9.15 Web Inspector JavaScript Debugger

When debugging an application and JavaScript execution halts at a breakpoint, you can control how the debugger continues execution of the code using buttons located at the top of the debug window; these buttons are highlighted in Figure 9.16.

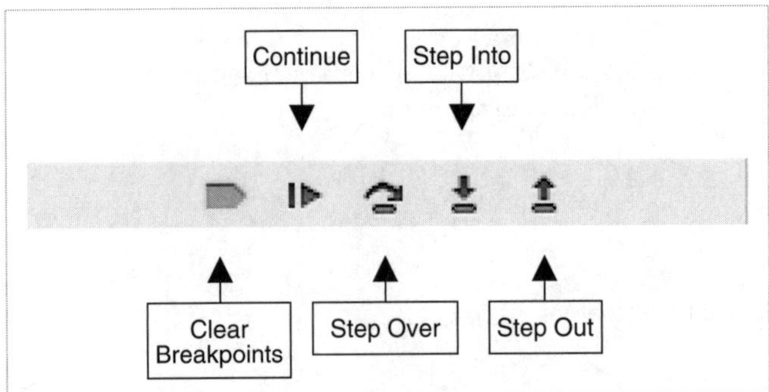

Figure 9.16 Web Inspector JavaScript Debugger Icons

You can remove all breakpoints so your JavaScript code executes without interruption by clicking the Clear Breakpoints button. By clicking the Continue button, you're instructing the debugger to continue execution until the next breakpoint is encountered. Use the Step Over button when the debugger is stopped on a line of code that is making a call to a subroutine and you want the subroutine to execute without debugging. The debugger will execute the subroutine, then halt at the line of code that follows the call to the subroutine. The Step Into button does the opposite—it executes the subroutine and halts execution at the first line of executable code in the subroutine. When you're done looking at the subroutine's code, click the Step Out button to finish executing the subroutine's code and return to the calling function.

While debugging the code, you can hover the mouse over any of the variables in the application and view the current value for the object as shown in the middle of Figure 9.17. You can also use the object inspector pane on the right side of the window to edit the current values associated with an object; this is highlighted in the upper-right corner of Figure 9.17. You can use this feature to simulate error conditions or change the values to adjust the flow of the application to allow you to test conditions that might not normally appear during testing.

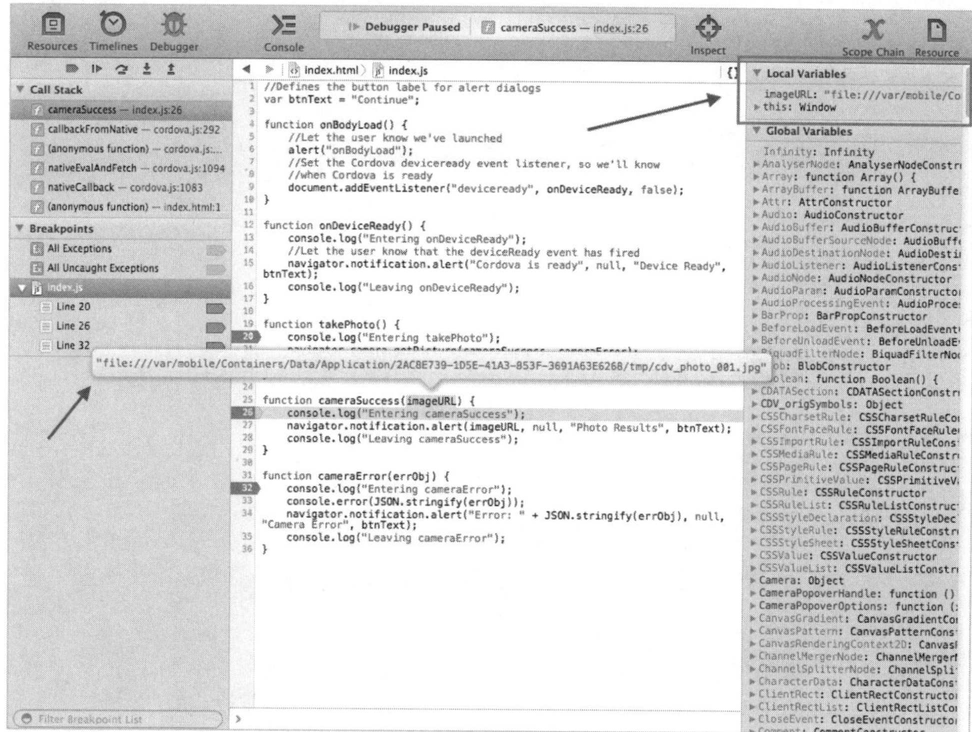

Figure 9.17 Web Inspector Viewing and Editing Variable Values

I've only skimmed the surface of what you can do with the Web Inspector. Before you go too far with iOS development for Cordova, spend some time with this tool to understand all it can do for you. You'll likely save time and frustration by using a tool like this for your testing and troubleshooting.

Wrap-Up

In this chapter, I've shown you how to test and debug your iOS Cordova applications in an iOS simulator and on a physical device. Using these tools should help simplify the development process and allow you to more quickly identify issues with your applications. Don't forget that when you're testing and debugging native plugins (described in Chapter 16, "Creating Cordova Plugins"), you'll likely use both of these tools during your debugging efforts.

10

Ubuntu Development with Cordova

One of the latest additions to the Cordova family is support for the Ubuntu Touch OS. The team at Canonical (www.canonical.com), the makers of the Ubuntu Linux distribution, jumped in and have implemented pretty complete support for Apache Cordova. In this chapter, I show you how to set up and use a Cordova development environment for Ubuntu Touch devices.

Installing the Cordova CLI on Ubuntu

Even though I walked you through all of the steps required to install the Cordova CLI in Chapter 3, "Configuring a Cordova Development Environment," that chapter covered only the Windows and OS X installations. The Ubuntu development environment is pretty straightforward to install and doesn't have any of the extra software installation requirements you found in Chapter 3. For that reason, I decided to cover the installation of the Cordova development environment for Ubuntu separately.

The Cordova tools for Ubuntu are supported only on Linux; if you try to execute any of the Cordova commands for Ubuntu Touch on any other operating system, you will receive an error. So, in order to work with Ubuntu Touch devices and Cordova, you're going to need a system (or virtual machine) running the Ubuntu operating system. The tools may install on other flavors of Linux, but since the tools are from Ubuntu, I decided to try them only on a system running Ubuntu.

Before we get started, I want to share a couple of links with you first. The instructions for how to configure a development environment for Ubuntu Touch can be found in the Ubuntu Platform Guide at http://goo.gl/tIynPO. The Ubuntu team also maintains a Cordova Guide which can be found at http://goo.gl/fN6v0N. There's even a simple Cordova Camera Application Tutorial located at http://goo.gl/yPCGQv.

To perform the installation, I started by downloading a copy of the latest version of the Ubuntu Linux operating system from www.ubuntu.com/download. I used the 64-bit version and installed the OS on one of my lab systems using the default options.

You could install Cordova by following the steps outlined in Chapter 3. Those steps include installing Git and NodeJS, then installing the Cordova CLI using NPM by opening a terminal window and executing the following command:

```
npm install -g cordova
```

The problem is that this will seem to work, but after the installation completes, the `cordova` command will simply not execute. What you need to do is follow the instructions provided in the Platform Guide linked above. First, you must configure the system with details on the Personal Package Archive (PPA) where the Ubuntu Cordova CLI files are maintained. To do this, open a terminal window and execute the following commands:

```
sudo add-apt-repository ppa:cordova-ubuntu/ppa
sudo apt-get update
```

These commands will configure the system for the cordova-ubuntu repository, so the system can install applications from it. The `apt-get update` command refreshes the local cache of applications so we'll be able to install the Cordova CLI from the repository. With those steps completed, you install the Cordova Ubuntu tools using the following command:

```
sudo apt-get install cordova-cli
```

That's it—that's all you have to do to install the Cordova CLI and tools for Ubuntu. Be prepared for this process to take a while as there's a lot to install. The system will grind and twist for a while and install a whole bunch of stuff needed by the tools. The cool thing about this is that one command installs everything you need, including the tools for testing and debugging your applications.

When the process completes, you can use any of the Cordova CLI commands outlined in Chapter 4, "Using the Cordova Command-Line Interfaces," to create and manage an Ubuntu application project. To create the simple Lunch Menu application I've used as an example before, you would open a terminal window, navigate to the folder where you want the project created, and issue the following commands:

```
cordova create lunchmenu com.ac4p.lunchmenu "Lunch Menu"
cd lunchmenu
cordova platform add ubuntu
cordova plugin add org.apache.cordova.console
cordova plugin add org.apache.cordova.dialogs
cordova plugin add org.apache.cordova.device
```

At this point, you can edit or copy in the web application code in the project's www folder and begin testing. I'll show you how to run and debug your Ubuntu Cordova application in the next section.

Debugging Ubuntu Applications

When it comes to executing your Cordova application, the Ubuntu platform works the same way as other platforms. Simply open a terminal window, navigate to the Cordova project folder, and execute the following command:

```
cordova run
```

That command will execute the application for all platforms that are associated with the project. If Ubuntu is the only platform in your project, executing this command will build the application and launch it; I'll explain more about what happens in a minute. If you have multiple platforms added to your project and you want to run only the Ubuntu Touch version, simply execute the following command:

```
cordova run ubuntu
```

If there's no device available, the CLI will actually build a desktop version of the app and launch it in the desktop browser. You can see an example of this in Figure 10.1; here I've launched a sample debug application I created to help show off the capabilities of debugging tools.

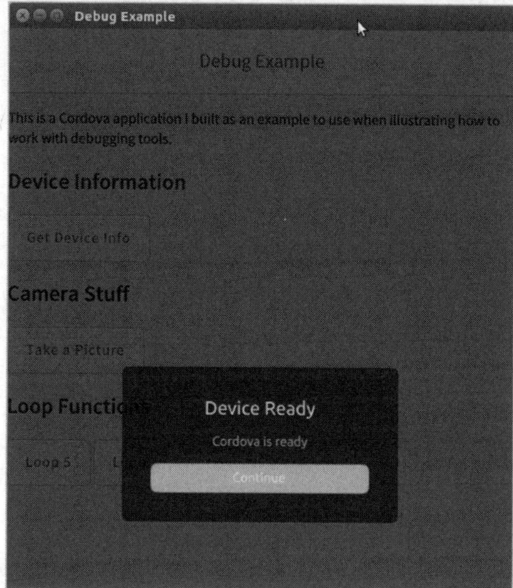

Figure 10.1 Ubuntu Touch Simulator

If you take a look at Figure 10.2, you'll see some more interesting things. First of all, as soon as the application starts running in the simulator, whenever the application writes to the console, the content is automatically displayed in the terminal window as shown in the figure. This makes it much easier for you to see the application's output; you don't have to open another tool. To regain control of the terminal window, you can press Ctrl-C in the terminal window or close the simulator window.

```
File Edit View Search Terminal Help
g/platforms/ubuntu/native/com.ac4p.debug/qml
In order to build debian package, execute
cd /home/johnwargo/dev/debug/platforms/ubuntu/native/com.ac4p.debug; debuild
pushd /home/johnwargo/dev/debug/platforms/ubuntu/native/prefix
/home/johnwargo/dev/debug/platforms/ubuntu/native/prefix /home/johnwargo/dev/deb
ug
QTWEBKIT_INSPECTOR_SERVER=9222 ./cordova-ubuntu www/
Warning:
WARNING: This project is using the experimental QML API extensions for QtWebKit
and is therefore tied to a specific QtWebKit release.
WARNING: The experimental API will change from version to version, or even be re
moved. You have been warned!

Warning: Inspector server started successfully. Try pointing a WebKit browser to
 http://127.0.0.1:9222
Warning: QFSFileEngine::open: No file name specified
Warning: file:///usr/lib/x86_64-linux-gnu/qt5/qml/Ubuntu/Components/TextField.qm
l:925:9: QML Image: Cannot open: file:///usr/lib/x86_64-linux-gnu/qt5/qml/Ubuntu
/Components/Themes/Ambiance/artwork/clear.svg
adding proxy for Device
Entering onDeviceReady
Cordova: 3.7.0-dev-8f41e8d
Leaving onDeviceReady
```

Figure 10.2 Ubuntu Terminal Window

Another interesting option available to you is also shown in Figure 10.2. In the middle of the figure you should see text instructing you on how to debug the Cordova application while it's running in the browser:

```
Warning: Inspector server started successfully.
Try pointing a WebKit browser to http://127.0.0.1:9222
```

The CLI has automatically launched a debug process for you and connected it to the simulator. So, when you open a compatible browser and point it to the specified URL, you will see a screen similar to what is shown in Figure 10.3. Ubuntu ships Firefox by default, but last I checked it wasn't running WebKit, so I installed the Google Chrome browser to use for testing the application.

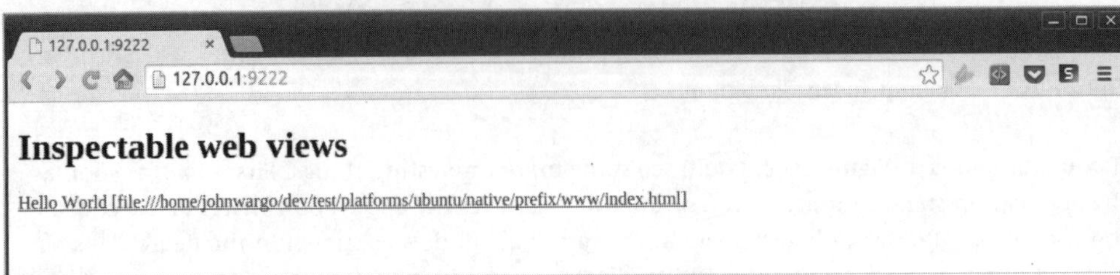

Figure 10.3 Ubuntu Debugger Window

Since there's only one inspectable application running in the simulator, that's all that shows up in the figure. I tried running another application on the simulator from another terminal window, but it opened a separate simulator process and failed when I tried to open the Web Inspector server.

When you click the link shown in Figure 10.3, the browser will open the standard web debugger window you've already seen in Chapters 5, 7, and 9. Figure 10.4 shows the Web Inspector window for my sample debug application.

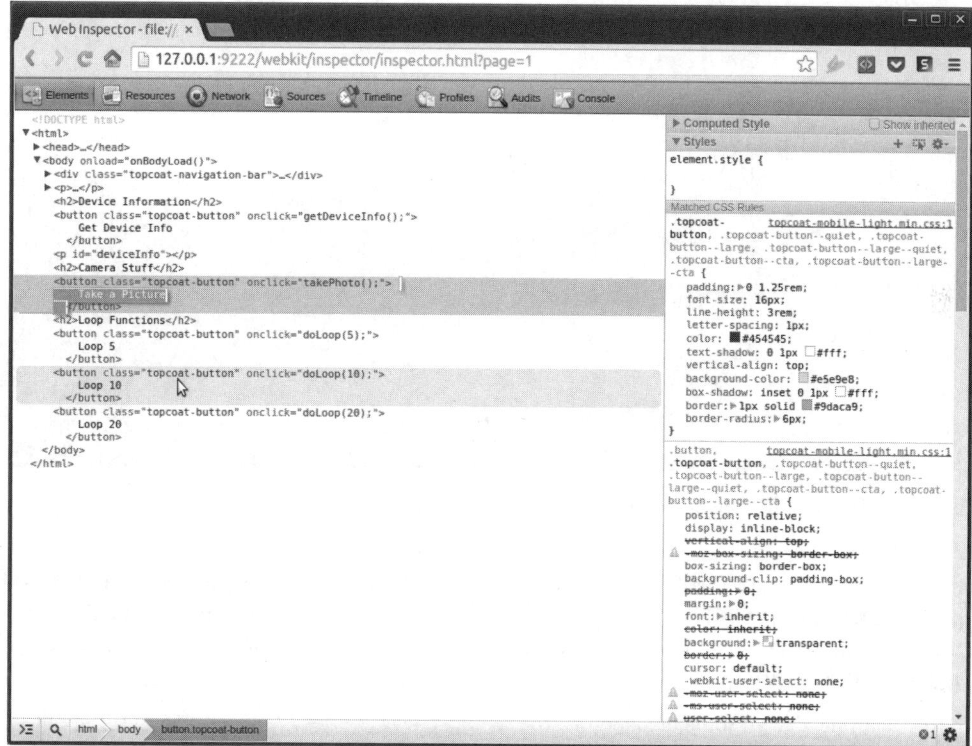

Figure 10.4 Ubuntu Web Inspector: Elements Tab

In the Elements pane, you can view the application's HTML content and even make changes to the content as I've shown in the figure. On the right side of the page are style and property panes you can use to edit the page's content and styling; the changes are immediately reflected in the simulator.

The Sources pane is used to display a pane you can use to interact with the application's code. Before you can begin poking around in the application's code, you must first enable debugging as shown in Figure 10.5. Select the option that makes the most sense for you and click the Enable Debugging button to continue. I always select Always enable; I can't think of a reason to do otherwise.

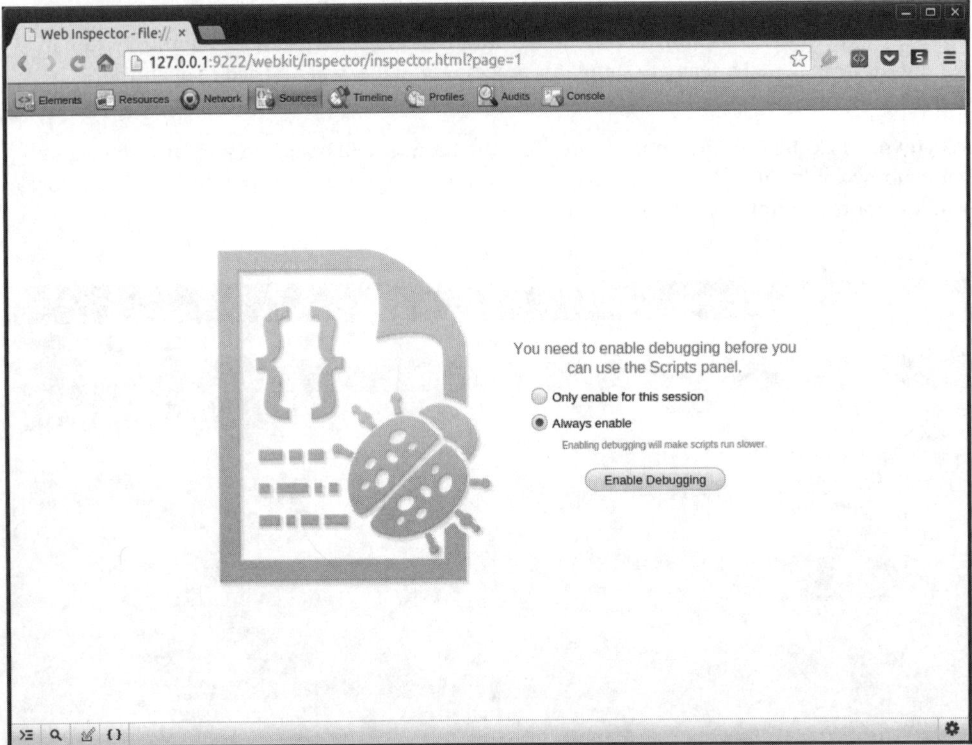

Figure 10.5 Ubuntu Web Inspector: Sources—Enabling JavaScript Debugging

At this point, the browser will open the pane shown in Figure 10.6. What you'll see is a navigator on the left that allows you to access the application's source code files, a main pane that lists the code from the selected file, and a properties pane on the right that allows you to interact with the code at runtime.

In this example, I've set some breakpoints, the symbols next to lines 32, 47, and 66 in the application's index.js file. Before the application executes one of those lines, the debugger will intercept execution so you can step through the code, evaluate expressions, view properties, and more.

When application execution is halted at a breakpoint, you use the buttons highlighted in Figure 10.7 to manage the execution of the halted code.

The Run button instructs the debugger to continue execution until the next breakpoint is encountered. The Step Over button causes the debugger to execute the subroutine, then halt at the line of code that follows the call to the subroutine. The Step Into button does the opposite: it executes the subroutine and halts execution at the first line of executable code in the

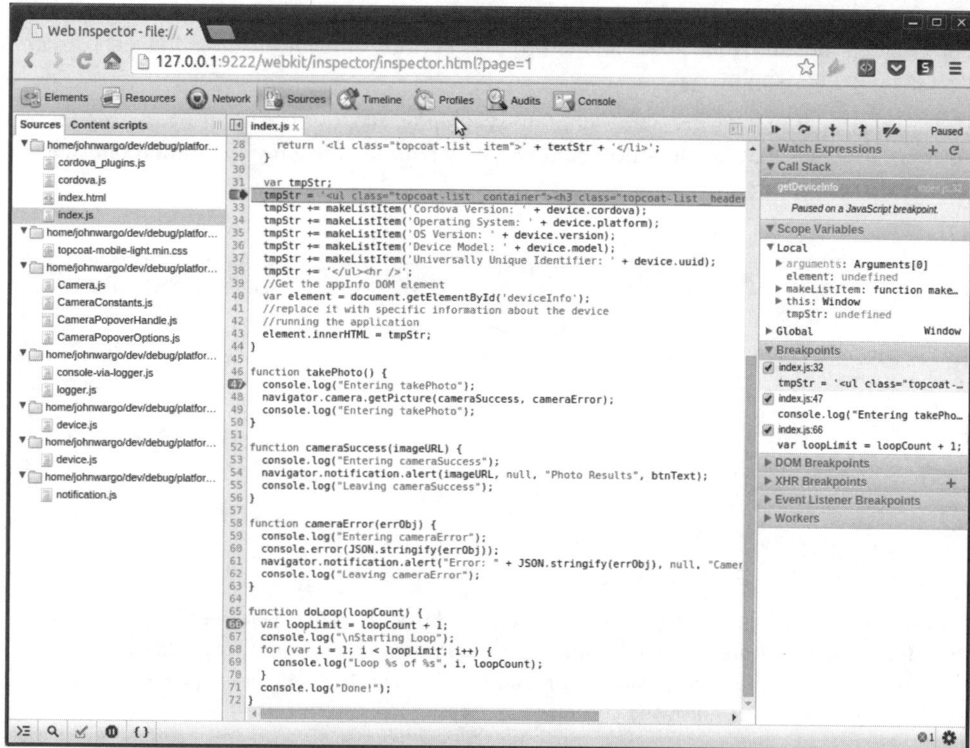

Figure 10.6 Ubuntu Web Inspector: Sources

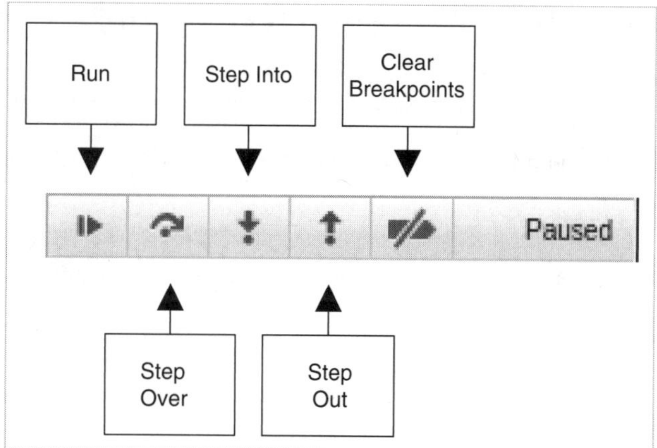

Figure 10.7 Ubuntu Web Inspector: JavaScript Source Execution Buttons

subroutine. When you're done looking at the subroutine's code, click the Step Out button to finish executing the subroutine's code and return to the calling function. To clear all breakpoints, click the Clear Breakpoints button.

The Console pane allows you to view all of the content written to the console by the application as shown in Figure 10.8. You'll notice that I've got an error in one of my application's meta tags; I've since fixed the error.

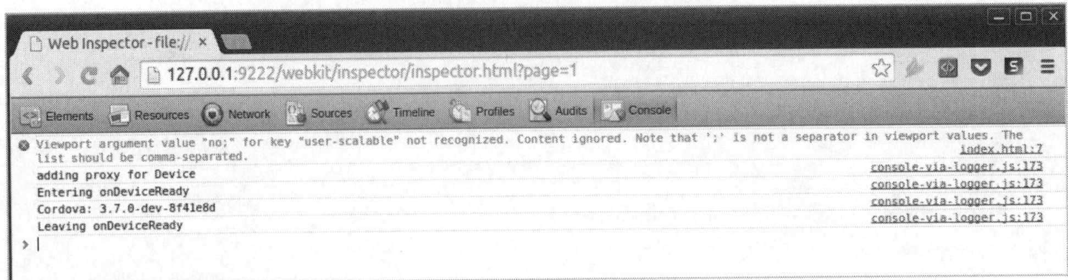

Figure 10.8 Ubuntu Web Inspector: Console

You will, of course, want to run the application on a physical device. Before you can do a build for a device, you must install a click chroot. Click chroot is a cross-compilation environment that allows you to build ARM binaries from an Intel desktop. To create one, open a terminal window and execute the following command:

```
click chroot -a armhf -f ubuntu-sdk-14.10 create
```

Be prepared to wait a while as this process takes a very long time.

You can also create a click chroot and install the Cordova build dependencies simultaneously:

```
sudo click chroot -a armhf -f ubuntu-sdk-14.10 maint apt-get install libicu-
dev:armhf qtfeedback5-dev:armhf qtpim5-dev:armhf qtsystems5-dev:armhf
```

With this in place, you can build the application for the phone using

```
cordova build --device
```

To run the application on a connected device, use the following command:

```
cordova run --device
```

To run the application on a device in debug mode, use the following:

```
cordova run --device --debug
```

The CLI will build the application, then start looking for target devices to run the application on. The folks at Canonical were nice enough to loan me a device to use for testing purposes, but I wasn't able to get it to work. Apparently there's a new version of the CLI coming that fixes the problems I encountered, but I was not able to test that version in time.

Wrap-Up

In this chapter, I showed you how to get started developing Cordova applications for the Ubuntu Touch platform. Support for Ubuntu is pretty new, so I expect to see a bunch of new capabilities coming to the tools.

11

Windows Development with Cordova

Cordova provides good support for the Windows platform, supporting Windows 8.x and Windows Phone 8.x. In this chapter, I show you how to use the Microsoft development tools to build and test Cordova applications for the Windows platform. What's unique about this chapter is that it covers smartphone as well as desktop OS development as Cordova supports both for the Windows platform. The Cordova project currently supports two Windows targets: windows (targets Windows 8, Windows 8.1, and Windows Phone 8.1) and wp8 (targets Windows Phone 8).

Windows development is done using Microsoft Visual Studio. A free version of Visual Studio is available from Microsoft and is pretty easy to use. I'll also cover some new tools from Microsoft that make cross-platform development for Cordova easier.

Windows versus WP8 Projects and Cordova

Before we get too far into this topic, I want to fill you in on how the different Windows platforms are supported by Cordova. Cordova supports Windows Phone 8 as well as another platform Cordova calls simply windows. You're creating a project for Windows Phone 8 when you issue the following Cordova CLI command:

```
cordova platform add wp8
```

When you open the project in Visual Studio, you'll see something similar to what is shown in Figure 11.1.

Notice that the Cordova project (the Debug.csproj file shown in the figure) is a C# project. Even though the default project type in Visual Studio for Windows Phone 8 applications was a JavaScript project, for Windows Phone 8 on Cordova, the development team implemented the Cordova container as a C# application instead. What this means for Cordova developers is that you won't be able to use the JavaScript debugging capabilities of Visual Studio to debug your

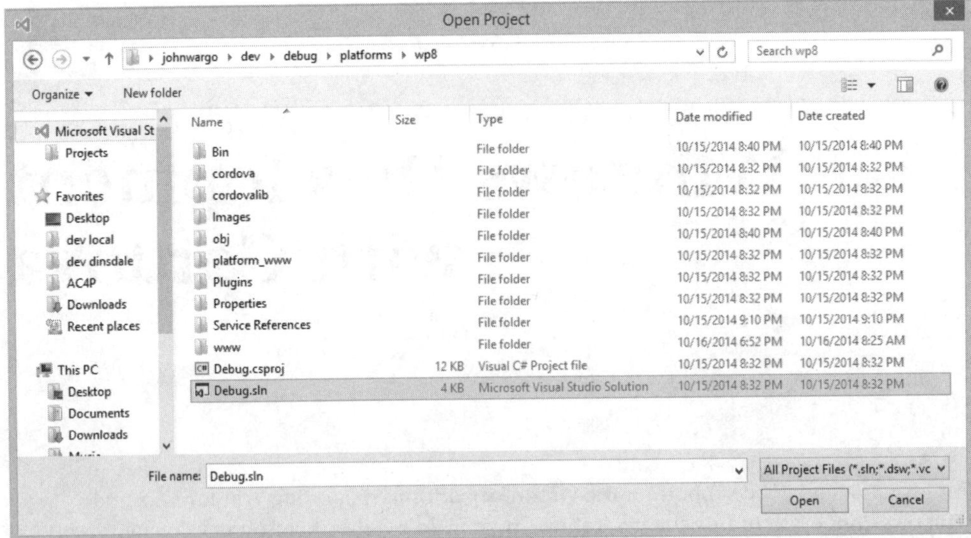

Figure 11.1 Visual Studio: Opening a Cordova Windows Phone 8 Project

application. Instead, you'll have to use something like weinre (described in Chapter 5, "The Mechanics of Cordova Development") to debug your applications.

Microsoft has since shifted to a universal app approach (http://goo.gl/d5suuO) for Windows applications that allows you to support multiple Windows targets for a single project. The Cordova windows platform creates a universal Windows app project for your Cordova application when you use the CLI to add a platform to your project using the following command:

```
cordova platform add windows
```

The project will support both Windows 8 and Windows 8.1 (desktop operating systems) as well as Windows Phone 8.1. When you open the project in Visual Studio, you will see a dialog similar to the one shown in Figure 11.2.

In this example, notice that there are multiple projects in the platform folder and they're all JavaScript projects. The CordovaApp.Phone.jsproj is the project file for the Windows Phone 8.1 project, and the other .jsproj files are for Windows 8.1 desktop (CordovaApp.Windows.jsproj) and Windows 8 desktop (CordovaApp.Windows80.jsproj).

For these projects, you'll be able to leverage the JavaScript debugging capabilities of Visual Studio to help troubleshoot your Cordova applications. I'll show you more about how those work later in the chapter.

You're going to select the target platforms for your application based on the specific requirements for your application, but there's a huge difference between the debugging capabilities

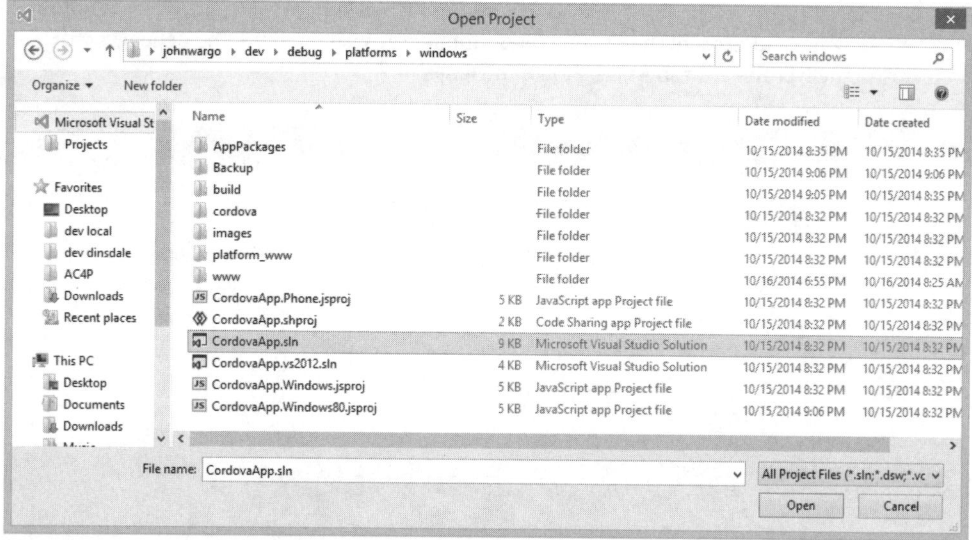

Figure 11.2 Visual Studio: Opening a Cordova Windows 8 Project

available to Cordova Windows 8.1 projects and what's available for Windows Phone 8 applications. I am going to cover only the Cordova windows platform support in this chapter as I imagine the Cordova team will drop support for Windows Phone 8 sometime soon.

Windows Phone Limitations and Security Restrictions

Now that you understand a bit about the different platform options available to you, I need to let you know about some limitations of running Cordova applications on the Windows platform.

JavaScript `alert` Not Supported

As you know, I use the JavaScript `alert` method in my applications to help me troubleshoot problems with the applications. Cordova fails silently when there's a JavaScript error in an application, so while doing initial testing of an application, I always put in a call to `alert` just so I can tell that the web application body has loaded:

```
function onBodyLoad() {
  console.log("Entering onBodyLoad");
  alert("onBodyLoad fired");
  document.addEventListener("deviceready", onDeviceReady, false);
}
```

Well, that doesn't work as the JavaScript `alert` method is not supported in universal Windows apps. When you try to execute the `onBodyLoad` function in Visual Studio, the debugger will wake up and deliver the error message shown in Figure 11.3.

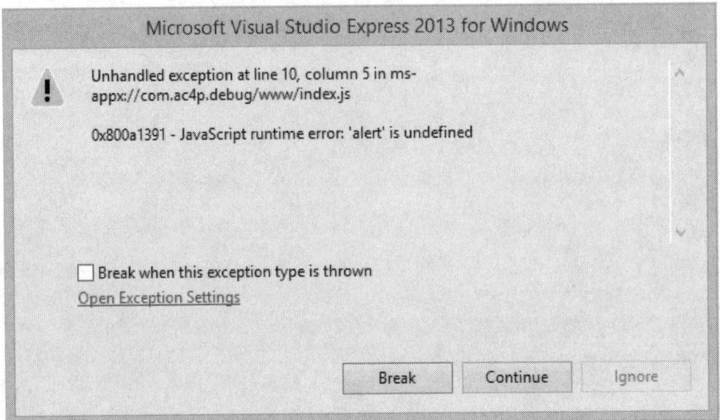

Figure 11.3 JavaScript Error Executing `alert`

Microsoft's answer on this topic is that a Windows app is not a browser, and `alert` is a function of the browser. Microsoft suggests that you use the `MessageDialog` class described at http://goo.gl/AeAD4X, and this book's technical reviewer, Ashwin Desai, gave me the following example:

```
function myAlert(message) {
  if (typeof (Windows) !== 'undefined') {
    new Windows.UI.Popups.MessageDialog(message, 'Alert').showAsync().done();
  } else {
    alert(message);
  }
}
```

Application Security Model Limitations

Because Windows, more than any other mobile platform, is heavily used in corporate environments, Microsoft has implemented a suite of security enhancements that are designed to protect customers from malicious software. On Windows 8.1, Cordova creates a universal Windows app based on the Visual Studio JavaScript template for Windows Store apps. For these apps, the Cordova app does not contain a WebView; instead, the app's web content runs in the WWAHost process on the device. The WWAHost process implements a sandbox around the web application content, and that causes some issues for dynamic Cordova applications. You can read about some of the restrictions at http://goo.gl/z75Oor.

The biggest impact on Cordova developers seems to be from third-party JavaScript libraries trying to inject dynamic content into a Cordova application. To help accommodate developers using these tools, Microsoft released the JavaScript Dynamic Content shim for Windows Store apps which can be found at http://goo.gl/pWTGyu. All you need to do is add a reference to the shim's JavaScript file, winstore-jscompat.js, toward the beginning of your Cordova application's code (before any other scripts are loaded or executed), and it will relax the manner in which checks are performed by the WebView.

Many of these restrictions are expected to go away with Windows 10.

Windows Development System Requirements

Before we start talking about the tools, it's important to understand a bit about the development environment you will need to create Windows applications for Apache Cordova. The Cordova team recently dropped support for Windows 7 and Windows Phone 7 applications, so you can really only create Windows 8.x applications using the current version of Apache Cordova.

The Android developer tools will run on Windows 7 or Windows 8, and for iOS development you must have a system running Macintosh OS X. In order to develop applications for the latest version of Windows, you will need to have a system running Windows 8 (you can build Windows 8 apps on Windows 8; you'll need to be running Windows 8.1 in order to build apps for Windows 8.1).

As a developer, you have several options. You can use two systems—one running Windows 8.1 and the other running OS X—or you can run both environments on an OS X system using virtualization software like VMware Fusion. You can install Xcode and the iOS development tools on the OS X system, install the Android tools on either OS X or Windows, then install the Microsoft tools on the Windows 8.1 system. Understand, though, that there's no way to configure one developer workstation and a single OS for Cordova development for all of the supported platforms. If you add Ubuntu Touch development to the mix, described in Chapter 10, "Ubuntu Development with Cordova," you'll need yet another OS (physical or virtual) to develop applications.

For this book, I did most of the development on a Mac Mini and did all of my Windows testing on separate VMware Fusion VMs running on the Mini. One VM ran Windows 7 and another Windows 8.1 (both legal licenses, of course). I installed the iOS, Android, and Firefox OS tools on the OS X partition and Android, Firefox OS, and Windows tools on the Windows virtual machines.

The problem with Windows Phone development, though, is that the device simulators have some pretty hefty requirements. When I wrote *PhoneGap Essentials*, I couldn't even get the simulators to run in a VM; I had to do all of my Windows Phone development on one of my lab machines. For this book, I was able to configure the virtual environment so that the simulators will run. Microsoft provides some pretty detailed instructions for how to configure VMware Fusion to run Visual Studio and the device simulators at http://goo.gl/fqms6P. Unfortunately, those instructions are for when you're creating a brand-new Windows 8.1 VM in Fusion; for my development environment, the VMs already existed, so I had to refer to the article at http://goo.gl/aBuJ7d for information on how to make the necessary changes to an existing VM. Either way, problem quickly solved; thanks, Microsoft!

Windows Phone Development Tools

To build Cordova applications for Windows 8.x, you will need to install Microsoft Visual Studio. For developing Windows Phone applications, you'll need the Windows Phone SDK. There are different versions of Visual Studio available to you. Visual Studio Express is free and includes the tools you need to create Windows Phone applications. You can download Visual Studio Express from the Windows Phone Dev Center located at http://goo.gl/FeXc2r. Download the software and install it on your development workstation, running Windows 8.1, of course. When you launch Visual Studio for the first time, you will be prompted to register with Microsoft for a free developer license as shown in Figure 11.4.

Figure 11.4 Microsoft Visual Studio—Get a Developer License for Windows 8.1

To obtain a license, you'll have to have an existing Microsoft account or create a new one. If you don't have one, don't worry—the account is free; all you'll need to do is register to get one. After you have logged in with your Microsoft account, Visual Studio will obtain a license, then display the confirmation dialog shown in Figure 11.5. At this point, Visual Studio Express is installed and all ready to go.

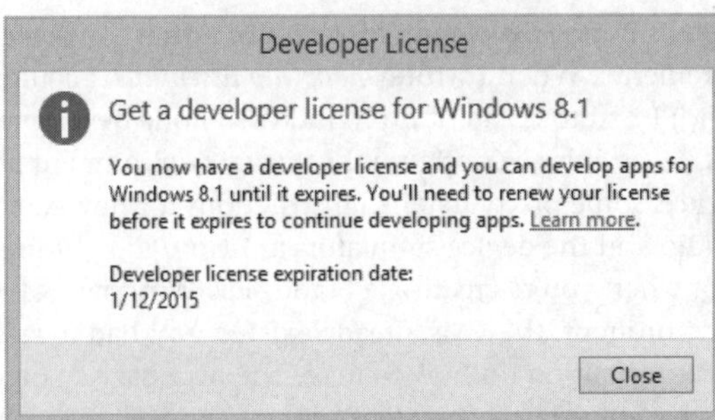

Figure 11.5 Microsoft Visual Studio—Developer License Confirmation

Another option is to use the commercially licensed Visual Studio Professional. You may wonder why you would want to use the Professional version of Visual Studio when the Express edition is free; that's because the hybrid development tools Microsoft provides work only with Visual Studio Professional (today). To use Visual Studio Professional, you'll need to acquire a license, then install the software on your development system.

Windows App Store Setup

Next, there are some administrative steps you must follow in order to be able to deploy Windows Phone applications into the Windows Phone Store or onto a physical device. To help you get started with the process, take a look at "How to Deploy and Run an App for Windows Phone 8" on Microsoft's web site at http://goo.gl/AoSCk6.

First you'll need to create a Microsoft account. Accounts are free and can be obtained at https://signup.live.com. Next, you'll need to register as a member of the Windows Phone Dev Center at https://dev.windowsphone.com/join. Joining the program isn't free, but it doesn't cost that much. With your registration, you get the ability to deploy your applications to a physical device and into the Windows App Store.

Configuring a Windows Phone Device for Application Testing

The Visual Studio development environment allows you to easily deploy and test Windows Phone applications onto a Windows Phone emulator. However, you should always test your Cordova applications on a physical device before publishing them to an app store. For Windows Phone development, before you can test your applications on a physical device, you must first register the device for development with Microsoft. The registration process is pretty simple; you can find Microsoft's instructions for the process at http://goo.gl/NloJmR.

To register a Windows Phone device, first you will need to power on the device and connect it to your Windows 8 desktop via a USB cable. Since each registered device has to have a unique name, open Windows Explorer on your desktop system and change the name of the device to something you know is unique, perhaps using your initials in the device name as shown in Figure 11.6.

In Windows 8 or later, bring up the All Apps view and under Windows Phone 8 SDK open the item labeled Windows Phone Developer Registration. You will see a screen similar to the one shown in Figure 11.7.

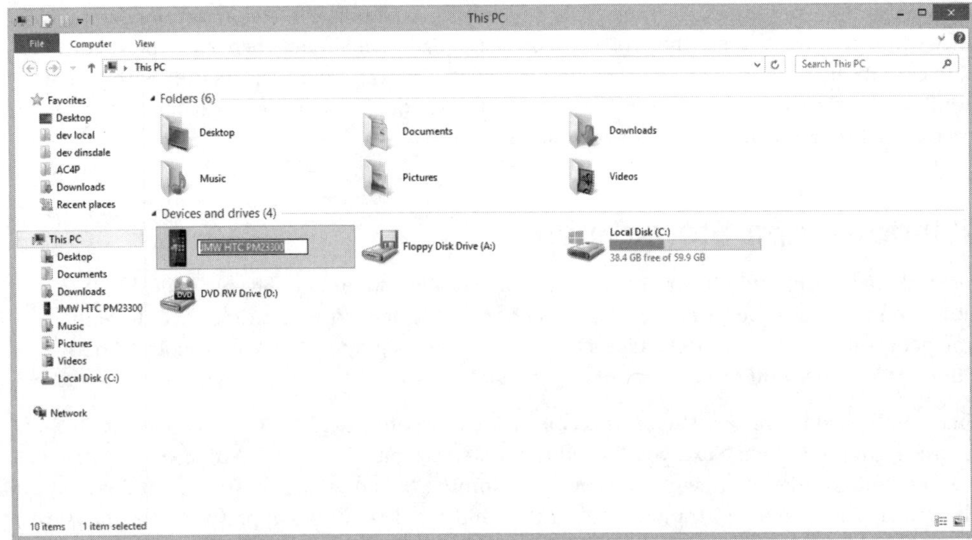

Figure 11.6 Setting a Windows Phone Device Name in Windows Explorer

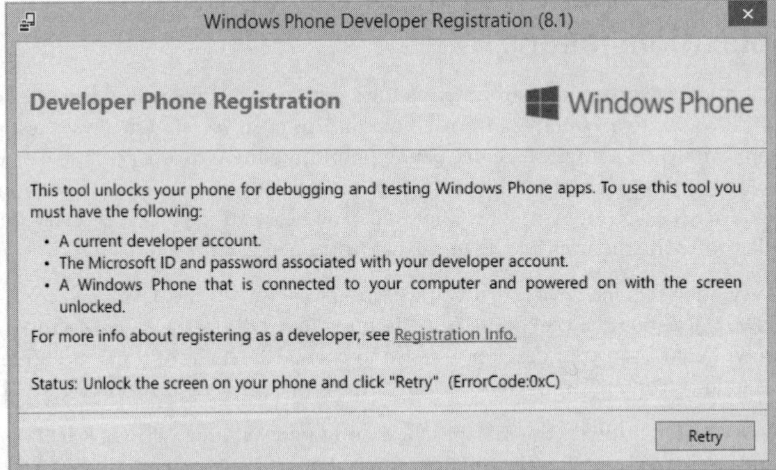

Figure 11.7 Windows Phone Developer Registration: Locked Device

In this example, my Windows Phone device is locked, so I have to unlock the device and click the Retry button to allow it to connect to the device. With this completed, you should see a screen similar to the one shown in Figure 11.8.

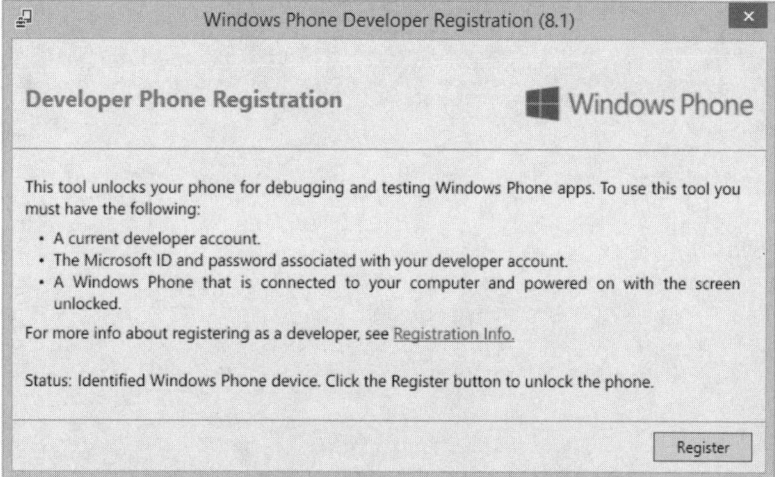

Figure 11.8 Windows Phone Developer Registration: Connected Device

When you click the Register button, you will be prompted to log in with your Microsoft account. Once you are logged in, you will see the screen shown in Figure 11.9. At this point, the device is registered with Microsoft and can be used to test your Windows applications.

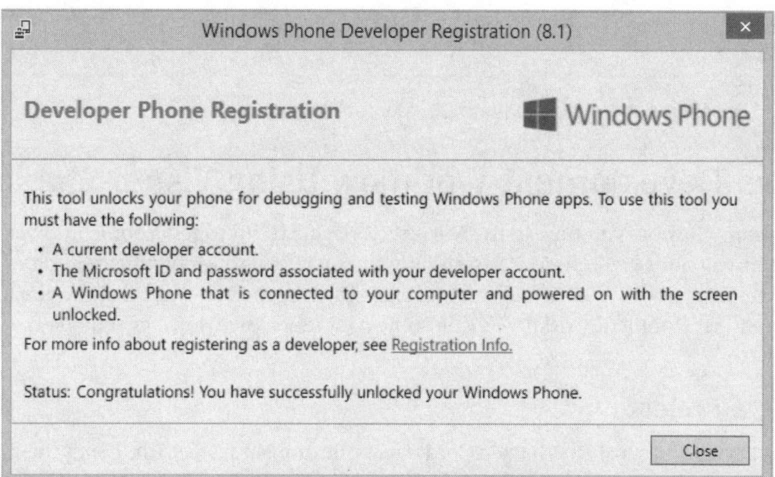

Figure 11.9 Windows Phone Developer Registration Completed

You can manage your registered devices from the Account summary page of the Windows Phone Dev Center located at http://goo.gl/kKbXmb as shown in Figure 11.10. Microsoft allows you to register only three devices for development, so if you have to support testing an application across a wide range of devices, you may be spending a lot of time on this page. To remove a registered device, click the Remove link to the right of the device you wish to remove.

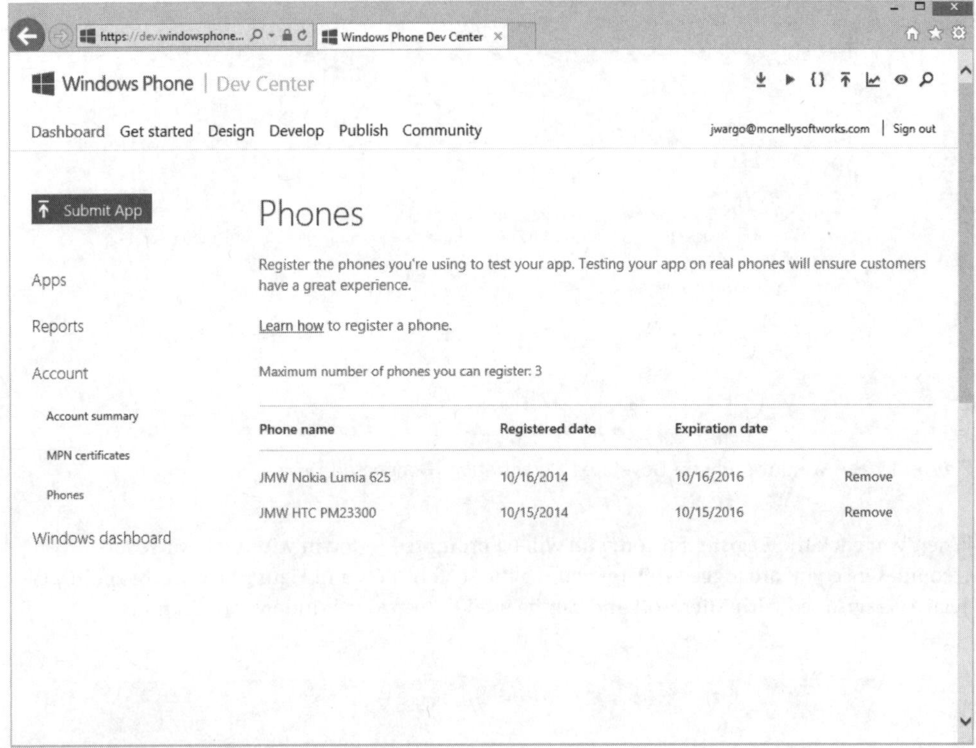

Figure 11.10 Microsoft Windows Phone Dev Center Phones Page

Cordova Development Workflow Using Visual Studio

In this section, I'll show you how to use Microsoft Visual Studio to test your Cordova applications. The instructions given here are essentially the same regardless of whether you're running Visual Studio Express or Visual Studio Professional. Later in the chapter, I'll show you a dramatically different development workflow using some cool tools Microsoft has provided.

Creating a Project

Before you begin, you must first have a Cordova application to work with. Using the Lunch Menu application example I've shown elsewhere in this book, create a new Cordova application project by opening a terminal window, navigating to the folder where you want the project created, then issuing the following commands:

```
cordova create lunchmenu com.ac4p.lunchmenu "Lunch Menu"
cd lunchmenu
cordova platform add windows
cordova platform add wp8
```

In this case, I've created the Lunch Menu application and added both universal Windows app (`windows`) and Windows Phone 8 (`wp8`) platforms to the project. I've added the platforms through separate commands just for demonstration purposes; I could just as easily have added both platforms in a single command using

```
cordova platform add windows wp8
```

At this point, you'll have a Cordova project all ready to be opened in Visual Studio so you can test the application. You'll be able to run the Windows application directly from Visual Studio. For the Windows Phone application, you'll be able to run the application on device simulators or physical devices connected to the development system (properly registered, of course, as described in the previous section).

When working with Windows applications, as with all other Cordova projects, you'll be editing the web application code for your project in the project's www folder—be sure to execute the `cordova prepare` command before trying to work with the project in Visual Studio:

```
cordova prepare
```

The CLI will copy the web content over into the platforms/wp8/www and platforms/windows/www folders. You can see an example of the files that are created in Figure 11.11.

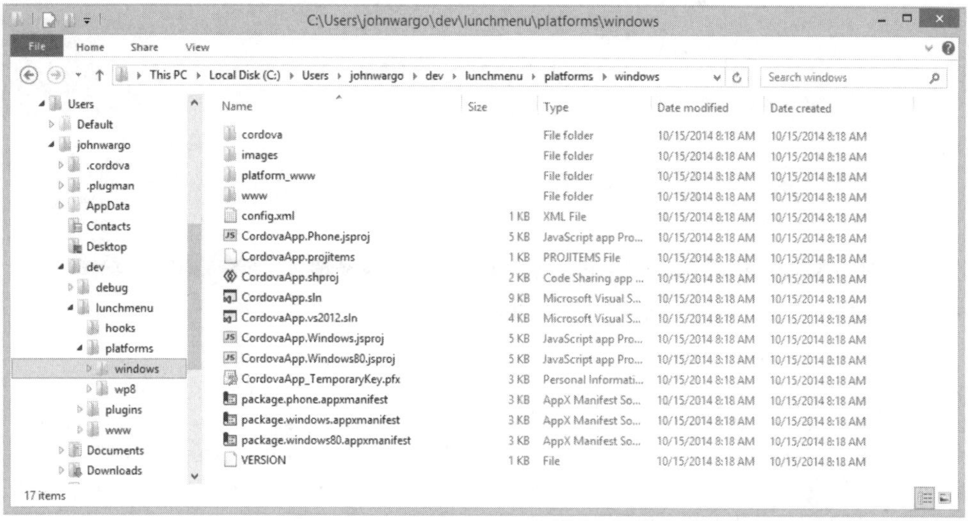

Figure 11.11 Cordova Windows Phone 8 Platform Folder

For the remainder of this section, I will focus on universal Windows app development using Visual Studio. The steps are essentially the same for Windows Phone 8 applications, except for the debugging capabilities I will show.

Opening a Cordova Project

Now that you have created a Cordova project for Windows Phone 8, open Visual Studio. When the development environment opens, it will display a screen similar to the one shown in Figure 11.12.

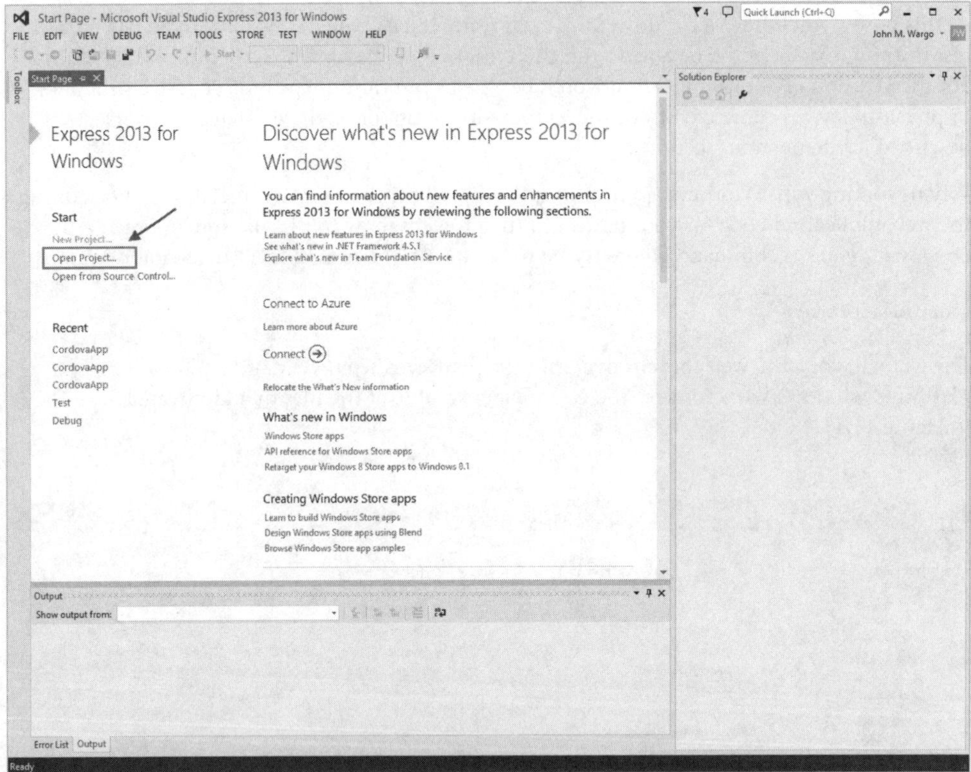

Figure 11.12 Visual Studio Express 2013 Startup Page

To open the Cordova project, click the Open Project link shown on the left of Figure 11.12, or open the File menu and select Open Project. Visual Studio will display the Open Project dialog shown in Figures 11.1 and 11.2 (depending on which platform you will be working with). Select the Microsoft Visual Studio Solution file (the file with the.sln extension) as shown in the figures and click the Open button to continue.

For some reason, the default Windows solution has the Windows 8 project selected as the default startup project. Because of this, when you open a Windows 8 solution in Visual Studio 2013, you may be prompted to upgrade the project as shown in Figure 11.13.

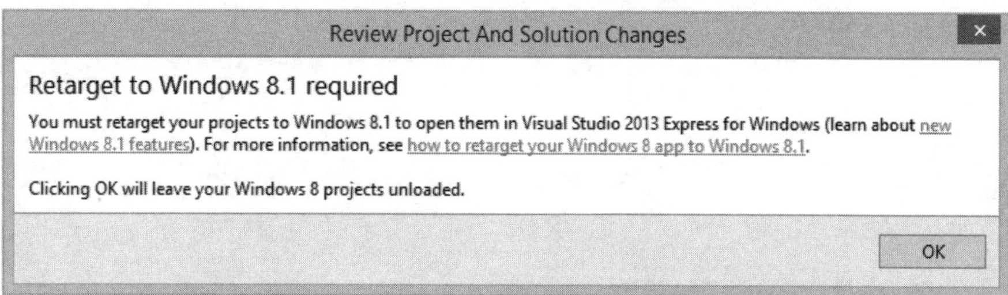

Figure 11.13 Visual Studio 2013: Retarget to Windows 8.1

Since that project is targeted at Windows 8, you really won't want to retarget it to Windows 8.1. You can open the project in an older version of Visual Studio in order to build the project for Windows 8. The project already has Windows 8.1 and Windows Phone 8.1 projects, so you can get around this warning by right-clicking one of those projects and selecting Set as StartUp Project as shown in Figure 11.14. That will change the default project and eliminate the warning.

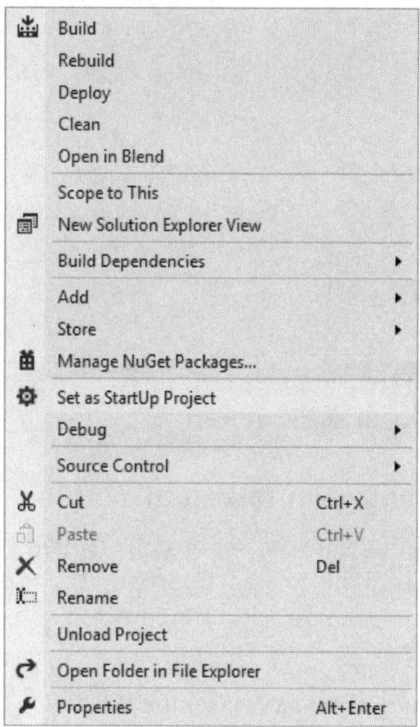

Figure 11.14 Visual Studio 2013: Project Options Menu

When the project opens, the Solution Explorer will show you all of the files in the project as shown in the right side of Figure 11.15. From here you can open the different web content files generated by the CLI; keep in mind, though, that the files shown here are copied from the Cordova project's www folder. Any changes you make to the web application content here will need to be copied back to the Cordova project's www folder before they can be applied to other platform projects. In this example, I've opened the Windows Phone 8 project's index.js file and set some breakpoints.

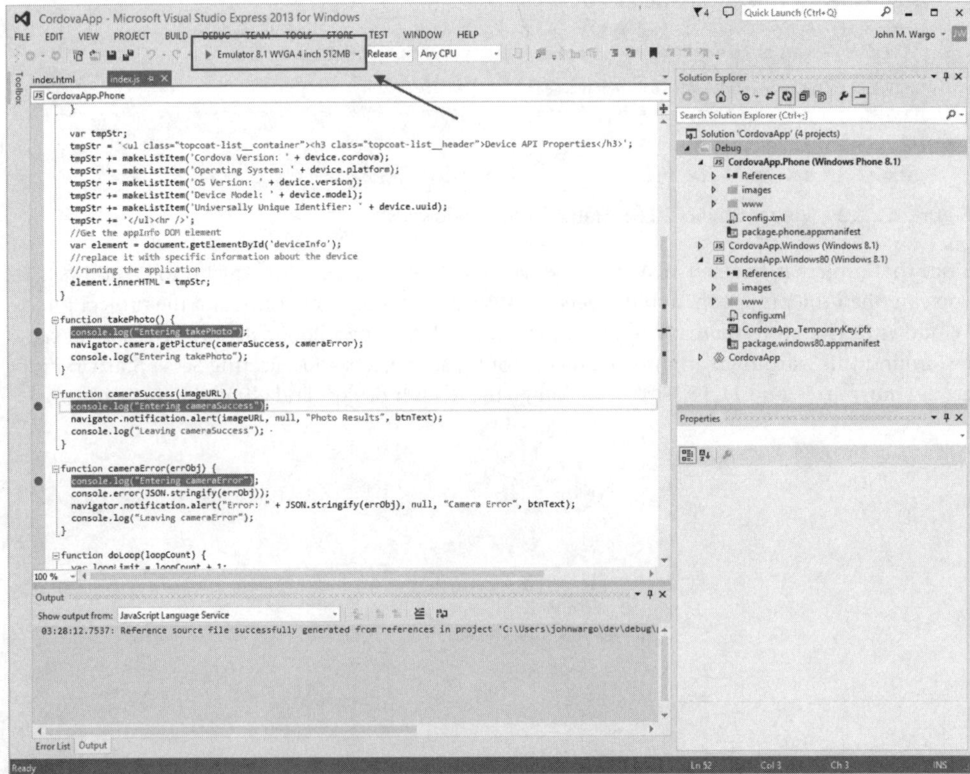

Figure 11.15 Visual Studio 2013: Solution Files

Running a Cordova Application in Visual Studio

To test applications in Visual Studio, use the options highlighted at the top of Figure 11.15. Click the Play symbol to the left of the device name to run the application. The drop-down list to the right of the Play icon allows you to select the emulator or a physical device where the application will run.

To run the application on a physical device, make sure the device is powered on, unlocked, and connected to the development system using a USB cable. When running on an emulator, the emulator window will open, start the emulated OS, and run the application as shown in Figure 11.16. The emulator looks and works like a regular device. You can swipe, click, and work with the application just as you would on a physical device.

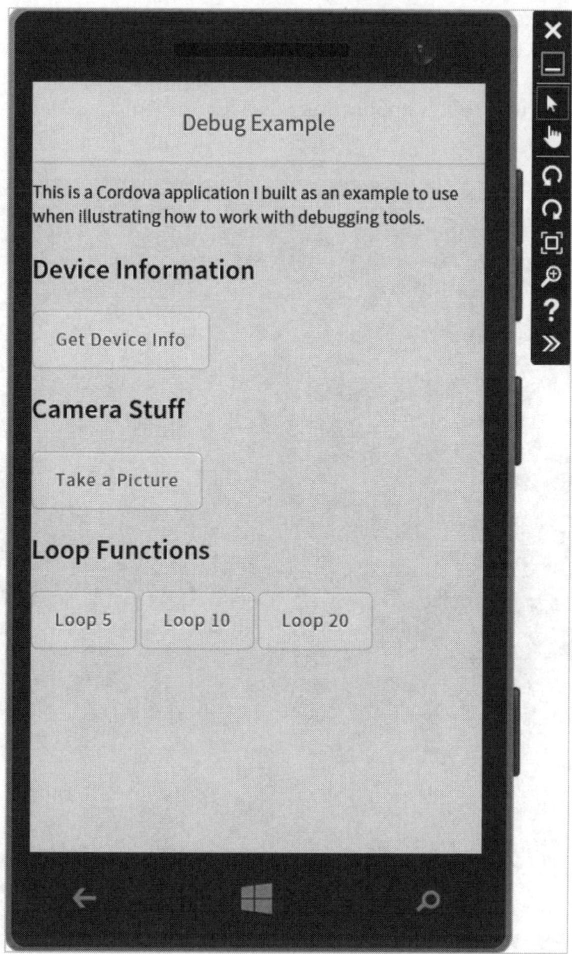

Figure 11.16 Windows Phone 8 Emulator

Controlling the Windows Phone Emulator

The icons to the right of the figure provide developers with some additional control over the emulator. You can change the orientation of the device, expand the size of the emulated device, or change the zoom level. The double bracket (>>) at the bottom of the list is used to open an Additional Tools window that provides the developer with some additional capabilities for manipulating the emulator. I'm going to cover only a few here; poke around in the emulator to see what else it can do.

The Accelerometer pane of the Additional Tools window is shown in Figure 11.17; it allows a developer to manipulate the orientation of the emulator along three axes. You can hold the primary mouse button down over the dot in the middle of the device image and move it around to position the emulated device. You can also select preset orientations or play back recorded orientation changes. This is a simple way to test mobile applications that leverage the accelerometer and an excellent way to test applications that use the Cordova Device Motion API.

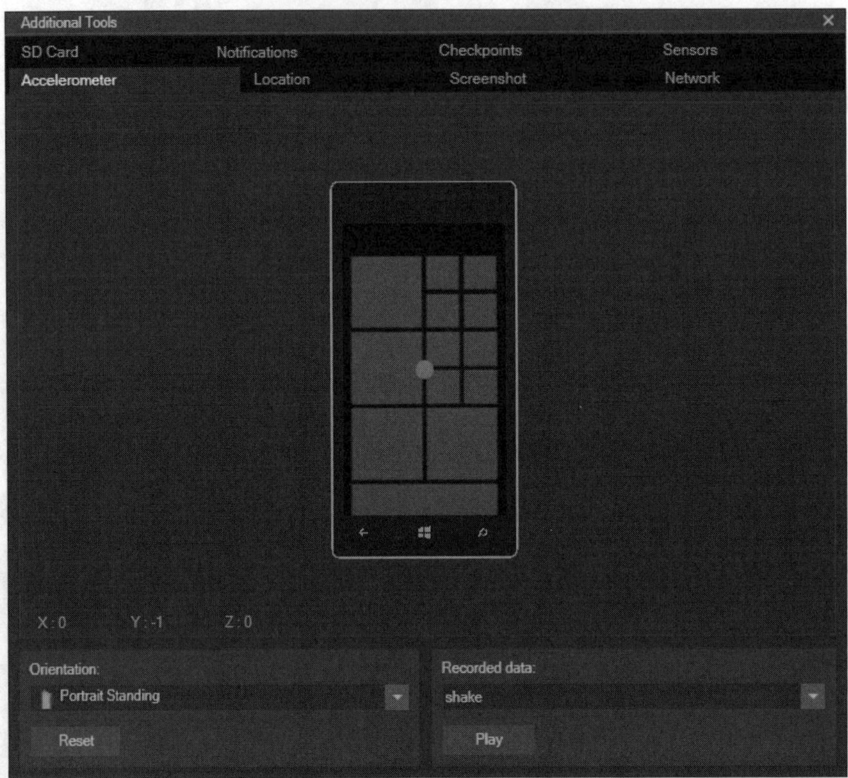

Figure 11.17 Emulator Additional Tools: Accelerometer

Figure 11.18 shows the Location pane; from here you can manipulate the emulator's location. You can search for a specific location or address and push it into the emulated device's GPS coordinates. You can also play back recorded trips. This is a simple way to test mobile applications that leverage the device's geolocation capabilities and an excellent way to test applications that use the Cordova Device Orientation (Compass) API.

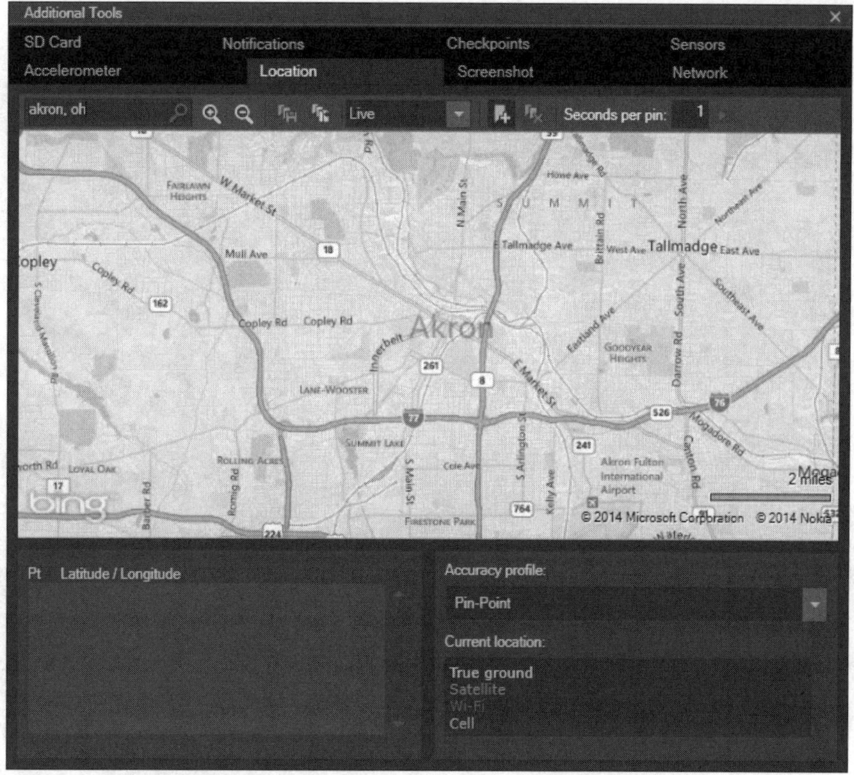

Figure 11.18 Emulator Additional Tools: Location

When writing documentation for your application, you can easily grab device screen shots using options in the Screenshot pane shown in Figure 11.19.

Capture a screen shot by clicking the Capture button, then save the file to disk using the Save button.

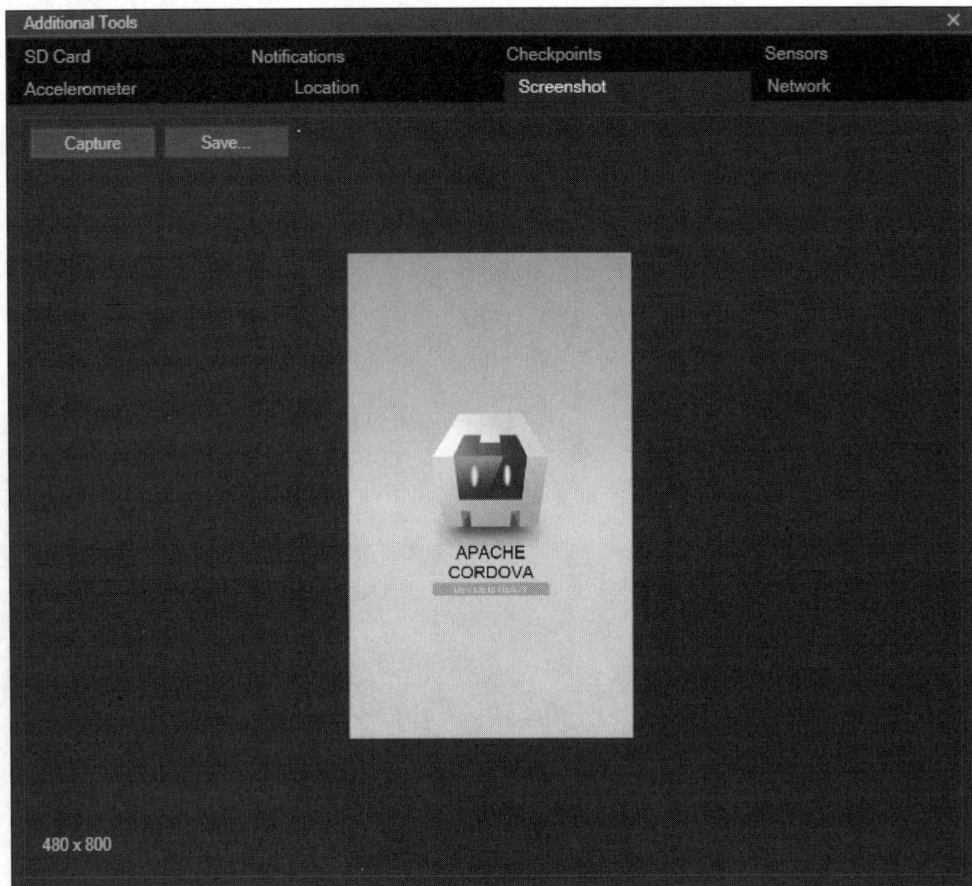

Figure 11.19 Emulator Additional Tools: Screenshot

Debugging Cordova Applications Using Visual Studio

Microsoft Visual Studio offers a robust set of debugging capabilities. Since a Cordova project for the windows platform is a universal Windows app project and the default application type for universal Windows apps is a JavaScript project, the debugging capabilities of Visual Studio can be leveraged. As a developer, you'll have full access to all the developer and debugging tools Visual Studio offers. And, when I talk about the Visual Studio Tools for Apache Cordova later in the chapter, you'll see that Microsoft has figured out how to apply these tools to Android and iOS projects as well.

When you open a source file in Visual Studio, you can click in the margin to set breakpoints in the application's JavaScript code as shown in Figure 11.20. Then, while the application is running in a simulator or on a physical device, when the application hits one of those breakpoints, the application will halt and you can use capabilities of the Visual Studio debugger to step through the code, set watches, view the contents of local variables, and more.

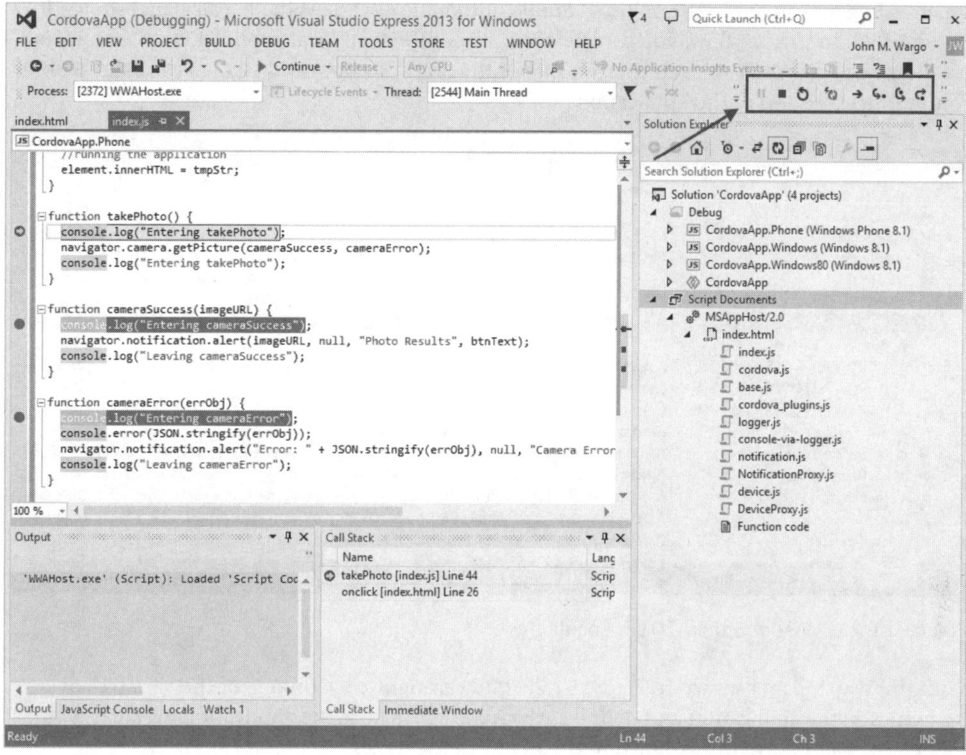

Figure 11.20 Visual Studio 2013: Debugging Session

When the application halts when it hits a breakpoint, you can use the debugging controls highlighted in the upper-right corner of Figure 11.20 to control how the application runs from there. Figure 11.21 describes the purpose of each control.

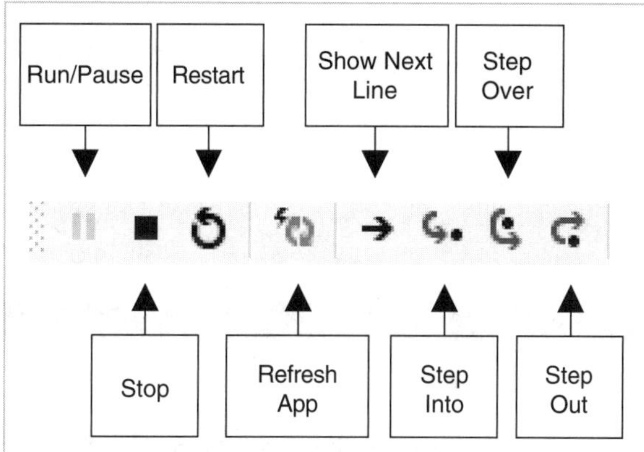

Figure 11.21 Visual Studio 2013: Debugging Controls

When debugging an application, Visual Studio automatically opens the Locals panel shown in Figure 11.22. In this window, you can view the properties of all local application objects, including global objects. You can even click on one of the object's values and change the value before continuing execution of the application.

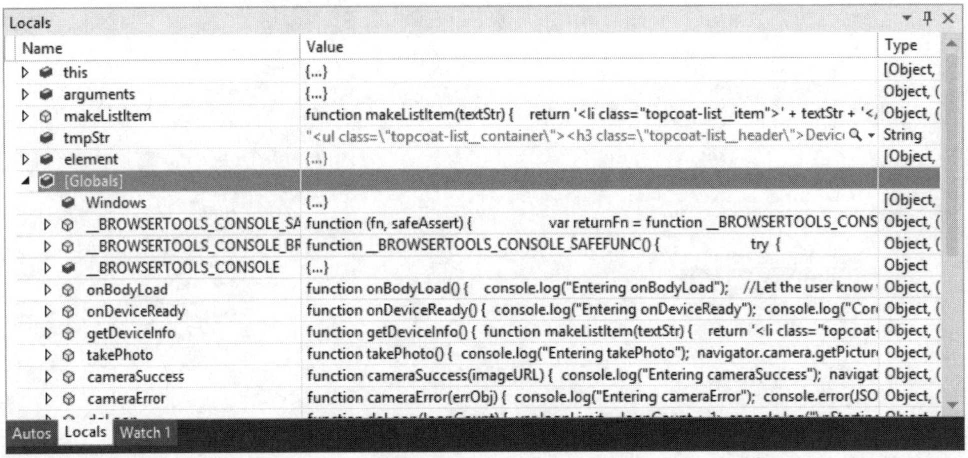

Figure 11.22 Visual Studio 2013: Locals Panel

With the Watch panel shown in Figure 11.23, you can right-click on one of the variables or properties in the application and define a watch for it. Then, as the application executes, you can see the value currently assigned to the object in the panel.

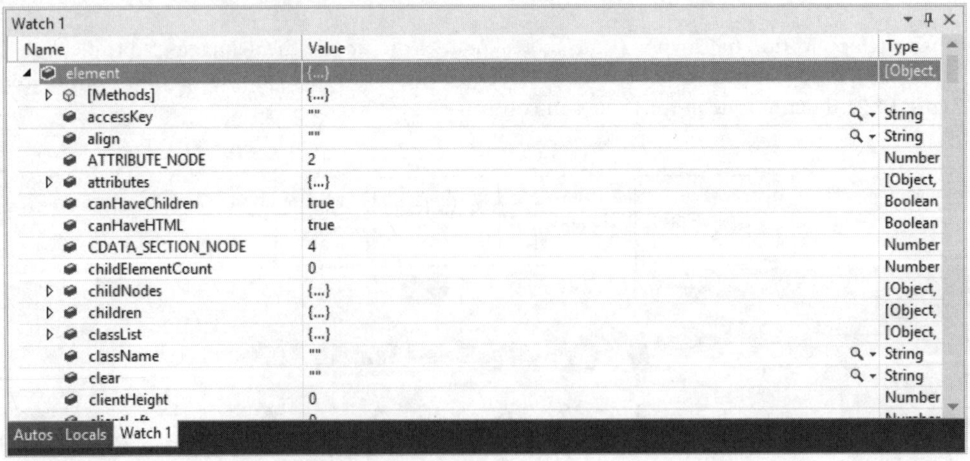

Figure 11.23 Visual Studio 2013: Watch 1 Panel

There's a lot more you can do with the debugging capabilities of Visual Studio; as this is a book on Apache Cordova and not Visual Studio, I'll leave it up to you to dig more into the capabilities. For more information, see Mario Hewardt, *Advanced .NET Debugging* (Boston: Addison-Wesley, 2009), and Mario Hewardt, *Advanced .NET Debugging LiveLessons* (Boston: Addison-Wesley, 2011).

Using Visual Studio Tools for Apache Cordova

Now that I've shown you the out-of-the-box capabilities of the Microsoft Windows development tools you can use with your Cordova applications, it's time to show you some tools Microsoft has produced that are specially tailored for Cordova applications.

A while back, Microsoft announced the Multi-Device Hybrid Apps Extension (MDHAE) for Visual Studio; the tools are still in beta, but they're cool enough and functional enough that I can cover them here. The tools are currently in Community Preview 2, and I'm not sure whether they will be released by the time you read this. I'm pretty excited about these tools as they solve a lot of problems for Cordova developers and they're from Microsoft of all places, a company that is well known for its professional-grade development tools.

> **Note**
>
> After I wrote this, Microsoft renamed the plugin to Visual Studio Tools for Apache Cordova and released Community Preview 3. Some of the options described herein may have changed by the time you read this.

You can read more about the tools at http://goo.gl/5S4lOR. Go to that link or search the Internet for "Microsoft Multi-Device Hybrid" to download the installer. I'll describe how to install and use the tools in this section, but you can also find details, and perhaps another perspective, at http://goo.gl/dtMq2C.

Visual Studio runs only on Microsoft Windows (today), and the extension works only with the commercial license for Visual Studio (not Express). So you will be able to install this extension only on Windows and only after you have already installed a working version of a compatible version of Visual Studio Professional. Once you've downloaded the extension, launch the installer and follow the prompts to install it on your development workstation.

One of the most interesting aspects of the extension for Cordova developers is that it installs a complete, functional Cordova development environment along with the extension. When you start the installation, one of the first things you'll see, after agreeing to the license terms, is the dialog shown in Figure 11.24. Notice that Ant, Git, Java, Node, the Android SDK, and more are preselected for installation. This essentially makes everything I covered in Chapter 3, "Configuring a Cordova Development Environment," obsolete.

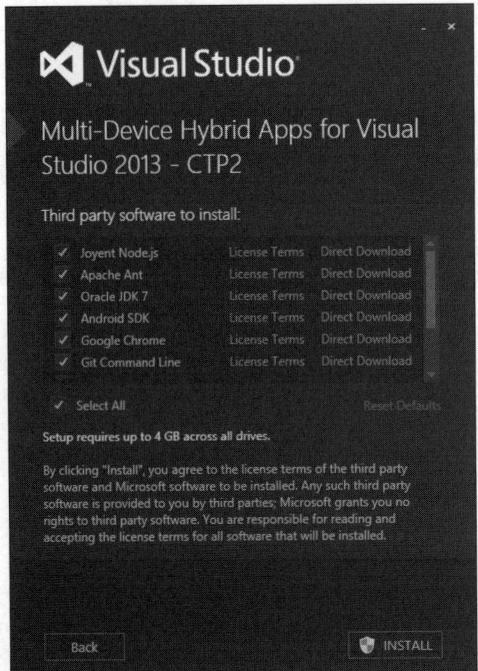

Figure 11.24 Multi-Device Hybrid Apps Extension Installation: Default Settings

Now, before you go off and rip out everything you did in Chapter 3, let me explain the implications of this. The MDHAE installation installs all of this stuff because it needs all of the tools in order to do what it does. It also installs a copy of the Cordova CLI, but it installs an older copy of the CLI than you may have installed in Chapter 3. So, the MDHAE components are tightly connected, and you can install them as your only Cordova developer tool chain, or you can install them alongside an existing installation of the Cordova development tools.

If you let the installer install everything as shown in the figure, you'll end up with a complete development environment that works seamlessly within Visual Studio. For my installation, I knew I wanted to use the latest version of the Cordova CLI, and I already had many of the tools installed, so I deselected the stuff I already knew I had installed as shown in Figure 11.25. Because I took a custom approach, there was some additional configuration that I had to do; I'll show you this in a little while.

Once you've completed the installation, you should have some new project options available to you in Visual Studio. To see this, open Visual Studio and create a new project by opening the File menu and selecting New. In the dialog that appears, select the JavaScript project type and you should see a new option, the Blank App (Apache Cordova) option shown in Figure 11.26.

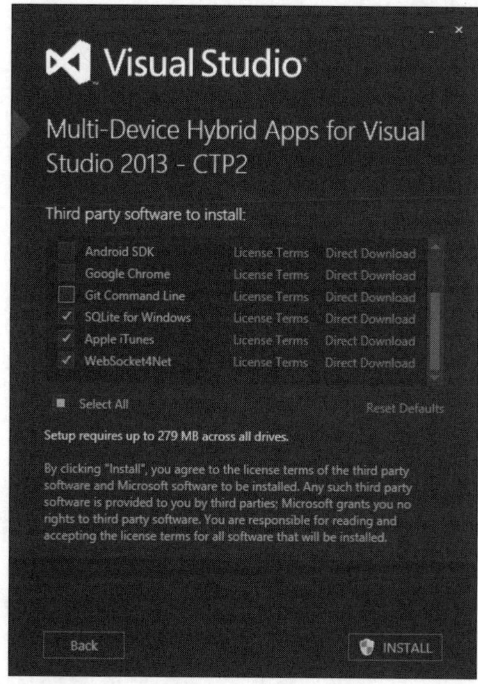

Figure 11.25 MDHAE Installation: Customized Installation

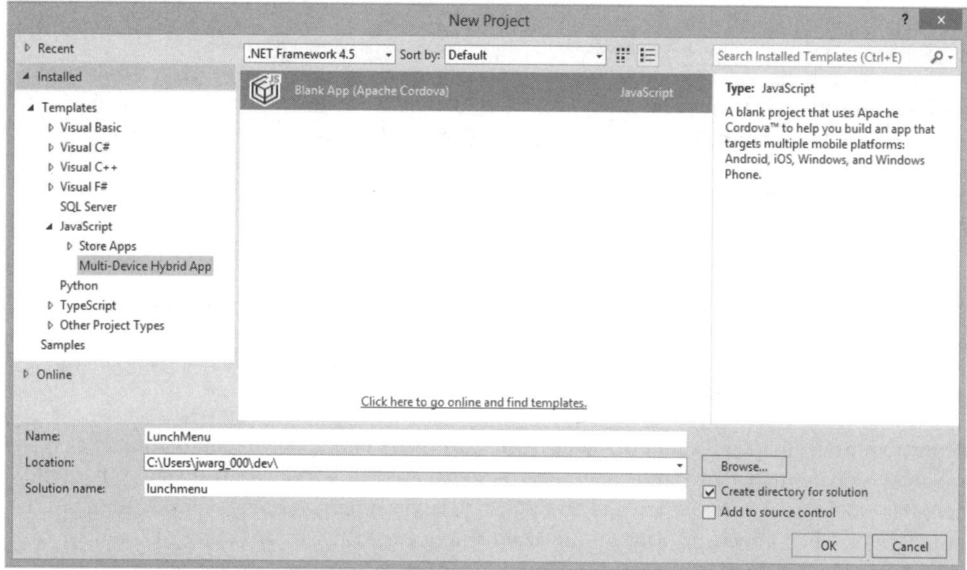

Figure 11.26 Visual Studio: New Project Dialog

Populate the project properties in the bottom of the dialog and click the OK button to create the project; Visual Studio will create the project, then open it for you.

Since I didn't allow the MDHAE to install some of the required components, as I had already installed them, Visual Studio will create the project, but when it opens the project, it will display the warning page shown in Figure 11.27. This happens because there are some additional steps that must be performed first. Remember, this is happening only because of the way I installed the tools. If you followed the default installation, you shouldn't see this warning.

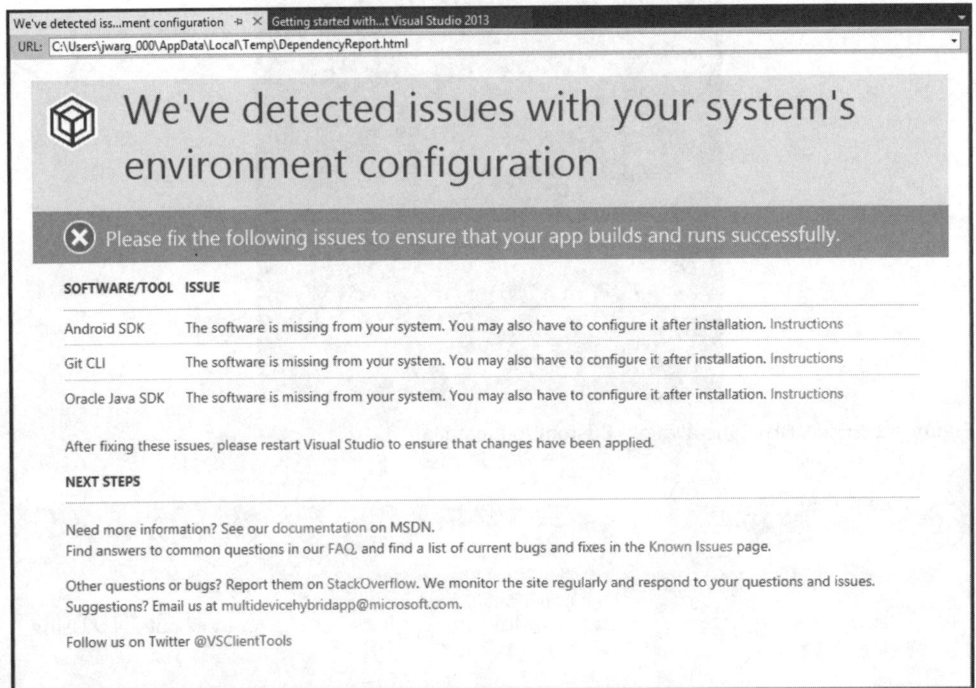

Figure 11.27 Visual Studio: MDHAE Configuration Error

It's telling me that it can't find the Android SDK, Git, and Java; I know I have those tools installed, so this can be easily fixed. After each warning message, there's a link to instructions you can follow to resolve the warning. In my case, they all led me to the Visual Studio Options dialog shown in Figure 11.28.

Remember from Chapter 3 that I had you set the `ANT_HOME` and `JAVA_HOME` environment variables. Apparently I could have added `ADT_HOME` and `GIT_HOME` variables as well. What I did here was close Visual Studio, then add an `ADT_HOME` environment variable pointing to my ADT installation. When I opened Visual Studio again and opened the Options dialog, I could see that the fix worked.

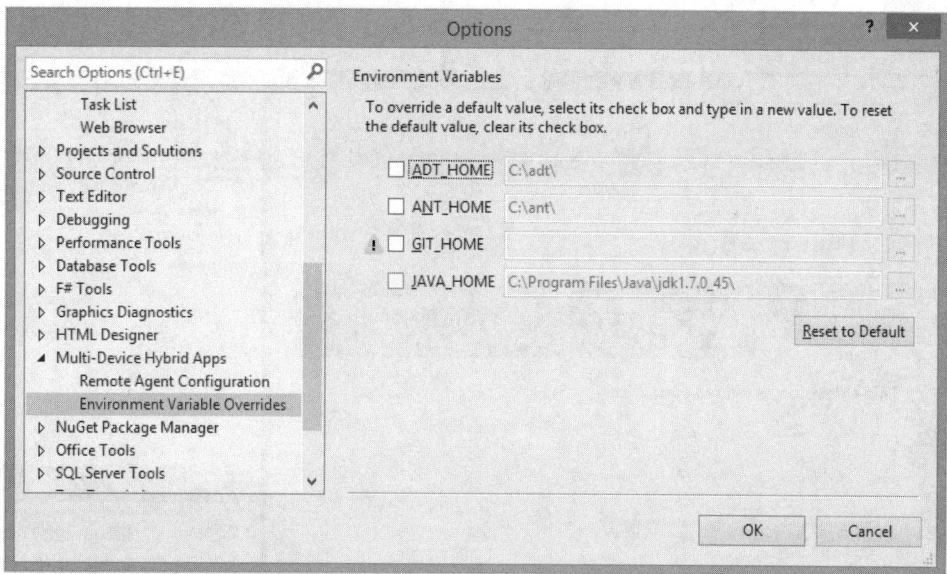

Figure 11.28 Visual Studio: Options—Environment Variables Overrides

Next, I could have done the same with a `GIT_HOME` variable, pointing it to my Git installation, or I could check the override checkbox and populate the input field with the path pointing to my Git installation.

With those changes in place, I can open Visual Studio, open the Lunch Menu application I created, and see a screen similar to the one shown in Figure 11.29. At this point, what I have is a regular Visual Studio project with some additional stuff in it that I will describe next.

The MDHAE doesn't create the standard Cordova project folder as shown in Chapter 4, "Using the Cordova Command-Line Interfaces," and Chapter 5; if you look at Figure 11.30, you'll see the project folder it created. Notice that the project doesn't have a www folder; everything is simply stored in the project folder. You do have the merges folder, though, and, although I didn't test it, you could probably add a hooks folder (described in Chapter 6, "Automation and the Cordova CLI") here as well.

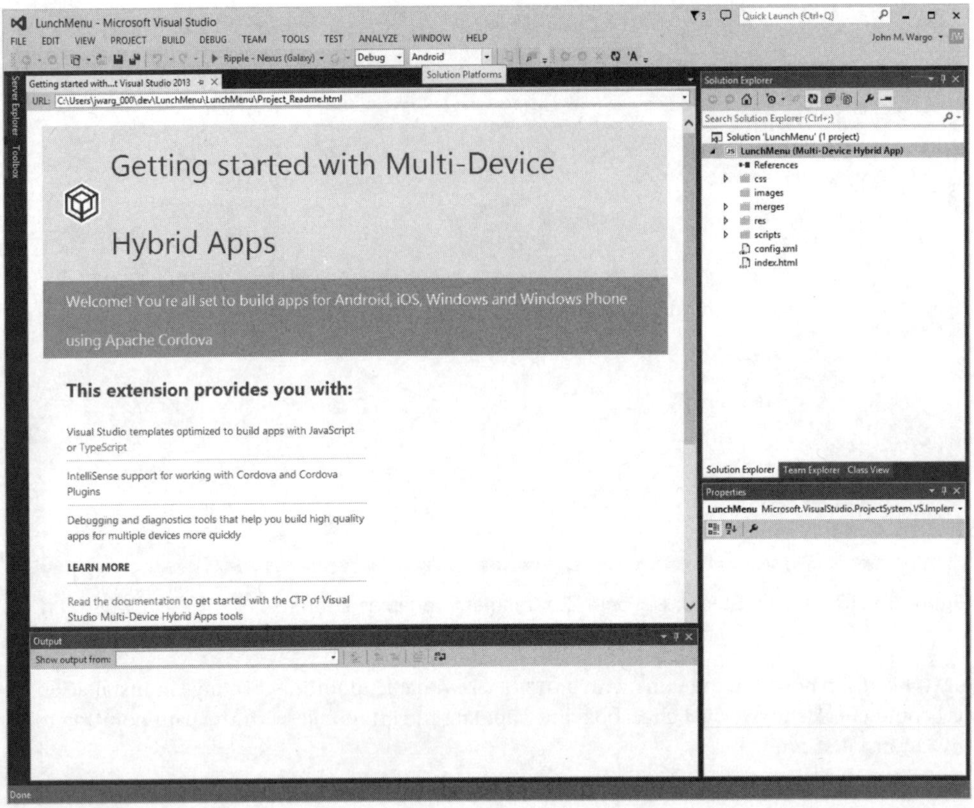

LunchMenu - Microsoft Visual Studio
FILE EDIT VIEW PROJECT BUILD DEBUG TEAM TOOLS TEST ANALYZE WINDOW HELP
Quick Launch (Ctrl+Q)
John M. Wargo
Ripple - Nexus (Galaxy)
Debug
Android
Solution Platforms
Getting started with...t Visual Studio 2013
URL: C:\Users\jwarg_000\dev\LunchMenu\LunchMenu\Project_Readme.html
Getting started with Multi-Device
Hybrid Apps
Welcome! You're all set to build apps for Android, iOS, Windows and Windows Phone
using Apache Cordova
This extension provides you with:
Visual Studio templates optimized to build apps with JavaScript or TypeScript
IntelliSense support for working with Cordova and Cordova Plugins
Debugging and diagnostics tools that help you build high quality apps for multiple devices more quickly
LEARN MORE
Read the documentation to get started with the CTP of Visual Studio Multi-Device Hybrid Apps tools
Output
Show output from:
Solution Explorer
Search Solution Explorer (Ctrl+;)
Solution 'LunchMenu' (1 project)
LunchMenu (Multi-Device Hybrid App)
References
css
images
merges
res
scripts
config.xml
index.html
Solution Explorer
Team Explorer
Class View
Properties
LunchMenu Microsoft.VisualStudio.ProjectSystem.VS.Implem
Server Explorer
Toolbox
Done

Figure 11.29 Visual Studio: New Hybrid Project

LunchMenu
File
Home
Share
View
This PC ▸ Boot (C:) ▸ Users ▸ jwarg_000 ▸ dev ▸ LunchMenu ▸ LunchMenu
Search LunchMenu
dev
acac
debug
empty
LunchMenu
LunchMenu
bin
bld
css
images
merges
res
cert
icons
screens
scripts
Name
Date modified
Type
Size
bin 11/3/2014 7:47 PM File folder
bld 11/3/2014 7:47 PM File folder
css 11/3/2014 7:47 PM File folder
images 11/3/2014 7:47 PM File folder
merges 11/3/2014 7:47 PM File folder
res 11/3/2014 7:47 PM File folder
scripts 11/3/2014 7:47 PM File folder
config.xml 11/3/2014 7:47 PM XML File 1 KB
index.html 11/3/2014 7:47 PM Firefox HTML Doc... 1 KB
LunchMenu.jsproj 11/3/2014 7:47 PM JSPROJ File 12 KB
LunchMenu.jsproj.user 11/3/2014 7:53 PM Visual Studio Proj... 1 KB
Project_Readme.html 7/27/2014 4:30 PM Firefox HTML Doc... 33 KB
12 items
1 item selected

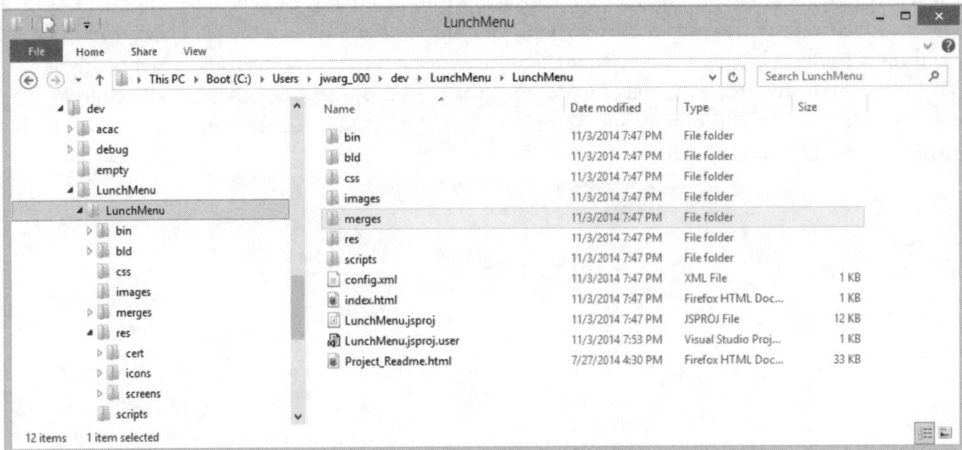

Figure 11.30 Hybrid Application Folder Structure

As with the typical Cordova project, the project's config.xml file describes the project to the CLI; I described many of the settings in Chapter 5. You can edit the file in Visual Studio by double-clicking it, which will open the editing pane shown in Figure 11.31. The Application pane, shown in the figure, contains general settings for the application and allows you to configure which orientations the application supports as well as to enable full-screen operation.

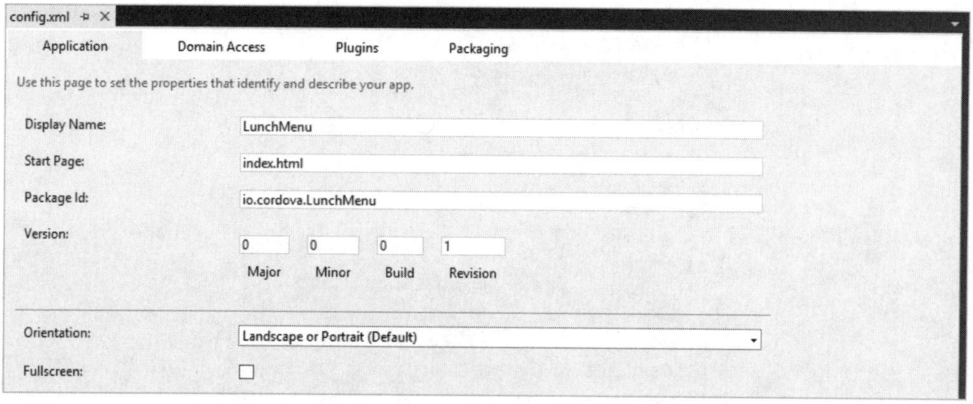

Figure 11.31 Visual Studio: config.xml Application Tab

The Domain Access pane shown in Figure 11.32 allows you to define the endpoint whitelist for the application, giving you control over what remote resources the application can connect to.

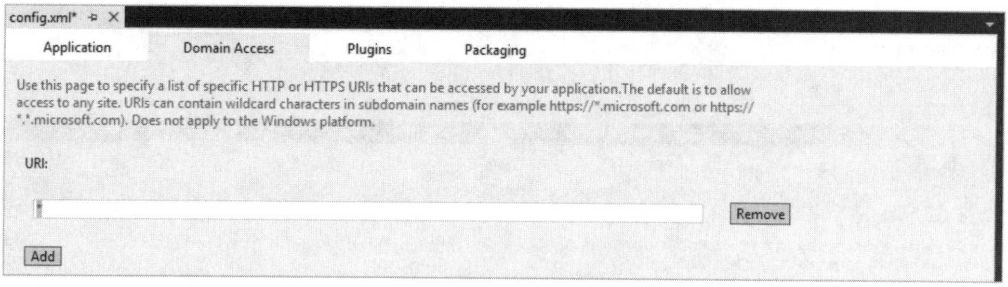

Figure 11.32 Visual Studio: config.xml Domain Access Tab

The Plugins tab shown in Figure 11.33 allows you to specify the Cordova plugins you want to add to the project. The HDMAE doesn't add the plugins when you make changes here; instead, it stores this information in the config.xml, then adds the plugins using the Cordova CLI during the build process for each target platform.

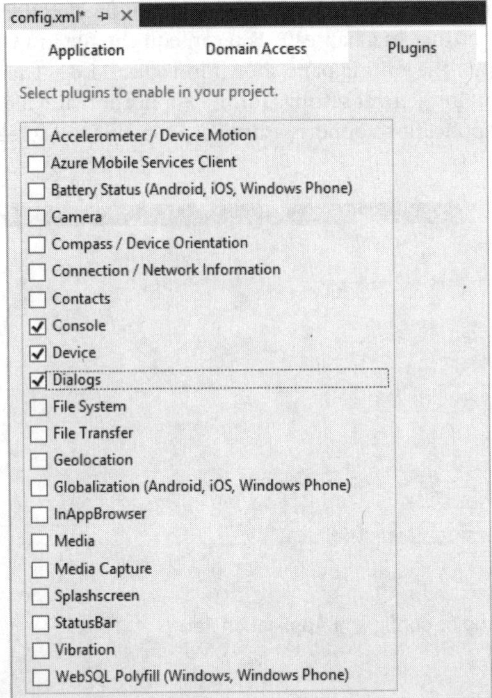

Figure 11.33 Visual Studio: config.xml Plugins Tab

The Packaging tab shown in Figure 11.34 hosts some additional settings for Windows 8 and Android projects.

config.xml*
Application | Domain Access | Plugins | Packaging

Windows 8

Use this page to set the properties for the Windows Store version of your app. For all other platforms, you may refer to the documentation. http://go.microsoft.com/fwlink/?LinkID=397716

Display Name: Lunch Menu

Package Id: com.ac4p.lunchmenu

Version: 0 0 0 1
Major Minor Build Revision

Android

Version Code:

Figure 11.34 Visual Studio: config.xml Packaging Tab

In the project folder, there are a few other files of interest. The getting-started guide shown in Figure 11.29 is the Project_Readme.html shown in Figure 11.30. You can open it at any time directly from the project folder.

The MDHAE doesn't use the default web application project files the Cordova CLI provides; instead, it provides its own. Listing 11.1 shows the contents of the project's index.html file. This is the app's startup page, and it's a really simple page that displays nothing but a text string.

Listing 11.1 index.html

```
<!DOCTYPE html>
<html>
<head>
  <meta charset="utf-8" />
  <title>LunchMenu</title>
  <!-- LunchMenu references -->
  <link href="css/index.css" rel="stylesheet" />
</head>
<body>
  <p>Hello, your application is ready!</p>
  <!-- Cordova reference, this is added to your app when it's built. -->
  <script src="cordova.js"></script>
  <script src="scripts/platformOverrides.js"></script>
  <script src="scripts/index.js"></script>
</body>
</html>
```

Of interest is the platformOverrides.js file. Notice the merges folder in Figure 11.30; the hybrid project includes a mechanism for having custom JavaScript code for each target platform through this overrides file. The platformOverrides.js in the project folder is essentially empty, but the merges folder contains a folder for each target platform and a platformOverrides.js file with platform-specific code. Take a look at each merges folder to see what overrides are included with the project.

The project's index.js file is different from the default Cordova project as well; you can see this in Listing 11.2. The JavaScript code sets up the deviceready event listener as well as ones for pause and resume, plus it includes a link pointing to the documentation for the application.

Listing 11.2 index.js

```
// For an introduction to the Blank template, see the following
// documentation:
// http://go.microsoft.com/fwlink/?LinkID=397704
// To debug code on page load in Ripple or on Android
// devices/emulators: launch your app, set breakpoints,
// and then run "window.location.reload()" in the JavaScript Console.
```

```
(function () {
  "use strict";

  document.addEventListener('deviceready', onDeviceReady.bind(this), false);

  function onDeviceReady() {
    // Handle the Cordova pause and resume events
    document.addEventListener('pause', onPause.bind(this), false);
    document.addEventListener('resume', onResume.bind(this), false);

    // TODO: Cordova has been loaded. Perform any initialization that
    //requires Cordova here.
  };

  function onPause() {
    // TODO: This application has been suspended. Save application
    //state here.
  };

  function onResume() {
    // TODO: This application has been reactivated. Restore
    //application state here.
  };
})();
```

At this point, you have an application all ready to run. You should update the index.html, index.js, and other application files to suit your application's needs. When it comes time to run the application, you can execute it using the Visual Studio Run button I showed earlier in the chapter. If you look at Figure 11.35, you'll see that there are a few more options than were available previously—there are now options for the Ripple Emulator as well as options for executing on a generic device and Android emulators.

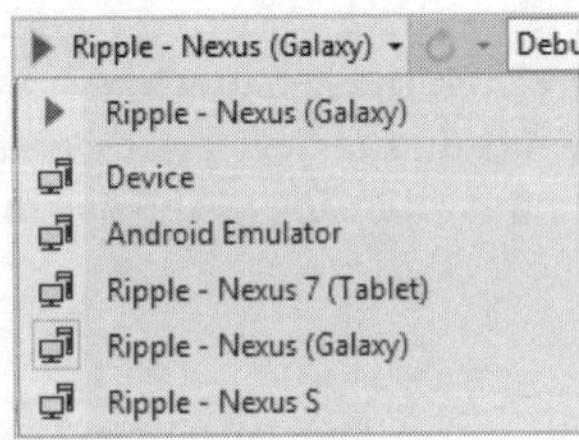

Figure 11.35 Visual Studio: Run Menu

This is part of the real power behind this tool. By doing one simple installation and creating a project in Visual Studio, I now have access to debug my Cordova application on a Windows device or emulator (phone or desktop), Android, and Ripple.

To demonstrate Ripple integration, I clicked the Ripple—Nexus (Galaxy) option and Visual Studio opened the Ripple Emulator window shown in Figure 11.36. You can learn more about Ripple in Chapter 5.

Figure 11.36 Ripple Emulator

Back in Visual Studio, if I pick Device in the Run menu, I can select from a multitude of devices from the device drop-down window shown in Figure 11.37.

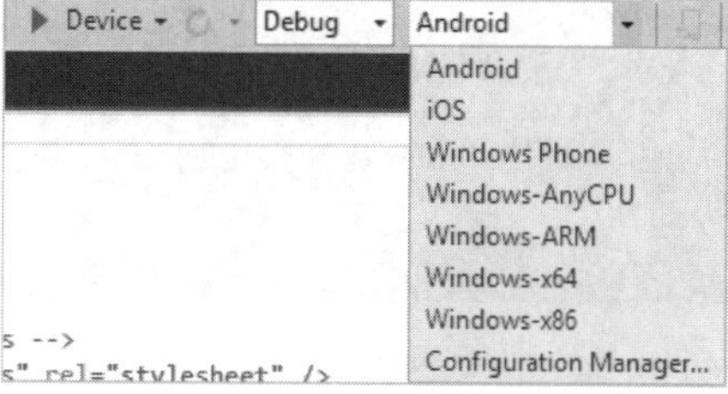

Figure 11.37 Visual Studio Run Menu: Target Options

Now, here's where it gets interesting. Notice that iOS is listed in Figure 11.37; that's because through this tool Visual Studio has the ability to build and deploy to iOS devices as well. Pretty cool, eh? Microsoft accomplishes this using a remote agent running on a Macintosh computer; you can read more about how to install the agent at http://goo.gl/GVb2tk, but I'll show you how here.

The agent must be installed on a network-connected Macintosh that is visible from the system running Visual Studio. You can run Visual Studio on a Windows VM and connect to the host Macintosh computer, or you can have two systems, one running OS X and another running Windows.

To install the agent, log on to your Macintosh computer, open a terminal window, and execute the following command:

```
sudo npm install -g vs-mda-remote --user=$USER
```

There's a lot of stuff that gets installed, so it might take a while, but when it's all done you should see the terminal output shown in Figure 11.38. Notice that it installed Cordova 3.5.0; that's because it's configured to use its own Cordova files to operate, instead of what you may already have installed, and it locks you into an older version of the CLI than is currently available. This is probably the only drawback I see with using this tool. According to Microsoft, this limitation is going away with a future release of the tools.

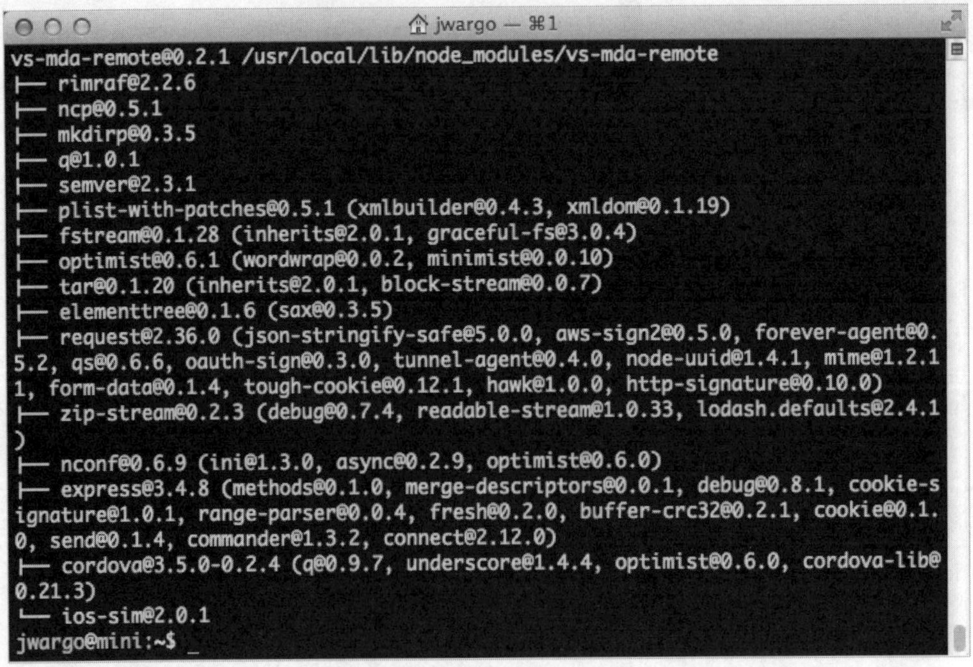

```
jwargo — ⌘1
vs-mda-remote@0.2.1 /usr/local/lib/node_modules/vs-mda-remote
├── rimraf@2.2.6
├── ncp@0.5.1
├── mkdirp@0.3.5
├── q@1.0.1
├── semver@2.3.1
├── plist-with-patches@0.5.1 (xmlbuilder@0.4.3, xmldom@0.1.19)
├── fstream@0.1.28 (inherits@2.0.1, graceful-fs@3.0.4)
├── optimist@0.6.1 (wordwrap@0.0.2, minimist@0.0.10)
├── tar@0.1.20 (inherits@2.0.1, block-stream@0.0.7)
├── elementtree@0.1.6 (sax@0.3.5)
├── request@2.36.0 (json-stringify-safe@5.0.0, aws-sign2@0.5.0, forever-agent@0.
5.2, qs@0.6.6, oauth-sign@0.3.0, tunnel-agent@0.4.0, node-uuid@1.4.1, mime@1.2.1
1, form-data@0.1.4, tough-cookie@0.12.1, hawk@1.0.0, http-signature@0.10.0)
├── zip-stream@0.2.3 (debug@0.7.4, readable-stream@1.0.33, lodash.defaults@2.4.1
)
├── nconf@0.6.9 (ini@1.3.0, async@0.2.9, optimist@0.6.0)
├── express@3.4.8 (methods@0.1.0, merge-descriptors@0.0.1, debug@0.8.1, cookie-s
ignature@1.0.1, range-parser@0.0.4, fresh@0.2.0, buffer-crc32@0.2.1, cookie@0.1.
0, send@0.1.4, commander@1.3.2, connect@2.12.0)
├── cordova@3.5.0-0.2.4 (q@0.9.7, underscore@1.4.4, optimist@0.6.0, cordova-lib@
0.21.3)
└── ios-sim@2.0.1
jwargo@mini:~$ _
```

Figure 11.38 Terminal: Remote Agent Installation

With the remote agent installed, you'll have to manually start it when you want to use it. To start the agent, open a terminal window (or use the one that's already open) and issue the following command:

```
vs-mda-remote --buildDir <build-directory>
```

The `build-directory` parameter refers to the target folder the remote agent will use as its working directory. Visual Studio will pass it files, which it will write to this folder before kicking off a build. So, for my development workstation I used the following:

```
vs-mda-remote --buildDir /Users/jwargo/builds
```

When you execute the command, the agent will launch, then display the configuration information shown in Figure 11.39. Don't close the terminal window; you'll need to have it running in order to be able to run iOS applications from Visual Studio.

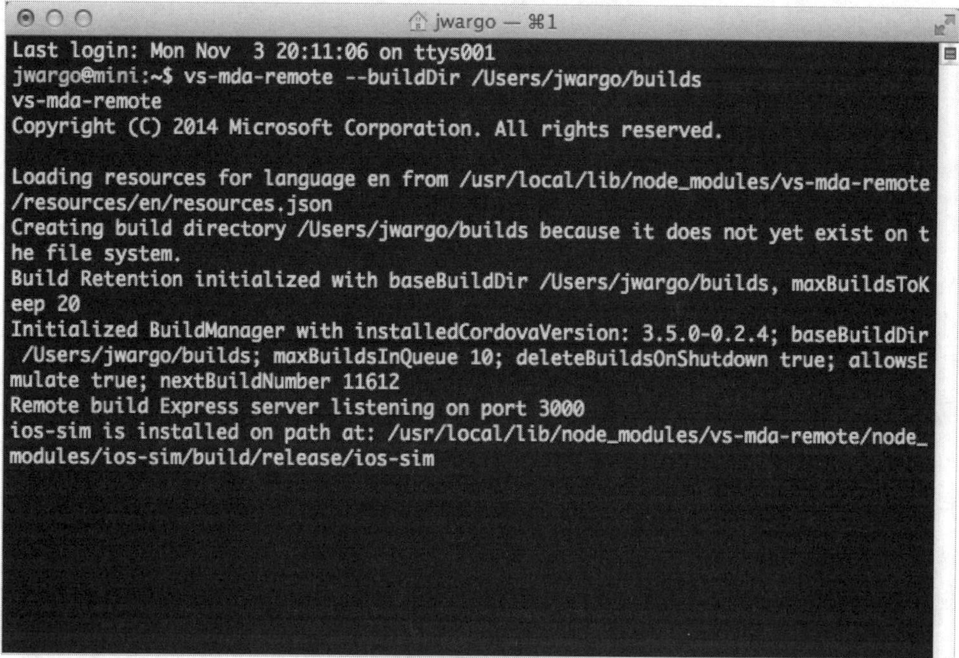

Figure 11.39 Terminal: Remote Agent

Notice in the figure that the Remote build Express server (the remote agent) is listening on port 3000. You'll need that port as well as the system's IP address in order to configure Visual Studio. To get the IP address, open the Macintosh Settings application, then select the Network option; you should see a screen similar to the one shown in Figure 11.40. In this example, my Macintosh has a wired Ethernet connection and I've highlighted the system's IP address in the figure.

Figure 11.40 Macintosh Settings: Network Information

You can also get the IP address from the terminal (not the one running the remote agent; you need to leave that terminal window alone until you're done with it); simply execute the following command:

```
ifconfig | grep "inet " | grep -v 127.0.0.1
```

You can see the output from this in Figure 11.41. The command filters the lines beginning with `inet` and skips lines that refer to `localhost` (127.0.0.1).

```
jwargo — ⌘2
jwargo@mini:~$ ifconfig | grep "inet " | grep -v 127.0.0.1
        inet 192.168.1.148 netmask 0xffffff00 broadcast 192.168.1.255
        inet 192.168.225.1 netmask 0xffffff00 broadcast 192.168.225.255
        inet 172.16.193.1 netmask 0xffffff00 broadcast 172.16.193.255
jwargo@mini:~$ _
```

Figure 11.41 Terminal: Determining the Device IP Address

Write down the port number and IP address and switch back to the system running Visual Studio. Open the Tools menu and select Options, then navigate to the Remote Agent Configuration shown in Figure 11.42. Enable remote iOS processing by setting that value to true as shown in the figure, then populate the Macintosh system's IP address in the Host field and the port in the Port field and click the OK button.

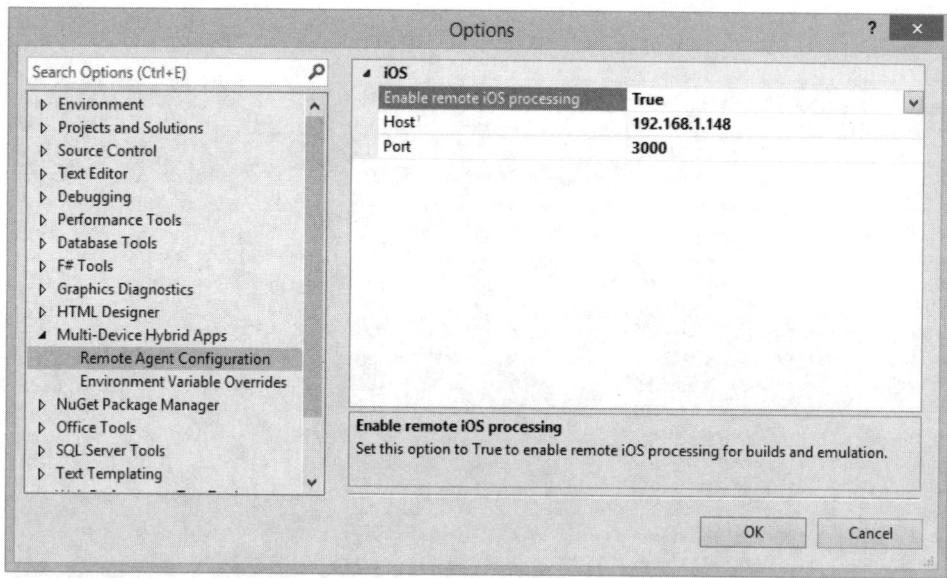

Figure 11.42 Visual Studio: Remote Agent Configuration Options

When this is complete, you can select iOS in the device list shown in Figure 11.37, then the Run menu will have a few extra options in it as shown in Figure 11.43. The Ripple options should be there regardless of whether or not you configured the remote agent, but now you have the ability to run on an iOS device or simulator.

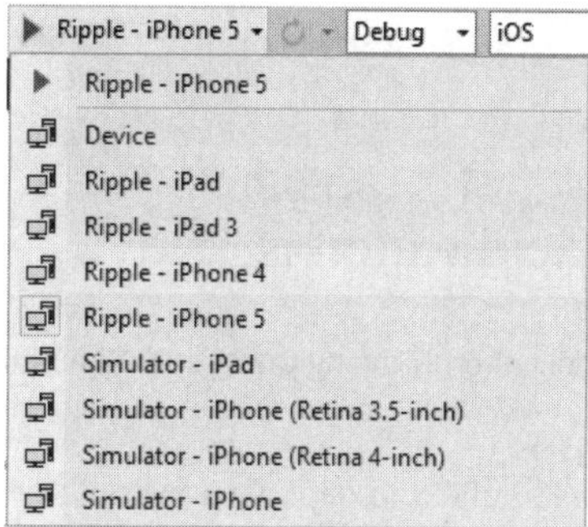

Figure 11.43 Visual Studio: iOS Run Options

Select Simulator—iPhone, for example, and Visual Studio will kick off a remote build on the Macintosh system running the remote agent. The remote agent terminal window will update, showing you what it's doing during this process as shown in Figure 11.44.

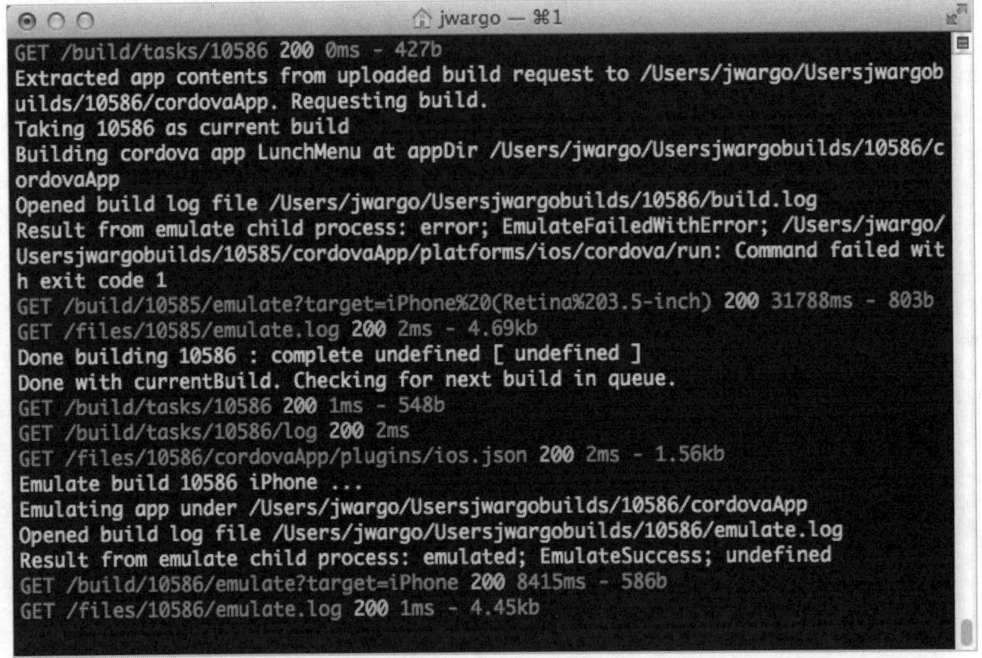

jwargo — ⌘1
GET /build/tasks/10586 200 0ms - 427b
Extracted app contents from uploaded build request to /Users/jwargo/Usersjwargob
uilds/10586/cordovaApp. Requesting build.
Taking 10586 as current build
Building cordova app LunchMenu at appDir /Users/jwargo/Usersjwargobuilds/10586/c
ordovaApp
Opened build log file /Users/jwargo/Usersjwargobuilds/10586/build.log
Result from emulate child process: error; EmulateFailedWithError; /Users/jwargo/
Usersjwargobuilds/10585/cordovaApp/platforms/ios/cordova/run: Command failed wit
h exit code 1
GET /build/10585/emulate?target=iPhone%20(Retina%203.5-inch) 200 31788ms - 803b
GET /files/10585/emulate.log 200 2ms - 4.69kb
Done building 10586 : complete undefined [undefined]
Done with currentBuild. Checking for next build in queue.
GET /build/tasks/10586 200 1ms - 548b
GET /build/tasks/10586/log 200 2ms
GET /files/10586/cordovaApp/plugins/ios.json 200 2ms - 1.56kb
Emulate build 10586 iPhone ...
Emulating app under /Users/jwargo/Usersjwargobuilds/10586/cordovaApp
Opened build log file /Users/jwargo/Usersjwargobuilds/10586/emulate.log
Result from emulate child process: emulated; EmulateSuccess; undefined
GET /build/10586/emulate?target=iPhone 200 8415ms - 586b
GET /files/10586/emulate.log 200 1ms - 4.45kb

Figure 11.44 Terminal: iOS Build Results

After the remote build completes, the remote agent will launch the device simulator, then deploy and launch the application as shown in Figure 11.45.

Figure 11.45 Lunch Menu Application Running on an iOS Simulator

What you're seeing here is an iOS build and deploy to a simulator initiated by Visual Studio running on a Windows system. As I write this, you can't remotely debug this application from Visual Studio, but you can use the Visual Studio debugger to do real-time debugging of the application running on Android and Windows as I described earlier in the chapter. At PhoneGap Day 2014, Microsoft announced that the next release of the hybrid tools would support remote debugging of iOS applications, so perhaps by the time you read this it will have become a reality.

Wrap-Up

In this chapter, I showed you how to use the free developer tools from Microsoft to test your Cordova applications for Windows Phone 8 and several other mobile device platforms as well. As I've described, this is pretty powerful stuff. Now, with a single installation and the robust Visual Studio, you can build, deploy, test, and debug cross-platform Cordova applications from a single IDE.

12

Using PhoneGap Build

Before the Cordova CLI became available, building Cordova applications for multiple device platforms was a challenge. You had to install the native SDK for each mobile device platform you were supporting and copy your Cordova application's web application content from project to project. You couldn't build or test multiple apps simultaneously. The CLI fixes much of that, but there are still limitations.

The PhoneGap Build service provides the means to build PhoneGap applications in the cloud, without the need to install a bunch of software on a developer workstation. All you have to do is write your web applications using your web content editor of choice, then upload the files to the cloud and let PhoneGap Build do the rest. You still need to have at least a Macintosh computer to create the appropriate mobile OS application signing keys, but the work required to set up a development environment is greatly reduced.

In this chapter, I show you how to set up and use the PhoneGap Build service to package your Cordova applications and share those applications with others. There's a lot to PhoneGap Build, so I couldn't cover it all here. This chapter focuses on the Build service and how to use it, not the device platform-specific intricacies.

What Is PhoneGap Build?

PhoneGap Build (https://build.phonegap.com/) is a cloud-based build service for PhoneGap applications. It is a commercial offering from Adobe; there's a free version of the service plus for-fee options that offer more capabilities.

With Build, a developer loads web application content into an Application definition on the Build server, and the service will automatically build a native application for each of the supported mobile device platforms. Figure 12.1 illustrates how the Build service works.

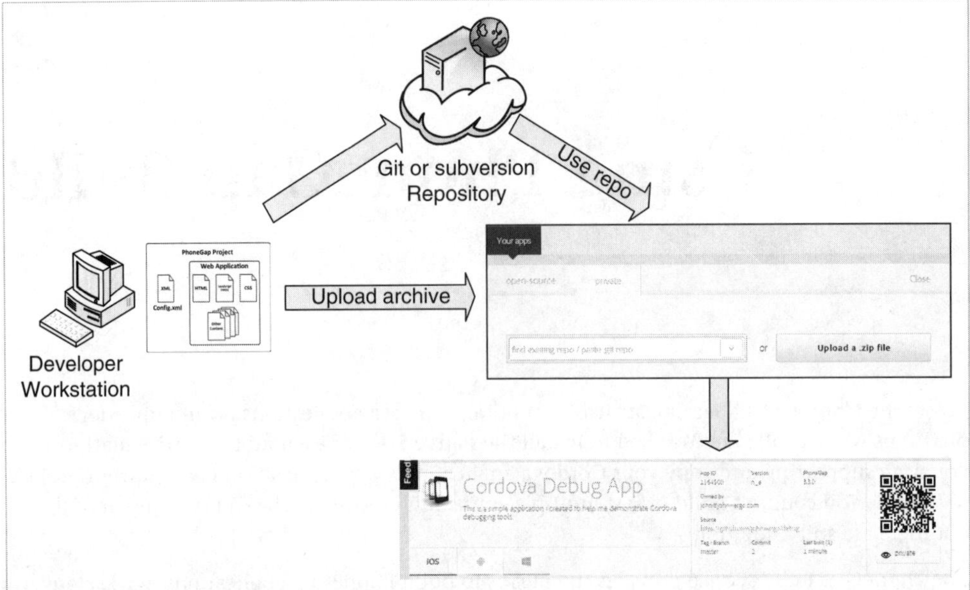

Figure 12.1 PhoneGap Build Overview

PhoneGap Build used to support a wider range of target platforms but currently supports packaging applications for only the following mobile device platforms:

- Android
- iOS
- Windows Phone 8

There are many features of the service, many of which will be described later in the chapter. For developers evaluating using the service, there are a few key ones that will be discussed in the following sections.

Quick Prototyping

PhoneGap Build enables a developer to quickly build a web application and deploy it into native applications for multiple mobile device platforms without having a complete, local development environment. This gives designers a quick way to flesh out a concept without having to spend time downloading and configuring mobile SDKs. While this prototyping can be easily done using a mobile web browser, if it is a requirement that the application be distributed in the Cordova (or PhoneGap) container, PhoneGap Build helps jump-start the process.

Once a concept has been validated, the web application source code can be passed on to a developer to add data integration and other complex aspects of the application later. The developer can continue to use the Build service or can switch over to the CLI and local copies of the native SDKs for continued development.

Collaboration

While version control systems allow developers to collaborate on their development projects on-premise or in the cloud, Build allows you to configure a project so others can work on the same PhoneGap Build project with you. You have the ability to define testers who get read-only access and developers who get read/write access.

This feature allows you to provide a private, hidden area of Build where you can collaborate with others and provide them with access to build results so they can easily test your applications as you develop them.

Content Refresh through Hydration

One of the reasons why many developers use Build is so that they can provide testers with a quick and simple mechanism for updating an application they are testing. Mobile application testers are used to having to update native applications on their test devices as they move from app version to app version, but PhoneGap Build makes this process simpler through a feature called Hydration (http://goo.gl/5cCZcK).

When a developer enables Hydration on a PhoneGap Build application, the Build service creates a version of the application that, instead of having its web content packaged within the application, receives its web content directly from the Build server. This feature significantly improves application build time and allows web content updates to be repeatedly deployed to the PhoneGap application over the air, whenever the application launches and a new version is available.

When a developer uploads a new version of the web application content to the Build service, the content is packaged for delivery (instead of the whole native application being packaged). The next time users open the application, the application will notify them that a new version of the application's content is available. Users can download the update or continue to work with the version of the application they already have.

The Hydration feature is really designed to support the testing process for mobile applications; you shouldn't try to use this feature with your production applications. For enterprise applications that need this feature, you may want to take a look at the SAP Mobile Platform (SMP); its Hybrid SDK (Kapsel) provides an over-the-air web content update for production applications.

Hydration is supported in PhoneGap 2.0 and higher, and the capability is available for Android and iOS applications.

Using PhoneGap Build

In this section, I'll show you how to use the PhoneGap Build service. I'll start by showing you how to create a PhoneGap Build account, and then I'll walk you through a quick example of creating a PhoneGap application using Build and show you how to leverage more of the configuration options for the service. It all starts by opening your browser of choice and pointing it to the Build service at http://build.phonegap.com/ as shown in Figure 12.2.

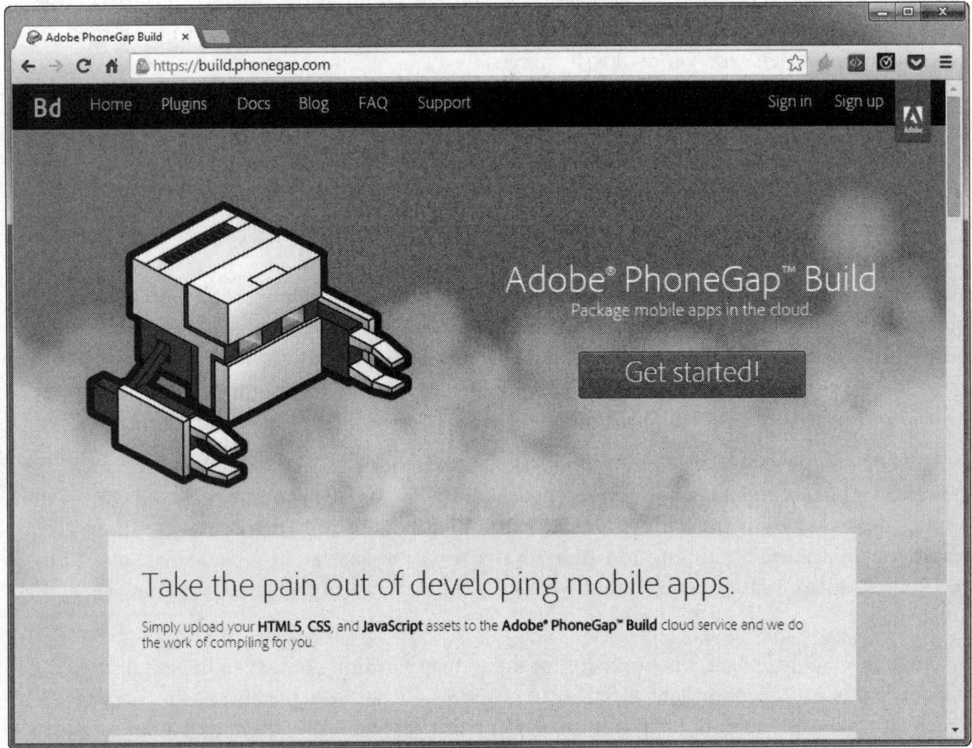

Figure 12.2 PhoneGap Build Web Site

If you have an existing Adobe Creative Cloud account, you can sign in using the credentials you already have. If not, you can create a new account or sign in using your GitHub account credentials. Once you're in, you'll be able to select your plan from the available choices. The free plan is limited to one private app, but the paid options are more flexible.

A Quick Example

Before I show you all of the intricacies of PhoneGap Build, I thought I'd throw together a quick example. At the barest minimum, all PhoneGap Build needs to have in order to create a mobile application for each supported mobile device platform is just a single HTML file. To prove this, I created a quick HTML5 application, shown in Listing 12.1.

Listing 12.1 Simple index.html File

```
<!DOCTYPE HTML>
<html>
<head>
  <title>PhoneGap Build Example</title>
</head>
<body>
  <h1>PhoneGap Build Example</h1>
  <p>This is a simple Apache Cordova application to use to demonstrate uploading an index.html file to PhoneGap Build. Not very exciting, is it?</p>
</body>
</html>
```

Next, I signed into the PhoneGap Build web site. If you don't have any applications defined on the system, PhoneGap Build will open to a page where you can create your first application. Otherwise, click the + new app button on the Build home page to create a new application.

In either case, the Build service will open the page shown in Figure 12.3; here you can either provide a URI for a Git repository or upload a file. In this case, the upload button is mislabeled

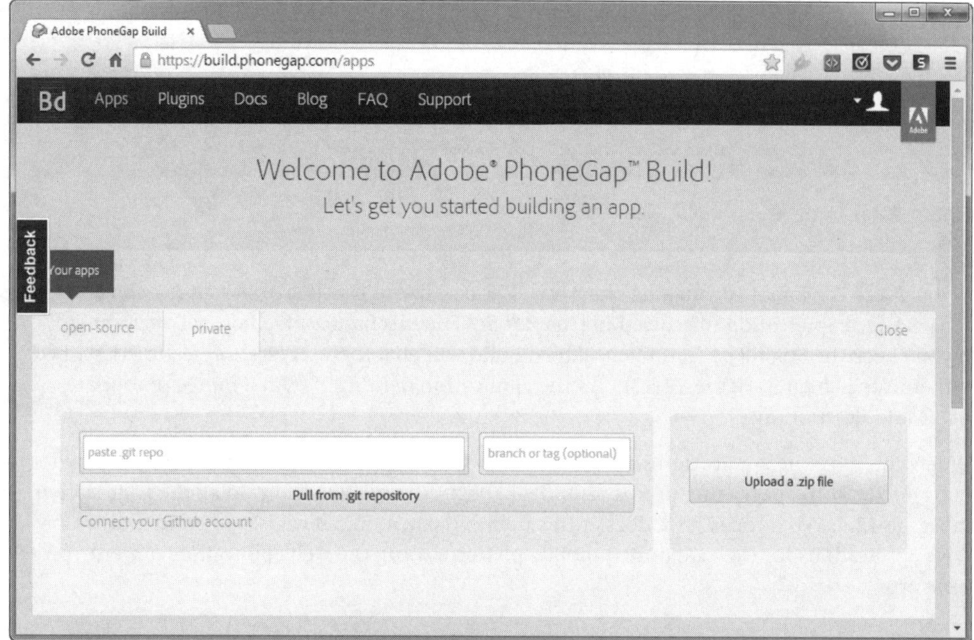

Figure 12.3 PhoneGap Build: Creating a New Application

(and I've suggested to the Adobe folks that they fix this; more than a year later they still haven't) because you can upload more than a .zip file—you can also upload an .html file like the one I just showed you. Regardless of which approach you want to use, you have to make sure Build has access to the application file(s) you want packaged into a Cordova application.

For this example, I simply clicked the Upload a .zip file button and pointed to the .html file I created. As soon as I finish that process, the Build service will open the new page shown in Figure 12.4. Since I didn't provide a configuration file (more on that later), Build sets a default application name of PG Build App as shown in the figure. You should change the application name and provide a brief description of your application so you and others will be able to easily recognize it later.

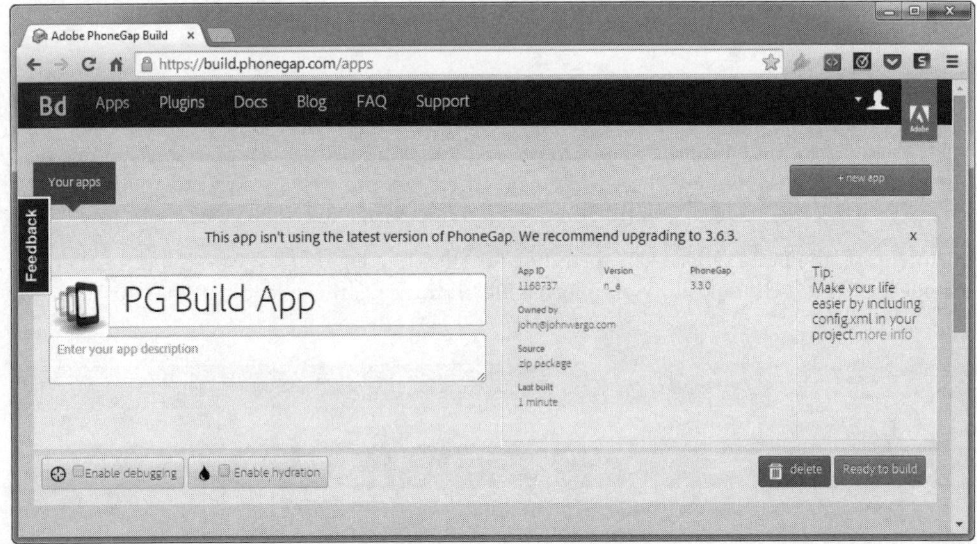

Figure 12.4 PhoneGap Build: New Application

If you check the Enable debugging checkbox, PhoneGap Build will enable weinre debugging in the packaged application (discussed in Chapter 5, "The Mechanics of Cordova Development"). If you check the Enable hydration checkbox, Build will enable the Hydration feature described earlier in the chapter. Figure 12.5 shows the application definition with a more appropriate name and description.

When you have the application settings set the way you want them, click the Ready to build button to start the packaging process. Build will begin the process and display the page shown in Figure 12.6. What the service does at this point is spawn off a few tasks to build native Cordova applications for each supported mobile platform using the web application content you have provided.

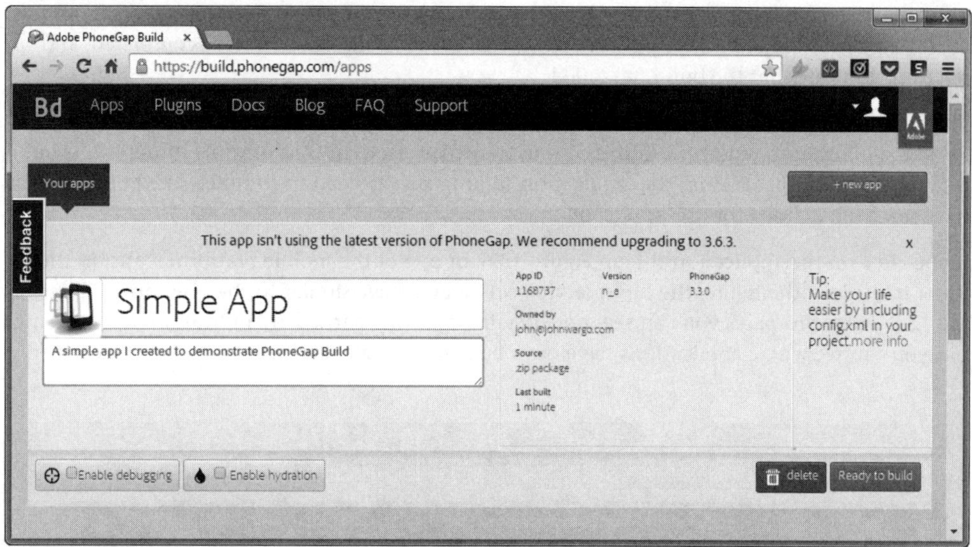

Figure 12.5 PhoneGap Build: New Sample Application

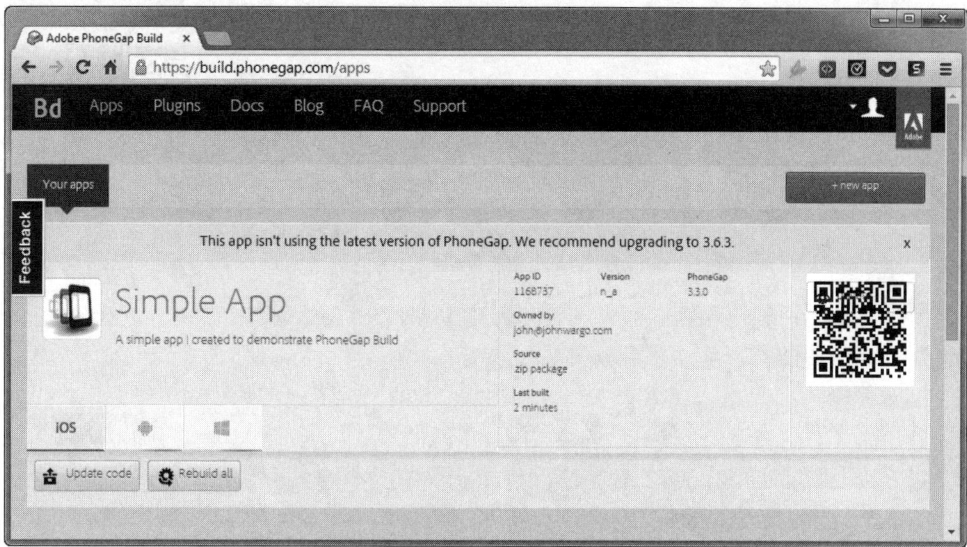

Figure 12.6 PhoneGap Build: Sample Application Being Built

The page will show the platform icon for each supported mobile device platform; you should be able to easily recognize them. Applications with blue icons (not shown) have completed, and red icons indicate that the build has failed.

The build process fails sometimes because of glitches with the Build service. Simply click the Rebuild all button to redo the build, and it usually fixes itself. In this example, though, the build is failing for a specific reason: the application signing keys needed to complete the build process have not been defined for this application.

If you click on the application title in Figure 12.6, or one of the mobile platform icons on the lower-left side of the figure, the Build service will open a page similar to the one shown in Figure 12.7. From this page, you can see more details about the particular application. In this example, you can see where applications have been built successfully and where the build has failed.

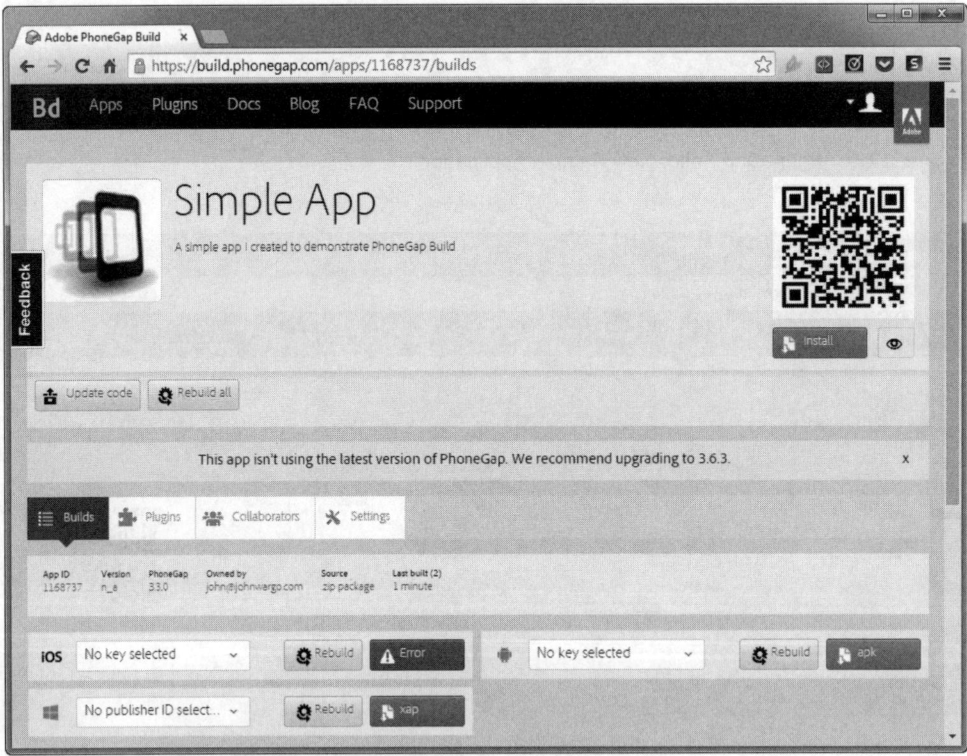

Figure 12.7 PhoneGap Build: Application Details

When you click any of the Error buttons, the page will expand an area beneath the button and display the error that caused the build to fail; an example of the iOS failure is shown in Figure 12.8; the iOS build failed because of signing key problems.

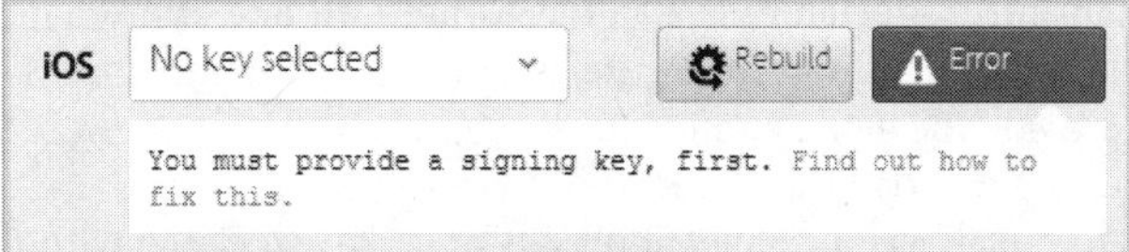

Figure 12.8 PhoneGap Build: iOS Build Error Details

Most mobile device platforms have some sort of signing process that must be completed before an application can be deployed to a device or into an app store. Apple is much more restrictive than other platforms, so you can't accomplish anything here without providing keys. Most other platforms either don't require a key or allow you to build with or without one.

To resolve the build issue, provide the necessary signing key(s) and rebuild the application. To do this, click the appropriate drop-down menu next to the operating systems that have failed as shown in Figure 12.7 and add your keys to the project as shown in Figure 12.9.

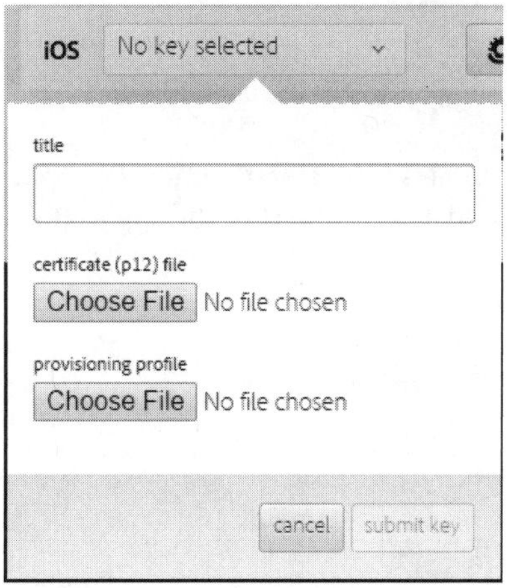

Figure 12.9 iOS Signing Key Options

When you create the keys, you're able to provide a title for the key set. This allows developers who work for multiple customers to define signing key settings for different projects or customers and select the appropriate key(s) depending on the scenario.

When you have the appropriate keys added to the project, simply click the individual Rebuild buttons or the Rebuild all button to start the process of rebuilding the application.

On the same page are additional options for the application. The Plugins tab shown in Figure 12.7 (but not displayed) allows you to view information about the plugins that have been added to the application. You will learn how to add plugins to your project later in the chapter.

The Collaborators tab shown in Figure 12.10 allows you to list one or more people who work with you on the project. As shown in the figure, to add a collaborator, click the Add a collaborator button, then provide the email address for the collaborator and identify whether the user will only be allowed to download the application (testers) or can make updates to the application (developers). The collaborators' email addresses must be associated with PhoneGap Build accounts in order for them to access the system.

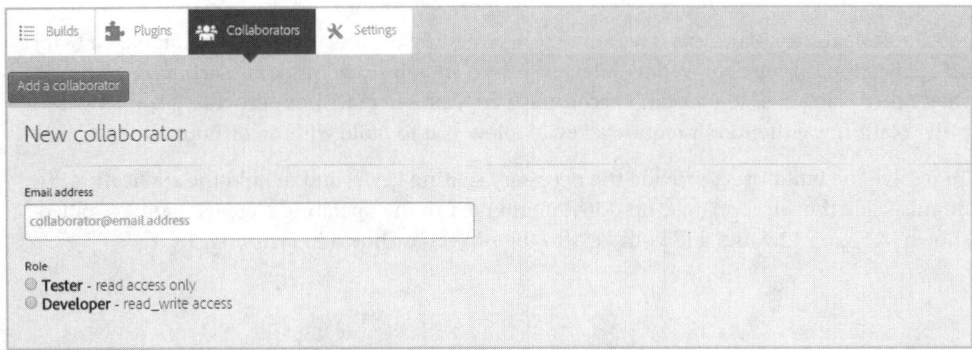

Figure 12.10 PhoneGap Build Application: Collaborators

The application Settings tab contains general settings for the application. The Basic area shown in Figure 12.11 allows you to update the source for the application as well as to set some properties of the application.

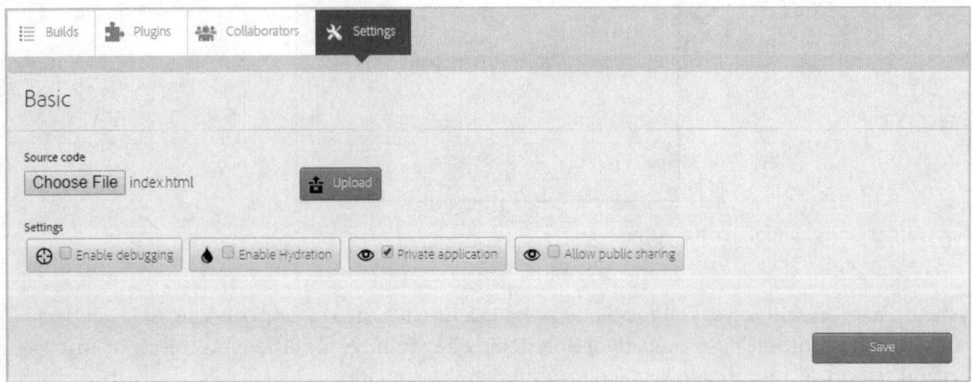

Figure 12.11 PhoneGap Build Application: Basic Settings

The Configuration section of the Settings page shown in Figure 12.12 allows you to set some application properties. The values shown here can be entered manually by the developer as I've done here, but later, when we talk about the application's config.xml, you'll see that these values can also be defined with the application content and uploaded to the service.

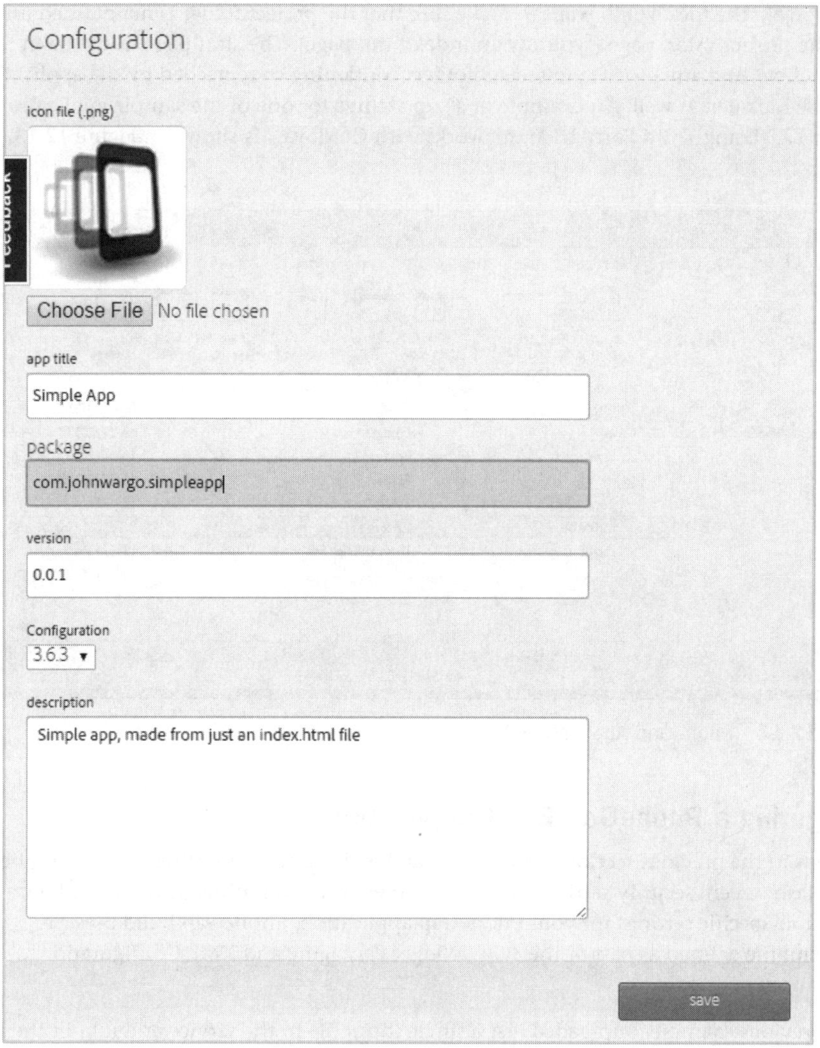

Figure 12.12 PhoneGap Build Application: Application Configuration

In the example I've shown, I've simply uploaded an index.html file containing my application's simple content. Very few Cordova or PhoneGap applications consist of an index.html file and nothing more. For most applications, you'll package all of the web application content into a .zip file and upload that to the Build service for packaging. I would show you how that works here, but there's really not much to it—you zip the files up, using whatever tools you want to use to do the packaging, and upload the .zip file instead of the .html file as I showed earlier. Everything else is the same.

When you zip the files, you'll want to make sure that the project folder is maintained underneath the project's start page (typically an index.html page). The start page has to be in the root of the archive, and any other required subfolders containing code needed by the application should be included as well. An example of a .zip archive for one of the sample applications from Chapter 17, "Using Third-Party UI Frameworks with Cordova," is shown in Figure 12.13.

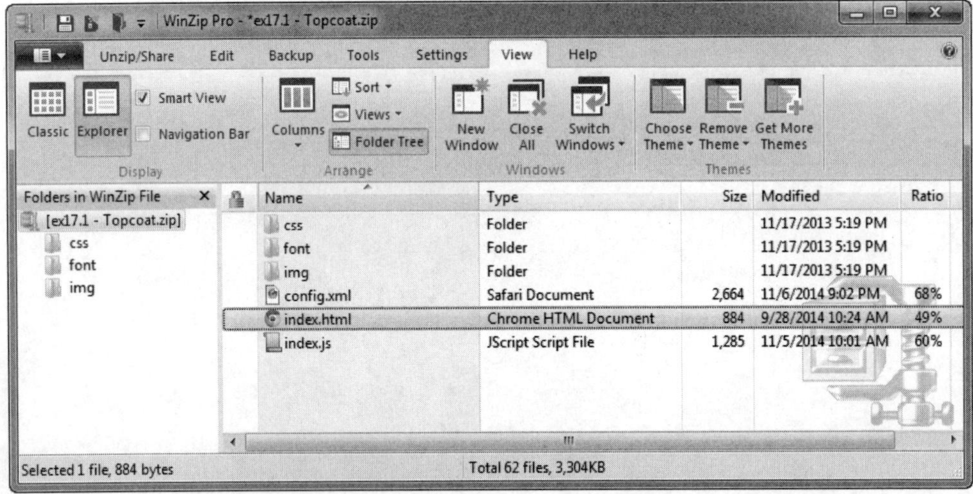

Figure 12.13 PhoneGap Application Archive

Configuring a PhoneGap Build Application

As shown in the previous section, PhoneGap Build will use default settings such as application icon, splash screen, security settings, and more unless you tell it differently. To configure application-specific settings for your PhoneGap application, PhoneGap Build uses the config.xml file defined as part of the W3C Widget Packaging and XML Configuration specification.

In the previous example, I uploaded just a single .html file to the service and it built the application for me. If I create a properly configured config.xml and include it in a .zip file with all of the web application's content, the service will use the config.xml file to set many of the properties and security settings for the application. The .zip file can contain just the index.html I used in the previous example, or it can be a complete web application with .html files, JavaScript code, CSS files, and more as I showed in Figure 12.13. It doesn't matter what the complexity of the app is, as long as it is packaged into a .zip file with the config.xml; the Build service should be able to package it into native Cordova applications for you.

The CLI will generate a config.xml file for you automatically when it creates a Cordova project. Listing 12.2 shows the config.xml file created by the CLI for the Hello World #3 application highlighted in Chapter 2, "Anatomy of a Cordova Application."

Listing 12.2 Default Cordova Project config.xml File

```
<?xml version='1.0' encoding='utf-8'?>
<widget id="com.ac4p.ex23" version="0.0.1"
  xmlns="http://www.w3.org/ns/widgets"
  xmlns:cdv="http://cordova.apache.org/ns/1.0">
    <name>Ex2.3</name>
    <description>
        A sample Apache Cordova application that responds to the deviceready event.
    </description>
    <author email="dev@cordova.apache.org" href="http://cordova.io">
        Apache Cordova Team
    </author>
    <content src="index.html" />
    <access origin="*" />
</widget>
```

The example config.xml file lists a limited amount of information needed to describe the application and a little bit about the application's preferences. If you updated the application name and author information in that file, packaged the config.xml into an archive, and uploaded it to PhoneGap Build, you would see that the new application project would be created using those settings.

The PhoneGap Build config.xml file can be pretty complicated. It has to contain settings that apply across multiple device platforms such as settings for application icons, splash screen graphics, and more. It also has to accommodate specific security settings that need to be enabled depending on which PhoneGap APIs are used. I'm not going to go into the details of all of the possible settings for the config.xml; they're all clearly documented in the PhoneGap Build Docs located at http://docs.build.phonegap.com/ and updated regularly when new capabilities are added.

It's never fun to edit an XML file, and since the PhoneGap Build service supports so many options, it's hard to make sure that you have all of the settings you need and that they're set correctly. To simplify this for you, an industrious developer published an application called ConfiGAP (http://configap.com/) that provides a simple interface you can use to define all of the settings you need in a PhoneGap Build config.xml file. The application is free and can be downloaded from the provided URL. The application is an Adobe Air application, so you'll need to have Air (http://get.adobe.com/air) installed in order to run the application.

When you run the application, you're prompted to either create a new config.xml or open an existing one. When you select the appropriate option, you will be presented with a screen similar to Figure 12.14. From this panel, you can set general settings for the application, some of the same settings I showed in Figure 12.2.

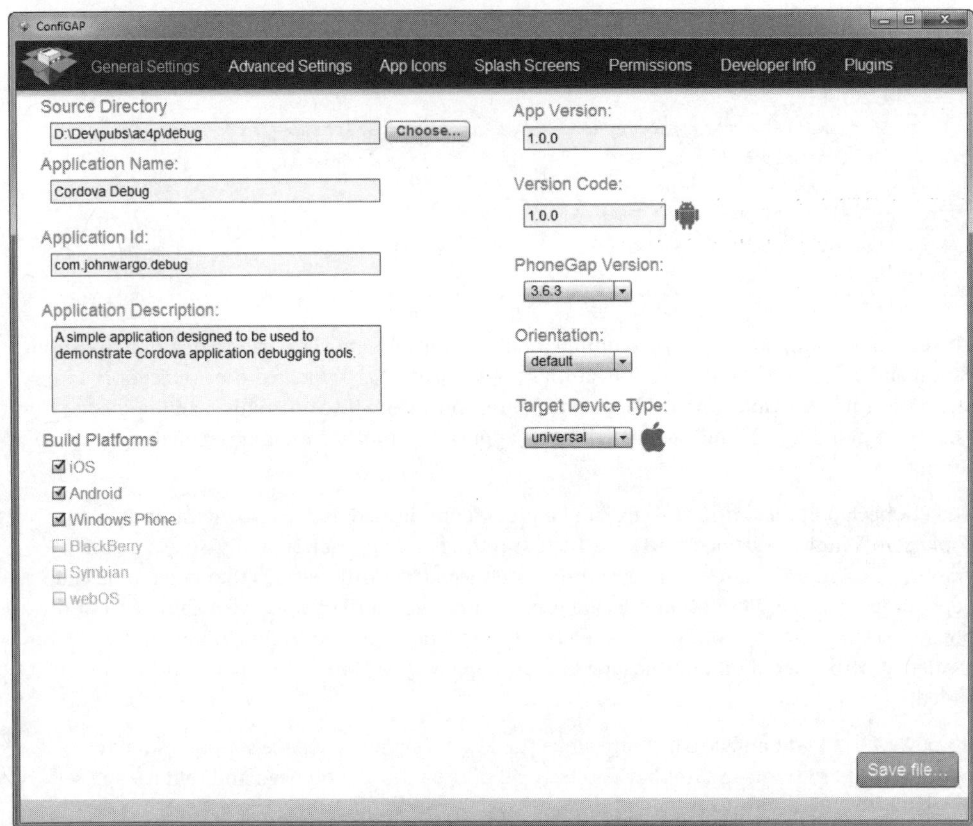

Figure 12.14 ConfiGAP: General Settings

Across the top of the window are tabs you can select to access other settings. Figure 12.15 shows the contents of the Advanced Settings tab; you would use these settings to control how the application renders and operates on a mobile device.

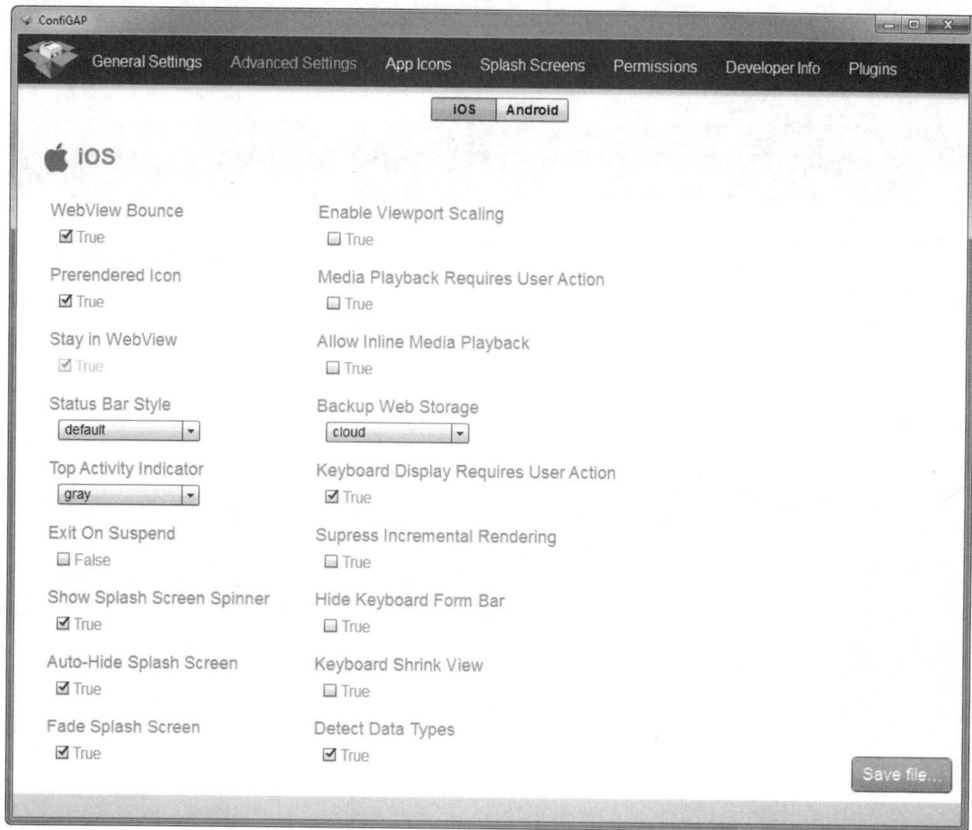

Figure 12.15 ConfiGAP: Advanced Settings

One of the things the Cordova CLI does for you that you used to have to do manually is manage the permissions settings for device-side capabilities exposed by the Cordova APIs. When a developer adds a plugin to an application that utilizes the Camera or some other native capability, the device OS expects that the developer has identified that he or she is using the API so that it can tell during installation what it needs to prompt the user for permission. If the permissions are not set correctly, even though you might have a plugin such as Camera added to the application, the camera functionality won't work.

The ConfiGAP Permissions tab, shown in Figure 12.16, includes options for setting the necessary API permissions as well as allowing you to define the domain whitelist described in Chapter 5.

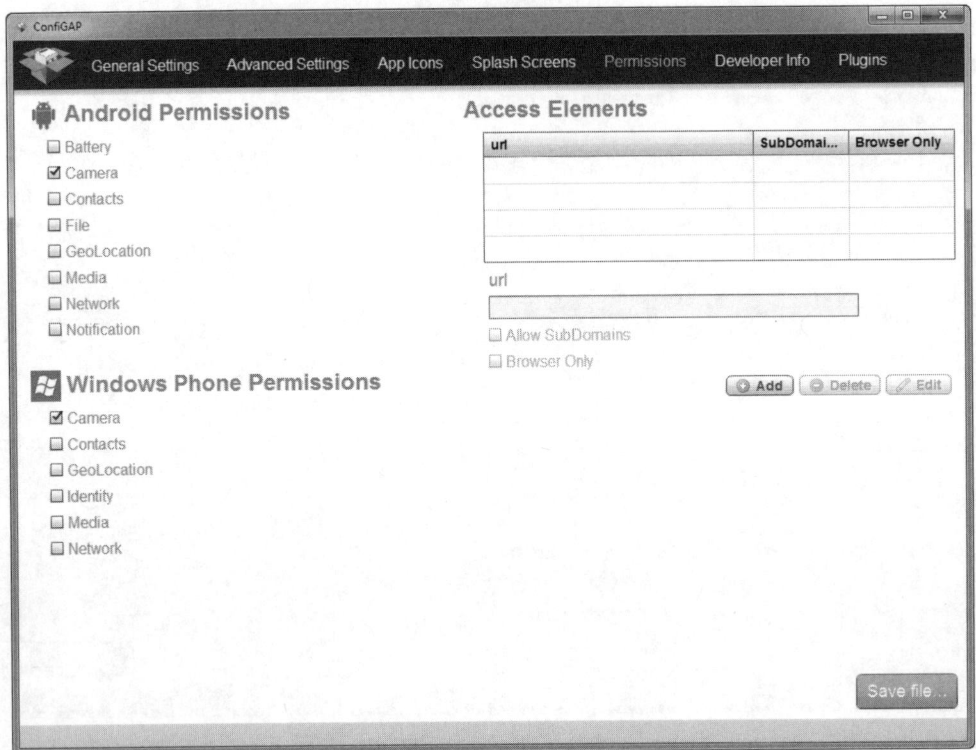

Figure 12.16 ConfiGAP: Permissions Settings

And finally, Figure 12.17 shows the content of the Plugins tab; here you can enable the plugins that will be added to your project by the build process. I'll explain how plugins work with the PhoneGap Build service in the next section.

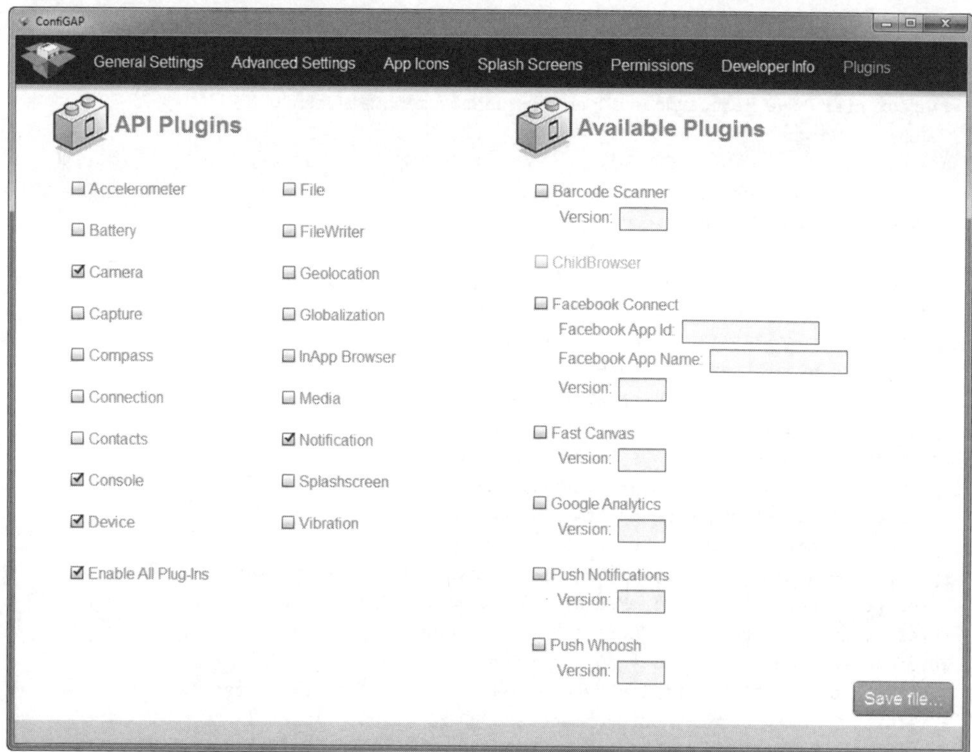

Figure 12.17 ConfiGAP: Plugin Settings

Listing 12.3 shows the complete config.xml file generated by ConfiGAP; all of the settings I enabled in the application are represented here.

Listing 12.3 PhoneGap Build config.xml File Generated by ConfiGAP

```
<?xml version="1.0" encoding="UTF-8" ?>
<widget xmlns="http://www.w3.org/ns/widgets"
  xmlns:gap="http://phonegap.com/ns/1.0" id="com.johnwargo.debug"
  versionCode="1.0.0" version="1.0.0">
  <name>Cordova Debug</name>
```

```
<description>
  A simple application designed to be used to demonstrate Cordova
  application debugging tools.</description>
<author href="www.johnwargo.com" email="user@somedomain.com">
  John M. Wargo
</author>
<preference name="phonegap-version" value="3.6.3" />
<preference name="orientation" value="default" />
<preference name="fullscreen" value="false" />
<preference name="target-device" value="universal" />
<preference name="webviewbounce" value="true" />
<preference name="prerendered-icon" value="true" />
<preference name="stay-in-webview" value="true" />
<preference name="ios-statusbarstyle" value="default" />
<preference name="detect-data-types" value="true" />
<preference name="exit-on-suspend" value="false" />
<preference name="show-splash-screen-spinner" value="true" />
<preference name="auto-hide-splash-screen" value="true" />
<preference name="EnableViewportScale" value="true" />
<preference name="MediaPlaybackRequiresUserAction" value="false" />
<preference name="AllowInlineMediaPlayback" value="false" />
<preference name="BackupWebStorage" value="cloud" />
<preference name="TopActivityIndicator" value="gray" />
<preference name="KeyboardDisplayRequiresUserAction" value="false" />
<preference name="HideKeyboardFormAccessoryBar" value="false" />
<preference name="SuppressesIncrementalRendering" value="false" />
<preference name="android-minSdkVersion" value="17" />
<preference name="android-targetSdkVersion" value="17" />
<preference name="android-installLocation" value="internalOnly" />
<preference name="SplashScreenDelay" value="5000" />
<preference name="ErrorUrl" value="" />
<preference name="BackgroundColor" value="0x000000" />
<preference name="KeepRunning" value="true" />
<preference name="DisallowOverscroll" value="false" />
<preference name="LoadingDialog" value="," />
<preference name="LoadUrlTimeoutValue" value="20000" />
<preference name="disable-cursor" value="false" />
<gap:platform name="ios" />
<gap:platform name="android" />
<gap:platform name="winphone" />
<feature name="http://api.phonegap.com/1.0/camera" />
<gap:plugin name="org.apache.cordova.camera.CameraLauncher" />
<gap:plugin name="org.apache.cordova.console" />
<gap:plugin name="org.apache.cordova.device.Device" />
<gap:plugin name="org.apache.cordova.dialogs.Notification" />
</widget>
```

You could make a custom config.xml file for each project, or you can create one base config.xml file and edit it as needed per project.

Adding Plugins to a PhoneGap Build Project

As described in Chapter 1, "The What, How, Why, and More of Apache Cordova," Cordova (and PhoneGap, of course) applications are all about access to native capabilities. These capabilities are typically exposed to an application through plugins. I'm not sure what limitation drives this, but PhoneGap Build supports only a subset of the available plugins. You can find a list of the supported plugins in the PhoneGap Build plugins repository (https://build.phonegap.com/plugins).

The repository contains a good-size catalog of plugins, plus you can submit your own for approval. In order for PhoneGap Build to be able to accept your plugin, you must agree to a license and your plugin must conform to the following requirements:

- Must be a Cordova plugin compatible with Plugman (described in Chapter 4, "Using the Cordova Command-Line Interfaces")
- Must be licensed under the Apache 2.0 or MIT license
- Must be distributed as source code only and contain no binary code
- Can be no larger than 15MB

Plugins are added to a PhoneGap Build project through the config.xml file as described at http://goo.gl/g3iBOM. For each plugin, you must add a `gap` entry as shown in the following example:

```
<gap:plugin name="plugin_name" />
```

As an example, to add the Cordova Device plugin to an application, you would add the following entry to the project's config.xml:

```
<gap:plugin name="org.apache.cordova.device.Device" />
```

You can see an example of this entry in a real config.xml in Listing 12.3.

You can also specify a specific version of a plugin by adding a version attribute to the XML element:

```
<gap:plugin name="plugin_name" version="plugin_version" />
```

So, to lock the Device plugin example to a specific version, use

```
<gap:plugin name="org.apache.cordova.device.Device" version="0.2.22" />
```

As you'll see in Chapter 16, "Creating Cordova Plugins," the plugin reference in the config.xml can include additional parameters that are used to configure the plugin:

```
<gap:plugin name="com.johnwargo.myplugin">
  <param name="Param1" value="42" />
  <param name="DebugMode" value="true" />
</gap:plugin>
```

With the appropriate entries added to the config.xml and the plugin listed as an approved plugin in the Plugin Registry, the PhoneGap Build service should be able to add the plugin(s) to the application and complete the build process.

Deploying PhoneGap Build Applications

When the build process completes, it will provide you with access to the packaged applications for each of the supported mobile device platforms. You can deploy these applications to mobile devices in different ways, depending on what is supported by the device manufacturer and even the mobile carrier. In this section of the chapter, I'll show you in general how to deploy the applications; you will have to refer to the specific documentation for each mobile device platform to determine which options are appropriate for the platform.

The simplest way to deploy an application built using PhoneGap Build is to grab a compatible device and use a code-scanning application on the device to scan the Quick Response (QR) code shown in the upper-right corner of Figure 12.7. The code-scanning application will convert the scanned code into a URL and open the web page on the mobile device. All the user has to do is follow the instructions on the web page to initiate the application download and installation.

Each mobile device platform has restrictions on what can be loaded directly onto a device, so you may have to change settings on the device to allow the application installation. Android, for example, has an issue with downloading applications from unknown sources, but a quick configuration change can enable it. The setting is typically in the Security area of the Settings application and should refer to Unknown Sources. You can see an example of the setting in Figure 12.18.

In some cases, you will want to have access to the native application executable file. In this case, you can download the packaged application directly to your development system. If you take another look at Figure 12.7, you'll see that there are buttons to the right of each mobile device platform shown at the bottom of the figure. If you click the button for a particular mobile device platform, the browser will download the appropriate files for the platform, downloading an .apk file for Android, a .xap file for a Windows application, and so on.

You can also click the Install button immediately below the QR code shown in Figure 12.7 to be taken to another page where you can download all of the application files directly as shown in Figure 12.19.

Once you have the application files downloaded, you can distribute the applications to others and deploy the applications directly to supported devices.

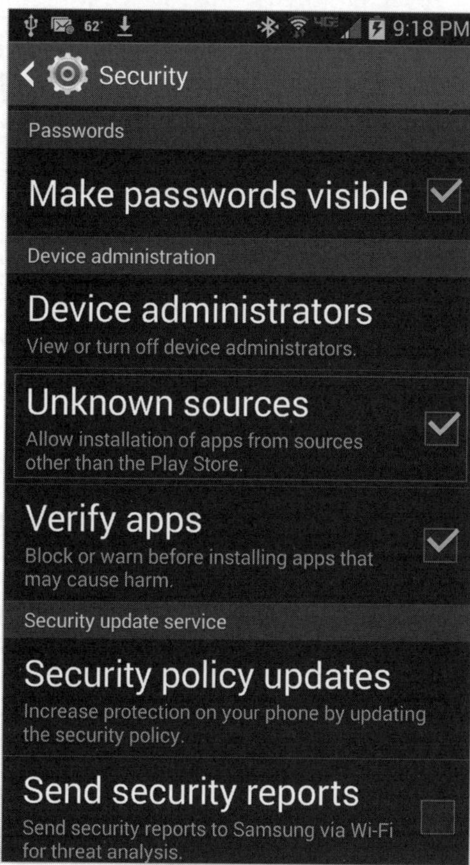

Figure 12.18 Enabling Unknown Sources on Android

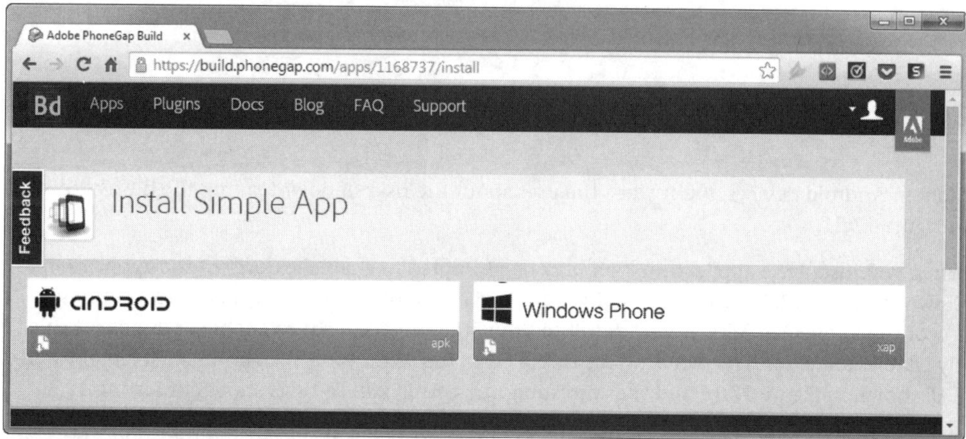

Figure 12.19 PhoneGap Build: Install Page

To test these applications on one or more device simulators, you can open the mobile browser on the simulator, then navigate and log in to the PhoneGap Build service using your credentials. If the simulator supports it, you can click the Install link and download the application's files directly to the device from the site as shown in Figure 12.20.

Figure 12.20 PhoneGap Build Accessing an Application from the Mobile Browser

Modern Android devices might warn the user about the risks of downloading the file as shown in Figure 12.21.

When you install the application, you may be prompted to enable features of the application as shown in Figure 12.22. Even though I've built only a simple application that doesn't even use any of the PhoneGap APIs, since I didn't tell the Build service what to enable or disable, it simply enables all features by default. This is related to the settings on the Permissions tab of ConfiGAP shown in Figure 12.16 and the corresponding config.xml settings shown in Listing 12.3.

The user will need to step through the pages here before being able to install the application.

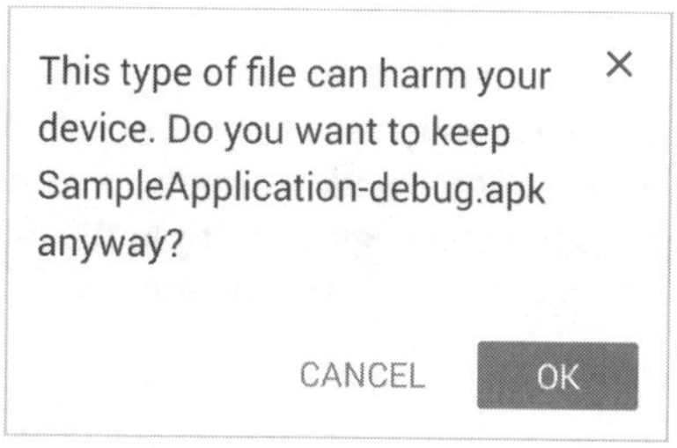

This type of file can harm your device. Do you want to keep SampleApplication-debug.apk anyway?

CANCEL OK

Figure 12.21 Android Application Security Prompt

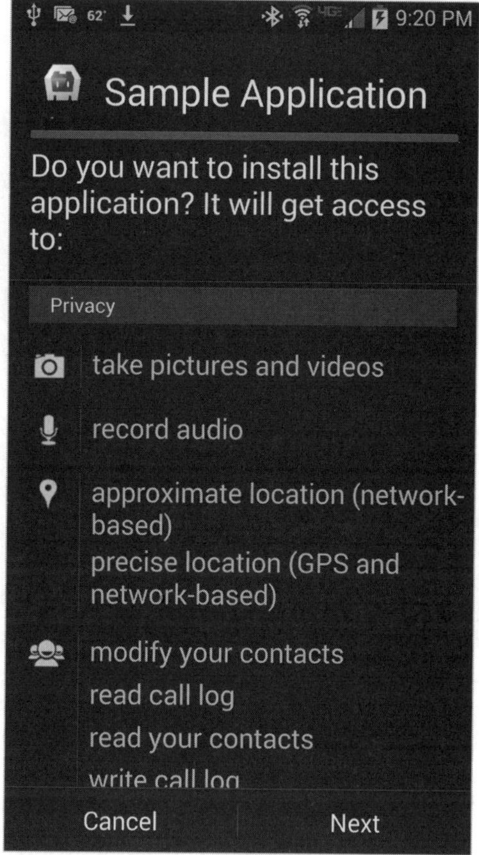

Figure 12.22 Android Installation Prompt

Wrap-Up

In this chapter, I showed you how you can use the PhoneGap Build service to package and deploy your web applications into the PhoneGap container. You should look at leveraging this service if you don't want to worry about managing multiple SDK installations or if you need an easy way to build and share your applications with a distributed audience of testers.

13

Using the PhoneGap CLI

The PhoneGap CLI is a command-line tool developers use to create and manage PhoneGap application projects. You can use the CLI to interact with local development projects, just as you do with the Cordova CLI (described in Chapter 4, "Using the Cordova Command-Line Interfaces"), but you can also use it to work with the PhoneGap Build service from the command line. In this chapter, I show you how to use the PhoneGap CLI for your projects, focusing most of my attention on how the PhoneGap CLI differs from the Cordova CLI.

PhoneGap CLI Rebirth

When I first started working with the Cordova CLI, it had everything I needed for the projects that I was working on. I wasn't using the PhoneGap Build service for anything except to describe it for my books, so I focused on the Cordova CLI instead. I saw the PhoneGap CLI demonstrated at my first PhoneGap Day, and from what I remembered of it, it looked just like the Cordova CLI with some extra stuff tacked on. That, as you should remember from Chapter 4, is how I regularly described it.

It wasn't until I started working on this chapter that I actually spent some real time with the PhoneGap CLI, and I quickly learned that it was nothing like I had previously described it. The PhoneGap CLI could be used to create and manage PhoneGap projects, just as the Cordova CLI was used to do the same with Cordova projects, but the two CLIs did things in a completely different way. Sigh; I truly can't understand why the PhoneGap team did this, but my testing proved this to be true.

OK, so for this chapter I had to learn a completely different CLI and then write about it—no big deal; I'm an experienced writer, so how bad could it be? When I started poking around with the CLI help, I really struggled to understand how this thing actually worked. There was more built-in help available for the PhoneGap CLI than for the Cordova CLI, so that was good, but it really wasn't very useful. It told me what the commands did, but not why I would use them; there was no description of the developer workflow.

I went to the PhoneGap web site and poked around there, only to find that the PhoneGap CLI help page was the Cordova CLI help page. Completely useless. I was able to switch the online docs page back to earlier versions and found that four versions back the CLI docs actually made a reference to the PhoneGap CLI rather than the Cordova CLI, but the documentation was still incomplete and there was no description of the complete developer workflow, especially using the PhoneGap Build service.

I started tweeting about this and emailing people I knew at Adobe who were working on this, and they acknowledged that there was work to be done. Eventually I learned that the CLI was due for an overhaul. A few days later, a completely new PhoneGap CLI was released that aligned very closely with the Cordova CLI. Whew. You can read all about this new version at http://goo.gl/fOIBaP. So, you can now use the information available in Chapter 4 on the `cordova` command with `phonegap`. What you'll find in this chapter is coverage of places where the PhoneGap CLI differs from the Cordova CLI.

The PhoneGap CLI operates the same way as the Cordova CLI demonstrated in Chapter 4. You open a terminal window, navigate to where you want a project created or to an existing PhoneGap project folder, and execute one or more commands by typing the text of the command and pressing the keyboard's Enter key. With the latest release, the PhoneGap CLI has access to the entire Cordova CLI command structure plus some extra commands.

Getting Help

The easiest way to learn about the capabilities of the PhoneGap CLI is to use the built-in documentation included with the CLI. To have the PhoneGap CLI display its help options in the terminal window, execute one of the following commands:

```
phonegap
phonegap -h
phonegap help
phonegap --help
```

For help with a particular `command`, you can use any one of the following:

```
phonegap <command> -h
phonegap <command> help
phonegap <command> --help
phonegap help <command>
```

As an example, to learn more about the `phonegap create` command options, you would execute one of the following:

```
phonegap create -h
phonegap create help
phonegap create --help
phonegap help create
```

For the `create` command, this does cause a slight problem. Remember from Chapter 4 that there are multiple forms of the `create` command: one where you simply provide the target project folder and the CLI uses some default settings and another where you provide all of the options on the command line. So, to create a project in a folder called help, you should be able to issue the following command:

```
phonegap create help
```

Unfortunately, this doesn't work. What you'll see when you issue this command is the command-specific help content for the `create` command. To create a project in a target folder called help, you must use the full version of the command:

```
phonegap target_folder appID appName
```

So, for my project called "help," the command would look like the following:

```
phonegap help com.ac4p.help Help
```

Project Management

As described in the sidebar, you can use the same Cordova CLI commands with the PhoneGap CLI, simply replacing `cordova` with `phonegap` in each command. With that in mind, the typical new project workflow will look something like the following:

```
phonegap create target_folder
cd target_folder
phonegap platform add platform_list
phonegap plugin add plugin
phonegap prepare
phonegap run platform
```

So, to create the Lunch Menu app we've discussed in previous chapters, use the following:

```
phonegap create lunchmenu
cd lunchmenu
phonegap platform add android ios windows
phonegap plugin add org.apache.cordova.console
phonegap plugin add org.apache.cordova.dialogs
phonegap plugin add org.apache.cordova.device
phonegap prepare
phonegap run android
```

That's it. With the latest version of the PhoneGap CLI, it should look and feel just like the Cordova CLI we've used throughout the book. All the other commands you learned in Chapter 4 should work here.

Anatomy of the Default PhoneGap Application

When you run this quick sample application, the application will render the page shown in Figure 13.1; this is almost the same sample app we've seen before in Figure 2.6, only showing the PhoneGap logo instead of the Cordova logo and slight changes in the page text.

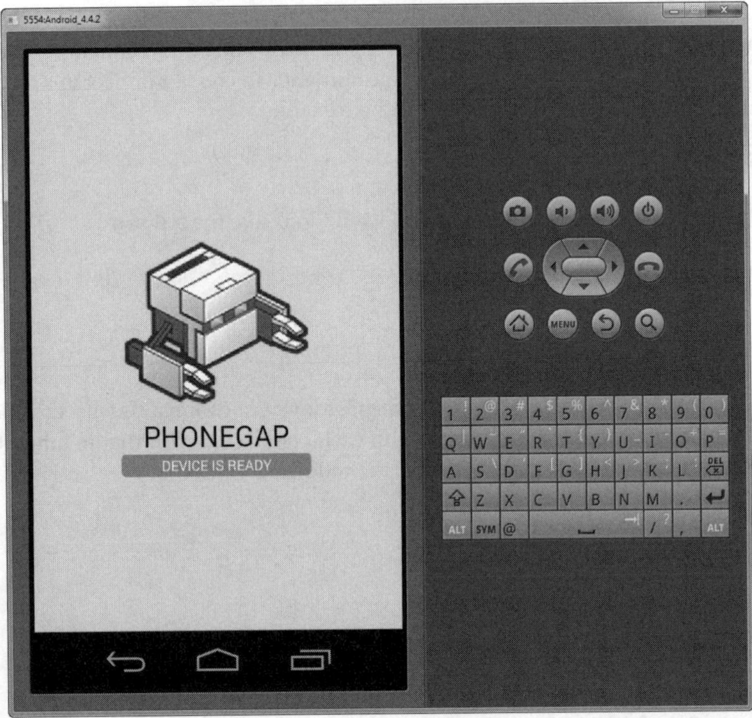

Figure 13.1 PhoneGap Sample App Running in the Android Emulator

I haven't added any of my own code to this project; I simply used the default project that PhoneGap uses. If you compare the application to the default Cordova application, there are some very small differences.

For the project's config.xml file (described in Chapter 5, "The Mechanics of Cordova Development"), Figure 13.2 shows a line-by-line comparison of the default file for this PhoneGap project and the default Cordova project. As you can see from the figure, mostly minor, descriptive differences appear between the files. The only major difference is the addition of the `preferences` element for the PhoneGap project. Preferences elements are used by the PhoneGap Build service and described briefly in Chapter 12, "Using PhoneGap Build."

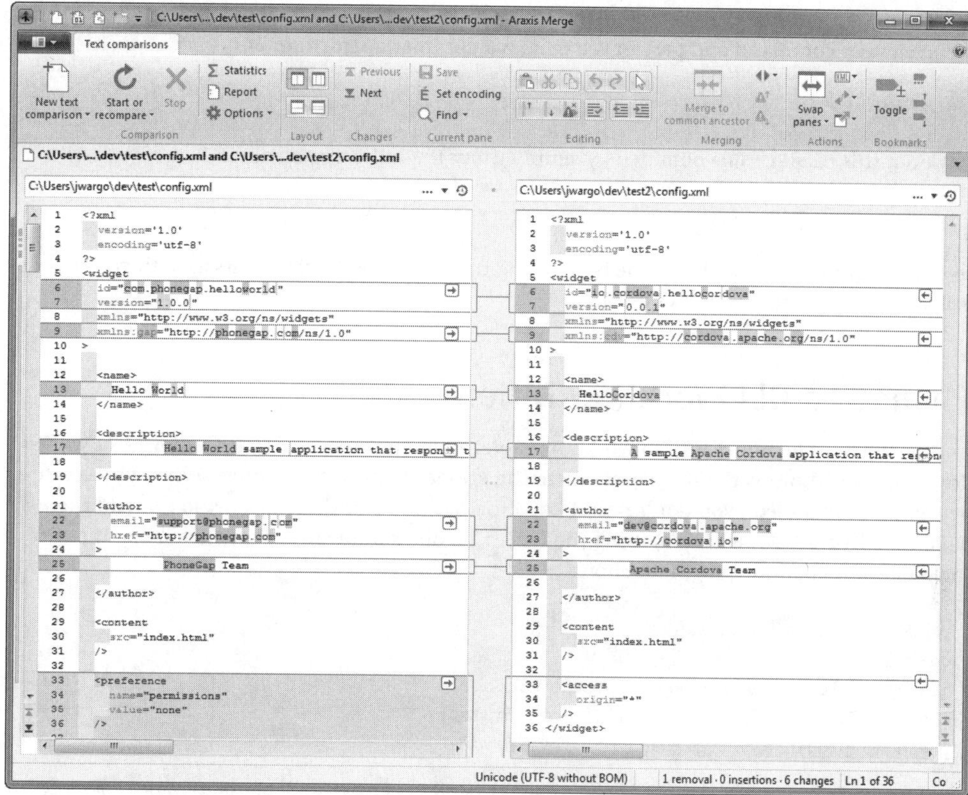

Figure 13.2 Comparison of PhoneGap and Cordova config.xml Files

The only other differences between the two applications are that the PhoneGap version of the application has the call to initialize the application in a script tag in the index.html file:

```
<script type="text/javascript">
  app.initialize();
</script>
```

The same call in the Cordova version of the application is simply appended to the end of the index.js file.

If there happens to be a Cordova CLI command that isn't directly supported by the PhoneGap CLI, you can use the PhoneGap CLI to pass the command on to the Cordova CLI like so:

```
phonegap cordova command command_parameters
```

So, to use the `cordova create` command from the PhoneGap CLI, you would simply execute the `phonegap` command and pass in the `cordova` command structure:

```
phonegap cordova create lunchmenu com.ac4p.lunchmenu "Lunch Menu"
```

However, this result can be obtained by simply using the following command:

```
cordova create lunchmenu com.ac4p.lunchmenu "Lunch Menu"
```

So I'm not quite sure what the value is of typing those extra eight characters as both commands deliver the same result as far as I can tell.

PhoneGap CLI Workflow Differences

As I've shown, the PhoneGap CLI workflow is pretty much the same as the Cordova CLI workflow. There are, however, some places where the PhoneGap workflow differs. When you create a new PhoneGap project, you don't need to add the platforms to the project; you can add them at build time instead. For example, using the Lunch Menu example from earlier, you could create the project and add the plugins as shown:

```
phonegap create lunchmenu
cd lunchmenu
phonegap plugin add org.apache.cordova.console
phonegap plugin add org.apache.cordova.dialogs
phonegap plugin add org.apache.cordova.device
```

Then, after you have added your web application content and you're all ready to test, you can add the Android platform to the project using the following command:

```
phonegap run android
```

Here the PhoneGap CLI will first add the platform (or platforms if you provided several on the command line), then execute `prepare` before starting the build process. This isn't a huge benefit as you're still adding each platform as needed; I believe this was added to support interacting with the PhoneGap Build service described in the following section.

> **Note**
>
> On the Cordova dev list recently, a developer requested that this same feature be added to the Cordova CLI. Michael Brooks from the PhoneGap team said he would add it, so you may be able to use this same feature with the Cordova CLI by the time you read this.

Interacting with the PhoneGap Build Service

So far, everything we've done has targeted a local PhoneGap project. That's fine, since you have to first create a local project and populate it with the necessary plugins and web application content before you can upload it to the PhoneGap Build service.

With earlier versions of the PhoneGap CLI, you instructed the CLI to work with a local project by prefacing every command with `local`. With the current version, the `local` parameter is being deprecated, and going forward the PhoneGap CLI will assume you're working with a local project until you tell it otherwise.

From a workflow standpoint, you can either create your project locally, then build and test using the local SDKs, or you can create the project locally and use the PhoneGap Build service to complete the build process for you. For the PhoneGap Build workflow, when you have your local project all ready to go, you use the `phonegap remote` command to switch the CLI context from the local project to the PhoneGap Build service.

Before you can work with the PhoneGap Build service from the command line, you must first log in to the service. The system will prompt you to log on the first time you try to use the `remote` command, or you can initiate the login process by opening a terminal window and issuing the following command:

```
phonegap remote login
```

In the following example, you can see the entire command-line process for creating the sample Lunch Menu application:

```
C:\Users\jwargo\dev>phonegap create lunchmenu com.ac4p.lunchmenu "Lunch Menu"
Creating a new cordova project with name "Lunch Menu" and id
"com.ac4p.lunchmenu" at location "C:\Users\jwargo\dev\lunchmenu"

Using custom www assets from https://github.com/phonegap/phonegap-app-hello-worl
d/archive/master.tar.gz

C:\Users\jwargo\dev>cd lunchmenu

C:\Users\jwargo\dev\lunchmenu>phonegap plugin add org.apache.cordova.console
Fetching plugin "org.apache.cordova.console" via plugin registry

C:\Users\jwargo\dev\lunchmenu>phonegap plugin add org.apache.cordova.dialogs
Fetching plugin "org.apache.cordova.dialogs" via plugin registry

C:\Users\jwargo\dev\lunchmenu>phonegap plugin add org.apache.cordova.device
Fetching plugin "org.apache.cordova.device" via plugin registry
```

At this point, the project has been created and all I have to do is populate the project with the appropriate web application content. Once the project is all ready, I can use the PhoneGap CLI `build` and `run` commands to build the app and test it using a simulator or physical device.

However, in this example I want to use the PhoneGap Build service to manage the build process, so I can initiate a remote build of the application using the following command:

```
phonegap remote build platform_list
```

To build for a single platform, I would provide the platform name at the end of the command:

```
phonegap remote build android
```

To build for multiple platforms, simply append the platform list to the end of the command:

```
phonegap remote build android ios windows
```

The CLI will return the following results:

```
C:\Users\jwargo\dev\lunchmenu>phonegap remote build android
[phonegap] compressing the app...
[phonegap] uploading the app...
[phonegap] building the app...
[phonegap] Android build complete
```

What happened is that the CLI packaged the web application in a .zip archive, created a new (or updated an existing) project on the Build service, and kicked off the Android build process. If I'd provided additional platforms with the command, the Build service would have started the build process for each platform.

On OS X, this worked without a hitch. On Windows, however, it may fail and display the error dialog shown in Figure 13.3.

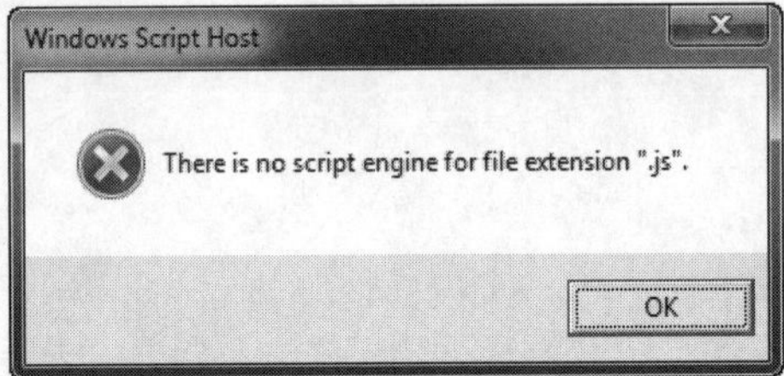

Figure 13.3 PhoneGap CLI Error

I had configured my development system so that JavaScript files open automatically in my editor of choice, and apparently the PhoneGap CLI has an issue with that. To get around this problem, I had to start the Windows terminal application with administrator privileges and issue the following command:

```
assoc .js=JSFILE
```

This resets some internal file associations and allows the PhoneGap CLI to complete its work.

At the conclusion of the process, you can log in to the PhoneGap Build service and see the application listed as shown in Figure 13.4.

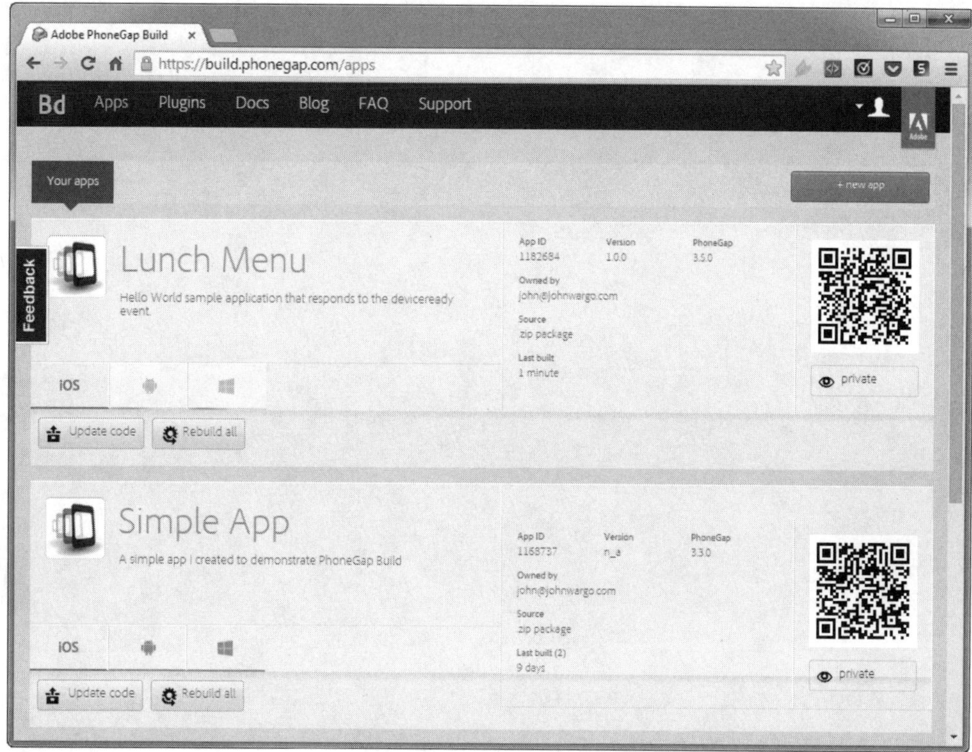

Figure 13.4 Lunch Menu Application on the PhoneGap Build Service

From here on in, the Build service operates as described in Chapter 12. The PhoneGap CLI provides an easier way to upload updates and initiate the build process from the CLI.

Wrap-Up

In this chapter, I showed you how to use the PhoneGap CLI to manage PhoneGap application projects. I highlighted some of the differences from the Cordova CLI, then showed how to use the CLI to upload projects to the PhoneGap Build service. With these tools in hand, you now have additional tools to use with your hybrid application projects and an easier way to upload updates to your application to the Build service.

14

Working with the Cordova APIs

So far I've shown you a lot about Cordova, how to set up a Cordova development environment and use the tools provided by the Cordova team and the mobile platform vendors. Now it's time, in this chapter and the two that follow, to talk more about how to build Cordova applications. In this chapter, I introduce you to the Cordova APIs and show you how to use them in your applications.

I don't go too deeply into each API. The Cordova documentation is a lot better than it used to be, but I show you at a high level how the APIs work and how to use them in your applications. There's simply not enough room here to do more, especially considering how useful the API docs are today. If you are looking for more detailed coverage of APIs as well as more complete examples, you will find them in this book's companion, the *Apache Cordova API Cookbook* (www.cordovacookbook.com).

In the next chapter ("Cordova Development End to End"), I describe the end-to-end Cordova development process with a complete example. In Chapter 16, "Creating Cordova Plugins," I show you how to write your own Cordova plugins and use them in your applications.

The Cordova Core APIs

Hybrid applications become much more powerful when they can do things that simply cannot be done within the mobile browser directly. As mentioned in the first chapter, one of the purposes behind Cordova was to provide mobile web applications running within the Cordova container access to native APIs. Cordova provides access to only a subset of the APIs available on a mobile device; the current suite of core Cordova APIs consists of

- Battery Status
- Camera
- Console

- Contacts
- Device
- Device Motion (Accelerometer)
- Device Orientation (Compass)
- Dialogs
- FileSystem
- File Transfer
- Geolocation
- Globalization
- InAppBrowser
- Media
- Media Capture
- Network Information (Connection)
- Splashscreen
- StatusBar
- Vibration

In some cases, an API mimics a capability that is already provided in modern mobile browsers. In most cases, applications simply use the existing API exposed through the native browser WebView embedded in the Cordova container. For devices whose browser does not expose the API, the Cordova team will implement the API so it is available across all supported mobile device platforms. You can see examples of this in the Geolocation and File APIs; they're pretty much standard on most mobile devices, so there's little the Cordova team has to do with them. As an example, take a look at the documentation for the Geolocation API:

> This API is based on the W3C Geolocation API Specification. Some devices (Android, BlackBerry, bada, Windows Phone 7 and webOS, to be specific) already provide an implementation of this spec. For those devices, the built-in support is used instead of replacing it with Cordova's implementation. For devices that don't have geolocation support, the Cordova implementation adheres to the W3C specification.

Because the File API is a standard that is already available in the mobile browser, I'm not going to cover it in this chapter. The Geolocation API falls into the same category, but in the hardware section of the chapter, I'll be covering other APIs that work just like it, so Geolocation will get some coverage there as well. The Contacts API is also based on a standard, but I'll give it some coverage here as it's unique in how it works compared to other Cordova APIs.

As mentioned in previous chapters, instead of APIs being readily available to any Cordova application, most of the core APIs are implemented as plugins. So, before your Cordova application can use any of the Cordova APIs, you will usually need to add the associated plugin to your project. To do this, open a terminal window, navigate to a Cordova project folder, and issue a command similar to the following:

```
cordova plugin add <path_to_plugin>
```

So, for example, to use the Camera API in your Cordova application, you must add the camera capabilities using the following command:

```
cordova plugin add org.apache.cordova.camera
```

This will pull the Camera plugin from the public plugin repository (currently www.npmjs.org). If you want to use the Camera plugin from a local installation, you can pass in instead the local file path pointing to where the plugin files are located as shown here:

```
cordova plugin add d:\plugin_folder\plugin_id
```

You can find more information about how to use the CLI to manage plugins in Chapter 4, "Using the Cordova Command-Line Interfaces."

Working with the Cordova API Documentation

To access the Cordova API documentation, point your browser of choice to www.cordova.io, then click the Documentation link at the top of the page. When I select that link, I am redirected to http://cordova.apache.org/docs/en/4.0.0/, which points to the appropriate language (English) version and to the latest and greatest released version of the framework.

On the Documentation page, use the drop-down menu in the upper-right corner to switch to the documentation for previous Cordova versions. The drop-down provides access to the documentation for the current Cordova version, previous versions, and even one future release of the framework called Edge. The Cordova dev team is working hard at adding support for additional languages, so you will see languages other than English represented in the docs.

At the bottom of the main docs page is a link to the Plugin APIs documentation. Click on that link to view the list of Cordova APIs. When working with the APIs, you will want to pay special attention to the "Quirks" section of the documentation for each exposed API; an example is the Camera API page shown in Figure 14.1.

Many of the APIs display different behavior on certain hardware platforms. As hard as the Cordova development team works to ensure consistency across all platforms, on some platforms an API needed to implement some feature simply isn't available or doesn't work as needed for the Cordova API. If you're trying something with a Cordova API and it is not working the way you expect, check out the quirks for that particular API.

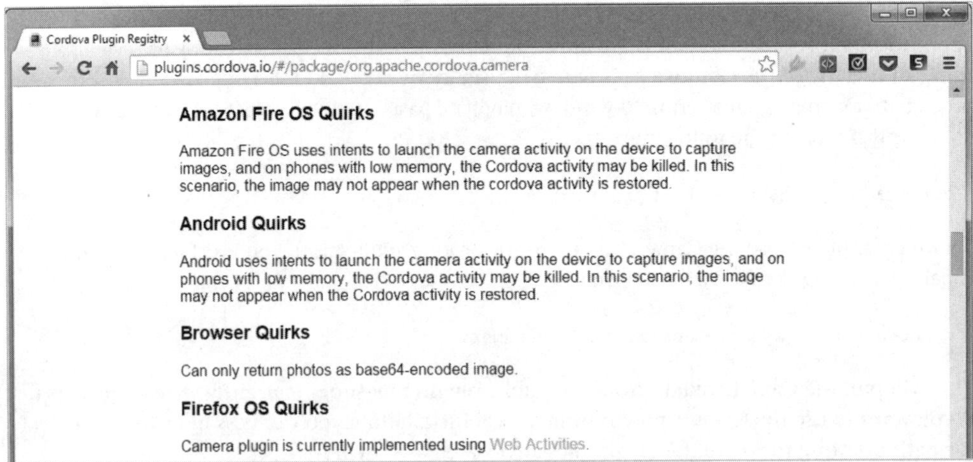

Figure 14.1 Cordova Documentation: API Quirks

Checking API Availability

If you try to use one of the Cordova APIs and the API isn't available, either because you forgot to add the appropriate plugin or because the API hasn't been implemented for the particular platform, you usually won't see any error messages as the Cordova container doesn't surface errors. To get around this, one of the approaches you can use is to manually check for the existence of the API before trying to use it. Listing 14.1 shows a sample application I created to highlight this approach.

Listing 14.1 index.html File

```
<!DOCTYPE html>
<html>
<head>
  <title>Test Application</title>
  <meta charset="utf-8" />
  <meta name="format-detection" content="telephone=no" />
  <meta name="viewport" content="user-scalable=no, initial-scale=1,
    maximum-scale=1, minimum-scale=1, width=device-width,
    height=device-height" />
  <script src="cordova.js"></script>
  <script>
    function onBodyLoad() {
      document.addEventListener("deviceready", onDeviceReady, false);
    }
```

```
    function onDeviceReady() {
      navigator.notification.alert("Cordova is ready!");
    }

    function doTest() {
      if (navigator.camera) {
        navigator.notification.alert("Houston, we have a Camera!");
      } else {
        navigator.notification.alert("No Camera, sorry.");
      }
    }
  </script>
</head>
<body onload="onBodyLoad()">
  <h1>Test Application</h1>
  <p>This is a Cordova application that illustrates how to check for Cordova API
availability.</p>
  <button onclick="doTest()">Click Me!</button>
</body>
</html>
```

In the application, the `doTest` function includes the following code:

```
if (navigator.camera) {
  navigator.notification.alert("Houston, we have a Camera!");
} else {
  navigator.notification.alert("No Camera, sorry.");
}
```

What this is doing is checking to see if the `camera` object exists. If it does, the application does whatever it wants to do with the Camera API. If the check fails, the application displays an alert (described later in the chapter) that lets the user know the Camera functionality isn't available.

What you can do is maintain a list of the different key APIs your application needs, then in the function that executes when the deviceready event fires (described in Chapter 2, "Anatomy of a Cordova Application") check to see that the API is available. Then, for APIs that aren't available, you can tell the user or, more appropriately, disable the application capabilities that utilize the unsupported APIs.

Catching Errors

One of the biggest sources of frustration for me as a Cordova developer is that I'll do something in my application's code and nothing will happen when the application runs. As I've described before, the Cordova container fails silently when it encounters an error in the application's JavaScript. When this happens, you might see something written to the console indicating the source of the error, but most often you won't. To get around this problem, you can add an `onerror` function to the application:

```
window.onerror = function (msg, url, line) {
  var idx = url.lastIndexOf("/");
  if (idx > -1) {
    url = url.substring(idx + 1);
  }
  //Build the message string we'll display to the user
  var errStr = "ERROR in " + url + " (line #" + line + "): " + msg;
  //Write the error to the console
  console.error(errStr);
  //Tell the user what happened
  alert(errStr);
  return false;
};
```

Put this code anywhere within your application's JavaScript code, but outside of any functions, and when an error is encountered, an error message is written to the console and the same error message is displayed in a dialog.

My biggest issue with testing new Cordova applications is that I often forget to add one or more critical plugins to the project. Using the `onerror` code shown above, I at least get an indication that a particular API isn't available when I run the application for the first time.

You may be wondering why I didn't use the Cordova `alert` method in this code. That's because if an error occurred before the deviceready event fired, the Cordova alert dialog wouldn't show because Cordova wouldn't have initialized all of its plugins yet, especially the Dialogs plugin.

Setting Application Permissions

Because most of the Cordova APIs leverage native APIs and many of them have security restrictions placed on them, in order to protect the user and/or device, developers using some Cordova APIs must set special configuration settings for their applications before deploying them to devices. These settings configure the native application container so that it informs the mobile OS during installation that it uses specific restricted APIs. This causes the mobile OS for some platforms to prompt the user of the application during installation to allow or disallow the restricted API or APIs for the application.

As an example of how this will appear to users, take a look at Figure 14.2, which shows the security prompt displayed when installing the default HelloCordova application (described in Chapter 2) on an Android device.

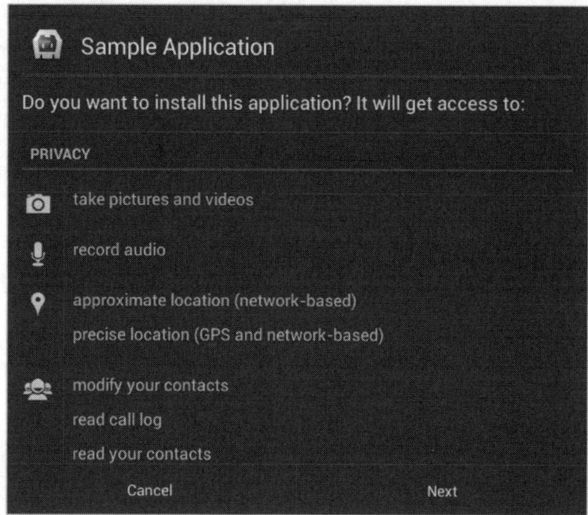

Figure 14.2 Android Application Permissions Settings Dialog

> **Warning**
>
> On many mobile device platforms, if a particular API or feature isn't enabled for a Cordova application as shown in this section, or if the user disables the feature by canceling the dialog shown in Figure 14.2, the portion of the application that uses the feature will simply fail silently when the application runs.
>
> You would think that the application would throw some sort of error when it tries to use a disabled or restricted API, but that's not the case—the application simply stops the execution of the JavaScript code and you're left scratching your head as to why the feature isn't working. If you've implemented a feature and it's simply not working and not telling you why, be sure to check your application permissions.

The good news is that the Cordova CLI manages setting application permissions for you. If there are special settings you must set in order to use a specific feature, you can find the information you need in the API docs. Figure 14.3 shows a portion of the documentation page for the Contacts API. Here you can see the specific application permissions that must be set on Firefox OS to enable a particular feature.

OK, now that I've covered all of the background information, let's start talking about the APIs.

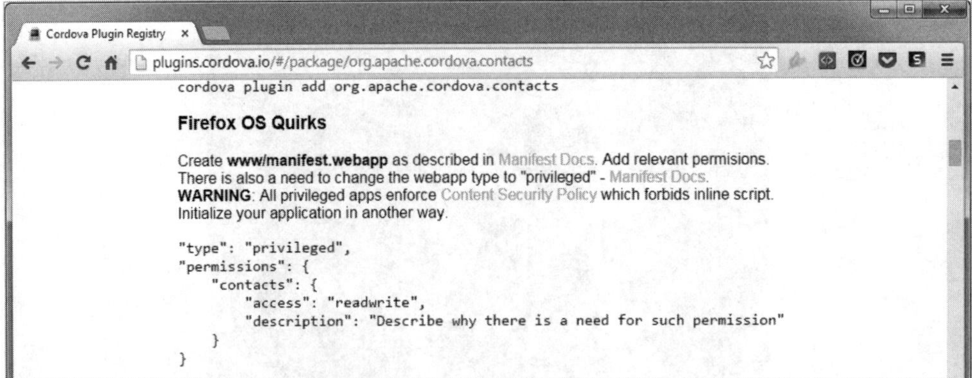

Figure 14.3 Cordova API Documentation—Permission Settings

Cordova Objects

Some of the Cordova APIs are not necessarily APIs; instead, they're useful objects that are exposed to a Cordova application through the plugin. In this section, I'll describe the `connection` and `device` objects and show you how to use them in your Cordova applications.

Connection Type

There are times when a mobile application needs to know what type of network connection it has available to it. With many mobile carriers capping data usage, the application should be careful when doing large updates to make sure it is doing so, for example, on a lower-cost (free) Wi-Fi connection rather than a cellular connection. As a best practice, mobile developers should categorize an application's data usage patterns and write their code in order to minimize the impact on the device and the device user's data plan costs.

To accommodate this, the Cordova framework exposes a `connection` object that can be used to determine the network connection type currently in effect. To leverage the information exposed by the `connection` object, you must first add the Network Information plugin to a project by opening a terminal window, navigating to the Cordova project folder, and issuing the following command:

```
cordova plugin add org.apache.cordova.network-information
```

With that in place, a Cordova application can determine the connection type by executing the following JavaScript code:

```
var ct = navigator.connection.type;
```

Next, you can compare the value of `ct` against the possible connection types exposed through the following properties:

- `Connection.CELL`
- `Connection.CELL_2G`
- `Connection.CELL_3G`
- `Connection.CELL_4G`
- `Connection.ETHERNET`
- `Connection.NONE`
- `Connection.UNKNOWN`
- `Connection.WIFI`

So, if you want to make sure the application has a network connection before you do something networky, your application can do something like this:

```
ct = navigator.connection.type;
if (ct != Connection.NONE) {
  console.log("You have a connection");
  //do whatever you want to do with the connection

} else {
  //Warn the user that they can't do that without a
  //network connection
  alert("No connection available!");
}
```

> **Warning**
>
> Your application has to query the `connection` object every time it wants to know what the current network status is. The `ct` variable shown in the previous example won't maintain a valid status value as the network status changes. When I cover events later in the chapter, you will see how you can monitor network connectivity.

If you are looking for a specific network type, your application can do something like this:

```
ct = navigator.connection.type;
if (ct == Connection.WIFI) {
  console.log("You have a WI-FI connection");
  //do whatever you want to do over the connection

} else {
  //Warn the user that they can't do that without a WI-FI
```

```
    //network connection
    alert("Function requires WI-FI network connection!");
  }
```

An application can also monitor the network status in real time using the online and offline events described later in the chapter.

device

The Cordova framework also exposes a `device` object that can be used to determine a limited amount of information about the device. The available `device` properties are shown in the following list:

- `device.cordova`
- `device.platform`
- `device.uuid`
- `device.version`
- `device.model`

To leverage the information exposed by the `device` object, you must first add the Device plugin to your project by opening a terminal window and issuing the following CLI command from the Cordova project folder:

```
cordova plugin add org.apache.cordova.device
```

To see an example of the `device` object in action, take a look at the Hello World #3 application described in Chapter 2.

Alerting the User

There are often times when developers will want to notify their application users of some activity. A web application can display some information on a page within the application or even open up an HTML popup, but in both cases, the management of the notification (and its removal from view) is the responsibility of the developer. To make this easier, the Cordova API includes some JavaScript functions a developer can use to provide a notification to users. There are two types of notifications: what I call hardware notifications and visual notifications. Each will be described in the following two sections.

Hardware Notifications

Any modern smartphone provides APIs that allow a developer to have an application make the device beep or vibrate; Cordova exposes similar methods an application can call to make the device beep or vibrate as well.

To leverage hardware notifications in your Cordova applications, you must first add the Vibration plugin to your project by opening a terminal window and issuing the following CLI command from the Cordova project folder:

```
cordova plugin add org.apache.cordova.vibration
```

`beep`

To cause a mobile device to beep, a Cordova application should make a call to the `navigator.notification.beep` method. To have the device vibrate, a Cordova application should make a call to the `navigator.notification.vibrate` method. Each takes a parameter that controls how many times or for how long the notification lasts as shown in the examples below.

The `beep` method accepts a parameter that controls how many times the device beeps when the method is called:

```
navigator.notification.beep(quantity);
```

To have a device beep three times, simply pass in a 3 as shown in the following example:

```
navigator.notification.beep(3);
```

`vibrate`

The `vibrate` method accepts a duration parameter instead that controls how long the vibration lasts:

```
navigator.notification.vibrate(duration);
```

Duration is expressed in milliseconds, so to make the device vibrate for half a second, you would pass a value of 500 to the `vibrate` method as shown in the following example:

```
navigator.notification.vibrate(500);
```

To make the device vibrate for a second, do the following:

```
navigator.notification.vibrate(1000);
```

Visual Notifications

Cordova exposes a number of methods a web application can call to allow the application to interact with the user. Web developers have always had access to the synchronous JavaScript `alert()`, `confirm()`, and `prompt()` methods that can be used to interact with the user, but the Cordova versions of these functions are asynchronous and allow for additional control over the content in the dialog that is displayed to users.

To leverage visual notifications in your Cordova applications, you must first add the Dialogs plugin to your project by opening a terminal window and issuing the following CLI command from the Cordova project folder:

```
cordova plugin add org.apache.cordova.dialogs
```

`alert`

To display an alert dialog in a web application, a web developer could execute the following JavaScript code:

```
alert("This is a JavaScript alert.");
```

When the code runs in a Cordova application, you will see something similar to what's shown in Figure 14.4.

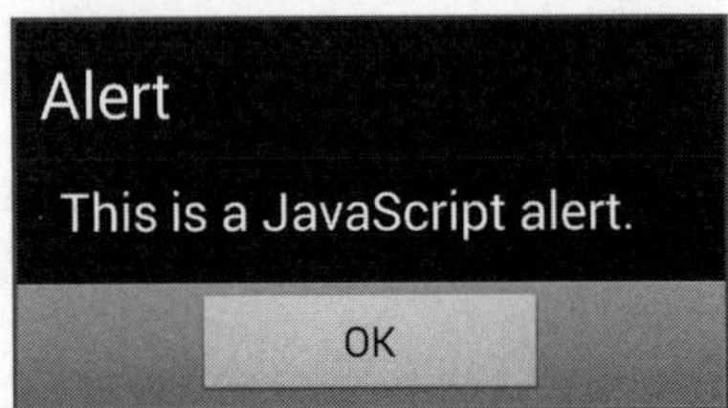

Figure 14.4 JavaScript `alert` Results

Cordova exposes its own `alert` method that you can execute using the following code:

```
navigator.notification.alert("This is a Cordova Alert.",
  myCallback, "Alert Test", "Click Me!")
```

When the code runs, you will see a dialog similar to the one shown in Figure 14.5.

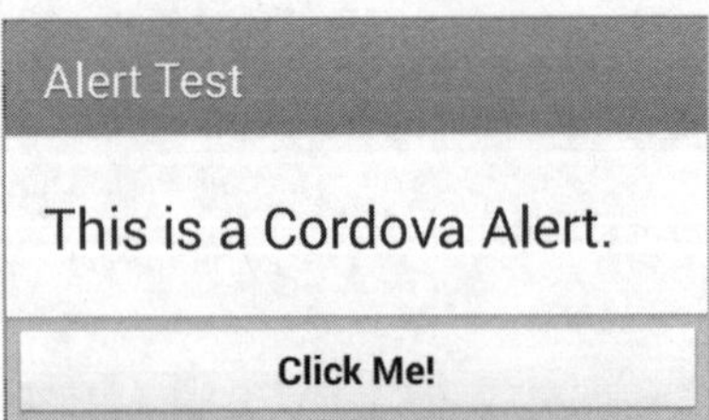

Figure 14.5 Cordova `alert` Results

Notice that I was able to set the title for the dialog as well as the text on the button the user taps to close the dialog.

I mentioned that the JavaScript `alert` is synchronous and the Cordova `alert` is asynchronous; this means that the JavaScript `alert` will stop application execution until the user taps the OK button. The Cordova `alert` will display and program execution will continue.

Now, in that example, I didn't tell you a lot about the format of the call to `alert`; in the following example, you can see the descriptive names of the parameters:

```
navigator.notification.alert(message, [callback], [title], [buttonLabel])
```

Note

In this example, the brackets around a parameter indicate that the parameter is optional.

Notice the `callback` parameter; it's there to allow you to define the function that is executed when the user taps the button on the alert dialog. The way you use the Cordova alert is to execute the `alert` method, then use the `callback` function to continue program execution after the user taps the button. Any code you have after the call to `alert` is executed by the container, perhaps finishing out the code in a JavaScript function. The application will continue to run or may sit idle until the user taps the button, then the code in the `callback` function is executed.

If you want, you can pass in a `null` value for the `callback` parameter:

```
navigator.notification.alert("This is a Cordova Alert.",
  null, "Alert Test", "Click Me!")
```

In this scenario, by not telling `alert` what function to call after the user taps the button, the Cordova container will render the specified alert dialog, then continue executing the JavaScript code that follows the call to `alert` and not act when the user taps the button.

The values for `callback`, `title`, and `buttonLabel` are optional; the value for `title` passed to the method will be used as the title for the dialog, and the `buttonLabel` value will be used as the text on the single button on the dialog.

`confirm`

The Cordova `confirm` method is similar to `alert` except that it allows you to specify more than one button label, and the `callback` function is passed a numeric value indicating which button was tapped by the application user. Here's the method signature:

```
navigator.notification.confirm(message, [callback], [title],
  [buttonLabels]);
```

The following code snippet shows how to use the Cordova `confirm` method:

```
navigator.notification.confirm('Do you want to continue?',
  doContinue, 'Please confirm', 'Yes, No');

function doContinue(buttonNum){
  navigator.notification.alert('You chose option #' +
    buttonNum + '?', null, 'Really?', 'Yes');
};
```

The value passed to the callback function is a numeric value indicating which button was tapped. The callback function will receive a 1 if the first button was clicked, a 2 for the second button, and so on. Figure 14.6 shows `confirm` in action on an Android device.

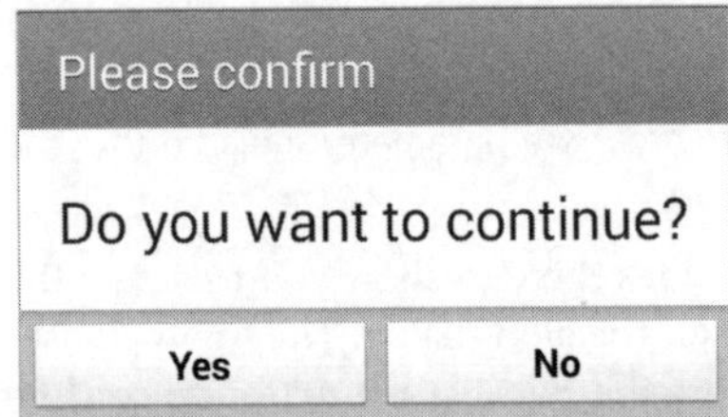

Figure 14.6 Cordova `confirm` Dialog

Figure 14.7 shows the results of the `doContinue` function being executed, indicating that the Yes button was tapped in Figure 14.6.

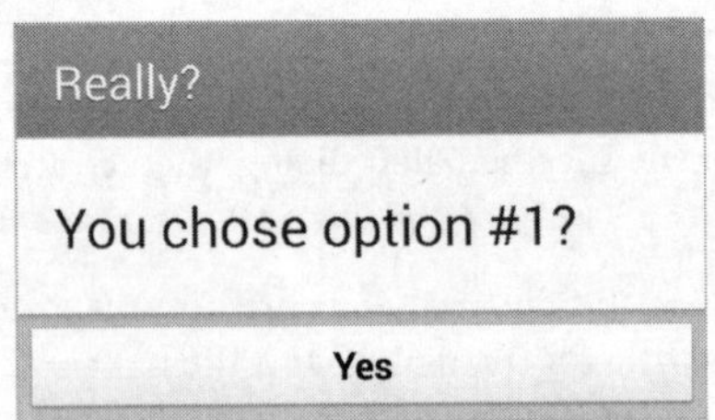

Figure 14.7 Showing `confirm` Results

`prompt`

Often a Cordova application will need to collect information from the application user outside of a web form; Cordova provides the `prompt` method to accommodate this requirement. The method works just like the other methods discussed in this section and has the following method signature:

```
navigator.notification.prompt(message, [callback], [title],
  [buttonLabels], [defaultText]);
```

To use `prompt` in your Cordova applications, make a call to the `prompt` method as shown here and provide the necessary callback function to process the user's input:

```
navigator.notification.prompt('Please enter your nickname',
  gotData, 'Nickname?', ['Cancel', 'OK'], 'Jimmy');
```

```
function gotData(res) {
  navigator.notification.alert('You chose option #' +
    res.buttonIndex + '\nYou entered: ' + res.input1, null,
    'Results', 'OK');
};
```

> **Note**
>
> Notice that `prompt` uses a different format for button labels than `confirm`. `prompt` expects an array of strings as shown in the previous example, and `confirm` expects a single string with the button labels separated by a comma.

Figure 14.8 shows the example code in action on an Android device.

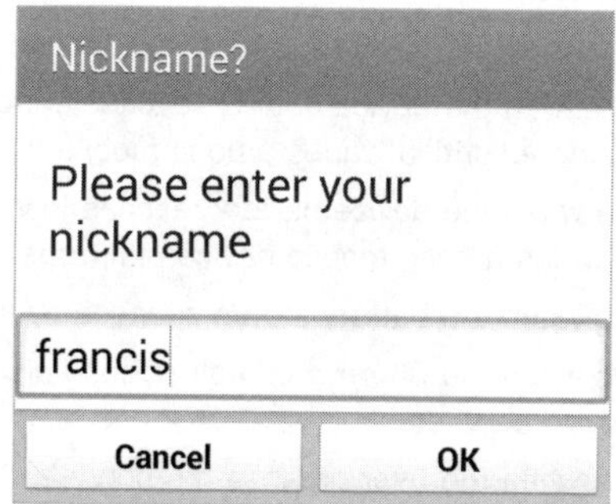

Figure 14.8 Cordova `prompt` Dialog

Figure 14.9 shows the results displayed by the `gotData` function.

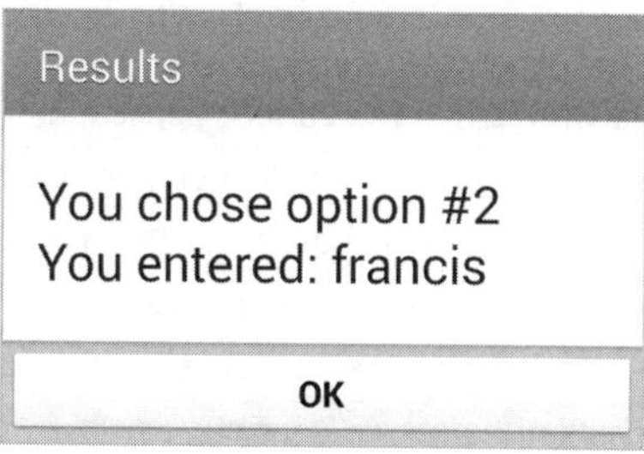

Figure 14.9 Cordova `prompt` Results

Cordova Events

The Cordova framework exposes a set of events a developer can use to react to certain things that happen on the device running the Cordova application. In some cases, the exposed events deal with hardware-related activities such as changes in the battery status or a physical button being pressed by the user. In other cases, the exposed events deal with application status changes such as the application being paused or resumed. The purpose of these events is to expose to a web application the same device status events that are available to native applications.

The complete list of supported events is provided in Table 14.1.

Table 14.1 Cordova Events

Cordova Event	Description
backbutton	Fires when the device's back button is pressed by the user.
batterycritical	Fires when the device battery reaches critical status. What is considered critical varies among mobile device platforms.
batterylow	Fires when the device battery reaches low status. What is considered low varies among mobile device platforms.
batterystatus	Fires when the battery status changes by at least 1% (up or down).
deviceready	Fires when the Cordova container has finished initialization and is ready to be used.
endcallbutton	Fires when the user presses the phone's end call button.
menubutton	Fires when the user presses the device's menu button.
offline	Fires when a device that has a network connection loses that connection.
online	Fires when a device goes online, when it switches from not having network connectivity to having network connectivity.
pause	Fires when the Cordova application is suspended. This typically happens when the device user switches to another application and the native OS pushes the current application to the background.
resume	Fires when a paused application is brought to the foreground.
searchbutton	Fires when the device user presses the search button.
startcallbutton	Fires when the device user presses the start call button.
volumedownbutton	Fires when the device user presses the volume decrease button.
volumeupbutton	Fires when the device user presses the volume increase button.

> **Regarding Buttons**
>
> Older devices had physical menu buttons and physical buttons to start and end phone calls. On newer devices, those buttons have been removed and replaced with virtual buttons that appear only when needed (like the menu and search buttons) or are specific to an application (like the phone buttons).

The majority of the listed events are built into the Cordova container. Only battery status is implemented as a plugin. To enable an application to monitor battery events, you must first add the Battery Status plugin to your project by issuing the following CLI command from the Cordova project folder:

```
cordova plugin add org.apache.cordova.battery-status
```

The deviceready event was discussed at length in Chapter 2; to see examples of that event in action refer to the Hello World #2 applications highlighted in that chapter.

To monitor one of these events, you simply have to have an application register a listener for it:

```
document.addEventListener("eventName", eventFunction, false);
```

As an example, to listen for the loss of network connectivity, you would register an offline event listener using the following code:

```
document.addEventListener("offline", isOffline, false);

function isOffline() {
  //Do whatever you want to do when the device goes offline

}
```

The `isOffline` function is called whenever the Cordova application that has a network connection detects that it has lost the network connection. No information is passed to the callback function; all your application knows is that the event has fired.

Battery event listeners are defined a little differently:

```
window.addEventListener("batterystatus", batteryCallback, false);
```

For battery events, the callback function is passed an object that can be queried to determine which battery event fired, the current battery charge level, whether the device is plugged in, and more. The object consists of the following values:

```
{
  "cancelBubble": false,
  "returnValue": true,
```

```
    "srcElement": null,
    "defaultPrevented": false,
    "timeStamp": 1416348013457,
    "cancelable": false,
    "bubbles": false,
    "eventPhase": 0,
    "currentTarget": null,
    "target": null,
    "type": "batterystatus",
    "isPlugged": true,
    "level": 50
  }
```

You can display information about the battery status in the console using the following:

```
function batteryCallback(batInfo) {
  console.log('%s event fired', batInfo.type);
  console.log(JSON.stringify(batInfo));
}
```

> **Warning**
>
> The events might not fire exactly when you expect them to on different mobile platforms. Be sure to test your application on different physical devices to make sure your application works as expected.

Hardware APIs

Cordova exposes a few APIs that allow developers to build applications that interact with common hardware components found in most modern smartphones. These APIs help make Cordova applications feel more like native applications as they let a Cordova application interact with the outside world in some way.

There's no specific grouping of these APIs in the Cordova documentation; bundling them together under the banner of hardware APIs is just my way of keeping things organized. The APIs that will be discussed in this section are

- Accelerometer
- Camera
- Compass
- Geolocation
- Media Capture

The Accelerometer, Compass, and Geolocation APIs all work in essentially the same manner; your application can measure the current value for the particular metric, or you can set up a watch that allows your application to monitor the particular metric as it changes over time. Both the Camera and Media Capture APIs allow you to capture photographs using the device camera, but they operate differently, plus the Media Capture API allows you to record video and audio files as well.

The World Wide Web Consortium has worked on defining specifications for some of these capabilities. The Compass API is defined at http://goo.gl/d1ptMV, the Geolocation API specification is defined at http://goo.gl/5q1bZc, and the Device Orientation specification is defined at http://goo.gl/Ivb6dA.

What you'll find is that some of the Cordova APIs align closely with the W3C specifications and others do not. For example, the Cordova Compass API has a `getCurrentHeading` method while the W3C specification uses `getCurrentOrientation`. I assume that the Cordova APIs will align with the standards over time; you will need to monitor progress and update your applications accordingly.

In the sections that follow, I will show you a little about how each of the APIs operates. Some of the APIs support a lot of options, so deep coverage is beyond the scope of this book; you can find complete examples of how to use each of these APIs in *Apache Cordova API Cookbook* (www.cordovacookbook.com).

Accelerometer

The Cordova Accelerometer API allows an application to determine the device's orientation in a three-dimensional space (using a three-dimensional Cartesian coordinate system of x, y, and z). To enable an application to use the Accelerometer API you must first add the Device Motion plugin to your project by opening a terminal window, navigating to a Cordova project folder, and issuing the following command:

```
cordova plugin add org.apache.cordova.device-motion
```

The API exposes three methods:

- `accelerometer.getCurrentAcceleration`
- `accelerometer.watchAcceleration`
- `accelerometer.clearWatch`

The `getCurrentAcceleration` method allows an application to query the device's current orientation. The `watchAcceleration` and `clearWatch` methods are used to allow an application to capture device orientation over a period of time, taking repeated measurements from the accelerometer at a specific time interval.

To measure the device's current orientation, you would use something like the following:

```
navigator.accelerometer.getCurrentAcceleration(onSuccess, onFailure);
```

In this example, the call to `getCurrentAcceleration` includes the names of two functions: `onSuccess` is executed after the orientation has been measured, and `onFailure` is executed if an error occurs. Here are examples of some functions that can be used for this purpose:

```
function onSuccess(res) {
  x = res.x;
  y = res.y;
  z = res.z;
  var d = new Date(res.timestamp);
  timestamp = d.toLocaleString();
}

function onFailure() {
  alert('I have no idea why this failed, but it did.');
}
```

The `onSuccess` function is passed an object that represents the different parts of the accelerometer measurement. The x, y, and z values represent the device's orientation in a three-dimensional coordinate system, and the timestamp value indicates the date/time when the measurement was made. If you write those values out to an application's screen, you will see something similar to what is shown in Figure 14.10, captured on an Android device.

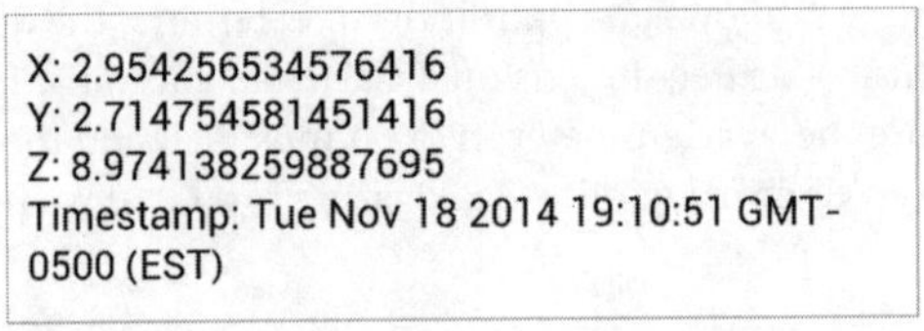

X: 2.954256534576416
Y: 2.714754581451416
Z: 8.974138259887695
Timestamp: Tue Nov 18 2014 19:10:51 GMT-0500 (EST)

Figure 14.10 Accelerometer Measurement Results

On an Android device, with the device lying flat on a tabletop, the accelerometer will return approximately the following values: z: 0, y: 0, z: 10. As the device is flipped so it's standing on its left edge, the values will adjust to approximately x: 10, y: 0, z: 0. If you instead move the device so it's standing on its bottom edge, the values will adjust to approximately x: 0, y: 10, z: 0. Standing the device on its top edge will result in approximate accelerometer values of x: 0, y: –10, z: 0. An application uses these values to determine how a user is holding the device, which is most useful for games and interactive applications.

Unfortunately, Cordova doesn't tell you anything about any errors that occur, when the `onFailure` function is called and nothing is passed to it (an error code or error message), that can be used to identify the source of the error. So, it either works or it doesn't; but as the app is talking directly to a physical device API that doesn't have much complexity, if you try to determine the orientation and the call fails, it's most likely because the device doesn't have an accelerometer.

getCurrentAcceleration is useful if you want a quick check of a device's orientation before doing something within your application. If you want to monitor a device's orientation over time, in a game, for example, getCurrentAcceleration isn't that useful. To use it in a game, you would have to write code that manually checks the orientation periodically. To help developers in this situation, the Cordova API allows a developer to periodically read the accelerometer by watching it using the accelerometer.watchAcceleration method.

To use accelerometer.watchAcceleration, an application sets up a watch using the following code:

```
var options = {frequency : 1000};
watchID = navigator.accelerometer.watchAcceleration(onSuccess,
  onFailure, options);
```

In this particular example, the code uses the same onSuccess and onFailure functions from the previous example.

The options object defines the frequency of the accelerometer measurement in milliseconds. So, to measure the current accelerometer values every second you would use 1000 as shown in the example. To measure every half-second, use a frequency of 500.

In the code, the result of the call to watchAcceleration is assigned to a variable called watchID that is used later to cancel the watch as shown in this example:

```
navigator.accelerometer.clearWatch(watchID);
```

With all of this in place, the application will read the accelerometer every second and pass the values to the onSuccess function to process the results.

Compass

The Compass API allows a developer to read the mobile device's heading (using the device compass if available). The API works almost the same as the Accelerometer API; you can either query the heading value once or define a watch to periodically measure the heading value. The only differences between the two are in the results object that is passed to the onSuccess function and options that can be set when creating the watch.

To enable an application to read the heading, you must first add the Device Orientation plugin to your project by opening a terminal window, navigating to a Cordova project folder, and issuing the following command:

```
cordova plugin add org.apache.cordova.device-orientation
```

Like the Accelerometer API, the Compass API exposes three methods:

- `compass.getCurrentHeading`
- `compass.watchHeading`
- `compass.clearWatch`

The `getCurrentHeading` method allows an application to query the compass's current orientation. The `watchHeading` and `clearWatch` methods are used to allow an application to capture the compass heading over a period of time, taking repeated measurements from the compass at a specific time interval.

To measure the compass's orientation, you would use the following:

```
navigator.compass.getCurrentHeading(onSuccess, onFailure);
```

In this example, the call to `getCurrentHeading` includes the names of two functions: `onSuccess` is executed after the heading has been measured, and `onFailure` is executed when an error occurs. Here are examples of functions that can be used for this purpose:

```
function onSuccess(res) {
  magneticHeading = res.magneticHeading;
  trueHeading =res. res.trueHeading;
  headingAccuracy = res.headingAccuracy
  var d = new Date(res.timestamp);
  timestamp = d.toLocaleString();
}

function onFailure(err) {
  alert("Error: " + err.code);
}
```

The `heading` object (`res` in the example) returned to the `onSuccess` function has the properties described in Table 14.2.

Table 14.2 Compass Results Values

Property	Description
`magneticHeading`	The compass heading in degrees from 0 to 359.
`trueHeading`	The compass heading relative to the geographic North Pole in degrees from 0 to 359. A negative value indicates that the true heading cannot be determined.
`headingAccuracy`	The difference in degrees between the magnetic heading and the true heading values.
`timestamp`	The date and time when the measurement was made (number of milliseconds since midnight, January 1, 1970).

When an error occurs, the `onFailure` function is passed an error code that can be queried to determine the cause of the error. Possible values are `CompassError.COMPASS_INTERNAL_ERR` and `CompassError.COMPASS_NOT_SUPPORTED`.

To use `compass.watchHeading`, an application sets up a watch using the following:

```
var options = {frequency : 1000};
watchID = navigator.compass.watchHeading(onSuccess, onFailure, options);
```

In this particular example, the code uses the same `onSuccess` and `onFailure` functions from the previous example. The `options` object defines the `frequency` of the heading measurement in milliseconds. So, to measure the current heading values every second you would use 1000 as shown in the example. To measure every half-second, use a `frequency` of 500.

You can also specify a `filter` value that defines a minimum degree value change that must occur before the watch is fired. As compass values fluctuate pretty rapidly, you will want to set a `filter` to reduce the number of times the heading measurement is made (and returned to your program) so your program can respond only to more dramatic changes in heading.

In the code, the result of the call to `watchHeading` is assigned to a variable called `watchID` that is used later to cancel the watch as shown in this example:

```
navigator.compass.clearWatch(watchID);
```

With all of this in place, the application will read the compass every second and pass the values to the `onSuccess` function to process the results. To see a complete application using the Compass API refer to Chapter 15, "Cordova Development End to End."

Geolocation

The Cordova Geolocation API allows an application to determine the physical location of the device running the application. The API is based on the W3C's Geolocation API and works almost the same as the Accelerometer and Compass APIs; you can either query the location once or define a watch to periodically measure the current location. The only differences between them are in the object that is passed to the `onSuccess` function and options that you can set when creating a watch.

To enable an application to determine the device's location, you must first add the Geolocation plugin to your project by opening a terminal window, navigating to a Cordova project folder, and issuing the following command:

```
cordova plugin add org.apache.cordova.geolocation
```

The Geolocation API exposes three methods:

- `geolocation.getCurrentPosition`
- `geolocation.watchPosition`
- `geolocation.clearWatch`

The `getCurrentPosition` method allows an application to determine the device's current location. The `watchPosition` and `clearWatch` methods are used to allow an application to periodically calculate the device's location, making repeated calculations at a specific time interval.

When the Geolocation API returns a `location` object, the object exposes `coordinates` and `timestamp` properties. The `timestamp` property contains the date and time when the measurement was made in number of milliseconds since midnight, January 1, 1970. The `coordinates` property is another object that includes the properties described in Table 14.3.

Table 14.3 Coordinates Properties

Property	Description
`accuracy`	The accuracy of the latitude and longitude coordinates in meters.
`altitude`	The device's height in meters above the ellipsoid (http://goo.gl/I91hDW).
`altitudeAccuracy`	The accuracy of the altitude coordinate in meters.
`heading`	The device heading (direction of travel) in degrees.
`latitude`	The latitude portion of the location in decimal degrees.
`longitude`	The longitudinal portion of the location in decimal degrees.
`speed`	The device's current speed in meters per second.

Refer to the Accelerometer and Compass sections for details on how this API works.

Camera

The Cordova framework provides two APIs for working with the device camera. One is the Camera API that provides developers with direct access to the native camera APIs, and the other is the Media Capture API described in the next section. The difference between the two options is that the Camera API exposes only the ability to take pictures with the camera, while the Media Capture API provides an interface to the camera that includes photos as well as videos plus the ability to record audio files. In this section, I will show you how to use the Camera API to capture pictures from a Cordova application; refer to the Media Capture API section for information on the other options.

To enable an application to take photos using the Camera API, you must first add the Camera plugin to your project by opening a terminal window, navigating to a Cordova project folder, and issuing the following command:

```
cordova plugin add org.apache.cordova.camera
```

From a programming standpoint, getting a Cordova application to take a picture is pretty simple; all you have to do is have the program call the Camera API using the following code:

```
navigator.camera.getPicture(onCameraSuccess, onCameraError);
```

To show how this works, I created a simple Camera application that makes that call to `getPicture`, then displays the data returned from the camera. You can see a screen shot of the application in Figure 14.11.

Figure 14.11 Camera Demo Application

As soon as you click the Take Photo button, the device's native camera application opens as shown in Figure 14.12. Manipulate the camera and image any way you want, then take the picture; in this example, you would click the camera image on the right. What you will see here will vary depending on the mobile device platform on which the application is running.

Figure 14.12 Device Camera Application—Confirming Photo

Notice in Figure 14.12 that there isn't a way to cancel taking the photo. Even if you decide not to capture a photo, you will have to snap one here, then you can cancel it in the next step.

Depending on the mobile device, you may be prompted to approve the photo as shown in Figure 14.13. In this example, you can tap Save to select the photo and return to the Cordova application or tap Discard to cancel returning the photo information to the Cordova application. On some devices, you will see graphical icons representing the select, cancel, and retake options the camera might expose.

Figure 14.13 Device Camera Application—Approving a Photo

When you accept a photo (by tapping the Save button in this example), the device camera application will close and return information about the selected photo to the Cordova application as shown in Figure 14.14. In this case, since I didn't tell `getPicture` anything about how to take the picture or what to do with it, the API used its default settings and simply returned a file URI pointing to the image file. At this point, the Cordova application can access the file using the URI it received from the API and render the image on the screen, upload it to a server, or do anything else it wants.

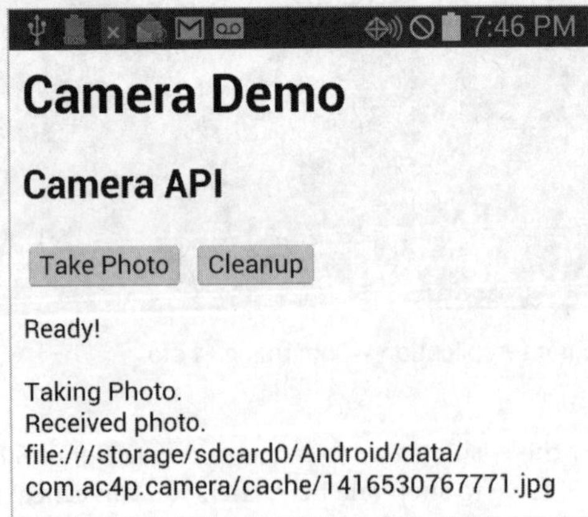

Figure 14.14 Camera Demo Application—Photo Results

If you choose to cancel the photo you've taken, the Camera API will return an error message of Camera Cancelled to the Cordova application.

Now that's not all there is to the Camera API; I was just showing you the API's default behavior. You can also call `getPicture` and pass in an options object that tells the API what to do and how to do it. Here's an alternate way to call `getPicture`:

```
navigator.camera.getPicture(onCameraSuccess, onCameraError,
  cameraOptions);
```

The `cameraOptions` shown in the example is a JavaScript object that contains the following properties:

```
var options = {
  quality : 75,
  destinationType : Camera.DestinationType.DATA_URL,
  sourceType : Camera.PictureSourceType.CAMERA,
  allowEdit : true,
  encodingType: Camera.EncodingType.JPEG,
  targetWidth: 100,
  targetHeight: 100,
  popoverOptions: CameraPopoverOptions,
  saveToPhotoAlbum: false
};
```

> **Warning**
>
> Different platforms ignore some of these properties, so be sure to check the "Quirks" section in the Cordova documentation before using them in your applications.

A developer will use some or all of these properties to control the picture capture process using the Camera API. Each of the possible options is described in Table 14.4.

> **Note**
>
> The camera options `targetHeight` and `targetWidth` properties have always perplexed me; when I wrote *PhoneGap Essentials* almost three years ago, I wrote the following:
>
> > The `targetHeight` & `targetWidth` parameters are supposed to control the height and width of the image obtained using `getPicture`. In my testing though, the parameters did not affect the resulting picture. The documentation says as well that the parameters must be used in conjunction with each other and that aspect ratio is maintained. This further reinforces that these options cannot work as documented (which my testing has proven) since it doesn't make sense that you have to set both height and width while at the same time maintaining an aspect ratio for the picture. If it truly was maintaining aspect ratio, then I'd expect that only one of the values would need to be provided.
>
> About a year ago I posted a question about this on the Cordova dev list, and from the responses I got back it was clear that it wasn't known how this should work. So, I tested all of the possible options and published the results to https://github.com/johnwargo/camera_res_test. The Cordova dev team is looking at this and will implement a fix someday.

Table 14.4 Camera Options

Property	Description
allowEdit	Boolean value. Specifies whether the photo can be edited by the user before being returned to the Cordova application. Not all mobile device platforms support this option, nor will many users expect this depending on your application.
cameraDirection	Numeric value. Directs the API on which camera (front or back) to use to take the photo. Use `navigator.camera.Direction.FRONT` for a front-facing camera (screen side) and `navigator.camera.Direction.BACK` to use the camera on the back of the device.
correctOrientation	Boolean value. Instructs the API to rotate the image to correct for the orientation of the device when the picture was taken.
destinationType	Numeric value. Specifies how the API will return the captured image. Options are `Camera.DestinationType.FILE_URI`, which is the default option and illustrated in the earlier example, `Camera.DestinationType.DATA_URL`, which returns the image as a base64-encoded string, and `Camera.DestinationType.NATIVE_URI`, which returns a native URI for the image file. Be careful using `DATA_URL` as JavaScript simply isn't capable of dealing with the entire image as an encoded string. Your app may crash if a high-resolution image is returned as a string to your program.
encodingType	Numeric value. Specifies the output format for the photo. Specify `Camera.EncodingType.JPEG` to have the API return a JPEG image or `Camera.EncodingType.PNG` to have the API return a PNG file.
mediaType	Numeric value. When `SourceType` is set to `PHOTOLIBRARY` or `SAVEDPHOTOALBUM`, this property specifies what type of file can be selected by the application user. Use `Camera.MediaType.PICTURE` to allow selection of photos only, `Camera.MediaType.VIDEO` to allow video files to be selected, and `Camera.MediaType.ALLMEDIA` to allow any supported media file to be selected. When `VIDEO` is selected, the API will return only a file URI; otherwise the API will return the image information in the format specified by the `destinationType` property.
quality	Numeric value. Used to control the quality of the captured image as a percentage of image quality from 0 to 100%. A value of 100 refers to full image quality with no compression. One of the reasons you would reduce the quality is to reduce the overall file size for the captured photo to make it easier to manipulate within your application.
saveToPhotoAlbum	Boolean value. Instructs the API to save images to the device's photo album after capture.

Table 14.4 Camera Options (continued)

Property	Description
`sourceType`	Numeric value. Specifies where the image should come from. Possible values are `Camera.PictureSourceType.CAMERA` (default), `Camera.PictureSourceType.PHOTOLIBRARY`, and `Camera.PictureSourceType.SAVEDPHOTOALBUM`. The behavior of this option will vary depending on the mobile device the application is running on as some devices do not expose photo libraries or photo albums.
`targetHeight`	Numeric value. Used to specify the target height of the captured image (in pixels). This is a weird one; see the note on page 343 for more information.
`targetWidth`	Numeric value. Used to specify the target width of the captured image (in pixels). This is a weird one; see the note on page 343 for more information.

Since the camera is a separate, independent application and an application user could take several photos before finally getting the one he or she wants to return to the Cordova application, there could be quite a few photos left lying around. In *PhoneGap Essentials*, I described how a developer could go into the file system and clean up the orphan photos manually. Since then, the Cordova team has added a `cleanup` method that can be used to clean up the orphaned photos. To use this method, call the method and pass in the names of success and failure callback functions as shown in the following example:

```
navigator.camera.cleanup(onCameraCleanupSuccess, onCameraCleanupError);
```

Unfortunately the method is currently supported only on iOS. When you try to perform the cleanup on an Android device, you will receive an Invalid Action error message.

Capturing Media Files

The Media Capture API is like the Camera API in that you can use it to capture photographs, but you can also use it to capture video and audio files. The API was originally based on the W3C Media Capture API (http://goo.gl/zypViK), but at the time, the PhoneGap team didn't or wasn't able to implement some of the API's features. The W3C stopped work on that specification as the Device API Working Group focused instead on the Media Capture and Streams API (http://goo.gl/B3d7g7) that isn't like the Media Capture API at all.

To enable an application to use the Media Capture API, you must first add the Media Capture plugin to your project by opening a terminal window, navigating to a Cordova project folder, and issuing the following command:

```
cordova plugin add org.apache.cordova.media-capture
```

The API exposes the following methods:

- capture.captureAudio
- capture.captureImage
- capture.captureVideo
- MediaFile.getFormatData

The first three work exactly the same; I'll show you how in a minute. The getFormatData is supposed to allow you to retrieve information about a media file, but because of limitations on mobile devices, very little or no information is available through this method.

Using the Media Capture API is pretty simple: you make a call to one of the three capture methods (audio, image, video) using the following method signature:

```
navigator.device.capture.captureAudio(onSuccess, onFailure, options);
```

Like many of the other APIs I've discussed in this chapter, the onSuccess and onFailure functions are called after the capture has completed successfully or when it fails.

The onSuccess function is passed a fileList object that can be iterated through to access the path pointing to each captured file as shown in the following example:

```
function onSuccess(fileList) {
  var len, I, path;
  //See how many files are listed in the array
  len = fileList.length;
  //Make sure we had a result; it should always be
  //at least greater than 0, but you never know!
  if(len > 0) {
    //Media files were captured, so let's process them...
    for( i = 0, len; i < len; i += 1) {
      //get the path to the file
      path = fileList[i].fullPath;
      //do something with the file here

    }
  } else {
    //This will probably never execute
    alert("Error: No files returned.");
  }
}
```

Once you have the path to each media file, you can upload the file to a server, play or display it within the app, and more.

When called, the onFailure function will be passed an object that can be queried to determine the error code as shown in the following example:

```
var onError = function(err) {
  alert('Capture error: ' + err.code);
};
```

The possible error codes are

- CaptureError.CAPTURE_INTERNAL_ERR
- CaptureError.CAPTURE_APPLICATION_BUSY
- CaptureError.CAPTURE_INVALID_ARGUMENT
- CaptureError.CAPTURE_NO_MEDIA_FILES
- CaptureError.CAPTURE_NOT_SUPPORTED

The optional options parameter controls how many media files are captured and, for audio captures, a duration property dictates the length of the audio capture:

```
var options = { limit: 3, duration: 10 };
```

Some platforms ignore some options, so be sure to check the "Quirks" section of the Cordova Media Capture API documentation and test on an appropriate sampling of devices to make sure you understand how this API works. The limit option works on my Android device, but my iPhone ignores it and captures only one file no matter what is passed in limit.

Globalization

Many mobile applications target audiences who speak and read different languages. If you create a popular Cordova app, it probably won't be long before you need to make it available in multiple languages. To make the globalization of a mobile application easier for developers, the Cordova team added a Globalization API that allows an application to query the OS for locale settings. Developers can use this API to determine the user's preferred language, then load the content in the appropriate language, but can also use methods in the API to better understand how to display dates, times, numbers, and currency appropriately for the user's preferred language.

To enable an application to leverage this API, you must first add the Globalization plugin to your project by opening a terminal window, navigating to a Cordova project folder, and issuing the following command:

```
cordova plugin add org.apache.cordova.globalization
```

The globalization methods all work in a similar manner; like most of the Cordova APIs, they're asynchronous, so you call the method and pass in success and failure functions as shown in the following example:

```
navigator.globalization.getPreferredLanguage(onSuccess, onFailure);
```

The success function is passed an object your application can query to access the value or values that are returned from the method. For most generic methods like the `getPreferredLanguage` method highlighted above, the method returns a string value that can be accessed as shown in the following example:

```
function onSuccess(lang) {
  alert("Preferred language: " + lang.value);
}
```

In this example, when the call to `getPreferredLanguage` is made, the `onSuccess` function executes and will display the dialog shown in Figure 14.15.

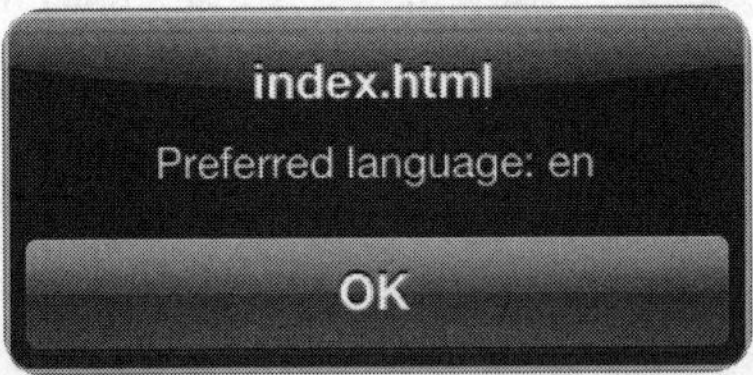

Figure 14.15 Results of `getPreferredLanguage`

Finishing out the `getPreferredLanguage` example, the failure function is passed an object that can be queried to determine an error code and an error message as shown in this example:

```
function onFailure(err) {
  alert("Error: " + err.code + " - " + err.message);
}
```

The possible error codes are

- `GlobalizationError.UNKNOWN_ERROR`
- `GlobalizationError.FORMATTING_ERROR`
- `GlobalizationError.PARSING_ERROR`
- `GlobalizationError.PATTERN_ERROR`

Table 14.5 lists all of the Globalization API methods as well as the parameters passed to the method and the results that are returned.

Table 14.5 Globalization Methods and Parameters

Method	Accepts	Returns
`dateToString`	JavaScript Date value, options	String value representing Date formatted based on options and user's current language settings.
`getCurrencyPattern`	Currency code	Pattern object that describes currency format and components of a currency value based on the user's current language settings.
`getDateNames`	Options	An array of month or day names, narrow or wide versions, depending on options and user's current language settings.
`getDatePattern`	Options	Pattern object that describes the format of a date value based on the user's current language settings.
`getFirstDayOfWeek`		Numeric value indicating the first day of the week based on the user's current calendar settings.
`getLocaleName`		String representation of the user's current locale as an ISO 3166 country code (http://goo.gl/6Xaf3J).
`getNumberPattern`	Options	Pattern object that describes the format of a numeric value based on the user's current language settings.
`getPreferredLanguage`		String representation of the user's preferred language as an ISO 639-1 two-letter code (http://goo.gl/EKwnmn).
`isDayLightSavingsTime`	Date	String value indicating whether or not Daylight Savings Time is in effect.
`numberToString`	Number, options	String value representing the number formatted using options and user preferences.
`stringToDate`	String, options	Parses a date string into individual components based on options and user's preferences.
`stringToNumber`	String, options	Parses a number string into individual components based on options and user's preferences.

As you can see from the table, some of the methods accept a `properties` object that allows a developer to control how a method operates. For example, to use the `dateToString` method to convert a date object into a string, a Cordova application would do the following:

```
var d = new Date();
navigator.globalization.dateToString(d, onSuccess, onFailure);
```

The `onSuccess` function is called after the date conversion has completed and is passed an object that can be queried to display the result as shown in the following example:

```
function onSuccess(res) {
  alert("Result: " + res.value);
};
```

When the application runs, on the Android platform it will display results similar to what is shown in in Figure 14.16.

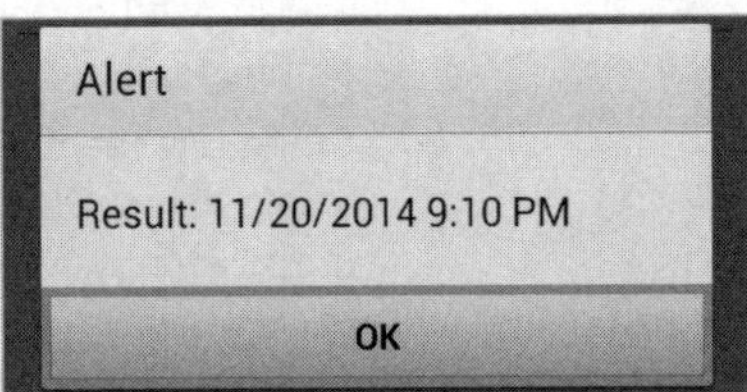

Figure 14.16 Displaying Results from `dateToString` Using Default Options

The `dateToString` method also supports an `options` parameter that a developer can use to change the format of the output as shown in the following example:

```
var d = new Date();
var options = {
  formatLength : 'short',
  selector : 'date'
};
navigator.globalization.dateToString(d, onSuccess, onFailure,
  options);
```

In this example, the `options` object is specifying `formatLength` and `selector` properties that are used to control how long the resulting string is and whether it should include date and/or time values (in this case I'm asking for only date). When I executed that code more than a year ago, my Android device displayed the dialog shown in Figure 14.17. When I executed the code today, the device displayed the result that is shown in Figure 14.16. Clearly something has changed with the API implementation on Android. Because of this, you'll need to make sure you validate the results on a range of devices just to make sure the API works the way you expect it to.

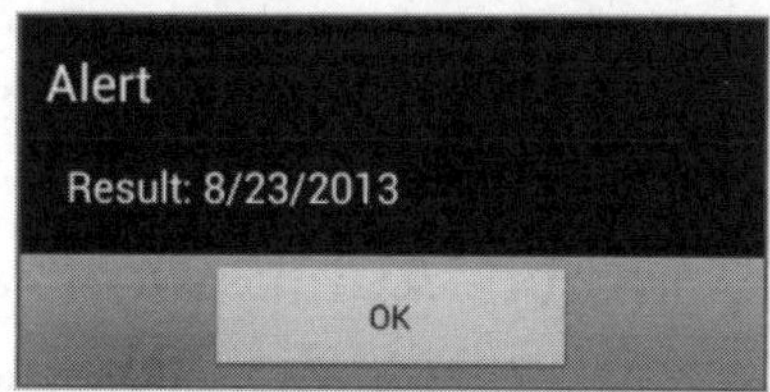

Figure 14.17 Displaying Results from `dateToString` with Options (Short Date)

You can use an `options` object that specifies `long` format, as shown in the following example:

```
var options = {
  formatLength : 'long',
  selector : 'date
}
```

Using `long` date format will change the application's output to what is shown in Figure 14.18.

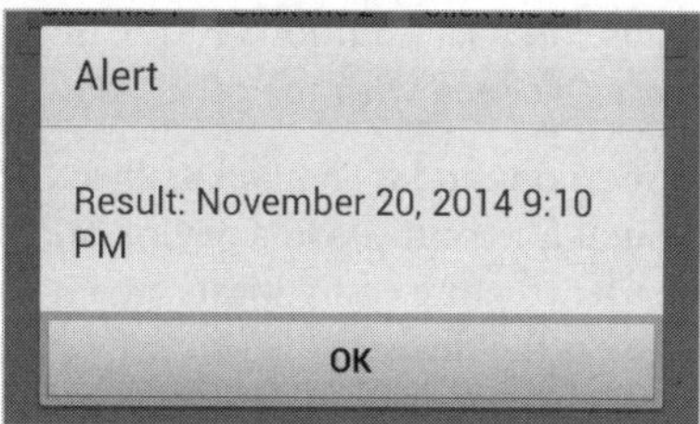

Figure 14.18 Displaying Results from `dateToString` with Options (`long` Date)

> **Warning**
>
> In my testing, on iOS I get the same results no matter what I pass in for options.

In this example, the success function is passed an object with only a single property, `value`, but several methods will return an object with multiple properties. The `stringToDate` method, for example, returns an object with separate properties for each date component as shown here:

```
{
  "month":7,
  "second":0,
  "millisecond":0,
  "day":20,
  "year":2014,
  "hour":9,
  "minute":47
}
```

When you use the Globalization API in your applications, refer to Table 14.5 and the corresponding Cordova documentation to understand exactly what any method accepts and what is returned.

Working with the Contacts Application

The Cordova Contacts API allows a developer to build an application that interacts with the address book or contacts application on a mobile device. The Cordova Contacts API is based on the W3C Contacts API (http://goo.gl/2unFyr). You would use this API if you wanted to build an application that read from the contacts list and used contact data within the application or used data from within the application to write a new contact to the contacts list.

To enable an application to access a device's contact list, you must first add the Contacts plugin to your project by opening a terminal window, navigating to a Cordova project folder, and issuing the following command:

```
cordova plugin add org.apache.cordova.contacts
```

The Contacts API is sometimes challenging to use because the contacts capabilities available on each mobile platform differ; so some of the contact fields you might use on an Android device will differ from what you would use on iOS. Additionally, the implementation of the Contacts API is a little different from what we've seen with the other APIs.

The Contacts API exposes three methods and a `contacts` object. The methods are used to create new `contacts` objects, search for contacts on a device, and display a contact picker your application can use to allow the user to more easily locate a contact. The `contacts` object is the representation of a contact record on the device.

To create a new contact, an application makes a call to the API's `create` method as shown in the following example:

```
var newContact = navigator.contacts.create();
```

Unlike the other API methods we've discussed so far, this particular call is synchronous, so instead of having to provide success and failure callbacks, this operation happens immediately. This method call doesn't actually create a contact in the device's contacts application; instead, all it does is create a new `contact` object, using the Contacts object's constructor. In this example, it's creating a new, empty `contact` object called `newContact`; nothing is saved to the contacts application until you call the object's `save` method which I'll describe a little later.

You can also populate the `contact` object during the creation process by passing in a `contact` object to the `create` method as shown in the following example:

```
var newContact = navigator.contacts.create ({"displayName": "John M. Wargo"});
```

In this example, I'm populating the `contact` object's `displayName` property when I create the new `contact` object. The `contact` object consists of the following properties; you can set some or all of these properties for a contact:

- `addresses`: an array containing of all the contact's different addresses
- `birthday`: the contact's birthday
- `categories`: an array containing all of the user-defined categories associated with the contact
- `displayName`: the display name for the contact
- `emails`: an array containing all of the email addresses for the contact
- `id`: a globally unique identifier for the contact
- `ims`: an array containing all of the contact's Instant Messaging addresses
- `name`: an object representing each of the components of the contact's name
- `nickname`: the nickname for the contact
- `note`: any notes associated with the contact
- `organizations`: an array containing all of the organizations associated with the contact
- `phoneNumbers`: an array containing all of the phone numbers associated with the contact
- `photos`: an array containing images associated with the contact
- `urls`: an array containing the web pages associated with the contact

Notice that some of the properties are arrays of other properties. A contact can typically have two or more mailing addresses, home and work at a minimum. Additionally, many contacts have more than one email address, so the `contact` object has to be able to accommodate a dynamic number of properties.

> **Note**
>
> I could spend about ten pages here describing all of the different arrays that are associated with the `contact` object, but that's really beyond the scope of this chapter. Instead, let me show you how to save the contact, then I'll show you how to search for contacts and dump the contact information to the console so you can more easily see how the `contact` object looks in the real world on different devices. If you need more detailed examples of how to use this API, don't forget that there's an entire chapter dedicated to this topic in my *Apache Cordova API Cookbook* (www.cordovacookbook.com).
>
> There are some inconsistencies in how different mobile devices store contact information, so seeing this in real-world scenarios is better anyway.

You can populate the contact object when you create the object as shown in the earlier example, or you can create the contact object, then populate the object's properties as shown in the following:

```
var newContact = navigator.contacts.create();
//Populate the contact object with values
var fullName = "John M. Wargo";
newContact.displayName = fullName
newContact.nickname = "John";

//Populate the Contact's Name entries
var tmpName = new ContactName();
tmpName.givenName = "John";
tmpName.familyName ="Wargo";
tmpName.formatted = fullName;
//Then add the name object to the contact object
newContact.name = tmpName;
```

In this example, I've created a new contact object, then started populating it with values. When it comes to populating the contact's name information, the code populates a ContactName object (defined within the Contacts object), then adds it to the newContact object. The ContactName object includes the following properties:

- familyName
- formatted
- givenName
- honorificPrefix
- honorificSuffix
- middleName

There are many different object types and arrays of objects that can be added to a contact record; this is only a small example of what can be done. Be sure to use the Contacts API documentation for details on all of the supported options.

Once you have all of the contact object properties set, you must call the contact object's save method to write the changes to the actual contact record:

```
newContact.save(onSuccess, onFailure);
```

The `save` method accepts the typical success and failure functions that you've seen with most of the other Cordova APIs. The failure function is passed an object you can use to identify the cause of an error and respond accordingly as shown in the following example:

```
function onFailure(err) {
  console.log("Error Saving Contact: " + err.code);
};
```

To manipulate an existing contact, you can use the Contacts API `find` method to locate the record as shown in the following example:

```
navigator.contacts.find(contactFields, onSuccess, onFailure, options);
```

In this example, the `contactFields` object represents an array of field names:

```
var contactFields = ["displayName", "name", "phoneNumbers", "emails", "addresses"]
```

The `find` method defines the field values that are returned in the search results; it does not define which fields are searched. Not what you expected, right? Me too!

The `options` object defines parameters around how the search is performed; a sample `options` object is shown here:

```
var options = {filter: "Wargo", multiple: true};
```

The `filter` property is used to provide the `find` method with the search string to use when searching records. The `multiple` property is a Boolean value that controls whether only a single (`false`) contact is returned or multiple (`true`) contacts are returned.

Let's take a look at a complete example. The following code sample shows how to call `find` and pass in a list of contact fields and search options. In the `onSuccess` function, the code simply writes the contact details to the console.

```
function findContact() {
  var contactFields = ["displayName", "name", "phoneNumbers", "emails", "addresses"];
  var contactOptions = {
    filter : "Wargo",
    multiple : true
  };
  navigator.contacts.find(contactFields, onSuccess, onFailure, contactOptions);
}

function onSuccess(contacts) {
  for (var i = 0; i < contacts.length; i++) {
    console.log("Contact[" + i + "]: " + JSON.stringify(contacts[i]));
  }
}
```

Remember that I mentioned that there was a way to see how every aspect of a contact record was structured? Well, the following chunk of JSON is the result (slightly modified to hide my real identity) of the previous example code running against the contacts database on my personal Android device. You can run the application, search for a particular contact, then grab the JSON text returned from the call to `find` and analyze it to see how to populate these fields within your application.


```
{"id":"1370", "rawId":"109", "displayName":"Wargo, John M.",
"name":{"middleName":"M.", "familyName":"Wargo", "formatted":"John M. Wargo",
"givenName":"John"}, "nickname":"John", "phoneNumbers":[{"type":"mobile",
"value":"(555) 555-3333", "id":"58", "pref":false}, {"type":"work", "value":
"(555) 555-4444", "id":"59", "pref":false}, {"type":"home", "value":"(555) 555-
6666", "id":"12860", "pref":false}], "emails":[{"type":"custom", "value":john@
somedomain.com ,"id":"901", "pref":false}], "addresses":[{"region":"CA",
"streetAddress":"99 Cordova lane ", "id":"902", "formatted":"99 Cordova Lane\
nSan Francisco, CA 99215\nUnited States of America", "postalCode":"99215",
"locality":"San Francisco", "type":"home", "pref":false, "country":"United
States of America"}, {"region":"CA", "streetAddress":"One Sybase Drive",
"id":"12861", "formatted":"One Sybase Drive\nDublin, CA 94568\nUnited States of
America", "postalCode":"94568", "locality":"Dublin", "type":"work", "pref":false,
"country":"United States of America"}], "ims":null, "organizations":null,
"birthday":null, "note":null, "photos":null, "categories":null, "urls":
"www.johnwargo.com"}
```


You can see, for example, how phone numbers are managed within the contacts application in this example:

```
"phoneNumbers":[
  {"type":"mobile", "value":"(555) 555-3333", "id":"58", "pref":false},
  {"type":"work", "value":"(555) 555-4444", "id":"59", "pref":false},
  {"type":"home", "value":"(555) 555-6666", "id":"12860", "pref":false}
]
```

Each phone number has a specific type, value, ID, and preferred status value. The ID should be created automatically by the device-side API when adding the phone number to the contact record.

The Cordova team recently added a mechanism an application can use to allow the user to pick a contact that is used by the application. When an application executes the following:

```
navigator.contacts.pickContact(onSuccess, onFailure);
```

the application will display a dialog similar to the one shown in Figure 14.19. If your application needs to prompt the user for a contact, it may be easier to use `pickContact` than to display an input field and use the value a user types to try to locate the contact. With `pickContact`, the user does all the work for you; all you have to do is process the result within your application.

The dialog displays the list of all contacts stored in the device's contacts application. When the user makes a selection, the success callback function is passed an object representing the selected contact, just as the `find` method does. Notice that the user can filter the results by typing in a portion of the contact's name.

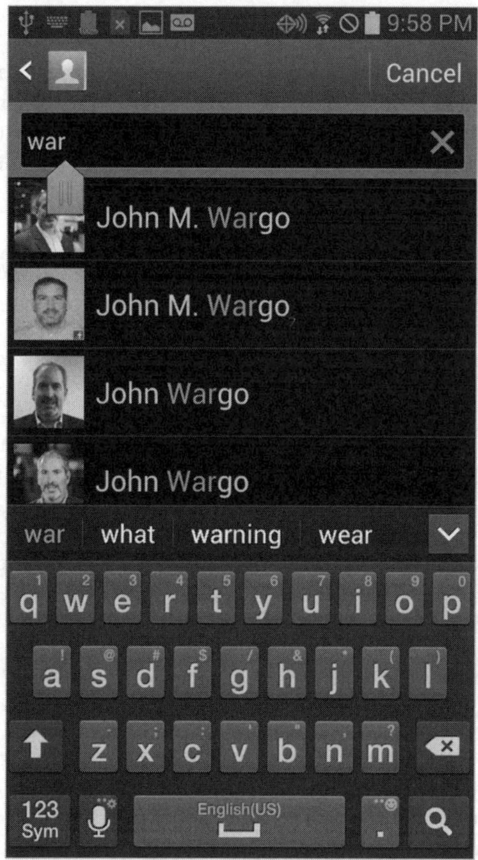

Figure 14.19 Contact Picker

Different mobile device platforms manage contact data differently, so be sure to test the contact format on each mobile device you will be supporting—you might have to deal with each platform differently.

Once you have a `contact` object returned from the call to `find`, you can change the properties of the object and write the changes back to the contacts application using the `save` method discussed earlier. To remove the contact, first get a handle to the `contact` object and make a call to `remove` as shown here:

```
foundContact.remove(onSuccess, onFailure);
```

There's a lot more to the Contacts API; I've only touched the surface. Be sure to leverage the Cordova documentation for more information.

Playing/Recording Media Files

The Cordova APIs include a Media API an application can use to record and play media files. This is the API you would use to play audio files in the background of a smartphone or tablet video game, for example. You could also use this API to build an application that records voice notes for playback, but most smartphones already have a dedicated app for this. At SAP, we're using this API to enhance a web-based customer relationship management (CRM) application running in a Cordova container with voice note capabilities.

To enable an application to work with media files, you must first add the Media plugin to your project by opening a terminal window, navigating to a Cordova project folder, and issuing the following command:

```
cordova plugin add org.apache.cordova.media
```

The Media API is like most of the other Cordova APIs in that the API's methods are asynchronous, but what triggers the callback functions is a little different. To use this API, an application starts by creating a `Media` object:

```
var mediaObj = new Media(srcFile, onSuccess, onFailure, onStatus);
```

The code creates a `mediaObj` object that points to the media file specified in the `srcFile` parameter shown in the example. The application doesn't open or connect to the file yet; it merely creates an object that refers to the file, nothing more. Other methods I'll show in a little while are used to actually play the file.

The `onSuccess` and `onFailure` functions shown in the example are the success and failure callback functions you should be familiar with by now, but they don't fire when you might expect. Since the code I've shown is only creating an object, there are no real callback functions that need to be executed as part of that process. The `onSuccess`, `onFailure`, and `onStatus` callback functions shown in the example are involved when any of the following methods are called against the `media` object just created:

- `getCurrentPosition`
- `getDuration`
- `pause`
- `play`
- `release`
- `seekTo`
- `setVolume`
- `startRecord`
- `stop`
- `stopRecord`

So, to play a media file called soundtrack.mp3, an application would use

```
srcFile = 'soundtrack.mp3';
var mediaObj = new Media(srcFile, onSuccess, onFailure, onStatus);
mediaObj.play();

function onSuccess() {
  console.log("Media: Success");
}

function onFailure(error) {
  alert('Media Error: ' + error.code + ': ' + error.message);
}

function onStatus(statCode) {
  console.log("Media Status: " + statCode);
}
```

To stop a media file from playing, simply call `mediaObj.stop()`. This example is using my example `mediaObj`; you would use whatever object you used to define your local `Media` object.

As you can see in the example, the `onStatus` function is passed a status code parameter that allows an application to understand what's currently going on with media playback or recording. The supported codes are

- `Media.MEDIA_NONE`
- `Media.MEDIA_STARTING`
- `Media.MEDIA_RUNNING`
- `Media.MEDIA_PAUSED`
- `Media.MEDIA_STOPPED`

With all of the methods and callbacks available with the Media API, you can build a complete media player application, or you can simply load up an audio file and play it without any UI; the API provides the flexibility a developer needs to do either.

> **Warning**
>
> The location where a Cordova application stores the media files packaged with the application varies among the different mobile device platforms. Android files are located in the /android_asset folder whereas on iOS, files are located within the root of the application's file area.

InAppBrowser

The InAppBrowser is a more recent addition to the Cordova APIs. It allows a web application to load content into a separate window. Originally created as independent Cordova plugins called

ChildBrowser for Android and iOS, it was added to the Cordova project as InAppBrowser, then expanded to support other mobile device platforms. It turns out that this plugin is pretty popular with Cordova developers as developers often need to open ancillary windows with content, and this plugin enables that to be done pretty easily.

Say, for example, that you want to show your application users additional web content. You could easily load additional content within your application and manage transitions to and from the content within your application. This is something that jQuery Mobile and other frameworks (demonstrated in Chapter 17, "Using Third-Party UI Frameworks with Cordova") can manage pretty well. Sometimes, however, you will want a different experience for your users. You could load the content in the system browser, but on iOS, for example, the user would have to perform manual steps to navigate back to your application after looking at the content in the browser. InAppBrowser loads web content in such a way that your application users can more easily return directly to the main application.

> **Warning**
>
> The InAppBrowser can be a bit flaky, not always doing things the way you expect them to work. The Cordova dev team periodically discusses a complete rewrite of this thing or possibly abandoning it, but nothing ever happens. I think a re-architecture and new implementation would be a good thing for everyone.

To enable an application to use the InAppBrowser, you must first add the InAppBrowser plugin to your project by opening a terminal window, navigating to a Cordova project folder, and issuing the following command:

```
cordova plugin add org.apache.cordova.inappbrowser
```

Loading Content

With the plugin added to your project, you can now open web content in a window using the following:

```
var ref = window.open('http://www.johnwargo.com', '_blank',
  'location=yes');
```

In this example, the application will open my personal web site and return an object that represents the browser window. You can later use the returned object to interact with the browser window.

You could also create the browser window but not display it by using the following:

```
var iabRef = window.open('http://www.johnwargo.com', '_blank',
  'hidden=yes');
```

Later on, when you're ready to display the browser window, use

```
iabRef.show();
```

Notice that there are no callback functions that we're used to seeing with the other Cordova APIs.

Of the parameters passed to the call to `window.open`, the `_blank` tells the application to open the content in its own window; you could also use `_self`, which tells it to open the page within the current window, and `_system`, which tells it to open the content in the system's default web browser (leaving the current application context).

The problem with a target of `_self` is that the page that is being loaded replaces the current web content for the application. For application users this means that there's no going back—there isn't an iOS button to use for that anyway, and on Android the device's Escape button won't take you back either.

The `'location=yes'` tells the InAppBrowser to display the target location within the browser window. There are several other options that can be used when loading a page, but the options vary depending on the mobile device platform; refer to the Cordova documentation for more details.

If you run the example on an Android device, you will see a screen similar to the one shown in Figure 14.20; I've cropped the screen to show only the top portion of the window. In this case, the browser window opens with an address bar a user can use to navigate to other sites as well. The user should tap the Done button (not shown) to return to the original program.

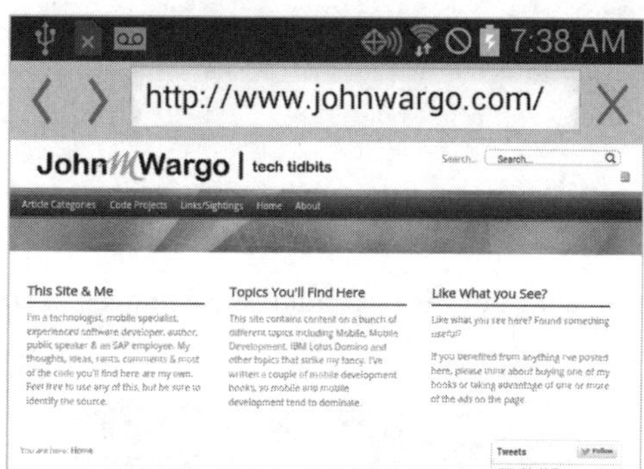

Figure 14.20 InAppBrowser Opening an External Web Page with an Address Bar on Android

When the same application is executed on an iOS device, the user will see the web page and at the bottom iOS will display the page address (without the ability to manipulate it or navigate to other sites) plus the Done button to close the window as shown in Figure 14.21.

Figure 14.21 InAppBrowser Opening an External Web Page with an Address Bar on iOS

Figure 14.21 highlights one of the key benefits of using InAppBrowser on an iOS device. When done reading the content, all the user has to do here is tap the Done button to return to the main application. If the page were loaded by spawning the system browser to open the page, the user would have to double-tap the device's Home button to bring up a list of running applications, then tap on the application name to return to the application—not the best user experience.

To turn off display of the page address, open a page with the following code:

```
var ref = window.open('http://www.johnwargo.com', '_blank',
  'location=no');
```

On Android, the page will load as in the previous examples but will not display the address bar as shown in Figure 14.22.

Figure 14.22 InAppBrowser Opening an External Web Page without an Address Bar on Android

On iOS, the Done button remains, but the page address is removed as shown in Figure 14.23.

Figure 14.23 InAppBrowser Opening an External Web Page without an Address Bar on iOS

You can also use InAppBrowser to load local content as shown in the following example:

```
var ref = window.open('help.html', '_blank');
```

In this case, I've added an HTML file called help.html to the Cordova project's www folder. The Cordova `prepare` command makes sure the file is copied over to the right location for each supported mobile platform project and available to be loaded by the application as needed. You can see an example of the page loading on an Android device in Figure 14.24.

Figure 14.24 InAppBrowser Opening a Local Web Page

To close an InAppBrowser window, simply call the `close` method on the window object:

```
ref.close();
```

As fun and interesting as it is to load web content into another window, there are also ways that an application can interact with the window. In the next few sections, I will highlight the different ways of interacting with the browser window from within a Cordova application.

Browser Window Events

There are many scenarios where an application will want to know what is going on within an InAppBrowser window. To accommodate those requirements, the InAppBrowser API fires different events at different times in the InAppBrowser window lifecycle. The supported events are

- loadstart: fires when the InAppBrowser begins to load a URL
- loadstop: fires when the InAppBrowser completes loading a URL
- loaderror: fires when the InAppBrowser encounters an error while loading a URL
- exit: fires when the InAppBrowser window is closed (either by the user or by the application calling the `close` method)

To flesh out my example from earlier, here's a block of code that opens a local HTML file using InAppBrowser, then defines event listeners for each of the new window's events:

```
var ref = window.open('help.html', '_blank');
ref.addEventListener('loadstart', onEvent);
ref.addEventListener('loadstop', onEvent);
ref.addEventListener('loaderror', onLoadError);
ref.addEventListener('exit', onEvent);
```

Notice that instead of having a separate event callback function for each, I have implemented only two callback functions, one for errors and another for everything else. This is because when anything but an error event fires, the callback function is passed an `event` object that describes the event that was fired as is illustrated in the following code:

```
function onEvent(event) {
  console.log('Type: ' + event.type);
  console.log('URL: ' + event.url);
  //do something based on event.type

}
```

Developers can query `event.type` and do whatever is appropriate for the particular event that has fired and dramatically simplify the code being executed.

When an error occurs, the error callback function is passed an object that includes code and message properties as illustrated in the following code. Developers can then query `event.code` and display an appropriate error message or perform the appropriate recovery steps as needed:

```
function onLoadError(event) {
  console.log('onLoadError: ' + event.code + ' - ' + event.message));
}
```

Execute Scripts

There are times when simply loading web content in a separate window isn't enough; you might need to modify content or execute some JavaScript within the page. To accommodate this need, the InAppBrowser includes a method that allows an application to execute JavaScript code within the InAppBrowser window. To make use of this feature in your application, you have your application execute the `executeScript` method:

```
ref.executeScript(scriptInfo, onSuccess);
```

The `onSuccess` function passed to the method is the standard success callback function you've seen used throughout this chapter; in this case, the function is executed after the code has been injected into the web page loaded in the InAppBrowser. The `scriptInfo` parameter in the example defines what JavaScript code is executed and where the code is obtained from: either passed directly to the method or loaded from a file.

To execute a specific piece of JavaScript code, you would pass in a JavaScript object with a property of `code` and a value that consists of a string containing the JavaScript code being executed:

```
{code : "$('#heading').replaceWith('<h2>This is some injected text</h2>');"}
```

In this example, the code is using the jQuery `replaceWith` function to replace some of the content within the loaded web page.

You can't execute your JavaScript code until the page has finished loading, so you will most likely add the call to `executeScript` to some part of your code that you know will execute after the page has completed loading like the loadstop event listener:

```
var ref = window.open('help.html', '_blank', 'location=no');
ref.addEventListener('loadstop', function() {
  ref.executeScript({
    code : "$('#heading').replaceWith('<h2>This is some injected text</h2>');"
  }, onSuccess);
});
```

To illustrate this example, I added a div called `heading` to the top of the local help.html file I used in a previous example. Then, when the example code provided above executes, after the page loads, you will see the div's content update as shown in Figure 14.25.

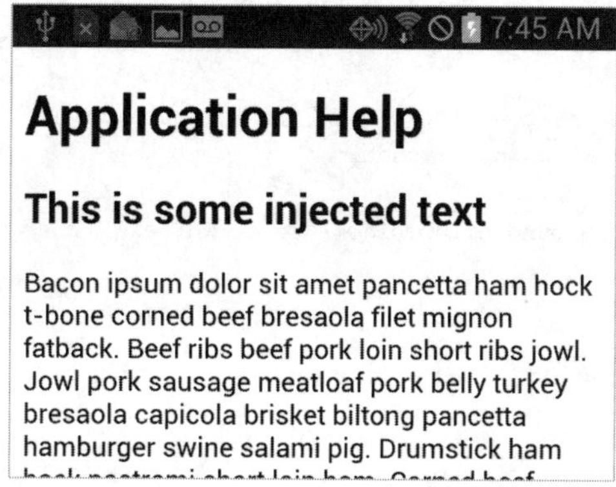

Figure 14.25 InAppBrowser Showing the Results of `executeScript`

Instead of passing in your JavaScript code directly to the `executeScript` method, you can save your code to a file and pass the file name to `executeScript` via the `scriptInfo` parameter as shown here:

```
{file : "myscript.js"}
```

The end result is the same; only the source of the JavaScript code changes in the example code shown earlier.

Insert CSS

Along with the ability to execute a script within an InAppBrowser window, you can also use a method exposed by the InAppBrowser to insert CSS into its window. Say, for example, the page you've loaded into the InAppBrowser window came from an external source and you wanted to change the styling of the page to match the rest of your application; you can easily change the CSS for the page on the fly. To do this, code the application to call the InAppBrowser's `insertCSS` method and pass in either the CSS or a reference to a CSS file you want inserted as shown in the following example:

```
ref.insertCSS(cssInfo, onSuccess);
```

The `onSuccess` function passed to the method is the standard success callback function you've seen used throughout this chapter. The `cssInfo` parameter in the example defines what CSS is inserted and where the CSS is obtained from: either passed directly to the method or loaded from a file.

To pass in a specific piece of CSS, you would pass in a JavaScript object with a property of `code` and a value that consists of a string containing the CSS being inserted as shown here:

```
{code : "body {background-color:black; color:white}"}
```

You can't insert your CSS until the page has finished loading, so you will most likely add the call to `insertCSS` to some part of your code that you know will execute after the page has completed loading, like the loadstop event listener shown in the following example:

```
var ref = window.open('help.html', '_blank', 'location=no');
ref.addEventListener('loadstop', function() {
  ref.insertCSS({
    code : "body {background-color:black; color:white}"
  }, onSuccess);
});
```

Figure 14.26 shows the page loaded with the modified CSS; notice how I switched page colors, making the background black and the text color white.

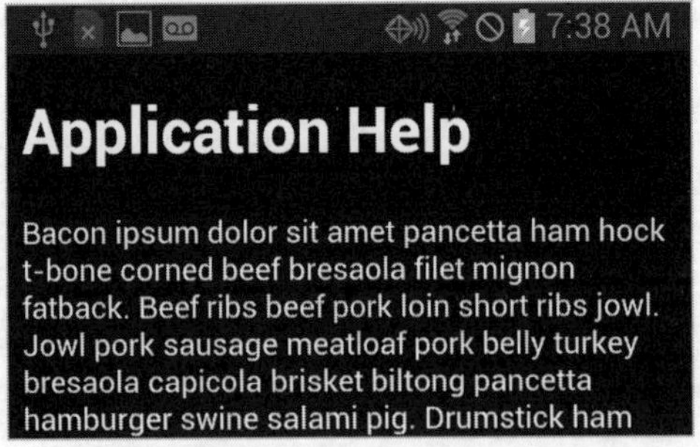

Figure 14.26 InAppBrowser Showing the Results of `insertCSS`

Instead of passing in your CSS directly to the `insertCSS` method, you can save your CSS to a file and pass the file name to `insertCSS` via the `cssInfo` parameter as shown here:

```
{file : "mystuff.css"}
```

The end result is the same; only the source of the CSS changes in the example code shown earlier.

Splashscreen

Cordova provides a Splashscreen API an application can use to display a custom splash screen when a Cordova application launches. To enable an application to use the Splashscreen API, you must first add the Splashscreen plugin to your project by opening a terminal window, navigating to a Cordova project folder, and issuing the following command:

```
cordova plugin add org.apache.cordova.splashscreen
```

There's a bit of work a developer needs to do to create the appropriate splash screen graphic files configured and scaled to support the variety of mobile device platforms as well as the multiple form factors per mobile OS. On the Android platform, there are some config.xml settings you can use to control the splash screen.

From a coding standpoint, once you have the appropriate graphics created and added to your Cordova and platform projects, you can display and hide your application's splash screen using the following code:

```
function showSplash() {
  navigator.splashscreen.show();
  setTimeout(hideSplash, 2000);
}

function hideSplash() {
  navigator.splashscreen.hide();
}
```

In this example, the `showSplash` function displays the splash screen, then sets up a timer to have the splash screen hide itself after 2 seconds.

StatusBar

A relatively new Cordova plugin is the StatusBar plugin. The plugin has been around for a while but was only recently added to the Cordova core set of plugins. The plugin allows you to control the status bar displayed at the top of any mobile device screen. Native developers have the ability to control whether their applications run in full screen (hiding the status bar) or with the status bar showing. The plugin was created so that Cordova developers would have an easy way to achieve the same thing.

To enable an application to use the StatusBar plugin, you must first add the plugin to your project by opening a terminal window, navigating to a Cordova project folder, and issuing the following command:

```
cordova plugin add org.apache.cordova.statusbar
```

With this in place, you're ready to start customizing the way your application displays on the screen. The plugin is supposed to work on Android, iOS, and Windows (today), but there are many features of the plugin that work only on iOS and Windows.

Some of the iOS settings can be applied to the application by making changes to the application's config.xml file. To have the status bar overlay the application's WebView, add the Boolean `StatusBarOverlaysWebView` preference to the config.xml:

```
<preference name="StatusBarOverlaysWebView" value="true" />
```

You can also set the background color for the status bar using the `StatusBarBackgroundColor` preference:

```
<preference name="StatusBarBackgroundColor" value="#000000" />
```

Use the `StatusBarStyle` preference to set the style for the status bar; you can see some examples of this in use later in the section:

```
<preference name="StatusBarStyle" value="lightcontent" />
```

You can programmatically hide or unhide the status bar within your application's JavaScript code. However, if you want to have the status bar hidden at startup, you have to modify the application's Xcode project info.plist file to include Status bar is initially hidden set to Yes and View controller-based status bar appearance set to No.

This plugin exposes a global object called `StatusBar` you can use to control the status bar.

To show the status bar, use

```
StatusBar.show();
```

On an iOS 8 device, you will see something similar to what is shown at the top of Figure 14.27.

To hide the status bar, use

```
StatusBar.hide();
```

The status bar will disappear as shown in Figure 14.28.

On iOS, the status bar can overlay the application's WebView, causing the application's content to scroll underneath the status bar as shown in Figure 14.29. Notice how the application's header bar becomes unreadable when it's underneath the overlaid status bar.

To enable this feature, use

```
StatusBar.overlaysWebView(true);
```

To disable it, use

```
StatusBar.overlaysWebView(false);
```

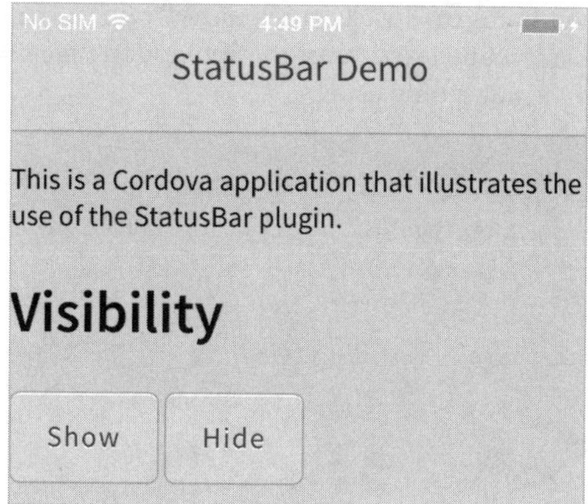

Figure 14.27 Showing the Status Bar

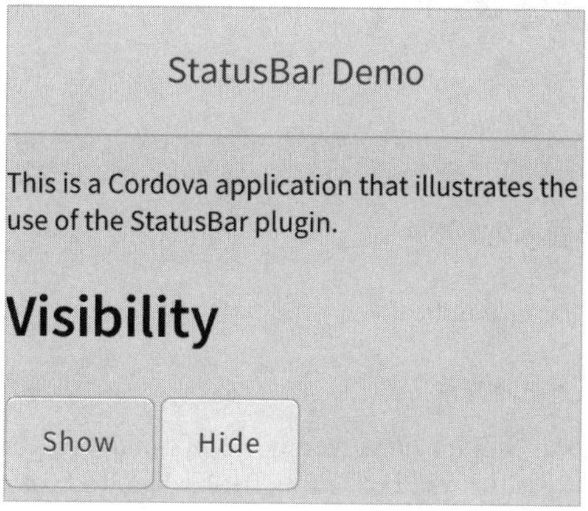

Figure 14.28 Hiding the Status Bar

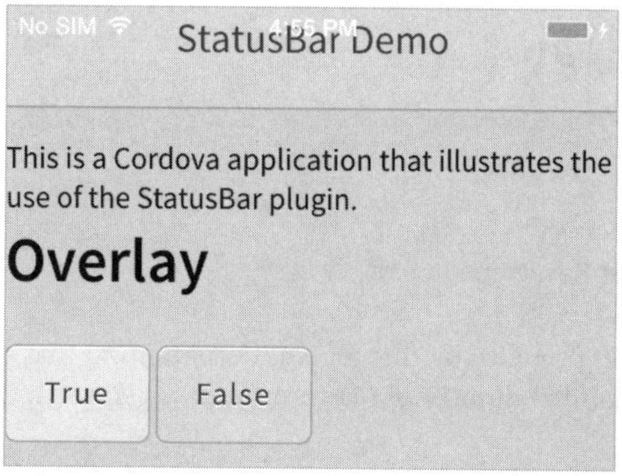

Figure 14.29 Status Bar Overlay Mode

For some reason, the default status bar style isn't set correctly on iOS. If you look at Figure 14.27, you'll see that the status bar is white text against the application's grey background. You can switch the status bar to its default setting using

```
StatusBar.styleDefault();
```

The status bar will display black text against the application's background as shown in Figure 14.30.

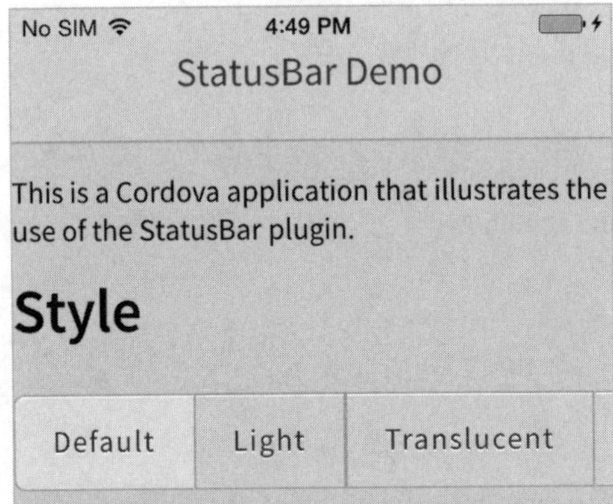

Figure 14.30 Default Status Bar Style

You can even set specific background colors in the status bar using

```
StatusBar.backgroundColorByName('orange');
```

In Figure 14.31 I've done this, but for some reason it is not updating correctly. The black background you see in the figure is the result of setting the background color to orange.

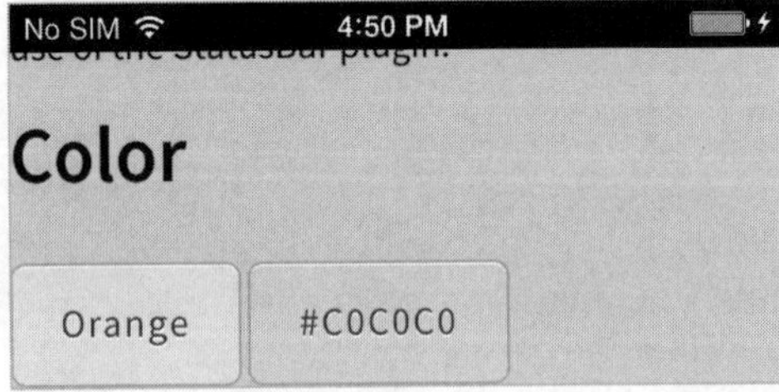

Figure 14.31 Status Bar Background Color

There are more capabilities provided by this plugin. Keep in mind that some of the capabilities are supported on only a limited number of platforms and as I showed, they didn't work very well in my testing.

Wrap-Up

There was a lot going on in this chapter; I introduced most of the Cordova APIs and showed you how to leverage them in your Cordova applications. I didn't go into a lot of detail for each but tried to show you enough for you to understand how the APIs work and get you started with the way they're invoked and what the responses look like. You will need to spend some time digging into the Cordova documentation for additional information about all of the options supported by each API. Your best and most complete overview for the Cordova APIs and how they operate on different devices can be found in my *Apache Cordova API Cookbook* (www.cordovacookbook.com).

15

Cordova Development End to End

At this point in the book, I've shown you a lot about Cordova programming, but I've not done a complete walk-through of the process using a real application as an example. So, in this chapter, I show you the steps needed to create and test a complete application from start to finish (and cover some new topics as well).

About the Application

In *PhoneGap Essentials*, I created at least one complete sample application for each Cordova API; it was a great way to highlight all of the options for each API. For *Apache Cordova 3 Programming*, I took one of the applications from that book and built it into a more complete example in order to demonstrate the end-to-end process. The application was a simple one I created to demonstrate how to implement the Compass API into an application. In this edition of the book, I have updated the material for Cordova 4.

The application displays a simple screen showing an image representing a compass dial. As the user rotates the device along a horizontal axis, the compass image rotates and the heading is displayed on the page below the compass image. The original application's screen is shown in Figure 15.1.

An interesting example, but not very pretty. In this chapter, I update the application's UI using jQuery Mobile, plus I use the Cordova merges folder capability to use different compass graphics for Android and iOS. I added a custom icon for the application as well.

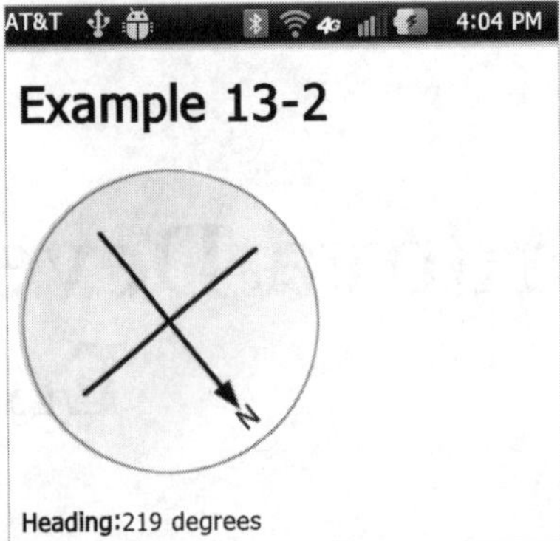

Figure 15.1 Sample Compass Application

Creating the Application

To create the application, I opened a terminal window and navigated to the system's dev folder, then issued the following command:

```
cordova create compass com.ac4p.compass Compass
```

The Cordova CLI will create the project folder, then download the default HTML project files for the www folder:

```
Creating a new cordova project with name "Compass" and id "com.ac4p.compass" at
location "C:\Users\jwargo\dev\compass"
Downloading cordova library for www...
Download complete
```

If I'd used the `--copy-to` or `--link-to` command-line switch, the CLI would have used local project files I already had available, so nothing would have been downloaded from the Internet. The second time I ran this command, nothing would be downloaded since a copy of the web application files would already have been available in my system's home folder.

Next, I need to change into the new project folder, then add the mobile device platforms I want to support:

```
cd compass
cordova platform add android ios
```

The Cordova CLI will connect to the NPM repository (www.npmjs.org), then pull down a mobile application project for each target platform. The project files are extracted to the project's platforms folder.

```
npm http GET https://registry.npmjs.org/cordova-android/3.6.4
npm http 200 https://registry.npmjs.org/cordova-android/3.6.4
npm http GET https://registry.npmjs.org/cordova-android/-/cordova-android-3.6.4.tgz
npm http 200 https://registry.npmjs.org/cordova-android/-/cordova-android-3.6.4.tgz
Creating android project...
Creating Cordova project for the Android platform:
    Path: platforms/android
    Package: com.ac4p.compass
    Name: Compass
    Android target: android-19
Copying template files...
Project successfully created.
npm http GET https://registry.npmjs.org/cordova-ios/3.7.0
npm http 200 https://registry.npmjs.org/cordova-ios/3.7.0
npm http GET https://registry.npmjs.org/cordova-ios/-/cordova-ios-3.7.0.tgz
npm http 200 https://registry.npmjs.org/cordova-ios/-/cordova-ios-3.7.0.tgz
Creating ios project...
```

At this point, what I have is a new Cordova project with support for the Android and iOS mobile device platforms. Notice that even though I'm using the Cordova 4 CLI, the platforms have not yet been upgraded.

I know that the application is going to need to leverage at least one Cordova core plugin, perhaps more, so it's time to start adding plugins. Knowing that I like to have my Cordova applications write content to the console as they run, at least during the initial testing phase, I know I will need to add the Console plugin to the project:

```
cordova plugin add org.apache.cordova.console
```

The Cordova CLI will connect to NPM, pull down the Console plugin code, and install it in the plugins folder:

```
Fetching plugin "org.apache.cordova.console" via plugin registry
npm http GET http://registry.cordova.io/org.apache.cordova.console
npm http 200 http://registry.cordova.io/org.apache.cordova.console
npm http GET http://cordova.iriscouch.com/registry/_design/app/_rewrite/org.apache
.cordova.console/-/org.apache.cordova.console-0.2.11.tgz
npm http 200 http://cordova.iriscouch.com/registry/_design/app/_rewrite/org.apache
.cordova.console/-/org.apache.cordova.console-0.2.11.tgz
Installing "org.apache.cordova.console" for android
Installing "org.apache.cordova.console" for ios
```

I will also have the application display alerts, as needed, during testing, so I will add the Dialogs plugin to the project:

```
cordova plugin add org.apache.cordova.dialogs
```

The Cordova CLI will connect to NPM, pull down the Dialogs plugin code, and install it in the plugins folder:

```
Fetching plugin "org.apache.cordova.dialogs" via plugin registry
npm http GET http://registry.cordova.io/org.apache.cordova.dialogs
npm http 200 http://registry.cordova.io/org.apache.cordova.dialogs
npm http GET http://cordova.iriscouch.com/registry/_design/app/_rewrite/org.apache
.cordova.dialogs/-/org.apache.cordova.dialogs-0.2.10.tgz
npm http 200 http://cordova.iriscouch.com/registry/_design/app/_rewrite/org.apache
.cordova.dialogs/-/org.apache.cordova.dialogs-0.2.10.tgz
Installing "org.apache.cordova.dialogs" for android
Installing "org.apache.cordova.dialogs" for ios
```

Notice that the versions are different between the two plugins; this is because plugins are released independently (they used to all be released in a bunch). Notice too that the plugin versions don't align with the Cordova 4 release. Again, this is because plugins are on their own release schedule.

I am not going to show the CLI output for the remaining plugins as it's more of what you've already seen. During troubleshooting, I like to write the Cordova version, which is exposed through the Device plugin API, to the console, so I'll need the Device plugin added to the project as well:

```
cordova plugin add org.apache.cordova.device
```

And finally, since I want the application to use the compass, I will need to add the Device Orientation plugin to the project:

```
cordova plugin add org.apache.cordova.device-orientation
```

With my project in place and all of my plugins added, I'm ready to write some code. I will do all of my code editing in the project's www folder shown in Figure 15.2.

The first thing I should do, though, is populate the application's config.xml file with important information about the application. At the top of the file list shown in Figure 15.2 is the config.xml; I opened the file in my text editor of choice and populated it with my information as shown in Figure 15.3.

The `name` element is populated automatically using the value provided when creating the project with the `cordova create` command; any additional values are added manually by the developer. The value defined in the `name` element is the name of the application as it will appear on the device home screen on each target platform. I used `Compass` here because it accurately describes the application and will easily fit within the available space on the home screen. The application's name typically appears beneath the application's icon on the home screen, and there is usually only a certain amount of space available before the device truncates the text. So, when you assign the application name, you will want to make sure it's short enough to display correctly on all platforms.

Next, I changed the `author` information in the file so that it contained my information instead of the generic settings provided by the Cordova developers.

With the config.xml file updated, I saved my changes, and now it's time to write some code.

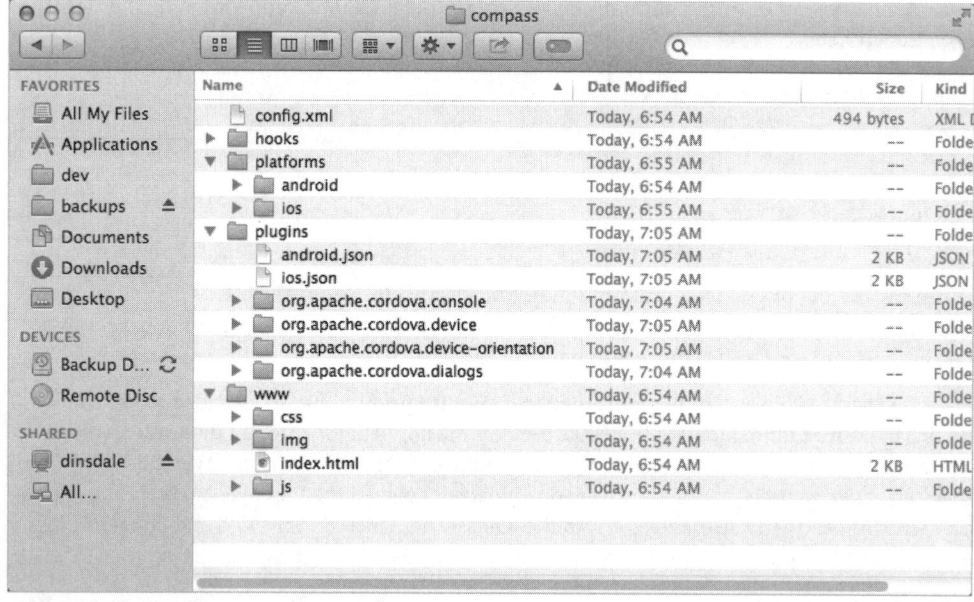

Figure 15.2 Compass Project www Folder

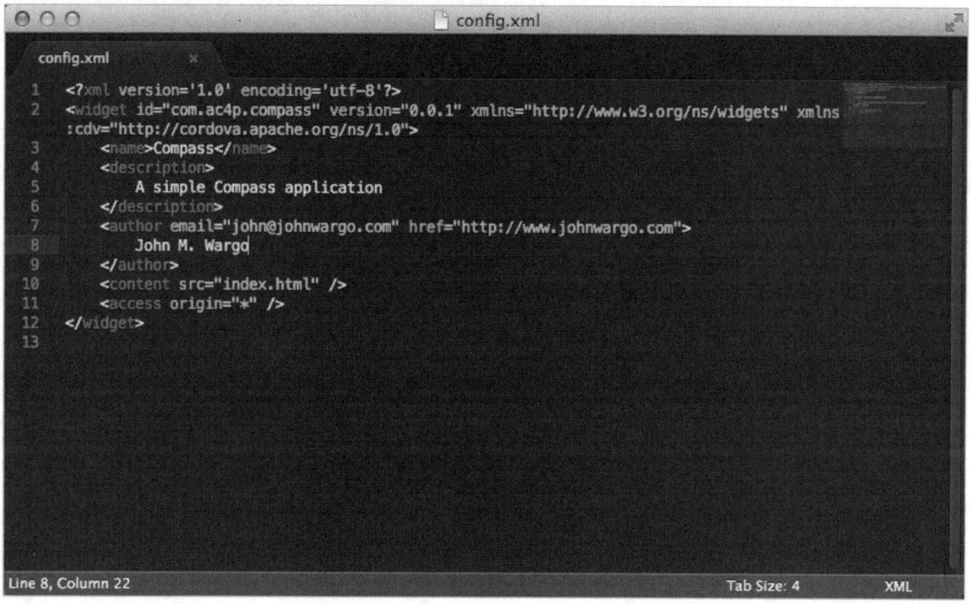

```
config.xml

<?xml version='1.0' encoding='utf-8'?>
<widget id="com.ac4p.compass" version="0.0.1" xmlns="http://www.w3.org/ns/widgets" xmlns
:cdv="http://cordova.apache.org/ns/1.0">
    <name>Compass</name>
    <description>
        A simple Compass application
    </description>
    <author email="john@johnwargo.com" href="http://www.johnwargo.com">
        John M. Wargo
    </author>
    <content src="index.html" />
    <access origin="*" />
</widget>

Line 8, Column 22                                   Tab Size: 4        XML
```

Figure 15.3 Compass Application config.xml File

The original version of this application had a very simple look to it, represented by the HTML code shown here:

```
<body onload="onBodyLoad()">
  <h1>Example 13-2</h1>
  <img src="compass.png" id="compass" />
  <br />
  <p id="headingInfo"></p>
</body>
```

When I wrote the original application, I didn't make any effort to make it look nice; I simply plunked in the HTML code I needed and that was it. I didn't do any styling of the page, nor did I do anything to center the compass graphic on the page.

For this version of the application, I wanted to spruce it up a little bit, so I decided to use jQuery Mobile to create a more mobile-phone-like look for the app. The first thing I did was download the latest versions of jQuery (www.jquery.com) and jQuery Mobile (www.jquerymobile.com) from their respective web sites. Once they were downloaded, I copied the files over to the Cordova project's www folder, then added references to the jQuery and jQuery Mobile CSS and JavaScript files to the `head` portion of the application's index.html:

```
<link rel="stylesheet" href="css/jquery.mobile-1.4.5.min.css" />
<script src="js/jquery-1.11.1.min.js"></script>
<script src="js/jquery.mobile-1.4.5.min.js"></script>
```

> **Note**
>
> For this project, I placed any CSS files into the Cordova project's www/css folder and any JavaScript resources into the Cordova project's www/js folder.

I could have easily used hosted versions of these files and pulled them down when the application first launched, but I prefer to have all of an application's assets packaged with the Cordova application. This topic is discussed further in Chapter 17, "Using Third-Party UI Frameworks with Cordova."

The application will need to be able to rotate the compass image; I accomplished this using jQuery Rotate, a free jQuery plugin I found at http://goo.gl/b3brTA . To add the plugin, I downloaded the plugin's JavaScript file to the Cordova project's www folder, then added a reference to the file in the application's index.html file:

```
<script src="js/jQueryRotateCompressed.js"></script>
```

The application's complete index.html file is shown in Listing 15.1.

Listing 15.1 index.html

```
<!DOCTYPE html>
<html>
<head>
  <title>Compass</title>
  <meta http-equiv="Content-type" content="text/html; charset=utf-8">
  <meta name="viewport" id="viewport" content="width=device-width,
    height=device-height, initial-scale=1.0, maximum-scale=1.0,
    user-scalable=no" />
  <link rel="stylesheet" href="css/jquery.mobile-1.4.5.min.css" />
  <script src="js/jquery-1.11.1.min.js"></script>
  <script src="js/jquery.mobile-1.4.5.min.js"></script>
  <script src="js/jQueryRotateCompressed.js"></script>
  <script src="js/index.js"></script>
  <script src="cordova.js"></script>
</head>

<body onload="onBodyLoad()">
  <div data-role="page">
    <div data-role="header">
      <h1>Compass</h1>
    </div>
    <div data-role="content">
      <div style="text-align:center;">
        <img src="images/compass.png" id="compass" />
        <br />
        <p id="headingInfo"> <strong>Heading:</strong> 0 Degrees</p>
      </div>
    </div>
    <div data-role="footer" data-position="fixed">
      <h3>www.cordova4programming.com</h3>
    </div>
  </div>
</body>
</html>
```

jQuery Mobile uses `data-role` attributes within elements to style those particular elements with the appropriate look. So, in Listing 15.1, I've created a `header` div on the page and assigned it a `data-role` of `header` and created a `footer` div on the page and assigned it a `data-role` of `footer`. The `data-position="fixed"` forces the footer to remain on the bottom of the application screen when scrolling.

Next, I moved the content for the page into a div assigned with a `data-role` of `content`. In order to have the compass graphic and heading text centered on the page, I added a new div and styled it with a `style="text-align:center;"` as shown in the code.

With that code in place, the look of the application is changed dramatically as shown in Figure 15.4. In this example, I haven't packaged the application and deployed it to a mobile device; I've simply opened the application's index.html page in the desktop browser so I can see how it looks. I could also have used the Ripple Emulator (described in Chapter 5, "The Mechanics of Cordova Development") to quickly view how the application would look on multiple simulated devices, and I could have simulated the compass heading as well.

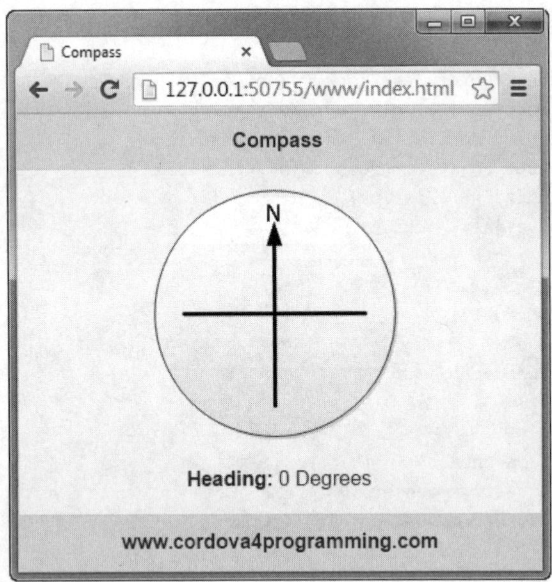

Figure 15.4 The Compass Application with a jQuery Mobile Look

Now that I have the application's user interface updated, it's time to start taking a look at the application's JavaScript code. In my original sample application, the JavaScript was embedded inside of the application's index.html file. As I described in Chapter 5, it's easier to work with some of the debugging tools if the HTML and JavaScript are in separate files, so I split out the JavaScript code into its own index.js file.

Since I know that my code isn't going to work right away, and since a Cordova application fails silently most of the time, the first thing I did was add an `onerror` function to the application:

```
window.onerror = function (msg, url, line) {
  var idx = url.lastIndexOf("/");
  if (idx > -1) {
    url = url.substring(idx + 1);
  }
  //Build the message string we'll display to the user
  var errStr = "ERROR in " + url + " (line #" + line + "): " + msg;
  //Write the error to the console
  console.error(errStr);
```

```
    //Tell the user what happened
    alert(errStr);
    return false;
  };
```

This function catches any errors encountered in the application's JavaScript code, then writes the error to the console and displays an alert dialog with the same information. This allows me to quickly catch any syntax errors when the application is running and also allows me to quickly tell when I've called a plugin API without adding the plugin to my project (which I happen to do all the time).

Next comes the `onDeviceReady` function I've shown throughout the book. It is set up as an event listener for the Cordova deviceready event and fires after the Cordova container has finished initialization. In this function, I know that the Cordova container is ready, so I can create the compass watch needed for this application:

```
function onDeviceReady() {
  console.log("Entering onDeviceReady");
  console.log("Cordova: " + device.cordova);
  navigator.notification.alert("Cordova is ready");
  //Set up the watch
  //Read the compass every second (1000 milliseconds)
  var watchOptions = {
    frequency: 1000,
  };
  console.log('%s Creating watch: %s', appName, JSON.stringify(watchOptions));
  watchID = navigator.compass.watchHeading(onSuccess, onError, watchOptions);
  console.log("Leaving onDeviceReady");
}
```

The function defines a `watchOptions` object that is used to help set up a heading watch that will cause the application to update the heading periodically. The `watchOptions` object can have either a `frequency` property or a `filter` property assigned to it. Right now, the application is set up with the following:

```
var watchOptions = {
  frequency : 1000
};
```

A heading watch will cause the Compass API to report the device's heading every 1000 milliseconds (every 1 second). The `filter` property is used to define the amount of heading change (in degrees) before the Compass API will report a heading. In the following example, the `filter` property is instructing the Compass API to deliver a heading every time the heading changes more than 1 degree:

```
var watchOptions = {
  filter : 1
};
```

You can specify both properties as shown below, but as soon as you specify a `filter`, the `frequency` property is ignored by the Compass API:

```
var watchOptions = {
  frequency : 1000,
  filter : 1
};
```

With `watchOptions` defined, the function makes a call to `watchHeading` to set up the heading watch as shown here:

```
watchID = navigator.compass.watchHeading(onSuccess, onError,
  watchOptions);
```

As with all of the other Cordova APIs you've learned so far, the `onSuccess` function is executed whenever the Compass API sends a heading value, and the `onError` function is executed whenever there is an error encountered by the Compass API.

Whenever the `onSuccess` function is executed, the Compass API passes it a `heading` object that contains properties indicating the device's current heading as shown here:

```
{
  "magneticHeading": 39.87841796875,
  "trueHeading": 39.87841796875,
  "headingAccuracy": 0,
  "timestamp": 1416661340676
}
```

The `onSuccess` function uses the `magneticHeading` property of the `heading` object to determine the current heading, then uses that value to rotate the compass graphic by that number of degrees as shown in this function:

```
function onSuccess(heading) {
  console.log("Entering onSuccess");
  console.log('Received Heading');
  console.log(JSON.stringify(heading));
  var hv = Math.round(heading.magneticHeading);
  $('#headingInfo').html('<b>Heading:</b> ' + hv + ' Degrees');
  console.log('Rotating to ' + hv + ' degrees');
  $("#compass").rotate(-hv);
  console.log("Leaving onSuccess");
}
```

Notice that the compass graphic is being rotated in the opposite direction of the device's current heading. That is because the compass graphic has to rotate in the opposite direction from the device rotation so that the North point on the compass graphic always points to Magnetic North.

Finally, the application's `onError` function is executed whenever the watch encounters an error. The function uses an object passed to the function to identify the cause of the error and display an appropriate error message for the user. Notice that the `onError` function also cancels the watch as it makes little sense to continue watching the heading when the application is not able to measure it.

```
function onError(err) {
  var msg;
  console.log("Entering onError");
  console.error('Error: ' + JSON.stringify(err));
  //Remove the watch since we're having a problem
  navigator.compass.clearWatch(watchID);
  //Clear the heading value from the page
  $('#headingInfo').html('<b>Heading: </b>None');
  //Then tell the user what happened.
  switch (err.code) {
  case CompassError.COMPASS_NOT_SUPPORTED:
    msg = 'Compass not supported';
    break;
  case CompassError.COMPASS_INTERNAL_ERR:
    msg = 'Internal compass error';
    break;
  default:
    msg = 'Unknown heading error!';
  }
  console.error(msg);
  navigator.notification.alert(msg, null, "Compass Error", "Continue");
  console.log("Leaving onError");
}
```

Notice that I'm doing a lot of writing to the console, logging something every time the application enters or leaves a function. This enables me to better understand the flow of the application so I can more easily troubleshoot problems when they occur. As soon as the application is tested and found to be acceptable, I remove or comment out many of the places where the application writes to the console. You can even use capabilities provided by some build tools (described in Chapter 18, "Using Third-Party Tools with Cordova") to strip console entries out of your application automatically when you switch over from debug to production.

Listing 15.2 shows the complete contents of the application's index.js file.

Listing 15.2 index.js

```
var watchID;

window.onerror = function (msg, url, line) {
  var idx = url.lastIndexOf("/");
  if (idx > -1) {
```

```
    url = url.substring(idx + 1);
  }
  //Build the message string we'll display to the user
  var errStr = "ERROR in " + url + " (line #" + line + "): " + msg;
  //Write the error to the console
  console.error(errStr);
  //Tell the user what happened
  alert(errStr);
  return false;
};

function onBodyLoad() {
  console.log("Entering onBodyLoad");
  alert("onBodyLoad");
  document.addEventListener("deviceready", onDeviceReady);
  console.log("Leaving onBodyLoad");
}

function onDeviceReady() {
  console.log("Entering onDeviceReady");
  console.log("Cordova: " + device.cordova);
  navigator.notification.alert("Cordova is ready");
  //Set up the watch
  //Read the compass every second (1000 milliseconds)
  var watchOptions = {
    frequency: 1000,
  };
  console.log('Creating watch: %s', JSON.stringify(watchOptions));
  watchID = navigator.compass.watchHeading(onSuccess, onError,
    watchOptions);
  console.log("Leaving onDeviceReady");
}

function onSuccess(heading) {
  console.log("Entering onSuccess");
  console.log('Received Heading');
  console.log(JSON.stringify(heading));
  var hv = Math.round(heading.magneticHeading);
  $('#headingInfo').html('<b>Heading:</b> ' + hv + ' Degrees');
  console.log('Rotating to ' + hv + ' degrees');
  $("#compass").rotate(-hv);
  console.log("Leaving onSuccess");
}

function onError(err) {
  var msg;
  console.log("Entering onError");
```

```
    console.error('Error: ' + JSON.stringify(err));
    //Remove the watch since we're having a problem
    navigator.compass.clearWatch(watchID);
    //Clear the heading value from the page
    $('#headingInfo').html('<b>Heading: </b>None');
    //Then tell the user what happened.
    switch (err.code) {
    case CompassError.COMPASS_NOT_SUPPORTED:
      msg = 'Compass not supported';
      break;
    case CompassError.COMPASS_INTERNAL_ERR:
      msg = 'Internal compass error';
      break;
    default:
      msg = 'Unknown heading error!';
    }
    console.error(msg);
    navigator.notification.alert(msg, null, "Compass Error", "Continue");
    console.log("Leaving onError");
}
```

Using Merges

One of the things I haven't done yet is show you how to use the merges capability of the Cordova CLI. In Chapter 5 I explained how it works, but here I'll show you a real example.

The compass graphic in my original application was pretty lame; I created it in Microsoft Visio and simply wanted a circle with an arrow pointing north. I got what I wanted, but professional grade it wasn't. For this upgraded version of the application, I wanted something with more panache and found a graphic that, while not technically accurate for my compass, implied a compass theme, so I decided to use it.

To leverage the merges aspect of the CLI, I decided to make two versions of the image, one for Android and the other for iOS, using graphics from the PhoneGap web site placed in the center of the compass face. You can see the Android version in Figure 15.5 and the iOS version in Figure 15.6.

Once I had the different graphics, it was time to use them to create distinct versions of the application using the CLI. Notice in the application's code that the compass image is being pulled from images/compass.png. To enable me to use the CLI and merges, I had to create an images folder in both the Cordova project's merges/android and merges/ios folders. With those folders in place, all I had to do was copy the right image files to the right folders, making sure they had the same file name.

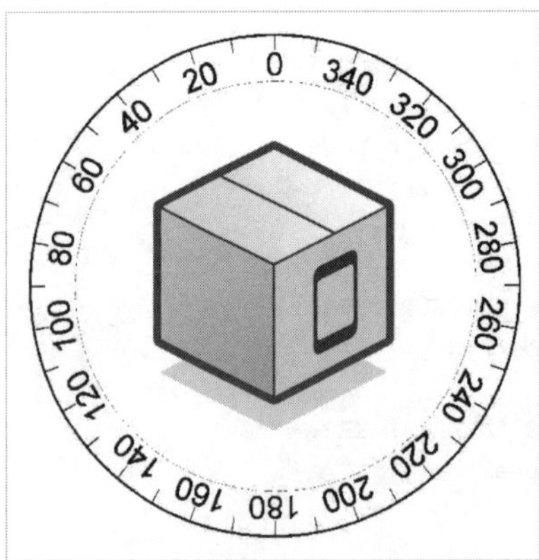

Figure 15.5 Updated Compass Image for Android

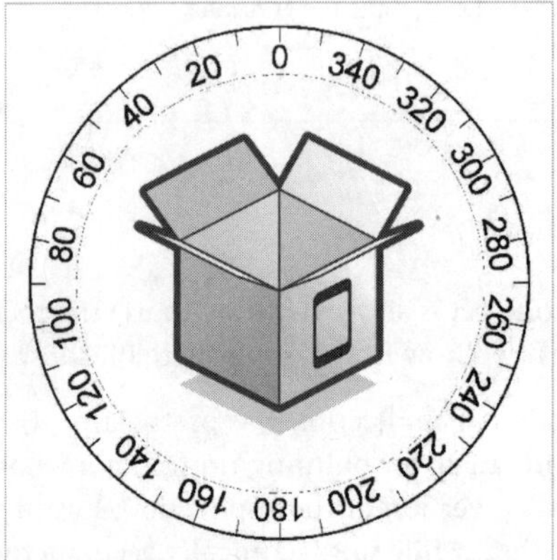

Figure 15.6 Updated Compass Image for iOS

Assuming my project is in a compass folder, I copied the Android version of the compass image into compass/merges/android/images/compass.png and copied the iOS version into compass/merges/ios/images/compass.png. Since I could run this Cordova application on any supported platform, I left the original lame version of the compass graphic in the Cordova application's www/images folder so that if the application ran on any platform beyond Android and iOS, it would still display a compass image.

During the build process, for the Android application, the Cordova CLI copies the file located at compass/merges/android/images/compass.png to compass/platforms/android/assets/www/images/compass.png. For the iOS application, the CLI copies the file located at compass/merges/ios/images/compass.png to compass/platforms/ios/www/images/compass.png. In both cases, the copied image overwrites the existing image I have in the project's www/images folder. For any platform except Android and iOS, the original graphic file is left untouched.

The result of this is that I can still maintain one set of code and only switch in the right resource files as needed depending on the platform. This same approach applies to HTML, CSS, and JavaScript files, and more. Any application resource can be customized using the merges capability.

You can see the results of this process in the next section. The use case I used here isn't perfect, but I hope you can see how, if you've themed your application differently for different platforms, this capability provides you with the means to easily manage the different resources for each platform.

Application Icons

Before I can deploy the fancy new Compass application I just created, I need to make some application icons for each supported platform. Now as this is a book about Apache Cordova and not native application development, I won't go into the details about how to create application icons and what icon file resolutions are required. That is a topic that should be covered in native development books for each target platform. The Cordova team has done a pretty good job documenting the application icon requirements at http://goo.gl/wY6B3N, so you can find some good information there.

I'm not a graphic artist, I'm simply not wired that way, so I normally have to rely upon others for my application graphics (which is why there are so few of them in this book). Since I knew I needed an icon for this chapter, I fired up Microsoft Visio and created a rough graphic to use here. The graphic is a simple square with rounded corners; then I placed a compass image Visio provided me in the middle of the square with the book's title underneath it. It's nothing special, but at least it's a custom image I can use; you can see the image in Figure 15.7.

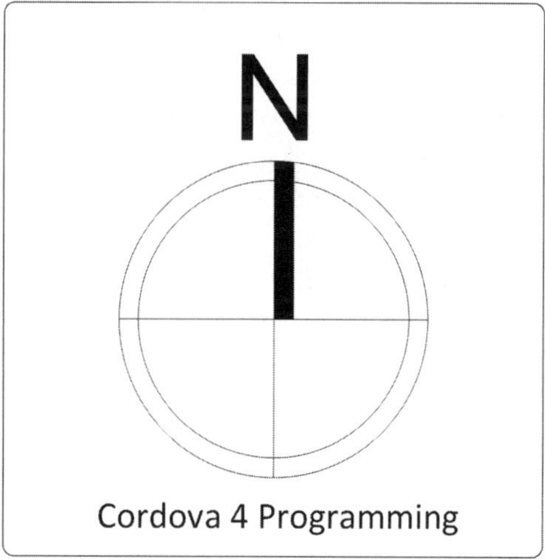

Figure 15.7 Compass Application Icon

Now that I had an icon I could use, I started looking for an easy way to convert this image to something I could use for my Cordova application. I quickly found a site called MakeAppicon (http://makeappicon.com); you drag an image file (1024 x 1024 pixels preferred) onto the site, provide an email address, and they will send you an archive with application icons for Android and iOS. Nice stuff.

For a Cordova project designed for multiple platforms, each platform has its own folder structure or project settings for application icons, so I didn't want to deal with extracting the icons from the MakeAppicon .zip file and copying them into the appropriate place for each target platform. Instead, I started looking for something that was Cordova aware.

A quick search pointed me to several Node-based tools that could generate icons for me, but none of them had been updated in a while and none of them worked very well. A modified search pointed me to the cordova-icon project at http://goo.gl/D47cTz. This one worked quite well for me, although it only provides icon files for Android and iOS.

To use the tool, you must first install ImageMagick using the instructions provided at www.imagemagick.org. Next, you install the cordova-icon Node module using the NPM. On Windows you install the module by opening a terminal window and executing the following command:

```
npm install -g cordova-icon
```

On Macintosh and Linux, you may need to install the module using `sudo`:

```
sudo npm install -g cordova-icon
```

To use the module, you need to copy an application icon file to the Cordova project folder as icon.png. Next, in the terminal window, navigate to the Cordova project folder and issue the following command:

```
cordova-icon
```

The module will read the project's config.xml file, determine which platforms are installed for the project, and generate the icon files:

```
Checking Project & Icon

  ✓  platforms found: ios, android
  ✓  icon.png exists
  ✓  config.xml exists

 Generating Icons for ios

  ✓  icon-40.png created
  ✓  icon-50.png created
  ✓  icon-50@2x.png created
  ✓  icon-60.png created
```

```
✓ icon-40@2x.png created
✓ icon-60@2x.png created
✓ icon-small.png created
✓ icon-76.png created
✓ icon-72.png created
✓ icon-small@2x.png created
✓ icon-72@2x.png created
✓ icon-60@3x.png created
✓ icon-76@2x.png created
✓ icon@2x.png created
✓ icon.png created

Generating Icons for android

✓ drawable-hdpi/icon.png created
✓ drawable-ldpi/icon.png created
✓ drawable-xhdpi/icon.png created
✓ drawable/icon.png created
✓ drawable-mdpi/icon.png created
```

That's it; at this point the project has application icons for Android and iOS copied over into the correct locations within the Cordova project structure. For many projects you'll likely need more than just icons for Android and iOS, but from looking at the code, I don't think it would be very hard to enhance this module to add support for other platforms.

Testing the Application

With the project all coded and ready to go, it's time to test the application. I usually start my testing with the device simulators, then switch to physical devices once I get the initial kinks out. So, with a terminal window open to the Compass project, issue the following command:

```
cordova prepare
```

The Cordova CLI will copy the web application content from the project's www folder into each target platform project folder. The content in any merges folders (the compass image in this case) will be copied over to the appropriate project folders as well.

Starting with the Android emulator, in the terminal window execute the following command:

```
cordova run android
```

The CLI will churn for a while building the native application for Android, then launch the emulator and display the screen shown in Figure 15.8. That's nice; the screen looks as I expect it to look, but how do I change the heading?

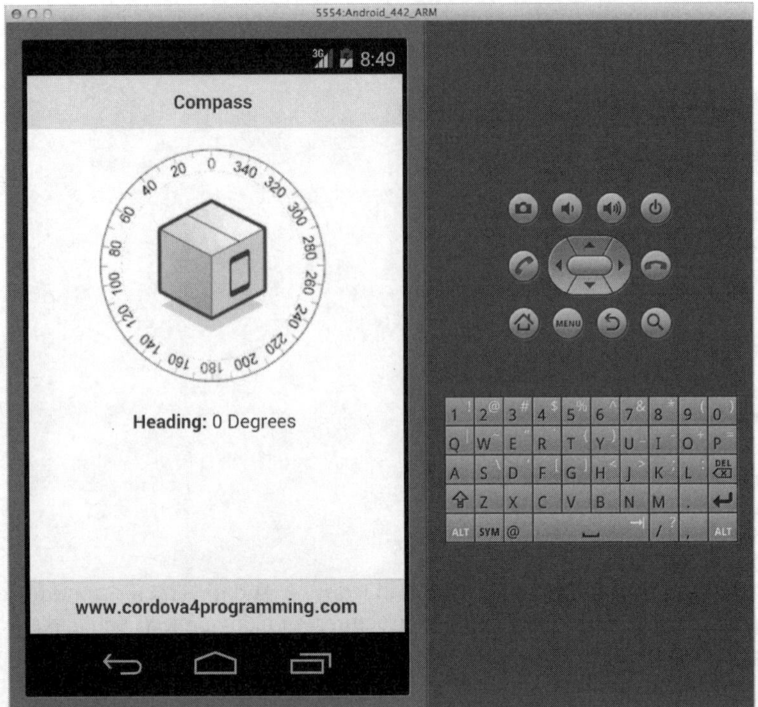

Figure 15.8 Compass Application Running on an Android Emulator

In the Android Monitor (described in Chapter 7, "Android Development with Cordova"), there's the Emulator Control option shown in Figure 15.9. There's an option for simulating geolocation data but not compass heading. Turns out that there's an Android SensorSimulator application you can run to simulate sensor data on an Android device or emulator. I didn't try it out, but you can read more about it at http://goo.gl/WY36jB. I have Android devices I can test the application on, so I didn't worry about that option.

My next step is usually to test the application on an iOS simulator. When I ran the application on an iOS device simulator, the application displayed the error message shown in Figure 15.10.

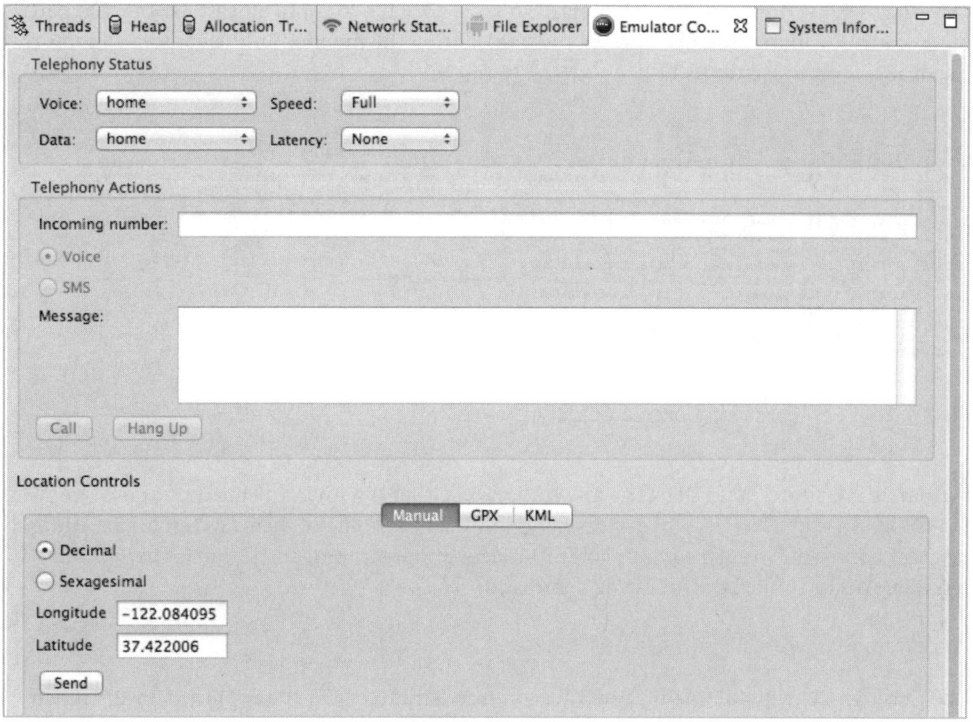

Figure 15.9 Android Monitor Emulator Control Tab

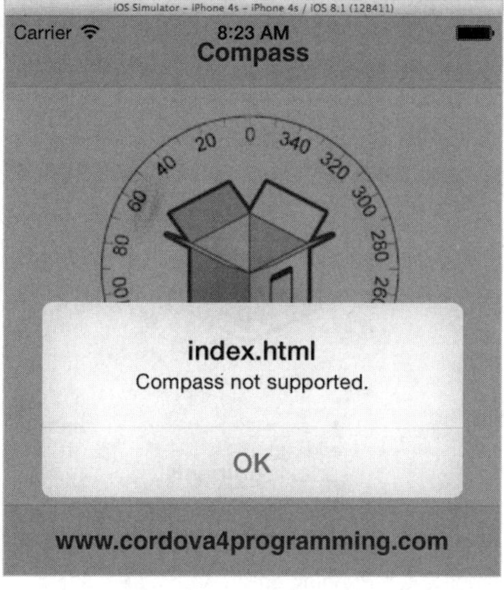

Figure 15.10 Compass Application Running on an iOS Simulator

The error is being displayed by the application's `onError` function, so at least I know that part of the code is working. You can also see the output from the function in the console window in Xcode as shown in Figure 15.11.

```
2014-11-22 15:11:51.299 Compass[10051:141869] Resetting plugins due to page load.
2014-11-22 15:11:51.443 Compass[10051:141869] Finished load of: file:///Users/jwargo/Library/Developer/CoreSimulator/Devices/
76AE8891-02E5-4BB7-8954-F384E10ABE85/data/Containers/Bundle/Application/9B90FF50-7EAB-4E8E-9311-2DD2F27E890B/Compass.app/www/
index.html
2014-11-22 15:11:52.989 Compass[10051:141869] Entering onBodyLoad
2014-11-22 15:11:52.989 Compass[10051:141869] Leaving onBodyLoad
2014-11-22 15:11:52.989 Compass[10051:141869] Entering onDeviceReady
2014-11-22 15:11:52.989 Compass[10051:141869] Cordova: 3.7.0
2014-11-22 15:11:53.020 Compass[10051:141869] Creating watch: {"frequency":1000}
2014-11-22 15:11:53.020 Compass[10051:141869] Leaving onDeviceReady
2014-11-22 15:11:53.991 Compass[10051:141869] Entering onError
2014-11-22 15:11:53.992 Compass[10051:141869] ERROR: Error: {"code":20}
2014-11-22 15:11:53.992 Compass[10051:141869] ERROR: Compass not supported
2014-11-22 15:11:54.025 Compass[10051:141869] Leaving onError
```

Figure 15.11 Application Console Output in Xcode

Well, that's not good; I can't test the application on either the Android emulator or iOS simulator. No worries; I have a bevy of devices here, so I'll test on some of them. To test on an Android device, I connected my Samsung Galaxy SIII to the computer using a USB cable, then in the terminal window issued the following command:

```
cordova run android
```

The Cordova CLI will do its stuff, and 30 seconds to a minute later the application will launch on the device. Figure 15.12 shows the application running; I've cropped the image to cut away the blank portion of the application screen. Success!

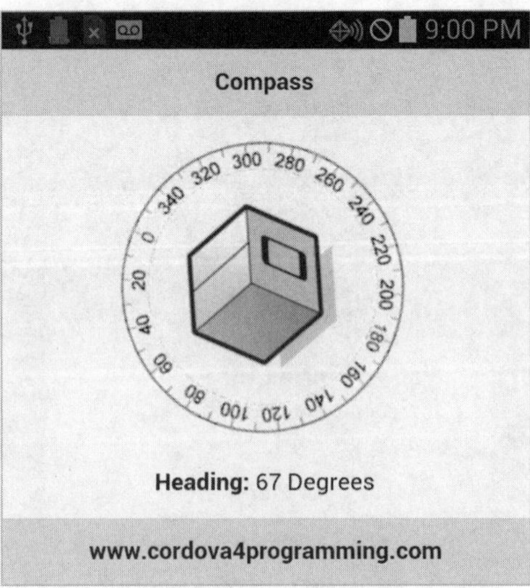

Figure 15.12 Compass Application Running on an Android Emulator

Next, to run the application on an iOS device, connect the device to the computer using a USB cable, then from terminal window, execute the following:

```
cordova run ios
```

The CLI will build the application, deploy it to the device, then launch it. As soon as the application starts, it tries to create the compass watch—this could potentially trigger the compass calibration process shown in Figure 15.13.

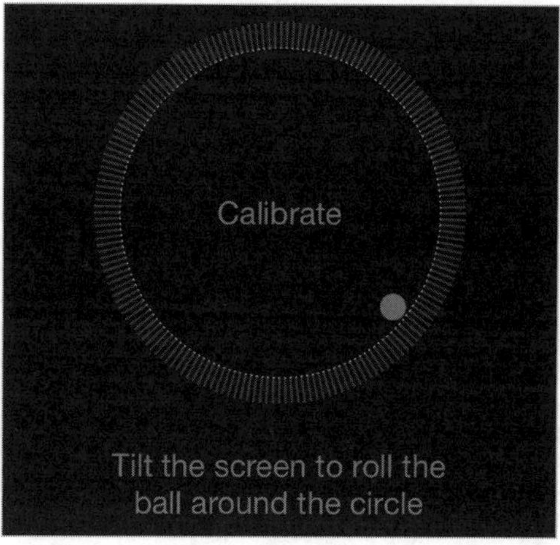

Figure 15.13 Compass Calibration on an iOS Device

Before the application can use the compass, the device has to be rolled and tilted until the ball sweeps through the entire circle on the screen.

When the application finally loads, it will display a screen similar to the one shown in Figure 15.14; I've cropped the image to cut away the blank portion of the application screen.

Notice that the compass graphics differ between the two devices (Figures 15.12 and 15.14) although I didn't code anything to make this happen; this is only one of the cool ways the Cordova CLI enhances cross-platform development.

Now Cordova development is about more than just Android and iOS development, so what about other platforms? To build the application for Windows, you'll have to create a project on a Windows system and complete most of the steps highlighted here. Microsoft provided me with a test device to use for this book, so I immediately tried the application on that device. Unfortunately, the device I was using didn't have a compass, so it didn't work. The good news, though, is that the Device Orientation plugin fired the `onError` function and let me know the compass wasn't supported (I had to go online to confirm the device didn't have a compass).

I grabbed another Windows Phone device and tested the application and it worked great.

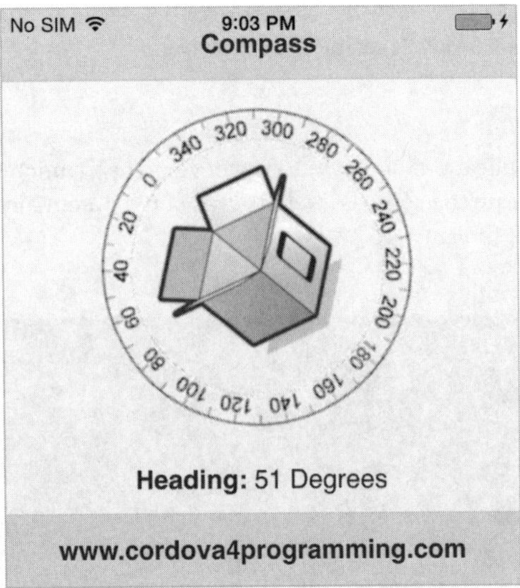

Figure 15.14 Compass Application Running on an iOS Device

I do happen to have a Firefox OS device, so I opened Firefox using the instructions I provided in Chapter 8, "Firefox OS Development with Cordova," and loaded the application. When I run the application on my device, I see the screen shown in Figure 15.15.

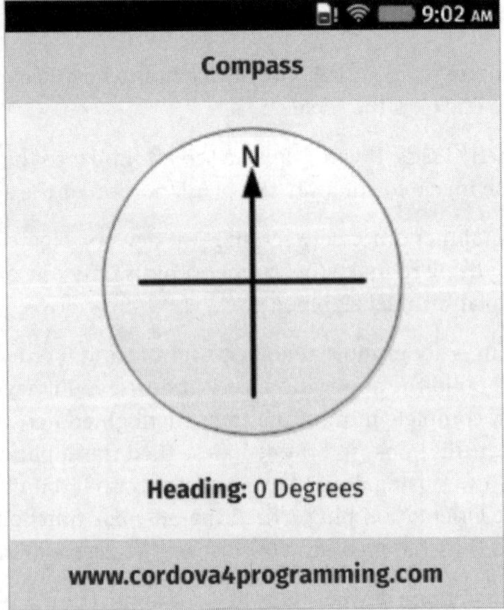

Figure 15.15 Compass Application Running on a Firefox OS Device

Notice the compass graphic; it's different from the ones shown in Figures 15.12 and 15.14. That's because I didn't provide a custom graphic for the Firefox OS platform, only Android and iOS, so any other platform gets the simple graphic from the original version of the application.

I noticed something interesting when I ran the application on the device: the heading did not update on the page, nor did the graphic rotate. I poked and prodded at the app, trying to figure out why it wasn't working, until I finally figured out that the device didn't have a compass. I had purchased a very limited-capability Firefox OS phone, and one of the limitations is that it didn't have a compass.

Remember, though, that I had code in the application that is supposed to let me know when the Compass API returns an error. Well, in the case of Firefox OS, the Device Orientation plugin doesn't expose that error, so there is no way for my application to know the API won't work on this particular device.

To confirm this, take a look at Figure 15.16; it shows the console output from the application. As you can see, the application is dutifully creating the compass watch, but nothing happens afterward.

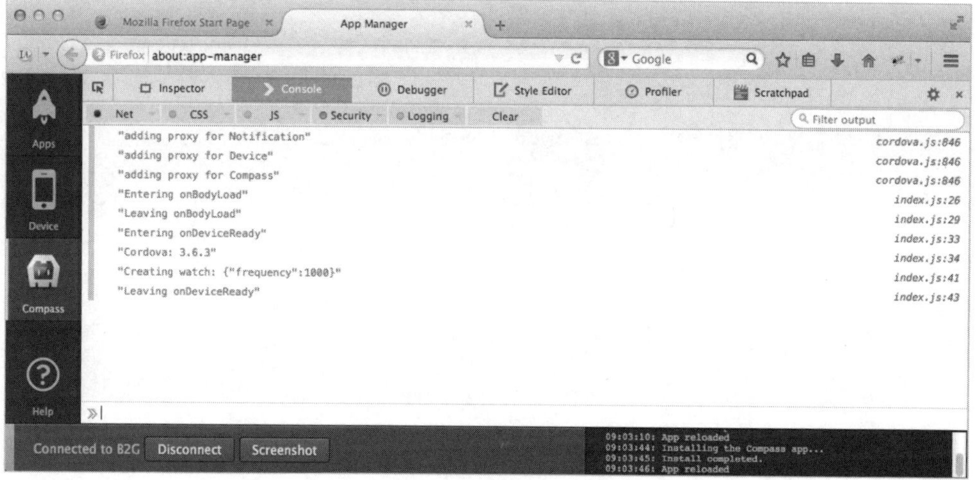

Figure 15.16 Firefox OS Debugging Tools

Clearly some of the device manufacturers, Microsoft and Mozilla in this case, have some work to do on their implementations of the Cordova plugins.

Wrap-Up

This chapter wraps up the Cordova programming story by demonstrating how to do cross-platform Cordova development from start to finish. In this chapter, you saw how to create a single application that uses different resources depending on the mobile platform running the application. I also showed you a complete Cordova web application and described each component. You've also seen more details about how to use the Compass API in your applications.

16

Creating Cordova Plugins

So far we've talked a lot about the tools and plugins that are part of the Cordova framework, but what if you want to do something within a Cordova application that isn't exposed through one of the existing plugins (either core plugins or third-party plugins)? Well, you will have to go it alone and build your own plugins. In this chapter, I show you how to create your own plugins for Apache Cordova.

Cordova plugins are not new. They've been around for a long time, but starting with Cordova 3.0 and through the capabilities provided by Plugman and the Cordova CLI, plugins changed dramatically. They became more prevalent, plus more standardized in their implementation.

In this chapter, I show you how to create two plugins, a JavaScript-only plugin and a native plugin for multiple target platforms (Android and iOS only, sorry). I will also show how to publish Cordova plugins to the Cordova Plugin Registry.

Anatomy of a Cordova Plugin

Before I jump into how to create a plugin, I thought I'd spend some time explaining the anatomy of a Cordova plugin—what makes a bunch of collected files a Cordova plugin. The Cordova documentation site has great introductory documents that describe how to create plugins. The Plugin Development Guide (http://goo.gl/v1qHBm) describes how to create the JavaScript interface for your plugins, and there are individual guides for creating the native plugin components for the different mobile platforms linked on the bottom of the page. You can find the Android guide at http://goo.gl/hLJukS and iOS at http://goo.gl/byrAD9.

A Cordova plugin is a set of files that together extend or enhance a Cordova application's capabilities. In general, a developer adds a plugin to a Cordova project (using the tools discussed in Chapter 4, "Using the Cordova Command-Line Interfaces") and interacts with the plugin through an exposed JavaScript interface. A plugin could do something without any coding by the developer, but in general you add the plugin to your project, then use it as you see fit by coding against the exposed API.

I mentioned that a plugin is a collection of files; it consists of a configuration file called plugin.xml and one or more JavaScript files plus (optionally) some native source code files, libraries, and associated content (HTML, CSS, and other content files) that are used by the plugin.

The plugin.xml describes the plugin and tells the CLI where to copy plugin components in the target mobile application projects. There are even settings in the plugin.xml that are used by the CLI to set platform-specific config.xml settings. There are a lot of available options within the plugin.xml file; I won't cover all of them here.

A plugin has to have at least one JavaScript source file; this one file is expected to define the methods, objects, and properties that are exposed by the plugin. Your application may wrap everything into one JavaScript file or may have several; it's all up to you. You can also bundle in additional JavaScript libraries (jQuery Mobile, lawnchair, mustache.js, handlebars.js, and so on) as needed.

Beyond those first two requirements, the rest of the plugin files are anything else you need to define your plugin. In general, a plugin will include one or more native source code files for each supported mobile device platform. On top of that, a plugin might include additional native libraries (in source code form or precompiled) or content (image files, style sheets, HTML files, who knows?).

The good thing about building your own plugins is that there are a whole bunch of examples readily available to you. You can access a plugin's source code by creating a new Cordova project (using the Cordova CLI, of course), adding several plugins, then opening the project's plugins folder and poking around at the code within each plugin's folder. Another option is to look for plugin projects on GitHub (that's where all of the Cordova core plugins are maintained). Just perform a search using the plugin ID (org.apache.cordova.console, for example), and one of the first few search results should point to the plugin's code on GitHub.

Creating a JavaScript-Only Plugin

A Cordova plugin does not have to have native code in it; instead, it can be completely composed of JavaScript code. I thought it would make sense to start with a simple plugin, something that shows what a plugin is all about, before digging into plugins with native code; this way you'll get a feel for the structure of a Cordova plugin without the distraction of native code. I'm calling the plugin I'm creating Meaning of Life, and I will abbreviate it to mol here. In the sections that follow, I'll expand on what we learned here and build a more complicated example plugin using native code.

> **Note**
>
> The plugin I create here isn't going to be very useful; it's merely designed to help teach you about the structure and format of a Cordova plugin. Here I'll create a plugin that calculates the meaning of life. This will make perfect sense to those of you who are aware of Douglas Adams's work; for the rest of you, in *The Hitchhiker's Guide to the Galaxy*, the "Answer to the Ultimate Question of Life, the Universe, and Everything" (shortened to Meaning of Life by me) is 42, so the one method exposed through the plugin will simply return 42 to the calling program. You can learn more about it at http://goo.gl/Chqm96.

Cordova provides a set of command-line tools for managing plugins called Plugman. I described how to install and use Plugman in Chapter 4. To create this plugin, I opened a terminal window, navigated to the folder where I wanted the plugin created, and issued the following command:

```
plugman create --name mol --plugin_id com.johnwargo.mol --plugin_version 0.0.1
```

Plugman will create a folder for the plugin project and populate it with a plugin.xml file and two folders as shown in Figure 16.1. The www folder contains the JavaScript interface files for the plugin, and the src folder is used to host native application code for the plugin. There won't be any native code for this plugin, so the src folder will go unused in this example.

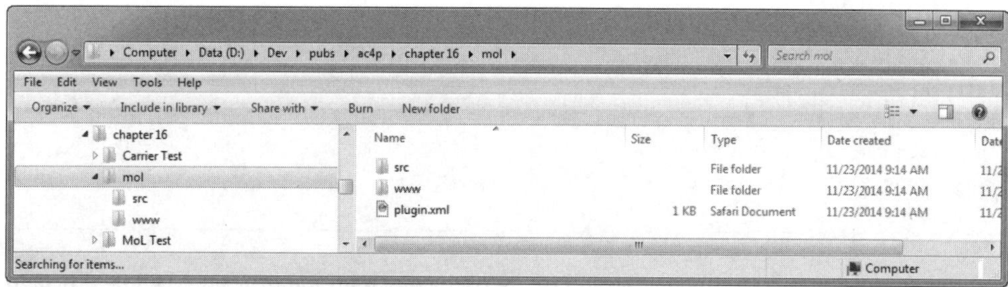

Figure 16.1 mol Plugin Folder Structure

plugin.xml File

The plugin's plugin.xml file is a configuration file that a developer uses to describe the plugin as well as the different software components and configuration settings for the plugin. You can read more about the different Cordova configuration files at http://goo.gl/sybkrq. Details about plugins and the plugin.xml file can be found at http://goo.gl/fbDxBw. Details on the Plugin specification are published at http://goo.gl/S4zCXX.

When you create a new plugin, Plugman creates the plugin.xml file for you, then populates it with some of the information passed on the Plugman command line. You can find the complete listing of this plugin.xml file in Listing 16.1.

Listing 16.1 Default plugin.xml File

```
<?xml version='1.0' encoding='utf-8'?>
<plugin id="com.johnwargo.mol" version="0.0.1"
  xmlns="http://apache.org/cordova/ns/plugins/1.0"
  xmlns:android="http://schemas.android.com/apk/res/android">
    <name>mol</name>
    <js-module name="mol" src="www/mol.js">
        <clobbers target="cordova.plugins.mol" />
    </js-module>
</plugin>
```

For this particular plugin, I want to add a better description of the plugin as well as my name, so I've updated the file and provided the complete listing in Listing 16.2.

Listing 16.2 Updated plugin.xml File

```
<?xml version='1.0' encoding='utf-8' ?>
<plugin id="com.johnwargo.mol" version="0.0.1"
  xmlns="http://apache.org/cordova/ns/plugins/1.0"
  xmlns:android="http://schemas.android.com/apk/res/android">
  <name>mol</name>
  <description>Answer to the Ultimate Question of Life, the Universe, and Everything
(42)</description>
  <license>Apache 2.0</license>
  <author>John M. Wargo</author>
  <keywords>42</keywords>
  <js-module name="mol" src="www/mol.js">
    <clobbers target="mol" />
  </js-module>
</plugin>
```

Some of the information in the plugin.xml file is for documentation purposes, to allow others to understand who created the plugin and why. The other options in the file are used to drive the Plugman or the Cordova CLI plugin installation process. You can find a listing of the different plugin.xml elements in Table 16.1.

There are additional supported elements for a plugin's plugin.xml file; these will be covered when I show how to create a native plugin later in the chapter.

Table 16.1 Cordova plugin.xml Elements

Component	Description
`plugin`	Defines the namespace, ID, and version for the plugin. Cordova 3 plugins should utilize the http://apache.org/cordova/ns/plugins/1.0 namespace. The ID for the plugin is a reverse-domain-style identifier. This is what will be displayed in the plugin list when you issue a `cordova plugins` command in a terminal window from a Cordova project folder.
`name`	Defines the human-readable name for the plugin.
`description`	Defines the human-readable description of the plugin.
`author`	Defines the name of the author who created the plugin.
`keywords`	Defines human-readable keywords associated with the plugin.
`license`	Defines the license for the plugin. In my example, I just used the default license that Cordova uses, but you can enter anything you want here, either a license description and/or a link to license terms.

Table 16.1 Cordova plugin.xml Elements (continued)

Component	Description
engines	Used to define the versions of Cordova the plugin supports. Add an additional engine element for each supported Cordova version: <engines> <engine name="cordova" version="4.0.0" /> <engine name="cordova" version="3.6.1" /> </engines> You can also use >, >=, <, and <= to indicate that a particular range of versions is supported: <engines> <engine name="cordova" version="<4.0.0" /> </engines> If you omit the engines element, the plugin will be available for any Cordova version. This element is not shown in the example as the plugin should work for any version of Cordova.
asset	Defines a file or folder that will be copied to the project's www folder during plugin installation. An asset can be any file or folder. One or more asset elements can be included in the plugin.xml file. For a file asset, use <asset src="www/compass.png" target="compass.png" /> For a folder asset, use <asset src="www/images" target="images" /> This element is not shown in the example since this plugin uses no additional assets.
js-module	Refers to the file name for a JavaScript file for which a script tag will be automatically added to a Cordova project's startup page (index.html by default). By listing your plugin's main JavaScript files within js-module tags, you eliminate some of the work developers have to do to use your plugin in their Cordova applications. The clobbers element specifies that the module.exports (mol in the case of this plugin) is automatically added to the window object, giving your plugin's methods scope at the window level.

The Plugin's mol.js File

When Plugman created the plugin project, it also created a base JavaScript file for the plugin. Since the plugin's name is mol, Plugman created a file called mol.js. This file describes the plugin's primary JavaScript interface that a Cordova application can call when using the plugin's capabilities. You can see the contents of the file Plugman created for this plugin in Listing 16.3.

Listing 16.3 Shell mol.js File

```
var exec = require('cordova/exec');

exports.coolMethod = function(arg0, success, error) {
```

```
    exec(success, error, "mol", "coolMethod", [arg0]);
};
```

Plugman assumes that the plugin will be executing native code, so it loads the Cordova `exec` library, then defines an `export` for a JavaScript method called `coolMethod`. Inside the exports structure, the code is executing a native method called `coolMethod` which you would have to provide for each target platform.

For this plugin, I don't have any native code to write (since this is a JavaScript-only plugin), so everything the plugin needs to do is shown in Listing 16.4. Here I export a function called `calculateMOL`; the function simply returns the value 42, the answer to the Ultimate Question of Life, the Universe, and Everything (as defined by Douglas Adams).

Listing 16.4 mol.js File

```
module.exports.calculateMOL = function () {
  return 42;
};
```

That's it; that's all there is to creating a simple, JavaScript-only Cordova plugin.

Now, remember that in the plugin's plugin.xml file there was this entry:

```
<js-module name="mol" src="www/mol.js">
  <clobbers target="mol" />
</js-module>
```

This tells Plugman or the Cordova CLI, when it's installing the plugin, to copy the mol.js file to each target platform project's www folder and to expose a `mol` object that that application can use. To use the plugin, all the application has to do is call `mol.calculateMOL()` and a value of 42 will be returned.

In this example, I've exposed only one method through the plugin. I could easily expose more by simply adding more exports to the mol.js file or adding additional .js files to the project that also export functions. I'll do this in the next example. You can see an example of how to do this with multiple files in the source code for the Console plugin at http://goo.gl/2zHOOc.

Now, the function I've created is not very Cordova-like. It's a JavaScript plugin and it works, but the majority of Cordova plugins are asynchronous; when a plugin API is called, at least one callback function is passed in, then the function is executed and passed the resulting value. To show you an example of an asynchronous version of the same API, I renamed the existing function `calculateMOLSync` and added a new `calculateMOL` to the mol.js file as shown in Listing 16.5.

Listing 16.5 Enhanced mol.js File

```
module.exports = {

  calculateMOLSync: function() {
```

```
    return 42;
  },

  calculateMOL: function(theCallback) {
    theCallback(42);
  }
};
```

With this in place, an application can call `calculateMOLSync()` to get the result returned immediately to the application or `calculateMOL(callback)` to get the result passed to the `callback` function. I'll show you an example of how both of these options work in the following section.

Testing the Plugin

To prove that the plugin works, I created a simple MOLTest application to exercise the plugin. To create the project, I opened a terminal window, navigated to my system's dev folder, then issued the following commands:

```
cordova create molTest com.ac4p.moltest MOLTest
cd molTest
cordova platform add android browser
cordova plugin add org.apache.cordova.console
cordova plugin add org.apache.cordova.dialogs
cordova plugin add org.apache.cordova.device
cordova plugin add "D:\Dev\pubs\ac4p\chapter 16\mol"
```

I've shown the output of most of those commands before (Chapter 4 and Chapter 15, "Cordova Development End to End"), so I won't show them again. When adding my custom plugin to the project, the CLI displays the following output:

```
Installing "com.johnwargo.mol" for android
Installing "com.johnwargo.mol" for browser
```

Notice that I'm adding the browser platform to this project as well. Since the plugin is JavaScript only, I can test this in the browser first before switching to one of the mobile platforms.

I've published the plugin to the Cordova Plugin Registry, so you can also add it to your project using the following command:

```
cordova plugin add com.johnwargo.mol
```

To see information about all of the installed plugins, issue the following command:

```
cordova plugins
```

The CLI will display the following output:

```
com.johnwargo.mol 0.0.1 "mol"
org.apache.cordova.console 0.2.11 "Console"
org.apache.cordova.device 0.2.12 "Device"
org.apache.cordova.dialogs 0.2.10 "Notification"
```

With those steps completed, all I had to do was open my HTML editor of choice and write the application. Listing 16.6 shows the application's index.html file; all that really happens there is that there's a single button on the page I can tap to check that the plugin is working. The application uses Topcoat to create a more pleasing UI for the application.

Listing 16.6 MOLTest Application index.html File

```
<!DOCTYPE html>
<html>

<head>
  <title>Meaning of Life Demo</title>
  <meta http-equiv="Content-type" content="text/html; charset=utf-8">
  <meta name="viewport" content="user-scalable=no, initial-scale=1,
    maximum-scale=1, minimum-scale=1, width=device-width" />
  <link rel="stylesheet" type="text/css" href="css/topcoat-mobile-light.min.css">
  <script src="index.js"></script>
  <script src="cordova.js"></script>
</head>

<body onload="onBodyLoad()">
  <div class="topcoat-navigation-bar">
    <div class="topcoat-navigation-bar__item center full">
      <h1 class="topcoat-navigation-bar__title">MoL Demo</h1>
    </div>
  </div>
  <p>Get the answer to the Ultimate Question of Life, the Universe, and Everything
(according to Douglas Adams).</p>
  <button class="topcoat-button--large" onclick="doMOLSync();">Synchronous</button>
  <button class="topcoat-button--large" onclick="doMOLAsync();">Asynchronous</button>
</body>

</html>
```

The guts of the application are in the project's index.js shown in Listing 16.7. The file contains the `doMOL` function that is executed when the user taps the button. The function makes a call to `mol.calculateMOL()` and displays the result in an `alert` dialog.

Listing 16.7 MOLTest Application index.js File

```
function onBodyLoad() {
  console.log("Entering onBodyLoad");
  document.addEventListener("deviceready", onDeviceReady);
  console.log("Leaving onBodyLoad");
}
```

```
function onDeviceReady() {
  console.log("Entering onDeviceReady");
  console.log("Cordova: " + device.cordova);
  navigator.notification.alert("Cordova is ready");
  console.log("Leaving onDeviceReady");
}

function doMOLSync() {
  console.log("Entering doMOLSync");
  var res = mol.calculateMOLSync();
  var msg = "Result: " + res;
  console.log(msg);
  navigator.notification.alert(msg, null, "MOL", "Continue");
  console.log("Leaving doMOLSync");
}

function doMOLAsync() {
  console.log("Entering doMOLAsync");
  var res = mol.calculateMOL(molCallback);
  console.log("Leaving doMOLAsync");
}

function molCallback(res) {
  console.log("Entering molCallback");
  var msg = "Result: " + res;
  console.log(msg);
  navigator.notification.alert(msg, null, "MOL", "Continue");
  console.log("Leaving molCallback");
}
```

That's all there is to it. When you run the application and tap the Synchronous button, you should see the results shown in Figure 16.2. You should, of course, receive the same result by tapping the Asynchronous button, only the result dialog is displayed by the `callback` function.

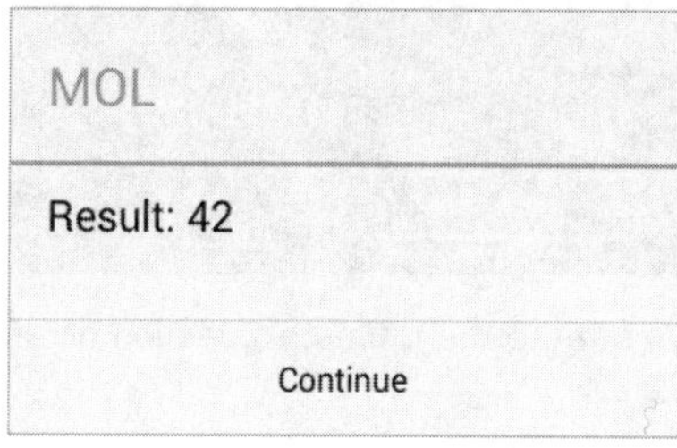

Figure 16.2 Calculating the Answer to the Ultimate Question of Life, the Universe, and Everything on an Android Device

Just so you'll believe me when I say that this JavaScript-only plugin will work on any supported Cordova device, Figure 16.3 shows the calculation results on the Firefox OS simulator.

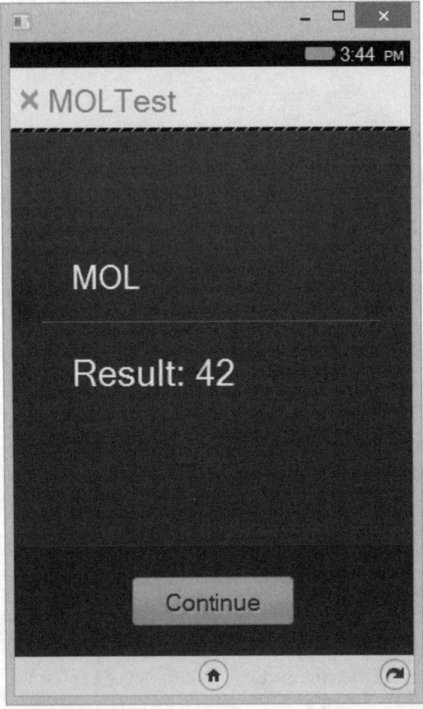

Figure 16.3 Calculating the Answer to the Ultimate Question of Life, the Universe, and Everything on a Firefox OS Device

Figure 16.4 shows the results of the calculation on a Windows Phone device.

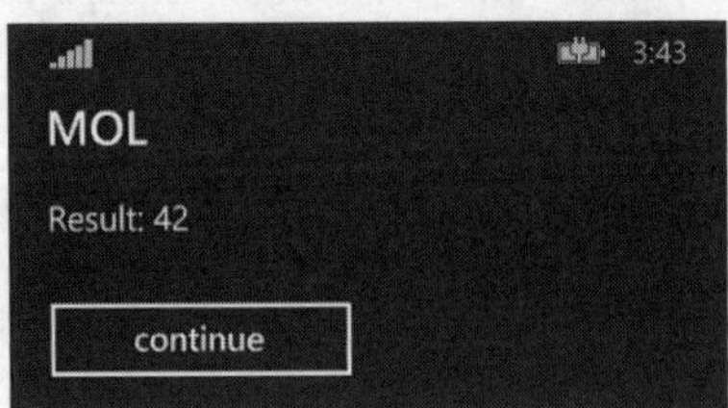

Figure 16.4 Calculating the Answer to the Ultimate Question of Life, the Universe, and Everything on a Windows Device

Success! Now let me show you a little bit about what happens with Cordova plugins when you add them to a project. Remember from Listing 16.5 that the index.html file has references to the index.js and cordova.js files. However, when you inspect the source code in a debugging tool (like the Chrome Developer Tools shown in Figure 16.5), you'll see that the index.html file has a bunch of additional script tags added to it. This happens at runtime and is performed by the Cordova container.

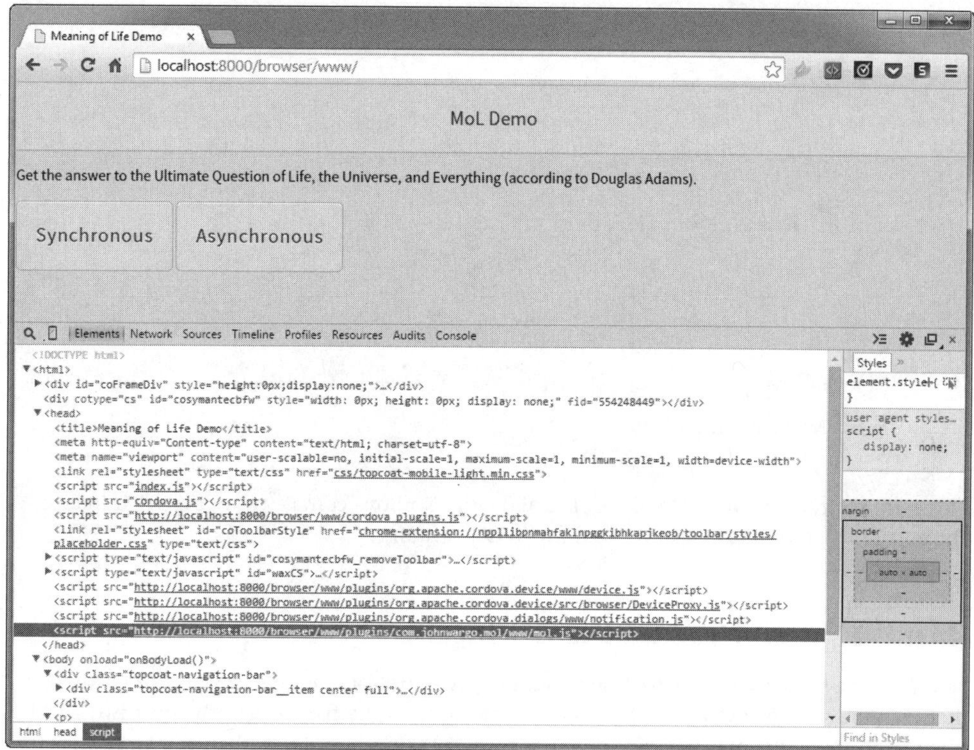

Figure 16.5 Chrome Developer Tools Showing the Application's Modified index.html File

When the container processes its list of plugins on startup, references to each of the plugins' JavaScript source code are added automatically to the application's startup file (the index.html in this case and by default). Remember the `js-module` element in the plugin.xml file? It's this configuration parameter that tells the Cordova container what file to add and what object it exposes to the application. All of this is done before the Cordova deviceready event is fired by the container and is why it might take a while for that event to fire.

If you look at the mol.js file, you'll see that it has been modified by the CLI when the plugin is installed in each platform's plugin folder. As you can see in Figure 16.6, a `cordova.define` wrapper has been placed around the `module.exports` shown in Listing 16.5.

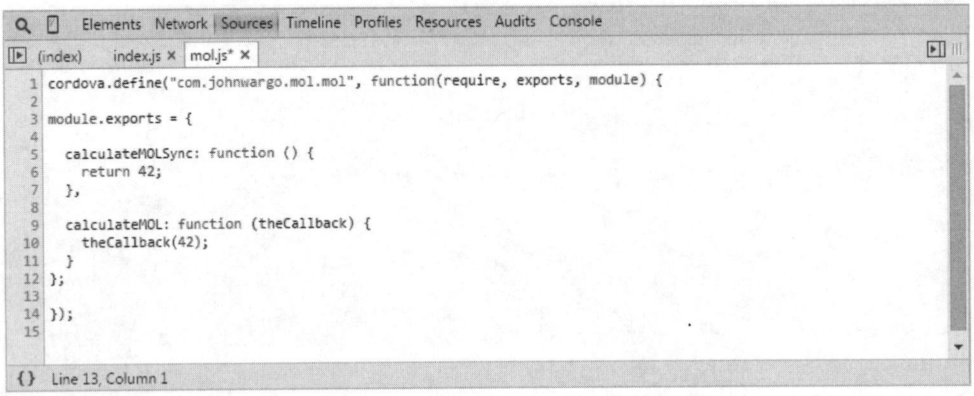

```
cordova.define("com.johnwargo.mol.mol", function(require, exports, module) {

module.exports = {

  calculateMOLSync: function () {
    return 42;
  },

  calculateMOL: function (theCallback) {
    theCallback(42);
  }
};

});
```

Figure 16.6 Modified mol.js File

This extra plumbing is added by the CLI to allow the Cordova container to properly initialize and expose itself to the application running in the container.

Creating a Cordova Native Plugin

Now that I've shown you how to create a simple, JavaScript-only plugin, it's time to go beyond that example and create a plugin for Cordova that contains native code. In the next two sections, I will show you how to create a simple native plugin for Android, then show you how to add the same functionality for iOS. The plugin I'll be creating isn't fancy; it simply exposes some native telephony APIs to a Cordova container. For this plugin, I just started poking around in the Android SDK documentation and found something interesting to expose, then coded the plugin. The reason I took this approach was to keep the native API code I was exposing through this plugin as clean as possible. The purpose of this chapter is to show you how to make plugins, not how to do native development, so that's why the plugin is not too complicated. What you'll see in the next couple of sections is how to structure your plugin; adding additional APIs or more sophisticated capabilities to your plugins will be easy once you know the basics of how native plugins work.

The plugin I'll be creating is called Carrier, and it exposes information provided by a smartphone's carrier: the carrier name plus the country code where the device is located or provisioned.

Native Development and the Plugin Workflow

For mobile apps, I'm not much of a native developer. I've done some native development for Android, BlackBerry, and other platforms, but I've simply not spent a lot of time writing native code. That's why Cordova is so interesting to me; it allows me to build cross-platform mobile apps using my web development skills (I've done a lot more web development). That's also why I'm the right guy to write Cordova development books, for the type of developer who's going to focus on web development and not go too deeply into native plugins. That web developer working with Cordova is the target audience for this book.

In this chapter, I show you how to create plugins, but not how to write a bunch of native code for mobile devices. There are a lot of books out there that will do that for you, just not this one. The native code I'll show here will be high-level—enough to allow the plugin to do something recognizable, but not so much that you can't see the plugin for the native code.

There's some documentation out there on Plugman, and a lot of documentation on how to structure a Cordova plugin's files and what code needs to go into the plugin. What I've struggled to find is a detailed workflow for developers building plugins. I know it's a personal preference thing, but you'd think developers would want to know how to work with the plugin's code, instead of just what the code needs to look like.

Should you create a separate folder structure for your plugin, then link it into a native project for compiling and testing; or should you create a native project, then add a plugin to it and do all of your work there? I really don't know. With that in mind, how then do you build a single plugin for multiple target platforms? Not something I know. All I can tell you is how I did it.

To create the plugins in this chapter, I created a separate folder for my plugin, then created a Cordova project for multiple targets and added my plugin to it for testing. If I were more of a native developer, I probably would have created a native project, squished my plugin project into it, and worked with the native debugger to get it all working, then copied out the native code for each platform into a common folder for my plugin for packaging and publishing.

It doesn't matter which option you choose, only that it works for you. No matter what, any option I could come up with still seemed a bit clunky to me—lots of moving parts. Before the next book, I'll query the Cordova dev team to learn their secrets of plugin development and share what I learn with you.

To create the plugin, I opened a terminal window, navigated to the folder where I wanted to create the plugin project, and issued the following commands:

```
plugman create --name carrier --plugin_id com.johnwargo.carrier
--plugin_version 0.0.1
```

Remember, the plugin is called Carrier, so I rightfully named the plugin project folder carrier as well.

As you saw with the JavaScript plugin, Plugman will create a project structure for the plugin, populating it with a simple plugin.xml file, two folders, and a shell JavaScript file that provides the API interface for the plugin.

Since I know I will be working with native code, I can use Plugman to add support for a limited number of platforms (only Android and iOS today unfortunately). To add support for any other platforms, you will need to create the necessary platform folder, populate the folder with source code files, and update the plugin.xml file with settings for the platform. This is surprising considering Plugman is more than a year old, but it is what it is.

To add support for Android and iOS, in the terminal window, execute the following commands:

```
cd carrier
plugman platform add --platform_name android
plugman platform add --platform_name ios
```

Here I'm changing into the plugin project folder that was just created and adding the two platforms individually. Remember from Chapter 4 that the Cordova CLI allows you to add multiple platforms with one command; unfortunately that doesn't work for Plugman. At the conclusion of the process, the plugin project's src folder will have two additional folders in it as shown in Figure 16.7. It's not shown here, but the android and ios folders shown in the figure have also been populated with the shell source code files needed for the plugin.

Figure 16.7 Carrier Plugin Folder Structure

In Listing 16.1 I showed the default plugin.xml file created by Plugman. Now that I've added two platforms to the plugin project, the plugin.xml file looks like what is shown in Listing 16.8. There are some problems with this file, but I'll fix them a little later and show you the results.

Listing 16.8 Carrier Plugin plugin.xml File

```
<?xml version='1.0' encoding='utf-8' ?>
<plugin id="com.johnwargo.carrier" version="0.0.1"
  xmlns=http://apache.org/cordova/ns/plugins/1.0
  xmlns:android="http://schemas.android.com/apk/res/android">
  <name>carrier</name>
  <js-module name="carrier" src="www/carrier.js">
    <clobbers target="cordova.plugins.carrier" />
  </js-module>
  <platform name="android">
    <config-file parent="/*" target="res/xml/config.xml">
      <feature name="carrier">
        <param name="android-package"
          value="com.johnwargo.carrier.carrier" />
      </feature>
    </config-file>
    <config-file parent="/*" target="AndroidManifest.xml" />
    <source-file src="src/android/carrier.java"
      target-dir="src/com/johnwargo/carrier/carrier" />
  </platform>
  <platform name="ios">
    <config-file parent="/*" target="config.xml">
      <feature name="carrier">
        <param name="ios-package" value="carrier" />
      </feature>
    </config-file>
    <source-file src="src/ios/carrier.m" />
  </platform>
</plugin>
```

In the project's www folder is a JavaScript file named for the plugin project, carrier.js in this case. The contents of the file are the same as what was shown in Listing 16.3.

JavaScript or Native Code First?

When creating a native Cordova plugin, you need to provide both JavaScript and native code for the plugin. The big question is, which do you create first? It depends.

Some plugin developers focus on the native code first, researching the capabilities being exposed by the plugin and crafting the native methods to expose them before crafting the JavaScript interface for the plugin. The developer could write the native code for one platform, then write the JavaScript interface before tackling additional platforms. Another option is to write the native code for all platforms, then when you have it all worked out, finalize everything with the JavaScript code.

I prefer to write the JavaScript interface first, then add the native code. For the plugin in this part of the chapter, I researched the available APIs for Android and iOS, analyzed the input and output I'd need, then crafted the JavaScript interface that matched. This is not rocket science, but it works for me.

Which approach should you take? Whichever one makes the most sense for the project at hand or the way your brain is wired. Enjoy!

Before I start on the native code, I need to first define the JavaScript interface that will be exposed to Cordova applications. The way this works is through the same type of JavaScript file I created for the mol plugin in the previous section. In the JavaScript file I created for this plugin I created a simple JavaScript object called `carrier` and defined within it one or more methods that can be called from a Cordova application. For this particular example, the Carrier plugin will expose the `getCarrierName` and `getCountryCode` methods.

Now, unlike the mol plugin, these JavaScript methods will not do any calculations and return any values directly; instead, they will make calls to a `cordova.exec` method that passes control to native code I've created for each target platform. This is the famous JavaScript to native bridge that allows Cordova applications to execute native APIs. When the native code is finished doing what it is supposed to be doing, it executes callback functions provided by the JavaScript code and passes back the results to the JavaScript code.

The method signature for `cordova.exec` is

```
cordova.exec(successCallback, errorCallback, 'PluginObject',
  'pluginMethod', [arguments]);
```

The `successCallback` and `errorCallback` parameters are the names of the functions that will be executed on success and failure of the particular plugin method call. The `'PluginObject'` parameter is a string that identifies the native object that contains the method being called, and the `'pluginMethod'` parameter is a string that identifies the method of the object that is executed. Last, the `arguments` parameter is an optional array of arguments that will be passed to the `pluginMethod` for it to use when performing whatever task it is performing.

In this example, the `getCarrierName` and `getCountryCode` methods don't require that any parameters be passed to them, so the `arguments` parameter will be empty and represented by empty brackets: `[]`.

Listing 16.9 shows the contents of the project's carrier.js file, the JavaScript interface file for the plugin. This file was created by Plugman; I simply adjusted it for the plugin. The code begins by defining the Cordova `exec` object by loading a code library through `require`. When this is done, the `exec` object can be used to invoke the JavaScript to native bridge. This library is a core part of the Cordova container and should be available to any Cordova plugin automatically.

With that in place, the `carrier` object is created and the two methods are defined. Each method calls `cordova.exec` and passes the necessary parameters (function names and object and method names) needed for the bridge to operate.

At the very end of the file is a `module.exports` assignment that allows the `carrier` object to be exposed to a Cordova application.

Listing 16.9 Carrier Plugin carrier.js File

```
var exec = require('cordova/exec');

var carrier = {
  getCarrierName: function (successCallback, errorCallback) {
    exec(successCallback, errorCallback, 'carrier', 'getCarrierName', []);
  },

  getCountryCode: function (successCallback, errorCallback) {
    exec(successCallback, errorCallback, 'carrier', 'getCountryCode', []);
  }
};

module.exports = carrier;
```

Let's take a look at one of the method definitions:

```
getCarrierName: function (successCallback, errorCallback) {
  exec(successCallback, errorCallback, 'carrier', 'getCarrierName', []);
},
```

The `getCarrierName` in the first line of the code defines one of the JavaScript methods exposed by the plugin. The method takes two parameters: success and error callback functions. If the method needed any additional parameters to operate, you would define them after the `errorCallback` parameter.

> **Note**
>
> Do you have to define the callback functions first and in that order followed by any additional parameters? No, not really. However, think about all of the Cordova APIs you experienced in Chapter 14, "Working with the Cordova APIs." Structuring an API method this way is the default way Cordova APIs are defined, so if you want your plugin to "feel" like the core Cordova plugins, you'll want to follow this convention.

As you can see from the code, all of the parameters are simply passed on to the Cordova JavaScript to native bridge through the execution of the `exec` method. The method signature for `exec` is fixed; if your plugin needs to pass additional parameters to the native code, you must pass them through the `arguments` parameter, the empty brackets `[]` shown on the `exec` line.

With that in place I am ready to begin coding the native parts of the plugin.

> **Note**
>
> You don't have to define the JavaScript interface for your plugin first. If you look at the different Cordova plugin tutorials available on the Internet, you will find that people do it either way: define the JavaScript interface first or write the native code first. It really doesn't matter. I researched the required native functions first, so I already had what I needed to craft the JavaScript interface.
>
> If you are working with a more complicated plugin, you may find it easier to work through all of the native functions and what they will require before crafting your plugin's JavaScript interface.

Creating the Android Plugin

With the JavaScript interface defined, it's time to start working on the native part of the plugin. In this case, I did things alphabetically, so I created the Android plugin first, then ported it to iOS later.

On Android, the information the plugin will be returning to the Cordova application will come from the Telephony API. To use this API, an application must import the `Context` and `TelephonyManager` classes:

```
import android.content.Context;
import android.telephony.TelephonyManager;
```

Then, the code must define an instance of the `TelephonyManager` class that exposes the methods we need to call to get the carrier name and country code:

```
tm = (TelephonyManager) getSystemService(Context.TELEPHONY_SERVICE);
```

To determine the carrier name, the plugin will make a call to `tm.getSimOperatorName()`, and to get the country code, it will make a call to `tm.getSimCountryIso()`.

Listing 16.10 lists the Java code used for the Android plugin; it defines a simple class called `CarrierPlugin` that exposes the `exec` method that is executed by the call to the JavaScript `cordova.exec` in Listing 16.9.

Listing 16.10 Carrier Plugin carrier.java File

```
package com.johnwargo.carrier;

//Cordova imports
import org.apache.cordova.CordovaInterface;
```

```
import org.apache.cordova.CallbackContext;
import org.apache.cordova.CordovaPlugin;
import org.apache.cordova.CordovaWebView;

//Android imports
import android.content.Context;
import android.telephony.TelephonyManager;

//JSON Imports
import org.json.JSONArray;
import org.json.JSONException;

public class carrier extends CordovaPlugin {

  // define some constants for the supported actions
  public static final String
    ACTION_GET_CARRIER_NAME = "getCarrierName";
  public static final String
    ACTION_GET_COUNTRY_CODE = "getCountryCode";

  public TelephonyManager tm;

  public void initialize(CordovaInterface cordova,
    CordovaWebView webView) {
    super.initialize(cordova, webView);
    // the plugin doesn't have direct access to the application
    // context, so you have to get it first
    Context context = this.cordova.getActivity().getApplicationContext();
    // Next we initialize the tm object
    tm = (TelephonyManager) context
      .getSystemService(Context.TELEPHONY_SERVICE);
  }

  @Override
  public boolean execute(String action, JSONArray args,
    CallbackContext callbackContext) throws JSONException {
    try {
      // First check on the getCarrierName
      if (ACTION_GET_CARRIER_NAME.equals(action)) {
        callbackContext.success(tm.getSimOperatorName());
        return true;
      } else {
        // Next see if it is a getCountryCode action
        if (ACTION_GET_COUNTRY_CODE.equals(action)) {
          callbackContext.success(tm.getSimCountryIso());
          return true;
        }
      }
```

```
      // We don't have a match, so it must be an invalid action
      callbackContext.error("Invalid Action");
      return false;
    } catch (Exception e) {
      // If we get here, then something horrible has happened
      System.err.println("Exception: " + e.getMessage());
      callbackContext.error(e.getMessage());
      return false;
    }
  }
}
```

The class defines two constants, `ACTION_GET_CARRIER_NAME` and `ACTION_GET_COUNTRY_CODE`, that are used in determining which method was called by the Cordova application. You could hard-code the comparison deeper within the Java code, but doing it this way makes it easier to change the names later.

Next, the class defines the `tm` object used to give the plugin access to the Telephony APIs.

The `initialize` method first calls `super.initialize`, which allows the `cordova` object to be initialized properly. Without this call, the Java code has no awareness of the Cordova container. The code then gets a handle to the current application context and uses that to wire the `tm` object into the services exposed by the Telephony API.

Next, the Java code overrides the `exec` method and implements the code that deals directly with the calls from the Cordova application. In this implementation, I've implemented a single operation that determines which action has been called (by comparing the action name passed by the call to `cordova.exec` to the constants I defined earlier) and acts accordingly.

If the `exec` method determines that the `getCarrierName` action was requested, it makes the call to the Android `getSimOperatorName` method and passes the results back to the Cordova application by calling `callbackContext.success()`. If the `getCountryCode` action was requested, it makes a call to the Android `getSimCountryIso()` and passes the results back to the Cordova application by calling `callbackContext.success()`.

If any part of this process fails, the code executes `callbackContext.error` and passes back an appropriate error message or error object indicating what went wrong.

> **Note**
>
> I could have done more error checking and provided more ways for the plugin to let the calling application know when things went wrong. Remember, though, I'm trying to demonstrate how to write a Cordova plugin, not highlight all the things you can do in native code. Be sure to spend some time with the source code of any of the Cordova core or third-party plugins; you'll see a lot more of what you can do in a plugin.

That's all there is to the code; I tried to make it as simple as possible in order to allow you to focus on the parts that are specific to Cordova plugins.

Before I can use the CLI to add this new plugin to a Cordova project, I have to update the plugin's plugin.xml with some additional information. Listing 16.11 shows the complete file contents for this plugin (so far, I'm omitting the iOS components and will cover them later). I've highlighted in bold the parts of the file that are different from the file created by Plugman (shown in Listing 16.8).

Listing 16.11 plugin.xml

```
<?xml version='1.0' encoding='utf-8' ?>
<plugin id="com.johnwargo.carrier" version="0.0.1"
  xmlns="http://apache.org/cordova/ns/plugins/1.0"
  xmlns:android="http://schemas.android.com/apk/res/android">
  <name>carrier</name>
  <description>A Cordova Plugin for retrieving Wireless Carrier information.</
description>
  <author>John M. Wargo</author>
  <keywords>carrier,telephony</keywords>
  <js-module name="carrier" src="www/carrier.js">
    <clobbers target="carrier" />
  </js-module>
  <platform name="android">
    <config-file parent="/*" target="res/xml/config.xml">
      <feature name="carrier">
        <param name="android-package"
          value="com.johnwargo.carrier.carrier" />
      </feature>
    </config-file>
    <config-file parent="/*" target="AndroidManifest.xml" />
    <source-file src="src/android/carrier.java"
      target-dir="src/com/johnwargo/carrier" />
    <config-file target="AndroidManifest.xml" parent="/*">
      <uses-permission
        android:name="android.permission.READ_PHONE_STATE" />
    </config-file>
  </platform>
  <platform name="ios">
    <!—some iOS Stuff I'll add and explain later-->
  </platform>
</plugin>
```

The file's `js-module` element defines the name of the JavaScript file that will be automatically loaded on application startup. It defines the JavaScript interface exposed to the Cordova application. The `clobbers` element specifies the JavaScript object that is assigned to the loaded

JavaScript object. In this example, shown here, I am directing that the Carrier plugin be exposed to the Cordova application through a `carrier` object:

```
<js-module name="carrier" src="www/carrier.js">
  <clobbers target="carrier" />
</js-module>
```

The Cordova application will access the `getCarrierName` method through the `carrier` object as shown here:

```
carrier.getCarrierName(onSuccess, onFailure);
```

In the plugin.xml file created by Plugman, the `clobbers target` was defined as `cordova.plugins.carrier`, so to use the plugin in a Cordova application, I would have had to use

```
cordova.plugins.carrier.getCarrierName(onSuccess, onFailure);
```

which is not simple enough for my needs.

The other part of the file that is different from the earlier example (Listing 16.1) is the `platform` section shown here:

```
<platform name="android">
  <config-file parent="/*" target="res/xml/config.xml">
    <feature name="carrier">
      <param name="android-package"
        value="com.johnwargo.carrier.carrier" />
    </feature>
  </config-file>
  <config-file parent="/*" target="AndroidManifest.xml" />
  <source-file src="src/android/carrier.java"
    target-dir="src/com/johnwargo/carrier" />
  <config-file target="AndroidManifest.xml" parent="/*">
    <uses-permission
      android:name="android.permission.READ_PHONE_STATE" />
  </config-file>
</platform>
```

It defines settings that are particular to specific mobile device platforms and contains settings that relate to the native code I've shown you in this section. There can be one or more platform elements in a plugin.xml file; the one shown next defines elements that apply to Android plugin components:

```
<platform name="android"></platform>
```

Within that element is a `source-file` element that points to one or more Android native source files that need to be installed by the CLI when the plugin is installed. In the following example, it is instructing Plugman or the CLI to copy the file called carrier.java located in the plugin source folder's src/android folder to the Cordova project's Android platform folder in the src/com/johnwargo/carrier folder:

```
<source-file src="src/android/carrier.java"
  target-dir="src/com/johnwargo/carrier" />
```

You don't have to copy the file to that deep of a folder structure, but it's the norm for Cordova plugins to be installed into a folder structure like that. Take a look at some of the Cordova core plugins and you will see what I mean.

The `config-file` element defines the changes that need to be made during plugin installation. In the following example, it is specifying that a feature named `carrier` should be added to the Android project's config.xml file and point to the Java class `com.johnwargo.carrier.carrier`:

```
<config-file parent="/*" target="res/xml/config.xml">
  <feature name="carrier">
    <param name="android-package"
      value="com.johnwargo.carrier.carrier" />
  </feature>
</config-file>
```

The last element in `platform` defines another configuration file setting. On Android, access to the Telephony API requires specific permissions. Any application that uses the API must add an entry to the application's AndroidManifest.xml file that lists the specific permissions required by the application. In this case, I have to add the `android.permission.READ_PHONE_STATE` permission to the manifest as shown here:

```
<config-file target="AndroidManifest.xml" parent="/*">
  <uses-permission android:name="android.permission.READ_PHONE_STATE" />
</config-file>
```

When you look at the settings screen for an application that uses this plugin, you will see the entry for "read phone status and identity" shown in Figure 16.8; that shows that the permission has been set correctly.

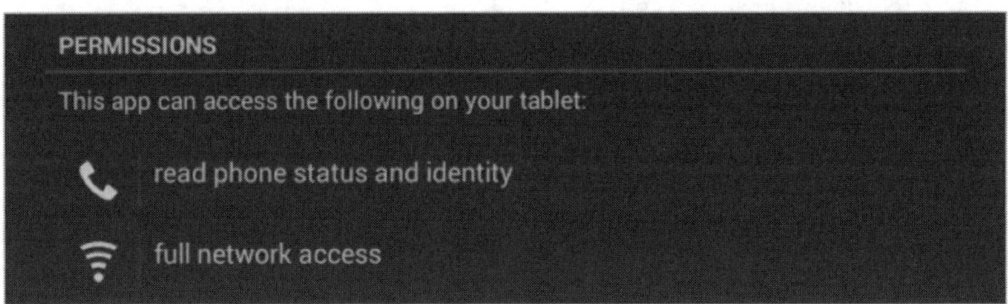

Figure 16.8 Android Application Permissions

If you do not set these permissions correctly, the part of the application that uses an API that requires the permission will fail without warning. If you forget to do this and wonder later why the Telephony API doesn't seem to be working, be sure to check the application permissions.

To test the application, I created the simple application shown in Listing 16.12. To create the application, I opened a terminal window, navigated to my system's dev folder, then issued the following commands:

```
cordova create carriertest com.ac4p.carriertest CarrierTest
cd carriertest
cordova platform add android
cordova plugin add c:\dev\plugins\carrier
```

I'll show you later how to publish the plugin to the Cordova Plugin Registry, but to use the published version of the plugin, you could add it to the project using

```
cordova plugin add com.johnwargo.carrier
```

With those steps completed, all I had to do was open my HTML editor of choice and enter the code shown in Listing 16.12. The application displays two buttons, one that makes a call to `getCarrierName` and another that makes a call to `getCountryCode`. The same `onSuccess` function is executed to display the results for both methods.

Listing 16.12 Carrier Plugin index.html

```
<!DOCTYPE html>
<html>

<head>
  <title>Carrier Demo</title>
  <meta http-equiv="Content-type" content="text/html; charset=utf-8">
  <meta name="viewport" content="user-scalable=no, initial-scale=1,
    maximum-scale=1, minimum-scale=1, width=device-width" />
  <link rel="stylesheet" type="text/css" href="css/topcoat-mobile-light.min.css">
  <script src="index.js"></script>
  <script src="cordova.js"></script>
</head>

<body onload="onBodyLoad()">
  <div class="topcoat-navigation-bar">
    <div class="topcoat-navigation-bar__item center full">
      <h1 class="topcoat-navigation-bar__title">Carrier Demo</h1>
    </div>
  </div>
  <p>This is a Cordova application that uses my fancy new Carrier plugin.</p>
  <div class="topcoat-button-bar">
    <div class="topcoat-button-bar__item">
```

```
      <button class="topcoat-button-bar__button--large"
        onclick="doGetCarrier();">Carrier Name</button>
    </div>
    <div class="topcoat-button-bar__item">
      <button class="topcoat-button-bar__button--large"
        onclick="doGetCountryCode();">Country Code</button>
    </div>
  </div>
</body>

</html>
```

The application uses the Topcoat CSS framework (http://topcoat.io) to give the application a cleaner UI; I'll describe Topcoat in Chapter 17, "Using Third-Party UI Frameworks with Cordova."

The application's JavaScript code is split out into the index.js file shown in Listing 16.13.

Listing 16.13 Carrier Plugin index.js

```
function onBodyLoad() {
  console.log("Entering onBodyLoad");
  document.addEventListener("deviceready", onDeviceReady);
  console.log("Leaving onBodyLoad");
}

function onDeviceReady() {
  console.log("Entering onDeviceReady");
  console.log("Cordova: " + device.cordova);
  navigator.notification.alert("Cordova is ready");
  console.log("Leaving onDeviceReady");
}

function doGetCarrier() {
  console.log("Entering doGetCarrier");
  carrier.getCarrierName(onSuccess, onError);
  console.log("Leaving doGetCarrier");
}

function doGetCountryCode() {
  console.log("Entering doGetCountryCode");
  carrier.getCountryCode(onSuccess, onError);
  console.log("Leaving doGetCountryCode");
}

function onSuccess(res) {
  console.log("Entering onSuccess");
```

```
  var msg = "Result: " + res;
  console.log(msg);
  navigator.notification.alert(msg, null, "Carrier Information", "Continue");
  console.log("Leaving onSuccess");
}

function onError(err) {
  console.log("Entering onError");
  console.error(JSON.stringify(err));
  var msg = "Error obtaining carrier information: " + err;
  navigator.notification.alert(msg, null, "Carrier Error", "Oops");
  console.log("Leaving onError");
}
```

When the application runs, it will display a screen similar to the one shown in Figure 16.9 (which I have cropped here for the sake of page real estate).

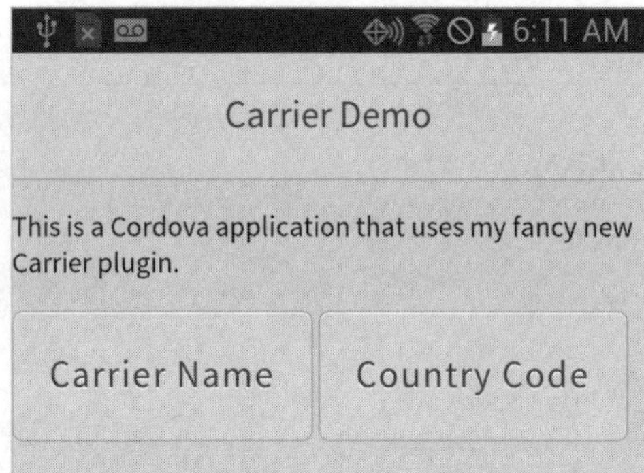

Figure 16.9 Carrier Demo Application

As you know, I like to start testing Cordova applications using simulators first. So, when I fired up this application on an Android emulator and tapped the Carrier Name button, the application displayed the message shown in Figure 16.10. Since the emulator isn't provisioned with a wireless carrier, the API doesn't have anything useful to return, so it simply returns "Android."

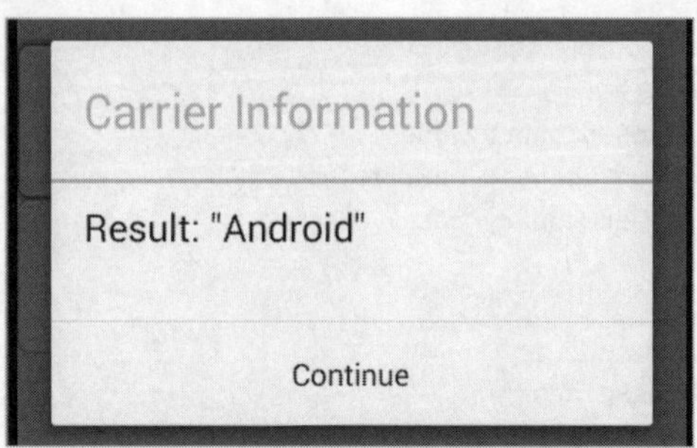

Figure 16.10 Results of `getCarrierName` on an Android Emulator

Now, I have an Android tablet, a Nexus 7, that is cellular enabled, but it's not a phone; Figure 16.11 shows what happens when I try to determine the provisioned carrier on the device. Unfortunately, since the tablet is not a phone, the Android Telephony APIs aren't going to help me. So, for a production plugin, not this simple sample I've created here, I'll have to check for a blank return value and return a message indicating that the device isn't telephony enabled.

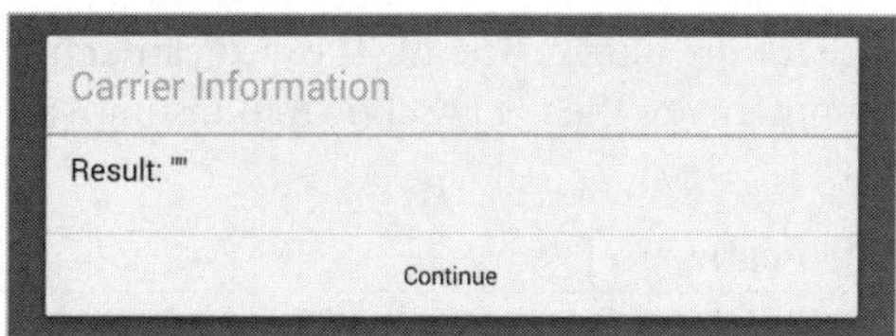

Figure 16.11 Results of `getCarrierName` on an Android Tablet

And finally to my Android smartphone. When I tap the Carrier Name button, the application will call the appropriate Telephony API and return my carrier's name as shown in Figure 16.12.

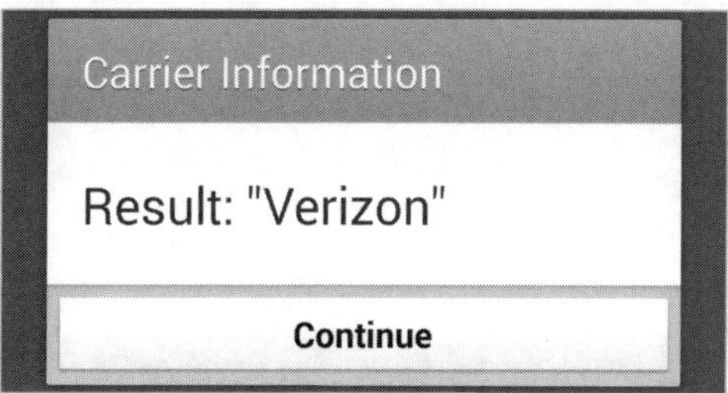

Figure 16.12 Results of `getCarrierName` on an Android Smartphone

When I tap the Country Code button, the device shows the message shown in Figure 16.13.

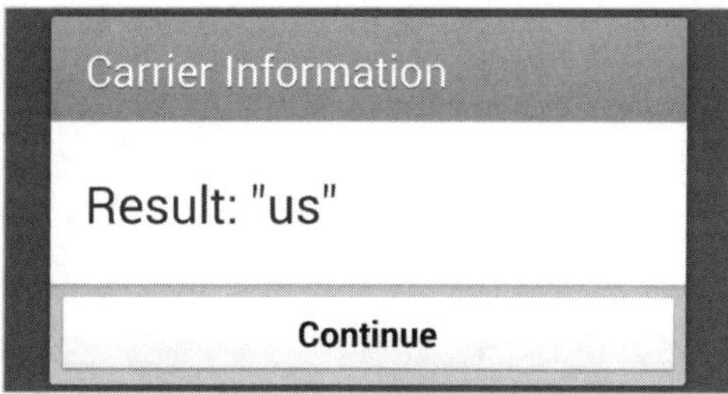

Figure 16.13 Results of `getCountryCode` on an Android Device

Clearly I have some work to do to make my plugin deal correctly with devices that aren't phones or aren't provisioned with a wireless carrier, but at least I now have a native plugin for Android and it's all ready to go.

Creating the iOS Plugin

In this section, I will show you how to implement the iOS version of the native Carrier plugin. For the iOS version of the plugin, things are a little simpler. On Android, when you call a plugin's methods, `cordova.exec` locates the native class and executes the methods on the class. For iOS, the plugin's methods are executed through URL commands exposed by the plugin.

When I created the plugin and added the iOS platform to the project, Plugman created a shell source code file for me to use for my plugin. The file is called carrier.h and it's located in the project's src/ios folder. The contents of the file are shown in Listing 16.14.

Listing 16.14 Carrier Plugin carrier.m File

```
/********* carrier.m Cordova Plugin Implementation *******/

#import <Cordova/CDV.h>

@interface carrier : CDVPlugin {
  // Member variables go here.
}

- (void)coolMethod:(CDVInvokedUrlCommand*)command;
@end

@implementation carrier

- (void)coolMethod:(CDVInvokedUrlCommand*)command
{
    CDVPluginResult* pluginResult = nil;
    NSString* echo = [command.arguments objectAtIndex:0];

    if (echo != nil && [echo length] > 0) {
        pluginResult = [CDVPluginResult
          resultWithStatus:CDVCommandStatus_OK messageAsString:echo];
    } else {
        pluginResult =
          [CDVPluginResult resultWithStatus:CDVCommandStatus_ERROR];
    }

    [self.commandDelegate sendPluginResult:pluginResult callbackId:command.
callbackId];
}

@end
```

The code imports the Cordova header file called CDV.h, defines an interface for the `coolMethod` method, then defines the implementation for the `carrier` object exposed through the plugin.

If you study the code, you'll see that it's showing how to process command arguments and return results for success and failure.

For this plugin, I need to define two methods to accommodate the `getCarrierName` and `getCountryCode` JavaScript functions the plugin exposes. In Listing 16.15, I've updated the file with the code we need for the iOS implementation of the plugin.

Listing 16.15 Updated Carrier Plugin carrier.m File

```
#import <Cordova/CDV.h>
#import <CoreTelephony/CTTelephonyNetworkInfo.h>
#import <CoreTelephony/CTCarrier.h>

@interface carrier : CDVPlugin {
  // Member variables go here.

}

- (void)getCarrierName:(CDVInvokedUrlCommand*)command;
- (void)getCountryCode:(CDVInvokedUrlCommand*)command;

@end

@implementation carrier

- (void)getCarrierName:(CDVInvokedUrlCommand*)command
{
    CTTelephonyNetworkInfo *netinfo = [[CTTelephonyNetworkInfo alloc] init];
    CTCarrier *carrier = [netinfo subscriberCellularProvider];
    CDVPluginResult* result = [CDVPluginResult resultWithStatus:CDVCommandStatus_OK
messageAsString:[carrier carrierName]];
    [self.commandDelegate sendPluginResult:result callbackId:[command callbackId]];
}

- (void)getCountryCode:(CDVInvokedUrlCommand*)command
{
    CTTelephonyNetworkInfo *netinfo = [[CTTelephonyNetworkInfo alloc] init];
    CTCarrier *carrier = [netinfo subscriberCellularProvider];
    CDVPluginResult* result = [CDVPluginResult resultWithStatus:CDVCommandStatus_OK
messageAsString:[carrier isoCountryCode]];
    [self.commandDelegate sendPluginResult:result callbackId:[command callbackId]];
}

@end
```

First, the code imports the library files the plugin needs to access the iOS Telephony APIs:

```
#import <CoreTelephony/CTTelephonyNetworkInfo.h>
#import <CoreTelephony/CTCarrier.h>
```

Next, the code defines the `carrier` interface as an implementation of `CDVPlugin`. What this does is let the iOS device know I'm exposing the code as a Cordova plugin. Next, the file defines the two methods used by the plugin: `getCarrierName` and `getCountryCode`. These are the methods that will be called by the plugin's JavaScript interface shown in Listing 16.9.

As you can see from the code, both methods leverage `CTTelephonyNetworkInfo`; for this plugin, neither of the methods accepts any parameters. For both methods, the plugin first defines a `netinfo` object that is assigned to an instance of the `CTTelephonyNetworkInfo` class as shown here:

```
CTTelephonyNetworkInfo *netinfo = [[CTTelephonyNetworkInfo alloc] init];
```

Next, a `carrier` object is created that provides the plugin with access to the cellular provider properties as shown here:

```
CTCarrier *carrier = [netinfo subscriberCellularProvider];
```

With that in place, the carrier name is exposed to the plugin through the `carrier` object's `carrierName` property. At this point, the plugin simply needs to return the value to the calling program. First the method sets the result of the operation and assigns the return value as shown here:

```
CDVPluginResult* result = [CDVPluginResult resultWithStatus:CDVCommandStatus_OK
messageAsString:[carrier carrierName]];
```

Then the method calls the appropriate callback function to complete the process:

```
[self.commandDelegate sendPluginResult:result callbackId:[command callbackId]];
```

That's it; that's all there really is to the code. For the `getCountryCode` method, it uses the same process, only returning the value of the `carrier` object's `isoCountryCode` property.

With the plugin's code in place, the last thing that has to happen is to update the plugin's plugin.xml file with the settings for the iOS portion of the plugin. To do this, I added a new `platform` section to the file; the elements and attributes for this section are shown here:

```
<platform name="ios">
  <config-file parent="/*" target="config.xml">
    <feature name="carrier">
      <param name="ios-package" value="carrier" />
    </feature>
  </config-file>
  <source-file src="src/ios/carrier.m" />
</platform>
```

This content defines the `carrier feature` that the plugin uses. It also specifies the `source-file` for the project, the carrier.m file shown in Listing 16.15.

Note that there are no permission settings to be set for this plugin; iOS doesn't require specific application settings to use telephony features as Android does. At this point I have everything defined that I need for the plugin. Listing 16.16 shows the complete listing for the plugin.xml file.

Listing 16.16 Complete plugin.xml File

```
<?xml version='1.0' encoding='utf-8' ?>
<plugin id="com.johnwargo.carrier" version="0.0.1"
  xmlns="http://apache.org/cordova/ns/plugins/1.0"
  xmlns:android="http://schemas.android.com/apk/res/android">
  <name>carrier</name>
  <description>A Cordova Plugin for retrieving Wireless Carrier information.</
description>
  <author>John M. Wargo</author>
  <keywords>carrier,telephony</keywords>
  <js-module name="carrier" src="www/carrier.js">
    <clobbers target="carrier" />
  </js-module>
  <platform name="android">
    <config-file parent="/*" target="res/xml/config.xml">
      <feature name="carrier">
        <param name="android-package"
          value="com.johnwargo.carrier.carrier" />
      </feature>
    </config-file>
    <config-file parent="/*" target="AndroidManifest.xml" />
    <config-file target="AndroidManifest.xml" parent="/*">
      <uses-permission
        android:name="android.permission.READ_PHONE_STATE" />
    </config-file>
    <source-file src="src/android/carrier.java" target-
dir="src/com/johnwargo/carrier" />
  </platform>
  <platform name="ios">
    <config-file parent="/*" target="config.xml">
      <feature name="carrier">
        <param name="ios-package" value="carrier" />
      </feature>
    </config-file>
    <source-file src="src/ios/carrier.m" />
  </platform>
</plugin>
```

To test the plugin, I used my existing test application and added the iOS platform to it. When I opened Xcode and tried to run the application, I received an error indicating that there was an undefined symbol in my project as shown in Figure 16.14.

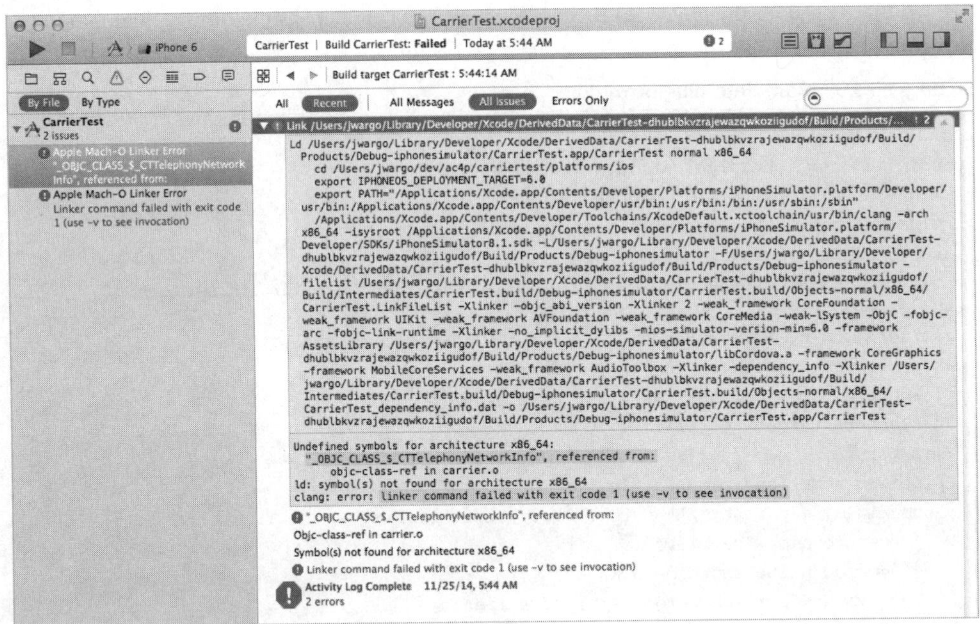

Figure 16.14 Xcode Build Error

This happens because the project didn't have the iOS `CoreTelephony` framework added to the project. To fix this, I had to click on the project name in the Xcode project navigator, open the Build Phases tab, and add the framework to the Link Binary With Libraries section as shown already completed in Figure 16.15.

To fix this, I clicked the plus sign highlighted at the bottom of Figure 16.15 and in the dialog that appeared, I started to type `telephony` as shown in Figure 16.16. When the `CoreTelephony.framework` entry appeared as shown in the figure, I clicked the Add button to add the framework to my project's configuration.

That's an ugly solution, isn't it? You can fix this for your users and keep them from seeing errors generated by the plugin's use of the Telephony APIs by adding the following line to the iOS portion of the plugin's plugin.xml file:

```
<framework src="CoreTelephony.framework" />
```

This configures the project with the right libraries, and the project should build without error.

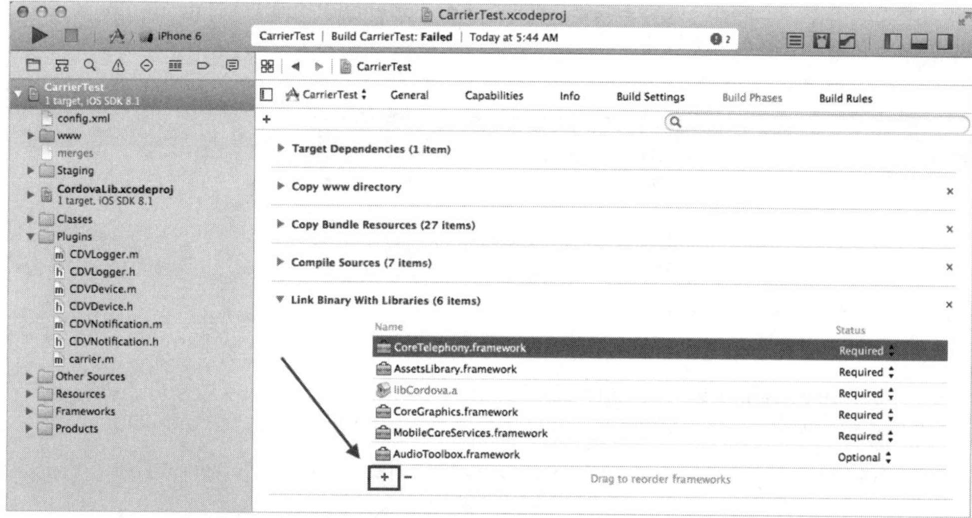

Figure 16.15 Xcode Project Build Phases Settings

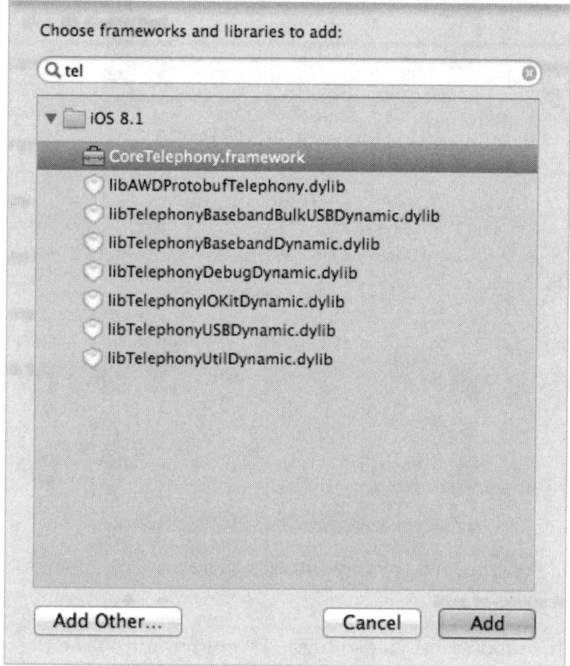

Figure 16.16 Xcode Add Framework Dialog

With that in place, I copied over my test project's index.html and ran the application on an iOS simulator as shown in Figure 16.17.

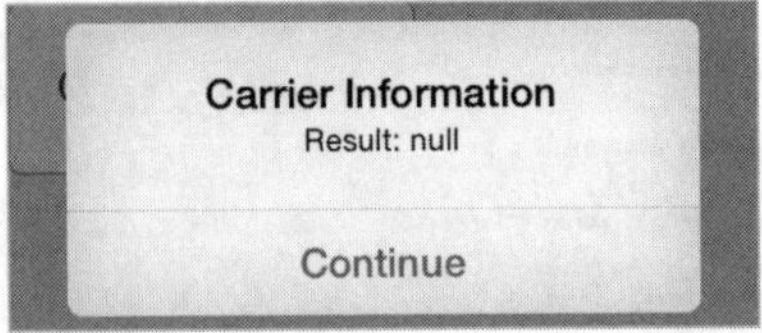

Figure 16.17 Results of `getCarrierName` on an iOS Simulator

Of course, since the simulator isn't provisioned for any carrier, the API doesn't know what to return and simply returns null. I get the same results for country code on the simulator.

When I run the application on my iOS device, I get the expected results shown in Figure 16.18.

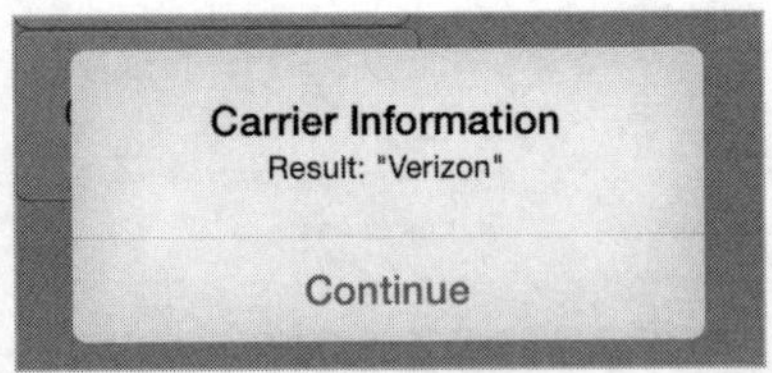

Figure 16.18 Results of `getCarrierName` on an iOS Device

When I try to get the country code on my iOS device, the plugin returns null, because I don't have a SIM in the device. When I try this on my iPad, which does have a SIM, I get the results shown in Figure 16.19.

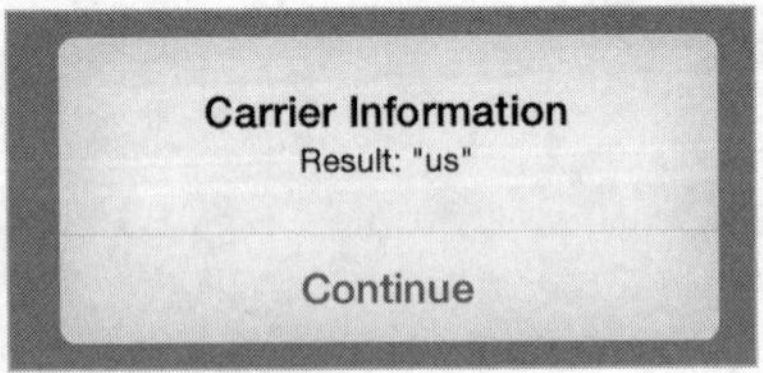

Figure 16.19 Results of `getCountryCode` on an iOS Device

If I were working with a production-grade plugin, I would want to tune the native implementations for Android and iOS so they deliver consistent results on the simulators. I could have coded the plugin's methods so they call the `onFailure` callback function and pass back an error message indicating that the carrier information was not available. Perhaps that is an enhancement you can make to the plugin.

Publishing Plugins

When it comes to deploying a custom plugin, you have several options. You can zip up the plugin folder, the folder containing your plugin's plugin.xml file plus all of the source files for the plugin, and distribute the .zip file to your users. All the user would have to do is extract the files into a folder and point to that folder when doing a `cordova plugin add` from a terminal window.

Cordova plugins, however, are best deployed through the Cordova Plugin Registry (CPR) at http://plugins.cordova.io. This is how the core Cordova plugins are deployed, and it's the place where most Cordova developers will expect to find your plugin. Fortunately it's pretty easy to publish plugins to the registry using Plugman.

To publish a plugin, you must first define a CPR user using the following:

```
plugman adduser
```

Plugman will prompt you for your username, password, and email address, then create an account for you on the registry.

Before you publish your plugin, you should first provide some documentation for the plugin and include it with the plugin's files. This is accomplished through the project's readme.md file. The .md extension for the file refers to the Markdown format (the opposite of markup) described at http://goo.gl/aVJGuS. The file should describe the plugin and list each method and property exposed by the plugin and any additional information users will need to know before they can use the plugin in their own projects. You can see an example of this in Figure 16.20; in the figure I show the plugin's readme in MarkdownPad, an editor (with preview) for Markdown files.

With the readme file in place, publish the plugin to the registry by opening a terminal window and executing the following:

```
plugman publish pluginfolder
```

In this example, the `pluginfolder` parameter is required; Plugman doesn't seem to know how to publish the plugin from the current folder.

So, if the terminal window is sitting right above the carrier plugin folder (called carrier), I could publish the plugin using

```
plugman publish carrier
```

If the terminal window is pointing to the plugin folder, you can publish the plugin to the registry using

```
plugman publish .
```

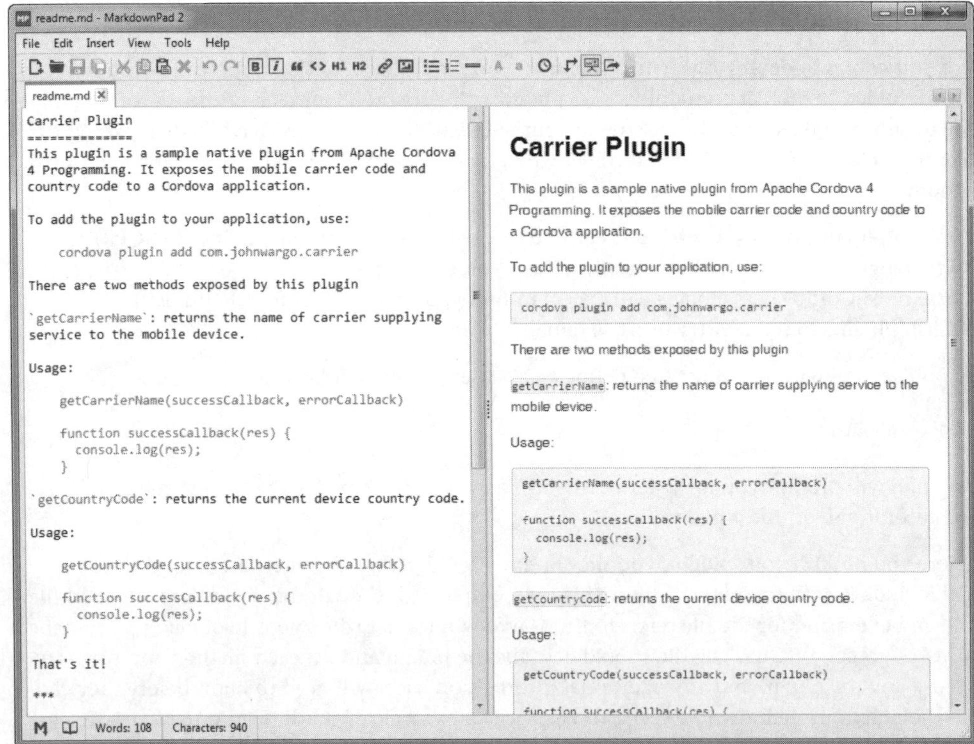

Figure 16.20 MarkdownPad: Carrier Plugin readme.md File

Plugman will update the terminal window as it publishes the plugin as shown in Figure 16.21.

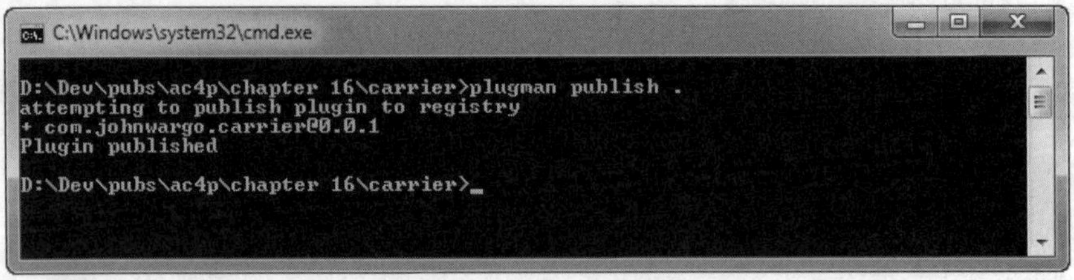

```
C:\Windows\system32\cmd.exe

D:\Dev\pubs\ac4p\chapter 16\carrier>plugman publish .
attempting to publish plugin to registry
+ com.johnwargo.carrier@0.0.1
Plugin published

D:\Dev\pubs\ac4p\chapter 16\carrier>_
```

Figure 16.21 Plugman: Publishing a Plugin

When Cordova 3 was first released, the Cordova team used GitHub to store plugins. The team recently moved away from GitHub to NPM (http://npmjs.org), so that's where the Cordova core plugins can be found, and the CPR stores plugins there as well.

During the publishing process, Plugman first creates a package.json file for the plugin using information in the plugin.xml file, publishes the plugin to NPM, deletes the package.json file, and updates the entry in the registry. If a problem is encountered with publishing the plugin, you may find the package.json file left lying around in your plugin folder.

Once the plugin has been published, you can view the plugin information in the registry as shown in Figure 16.22.

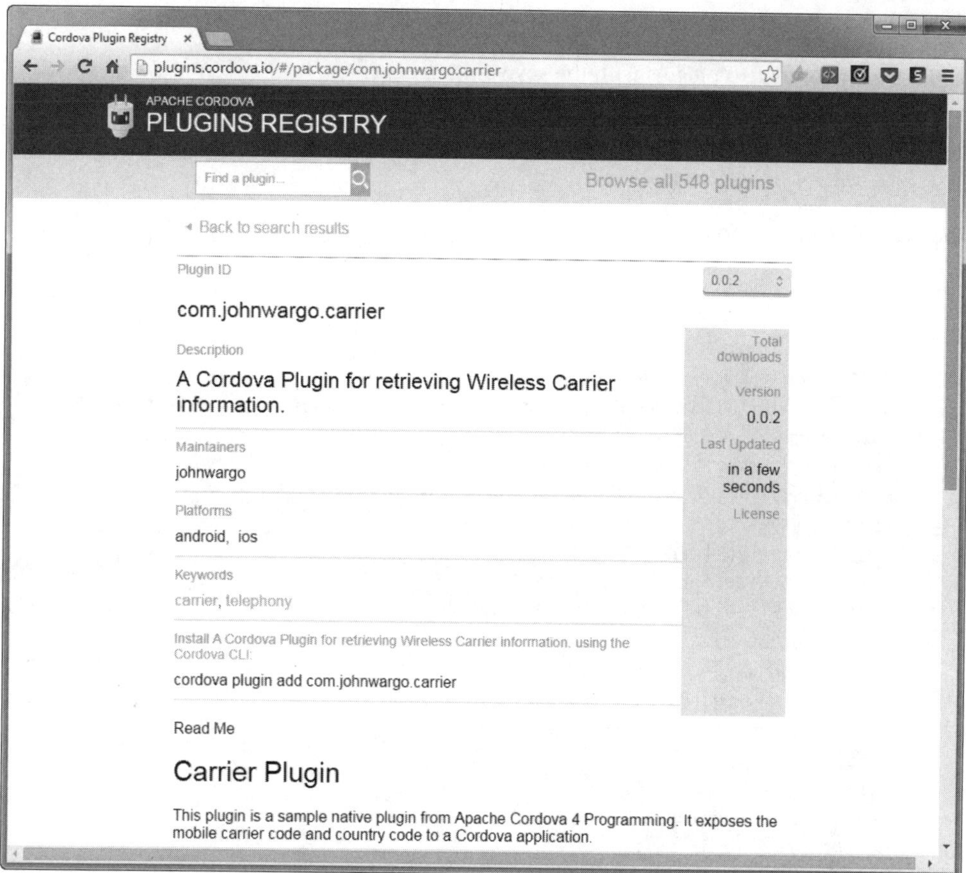

Figure 16.22 Cordova Plugin Registry: Carrier Entry

With the plugin published, all of the Cordova CLI and Plugman plugin-related commands work. For example, you can now add this plugin to your projects using the plugin ID:

```
cordova plugin add com.johnwargo.carrier
```

You can search for plugins using keywords:

```
cordova plugin search carrier
```

The CLI will return the following:

```
com.johnwargo.carrier - A Cordova Plugin for retrieving Wireless Carrier
information.
com.rensanning.cordova.carrier - CarrierPlugin Description
```

Notice that there are two plugins with the keyword `carrier`.

You can even view plugin information from the command line using

```
plugman info com.johnwargo.carrier
```

The CLI will return the following:


```
{ '0.0.3':
   { _id: 'com.johnwargo.carrier@0.0.3',
     _rev: '7-ab70bc82d8aa9c00d7aa1b7421cc3ee0',
     name: 'com.johnwargo.carrier',
     description: 'A Cordova Plugin for retrieving Wireless Carrier information.',
     'dist-tags': { latest: '0.0.3' },
     versions: [ '0.0.1', '0.0.2', '0.0.3' ],
     maintainers: [ [Object] ],
     time:
      { '0.0.1': '2014-11-25T12:31:38.708Z',
        '0.0.2': '2014-11-25T12:36:34.811Z',
        '0.0.3': '2014-11-25T17:08:22.601Z' },
     _attachments:
      { 'com.johnwargo.carrier-0.0.3.tgz': [Object],
        'com.johnwargo.carrier-0.0.2.tgz': [Object],
        'com.johnwargo.carrier-0.0.1.tgz': [Object] },
     version: '0.0.3',
     cordova_name: 'carrier',
     keywords: [ 'carrier', 'telephony' ],
     platforms: [ 'android', 'ios' ],
     engines: [],
     readmeFilename: 'readme.md',
     dist:
      { shasum: '1c091a315f25b59fd972016614318ce8c55a7cdd',
        tarball: 'http://cordova.iriscouch.com/registry/_design/app/_rewrite/com
.johnwargo.carrier/-/com.johnwargo.carrier-0.0.3.tgz' },
     _from: '.',
     _npmVersion: '1.3.4',
     _npmUser: { name: 'johnwargo', email: 'user@somedomain.com' },
     directories: {} } }
name: com.johnwargo.carrier
version: 0.0.3
```


As you can see, publishing your plugin to the registry is a pretty straightforward process and quickly exposes your plugin to a wide audience of developers.

Wrap-Up

In this chapter, I've shown you how to create Cordova plugins. With the information provided in this chapter, the Cordova documentation, and the core Cordova plugins as examples to study, you have the information you need to create your own custom plugins.

I only touched upon the surface of this topic; there is much more you can do with plugins. The plugin.xml supports a lot more options than what I covered here. For example, if your plugin depends on another plugin, you can configure the plugin.xml to have Plugman or the Cordova CLI install the required plugins for you. You can also link precompiled or custom libraries into your plugin. So, if your plugin leverages some proprietary code, you can still include it but protect it from prying eyes.

17

Using Third-Party UI Frameworks with Cordova

From time to time, people pop up on the Cordova dev list or the support forums asking about what UI capabilities Cordova provides and what HTML5 frameworks are compatible with Apache Cordova. The purpose of this chapter is to address all of those questions.

The quick answer to the first question is that Apache Cordova doesn't provide any UI capabilities. None. This was demonstrated in Chapter 2, "Anatomy of a Cordova Application." The Cordova framework doesn't do anything to enhance the UI of a Cordova application. There are several good reasons for this.

First of all, the definition of Apache Cordova directly from the Apache Cordova web site (www.cordova.io) says:

> Apache Cordova is a set of device APIs that allow a mobile app developer to access [a] native device function such as the camera or accelerometer from JavaScript.

There's nothing there that says anything about UI; Apache Cordova is all about access to native APIs through a JavaScript interface, nothing more. It does one thing and it does it really well. The framework provides access to device-specific features and applications and leaves it up to developers to theme their applications however they see fit. Web developers should use the capabilities provided by HTML, CSS, and even JavaScript to enhance the UI of their Cordova applications as needed.

Second, most of the developers I know are persnickety. They have cool jobs, they write cool apps that do cool stuff, and they use cool tools to do it all. Over the years, developers build a relationship with specific tools and frameworks, and if Cordova provided a UI framework, most developers simply wouldn't use it. Each developer has his or her own favorite, and there's really nothing you can do to change it.

There, I answered the first question pretty clearly, right? Now on to the second one.

A long time ago, web developers learned that they could rely upon third-party frameworks to give their applications a complete and interesting UI. There's a ton of them out there, so I'm not going to give you a list, but there are a lot of frameworks available that can simplify web development by providing a UI layer that the application's other stuff fits cleanly into. As smartphones became more popular, web developers found themselves needing to be able to build web applications that mimic the look-and-feel of native applications on these mobile platforms. Many open-source and commercial frameworks were created to accommodate this need.

So of all of the HTML5 frameworks out there, which ones are compatible with Apache Cordova?

All of them.

Yep, that's it—all of them. So the answer to the question "Can I use framework X for my Cordova applications?" (filling in any framework name for X) is yes. That was easy.

Remember, an Apache Cordova application is simply a web application running in a browser window embedded inside of a native mobile application. Since it's essentially the device's web browser that is running the web content and the web browser is compatible with HTML5, pretty much any HTML5 framework will work in a Cordova application.

There can be issues when you're running multiple frameworks in the same app, though. Frameworks such as MooTools (http://mootools.net) and jQuery (http://jquery.com), for example, conflict with each other when running in the same app. Cordova apps will run into this problem, not because of Cordova, but simply because of how the frameworks work. Of the two examples given here, both use the `$` as a shortcut to functions within the framework. When you run your application and use the `$` shortcut to do something, you really won't know whether MooTools or jQuery is responding. This is all documented pretty well (with a workaround) at http://goo.gl/R13BYx, so it is something that's easily fixed.

With all of those questions behind us, I thought I'd use the rest of the chapter to show you how to use some of the frameworks I've worked with. The options I describe here aren't necessarily the most common frameworks used, but they're the ones I already know and a few I wanted to learn about. In this chapter, we discuss how to enhance the UI of a Cordova application using the following frameworks:

- Adobe Topcoat
- jQuery Mobile
- Bootstrap
- OpenUI5
- Ionic
- Onsen UI

Adobe Topcoat is there because it's from Adobe, and since Cordova and PhoneGap are both from Adobe as well, I thought I'd highlight it. jQuery Mobile and Bootstrap are there because they're commonly used frameworks. I added OpenUI5 because that's an open-source framework from SAP (and I work for SAP). Ionic and Onsen UI are new frameworks that are specifically crafted to work with hybrid application frameworks like Cordova. I was going to add a section on Sencha Touch, but it is the most complicated of the available options and I ran out of time and space.

In each section that follows, I introduce you to a framework and show you how to use it to make a Cordova application. Don't forget, though, for all but the ones that are crafted specifically for Cordova development, there's nothing special about using them with your Cordova applications. For each of the examples in this chapter, I've taken the Hello World #5 application from Chapter 2 and enhanced the application's UI using the frameworks. I'm not going to go into detail for each framework. I just want to give you the high-level overview and let online help and any available books dedicated to the topic cover the frameworks in detail.

Adobe Topcoat

To make it easy for web developers to create good-looking Cordova applications, some developers at Adobe created a small, fast CSS library called Topcoat (http://topcoat.io) that you can use to apply a simple and clean UI to your Cordova applications. Topcoat is a clean wrapper around some common web application UI elements with a library of images and button styles you can use in your application. It's not a full HTML5 framework like Sencha Touch or jQuery Mobile, but it is very useful for creating clean, simple, fast UIs for your web applications.

As it's entirely CSS based, there are some things that it can't do that other frameworks easily can. An example of this is the slider control. Topcoat can easily style an HTML slider control so it matches the Topcoat theme, but frameworks like jQuery Mobile provide more functionality around the control. You can see examples of this in the sample applications from my *Apache Cordova API Cookbook* (www.cordovacookbook.com). In that book, I used Topcoat for as many of the applications as I could, but some of the more complicated applications needed the additional capabilities provided by jQuery Mobile.

To use Topcoat, download the framework's files from the Topcoat web site. The download is a .zip file, so extract the files to a folder on your development system, then copy the download's css, font, and img folders to your Cordova project's www folder.

Next, add the following line to the application's index.html file:

```
<link rel="stylesheet" type="text/css" href="css/topcoat-mobile-light.min.css">
```

Topcoat provides both light and dark themes for applications; I'll show you examples of both after I show you some code. This link tag loads the light, mobile version of the framework's CSS file into the application; there is also a desktop version. With that in place, all you have to do to use the framework is add some CSS tags to your application's HTML to make the application look beautiful.

If you take a look at Listing 17.1, you'll see the Hello World #5 application from Chapter 2 updated so it gets its UI from Topcoat. I'll explain the differences after you have finished looking at the code.

Listing 17.1 Hello World #5 index.html Using Adobe Topcoat

```
<!DOCTYPE html>
<html>

<head>
  <title>Hello World #5 - Topcoat Version</title>
  <meta charset="utf-8" />
  <meta name="format-detection" content="telephone=no" />
  <meta name="viewport" content="user-scalable=no, initial-scale=1,
    maximum-scale=1, minimum-scale=1, width=device-width,
    height=device-height" />
  <link rel="stylesheet" type="text/css"
    href="css/topcoat-mobile-light.min.css">
  <script src="index.js"></script>
  <script src="cordova.js"></script>
</head>

<body onload="onBodyLoad()">
  <div class="topcoat-navigation-bar">
    <div class="topcoat-navigation-bar__item center full">
      <h1 class="topcoat-navigation-bar__title">Hello World #5 - Topcoat Version</h1>
    </div>
  </div>
  <p>This is a Cordova application that makes calls to the Cordova Device API.</p>
  <p id="deviceInfo">Waiting for Cordova Initialization to complete.</p>
</body>

</html>
```

In the body section of the HTML, I made a few changes to give the application a topcoat (pun intended). I added a few divisions that add a toolbar to the top of the web page:

```
<div class="topcoat-navigation-bar">
  <div class="topcoat-navigation-bar__item center full">
    <h1 class="topcoat-navigation-bar__title">Hello World #5</h1>
  </div>
</div>
```

Topcoat doesn't have a footer style, so the bottom of the page will be plain. The application generates the device information list after the deviceready event has fired, so all of that code is in the application's index.js file shown in Listing 17.2.

Listing 17.2 Hello World #5 Application index.js Using Adobe Topcoat

```
function onBodyLoad() {
  console.log("Entering onBodyLoad");
  alert("Body Load");
```

```
  document.addEventListener("deviceready", onDeviceReady, false);
}

function makeListItem(textStr) {
  return '<li class="topcoat-list__item">' + textStr + '</li>';
}

function onDeviceReady() {
  console.log("Entering onDeviceReady");
  navigator.notification.alert("Cordova is ready!");
  console.log("Cordova: " + device.cordova);
  var tmpStr;
  tmpStr = '<ul class="topcoat-list__container"><h3 class="topcoat-list__
header">Device API Properties</h3>';
  tmpStr += makeListItem('Cordova Version: ' + device.cordova);
  tmpStr += makeListItem('Operating System: ' + device.platform);
  tmpStr += makeListItem('OS Version: ' + device.version);
  tmpStr += makeListItem('Device Model: ' + device.model);
  tmpStr += makeListItem('UUId: ' + device.uuid);
  tmpStr += '</ul>';
  //Get the appInfo DOM element
  var element = document.getElementById('deviceInfo');
  //replace it with specific information about the device
  //running the application
  element.innerHTML = tmpStr;
  console.log("Leaving onDeviceReady");
}
```

In the `onDeviceReady` function, the application creates some HTML and adds it to the page (replacing the contents of an existing div). The content being added begins with the definition of an unordered list that includes a simple `h3` header. Special Topcoat classes are added to the tags to allow Topcoat to apply its style to the page elements.

```
tmpStr = '<ul class="topcoat-list__container"><h3 class="topcoat-list__
header">Device API Properties</h3>';
```

In the `makeListItem` function, the code adds a list item tag to the device information that's being written to the unordered list. As in the previous example, a Topstyle class is added to the list item definition in order for Topcoat to be able to apply its styling:

```
function makeListItem(textStr) {
  return '<li class="topcoat-list__item">' + textStr + '</li>';
}
```

As you can see, using Topcoat to clean up the UI of your web application is really simple; all you have to do is add some class attributes to your existing page elements and you're all done. Figure 17.1 shows the application running on an Android device.

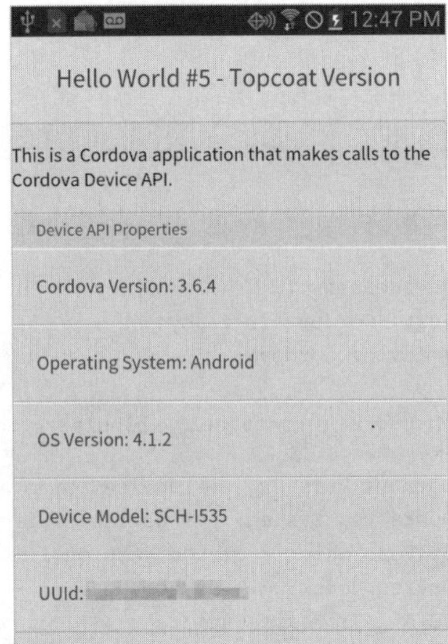

Figure 17.1 Topcoat Version of the Hello World #5 Application Running on an Android Device

Figure 17.2 shows the same application running on an iOS device. Notice that the application looks almost exactly the same; there are some scaling differences because of display differences between the devices, but they're essentially the same.

These HTML frameworks work very hard to make sure the application looks the same on all supported platforms, so you shouldn't be too surprised to see that the results are pretty much the same on Android and iOS devices.

Notice, however, that the Cordova version differs between the two devices. I created these screen shots after Cordova 4.0 was released, but the native platforms are lagging behind a bit, and since they're on different release streams, the versions will always be a bit out of alignment between platforms. This isn't a problem; it's simply the result of the CLI, platforms, and plugins all being on independent release schedules.

Topcoat supports light and dark themes; to switch to the dark theme, look for the following line in the beginning of the sample application:

```
<link rel="stylesheet" type="text/css" href="css/topcoat-mobile-light.min.css">
```

Replace it with the following:

```
<link rel="stylesheet" type="text/css" href="css/topcoat-mobile-dark.min.css">
```

When you run the modified application on an Android device, you'll see something similar to what is shown in Figure 17.3.

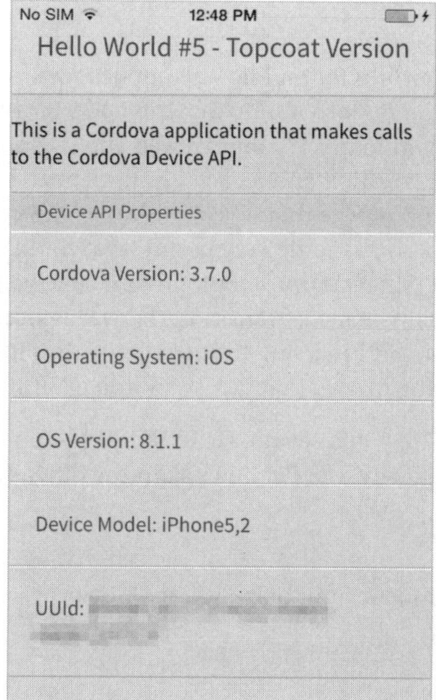

Figure 17.2 Topcoat Version of the Hello World #5 Application Running on an iOS Device

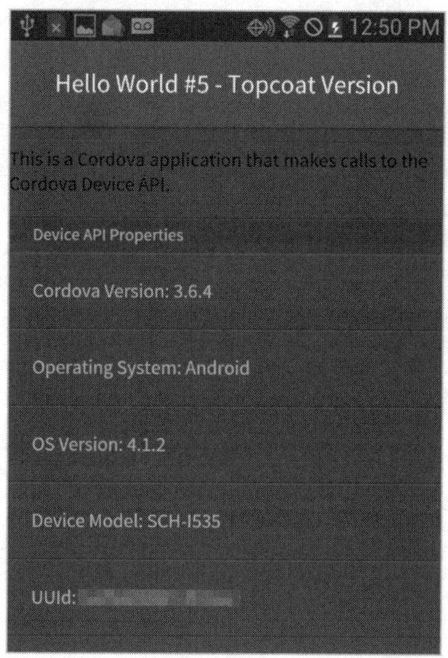

Figure 17.3 Topcoat Version of the Hello World #5 Application Running on an Android Device Using the Dark Theme

jQuery Mobile

One of the most popular frameworks for mobile web applications is the jQuery Mobile framework (http://jquerymobile.com). Built to mimic the Apple iOS Browser type of application, jQuery Mobile (jQM) enables you to quickly build a web application with toolbars top and bottom as well as drill-down navigation and a cool, clean, themable UI. One of the useful differences between Topcoat and jQM is that jQM has similar CSS code and images to make the application look pretty, but it also has some very useful JavaScript capabilities that enable you to do so much more. It's the jQM JavaScript libraries that enable you to make more compelling application UIs and automatically manage transitions between pages of your application. There's so much you can do with jQM, but I'm going to show you only a little bit of it here; there are a lot of jQM books available in the market that can show you all of the ins and outs of jQM.

If you take a look at Listing 17.3, you'll see the Hello World #5 application from Chapter 2 updated so it gets its UI from jQuery Mobile. I'll explain the differences after you have finished looking at the code.

Listing 17.3 Hello World #5 index.html Using jQuery Mobile

```
<!DOCTYPE html>
<html>

<head>
  <title>Hello World #5 - jQuery Mobile Version #1</title>
  <meta charset="utf-8" />
  <meta name="format-detection" content="telephone=no" />
  <meta name="viewport" content="user-scalable=no, initial-scale=1,
    maximum-scale=1, minimum-scale=1, width=device-width,
    height=device-height" />
  <link rel="stylesheet" href="css/jquery.mobile-1.4.3.min.css" />
  <script src="js/jquery-2.1.1.min.js"></script>
  <script src="js/jquery.mobile-1.4.3.min.js"></script>
</head>

<body onload="onBodyLoad()">
  <div data-role="page">
    <div data-role="header" data-position="fixed">
      <h1>Hello World #5 - jQuery Mobile Version</h1>
    </div>
    <div data-role="content">
      <p>This is a Cordova application that makes calls to the Cordova Device API.</p>
      <h3>Device API Properties</h3>
      <ul data-role="listview" id="devInfo"></ul>
```

```
    </div>
    <div data-role="footer" data-position="fixed">
      <h1>Apache Cordova 4 Programming</h1>
    </div>
  </div>
  <script src="index.js"></script>
  <script src="cordova.js"></script>
</body>

</html>
```

To use jQM in your web application, you will have to download libraries from two locations. jQM makes heavy use of utility functions from jQuery (http://jquery.com), so you'll first have to go to the jQuery web site and download the latest compatible version of jQuery. Next, you'll need the jQM CSS and JavaScript libraries that can be downloaded from http://jquerymobile.com/download. With that done, copy the downloaded files to your Cordova application's www folder. I typically put the CSS file in the css folder Cordova creates for me and the JavaScript files in the existing js folder. With the files in place, add the following lines to the application's index.html file:

```
<link rel="stylesheet" href="css/jquery.mobile-1.4.3.min.css" />
<script type="text/javascript" src="js/jquery-2.1.1.min.js"></script>
<script type="text/javascript" src="js/jquery.mobile-1.4.3.min.js"></script>
```

The min versions are compressed so comments, white space, line breaks, and so on are removed from the files. This allows the files to take up less space within the packaged application, helping to reduce the file size of the application, and allows these resources to load more quickly when the user launches the application.

All you have to do next to make use of the jQM features is to add special attributes to your web application content. Instead of using CSS classes as Topcoat does, jQM uses proprietary attributes added to the HTML tags as shown in the example here:

```
<div data-role="page">
  <div data-role="header" data-position="fixed">
```

```
    <h1>Hello World #5 - jQuery Mobile Version</h1>
  </div>
  <div data-role="content">
    <p>This is a Cordova application that makes calls to the Cordova Device API.</p>
    <h3>Device API Properties</h3>
    <ul data-role="listview" id="devInfo"></ul>
  </div>
  <div data-role="footer" data-position="fixed">
    <h1>Apache Cordova 4 Programming</h1>
  </div>
</div>
```

The most common one you'll encounter with jQM is the `data-role` attribute. In the example code I've shown, the `data-role` attribute is used to define the different parts of the page; you should be able to easily see in the code how I've defined the page, header, footer, and content sections of the HTML `body` content. When the application runs, the jQuery libraries are loaded, and they quickly scan the web page and replace the tagged HTML content with the appropriate settings and associated JavaScript code to implement the needed UI and user experience (UX).

The device information list is rendered within a jQuery ListView. To implement this in the application, I created an unordered list and assigned it a `data-role` of `listview`:

```
<ul data-role="listview" id="devInfo"></ul>
```

When the application runs, the list gets the correct styling as well as code that allows the user to smoothly scroll up and down through the list and tap on items to drill down into the details if needed. I didn't do that for this application, but in Chapter 10 of *Apache Cordova API Cookbook* (www.cordovacookbook.com) you'll find several examples of this.

With the page content in place, the application's JavaScript code does the rest; the complete listing of the application's index.js is provided in Listing 17.4.

Listing 17.4 Hello World #5 index.js Using jQuery Mobile

```
function onBodyLoad() {
  console.log("Entering onBodyLoad");
  alert("Body Load");
  document.addEventListener("deviceready", onDeviceReady, false);
}

function makeListItem(textStr) {
  return '<li>' + textStr + '</li>';
}

function onDeviceReady() {
  console.log("Entering onDeviceReady");
```

```
  navigator.notification.alert("Cordova is ready!");
  console.log("Cordova: " + device.cordova);

  var tmpStr;
  tmpStr = makeListItem('Cordova Version: ' + device.cordova);
  tmpStr += makeListItem('Operating System: ' + device.platform);
  tmpStr += makeListItem('OS Version: ' + device.version);
  tmpStr += makeListItem('Device Model: ' + device.model);
  tmpStr += makeListItem('UUId: ' + device.uuid);

  //Write the values to the Unordered list
  $('#devInfo').html(tmpStr);
  $('#devInfo').listview('refresh');
  console.log("Leaving onDeviceReady");
}
```

In the deviceready event listener, the application builds the unordered list as shown in the other examples, then writes the content to the page. jQuery provides a quick and easy way to manipulate the web page content through the `$` function. When it comes time to write the HTML to the page, the application executes the following code:

```
$('#devInfo').html(tmpStr);
$('#devInfo').listview('refresh');
```

The first line writes the content to the page. Since there weren't any list items on the page previously, jQM wasn't able to update the page content with all of the style information and JavaScript code, so in order to make the `listview` render like a jQM `listview`, you have to tell jQM to refresh the `listview` content as shown in the second line of code.

When you run the application on an Android device, you will see something similar to what is shown in Figure 17.4. Figure 17.5 shows the same application running on an iOS device.

Notice that the application looks similar across platforms. In a more complicated application, as you navigate deeper, the jQM framework will automatically add mobile device platform features to the application such as a back button on iOS and support for the Escape key and menu on Android devices.

The application's header, however, isn't rendering very well; this is because I've put too much information into that portion of the page. Even though there's enough space on the page for all of the content I've provided, jQM automatically allocates space in the header for buttons to the left and right of the header content—that's why the header text is truncated in these examples.

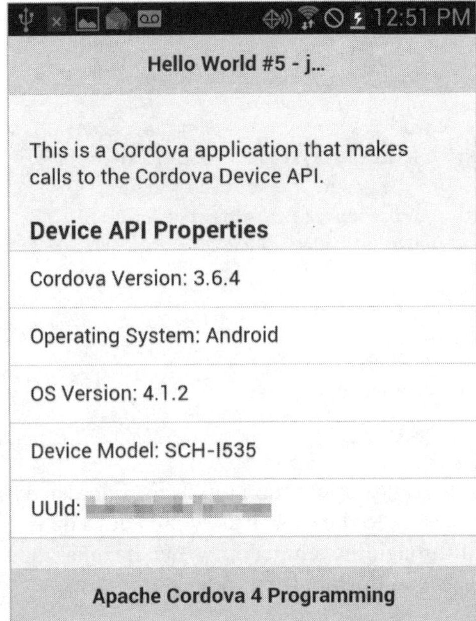

Figure 17.4 jQuery Mobile Version of the Hello World #5 Application Running on an Android Device

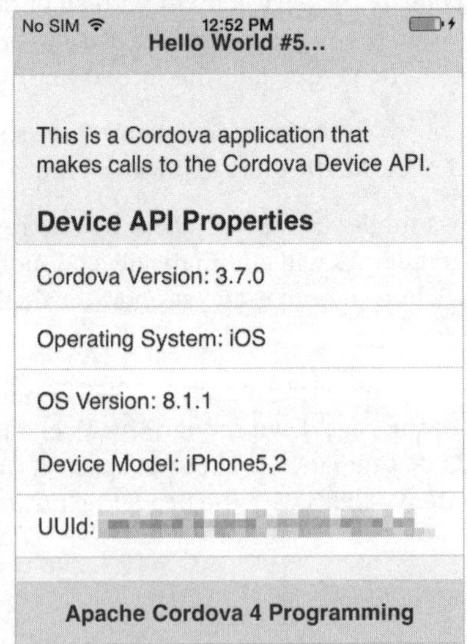

Figure 17.5 jQuery Mobile Version of the Hello World #5 Application Running on an iOS Device

When you were downloading the jQM files, you may have noticed that there were instructions for how to use CDN (content delivery network)-hosted files for your application. The instructions say to add the following lines to your application's HTML:

```
<link rel="stylesheet"
  href="http://code.jquery.com/mobile/1.4.3/jquery.mobile-1.4.3.min.css" />
<script src="http://code.jquery.com/jquery-1.11.1.min.js"></script>
<script src="http://code.jquery.com/mobile/1.4.3/jquery.mobile-1.4.3.min.js">
</script>
```

What this means is that the jQM files will be hosted on the Internet, and your application simply retrieves them as needed when the application launches. This keeps you from having to host the files on your own server or, in the Cordova case, package the files into your Cordova app. This is a good approach to take when you're running a hosted web application from a web server, but it might not work so well for you in a Cordova application.

When you use this approach in a hosted application, users don't really notice the difference. They type in your web site's URL or tap on a bookmark, and your application's files are retrieved from your web server and the jQM files are retrieved from, well, somewhere else. The desktop browser fires off multiple threads to retrieve resources simultaneously, so it's pretty fast. As far as the user is concerned, nothing's different; the site loads and renders as expected. There might be a slight problem if your web server is up and the CDN is down, but for the most part that's not going to happen that often.

Within a Cordova application, however, this could be a problem. Remember, in general, the Cordova application web application assets are packaged with the Cordova application. When the Cordova application launches, it usually has everything it needs locally (except perhaps for any network-based data that's loaded after the application has finished rendering). If you switch to using CDN-hosted resources, when the Cordova application launches, it will have the content it needs to render the application's UI, but it must make an external network request to get the jQM files it needs to render the UI with the appropriate styling and JavaScript code. So, when you launch the application, and if there's a delay in retrieving the files from the CDN, your web application won't look right until the app completes downloading those extra files. An example of this is shown in Figure 17.6; in this case you're seeing the application from Listing 17.2 before the jQM files have successfully downloaded. In this example, I've turned off the device radio to allow me to simulate the delay in retrieving the network-based files.

One of the benefits of using Cordova for your applications is that if all of the web application content is packaged within the Cordova container, the application can run when the mobile device radio is turned off. If, however, you choose to use CDN-hosted content, your application will run correctly only when connected to the network. For this reason, I suggest that you ignore the CDN option for your third-party libraries unless you can guarantee that the application will be used only when network connectivity is available.

These examples only lightly cover the capabilities of jQM; there's so much more you can do with this framework to enhance the user experience within your Cordova applications. Refer to

Figure 17.6 jQuery Mobile Version of the Hello World #5 Application Running on an Android Device with CDN-Hosted Files

the jQM online documentation or several of the new books on jQM for additional information about the capabilities provided by the framework, for example, Phillip Dutson, *Sams Teach Yourself jQuery Mobile in 24 Hours* (Indianapolis, IN: Sams Publishing, 2012).

Bootstrap

Bootstrap (http://getbootstrap.com) is a very popular front-end framework for building responsive, mobile-first web sites. Originally created by Twitter, it's now one of the most popular open-source projects in the world (according to the Bootstrap web site). Instead of providing a mobile-friendly UI like jQuery Mobile and Topcoat, Bootstrap is mostly about responsive design and layout. It includes some styling, but the primary reason developers use it for their web applications is its capability to quickly and easily deliver a responsive web application anywhere.

To use Bootstrap for your web applications, download the latest version of Bootstrap from the project's web site. When you extract the downloaded files, all you'll see in the target folder are three folders: css, font, and js. Copy all of the folders to your Cordova project's www folder and you're all set.

The Bootstrap team publishes several starter applications developers can use as a starting point for their mobile applications. The starter pages are listed as examples on the project's Getting Started page at http://goo.gl/59aDu7. For Listing 17.5, I grabbed the Starter template and updated it to accommodate the standard Hello World #5 application from Chapter 2.

Listing 17.5 Hello World #5 index.html Using Bootstrap

```
<!DOCTYPE html>
<html>

<head>
  <title>Hello World #5 - Bootstrap Version</title>
  <meta charset="utf-8" />
  <meta name="format-detection" content="telephone=no" />
  <meta name="viewport" content="width=device-width, initial-scale=1">
  <!-- Bootstrap core CSS -->
  <link href="css/bootstrap.min.css" rel="stylesheet">
  <!-- Custom styles for this template -->
  <link href="css/starter-template.css" rel="stylesheet">
</head>

<body onload="onBodyLoad()">
  <div class="navbar navbar-inverse navbar-fixed-top" role="navigation">
    <div class="container">
      <div class="navbar-header">
        <button type="button" class="navbar-toggle"
          data-toggle="collapse" data-target=".navbar-collapse">
          <span class="sr-only">Toggle navigation</span>
          <span class="icon-bar"></span>
          <span class="icon-bar"></span>
          <span class="icon-bar"></span>
        </button>
        <a class="navbar-brand" href="#">Hello World #5 - Bootstrap Version</a>
      </div>
      <div class="collapse navbar-collapse">
        <ul class="nav navbar-nav">
          <li class="active"><a href="#">Home</a>
          </li>
          <li><a href="#about">About</a>
          </li>
          <li><a href="#contact">Contact</a>
          </li>
        </ul>
      </div>
      <!--/.nav-collapse -->
    </div>
  </div>
```

```
  <div class="container">
    <div class="starter-template">
      <p class="lead">
        This is a Cordova application that makes calls to the Cordova Device API.
      </p>
      <h3>Device API Properties</h3>
      <p id="deviceInfo"></p>
    </div>

    <footer>
      <hr />
      <p>Apache Cordova 4 Programming</p>
    </footer>

  </div>
  <!-- /.container -->

  <!-- jQuery (necessary for Bootstrap's JavaScript plugins) -->
  <script src="js/jquery-2.1.1.min.js"></script>
  <!-- Include all compiled plugins (below), or include individual files as needed -->
  <script src="js/bootstrap.min.js"></script>
  <script src="index.js"></script>
  <script src="cordova.js"></script>
</body>

</html>
```

The first thing you might notice about this application is that I've changed the `viewport` meta tag. Since I'm going to be letting Bootstrap manage the layout of the page, I deleted my standard Cordova viewport settings and simply used the one from the Bootstrap Starter template:

```
<meta name="viewport" content="width=device-width, initial-scale=1">
```

Next, the application loads some of the required Bootstrap files. The bootstrap.min.css file is part of the Bootstrap distribution, while the starter-template.css file is specific to the Starter template I'm using.

```
<!-- Bootstrap core CSS -->
<link href="css/bootstrap.min.css" rel="stylesheet">
<!-- Custom styles for this template -->
<link href="css/starter-template.css" rel="stylesheet">
```

In this example, the application defines a toolbar and a content container for the application. The toolbar code defines a collapsible toolbar and populates it with a few options. For this application I'm not including any code for the other pages exposed through the toolbar.

```
<div class="navbar navbar-inverse navbar-fixed-top" role="navigation">
  <div class="container">
    <div class="navbar-header">
      <button type="button" class="navbar-toggle"
        data-toggle="collapse" data-target=".navbar-collapse">
        <span class="sr-only">Toggle navigation</span>
        <span class="icon-bar"></span>
        <span class="icon-bar"></span>
        <span class="icon-bar"></span>
      </button>
      <a class="navbar-brand" href="#">Hello World #5</a>
    </div>
    <div class="collapse navbar-collapse">
      <ul class="nav navbar-nav">
        <li class="active"><a href="#">Home</a></li>
        <li><a href="#about">About</a></li>
        <li><a href="#contact">Contact</a></li>
      </ul>
    </div>
    <!--/.nav-collapse -->
  </div>

</div>
```

The application's main content area is defined using the following code:

```
<div class="container">
  <div class="starter-template">
    <p class="lead">
      This is a Cordova application that makes calls to the Cordova Device API.
    </p>
    <h3>Device API Properties</h3>
    <p id="deviceInfo"></p>
  </div>
  <footer>
    <hr />
    <p>Apache Cordova 4 Programming</p>
  </footer>
</div>
<!-- /.container -->
```

Here the application defines a content area, a container that is managed by Bootstrap as the page layout changes when the user rotates the device. The application replaces the content in the `deviceInfo` div with the data from the Device API.

At the bottom of the file the template loads the jQuery libraries as well as the supporting JavaScript code for Bootstrap. This is loaded at the bottom of the file so that the UI can load before extra processing of the page can begin. Since we want the application UI to appear before Cordova does its initialization, I've added the cordova.js file here as well:

```
<!-- jQuery (necessary for Bootstrap's JavaScript plugins) -->
<script src="js/jquery-2.1.1.min.js"></script>
<!-- Include all compiled plugins (below), or include individual files as needed -->
<script src="js/bootstrap.min.js"></script>
<script src="cordova.js"></script>
```

The rest of the differences are all in the HTML body for the application. Bootstrap doesn't have any special list processing like Topcoat and jQuery Mobile, so for this version of the application I decided to simply write the device information to the screen as text. The complete listing for the application's JavaScript code is shown in Listing 17.6.

Listing 17.6 Hello World #5 index.js Using Bootstrap

```
function onBodyLoad() {
  console.log("Entering onBodyLoad");
  alert("Body Load");
  document.addEventListener("deviceready", onDeviceReady, false);
}

function makeListItem(label, value) {
  return '<strong>' + label + '</strong>' + value + '<br />';
}

function onDeviceReady() {
  console.log("Entering onDeviceReady");
  navigator.notification.alert("Cordova is ready!");
  console.log("Cordova: " + device.cordova);
  //Now populate the content
  var tmpStr;
  tmpStr = makeListItem('Cordova Version: ', device.cordova);
  tmpStr += makeListItem('Operating System: ', device.platform);
  tmpStr += makeListItem('OS Version: ', device.version);
  tmpStr += makeListItem('Device Model: ', device.model);
  tmpStr += makeListItem('UUId: ', device.uuid);

  //Write the values to the page
  $('#deviceInfo').html(tmpStr);

  console.log("Leaving onDeviceReady");
}
```

When you run the application on an Android tablet, you will see a screen similar to what is shown in Figure 17.7. In this case, the image shows the application layout in portrait mode. Because the application is displaying in portrait mode, there is not enough room for the toolbar content, so Bootstrap automatically collapses it and exposes it through the Menu button on the top right corner of the screen.

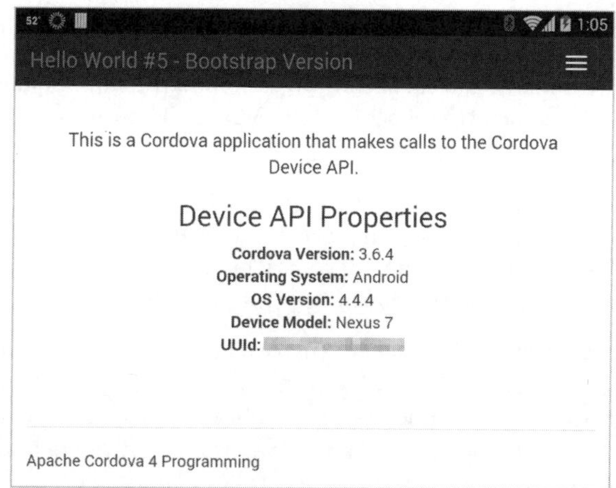

Figure 17.7 Bootstrap Version of the Hello World #5 Application Running on an Android Device in Portrait Mode

When you rotate the tablet to landscape mode, you will see a screen similar to what is shown in Figure 17.8. In this case, since there is enough room for the toolbar, the application expands the toolbar to display all of the options.

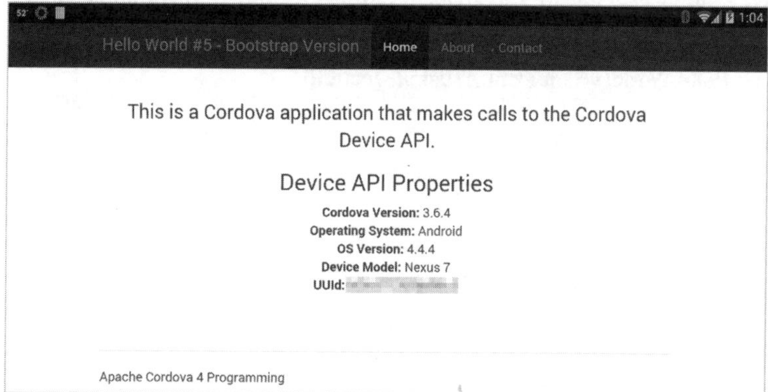

Figure 17.8 Bootstrap Version of the Hello World #5 Application Running on an Android Device in Landscape Mode

There's a lot more you can do with Bootstrap; I could, for example, have shown you a web application with multiple content areas and used Bootstrap to automatically format that content for a smartphone's smaller screen. As this is a Cordova book and not a Bootstrap book, I tried to get you what you need to see how Bootstrap works and how to get started.

SAP OpenUI5

SAP is a German enterprise software company producing Enterprise Resource Planning (ERP) and other business software for large and small companies around the world. I'm telling you this for two reasons: because I work for SAP and because you may not know what we do. SAP is one of the largest software companies in the world.

For years, SAP customers have complained about the user interface of our software products. The core ERP software from SAP was written 40 years ago, before robust graphical interfaces or the web browser. It's been updated since, of course, but it has never really gotten a high-performance, polished UI upgrade. This all changed with SAP UI5 and Fiori.

SAP UI5 is an HTML framework SAP created to enable a new suite of applications called SAP Fiori. *Fiori* is Italian for "flower," and for SAP and SAP customers it has become a design paradigm for focused web applications for desktop and mobile browsers. SAP UI5 is used to create applications with a clean and simple UI and is how SAP will be delivering beautiful applications to customers going forward.

In late 2013, SAP open-sourced SAP UI5 as OpenUI5 (http://sap.github.io/openui5), so now this beautiful framework is available for you to use for your web and/or Cordova applications. I'm not going to go too deeply into OpenUI5—there's a whole lot to it. I'm only going to use it to create a simple Cordova application for this chapter; you'll need to refer to the OpenUI5 web site for additional information on the framework's capabilities.

With SAP UI5 and OpenUI5, web applications start with a simple HTML-based shell, but the majority of an application's UI and UX is handled by JavaScript code included with the application. I created a simple example for this chapter; Listing 17.7 shows the example's index.html file.

Listing 17.7 Hello World #5 index.html Using OpenUI5

```
<!DOCTYPE html>
<html>

<head>
  <meta http-equiv='X-UA-Compatible' content='IE=edge' />
  <title>Hello World #5 - OpenUI5 Version</title>
  <script id='sap-ui-bootstrap' src='resources/sap-ui-core.js'
    data-sap-ui-theme='sap_bluecrystal' data-sap-ui-libs='sap.m'>
  </script>
  <script src="cordova.js"></script>
  <script src="index.js"></script>
```

```
</head>
<body id="body" class='sapUiBody' onload="onBodyLoad()"></body>
</html>
```

There's really not much to it; all it does is load some scripts and define an empty body for the web application. Everything else is done in JavaScript. Notice that no CSS files are loaded and the script tag has more to it than we've seen in any other example in the book. This is because the script file loaded by the application manages the bootstrapping of OpenUI5 and loads the appropriate themes and more during startup. The application knows what theme to apply to the page from the following:

```
data-sap-ui-theme='sap_bluecrystal'
```

Blue Crystal is the default theme for UI5; there are others and you can create your own.

The application loads its mobile UI files through the following:

```
data-sap-ui-libs='sap.m'
```

As you can see from Listing 17.7, the web application's `body` tag has an `id` and `class` assigned to it; it's through these that OpenUI5 creates and manages the application's UI. I added the call to `onBodyLoad` to enable me to do my Cordova stuff after the Cordova container has finished initializing.

Listing 17.8 shows the contents of the application's index.js file.

Listing 17.8 Hello World #5 index.js Using OpenUI5

```
"use strict";

function onDeviceReady() {

  function makeListItem(label, value) {
    return '<li><strong>' + label + '</strong>' + value + '</li>';
  }

  console.log("Entering onDeviceReady");
  navigator.notification.alert("Cordova is ready!");
  console.log("Cordova: " + device.cordova);

  //Now populate the UL content
  var tmpStr;
  tmpStr = makeListItem('Cordova Version: ', device.cordova);
  tmpStr += makeListItem('Operating System: ', device.platform);
  tmpStr += makeListItem('OS Version: ', device.version);
  tmpStr += makeListItem('Device Model: ', device.model);
  tmpStr += makeListItem('Universally Unique Identifier: ', device.uuid);
```

```
    //Write the values to the page
    $('#deviceInfo').html(tmpStr);

    console.log("Leaving onDeviceReady");
  }

  function onBodyLoad() {
    console.log("Entering onBodyLoad");
    alert("Body Load");
    document.addEventListener("deviceready", onDeviceReady, false);

    var app = new sap.m.App("myApp");
    var mainPage = new sap.m.Page("mainPage", {
      title: "Hello World #5 - OpenUI5 Version",
      content: new sap.ui.core.HTML({
        content: "<p>This is a Cordova application that makes calls to the Cordova
  Device API.</p><ul id=deviceInfo></ul>"
      }),
      footer: new sap.m.Bar({
        contentMiddle: [new sap.m.Label('footerTitle', {
          text: "Apache Cordova 4 Programming"
        })]
      })
    });
    app.addPage(mainPage);
    app.setInitialPage("mainPage");
    app.placeAt("body");
  }
```

The application's entire UI is created through the following code:

```
var app = new sap.m.App("myApp");
var mainPage = new sap.m.Page("mainPage", {
  title: "Hello World #5 - OpenUI5 Version",
  content: new sap.ui.core.HTML({
    content: "<p>This is a Cordova application that makes calls to the Cordova
Device API.</p><ul id=deviceInfo></ul>"
  }),
  footer: new sap.m.Bar({
    contentMiddle: [new sap.m.Label('footerTitle', {
      text: "Apache Cordova 4 Programming"
    })]
  })
});
app.addPage(mainPage);
app.setInitialPage("mainPage");
app.placeAt("body");
```

It essentially creates the same header, footer, and content area for the application that you've seen in other examples throughout this chapter. Once that's in place, after the Cordova container has finished initializing, the application's `onDeviceReady` function is executed to update the page with the device information.

For this example, I didn't use a listview to render the device information; I simply rendered the device information as an unordered list as shown in Figure 17.9. OpenUI5 supports listviews like Topcoat and jQuery Mobile, but since SAP is an enterprise company and enterprise apps are all about data, the OpenUI5 listview is focused on rendering data from a local or back-end data source to the screen.

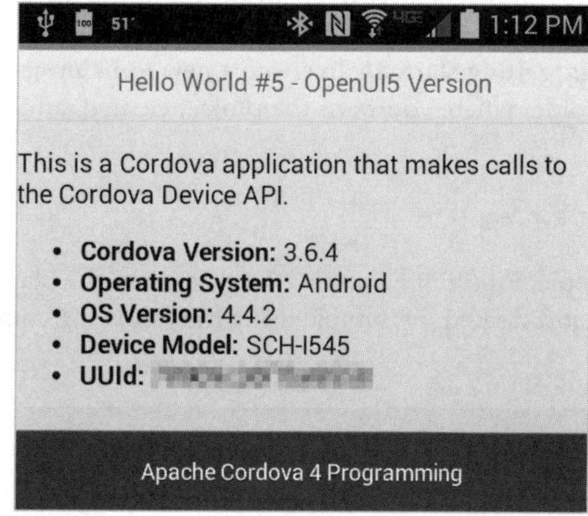

Figure 17.9 OpenUI5 Version of the Hello World #5 Application Running on an Android Device

In order for me to be able to use a listview for this application, I would have to define a data model, create and populate a local store with the device information, and let a listview render the store on the page. That was way more complicated than I wanted for this simple sample application, so I didn't take that route. For applications that need to render data, though, this is a very powerful feature. In case you're interested, Sencha Touch works the same way.

Ionic Framework

Ionic (http://ionicframework.com/) is an HTML framework designed specifically for hybrid applications. Created by Drifty (http://drifty.com/), Ionic is designed to be simple and very fast. Along with the UI framework, the Drifty team has given Ionic its own CLI wrapper around the Cordova CLI, so you have an easy way to start new Ionic projects using tools you are already familiar with. I saw a member of the Ionic team speak at PhoneGap Day 2014, and they seem pretty committed to Apache Cordova and apparently have plans to create the "world's first full-stack hybrid mobile platform."

To use Ionic for your Cordova applications, there's nothing to download; everything is done through the CLI. To install the Ionic CLI on Windows, open a terminal window and issue the following command:

```
npm install -g ionic
```

For Macintosh OS X, use the following:

```
sudo npm install -g ionic
```

When that process completes, you will have the `ionic` command at your disposal.

The Ionic team has created a suite of starter templates you can use for your Cordova applications. You can find the list of them on the Ionic Getting Started page at http://ionicframework.com/getting-started/. To create a new Ionic project, open a terminal window, navigate to the folder where you want the project created, and issue the following command:

```
ionic start appFolder appTemplate
```

So, for this chapter's example, I'll call it Example 17.6, I selected the blank template as a starting point for the application and created my sample using the following command:

```
ionic start ex176 blank
```

The Ionic CLI will use the Cordova CLI to create a new project and copy over some additional components Ionic uses for its builds and other stuff. You can see the folder structure it created for this project in Figure 17.10. As you can see from the figure, the project includes

Figure 17.10 Ionic Project Folder

configuration files for Bower, Gulp (described in Chapter 18, "Using Third-Party Tools with Cordova"), NPM, and more. It also includes support for Sass (http://sass-lang.com/). There's a lot going on here, more than we've seen for any other framework.

When the Ionic CLI has completed creating the project, it will display some additional information in the terminal window to help you understand what you can do next:

```
Your Ionic project is ready to go! Some quick tips:

 * cd into your project: $ cd ex176

 * Setup this project to use Sass: ionic setup sass

 * Develop in the browser with live reload: ionic serve

 * Add a platform (ios or Android): ionic platform add ios [android]
   Note: iOS development requires OS X currently
   See the Android Platform Guide for full Android installation instructions:
   https://cordova.apache.org/docs/en/edge/guide_platforms_android_index.md.html

 * Build your app: ionic build <PLATFORM>

 * Simulate your app: ionic emulate <PLATFORM>

 * Run your app on a device: ionic run <PLATFORM>

 * Package an app using Ionic package service: ionic package <MODE> <PLATFORM>

For more help use ionic --help or visit the Ionic docs: http://ionicframework.com/
docs
```

So, to add target platforms to the project, use

```
ionic platform add ios android
```

The Ionic CLI creates a simple index.html file for the project, one that automatically loads the libraries and frameworks needed by the application template. You can see a complete listing of the file, updated with some stuff I added, in Listing 17.9.

Listing 17.9 Hello World #5 index.html Using the Ionic Framework

```
<!DOCTYPE html>
<html>

<head>
  <meta charset="utf-8">
  <meta name="viewport" content="initial-scale=1, maximum-scale=1,
```

```
    user-scalable=no, width=device-width">
  <title>Hello World #5 - Ionic Version</title>

  <link href="lib/ionic/css/ionic.css" rel="stylesheet">
  <link href="css/style.css" rel="stylesheet">

  <!-- IF using Sass (run gulp sass first), then uncomment below and
    remove the CSS includes above
    <link href="css/ionic.app.css" rel="stylesheet">
    -->

  <!-- ionic/angularjs js -->
  <script src="lib/ionic/js/ionic.bundle.js"></script>

  <!-- cordova script (this will be a 404 during development) -->
  <script src="cordova.js"></script>

  <!-- your app's js -->
  <script src="js/app.js"></script>
</head>

<body ng-app="starter">
  <ion-pane>
    <ion-header-bar class="bar-stable">
      <h1 class="title">Hello World #5 - Ionic Version</h1>
    </ion-header-bar>
    <ion-content>
      <p id="deviceInfo">Waiting for Ionic Initialization to complete.</p>
    </ion-content>
  </ion-pane>
  <div class="bar bar-footer bar-stable">
    <div class="title">
      <a href="www.cordova4programming.com">www.cordova4programming.com</a>
    </div>
  </div>
</body>

</html>
```

Everything I added is within the file's `body` tag; Ionic uses `ion-pane`, `ion-header`, and `ion-content` to define the different parts of an application page. I changed the header for the page, then added the `deviceInfo` div to the `ion-content` section of the page.

With the page all set, I next updated the application's app.js file with my code to update the page content with the Cordova device information; you can see a complete listing of the file in Listing 17.10.

Listing 17.10 Hello World #5 app.js Using the Ionic Framework

```
// Ionic Starter App

//angular.module is a global place for creating, registering and
//retrieving Angular modules
//'starter' is the name of this angular module example (also set in
//a <body> attribute in index.html)
// the 2nd parameter is an array of 'requires'
angular.module('starter', ['ionic'])

.run(function ($ionicPlatform) {
  $ionicPlatform.ready(function () {

    function makeListItem(textStr) {
      return '<li class="item">' + textStr + '</li>';
    }

    // Hide the accessory bar by default (remove this to show the
    //accessory bar above the keyboard for form inputs)
    if (window.cordova && window.cordova.plugins.Keyboard) {
      cordova.plugins.Keyboard.hideKeyboardAccessoryBar(true);
    }
    if (window.StatusBar) {
      StatusBar.styleDefault();
    }

    console.log("Cordova: " + device.cordova);
    var tmpStr;
    tmpStr = '<ul class="list">';
    tmpStr += makeListItem('Cordova Version: ' + device.cordova);
    tmpStr += makeListItem('Operating System: ' + device.platform);
    tmpStr += makeListItem('OS Version: ' + device.version);
    tmpStr += makeListItem('Device Model: ' + device.model);
    tmpStr += makeListItem('UUId: ' + device.uuid);
    tmpStr += '</ul>';
    //Get the appInfo DOM element
    var element = document.getElementById('deviceInfo');
    //replace it with specific information about the device
    //running the application
    element.innerHTML = tmpStr;
  });
});
```

Instead of using the default Cordova deviceready event, Ionic exposes an ionicPlatform.ready event that is fired once Cordova and the Ionic framework have initialized. It's here that I've added my code to update the page with the Cordova device information. Ionic uses the `list` class to style the unordered list and the `item` class to style list items, so those are the only changes I had to make to the code compared to other versions of this app.

The Ionic CLI provides commands for running the application; I didn't check, but I'm assuming it uses Gulp and some of those other components to process the application's code during the prepare/build/run steps. To run the application on an Android device, open a terminal window, navigate to the Ionic application project folder, and issue the following command:

```
ionic run android
```

To run the application on a device simulator, use the `emulate` command:

```
ionic emulate ios
```

You can see an example of the application running on an iOS device in Figure 17.11.

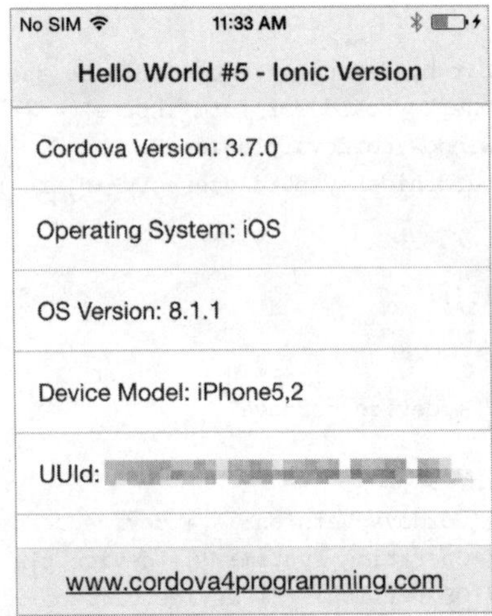

Figure 17.11 Ionic Version of the Hello World #5 Application Running on an iOS Device

Onsen UI

Another third-party framework specifically designed for Cordova applications is Onsen UI (http://onsenui.io). Onsen UI takes a slightly different approach when it comes to creating new projects; instead of providing a CLI like Ionic, Onsen UI simply provides downloadable Cordova projects to use as a starting point. The framework was created by Asial Corporation and works hand-in-hand with the company's Monaca cloud-based development environment.

Monaca seems to be a pretty robust hybrid application editor with remote debugging capabilities. I didn't get a chance to dig too deeply into this product, so I won't include any details on it for this edition of the book.

To get started with Onsen UI, download one of the starter project templates from http://goo.gl/OigfgY and extract the downloaded files to a folder on your development system. To work with the project, open a terminal window and navigate to the new project folder. You can use the Gulp-based capabilities included with the project by installing the required Node modules using

```
npm install
```

Since the project folder contains a complete Cordova project folder structure (including a project config.xml), you can immediately start using Cordova CLI commands against the project. Before you can run the application, you'll need to add platforms and plugins to the project using the `cordova platform add` and `cordova plugin add` commands, for example.

For the sample project for this chapter, I grabbed one of the starter projects—I think it was the Sliding menu project—and deleted all of the junk I didn't need from the project's index.html file. Next, I added the content I needed for the Hello World #5 application; you can see the complete source code in Listing 17.11.

Listing 17.11 Hello World #5 index.html Using the Onsen UI Framework

```
<!doctype html>
<html lang="en" ng-app="app">

<head>
  <title>Hello World #5 - Onsen UI Version</title>
  <meta charset="utf-8">
  <meta name="apple-mobile-web-app-capable" content="yes">
  <meta name="mobile-web-app-capable" content="yes">

  <link rel="stylesheet" href="lib/onsen/css/onsenui.css">
  <link rel="stylesheet" href="styles/onsen-css-components-blue-basic-theme.css">
  <link rel="stylesheet" href="styles/app.css" />

  <script src="lib/onsen/js/angular/angular.js"></script>
  <script src="lib/onsen/js/onsenui.js"></script>

  <script src="index.js"></script>
  <script src="cordova.js"></script>

  <script>
    var module = angular.module('app', ['onsen']);
  </script>

</head>

<body onload="onBodyLoad()">
  <ons-page>
    <ons-toolbar>
```

```
      <div class="center">Hello World #5 - Onsen UI Version</div>
    </ons-toolbar>
    <p>This is a Cordova application that makes calls to the Cordova Device API.</p>
    <ons-list id="deviceInfo">
    </ons-list>
  </ons-page>
</body>

</html>
```

The file loads all of the libraries required by Onsen UI; all I really did was add the content to the file's body element. It should look pretty similar to what you've seen in other examples in this chapter; the only real difference is in the device information list. Instead of using HTML unordered list (`ul`) elements like some of the other frameworks, Onsen UI uses proprietary `ons-list` elements to define the list and `ons-list-items` to define the list items. In the index.html file, I've defined an empty `ons-list` with an `id` of `deviceInfo`; in the application's JavaScript code, I'll populate that list with the appropriate content for the application.

Listing 17.12 shows the contents of the application's index.js file; it should look a lot like the other examples shown in this chapter. I'll explain the differences after you have had a chance to look at the code.

Listing 17.12 Hello World #5 index.js Using the Onsen UI Framework

```
function onBodyLoad() {
  console.log("Entering onBodyLoad");
  alert("Body Load");
  document.addEventListener("deviceready", onDeviceReady, false);
}

function makeListItem(textStr) {
  return '<ons-list-item>' + textStr + '</ons-list-item>';
}

function onDeviceReady() {
  console.log("Entering onDeviceReady");
  navigator.notification.alert("Cordova is ready!");
  console.log("Cordova: " + device.cordova);

  var tmpStr;
  tmpStr = '<ons-list-header>Device API Properties</ons-list-header>';
  tmpStr += makeListItem('Cordova Version: ' + device.cordova);
  tmpStr += makeListItem('Operating System: ' + device.platform);
  tmpStr += makeListItem('OS Version: ' + device.version);
  tmpStr += makeListItem('Device Model: ' + device.model);
  tmpStr += makeListItem('UUId: ' + device.uuid);
```

```
    //Get the appInfo DOM element
    var element = document.getElementById('deviceInfo');
    //replace it with specific information about the device
    //running the application
    element.innerHTML = tmpStr;
    ons.compile(element);
    console.log("Leaving onDeviceReady");
}
```

In the application's deviceready event listener function, the code populates the page's `ons-list` element with `ons-list-items`. The individual device information components are wrapped in the proprietary tags using

```
function makeListItem(textStr) {
  return '<ons-list-item>' + textStr + '</ons-list-item>';
}
```

The only other difference from the other examples shown in this chapter is the following line:

```
ons.compile(element);
```

What this does is refresh the contents of the `ons-list` on the page; if I didn't do this, the text would appear on the page, but it would not render into the list shown in Figure 17.12. In the figure, the application is running on an iOS device.

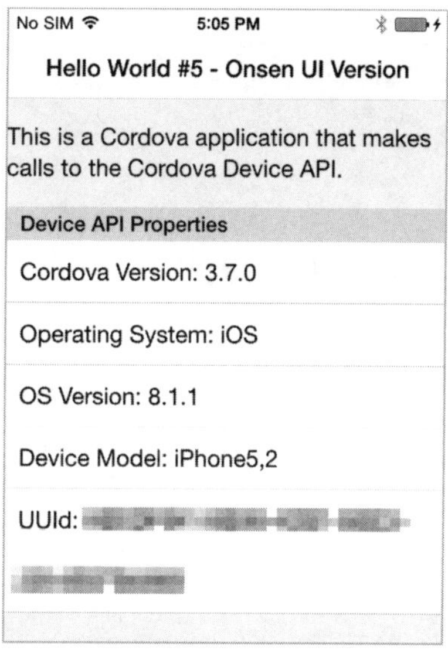

Figure 17.12 Onsen UI Version of the Hello World #5 Application Running on an iOS Device

Onsen UI provides a clean and simple framework for delivering visually pleasing hybrid UIs. When coupled with the code-editing and debugging capabilities of Monaca, it's a pretty slick solution for beginning or experienced Cordova developers.

Wrap-Up

In this chapter, I answered a couple of very important questions about the compatibility of third-party frameworks with Apache Cordova and showed you how to leverage several popular, a couple of not-so-popular, and two Cordova-specific HTML5 frameworks in your Cordova applications. Using the information provided herein, you'll be able to enhance the visual appeal of any Cordova application.

In the next chapter, I wrap up the book by covering third-party tools you can use to enhance your Cordova development experience.

18

Using Third-Party Tools with Cordova

Throughout the book, I've tried to show you as much as I can about the Cordova project, tools, APIs, mobile SDKs, and more. In this last chapter, I show you some additional tools you can use with your Cordova application projects. Herein I show you tools you can use to find errors in your JavaScript code before you even begin to test your applications, highlight some Cordova-aware code editors, introduce you to some Cordova development productivity enhancement tools, and demonstrate how to use build tools to optimize your Cordova applications.

There is a wide range of tools available to Cordova developers; I am only going to cover some tools I use myself or thought were interesting enough to learn about (so I could write about them here).

Code Validation Tools

If you're like me, you like to know whether there are errors in your Cordova applications' JavaScript code before you try to test them on simulators or physical devices. If you're using an HTML or JavaScript-aware IDE to code your application's JavaScript, you'll know right away when there are problems. Early on in the book I told you that you could use any code editor you want, and many of them may have an awareness of the language, but some do not.

When I worked on *Apache Cordova 3 Programming*, I used the open-source Aptana IDE to edit my sample application JavaScript code. I selected this tool because it allowed me to automatically format the code in such a way that it was easy to paste it into the manuscript. It is JavaScript aware, more or less, but didn't show me the errors in my code. Late in the process, I discovered JSLint and JSHint, command-line tools I could use to validate my code and point out any errors therein. I'll describe each of these tools in the following sections.

You can manually execute either one of these tools as part of your development process but can also use the hooks capabilities of the Cordova CLI (described in Chapter 6, "Automation and the Cordova CLI") to have them execute automatically during the prepare process.

As cool as these command-line tools are, though, I'll show you later how you can make executing them an automatic part of saving your code in Adobe Brackets.

JSLint

One of the early JavaScript validators is a program called JSLint (www.jslint.com) by Douglas Crockford. The program is available through a web interface, or you can install it as a Node module. Since Cordova uses Node and we want to be able to run this program from the command line, we'll install the Node module. To install JSLint on a Windows system, open a terminal window and execute the following command:

```
npm install -g jslint
```

On Macintosh OS X you will need to execute this command:

```
sudo npm install -g jslint
```

With the installation completed, you can navigate to a folder containing JavaScript files and validate them using the following command:

```
jslint <javascript_file_name>
```

For one of my sample applications, I could validate the application's index.js using the following command:

```
jslint index.js
```

JSLint will load, process the file, and update the console with the list of errors it found in the file:

```
index.js
 #1 Missing 'use strict' statement.
    alert("onBodyLoad"); // Line 6, Pos 3
 #2 Expected 'document' at column 5, not column 3.
    document.addEventListener("deviceready", onDeviceReady, false); // Line 9, Pos 3
 #3 'onDeviceReady' was used before it was defined.
    document.addEventListener("deviceready", onDeviceReady, false); // Line 9, Pos 44
 #4 Missing 'use strict' statement.
    console.log("Entering onDeviceReady"); // Line 13, Pos 3
 #5 Expected 'console' at column 5, not column 3.
    console.log("Cordova: " + device.cordova); // Line 14, Pos 3
 #6 'device' was used before it was defined.
    console.log("Cordova: " + device.cordova); // Line 14, Pos 29
 #7 Expected 'navigator' at column 5, not column 3.
    navigator.notification.alert("Cordova is ready", null, "Device Ready", btnText);
// Line 16, Pos 3
 #8 Expected 'console' at column 5, not column 3.
    console.log("Leaving onDeviceReady"); // Line 17, Pos 3
 #9 Missing 'use strict' statement.
    function makeListItem(textStr) { // Line 22, Pos 3
#10 Expected 'return' at column 9, not column 5.
    return '<li class="topcoat-list__item">' + textStr + '</li>'; // Line 23, Pos 5
```

JSLint found 44 errors in my short little file, then quit before finishing with the rest of the file. It didn't quit because it failed somehow. It basically figured that if the file had that many errors, it didn't need to keep going until I'd fixed most of them. The idea is that you should fix the errors, then repeat the process until all errors have been addressed.

From what I've read, Crockford believes in a very specific format for JavaScript code, and the terminal output proves it. For my manuscript, I configured my code formatter to use two spaces for indentation. JSLint, on the other hand, expects four spaces, so the linter is going to spit out an error for every indented line in my code. For this reason, and because JSLint is not as configurable as many people would like, the project was forked and JSHint was created as an alternative. I describe this tool in the following section.

JSHint

JSHint (http://jshint.com/) started as a fork of JSLint, designed to be more tolerant and more configurable than JSLint. To install JSHint on a Windows system, open a terminal window and execute the following command:

```
npm install -g jshint
```

On Macintosh OS X you will need to execute this command:

```
sudo npm install -g jshint
```

With the installation completed, you can navigate to a folder containing JavaScript files and validate them using the following command:

```
jshint <javascript_file_name>
```

For one of my sample applications, I could validate the application's index.js using the following command:

```
jshint index.js
```

In this file, the same file I used in the previous section, JSHint found only five errors:

```
index.js: line 6, col 22, Missing semicolon.
index.js: line 10, col 2, Unnecessary semicolon.
index.js: line 23, col 5, Expected an assignment or function call and instead saw an
expression.
index.js: line 23, col 11, Missing semicolon.
index.js: line 23, col 58, Expected an assignment or function call and instead saw
an expression.

5 errors
```

Figure 18.1 shows the process running in a terminal window.

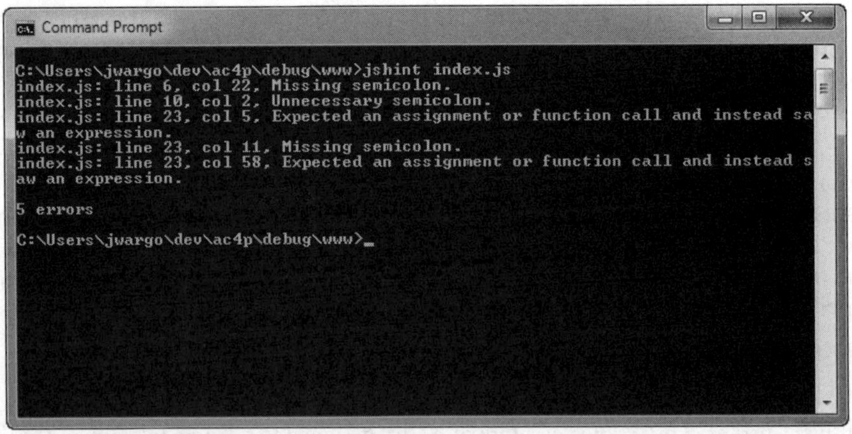

```
C:\Users\jwargo\dev\ac4p\debug\www>jshint index.js
index.js: line 6, col 22, Missing semicolon.
index.js: line 10, col 2, Unnecessary semicolon.
index.js: line 23, col 5, Expected an assignment or function call and instead sa
w an expression.
index.js: line 23, col 11, Missing semicolon.
index.js: line 23, col 58, Expected an assignment or function call and instead s
aw an expression.

5 errors

C:\Users\jwargo\dev\ac4p\debug\www>_
```

Figure 18.1 JSHint Running in a Terminal Window

As you can see, JSHint doesn't care about how I've formatted my code, only the technical accuracy of the code. It will be much easier for me to locate and fix the bugs in the file because there are simply fewer of them—only because of the tool I selected to validate my code.

Now, there are many times when developers will do something in their code that is technically accurate but JSHint won't have any way of knowing. One of the best examples I can think of is the Cordova APIs. When I'm coding a Cordova application, I can use the Cordova APIs in my code without having the API's JavaScript code handy. When the application is running in a Cordova container, the cordova.js file loads the APIs for me, and the associated JavaScript files will be in the container, placed there automatically by the Cordova CLI.

If you take a look at the JSHint documentation at www.jshint.com/docs/, you'll see that there are many configuration options you can use to tweak JSHint (and JSLint as well). The tweaks are generally applied by simply adding options to the JavaScript file. For example, to instruct JSHint that I want undefined and unused variables to be flagged, I can add the following to the beginning of my source code file:

```
/* jshint undef: true, unused: true */
```

Then, when JSHint runs, I will see the following output:

```
index.js: line 8, col 3, 'alert' is not defined.
index.js: line 11, col 3, 'document' is not defined.
index.js: line 15, col 3, 'console' is not defined.
index.js: line 16, col 29, 'device' is not defined.
index.js: line 18, col 3, 'navigator' is not defined.
```

In this example, `alert`, `console`, `document`, and `navigator` are built-in capabilities available in the browser and the Cordova WebView, so even though I don't have JavaScript files that reference them, they're still valid. To override JSHint and let it know that these variables are OK, I can add the following to my source code file:

```
/*global alert*/
/*global console*/
/*global device*/
/*global document*/
/*global navigator*/
```

This defines the objects so that JSHint will ignore them. The comments are ignored by JavaScript but processed by JSHint.

There's a whole lot more you can do with these tools; I've only touched the surface here. I simply wanted to let you know about some of the tools that can help you write better code. In the next section, I'll show you how those tools are exposed through code-editing tools so that you can validate your code as you write it.

Code Editors

As I mentioned before, when working on the code for my previous PhoneGap/Cordova books, I used Aptana Studio to edit the HTML and JavaScript source code. For this book, I decided to use the then-still-in-beta Adobe Brackets. About halfway through the book, I discovered WebStorm and spent some of my time with that editor as well.

Both editors support JSLint and JSHint, plus both can work directly with Apache Cordova and Adobe PhoneGap projects. In this section, I'll introduce you to each editor and show you how to use the Cordova-related special capabilities of each.

Adobe Brackets

In 2012, Adobe announced a new open-source project, the Brackets web code editor (http://brackets.io/). The editor is lightweight, JavaScript based, and uses plugins to enhance its capabilities. With the editor you get basic editing of web content (HTML, CSS, and JavaScript), syntax highlighting, and more. Through extensions, you can have support for JSLint, JSHint, Apache Cordova, and much more.

The editor is built using the Chromium Embedded Framework (CEF), and anyone can download the code to see how all of this stuff works. Brackets supports Windows, OS X, and Linux, so it's available on any platform a Cordova developer would use.

To use Brackets, download the installer from http://brackets.io and run it. Figure 18.2 shows the Brackets editor with a Cordova project open. On the left is the list of open files and below that the project folder structure. With Brackets, you can open individual files or you can open an entire folder and quickly switch between files. It even supports live preview, which is pretty useful when writing web applications.

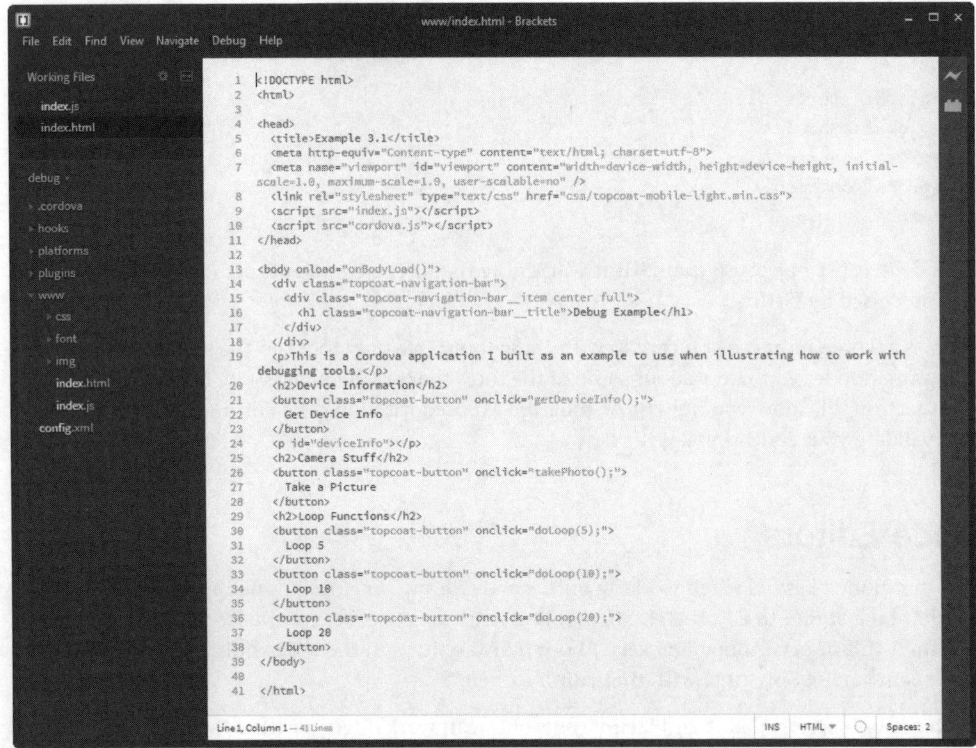

Figure 18.2 Adobe Brackets: Editing an HTML File

For JavaScript code editing, I always turn on the Auto Close Braces option (under the Edit menu) which causes Brackets to automatically add closing braces when editing JavaScript files. Beyond that one setting, all of the other interesting capabilities for me come through extensions.

To access Brackets extensions, open the File menu and select Extension Manager. A window will appear similar to the one shown in Figure 18.3. In this example, I'm using the extension search capabilities to locate and install the Beautify extension (http://goo.gl/yoo0t0). Beautify uses the JS Beautifier module to properly format source code.

To install an extension, select it from the list and click the Install button shown on the right side of Figure 18.3. For the Beautify extension, you can beautify any file by opening the Brackets Edit menu and selecting Beautify, or you can have Beautify run every time you save any file by enabling the plugin's Beautify on save option located in the same menu.

I have this extension enabled to beautify on every save; that way all of my source code files are always cleanly formatted. The extension works on HTML and JavaScript files and is so quick you won't even notice it running.

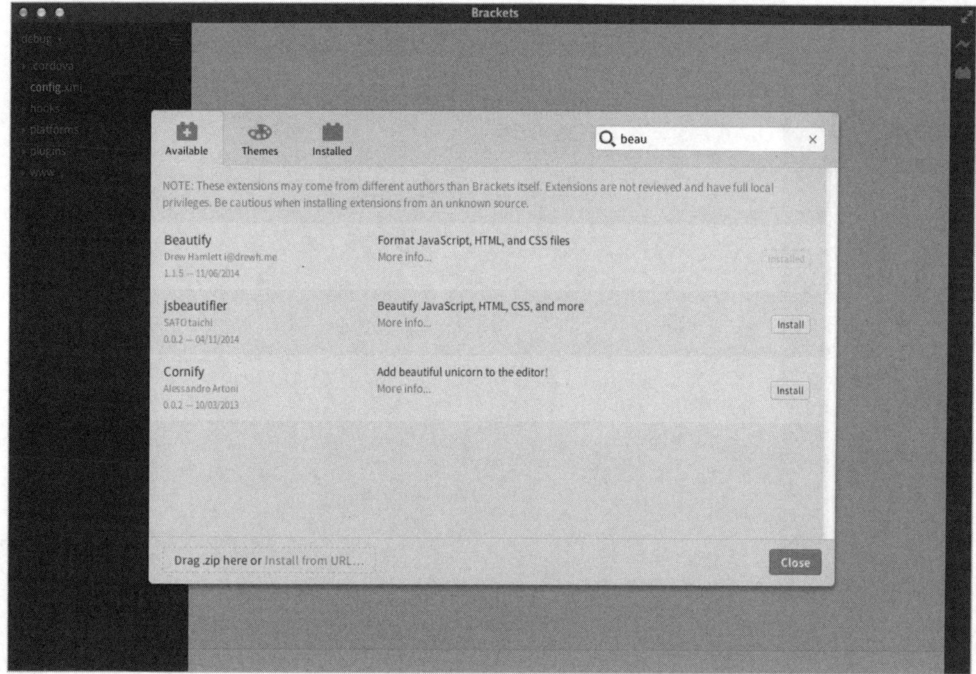

Figure 18.3 Adobe Brackets: Finding Extensions

For the manuscript, I like to indent the structure of the code by two spaces for each level. This provides my code with clear indentation but utilizes the minimum of real estate. Beautify defaults to indenting by tabs, but for the manuscript I had to use spaces. The extension offers a quick and easy way to change that setting. If you look in the bottom-right corner of Figure 18.2, you can see Spaces: 2. To switch from spaces to tabs, simply click the word Spaces. To switch from tabs to spaces, click Tabs (not shown). To adjust how many spaces are used for indentation, click on the 2 and type a new value. That's all there is to configuring Beautify.

There is also a JSHint extension for Brackets, so I use that to have Brackets automatically check for errors every time a file is saved. You can see an example of this in Figure 18.4. I've opened up a JSHint Problems report at the bottom of the Brackets window.

Notice the triangle on the bottom right of the screen—that indicates that there are problems with the code. Click the symbol to open or close the Problems report shown in the figure. This feature is another reason why I split out my Cordova application's web code into .html and .js files everywhere—it enables me to use JSHint more efficiently in Brackets.

> **Tip**
>
> Double-click on any of the lines in the JSHint Problems area to highlight the corresponding code line in the editor.

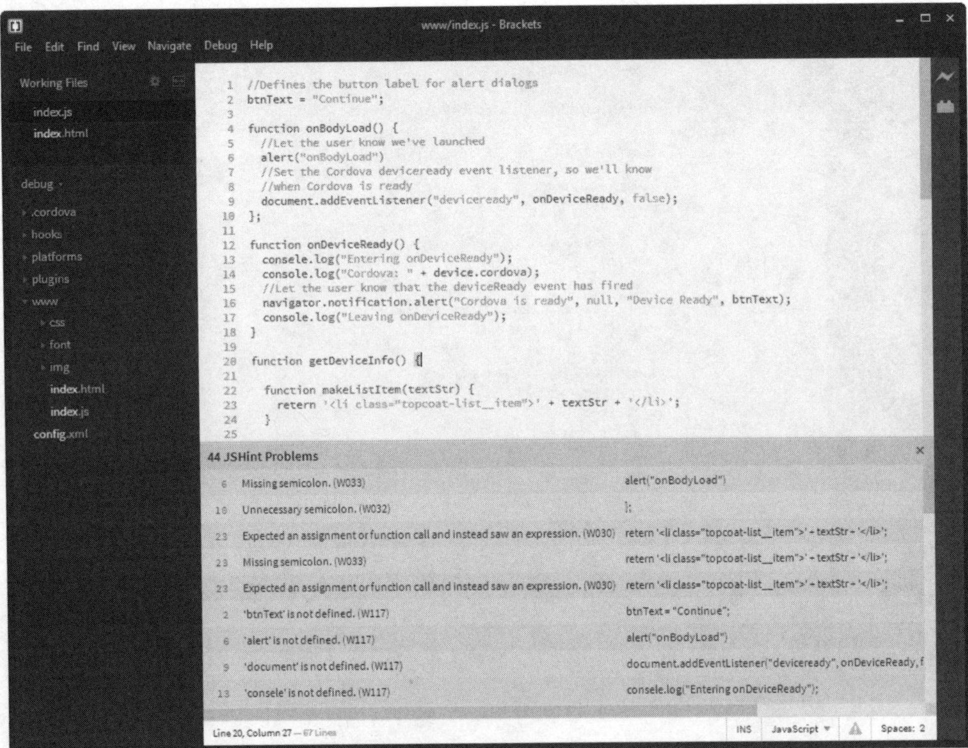

Figure 18.4 Adobe Brackets: JSHint Support

Cordova Plugin

Brackets doesn't have an awareness of Apache Cordova, but since it's an Adobe product, I knew that it could. There are currently two Brackets Cordova plugins available as shown in Figure 18.5. The first one is published by Ray Camden, a developer evangelist at Adobe, so I decided to select that one. Both plugins support only OS X, which is disappointing, but there's nothing I can do about it unless I want to make my own extension or submit fixes to Ray's.

After you install the extension, whenever the extension detects that you are working with a Cordova project, it enables some Cordova-aware features in the editor. The first thing you must do is open a Cordova project. To do this, open the Brackets File menu and select the Open Folder option. Navigate to a Cordova project folder and click the Open button as shown in Figure 18.6.

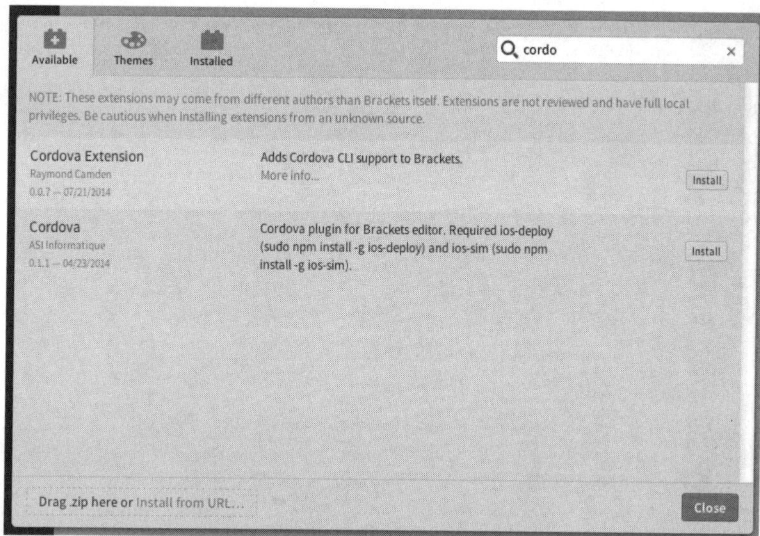

Figure 18.5 Adobe Brackets: Searching for Cordova Extensions

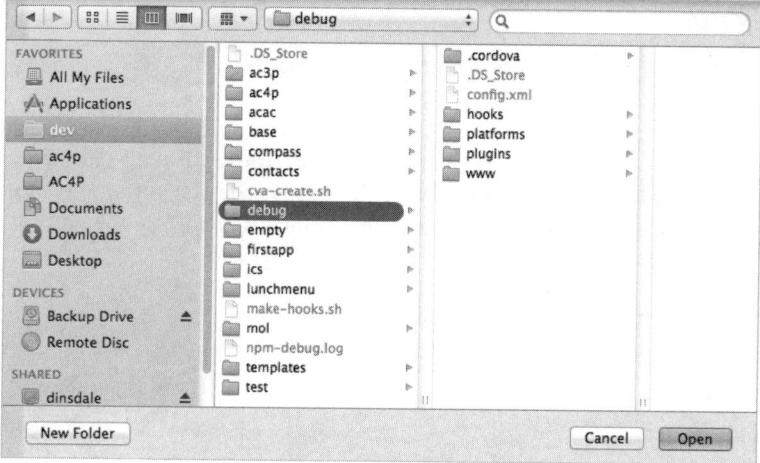

Figure 18.6 Adobe Brackets: Selecting a Cordova Project Folder

With the project selected, notice the Cordova icon shown in the upper-right side of Figure 18.7. When the button is enabled, you can click on it to open the panel shown at the bottom of the figure. From the Platforms tab shown in the figure, you can add or remove target platforms from the project by clicking true or false in the Enabled column. To execute the application project in a simulator or physical device, click the Emulate or Run option in the Build Options column.

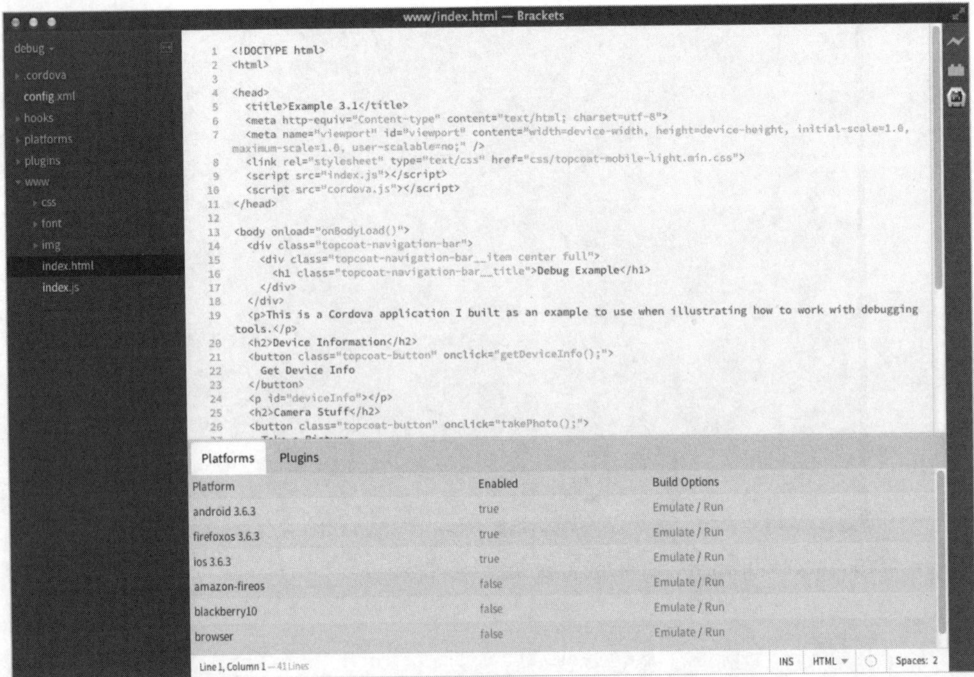

Figure 18.7 Adobe Brackets: Managing Cordova Platforms

You can manage plugins directly from this panel as well. Select the Plugins tab at the top of the panel and you will be shown a list of the plugins that are currently installed in the project. Click the Remove link to the right of the plugin version to remove the plugin from the project. To add plugins to the project, use the search field to locate the plugin, then click the Add Plugin button to add it to your project (see Figure 18.8).

Platforms Plugins

barco | Add Plugin

com.blackberry.community.barcodescanner
com.phonegap.plugins.barcodescanner
org.bloxlab.barcodescanner

	Version	Options
	0.3.2	Remove
Console (org.apache.cordova.console)	0.2.11	Remove
Device (org.apache.cordova.device)	0.2.12	Remove
Notification (org.apache.cordova.dialogs)	0.2.10	Remove

Line 1, Column 1 — 41 Lines INS HTML Spaces: 2

Figure 18.8 Adobe Brackets: Searching for Cordova Plugins

That's it; that's all there is to this plugin. It's not earth-shattering, but it's at least useful. I would like to see the ability to add new projects added to the extension.

PhoneGap Plugin

There's also a PhoneGap plugin for Brackets, but it's pretty lame. All it does is allow you to log in to the PhoneGap Build service as shown in Figure 18.9 and interact with your existing PhoneGap Build projects.

Figure 18.9 Adobe Brackets: PhoneGap Build Logon

After you have logged in, you can view your existing projects and initiate a rebuild or delete the project from the panel (Figure 18.10).

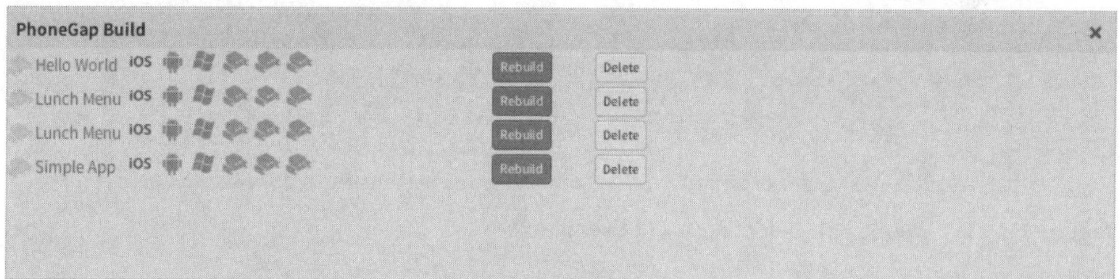

Figure 18.10 Adobe Brackets: PhoneGap Build Projects

For all the features I've described, I really like Adobe Brackets and it will probably remain my primary editor for web application projects. I also love the extensibility of the editor and hope I can find some time to write my own plugins or help enhance some existing ones.

WebStorm

As I worked on this manuscript, I noticed an email on the Cordova dev list describing the Cordova capabilities of the WebStorm JavaScript IDE (http://goo.gl/ZPaELr). WebStorm is from JetBrains, the company behind IntelliJ IDEA, the IDE under the covers in Google's Android Studio. Where Brackets is lightweight, quick, and nimble, WebStorm is not; it takes a really long time to start up and keeps grabbing focus as it completes its different startup scans.

WebStorm comes out of the box with support for Apache Cordova, Adobe PhoneGap, and Ionic. As long as WebStorm can detect your framework CLI installation, it will enable the features within the IDE.

When creating a new project, you can select PhoneGap/Cordova App as shown in Figure 18.11.

Figure 18.11 WebStorm: New PhoneGap/Cordova App Project

When you click the OK button, you will be prompted to select the CLI command you want to use for this new project. Select cordova.cmd (on Windows) as shown in Figure 18.12 to create a Cordova project. Select phonegap.cmd to create a PhoneGap project.

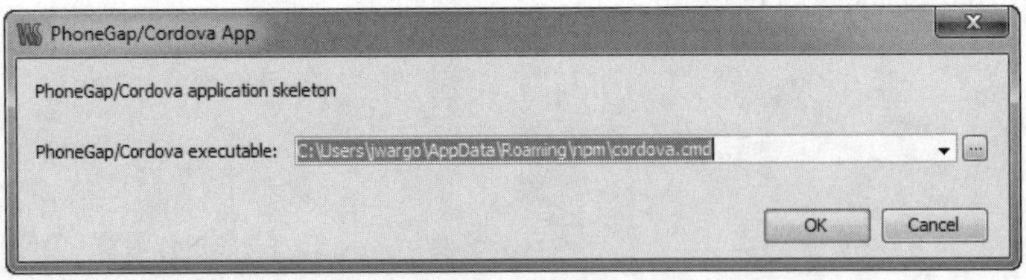

Figure 18.12 WebStorm: Selecting a CLI Executable

If you have an existing project open, WebStorm will ask whether you want the current window replaced as shown in Figure 18.13.

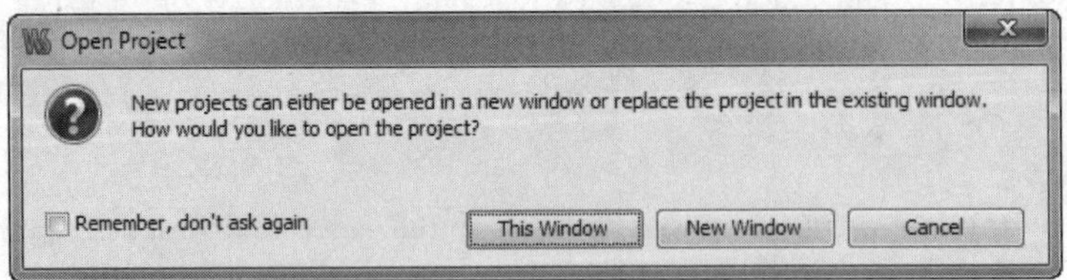

Figure 18.13 WebStorm: Open Options

To create the project, WebStorm invokes the appropriate CLI to create a new project. Figure 18.14 shows the new project in the editor. Notice the folder structure on the left; this is the same folder structure you have seen many times throughout this book. It was created using the CLI, so you can work with it here within the WebStorm IDE or switch out to a terminal window and work with the project via the appropriate CLI. Pretty cool stuff.

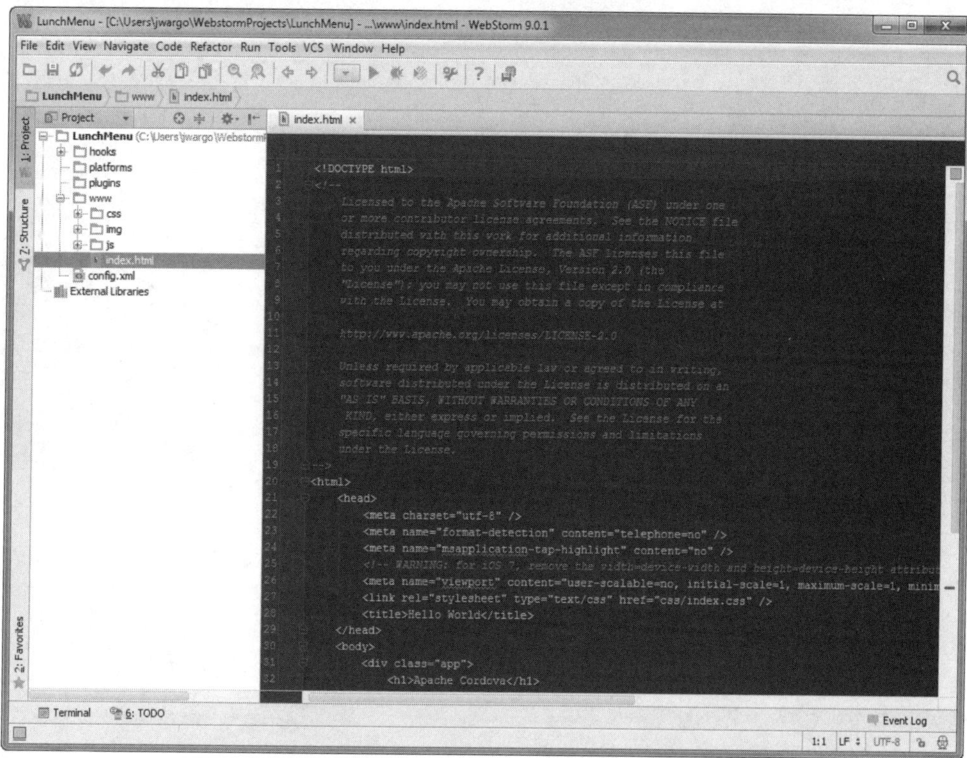

Figure 18.14 WebStorm: New Cordova Project

WebStorm can also manage the installation of Cordova plugins into the project as shown in Figure 18.15. Open the File menu and select Settings to open the dialog shown in the figure. Settings shows the list of plugins currently added to the project. To manipulate that list, use the buttons highlighted on the right side of the figure.

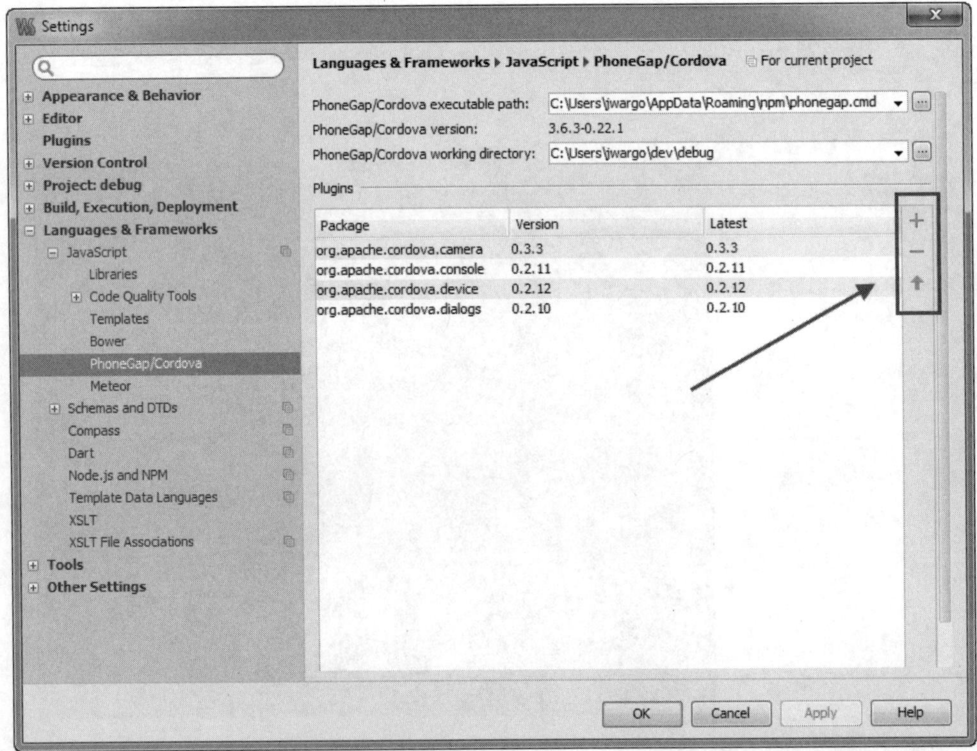

Figure 18.15 WebStorm: Project Settings

To add a plugin to the current project, click the plus sign (+) shown in the figure. WebStorm will open the Available Packages window shown in Figure 18.16. You can browse through the list of plugins from the Cordova Plugin Registry, or you can type a keyword in the search box to filter the results. When you select a plugin, click the Install Package button to add the plugin to your project.

Click the minus button (-) to remove a selected plugin. Use the up arrow, when enabled, to upgrade the selected plugin.

WebStorm also has support for running a hybrid application project directly from within the IDE. To enable this capability, you must first create one or more Run Configurations for your project. To do this, open the Run menu and select Edit Configurations. WebStorm will open the window shown in Figure 18.17. Click the plus sign (+) in the upper-left corner of the window to create a new configuration. WebStorm will prompt you to select the type of Run Configuration to create; select PhoneGap/Cordova from the list.

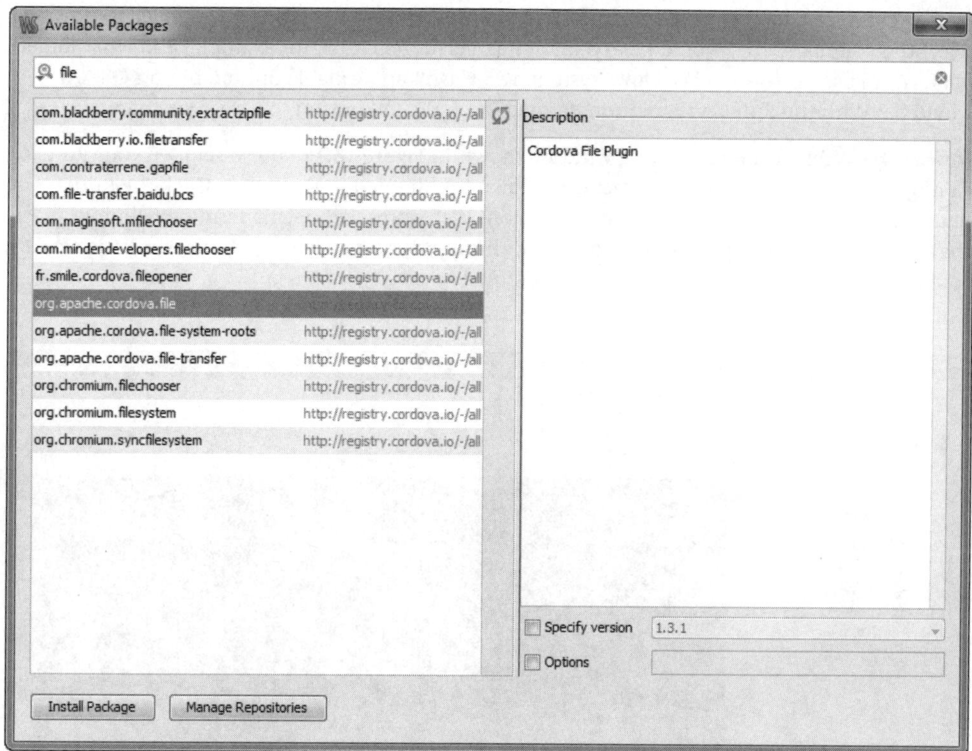

Figure 18.16 WebStorm: Available Packages

Figure 18.17 WebStorm: Run/Debug Configurations

I haven't dug into too many of the options in this dialog. For my testing all I needed to do was select the command that would be executed (`run` versus `emulate`, for example) and what target platform to use. As this is a Windows system, iOS wasn't an available option, but on OS X it would be. With the Run Configuration defined, click the OK button to save your changes.

Now in the WebStorm main editing window shown in Figure 18.18 you should see your Run Configuration listed in the Run Target drop-down highlighted in the figure. Click the Run button to launch the selected Run Configuration. WebStorm will open a terminal window at the bottom of the editing window and launch the appropriate Cordova, PhoneGap, or Ionic CLI commands to run your project as you have defined.

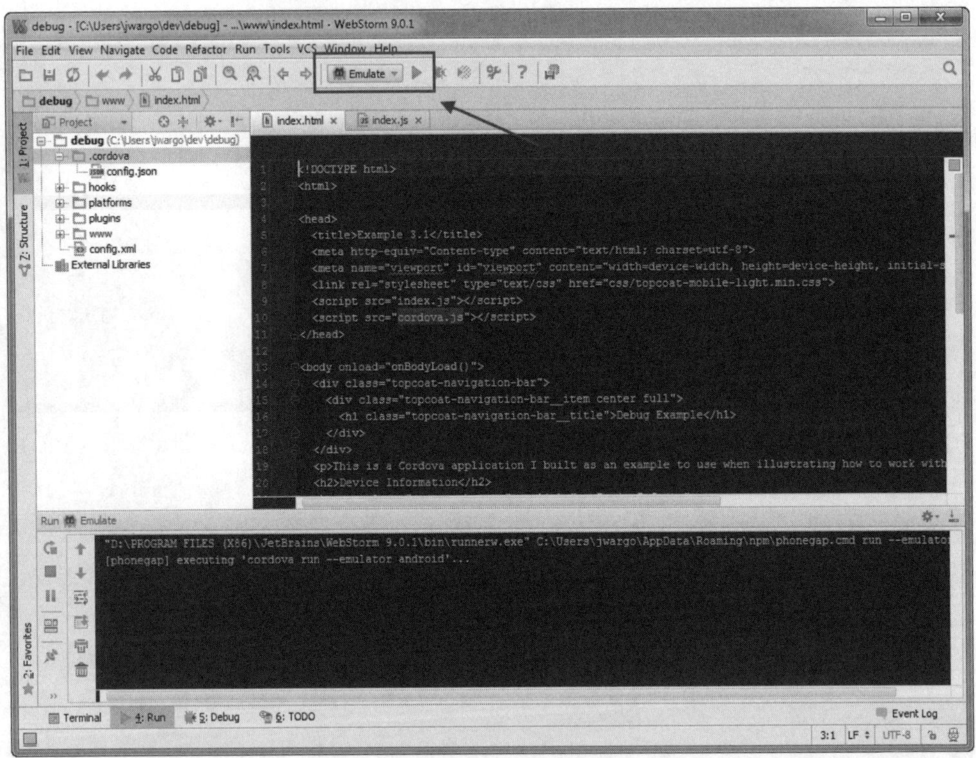

Figure 18.18 WebStorm: Running a Cordova Project

WebStorm would be incomplete if it didn't check your code for you as you typed. Built into the IDE is support for both JSLint and JSHint and more. To enable one of them, open the Settings window, expand Languages and Frameworks, and select the one that suits your requirements; you will see a panel open similar to the one shown in Figure 18.19.

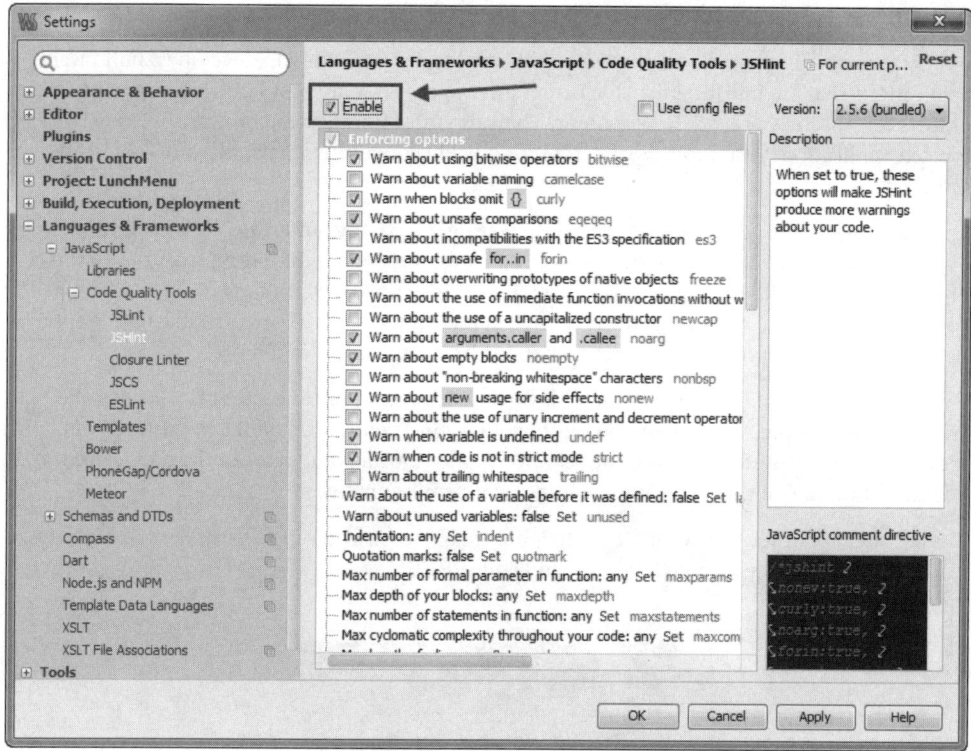

Figure 18.19 WebStorm: JSHint Options

In this example, I've opened the options for JSHint as I find JSLint to be too restrictive. To use this option, you must check the Enable checkbox highlighted at the top of the screen. Next, ignore or configure each JSHint option shown in the figure. WebStorm gives you access to most, if not all, capabilities of JSHint; you only have to decide which ones are important for you.

There's a lot more to this tool; I've only touched the surface of what it can do. Its awareness of hybrid development tools makes it a great choice for Cordova, PhoneGap, and Ionic developers.

Developer Productivity Enhancement Tools

As you have seen already in this chapter, individuals and companies have produced Cordova-aware tools. In the previous section, I showed you some code editors that have features designed to help hybrid developers; in this section, I'll show you some developer productivity enhancement tools available today.

There are quite a few products in this space, and I won't be able to cover all of them. I meant to take a look at the Intel XDK (http://goo.gl/DmfHXG) but didn't have time, and it's got so many features that it likely would have required its own chapter. Maybe in the next book. I will spend some time here covering AppGyver and a new Eclipse project called THyM.

AppGyver

AppGyver (www.appgyver.com) provides a set of tools designed to help developers build web applications that are indistinguishable from native apps. They are best known for Steroids, a set of tools for Apache Cordova development. They also offer Composer, a browser-based designer for web applications, and Prototyper, a tool for quickly converting image files into application prototypes.

Steroids consists of a command-line tool for creating, managing, and running hybrid web applications. The CLI is pretty sophisticated, doing a lot more hand-holding than the Cordova or PhoneGap CLI will do. It also tells you a lot more about what to do next. It offers a set of UI controls a developer can leverage to create web applications that look and feel like native applications. It includes support for a navigation bar, loading page, views, and more.

To simplify testing and debugging, Steroids offers a Scanner application that is a lot like the PhoneGap Developer App. When you create your hybrid application, you can serve it from your local development system and use the Scanner app to download updates to the application so you can run it in real time without needing a build environment.

The Scanner application is available in the public app stores; you can see an example of the Android version in the Google Play store in Figure 18.20.

Figure 18.20 AppGyver Scanner Application in the Google Play Store

When you install the application, you're prompted to enable a wide range of options as shown in Figure 18.21. The Scanner application comes preconfigured with many, if not most, Cordova plugins, so that's why you have to enable so many options.

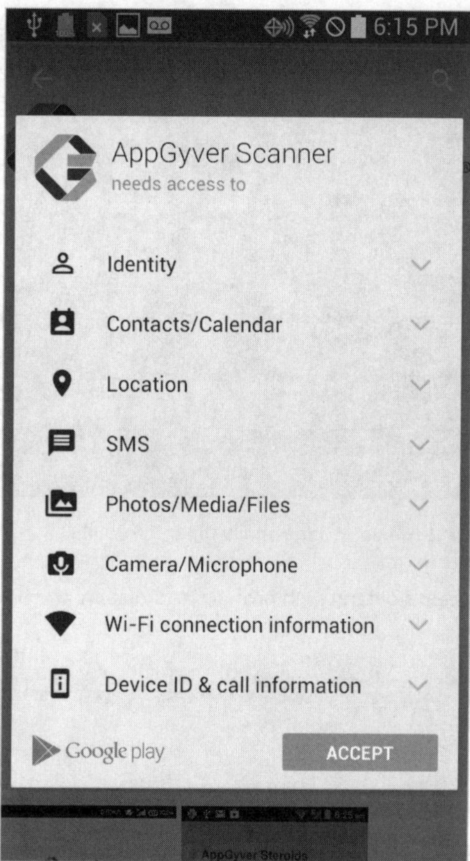

Figure 18.21 AppGyver Scanner Application Permissions

To manage hybrid projects using AppGyver, you use a terminal window and the `steroids` command. AppGyver provides a tutorial that walks you through how to work with projects, so I'm only going to cover a highlight here.

Once you have a hybrid project created, you can test it pretty quickly using the `steroids connect` command. When you execute the command, it will build the project, then host the application using a local server as illustrated in Figure 18.22.

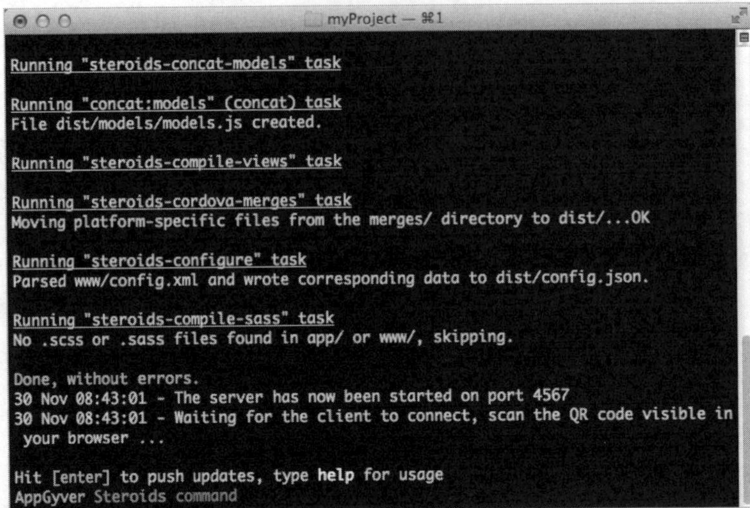

Figure 18.22 AppGyver `steroids connect` Command Results

It will then launch the system's default web browser and display the page shown in Figure 18.23.

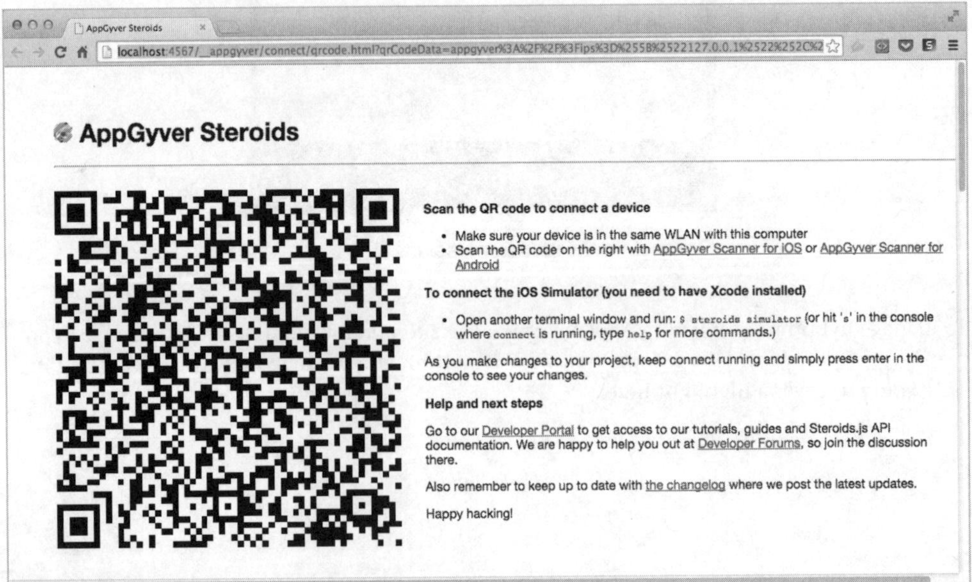

Figure 18.23 AppGyver Steroids Application QR Code

With this in place, launch the AppGyver Scanner application on a supported mobile device. You will see a screen similar to the one shown in Figure 18.24. Tap the Scan button in the middle of the screen, use the smartphone's camera to capture the QR code shown in Figure 18.23, and the hybrid application will download and launch automatically in the Scanner application.

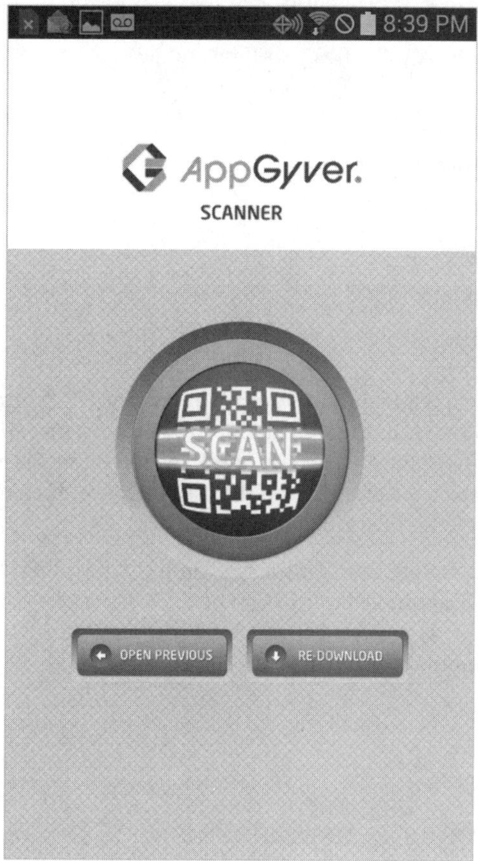

Figure 18.24 AppGyver Scanner Application Main Screen

As you test the application and make changes to the application's code, you can simply return to the terminal window (Figure 18.22) and press the keyboard's Enter key to refresh the content and reload it in the mobile application.

AppGyver is worth looking at from a UI and developer experience standpoint. The company seems to be well funded and has released some interesting products.

Eclipse THyM

The JBoss (www.jboss.org) tools team at Red Hat (www.redhat.com) created a suite of tools for mobile development and donated them to the Eclipse project as THyM, which stands for The Hybrid Mobile. The project adds cross-platform mobile development capabilities to the Eclipse IDE. Originally designed for Cordova development, the team added support for other distributions and frameworks. You can read about the project at www.eclipse.org/thym/.

Going forward, I'm going to skip the fancy spelling and just refer to the project as Thym.

The main parts of Thym are

- New hybrid project wizard
- Project import and export
- Config.xml editor
- Run options for Android and iOS
- Plugin Discovery wizard

Thym is installed as an Eclipse plugin; simply open an instance of Eclipse, open the Help menu, and select Install New Software. In the Available Software wizard that appears, add the Thym project download site http://download.eclipse.org/thym/snapshots to the Work with field as shown in Figure 18.25. Select the project from the list of options, then click the Next button to work through the remainder of the installation wizard.

With the plugin installed, Eclipse now has the new project type called Hybrid Mobile shown in the Eclipse New Project wizard in Figure 18.26. When you select this option, you'll be enabling the creation of a new Cordova project. Thym doesn't use the Cordova CLI to create projects; the new project capability is built into the plugin.

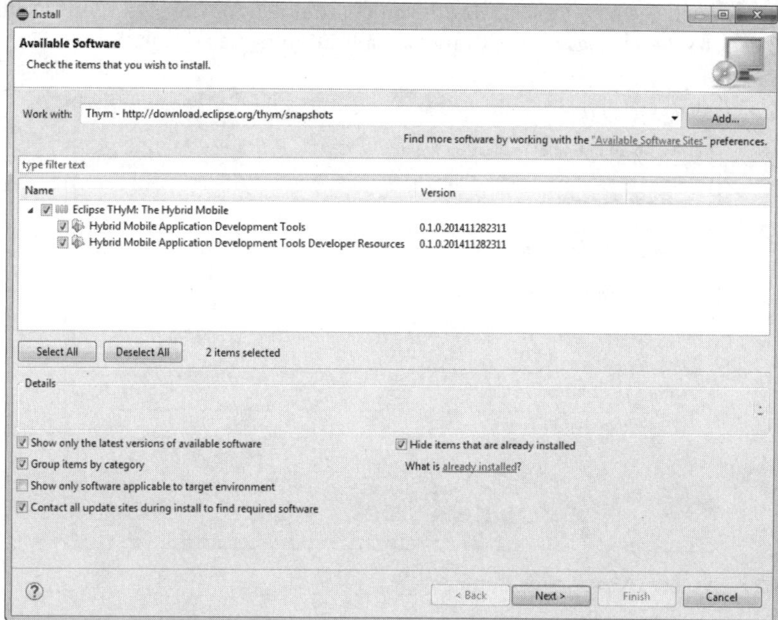

Figure 18.25 Eclipse: Installing Thym

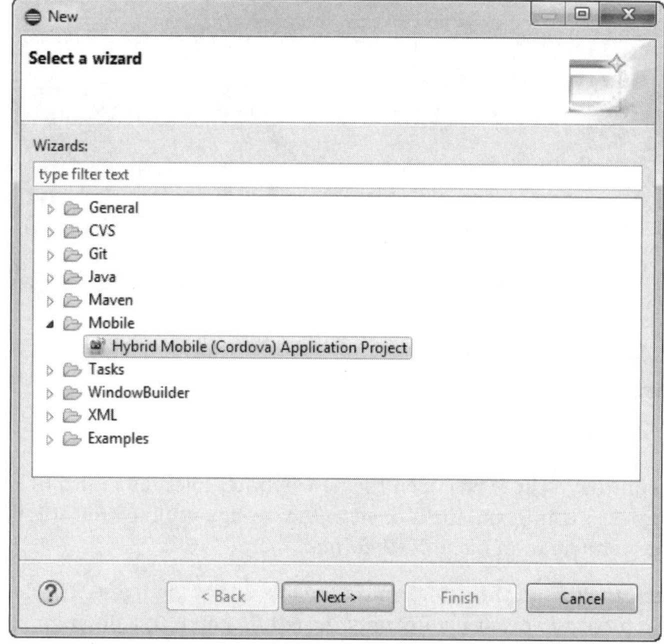

Figure 18.26 Eclipse: New Project

As you work through the New Project wizard, you're prompted for Cordova-specific settings. Figure 18.27 shows the settings for the Cordova application name and application ID.

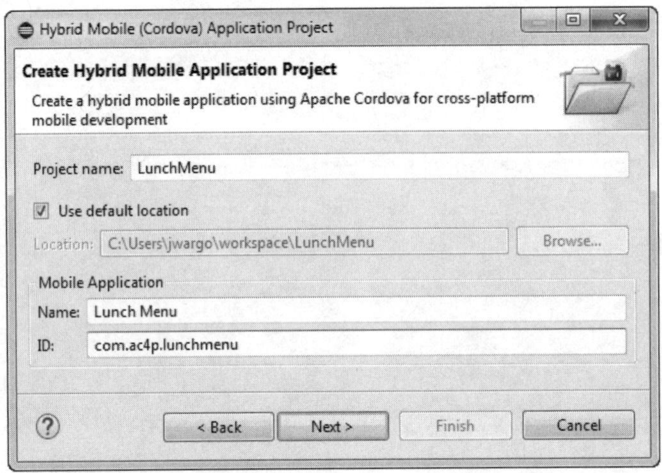

Figure 18.27 Eclipse: New Project Settings

Next, you'll be asked to select the hybrid framework version to use for this project as shown in Figure 18.28. You should be able to use PhoneGap and other distributions here as well. Simply click the Download button to install a new framework version.

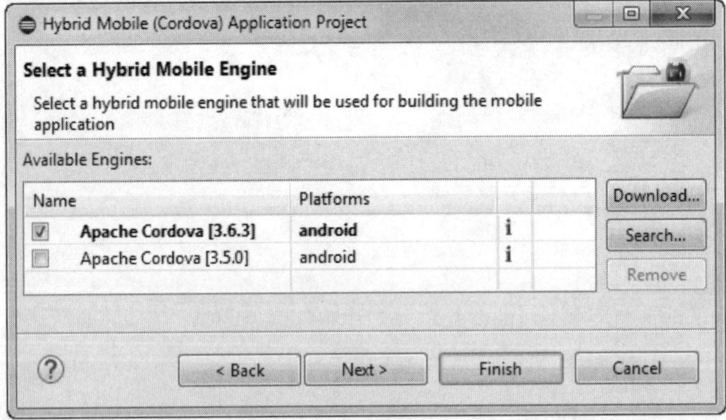

Figure 18.28 Eclipse: Hybrid Mobile Engine Selection

Once the wizard finishes, Eclipse will open the new hybrid project as shown in Figure 18.29. In this figure, the project's config.xml file is open in the configuration editor; this isolates you from having to edit the configuration file in XML format.

Notice the project structure in the navigator on the left side of the figure. This looks like the standard Cordova project folder structure, only the config.xml is in a different place. The platforms folder is missing as well, but that is taken care of by the plugin at runtime.

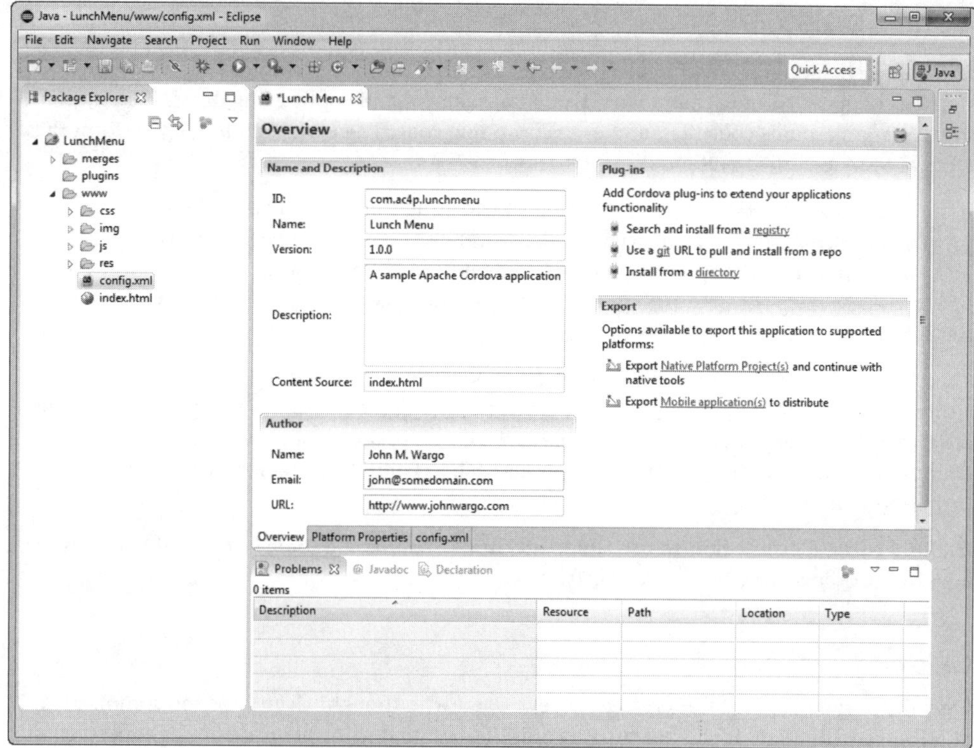

Figure 18.29 Eclipse: Project Properties

Thym adds some new run options to Eclipse as shown in Figure 18.30. Since this screen shot was taken on a Windows system, only Android options are shown. On OS X, you would see options for running on iOS devices and simulators as well.

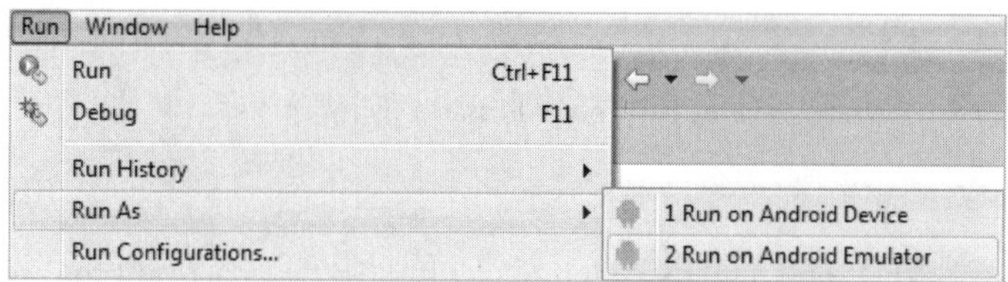

Figure 18.30 Eclipse Run Menu

Thym is brand-new and still has a long way to go, but it's a good starting point for providing the Eclipse IDE with hybrid development capabilities.

Build Tools

For some web development projects, there are tasks that must be performed as part of the build step that happens before deployment. Those tasks may include optimizing image files, minimizing or merging source code files, and even compiling code. The tools used to help perform these types of tasks are called build tools.

If, for example, you coded a web application's logic using something like CoffeeScript (http://coffeescript.org/) or Dart (www.dartlang.org), the code would need to be compiled into JavaScript before the application could be deployed. If you'd crafted a web application's CSS using Less (http://lesscss.org/) or Sass (http://sass-lang.com/), you would need to compile the code into CSS for deployment.

There is a plethora of free build tools available; for example, the Android Developer Tools use either Ant or Gradle, depending on the IDE you use. As Cordova uses JavaScript and Node, there are several Node-based build tools available as well. One of the most popular is Grunt JS (http://gruntjs.com/), along with other options such as Gulp (http://gulpjs.com/) and Brunch (http://brunch.io/).

In this section, I'll show how to use Gulp and Grunt to automate some of the build tasks associated with Cordova development projects.

Gulp

Gulp (http://gulpjs.com/) was created by developers who thought Grunt was too complicated, and I agree with them. It's a stream-based build system that gains performance enhancements by having the results of one operation streamed directly to the next step in the process instead of having to make an intermediate trip to disk.

Gulp projects are coded in JavaScript and Gulp, and its plugins can all be installed using Node. To use Gulp, you create a file called gulpfile.js in your project's root folder, then add JavaScript code to the file to perform specific build tasks. Let me show you how this works.

First, install Gulp by opening a terminal window and issuing the following command:

```
npm install -g gulp
```

On OS X or Linux, you may have to run the command using this:

```
sudo npm install -g gulp
```

Now all you have to do is populate the gulpfile.js with the code to perform the appropriate tasks for your project. At a minimum, the gulp file, gulpfile.js, needs to include the following:

```
var gulp = require('gulp');

gulp.task('default', function() {
  // place code for your default task here
});
```

Anything Gulp does is coded using JavaScript inside of that `gulp.task` method.

Now let me give you an example of how I use Gulp in a Cordova project. When I build a Cordova application, there are a few things I want to do to my code before I put it into production. First, I want to minimize all of the source code (HTML, JavaScript, and CSS) so it's smaller and loads faster in the container. Additionally, if I have any image files, I want to optimize them for mobile, reducing either the size or the quality of the images so they load quickly and render correctly on a mobile device. I may even want to concatenate my application's JavaScript files into a single, minified file. These are all tasks I can perform using Gulp.

Now, in order to do this, I can't code my application in the Cordova project's www folder as the Cordova CLI will expect to find all of its files there. What I want is to code in a different folder location, then use Gulp to process the files and copy them into the www folder before passing control over to the Cordova CLI to do its stuff.

So, what I did was added a folder called code to my Cordova application project folder structure, then placed my web application's files there. Then I created the gulp file shown in Listing 18.1 to preprocess the files and copy the results into the project's www folder.

Listing 18.1 gulpfile.js File

```
// include gulp
var gulp = require('gulp');
var shell = require('gulp-shell');

// include plug-ins
var jshint = require('gulp-jshint');
var changed = require('gulp-changed');
var imagemin = require('gulp-imagemin');
var minifyHTML = require('gulp-minify-html');
var concat = require('gulp-concat');
//Uncomment the following line before going to production
//var stripDebug = require('gulp-strip-debug');
var uglify = require('gulp-uglify');
var autoprefix = require('gulp-autoprefixer');
var minifyCSS = require('gulp-minify-css');

// JS hint task
gulp.task('jshint', function () {
  gulp.src('./code/js/*.js')
    .pipe(jshint())
    .pipe(jshint.reporter('default'));
});

// minify new images
gulp.task('imagemin', function () {
  var imgSrc = './code/img/**/*',
```

```
    imgDst = './www/img';
  gulp.src(imgSrc)
    .pipe(changed(imgDst))
    .pipe(imagemin())
    .pipe(gulp.dest(imgDst));
});

// minify new or changed HTML pages
gulp.task('htmlpage', function () {
  var htmlSrc = './code/*.html',
    htmlDst = './www';
  gulp.src(htmlSrc)
    .pipe(changed(htmlDst))
    .pipe(minifyHTML())
    .pipe(gulp.dest(htmlDst));
});

// JS concat, strip debugging and minify
gulp.task('scripts', function () {
  gulp.src(['./code/js/index.js', './code/js/*.js'])
    .pipe(concat('script.js'))
    //Uncomment the following line before going to production
    //.pipe(stripDebug())
    .pipe(uglify())
    .pipe(gulp.dest('./www/'));
});

// CSS concat, auto-prefix and minify
gulp.task('styles', function () {
  gulp.src(['./code/css/*.css'])
    .pipe(concat('styles.css'))
    .pipe(autoprefix('last 2 versions'))
    .pipe(minifyCSS())
    .pipe(gulp.dest('./www/'));
});

gulp.task('prepare', shell.task(['ls', 'cordova prepare']));

// default gulp task
gulp.task('default', ['imagemin', 'htmlpage', 'scripts', 'styles',
  'prepare'], function () {});
```

If you look at the code, you'll notice that there are a bunch of modules that are required by the gulp file. These are Gulp plugins, and each one takes care of a specific step in the process. One option is to manually install each module using the following commands:

```
npm install gulp-autoprefixer
npm install gulp-changed
npm install gulp-concat
npm install gulp-imagemin
npm install gulp-jshint
npm install gulp-minify-css
npm install gulp-minify-html
npm install gulp-strip-debug
npm install gulp-uglify
```

The modules are installing locally; notice that I didn't add the `-g` flag to each command, as each project may have different requirements. To make this easier, I created a package.json file that contains all the required modules as shown in Listing 18.2.

Listing 18.2 package.json File

```
{
  "name": "gulpdemo",
  "version": "1.0.0",
  "description": "Cordova Gulp Demo",
  "main": "gulpfile.js",
  "dependencies": {
    "gulp": "^3.8.10",
    "gulp-autoprefixer": "^0.0.7",
    "gulp-changed": "^0.3.0",
    "gulp-concat": "^2.2.0",
    "gulp-imagemin": "^0.5.0",
    "gulp-jshint": "^1.6.0",
    "gulp-minify-css": "^0.3.4",
    "gulp-minify-html": "^0.1.3",
    "gulp-shell": "^0.2.5",
    "gulp-strip-debug": "^0.3.0",
    "gulp-uglify": "^0.3.0"
  },
  "devDependencies": {},
  "author": "John M. Wargo",
  "license": "Apache"
}
```

Now, to use this in any project, I simply have to copy over my gulpfile.js and package.json files to the Cordova project folder, then create a folder called code, and I'm all set. Once the files are there, I can open a terminal window pointing to the folder and issue the following command:

```
npm install
```

This will automatically install all of the required Gulp plugin modules for me.

Now let's dig into the code for Listing 18.1. If you look at the very bottom of the file, you'll see the following code:

```
// default gulp task
gulp.task('default', ['imagemin', 'htmlpage', 'scripts', 'styles', 'prepare'],
  function () {});
```

This defines the default task Gulp performs when you issue the `gulp` command all by itself. In this example, the default process is performing the following steps:

1. Minimize image files.
2. Process HTML files.
3. Process JavaScript files.
4. Process CSS files.
5. Issue a `cordova prepare` command.

If you take a look through the remainder of the file, you will see that a separate function is defined for each of these tasks. Let's take a look at the code for processing JavaScript files:

```
// JS concat, strip debugging and minify
gulp.task('scripts', function () {
  gulp.src(['./code/js/index.js', './code/js/*.js'])
    .pipe(concat('script.js'))
    //Uncomment the following line before going to production
    //.pipe(stripDebug())
    .pipe(uglify())
    .pipe(gulp.dest('./www/'));
});
```

What this code does is process all of the .js files in the code/js folder, treating the index.js file as the primary file. Notice how all of the commands that follow begin with `.pipe`; that's because the results of one are piped into the next command in the list. So, for this example, the JavaScript files are first concatenated into a single file called script.js, then uglified (minified) and finally copied into the project's www folder. All of that is done with one line of code.

Notice that I have the call to `stripDebug` commented out; that particular function removes any code lines that call `console.debug`, the thought being that those are there for debug purposes and should not be included in production code.

If you look through the remainder of the file, you'll see that all of the functions are set up the same way, only processed a little differently depending on the type of file being processed.

You can have multiple tasks defined within a Gulp file; simply add additional commands the same way as the default option was added. To add a debug process that shrinks images but copies over the source files in their original format, unminified, I would add a debug option using

```
gulp.task('debug', ['imagemin', 'copyfiles', 'prepare'], function () {});
```

Then I would add a new function to the file called copyfiles that copied the files from code to www and I'd be all set. To invoke the command I would pass the command name to the `gulp` command using

```
gulp debug
```

The gulp file issues a `cordova prepare` when it's done processing all of the files, so to use this as part of my development process, I simply had to have a terminal window open to the project folder and issue the following commands:

```
gulp
cordova run android
```

This will prepare all of the files, then run the application on either an Android device or Android emulator. You can replace the `cordova run` command with whatever command is appropriate based on what it is you want to do. All I'm really showing is that I've replaced typing `cordova prepare` with `gulp`; otherwise the process remains the same.

Figure 18.31 shows Gulp in action, processing all of my application's files.

```
C:\Windows\system32\cmd.exe

C:\Users\jwargo\dev\gulpdemo>gulp
[14:53:52] Using gulpfile ~\dev\gulpdemo\gulpfile.js
[14:53:52] Starting 'imagemin'...
[14:53:52] Finished 'imagemin' after 10 ms
[14:53:52] Starting 'htmlpage'...
[14:53:52] Finished 'htmlpage' after 3.22 ms
[14:53:52] Starting 'scripts'...
[14:53:52] Finished 'scripts' after 5.09 ms
[14:53:52] Starting 'styles'...
[14:53:52] Finished 'styles' after 3.14 ms
[14:53:52] Starting 'prepare'...
code
config.xml
gulpfile.js
hooks
merges
node_modules
package.json
platforms
plugins
www
[14:53:57] Finished 'prepare' after 4.35 s
[14:53:57] Starting 'default'...
[14:53:57] Finished 'default' after 6.01 μs

C:\Users\jwargo\dev\gulpdemo>_
```

Figure 18.31 Gulp in Action

There is, of course, much more you can do with Gulp; I've only touched the surface here, but I hope I've provided you with enough information to get started with the tool. There are a ton of plugins available, so you can likely find one that can perform most any task you want performed.

Grunt

Grunt (http://gruntjs.com/) is a JavaScript-based build tool like Gulp. Grunt is more popular than Gulp, but mostly because it's been around longer. Gulp is faster and easier to use, but Grunt has a wider following.

To install Grunt, open a terminal window and execute the following command:

```
npm install grunt-cli
```

On OS X or Linux, you may have to run the command using this:

```
sudo npm install -g grunt-cli
```

This installs the Grunt CLI; you'll still need to install Grunt and any associated plugins in each project folder.

Using Grunt is just like using Gulp: you create a package.json file that includes all of your dependencies and use a gruntfile.js file to execute all of your project's Grunt commands. For this example, I created the simple gruntfile.js shown in Listing 18.3. It performs three actions on a project's source code files: minimizes the application's HTML files, minimizes the application's JavaScript files, and optimizes the application's image files.

Listing 18.3 gruntfile.js File

```
module.exports = function (grunt) {
  grunt.initConfig({
    //Process JavaScript files
    uglify: {
      jsFiles: {
        files: [{
          expand: true,
          cwd: 'code',
          src: '**/*.js',
          dest: 'www'
          }]
      }
    },

    //Process HTML files
    htmlmin: {
      htmlFiles: {
```

```
          options: {
            removeComments: true,
            collapseWhitespace: true
          },
          files: [{
            expand: true,
            cwd: 'code',
            src: '**/*.html',
            dest: 'www'
        }]
        }
      },

      //Process Image files
      imagemin: {
        imgFiles: {
          files: [{
            expand: true,
            cwd: 'code/img',
            src: ['**/*.{png,jpg,gif}'],
            dest: 'www/img'
        }]
        }
      }

    });

    //Load the needed grunt modules
    //Minifies JavaScript files
    grunt.loadNpmTasks('grunt-contrib-uglify');
    //Minifies HTML files
    grunt.loadNpmTasks('grunt-contrib-htmlmin');
    //optimizes image files
    grunt.loadNpmTasks('grunt-contrib-imagemin');

    // Default task(s).
    grunt.registerTask('default', ['uglify', 'htmlmin', 'imagemin']);
    grunt.registerTask('js', ['uglify']);
    grunt.registerTask('html', ['htmlmin']);
};
```

As with the Gulp example, the gruntfile.js defines the default task:

```
grunt.registerTask('default', ['uglify', 'htmlmin', 'imagemin']);
```

When `grunt` is executed without any additional parameters, this is the task that will execute.

To use this for your projects, copy the gruntfile.js and package.json file (shown in Listing 18.4) to your Cordova project folder, create a folder called code, and populate the folder with your application's code. To install the required modules, open a terminal window, navigate to the Cordova project folder, and issue the following command:

```
npm install
```

With the modules installed, to execute the default Grunt process, issue the following command:

```
grunt
```

Listing 18.4 package.json File

```
{
  "name": "gruntdemo",
  "version": "1.0.0",
  "description": "Cordova Grunt Demo",
  "main": "gruntfile.js",
  "author": "John M. Wargo",
  "license": "Apache",
  "devDependencies": {
    "grunt": "^0.4.5",
    "grunt-contrib-htmlmin": "^0.3.0",
    "grunt-contrib-imagemin": "^0.9.2",
    "grunt-contrib-uglify": "^0.6.0"
  }
}
```

That's all there is to it. Grunt will minify the HTML and JavaScript files, then process any image files. Figure 18.32 shows the default `grunt` command in action. In this example, a single JavaScript file was processed, the index.html was compressed from 522 bytes to 453 bytes, and no image files were processed (because my project doesn't have any).

I've also defined some additional tasks in the gruntfile.js, such as

```
grunt.registerTask('js', ['uglify']);
```

This task only processes the application's JavaScript files and can be executed using the following command:

```
grunt js
```

There is, of course, much more you can do with Grunt; I've only touched the surface here, but I hope I've provided you with enough information to get started with the tool. There are a ton of plugins available, so you can likely find one that can perform most any task you want performed.

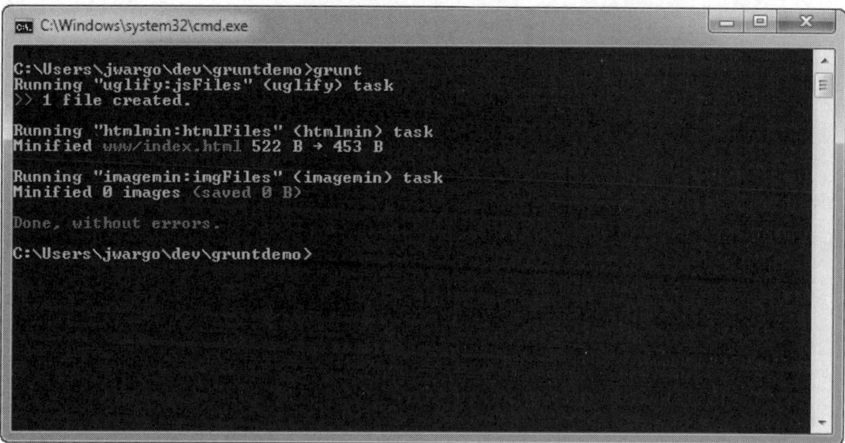

Figure 18.32 Grunt in Action

Wrap-Up

In this chapter, I covered different third-party tools you can use to simplify your Cordova development efforts. In some cases, they are tools I use myself, so I find them to be particularly useful. For others, what you learned about here were tools that I'm interested in but never really got a chance to play with (until now).

That's all there is for this book; I'm out of space (I exceeded the publisher's length estimate by about 100 pages) and I'm out of time (the manuscript is due tomorrow). I hope you enjoyed this book!

Index

A

B

C

H

I

J

K

L

M

N

O

P

Q

R

S

T

U

V

W

Z

Register the Addison-Wesley, Exam Cram, Prentice Hall, Que, and Sams products you own to unlock great benefits.

To begin the registration process, simply go to **informit.com/register** to sign in or create an account. You will then be prompted to enter the 10- or 13-digit ISBN that appears on the back cover of your product.

Registering your products can unlock the following benefits:

- Access to supplemental content, including bonus chapters, source code, or project files.
- A coupon to be used on your next purchase.

Registration benefits vary by product. Benefits will be listed on your Account page under Registered Products.

About InformIT — THE TRUSTED TECHNOLOGY LEARNING SOURCE

INFORMIT IS HOME TO THE LEADING TECHNOLOGY PUBLISHING IMPRINTS Addison-Wesley Professional, Cisco Press, Exam Cram, IBM Press, Prentice Hall Professional, Que, and Sams. Here you will gain access to quality and trusted content and resources from the authors, creators, innovators, and leaders of technology. Whether you're looking for a book on a new technology, a helpful article, timely newsletters, or access to the Safari Books Online digital library, InformIT has a solution for you.

THE TRUSTED TECHNOLOGY LEARNING SOURCE

Addison-Wesley | Cisco Press | Exam Cram
IBM Press | Que | Prentice Hall | Sams
SAFARI BOOKS ONLINE